Effective Reading Instruction, K–8

THIRD EDITION

Donald J. Leu
Syracuse University

Charles K. Kinzer
Vanderbilt University

Merrill,
an imprint of Prentice Hall

Englewood Cliffs, New Jersey   Columbus, Ohio

Library of Congress Cataloging-in-Publication Data

Leu, Donald J.
  Effective reading instruction, K–8/Donald J. Leu, Jr., Charles
K. Kinzer.—3rd ed.
    p. cm.
  Includes bibliographical references and index.
  ISBN 0-02-370065-3
    1. Reading (Elementary)—United States.   I. Kinzer, Charles K.
II. Title.
  LB1573.L445 1995
  372.4'1'0973—dc20   94-38994

Cover photo: © *Scott Cunningham / Cunningham / Feinknopf Photography*
Editor: *Linda James Scharp*
Developmental Editor: *Linda Ashe Montgomery*
Production Editors: *Laura Messerly and Linda Bayma*
Production Coordination: *Elm Street Publishing Services, Inc.*
Photo Editor: *Anne Vega*
Text Designer: *Elm Street Publishing Services, Inc.*
Cover Designer: *Julia Zonneveld Van Hook*
Production Buyer: *Pamela D. Bennett*

This book was set in ITC Century Book by The Clarinda Company and was printed and bound by Von Hoffmann Press, Inc. The cover was printed by Von Hoffmann Press, Inc.

©1995 by Prentice-Hall, Inc.
A Simon & Schuster Company
Englewood Cliffs, New Jersey 07632

Earlier editions © 1991 by Macmillan Publishing Company and © 1987 by Merrill Publishing Company.

Photo Credits: Anne Vega/Merrill and Prentice Hall: pages 10, 118, 151, 216, 225, 287, 308, 350, 355, 474. KS Studios/Merrill and Prentice Hall: pages 2, 194, 398. Charles K. Kinzer: pages 7, 16, 32, 35, 40, 54, 70, 86, 134, 160, 178, 204, 233, 245, 254, 250, 276, 291, 313, 339, 368, 372, 383, 423, 456, 468, 561, 577, 599, 606, 614. Scott Cunningham/Cunningham/Feinknopf Photography/Merrill and Prentice Hall: pages 26, 76, 494, 518. Barbara Schwartz/Merrill and Prentice Hall: pages 105, 124, 174, 270, 322, 450, 554, 566, 592. Tom Watson/Merrill and Prentice Hall: pages 333, 523, 546. Todd Yarrington/Merrill and Prentice Hall: pages 404, 429, 438.

Printed in the United States of America

10 9 8 7 6 5 4 3 2 1

ISBN: 0-02-370065-3

Prentice-Hall International (UK) Limited, *London*
Prentice-Hall of Australia Pty. Limited, *Sydney*
Prentice-Hall of Canada, Inc. *Toronto*
Prentice-Hall Hispanoamericana, S. A., *Mexico*
Prentice-Hall of India Private Limited, *New Delhi*
Prentice-Hall of Japan, Inc., *Tokyo*
Simon & Schuster Asia Pte. Ltd., *Singapore*
Editora Prentice-Hall do Brasil, Ltda., *Rio de Janeiro*

TO OUR FAMILIES—
*Alexandra, Debbie, Katie, Rita, and Sarah. Once again, with grati-
tude for your understanding and support as we developed these ideas
during three years of late nights and weekends on the computer.*

TO OUR PRESERVICE READERS—
*you are part of a very long and important chain that began with your
parents and teachers, includes your current professors, and will continue as you enter the noblest of professions—teaching.*

TO OUR UNDERGRADUATE AND GRADUATE STUDENTS—
*with appreciation for the opportunity to participate in your develop-
ment and for the ideas you shared which contributed to our own development.*

TO TEACHERS AROUND THE COUNTRY—
*with heartfelt thanks for allowing us to enter the special worlds you
create for children. Your insights have been especially helpful as we
seek to support the development of future teachers.*

PREFACE

Developed as the basic text for preservice teachers in an elementary reading methods course, this book was written to develop insightful teachers empowered to make logical, reflective decisions about reading instruction. It is an integrative text, based on the assumption that effective teachers of reading must understand both what to do during instruction and why it should be done.

Goals

This text translates the most consistent research findings into practice. It presents the major perspectives in reading education, describes a comprehensive range of instructional practices, and shows teachers how to select and modify practices that are consistent with their perspectives and the individual needs of their students. Our goal is to provide a text that facilitates the development of teachers who can be reasoned decision makers within the school-restructuring debate that currently impacts issues of teacher empowerment.

Previous editions noted that an explosion in reading research had occurred in the past decades. Research findings on socio-cultural aspects of literacy, readers' cognitive and linguistic processes, teacher behavior and teacher cognition, classroom environments, interest and attitude, and different text structures resulted in a knowledge base with clear instructional implications. More recently, while research efforts in these areas have continued, they have been augmented by research in multicultural issues, emergent literacy, whole language, reading/writing relationships, cooperative learning, and portfolio and alternative assessment strategies. At the same time, changes in instructional materials have taken place. Published reading programs now reflect a greater emphasis on children's literature, and technological advances continue to move far beyond drill and practice.

Research base

In order to address the changes that have occurred since the second edition was published, substantive revisions have been made in each chapter. Highlights of this edition follow.

Highlights, changes, additions

- Major sections on strategies for using multicultural literature and on the treatment of linguistically and culturally diverse students are included.

- A full chapter about reading/writing relationships and major sections in several chapters about emergent literacy and whole language are included.

- Throughout the text, major sections on using literature in reading instruction and on developing thematic units have been added. Thematic lists of appropriate children's literature appear in most chapters.

- Major sections on alternative assessment, product/process assessment, and portfolio assessment are included.

- Major sections on the important role of reader-response have been integrated throughout the text.

- An inclusive perspective has been integrated in the discussion of teaching children with special needs.

- Sections discussing cooperative learning and its potential value to teachers of reading have been added to several chapters.

- The section on computer literacy has been replaced with a broader focus on the use of technology, various types of software appropriate for reading instruction, and a discussion of technologies beyond microcomputers.

- Updated references provide a comprehensive and up-to-date resource for students who will become our future teachers of reading.

These and other changes ensure that the text is as current as possible.

Model lessons, sample activities

Becoming an insightful, reflective teacher is not easy. We have written this text to be considerate of the needs of learners on their way to becoming professionals in literacy education. Part of this support structure comes from model lessons provided for each major teaching procedure discussed and more than 300 sample activities and teaching strategies that are presented and highlighted for easier reference. These activities and strategies allow students to select and practice procedures in field-experience components that are common to most preservice reading methods courses. Learning should also be facilitated by the early discussion of several different definitions of reading and a clear statement of the definition used in this book. In addition, end-of-chapter summaries, questions, and activities have been chosen to provoke further thought about teacher decision making and to solidify important concepts presented in each chapter.

Special features

Special attention has been devoted to the layout and design elements of this text in order to further support the needs of students—from initial reading through practicum and student teaching experiences. A relevant quotation from preservice students, parents, children, or teachers captures each chapter's theme, followed by performance objectives that sharpen the reader's expectations and a list of key concepts that can function in a variety of ways. Instructors might use them in a prediscussion to build students' backgrounds, students might ask about definitions before they begin reading, or instructors and students together might focus on key concepts in postreading activities, perhaps constructing a concept or semantic map in class discussion.

To facilitate students' comprehension, key terms are highlighted in the text, and definitions appear as margin notes. In addition, major points are itemized at the end of each chapter. For easier access and reference during field experiences, model lessons and sample activities are highlighted by a unique design feature and a second color. Headings also have been clearly differentiated by a second color to promote previewing and studying.

All chapters include an element called *Exploring Diverse Points of View,* which presents issues being debated in the field and encourages students to think about their own responses to these issues. Instructors might use this feature in expanded class activities, for student research projects, or to promote student discussion. Each chapter also includes an important, highlighted element called *Opportunities to Celebrate Diversity,* which presents specific teaching suggestions to enhance preservice students' awareness of the need to actively promote student diversity within a classroom by recognizing the different cultural backgrounds and subsequent prior knowledge these students bring to their reading and writing experiences.

The end of each chapter contains a feature called *Making Instructional Decisions.* This is intended to encourage students' interaction with the text by providing projects, discussion questions, and hypothetical situations for student response. In addition, the brief annotated list for further reading at the end of each chapter allows interested readers to pursue a specific topic. These references also provide an initial source for literature searches as appropriate for class assignments. A comprehensive list of references cited concludes each chapter, and author and subject indexes appear at the end of the text.

Two additional features help make this text current and unique. First, extensive thematic lists of children's literature appear throughout the text, rather than only in specific chapters that relate to children's literature, as is common in many other reading texts. These lists allow students to choose appropriate literature selections during field experiences and allow instructors to more easily incorporate the use of literature in student assignments. Second, a multicultural perspective has been integrated throughout the text.

Each chapter ends with a section titled *Comments from the Classroom,* in which two experienced teachers, Judy Dill and Nikki Robinson, have written comments and shared successful strategies they have used in the classroom respective to the chapter content. These comments will allow preservice students to hear the voice of practicing professionals with regard to applying the chapter's concepts in real classrooms. Instructors

Teacher comments, instructional perspectives

should find these sections helpful in promoting a discussion of teacher decision making.

The text is divided into four major sections, the first of which contains three chapters. Chapter 1 provides an introduction to the field and presents various definitions of and perspectives toward reading. Developing and clarifying personal perspectives about how one reads and how reading is taught—what is called a "framework" for teaching literacy—is the subject of the second chapter. After exploring how a person reads and how reading ability develops, students identify how their own understanding of literacy will affect their teaching decisions every day. The third chapter presents the various materials and methods commonly used in reading instruction and describes the instructional frameworks within which they often appear. As a whole, the first section assists students in developing their own instructional framework as they identify their perspectives toward reading. This framework will be enhanced and modified as readers proceed through the book and through their own teaching careers.

The second section includes seven chapters that develop the reader's knowledge base about literacy and reading instruction. The first two chapters in this section present the central role of children's literature and the connection between reading and writing. This is followed by chapters that address beginning readers and how to support their emerging literacy, decoding, vocabulary, comprehension and response, and teaching content-area reading and study skills. Thus, this section includes separate chapters about using literature in a reading program, connecting reading and writing, and understanding the special reading and instructional demands of expository texts. While each chapter has a dominant focus, each recognizes that fluent reading of "real" materials is the goal of effective reading instruction.

The third section consists of two chapters about determining and meeting instructional needs. Chapter 11 discusses assessment in both individual and group situations, and includes assessment of materials as well as readers. The chapter considers issues related to product and process assessment, portfolio assessment, and informal assessment tools such as running records, think-alouds, and "kidwatching." More traditional, formal assessment tools are also discussed. Chapter 12 looks at the instructional needs of special populations, including the learning disabled and the gifted. Special attention is given to forming inclusive communities of learners in a classroom.

The fourth section concludes the book with chapters that present the importance of classroom organization and how technology can be used to advance literacy instruction. Chapter 13 discusses instructional organization both between and within classes and addresses management issues related to effective teaching. Chapter 14 examines the changing patterns resulting from the impact of technology on reading instruction. This chapter moves beyond microcomputers to consider software types, videodisc and CD-ROM technology, hypermedia, and simple, cost-effective uses of technology to facilitate disseminating information to parents and encouraging parental involvement.

The chapters in this text have been ordered in a logical instructional sequence. We suggest that Chapters 1, 2, and 3 be read first, regardless of any reordering of subsequent chapters. These first three chapters explain the instructional consequences of various instructional frameworks and begin the process of helping readers develop their own personal frameworks. However, all chapters have been written to stand alone.

Instructional sequence

Several ancillary materials have been developed for instructors who use this text. These materials can be requested from the publisher. An instructor's guide includes summaries of each chapter, as well as additional questions that are appropriate for cooperative learning activities, individual student projects, and prediscussion of chapters. The instructor's guide also contains blackline masters for each chapter, which incorporate many of the figures, diagrams, and summary lists in the text. These are intended for use with an overhead projector to facilitate class discussion. Finally, the instructor's guide includes an extensive test bank, complete with chapter questions, quizzes, and section tests. The test bank includes multiple-choice, true/false, short-answer, and essay questions and provides answer keys for multiple-choice and true/false questions.

Instructor's guide, blackline masters, test bank

The final ancillary is a videotape that includes examples of major methods and topics discussed in the text. For example, short segments demonstrate a big book activity, a ReQuest procedure, a language experience activity, a directed reading-thinking activity, and so on. Although the segments are relatively short, they should enhance and promote class discussion and provide instructors with points of departure for additional comments.

Videotape

Even as this third edition goes to press, new research is appearing that has great potential for improving reading education. Future revisions will continue to incorporate the best, most current knowledge about effective reading instruction and will attempt to present it in a useful manner. To this end, we welcome comments and suggestions from both instructors and students who use this text. Comments on the first two editions were most helpful to us in the revision process, and any recommendations for further improvements will be appreciated.

Request for comments

Working together has been an especially worthwhile experience for us. Neither the previous editions, nor this third edition, would have its depth of coverage without the combined knowledge of each author. The text is a joint effort in the fullest sense of a partnership—a coauthored text with both authors participating equally throughout the project. Author order was determined randomly.

A personal note

ACKNOWLEDGMENTS

It is impossible to recognize or thank individually each of the many friends and colleagues who have contributed to this revision, and we beg the indulgence of any we might inadvertently fail to acknowledge. As in any major project, the quality of the finished product results from the efforts, encouragement, and sacrifices of many individuals. We greatly appreciate all who have supported our work.

This revision has benefited from an extensive review. The number of reviewers, their variety of perspectives, and their sharing of time and ideas have made this text current, complete, and accurate. We especially thank the following distinguished reviewers who participated in this project and have our continuing gratitude for their professionalism and consideration: Carolsue Clery, Northern Illinois University; Judith Hillman, St. Michael's College; Maria J. Meyerson, University of Nevada, Las Vegas; William Oehlkers, Rhode Island College; Peter Quinn, St. John's University; Robert J. Rickelman, University of North Carolina, Charlotte; Robert T. Rude, Rhode Island College; Jay Samuels, University of Minnesota, Minneapolis; Sam Sebesta, University of Washington; Timothy Shanahan, University of Illinois, Chicago; James W. Wiley, Baylor University; and David B. Yaden, University of Southern California.

CONTENTS

CHAPTER 3

*Material and Method Frameworks: Applying Initial Insights
About Reading   70*

PART 2
Developing a Knowledge Base 117

CHAPTER 6
Facilitating Beginning Readers' Emerging Literacy   216

CHAPTER 9

Comprehension of Extended Text   350

PART 4
Instructional Patterns and Technologies   553

CHAPTER 13
Classroom Organization   554

CHAPTER 14
Supporting Literacy with Computers and Related Technologies   592

PART 1

Entering the World of Reading Instruction

CHAPTER

The Challenge and the Rewards

1

"I've heard that teaching reading is one of the most important things that teachers do and I'm a bit anxious. Even though I'm a good reader, I can't remember how I learned to read, and I've talked to teachers who all seem to use different philosophies and procedures to teach reading. There seems to be so much I don't know. And yet I love reading and want to help children to learn to read and to love it also."

An undergraduate student at the beginning
of a reading methods course.

Through your own experiences, you already know that teaching is a challenging and rewarding profession. Teachers often have a significant influence on their students' lives, and teachers of reading can have an especially lasting impact. The importance of reading is seen in every subject area and in nearly every aspect of life, and the decisions a teacher makes are critical to a student's success.

This chapter presents the importance of teacher decisions in reading instruction, discusses several views of the reading process and how these influence instructional decisions, and introduces the concept of literacy frameworks, which can help you become an effective decision maker when teaching reading. Chapter 1 includes information that will help you answer questions such as:

1. Why do different teachers reach different decisions about how to teach reading?
2. How do different definitions of "reading" influence how it is taught?
3. What is a personal framework of the reading process, and why is it important to a future teacher of reading?
4. What are instructional frameworks, and how do these affect teaching decisions in reading instruction?

KEY CONCEPTS

literacy framework	instructional decision making
definitions of the reading process	reading comprehension and response
interactive processes	reading process

TEACHING READING—A DECISION-MAKING PROCESS

Assume that you will be teaching a first-grade class in two years. Take this year's date and add fourteen. Your result is the year in which your future first-grade students will graduate from high school. Add four more years to that date, and you have the year that those students will graduate from college with an undergraduate degree, if they choose to attend and go straight through. Keep in mind that as you teach reading, the instructional decisions you make will support your students throughout their school years and their adult lives.

The importance of the instructional decisions you will make cannot be overemphasized, and in talking with teachers over the years we have consistently heard about the challenge, rewards, and importance of being a teacher of reading. Teachers have told us many times that seeing beginning readers develop excitement and maturity in reading reinforces their commitment to teaching and to their students. Yet they also say that

EXPLORING DIVERSE POINTS OF VIEW

During the past several years a tremendous change has taken place in education, partly because of the rapid spread of technology in our society in general and in our schools in particular. This ever-increasing emphasis on technology has resulted in speculation that a number of school subjects may need to be taught differently, if our students are to be educated most effectively. In fact, some say that school subjects such as reading and mathematics will become obsolete, because sophisticated and easy-to-use technology may soon read and calculate for us. The increasing acceptance and use of calculators in arithmetic classes and the potential of microcomputers with synthetic speech capabilities lend support to this line of thinking. Nonetheless, reading ability continues to concern parents, educators, and legislators alike. In fact, many primary-grade teachers measure their success against their students' literacy achievements. How should we resolve this seeming discrepancy between viewpoints? Will reading be increasingly de-emphasized, or will reading continue to be viewed as among the most important aspects of education?

teaching reading is a challenge because of the many decisions that need to be made during a lesson and in a class. Decisions about meeting students' individual needs, choosing materials for instruction, assessing, and reacting appropriately to students' reading behaviors in ways that improve their reading ability continually challenge and reward teachers.

As a teacher, you will sense the importance of reading as parents ask about their children's progress; as administrators provide in-service workshops on reading instruction; as you see your school's reading test scores reported in the local newspaper; and especially as you look at the faces of your students, who want very much to learn to read. Reading is a critical part of the elementary curriculum, and many people pay close attention to reading instruction and to students' progress in reading ability.

Teaching reading is also a challenge because reading is a complex developmental process. Consequently, teachers of reading must have an understanding of this complexity as well as an understanding of effective instructional strategies. As you learn how to teach reading, you will be developing answers to a number of important questions as well an understanding of the **reading process.** The match between understanding the reading process and instructional decisions is one we revisit throughout this text, and it will guide your decisions about which instructional strategies to choose and how to modify these strategies. Some of the questions you will confront and answer as you learn to teach reading effectively are:

reading process
Active and internal operations involved in reading.

What must readers know in order to comprehend complete stories, articles, and books? How can I help readers gain meaning from these and other kinds of writing?

What materials should be used to teach reading? How can I select and adapt appropriate materials for reading instruction?

How can I best organize my classroom? What organizational patterns can be used to provide for the range of individuals in my classroom?

What are the characteristics of effective teachers? What must I do to become an effective teacher of reading?

Because there are different definitions of reading, there are different answers to each of these questions. No single, definitive answer exists that can be applied to each situation.

An aspect related to the challenge of reading instruction is the diversity of the students found in any classroom. Some of your students will be far beyond their classroom peers in reading ability; others will be somewhat below the class average. All will have individual needs. Some will have difficulty with pronunciation in oral reading; others will need help understanding word meanings, and certain students will require assistance in interpreting or evaluating what is read. This diversity of needs and abilities makes teaching in general—and the teaching of reading in particular—challenging and exciting.

The final challenge for you as a teacher of reading will be to make appropriate instructional decisions while attending to the many events that take place during the course of a lesson. Learning to manage classroom activities to provide the best possible learning environment is an important part of becoming a teacher. Can you remember how you felt when you were learning to drive a car? You were confronted with important decisions that had to be made while you attended to many other things—the cars in front of and behind you, the actions of your passengers, the condition of the road, and so on. You probably drive skillfully now, and any uneasiness has likely disappeared. With a solid knowledge base and concentrated practice, you will also master both the decision-making process and the management functions that will make your classroom a haven for learning.

As a teacher of reading, you will face several challenges. To be successful, you will need a clear understanding of this complex subject, the ability to make informed decisions, and the management skill to accomplish your instructional goals in a busy classroom environment. Across the continent teachers are meeting these and other challenges, giving North America one of the highest literacy rates in the world. When we compare the percentage of people who can read now to the percentage of 50 years ago, it is clear that teachers are learning to teach reading and are doing so effectively. With the help of this text and your own work and practice, you can develop into a successful reading teacher who will be repeatedly rewarded as your students become eager readers.

How does a teacher make appropriate decisions in the classroom? The answer lies partly in a teacher's definition of the reading process, which is included in a teacher's literacy framework and helps guide decisions. In the next section we discuss definitions of the reading process and how respective definitions influence the choices and decisions that teachers

Reading can take place anywhere and for a variety of purposes. Group reading activities, especially if followed by discussion, benefit reading comprehension and learning.

make. We then introduce literacy frameworks and explain how they help teachers in the classroom decision-making process.

THE IMPORTANCE OF ESTABLISHING A PERSPECTIVE

Your view of reading—the factors involved, their relative importance, and the way the process takes place and develops—will have a direct and significant impact on your decision making. This, in turn, will affect how you teach reading. In fact, the relationship between a personal view of reading and teaching practices has been discussed for some time:

> If we think of reading primarily as a visual task, we will be concerned with the correction of visual defects and the provision of legible reading material. If we think of reading as word recognition, we will drill on the basic sight vocabulary and word recognition skills. If we think of reading as merely reproducing what the author says, we will direct the student's attention to the literal meaning of the passage and check his comprehension of it. If we think of reading as a thinking process, we shall be concerned with the reader's skill in making interpretations and generalizations, in drawing inferences and conclusions. If we think of reading as contributing to personal development and effecting desirable personality changes, we will provide our students with reading materials that meet their needs and have some application to their lives (Strang, McCullough, & Traxler, 1961, pp. 1-2).

Teachers are often left to discover their view of the reading process on their own; they are not told how various viewpoints will affect their instructional decisions. This text provides guidance in establishing and making explicit your view of reading. It also helps you incorporate your view into a framework that will guide your instructional decisions. This will allow you later to modify your viewpoint and instruction consciously as appropriate. First, however, let us look at how others have defined *reading* and how *reading* is defined in this text.

Some Definitions of Reading

As knowledge about the reading process has evolved, definitions of reading have become more complex. Although "getting meaning from print" is one way to define reading, such simplified definitions do not adequately present the complexity of the process, nor do they reflect the interaction of factors that enter into the reading act. Look at the following definitions. Consider them carefully, and think about the kinds of instructional choices each might imply.

> Learning to read is like learning to drive a car. . . . The child learns the mechanics of reading, and when he's through, he can read (Flesch, 1981, p. 3). [We should teach the child phonics] letter-by-letter and sound-by-sound until he knows it—and when he knows it he knows how to read (Flesch, 1955, p. 121).

If our conception of reading is largely equated with mechanics and pronunciation, then personal aspects such as motivation and background knowledge become less important. But is a knowledge of letters and sounds all there is to reading? In the case of a blind law student, the job of a paid reader is to read assigned class material to the student. Who would you say is reading—the sighted person who is pronouncing the material or the blind student who is comprehending it? Most people would agree that reading includes, but goes beyond, decoding symbols.

> Reading cannot occur unless the pupil can identify and recognize the printed symbol, and generally the pupil must also give the visual configuration a name. Even so, it is only one aspect of the reading process. Meaning, too, is an absolute prerequisite in reading. Perhaps too much emphasis in reading instruction has been placed on word identification and not enough on comprehension (Dechant, 1982, p. 166).

If we assume that reading goes beyond pronunciation and involves understanding, we can see that the process of reading is more than a mechanical skill; it is active and internal. In fact, teaching reading may be thought of as teaching thinking, because readers must organize information, recognize cause and effect, assess the importance of what is being read, and fit the material into their own beliefs and knowledge base.

psycholinguistic
Referring to the psychological and linguistic processes involved in language.

> Reading is a **psycholinguistic** guessing game. It involves an interaction between thought and language. Efficient reading does not result from

precise perception and identification of all elements, but from skill in selecting the fewest, most productive cues necessary to produce guesses [about meaning] which are right the first time (Goodman, 1976, p. 498).

Reading is the process of understanding written language. It begins with a flutter of patterns on the retina and ends (when successful) with a definite idea about the author's intended message . . . a skilled reader must be able to make use of sensory, **syntactic, semantic,** and **pragmatic** information to accomplish his task. These various sources of information interact in many complex ways during the process of reading (Rumelhart, 1994 p. 864).

syntactic
Referring to the ordering of words that makes meaningful phrases and sentences.

semantic
Referring to the meanings of words.

pragmatic
Referring to the social appropriateness of speech acts in certain contexts.

Definitions that present the reading process as a set of variables that all interact in order to bring about reading comprehension are called interactive definitions, and some theorists believe that any particular variable (such as the syntactic, semantic, and pragmatic information noted in Rumelhart's definition) can be used to support a reader if another variable is lacking. In other words, one variable can compensate for weakness in another (Stanovich, 1980, 1986).

In addition to definitions like those shown above (which describe the reading process in terms of language units and their interaction), other definitions focus on the social, communicative nature of reading and writing. For proponents of such views, learning is thought to take place as children see the importance of communication, at which time requisite teaching occurs. Harste (1990), for example, notes that "language is a social event" (p. 317), and Shanahan stresses its communicative purpose:

We read an author's words and are affected by the author's intentions. We write with the idea of influencing or informing others. . . . The fusion of reading and writing in the classroom offers children the possibility of participating in both sides of the communication process and, consequently, provides them with a more elaborate grasp of the true meaning of literacy (Shanahan, 1990, p. 4).

The relationship between reading and writing—between readers and writers—has been called interactive by some, transactional by others. For example, Rosenblatt (1985, 1988) has described this relationship as a transaction between the text and the reader, during which both are changed and become more than the sum of their parts. Rosenblatt's transactional view has had a major impact on reader-response theory; that is, thoughts about how readers react to a text—socially, psychologically, and morally.

For the individual, then, language is that part, or set of features, of the public system that has been internalized through that person's experiences with words in life situations. . . . The residue of the individual's past transactions in particular natural and social contexts constitutes what can be termed a linguistic-experiential reservoir. . . . this inner capital is all that each of us has to draw on in speaking, listening, writing, or reading. We "make sense" of a new situation. . . . by applying, reorganizing, revising, or extending public and private elements selected from our personal linguistic-experiential reservoirs (Rosenblatt, 1994, pp. 1060, 1061).

The definitions presented above view reading quite differently, ranging from a mechanical sounding-out process to an interaction between what is read and what is already known, to a social and emotional experience. Different instructional decisions result partly from these varied definitions of reading. For example, a teacher who defines reading as strictly sounding out letters usually spends more time at the early grade levels teaching letter-sound relationships and less time reading to students.

All definitions of reading are personal, based on an individual's view of the reading process and the way in which reading ability develops. The following definition has guided the writing of this text. We believe that an interactive view of the reading process—where the reader's knowledge interacts with information from the text—is more readily supported by current research. We have thus written this text from an interactive perspective that includes the importance of social aspects of literacy learning. We also know, however, that any definition of reading is only a guide and must change as our knowledge of the reading process grows.

Supporting children in their search to relate meaning from print is a valued teaching behavior independent of any individual definition of reading.

> Reading is a *developmental, interactive,* and *global process* that involves *learning.* It is a *personal process* specifically incorporating an individual's *linguistic knowledge* and can be both positively and negatively influenced by nonlinguistic *internal* and *external variables,* or factors.

The eight aspects of this definition that are italicized are briefly explained here and will become clearer in the remaining chapters of this text.

1. *Developmental process.* This aspect recognizes that reading ability develops over time and that readers read differently at different stages in their reading development. For example, a beginning reader attends more to individual letters, whereas a mature reader focuses more on words and general meaning.

2. *Interactive process.* This aspect recognizes that reading is an interaction involving the reader, the writer, and the text being read. Meaning is not only in the mind of the person doing the reading, nor is it only in the text being read. It is instead the interaction between the text being read and a reader's existing knowledge and expectations that determines the amount and type of comprehension that takes place. Because individual knowledge and expectations differ, different readers may interpret an identical text in different ways.

3. *Global process.* This aspect recognizes that comprehension can occur at different levels of complexity yet as part of a comprehensive and organized process. For example, comprehension can occur at a letter, word, phrase, sentence, or entire discourse level, but all of these levels must function in a coordinated manner and with some sophistication for reading to occur.

4. *Learning.* This aspect recognizes that reading ability develops over time; it also reflects our knowledge that instruction helps students learn to read. A reader must learn how to learn, acquiring certain strategies for reading as well as an understanding of when and how to use them.

5. *Personal process.* This aspect recognizes the social and emotional dimensions of reading. In addition to the different interpretations noted earlier, readers' differing backgrounds and knowledge result in different emotional, moral, and psychological reactions to what is read.

6. *Linguistic knowledge.* This aspect acknowledges that various language components influence reading ability: (1) phonic knowledge of sounds and their relationship to symbols; (2) semantic knowledge of meanings; (3) syntactic knowledge of word patterns; and (4) discourse knowledge of how different written products are structured. This aspect also recognizes the effect of **metacognitive knowledge** on comprehension. Metacognitive knowledge allows a reader to monitor comprehension as it occurs and to

metacognitive knowledge
A type of knowledge important for reading that includes the strategies used during reading and comprehension monitoring.

```
OPPORTUNITIES TO CELEBRATE DIVERSITY
```

In your classroom, you will encounter students with different dialects, backgrounds, abilities, concerns, motivations, interests, and reading levels. Try acknowledging diversity in a number of ways. If you recognize the developmental nature of reading, for example, you will acknowledge that students will differ in their reading ability and in their progress. Because our definition views reading as being a personal process, and because it recognizes the importance of linguistic knowledge and internal and external variables, it acknowledges that diverse linguistic backgrounds, cultures, and experiences will influence the reading behaviors of your students. Consider then how the diversity you encounter provides opportunities for meeting individual needs, as well as opportunities to learn from each other; use diversity to strengthen yourself and your students.

choose strategies that result in rereading or asking for help when necessary.

7. *Internal variables.* Factors such as physical and mental well-being, general intelligence, specific developmental handicaps, and interest in or attitude toward reading and what is being read also influence the reading process. This aspect includes knowledge of pragmatics (the acceptability of speech acts in certain social contexts) and something called "world knowledge," or general knowledge or experience. For example, knowing what might be said acceptably in certain situations helps a reader interpret what a character in a novel might be saying; such knowledge might help a reader identify sarcasm. To use another example, general knowledge of city life might boost comprehension of a story that is set in a large city.

8. *External variables.* This aspect recognizes that instructional and situational characteristics also influence the reading act. Such factors include the physical environment of the reader; the instructional program (including the materials used in instruction); the prereading home environment; teacher-student interactions in the classroom; and other influences that are neither controlled by nor inherent to the reader.

We view reading, then, as more than recognition or pronunciation of printed squiggles on a page; it is a process in which the reader and print interact. The material being read is a starting point from which the reader moves on, incorporating existing knowledge in order to reason, learn, react, and ultimately go far beyond the assimilated printed symbols. Thus, all the knowledge a reader already has can be used to aid comprehension. And because reading is a language activity, preexisting language and language-related abilities are key factors in understanding and interpreting what is read. We must remember that children come to school with a wealth of language on which reading instruction can build. At the very least children know how to speak; thus all the sounds of the English language are already known, even if their relationship to specific printed symbols is not. Furthermore, through the use of oral language, children know that communication is possible and that the goal of communication is to transmit meaning. It is crucial not to overlook these vital and highly developed communication skills in your classroom, whatever grade level you teach.

Throughout this text we will remind you that your view of reading will determine how you teach. As you read through the following chapters, look back periodically at the definition we have just presented. Add to it or delete from it as your knowledge changes. Specifying a definition and personal framework in order to develop and improve instructional strategies is an important part of being a reading teacher and will help you meet the challenges outlined here. Guiding you in this task is one of our major goals.

LITERACY FRAMEWORKS AND INSTRUCTIONAL DECISIONS

Teachers provide effective reading instruction in busy classroom environments by relying on different types of literacy frameworks. Frameworks help teachers decide what to teach and how to teach. Such frameworks consist of the materials, methods, and beliefs about reading that teachers use to make their instructional decisions. Literacy frameworks provide structure and reduce the number of conscious decisions that teachers must make during interactions with students.

Literacy frameworks guide teachers in planning and teaching their reading lessons in much the same way that road maps guide drivers in their travels or grocery lists guide shoppers at the supermarket. Consider how a road map provides a general sense of direction and goals as well as specific instructions along the way, and how this sense of direction and goals helps a driver who encounters an unexpected detour. Literacy frameworks provide a teacher a reference point from which instructional decisions can be quickly made when unexpected things are encountered in a reading lesson—perhaps a student who is not reaching certain expectations, or materials that might be inappropriate for one or more students. Literacy frameworks promote individual decisions that are consistent with overall instructional goals.

Three Types of Frameworks

Teachers use three types of frameworks to meet the instructional and organizational challenges of reading instruction:

1. frameworks based on a set of instructional materials, called *material frameworks;*

2. frameworks based on instructional methods, called *method frameworks;* and
3. frameworks based on an understanding of reading comprehension and response to what is being read, called *literacy frameworks.*

material framework
A framework used to teach reading; based on a published set of materials and lesson-planning information.

A **material framework** is based on the materials and lesson planning information available in a published set of instructional tools, whether a kit of graded activity cards, computer software, or a complete reading program. The lesson planning information that accompanies a set of materials often states how a teacher should make decisions about the sequence of instruction (the order students are presented with parts of the material); the type and manner of assessments to use (perhaps providing tests and suggesting when these should be given); and where to proceed, with regard to further instruction, based on student performance on the measures provided. Because the lesson planning information in the teacher's guide has a sequence of procedures and plans to follow, many decisions are already made or suggested. A material framework, based on a detailed description of how to teach reading (provided in a given set of instructional materials), reduces the number of instructional decisions that a teacher must make.

Adopting a material framework typically means becoming familiar with the teacher's manual for a particular reading program and following its directions quite closely. Many new teachers begin with a material framework because they have little time to develop or modify their own plans for instruction. Their willingness to accept the decisions of a teacher's manual does not suggest the absence of careful evaluation or conscious decision making. Rather, the guidelines provided by a set of materials provide the basis for a teacher's specific instructional decisions following a material framework.

method framework
A framework used to teach reading; based on procedural steps for teaching and options for completing each step.

Other teachers make instructional decisions primarily from a **method framework.** These teachers have one or more methods they think are most appropriate for teaching reading, and they implement these methods as appropriate to their instructional goals. Instructional methods all include certain procedural steps as well as options that may be selected at each step. Thus, instructional decision making revolves around the procedural steps that are specified by a particular method, and teachers' instructional decisions are clearly laid out to conform to these steps. A method framework is, therefore, based on the procedural steps of one or more instructional methods and the options that may be selected at each step. After a teacher learns and relies on a set of methods to teach reading and these become the basis for instruction across a wide variety of situations, we say that *a method framework has been established.* Figure 1-1 presents an example of one type of method framework, a **directed reading-thinking activity (DRTA).**

directed reading-thinking activity (DRTA)
A method framework used to assist students in predicting outcomes and drawing conclusions; involves predicting, reading, and proving.

A method framework provides a general description of the steps to follow during instruction and a general indication of the activities that

FIGURE 1-1

A procedural outline for a directed reading-thinking activity

1. *Predicting.* During this first step ask students what they expect to find when they read. At the beginning ask questions like, "What might a story with this title be about? Why?" Later in a story ask questions like, "What do you think will happen next? Why?" Each student should form a prediction and be able to support it.

2. *Reading.* During this second step ask students to read up to a specified point in the story and check their predictions. They may read either orally or silently.

3. *Proving.* During this third step ask students to evaluate their predictions within the context of a discussion. Ask questions like, "Was your prediction correct? Why or why not?" At the end of the discussion begin the procedural cycle again, and have students predict what will take place in the next portion of the story. Continue in a similar fashion until students finish reading the story.

might be used at each step. Nevertheless, it is not usually tied to a specific set of materials. Instead, a method framework may be used with almost any set of materials, from selections found in published reading programs to selections written by teachers or provided by students. If the teaching procedures suggested by particular materials differ from a teacher's preferred method, then the teacher following a method framework would substitute the preferred method and appropriate activities.

Often teachers employ several different method frameworks, using each for different instructional purposes. For example, a particular method or set of methods might be preferred for teaching decoding skills; another combination might be preferred for teaching study skills. Some of the more frequently used method frameworks include directed reading activities, language experience activities, and activities associated with deductive and inductive instruction. These and other common method frameworks are presented in chapter 3.

A **literacy framework** is the most powerful and flexible of the three frameworks discussed here. It is what most effective teachers strive toward. A literacy framework is more abstract than either a material framework, where teachers follow the suggestions and decisions as found in a teacher's manual, or a method framework, where teachers follow the procedures and options specified as part of a particular teaching method. A literacy framework, based on an understanding of reading comprehension and response, requires answers to these questions:

Literacy framework
Beliefs about the components of reading comprehension and response, the way in which people read, and the way in which reading ability develops.

1. What are the components of the reading process? How does reading take place; how do we read?
2. How does reading ability develop? How do we learn to read?

Answers to these questions form a teacher's beliefs about reading comprehension and response, and influence why, what, and how we teach. Experienced, effective teachers often arrive at their literacy framework after becoming knowledgeable about a wide range of materials and methods—after being exposed to many materials and methods and drawing their own conclusions about how reading takes place and develops. A literacy framework allows a teacher to make instructional decisions by knowing which material and method to choose in order to address one or more students' instructional needs. A literacy framework thus incorporates the knowledge base of a material and/or a method framework.

Literacy frameworks are used in two major ways: first, to select appropriate materials and methods and second, to adapt methods and materials that are inconsistent with beliefs about reading comprehension. Thus, a teacher with a literacy framework might adapt the lesson plans and activities in a set of materials and might select several different methods to teach a reading lesson. Each choice or decision would be deliberate and

All students bring different backgrounds and experiences to any reading task and these experiences are enhanced through interacting with all types of texts.

reasoned and would be consistent with that teacher's explanation of how a person reads and how reading ability develops.

Given the relative difficulty and complexity of developing a literacy framework, why should it be preferred to a material or a method framework? Teaching from a literacy framework is preferable for at least five important reasons.

1. A literacy framework provides a clear sense of direction, especially as you decide how and when to modify instructional resources. All teachers adapt and supplement available instructional materials, and a literacy framework guides the necessary decision making.

2. A literacy framework provides more strategies for meeting individual needs and for working with diverse and challenged learners. Within material or method frameworks individual needs are met by altering the pace of instruction and/or the amount of practice. Within a literacy framework individual needs can also be met by altering instructional materials, methods, and even what is taught.

3. A literacy framework helps explain why certain decisions are made during reading instruction, whereas frameworks based on materials or methods simply tell teachers what to do. Knowing why something is being done will allow you to alter instruction for particular students more effectively and to evaluate the success of an instructional activity more accurately.

4. Literacy frameworks can be used in many more situations than frameworks based on materials or instructional methods. For example, specific material and method frameworks are often helpful only if a teacher's preferred methods or materials are those favored by the school district in which they are to be used. A literacy framework can be used in any instructional situation.

5. Literacy frameworks offer more flexibility in instructional decision making than either material or method frameworks. The illustration in Figure 1-2 indicates that teachers making decisions based on literacy frameworks choose from the full range of methods and materials. Teachers with method frameworks are somewhat less flexible but are able to choose any materials that are appropriate to their chosen method(s). But teachers with material frameworks are completely constrained by their chosen instructional materials.

Developing a literacy framework is more difficult than developing a material or method framework, partly because of the broad knowledge base required. Nevertheless, such wide-ranging knowledge certainly results in a more effective teacher, and knowing in advance that you will probably develop a literacy framework as you teach will facilitate that development. Knowing where you are going always makes the journey

FIGURE 1-2

An illustration of the inclusiveness of a literacy framework

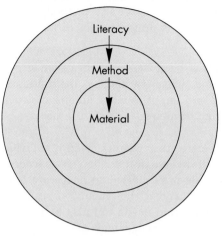

shorter and easier. Thus, learning about reading instruction from the perspective of a literacy framework should make your learning process more effective and efficient.

Decision Making and the Modification of Frameworks

Instructional frameworks are not static devices; they are, instead, modified as knowledge about materials, methods, and the reading process develops and changes. Teachers continually modify their frameworks according to what does and does not help children learn to read. Moreover, with adequate knowledge of the reading process—and their students—teachers can shift from one framework to another. Or they can use one framework predominantly, supplementing it with aspects of one or both of the other frameworks. Modification of instructional frameworks usually follows a cyclical routine, as described here and illustrated in Figure 1-3.

> *Step 1.* Teachers use frameworks to help them make instructional decisions. Teachers with a *material framework* generally follow the directions in a teacher's manual. Teachers with a *method framework* choose instructional activities for the various steps in a procedural outline. Teachers with a *literacy framework* select materials and methods consistent with their beliefs about how reading occurs and develops.

FIGURE 1-3

An illustration of the framework modification cycle

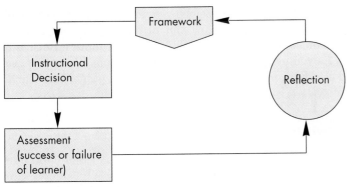

Step 2. Teachers evaluate the appropriateness of their instructional decisions. Successful activities are apparent in student performance, and both teachers and students share a feeling of accomplishment.

Step 3. Teachers reflect on their students' performance and on their instructional decisions.

Step 4. Teachers modify their frameworks based on the success or failure of instructional decisions. Those with a material or method framework tend to repeat successful activities the next time that lesson is taught; unsuccessful activities are dropped or modified. Teachers with a literacy framework find support for their beliefs in successful activities; unsuccessful lessons tend to alter beliefs about how reading occurs and develops.

Step 5. These confirmed or modified frameworks are used to make additional decisions, and the process repeats itself.

Figure 1-3 emphasizes the sequence of these steps. Assessment does not lead directly to instructional decisions. Instead, decisions are made by "filtering" the results of assessment through the framework as a result of reflection on what is noticed about students' growth and performance on tasks associated with instructional decisions.

The decision-making process described here is similar to the process used by researchers or scientists. Just as researchers use a theory to make predictions, teachers of reading use a framework to make instructional decisions. And as researchers test their predictions in an experiment, teachers evaluate the appropriateness of their instructional decisions. Finally, as researchers modify their theories based on the results of their experiments, teachers modify their frameworks based on the results of classroom lessons. Thus, although teachers are not true scientific researchers, they are involved in decision-making processes that share many similarities.

Frameworks are central to the decisions you will make as a teacher of reading. They reduce complexity, allow you to make decisions quickly, and most important, help you meet the challenges encountered in reading instruction. As you learn about ways to teach reading effectively, you will define and clarify your own framework, which will guide your teaching decisions.

WHAT ARE THE REWARDS?

Classroom teaching, particularly the teaching of reading, is not only challenging. It is also immensely rewarding. Good readers often forget how difficult it may have been to learn to read and how reading affects our everyday lives. We may also take for granted the many times our reading ability is used. Look around you right now. How many things need to be read? At home there may be a newspaper, TV guide, cereal box, or mail. At school there may be a bulletin board, posters, books, or class notes. Think of all the things you have already read so far today. If you view reading in the broadest terms, perhaps as making meaning from abstract symbols, then you may have read your watch, the morning paper, road signs, a map or some other set of directions, or the numbers and letters on a dollar bill. Reading touches all aspects of life.

It is also rewarding to know that reading ability influences our lifestyles positively. For example, teaching children to read well will be a key factor in determining their later employment opportunities. Reading can, moreover, positively impact depression and boredom, as well as provide role models and inspiration. It can answer our questions and give us directions. It can teach and transform, provide pleasure, and stimulate original thought. As a teacher of reading you will have a lasting impact on your students' personal and professional lives.

In school, reading cuts across every subject area. The ability to read a textbook, do research in the library, or read a teacher's notes on the chalkboard directly affects the quality of a student's learning. It is not surprising, then, that teachers and parents, as well as students, are greatly concerned that reading be effectively taught—and that teachers feel an immense sense of satisfaction as they see their students' growth in reading.

You will play a central role in helping children gain access to the pleasure and power of reading and thus will have a significant impact on their lives. Helping your students acquire needed skills and knowledge to develop into productive adults provides a feeling of reward and accomplishment that is rare in other professions. Perhaps it can best be described by one student, whose teacher made a number of instructional decisions that helped him enter the world of readers.

Darren's Reflections on Learning to Read

"You know the stories about parents who used to go through snowdrifts and walk ten miles to school? Well, I feel something like that! I used to have to get up early and ride the bus for what seemed like hours. And I know that lots of what we called "white kids" were doing the same. So my first grade wasn't anywhere close to my 'hood. And though I could (and still do) talk up a storm, I really wasn't much for reading. It's different now, but it wasn't important to me then. I remember Mom saying that my report cards and notes from the teacher would say that I needed to pay more attention.

I remember that I got more interested about halfway through the year. For one thing, Mom tells me she had a long conference with my teacher. But what I remember most was a book that my teacher started reading to us—*Charlotte's Web.* It was about a farm and pigs and spiders and animals, and I was a city kid, but the friendships in that story made me cry. There were a lot of people moving in and out of where Mom and I lived then, and my best friend had just moved away. That book really tore at me. I guess my teacher let Mom have it [the book], because she would read a bit to me, and we would talk about it every night.

My teacher would also find things for me to do that made more sense to me and that helped me read. Like I said, I talked a lot, and I also loved to draw. So I started drawing pictures and then writing down what they were about. And I got to talk more to my teacher, who would write down what I said and let me draw on those pages. My teacher put them in a notebook that I would take home and read to my Mom.

Looking back, I think that's what turned things around. The interest my teacher showed in me. Letting me do things that meant things to me, and taking the time to learn how I felt about things."

Comments from the Classroom

Judy Dill, first grade teacher
Because I have been teaching many years, I am often asked to explain how children learn to read. I try my best to explain that there is no one, prescribed way. Learning to read is a multifaceted process and, as each child is different with different abilities and learning styles, teachers must figure out what strategies work best with individual children.

One thing I have learned is that the most challenging part of teaching reading is to develop a love of reading. Children will not undertake the struggle to learn to read if they do not have a strong desire to do so.

A big key in getting children to learn to love reading is to tap into their interests. Obvious? Not always. It is easy to choose books you like and these are not always what children choose. As an example, this year my first grade class had a tremendous interest in dinosaurs. A science buff I am not. But we read books and poems and wrote songs about dinosaurs. Several children brought in models of dinosaurs and we researched their names and characteristics. The children then wrote and published their own stories and we all learned how fascinating these creatures are. And I was able to introduce some wonderful, enriching vocabulary including carnivore, herbivore, and paleontologist. My first graders loved learning these big words.

My advice to beginning teachers who want to open the world of reading for children is to ascertain where each child is developmentally. Then, match books to their interests—not yours. Be prepared to find that children's development and their interests will be as varied as flowers in a garden. The role of a teacher is to know what nourishment will allow each child to grow and flourish and how to nurture children so they blossom into good readers.

Source: Judy Dill teaches at Strong Elementary School in a consolidated school district in rural Maine. She served as director of a preschool for several years before moving on to teach kindergarten and then first grade for the past sixteen years. In a number of chapters in this text, Judy shares her perspectives on how teachers can facilitate literacy to help children emerge as readers and writers.

Major Points

- Reading ability is important. It is a key factor in the job opportunities and quality of life for each one of us.

- The teacher is a continual decision maker in the classroom, using observational skills to gather information with which to guide instruction.

- Reading is not a mechanical skill but is an interactive, problem-solving process. From this perspective the importance of reading and the teaching of reading will not become obsolete.

- A teacher's definition and perception of how one reads and how reading ability is developed determine how reading will be taught.

- Teaching reading to children in the elementary grades is one of the most rewarding tasks anyone can perform. Teachers of reading have the potential to help young children achieve one of their most important and exciting accomplishments.

1. Different teachers, using the same information about their students, often make different instructional decisions. How would you explain such differences?

2. Interview at least two teachers and two parents. Ask them (a) what they think reading is and (b) how important they think reading is now and will be in the future. Ask the teachers how their beliefs about reading and its importance influence their instructional decisions. Ask the parents what they would emphasize if they were teaching reading. What implications do any similarities or differences have for students and for teachers?

3. What are literacy frameworks and how are they modified? Which is the most powerful and flexible framework? Why?

Making Instructional Decisions

Aaron, I. E., Chall, J. S., Durkin, D., Goodman, K., & Strickland, D. (1990). The past, present, and future of literacy education: Comments from a panel of distinguished educators. Part I. *The Reading Teacher, 43,* 302–311.

Presents a discussion of trends in literacy and literacy education from various perspectives. The discussion continues in The Reading Teacher, 43, *370–381.*

Carroll, J. B. (1986). The nature of the reading process. In H. Singer & R. Ruddell (Eds.), *Theoretical models and processes of reading* (3rd ed., pp. 25–34). Newark, DE: International Reading Association.

Discusses the nature of reading. Points out that disagreement centers not on what is involved in reading but on the order of the steps that are involved.

Diehl, W. A., & Mikulecky, L. (1980). The nature of reading at work. *Journal of Reading, 24,* 221–227.

Discusses reading demands in different jobs. Points out how these differ from what is expected in school.

Further Reading

Guthrie, J. T. (1983). Where reading is not reading. *Journal of Reading, 26,* 382–384.
   Case studies of reading in 14 occupational settings.

Mason, J. A. (1992). Emergent literacy: Alternative models of development and instruction. In M. J. Dreher & W. H. Slayter (Eds.), *Elementary school literacy: Critical issues* (pp. 51–71). Norwood, MA: Christopher-Gordon.

   Discusses, in general terms, various reading models (process models, sociological models, cognitive models, and so on), and examines the instructional implications of each.

Pils, L. J. (1993). "I love you, Miss Piss." *The Reading Teacher, 46,* 648–653.

   An informative description of two first-grade students "at risk" of school failure and their growth in attitudes and abilities, with a focus on their teacher's influence.

Taylor, D. (1993). How do you spell *dream?* You learn—with the help of a teacher. *The Reading Teacher, 47,* 8–16.

   Presents an autobiographical account of school experiences and highlights the importance of teachers in children's lives.

References

Dechant, E. (1982). *Improving the teaching of reading* (3rd ed.). Englewood Cliffs, NJ: Prentice Hall.

Fingeret, A. (1983). A new perspective on independence and illiterate adults. *Adult Education Quarterly, 33,* 133–146.

Flesch, R. (1955). *Why Johnny can't read.* New York: Harper & Brothers.

Flesch, R. (1981). *Why Johnny still can't read.* New York: Harper & Row.

Goodman, K. S. (1976). Reading: A psycholinguistic guessing game. In H. Singer & R. Ruddell (Eds.), *Theoretical models and processes of reading* (2nd ed., pp. 497–508). Newark, DE: International Reading Association.

Harste, J. C. (1990). Jerry Harste speaks on reading and writing. *The Reading Teacher, 43,* 316–318.

Heath, S. B. (1980). The functions and uses of literacy. *Journal of Communication, 30,* 123–133.

Miller, P. (1982). Reading demands in a high-technology industry. *Journal of Reading, 26,* 109–115.

Rosenblatt, L. M. (1985). The literary transaction: Evocation and response. *Theory into Practice, 21,* 268–277.

Rosenblatt, L. M. (1994). The transactional theory of reading and writing. In R. B. Ruddell, M. R. Ruddell, & H. Singer (Eds.), *Theoretical models and processes of reading* (4th ed., pp. 1057–1092). Urbana, IL: Center for the Study of Reading.

Rosenblatt, L. M. (1988). *Writing and reading: The transactional theory* (Tech. Rep. No. 416). Urbana, IL: Center for the Study of Reading.

Rumelhart, D. (1994). In H. Singer & R. Ruddell (Eds.), *Theoretical models and processes of reading* (4th ed., pp. 864–894). Newark, DE: International Reading Association.

Samuels, S. J., & Kamil, M. L. (1984). Models of the reading process. In P. D. Pearson (Ed.), *Handbook of reading research* (pp. 185–224). New York: Longman.

Shanahan, T. (1990). Reading and writing together: What does it really mean? In T. Shanahan (Ed.), *Reading and writing together: New perspectives for the classroom* (pp. 1–18). Norwood, MA: Christopher-Gordon.

Stanovich, K. E. (1980). Toward an interactive compensatory model of individual differences in the development of reading fluency. *Reading Research Quarterly, 16,* 32–71.

Stanovich, K. E. (1986). Matthew effects in reading: Some consequences of individual differences in the acquisition of literacy. *Reading Research Quarterly, 16,* 360–407.

Strang, R., McCullough, C., & Traxler, A. (1961). *The improvement of reading* (3rd ed.). New York: McGraw-Hill.

CHAPTER

Developing a Literacy Framework

2

" . . . I think about reading differently now. I not only know what to do during reading instruction but, more importantly, I understand why I should do it. To me, this is the most important part of my preparation. My insights allow me to respond appropriately to each student as I work to support their learning . . ."

From the introduction to a student's final program portfolio in elementary teacher education.

Let us be very clear: there is no single *best* method for teaching reading. What appears to help students most is an insightful teacher, not a particular instructional practice; reading and children are both too complex for a single instructional practice to meet every instructional need. But what is an insightful teacher? An insightful teacher understands the nature of the reading process. An insightful teacher also understands how reading ability develops and knows how to draw upon many different methods to meet the unique needs of each child in the classroom. In short, an insightful teacher knows what to do and why it should be done. This chapter will help you develop the insights necessary to become an effective teacher of reading as you define your own literacy framework.

Chapter 2 includes information that will help you answer questions such as:
1. What is a literacy framework?
2. What are the components of reading comprehension and response?
3. How does one read?
4. How do children learn to read?
5. How can a literacy framework help me to make insightful decisions during reading instruction?

KEY CONCEPTS

affective aspects	interactive explanations
automaticity	metacognitive knowledge
decoding knowledge	reader-based explanations
discourse knowledge	specific skills explanations
emergent literacy	syntactic knowledge
holistic language learning explanations	text-based explanations
integrated explanations	vocabulary knowledge

WHAT ARE MY CURRENT BELIEFS ABOUT READING COMPREHENSION AND RESPONSE?

What should I teach my students about reading today? How should I teach it? As a classroom teacher, you will face these and many other important decisions. Each will be fundamentally influenced by the beliefs you have about reading and learning to read (Richardson, Anders, Tidwell & Lloyd, 1991). These beliefs can be a powerful tool for developing insights about your students and your teaching (Goodman, 1992, 1986; Spiegel, 1993). It is important for you to become aware of your beliefs about reading and to think about their appropriateness.

What are your beliefs about reading? To identify your current beliefs about how one reads, read the 15 statements in Figure 2-1. Mark the 5 statements in Figure 2-1 that best represent your current ideas about this issue. Then identify your beliefs about how children learn to read by looking at the 15 statements in Figure 2-2. Mark the 5 statements in Figure 2-2 that best represent your current ideas about this second issue. *Do this now before you read any further.* Think about your choices as you read the remainder of this chapter. At the end of this chapter, you will be asked to come back and determine how the choices you made here can help to define your literacy framework.

FIGURE 2-1

Beliefs about how one reads

1. When children cannot recognize a word during reading, a useful strategy is to help them try to sound it out.
2. Children's knowledge about the world is more important during reading than their ability to sound out words correctly.
3. To understand what they read, it is important that children be able to read most words correctly.
4. Before young children read about something, it is helpful for them to have an experience similar to that depicted in the reading passage.
5. When we ask children a question about a story they have read, usually there is one answer that is better than others.
6. When children cannot recognize a word during reading, a useful strategy for them is to read the sentence again, look at the first letter of the difficult word, and make a guess.
7. In the early grades, teachers should spend roughly equal amounts of time showing students how to sound out unfamiliar words and how to make reasonable guesses about unfamiliar words.
8. Reading is really the interaction between what an author intended to mean and the meaning a reader brings to that text.
9. Teachers should encourage each child to have a different interpretation and response to a story.
10. When we think about comprehension, it is important to keep in mind that the meaning an author intended is usually what we should encourage children to take away from their reading experience.
11. Teachers should always find out what children know about the topic of a story before asking them to begin reading.
12. Generally speaking, there is usually one interpretation of a story that the reader and writer both share.
13. During the reading process, guesses are often as important as accurate recognition of words.
14. Authors and readers understand a story in their own ways.
15. When children cannot recognize a word, a useful strategy for them is to read the sentence again and make a guess.

FIGURE 2-2

Beliefs about how children learn to read

1. It is important for teachers to provide clear explanations about significant aspects of reading.
2. Students should receive many opportunities to select and read materials unrelated to school learning tasks.
3. Reading instruction should include both teacher-directed and student-directed learning opportunities.
4. Students learn the most about reading when they engage in reading experiences that are personally meaningful, accomplish an important function, and are self-directed.
5. An effective reading program is one in which both students and teachers have a clear understanding of the crucial skills of reading that need to be learned.
6. Reading assessment should closely match the skills that have been developed in class.
7. Some children seem to learn about reading best when they determine their own literacy experiences; others seem to learn best through more structured experiences designed by a teacher.
8. Children should be read to frequently while they are young so that they acquire a feeling for what reading is like.
9. Teachers should create literacy experiences that are personally significant to students and provide them with authentic reasons to read and write.
10. Teachers need to consider regularly which children will benefit from more student-directed literacy experiences and which children will benefit from more teacher-directed literacy experiences.
11. Teachers should have a minimal list of literacy learning goals for each student to accomplish during the year.
12. Much of what children learn about literacy can be attributed directly to what a teacher has taught in the classroom.
13. Both students and teachers should be allowed to define the nature of literacy learning in classrooms.
14. Children learn much about literacy by watching their parents at home.
15. No single approach to literacy learning will fit each child perfectly. Teachers need to modify their programs to meet their child's unique needs.

DEFINING LITERACY FRAMEWORKS

literacy framework
Beliefs about how one reads and how children learn to read that may be used to develop insights and inform instructional decisions about reading.

A **literacy framework** may be used to organize your beliefs and inform instructional decisions about reading. Most important, a literacy framework provides the insight about reading instruction that will make you a more effective teacher as you work to help each of your students become more enthusiastic and proficient readers. A literacy framework helps you understand why you teach reading as you do.

TABLE 2-1

How each portion of a literacy framework may be used to inform instructional decisions about reading

Issues and beliefs in a literacy framework	Instruction decisions that are informed by your beliefs about each issue
1. How does one read?	**What should I teach?**
One reads by relying largely upon prior knowledge to help interpret the text.	I should teach the prior knowledge components of reading comprehension and response.
One reads by recognizing individual words.	I should teach those components that help children recognize individual words.
One reads by both relying upon prior knowledge and recognizing individual words.	I should teach both prior knowledge and word recognition components.
2. How do children learn to read?	**How should I teach?**
Children learn to read by engaging in purposeful, self-directed reading experiences in authentic contexts.	I should create learning environments for children to explore and develop their own, more holistic, literacy insights.
Children learn to read by receiving direct instruction in specific skills.	I should teach specific skills with direct instructional practices.
Children learn to read by directing their own reading experiences and by direct instruction in specific skills.	I should create learning environments for children to explore their own literacy insights and also teach specific skills when it is appropriate.

A literacy framework helps you to develop insights about two important issues in reading:

1. How does one read?
2. How do children learn to read?

By developing insights about these issues, you are in a powerful position to assist children. Table 2-1 summarizes how each portion of a literacy framework provides important insights and informs instructional decisions about reading. The first portion of your literacy framework, your beliefs about how one reads, informs you about *WHAT* children need to learn and *WHAT* you need to teach. Several different theories for how one reads have been proposed that explain why some components of the reading process are more important than others. Each theory has different consequences for what you should teach. For example, a teacher who believes that readers bring their own meaning to a passage would teach those components that are related to background knowledge. On the other hand, a teacher who believes that reading is a process of recognizing individual words would teach those components related to word recognition. Or, some teachers believe that readers bring their own meaning to a reading passage at the same time that they need to recognize individual words; these teachers would look for ways to develop all components of the reading process.

The second portion of a literacy framework, your beliefs about how children learn to read, informs decisions about *HOW* to teach reading. Several different theories have been proposed to account for the development of reading proficiency (McKenna, Robinson, & Miller, 1993; Weaver & Shonhoff, 1984), and each theory has different consequences for how reading is taught.

For example, a teacher who believes that students learn best when they are engaged in purposeful and self-directed literacy experiences wants to create many meaningful and functional opportunities for stu-

A literacy framework, which includes beliefs about how a person reads and how reading ability develops, helps a teacher of reading decide both what and how to teach.

------------------------ **EXPLORING DIVERSE POINTS OF VIEW** ------------------------

Because they are directly accountable to parents, school boards, and district superintendents, principals often discourage teachers from implementing their individual literacy frameworks during reading instruction. Instead, principals sometimes will require all teachers at a school to teach from a single point of view, using a single set of materials. They argue this makes it easier for students to make the transition from one grade to another because each teacher uses the same approach with the same materials. Others argue that every teacher teaches differently anyway, even with the same set of materials, and that it would be better to empower teachers by valuing the different insights each teacher brings to reading instruction. They also point out that children are much more flexible than we give them credit for and can adapt easily to different learning approaches. Finally, they suggest that teachers need to be able to respond to individual students' needs and that it is important to be flexible enough to do this. To what extent do you think that a teacher's individual literacy framework should be sacrificed for consistency in a school reading program? Do you think that a school where different literacy frameworks are used will confuse children about the nature of reading as they move from classroom to classroom? How would you resolve the tension between consistency and diversity in literacy frameworks?

dents to read. This type of teacher believes that students learn best in an **inductive** fashion. As a result, this teacher is likely to use method frameworks that permit students to direct many of their own reading and learning experiences. On the other hand, a teacher who believes that students learn best when they acquire specific reading skills wants to provide direct instruction in a number of specific skills. This type of teacher believes that students learn best in a **deductive** manner. As a result, this teacher is likely to use method frameworks that emphasize direct skill instruction. Finally, some teachers believe that students learn best by self-directing their reading experiences and by being taught specific aspects of reading. These teachers look for ways to integrate those experiences by using many different types of method framework.

inductive
Refers to learning that results from a student's self-discovery; uses experiences to generate a rule or principle.

deductive
Refers to learning that is explicit and teacher-directed; begins with a rule or principle and then demonstrates how it is applied.

Both parts of a literacy framework are important for you to consider. Your beliefs about how one reads will guide decisions about *what* to teach. And your beliefs about how students learn to read will help you decide *how* to teach. Your knowledge of each issue will empower you to make reasoned and insightful decisions that benefit your students.

UNDERSTANDING THE COMPONENTS OF READING

Before we consider the two issues that comprise your literacy framework, let's take a look at what the components of the reading process are. Most scholars and teachers agree that the eight components illustrated in Figure 2-3 contribute in a major way to reading comprehension and response (Anderson, Hiebert, Scott, & Wilkinson, 1985). While people may disagree about which components are most important, most would agree

FIGURE 2-3

Major components of reading comprehension and response

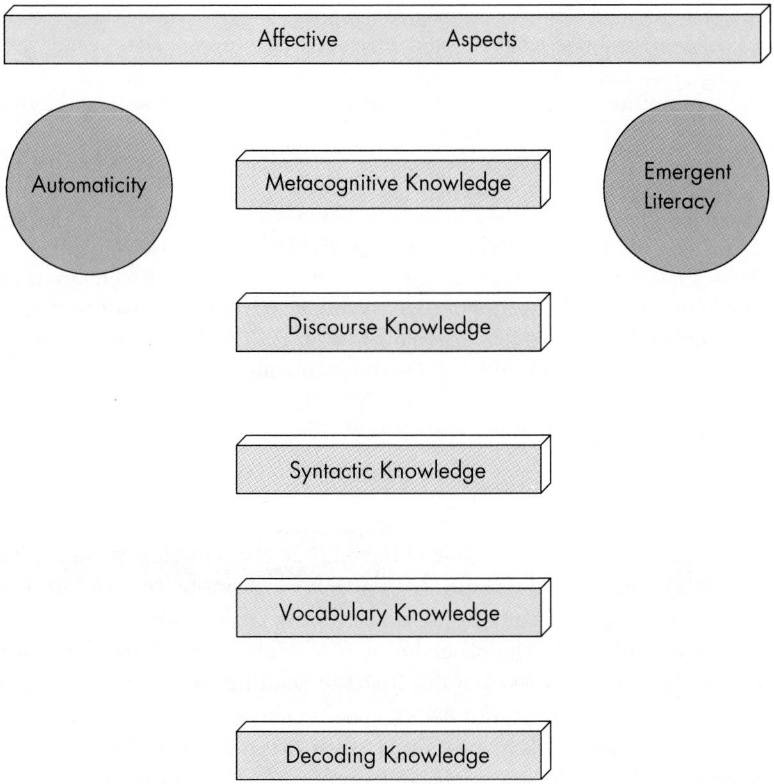

that these components define most of what we need to know in order to become proficient readers.

Much of reading instruction consists of activities designed to develop the components in Figure 2-3. For example, teachers often discuss the meanings of unfamiliar words before asking students to read a selection. Those teachers are helping students develop vocabulary knowledge, one component of the process, in order to assist the students' comprehension of the upcoming story or article. Similar instructional activities are used to develop each of the other components.

Affective Aspects

affective aspects
Elements such as interest and attitude that increase motivation and facilitate comprehension and response.

Traditionally, many teachers have assumed that reading instruction was limited to teaching important skills. For these teachers, students' success at reading was measured by how well they mastered a number of specific skills. Such a view, however, fails to recognize the importance of the **affective aspects** of the reading process. Reading is not just a cognitive process; it is also an affective process (Holdaway, 1979; Madden, 1988; Oldfather, 1993). Affective aspects of the reading process include a reader's general attitude and interest about reading. Students' attitude and interest about reading play an important role in the way they approach reading experiences and in the way they respond to them. For example, a child who views reading as a boring activity, unrelated to the more exciting things in life, is not likely to respond very well to an opportunity to read. Moreover, this child will not comprehend or respond to a passage as well as someone who views reading as an exciting activity and becomes engaged in almost any reading experience. All readers comprehend and respond better when they are interested in reading, and the difference is especially noticeable among less proficient readers. As teachers, we need to make certain that we make reading an exciting experience for everyone. Often this is done by providing students with opportunities to select their own reading experiences. By encouraging students to choose selections that are personally interesting, teachers seek to increase their students' attitude and interest about reading in general.

Providing time to browse in the library and to check out books can positively impact affective aspects of reading.

While it is clear that affective aspects include your students' general attitudes and interests about reading, it is also clear that affective aspects include a reader's attitude and interest toward a specific reading passage. A student, for example, may be very interested in reading a mystery about the appearance of a ghost and not be interested in reading an informational article about life in Australia. As a result, this student's comprehension and response would be much greater in the first selection. As teachers, we need to allow opportunities to pursue individual reading interests but we also want to expand those interests. By guiding students to read about new topics and by making those topics exciting, teachers also seek to develop a wider variety of reading interests. Teachers use activities such as the ones found at the beginning of Figure 2-4 to increase students' affective aspects.

Metacognitive Knowledge

metacognitive knowledge
A type of knowledge important for reading that includes the strategies used during reading and comprehension monitoring.

A second component that we use during reading is **metacognitive knowledge.** Metacognitive knowledge includes an awareness of the strategies necessary to read effectively (Baker & Brown, 1984; Palincsar & Ransom, 1988). As we read, we use many different strategies. For example, you may have decided to start reading this chapter by reading the summary at the end to get a sense of its content. Or perhaps you leafed through the pages, looking at the sequence of section headings. You may even have decided to read this page again if you got to the end of it and did not understand parts of what you had read. All of these strategies reflect your strategic knowledge.

Strategic knowledge is very useful for comprehension; it allows you to acquire information efficiently. It is not usually efficient to begin reading a chapter like this at the beginning. Before they read, good readers usually preview the material they will encounter and often begin by reading the summary at the end. Good readers also use many other strategies as they read. They stop to look at a figure or a table, sound out an unfamiliar word, reread a troublesome sentence, think about what they have read, and underline important information. Each of these decisions involves the use of strategic knowledge.

In addition to strategic knowledge, metacognitive knowledge also includes knowing how and when to monitor your understanding of a passage. This is referred to as *comprehension monitoring*. Readers monitor their comprehension to ensure the material they are reading makes sense. Comprehension monitoring allows the reader to check the text against a developing understanding of its meaning. It prevents the reader from reaching the end of a passage and being unable to remember what was read.

Thus, metacognitive knowledge is usually thought to include two elements: strategic knowledge and what most people call comprehension monitoring. Together these factors enable readers to take charge of their reading and be certain that the information they acquire makes sense.

FIGURE 2-4

Sample activities designed to support the development of affective aspects and metacognitive knowledge

Developing Affective Aspects

 Storybook Character Days. At different times during the year, designate a day as Storybook Character Day. Encourage your students to come dressed as their favorite character in a book they have recently read. Come dressed as a character yourself. Have a contest to see who can identify the greatest number of characters. Encourage the youngsters to talk about their characters and the books from which their characters come. Such an activity will increase interest in reading and will lead students to books they might not have considered reading before.

 Book Talks. At the beginning of every week, take five to ten minutes to introduce several new books to your students. You may wish to bring these from your own library, your local library, or your school's library. As you introduce each book, talk about it as if you were trying to "sell" it to your students. Tell them the title, the author, the general plot of the story, and something special about the book or author that will interest your students in reading the book (e.g., "If you are really interested in books about outdoor adventures, this is the book for you!"). After you have introduced all of the books, set them in a visible location in your room such as your reading corner.

Developing Metacognitive Knowledge

 Sharing Reading Strategies. As you engage students in reading experiences, periodically ask them what they did as they read. This might happen, for example, when you ask students a question about something in the story. After someone answers the question, ask them how they figured out the answer. Sharing reading and interpretation strategies is important because this type of knowledge is usually hidden to others.

 Think Alouds. Periodically, model your own reading strategies in a think aloud. To conduct a think aloud you should begin reading a passage and then share aloud each of your thoughts as you are reading. These might be questions you have about what is going to happen next, surprise at something happening in the story, or strategies that you use to monitor your understanding. Think alouds help your students to see what is happening inside your head as you read. Encourage students to conduct a think aloud as well.

The development of metacognitive knowledge is usually thought to be a later-developing skill (Harris & Sipay, 1990). Metacognition requires readers to step back from their reading and consider their own reading process, a hard task for young children who often struggle just to recognize the next word or understand the next sentence. Teachers use activities such as the ones in the second half of Figure 2-4 to teach metacognitive knowledge.

Discourse Knowledge

Discourse knowledge is also very important as we read. Discourse knowledge is knowledge about how different language forms are organized like a business letter, a memo, a newspaper article, or a story. Discourse knowledge tells you what kinds of things to expect while you are reading a familiar form. Consider, for example, what happens when you read the first four words of a book that begins, "Once upon a time. . . ." If you read a book that began in this fashion, your discourse knowledge would allow you to recognize many things. You would know, for example, that this is probably a fairy tale, not a chapter in a social studies book. Because you are familiar with the discourse structure of a fairy tale, you would also know that the location of this story is likely to be a kingdom "long ago and far away." In addition, you would know that there is apt to be a prince and princess as central characters, as well as a king and queen. Finally, you would know that there would probably be some conflict that the hero or heroine will resolve and that there will be a happy ending, perhaps with a message for young children. You can see how discourse knowledge is very important to reading. Knowing the discourse structure of a passage you are reading tells you many things about what you are likely to find in that passage.

Discourse knowledge often receives greater instructional emphasis at higher grade levels, as students encounter a wider variety of written forms. Teachers will sometimes teach discourse knowledge as described in Figure 2-5.

Syntactic Knowledge

In addition to affective aspects, metacognitive knowledge, and discourse knowledge, readers also use **syntactic knowledge** during reading. Syntactic knowledge refers to the knowledge of word order rules that determine meaning within sentences. The knowledge of sentence syntax, or word order, is crucial to the comprehension process as readers derive meaning from individual sentences (Irwin, 1986).

You can see the importance of syntactic knowledge for comprehension by doing an experiment with children at different age levels. Write the following sentence on the chalkboard and read it to children who are about five years old.

David, John's father, went outside.

Then ask children how many people went outside. Most five-year-olds will tell you that two people (David and John's father) or even three people (David, John, and father) went outside. Now do the same thing with ten-year-olds. Most ten-year-olds, because they have the appropriate syntactic knowledge, will tell you that only one person went outside. Ten-year-olds are usually familiar with the way in which an appositive phrase clarifies the meaning of the noun that directly precedes it, even if they do not know the label for this syntactic structure.

FIGURE 2-5

Sample activities designed to support the development of discourse and syntactic knowledge

Developing Discourse Knowledge

Teaching the Characteristics of a Fable. Read one fable aloud each day for several consecutive days. Discuss each fable. After students have listened to a number of fables, ask them to help you list the characteristics that are common to all. They may respond, for example, with the following observations: animals are the main characters, the animals talk and act like people, there is usually a lesson (moral) at the end of each story, the fables did not really happen. Write these observations on the board. Read, or have students read, another fable to see whether the same structural elements also appear in it. Discuss the ones they noticed. Finally, have students write or dictate a fable themselves, being sure to incorporate the structural elements of this type of writing.

Teaching the Discourse Structure of Newspaper Articles. Explain to students that most newspaper articles are written to inform readers about important current events. Explain that this form of writing usually tells who, what, when, where, and why. Write these words on the chalkboard. Read two short articles together, identifying each of these elements (who, what, when, where, and why) in the articles and underlining them. Provide students with a short article and have them underline each type of information on their own. Now divide the class into groups and provide each with a headline. Have each group write an appropriate newspaper article, including each type of information. Have them use a computer if one is available. Have one student from each group share the results with the class. Post the results on your bulletin board.

Developing Syntactic Knowledge

Conducting a Style Study. Help your students become familiar with the writing style of an outstanding author. Read a book together by this author. As you read, look for the syntactic characteristics of this author's style. It may be that the author often uses a sequence of descriptive adjectives or participial phrases to evoke more complete images in the mind of the reader. Perhaps your author uses the word "and" frequently during conversations to make these seem more natural and consistent with the way people speak. It may be that the author uses very short and compact sentences to paint a precise picture of what took place. Or perhaps the author uses a semicolon frequently. Find one very common syntactic characteristic and have students discuss why they think the author used this feature. Then have students respond to a short writing task that allows them to try using this same feature in their own writing. Afterwards, have students share their work in small groups. After each student shares a piece of writing, encourage students to make at least one positive comment about the writing that was shared.

Exposure to the language patterns that appear in children's literature increases students' understanding of syntactic knowledge.

Sometimes syntactic knowledge enables you to determine the grammatical function of a word and, as a result, its meaning and pronunciation. For example, consider your ability to read and understand the following sentence:

Sarah will *lead* the miners to the vein of *lead.*

In this sentence, syntactic knowledge enables you to determine the difference in meaning and pronunciation between two words that are spelled exactly the same but appear in different sentence positions. Syntax indicates that the third word (*lead*) is a verb meaning "to direct" and is pronounced "leed." It also determines that the last word (*lead*) is a noun meaning "a heavy metal" and is pronounced "led."

Children's oral language ability is fairly well developed when they come to school at five or six years of age. Nevertheless, a number of complex syntactic patterns are unfamiliar to most children, and they need to develop an understanding of how those patterns affect meaning. Understanding more complex syntactic patterns becomes especially important as readers mature and as their reading selections contain more complicated types of sentence structures. Teachers often use activities such as the last one in Figure 2-5 to help students develop new insights about syntactic knowledge.

Vocabulary Knowledge

Another component that is very important during the reading process is **vocabulary knowledge.** Vocabulary knowledge includes two types of knowledge: 1) the knowledge readers have of word meanings and 2) the knowledge readers use to determine the meanings of unfamiliar words from the surrounding context. Both elements are essential to the reading process, for we must understand the meanings of most of the individual words we read if we hope to understand an entire passage. Consider this first sentence in a brief passage:

> Joan's problem is with her ethmoid.

Unless you know the meaning of the final word in this sentence, you cannot understand the sentence. Your knowledge of word meanings is crucial to understanding what you read. This is one aspect of vocabulary knowledge.

Sometimes, however, the meaning of a word is not known but a reader is able to determine the meaning from surrounding information, or context. The context of the second sentence in this brief passage can help you determine the meaning of *ethmoid:*

> Joan's problem is with her ethmoid. She broke this bone at the point where the nose joins the skull.

The other words in this passage, not your knowledge of the word *ethmoid,* probably helped you discover that this word refers to a bone connecting the nose and the skull. Thus, knowing how to use context is a second element of vocabulary knowledge.

Helping students develop vocabulary knowledge is important at all grade levels (Harris & Sipay, 1990; Johnson & Pearson, 1984). It is particularly important as children explore less familiar subject areas that use specialized vocabularies. Before students read an article about the developmental stages of a butterfly, for example, the teacher might wish to show students how to use context to determine the meanings of words like *chrysalis, pupa,* and *metamorphosis*. This will support students as they seek to understand the article. Activities such as the first one described in Figure 2-6 might also be used to support the development of vocabulary knowledge.

Decoding Knowledge

Decoding knowledge is the knowledge readers use to determine the oral equivalent of a written word. When we sound out an unfamiliar word

vocabulary knowledge
The knowledge that readers have of word meanings; includes the ability to use context to determine word meanings.

decoding knowledge
The knowledge that readers use to determine the oral equivalent of a word.

FIGURE 2-6

Sample strategies to support the development of vocabulary knowledge and decoding knowledge

Developing Vocabulary Knowledge

A Synonym Tree. Make a synonym tree in your classroom and have students look for words that are similar in meaning to the words on your tree. On a bulletin board put up the outline of a large tree made from construction paper. Cut out blank word cards in the shape of a leaf. Write challenging words on the word cards (one per card). Then pin each card on the tree. As students discover synonyms in their reading, have them write them on blank word cards and pin them to the original words on the tree so that students can see the appropriate synonym pairs.

Developing Decoding Knowledge

Using an Inductive Method Framework. Use an inductive method framework to teach students that *-ake* usually represents the sound "ache." Inductive instruction allows students to induce a rule or principal from a set of data and then provides them with practice opportunities.

1. *Provide examples of the rule.* Present riddles in which the answers rhyme with *make* and end in *-ake*. For example, "I'm thinking of a word that rhymes with *make* and is something you eat at a party" (cake). "I'm thinking of a word that rhymes with *make* and is something that crawls in the grass" (snake). As students guess each riddle, write the answers on the board until you have four or five words that end in *-ake: cake, snake, rake, lake, bake.*
2. *Help students discover the rule.* Help students see that all of the words on the board end in *ake* and sound like "ache." Use the words on the board to help students induce the decoding generalization: the letters *-ake* usually represent the sound "ache."
3. *Provide guided practice.* Help students apply this generalization to read other, similarly spelled words such as *take, fake,* or *wake.*
4. *Provide independent practice.* Offer independent practice that allows students to use this generalization. This activity may include the reading of a short literary selection containing the *-ake* pattern or a writing experience where this pattern is likely to appear.

Make a Base Book. Cut ten or twelve strips of oaktag or posterboard about 2" long. Cut one strip 5" long. Use a paper punch to punch holes in each strip aligning the strips one on top of the other with the longest strip on the bottom. Fasten the strips together with a ring clip. On the longest strip, write a phonemic base such as -ake, -ong, -at, -ate, and so on. On the shorter strips write a variety of beginning sounds, single letters, and consonant blends. By spacing the letters carefully, students can flip the shorter strips to sound out rhyming words.

in order to recognize it, we are using decoding knowledge. Sometimes decoding knowledge is important for comprehension and response; at other times it is not. Decoding knowledge is important when recognizing the sound of a word can help a reader identify its meaning. This frequently happens for beginning readers, who know the meanings of many words they hear but are less familiar with the printed version of those words. Thus, knowing how to sound out a common word enables a beginning reader to determine its meaning. Nevertheless, decoding knowledge is not important when a word's sound does not help a reader identify the word's meaning. For example, just knowing how to decode an unfamiliar word like *taligrade* is, for most of us, probably not an aid to understanding its meaning.

Developing decoding knowledge is almost always included in instructional programs. It is an important part of beginning reading instruction (Adams, 1989; Anderson, Hiebert, Scott & Wilkinson, 1985; Chall, 1983; Cunningham, Hall & Defee, 1991). Teachers use activities such as those in the section of Figure 2-6 to develop decoding knowledge and help children recognize individual words.

Automaticity

Automaticity is also important in any explanation of how we read. Automaticity describes situations where we perform a complex activity without paying attention to any of the component parts of that activity. Consider, for example, the physical movements of a concert pianist during a performance. Playing a piece of music requires many complex sequences of movement. Proficient pianists have learned how to perform these movements automatically without attending to any of the components, such as finger movement. We say that concert pianists have developed automaticity with respect to their finger movements during a performance because they don't even think about this part of their activity. Similar explanations may be given to other complicated activities such as solving a long division problem, throwing a football, hitting a golf ball, or driving a car. In each, the person performs a complex task without attending to the components of that task.

Learning each of these complex tasks, though, requires you consciously to attend to each of the component parts at the beginning. You think about your grip on a football, keeping your left arm straight in a golf swing, or which direction you move the turn signal for a right-hand turn. Gradually, though, you learn to perform each action without attending to each of the components. That is, you develop automaticity with respect to each of the component parts.

Reading is also a complicated process like playing a piano or driving a car. As such, it requires attention to the many components of the process when one is first learning how to read. As one practices the many aspects of this process, these components become increasingly automatic. As you

automaticity
The ability to perform a complex task without attending to any of the components of that task.

become more automatic at reading, you are able increasingly to attend to the developing meaning of the material you read (Samuels & Eisenberg, 1981; Stanovich, 1980). You are also able to respond to what you have read with increasing complexity. Occasionally, you have to direct your attention to one of the lower levels to correct an error made during reading, to rethink what you have read when something doesn't make sense or when you are unfamiliar with a word you encounter. Most of your attention as a mature reader, though, can focus on your comprehension and your response, not on the components of the reading process. This explains why we can read without thinking about what we are doing.

Looking at reading as the development of automaticity will provide you with insights about a number of things in your classroom. You will understand why a student forgets to spell an easy word correctly when they are writing quickly, trying to capture the essence of a thought before they forget it. This child's limited attention is being devoted to the content of the writing, not the form. You will know that you can encourage this child to go back later and attend to the spelling and punctuation as they revise the piece. You will also understand why some beginning readers attempt to recognize the oral equivalent of a written word by sounding out individual letters. You will know that these readers do not yet have automatic decoding skills and seek ways to assist them. Understanding reading as an automatic process will provide you with many insights about your students.

Emergent Literacy Aspects

emergent literacy
A recent view of reading as a continuously emerging and evolving ability that results from children's experiences and experiments with language in literacy contexts.

A final component important to understanding the nature of the reading process is **emergent literacy.** Emergent literacy refers to a developmental point of view that assumes reading is a continuously emerging and evolving ability (Teale & Sulzby, 1986, 1989). According to an emergent literacy view, each of us, from a preschool-aged child to an adult, continues to emerge in our ability as a reader. Each of us is constantly learning something new about the reading process, though this will differ according to where we are in our development. You, for example, may have developed a richer understanding about the nature of reading from the information in this chapter. A preschooler who is read to at home each night may be discovering some of the more rudimentary aspects of reading such as how to hold a book, the names of several letters, or the left-to-right sequence in our writing system. Each of us, however, is always growing as a reader.

An important consequence from this point of view is that each child can benefit from learning about reading, so long as reading instruction is defined appropriately for that child's developmental level. For example, all youngsters will benefit from being read to no matter how young they are. Moreover, all youngsters beginning school are ready to engage in reading experiences such as read alouds or language experience stories,

FIGURE 2-7

Using predictable texts to support the development of emergent literacy

Reading Predictable Texts. Read predictable texts aloud to your young students. Predictable texts are story books that contain a repeated element—a sentence pattern, a rhyming pattern, or some other pattern—that makes the language highly predictable. Examples include *The Cat in the Hat, The Little Red Hen, Henny Penny, The House that Jack Built, The Gingerbread Boy,* and *Brown Bear, Brown Bear.* When you read predictable texts aloud to your students, they will quickly notice the repeated pattern. As they do, occasionally leave out the repeated pattern and have students complete it for you. Afterwards, place that book out on a table for your students to enjoy. Even your weakest readers will be able to read some of these books on their own as soon as they discover the predictable pattern.

regardless of whether they are ready for more demanding types of reading experiences. As teachers, an emergent literacy view suggests that we need to engage all of our students in appropriate types of reading experiences so that each may grow and develop as a reader.

As we consider how to create developmentally appropriate types of reading experiences for students it is important to understand the notion of **scaffolding,** or scaffolded instruction. Scaffolding refers to the intentional support provided to students as we engage them in literacy tasks they might not be able to accomplish on their own (Meyer, 1993). Scaffolding has been observed in studies of parents and children interacting in home settings (Bruner, 1983). Here, parents were found to provide temporary support for their children on challenging tasks. For example, parents might hold their child's hand as they showed them how to hold a crayon for writing. Or, parents might read a story aloud at bedtime to provide their very young child a sense of what books and reading are all about. This temporary support appears very important for assisting readers as they accomplish more challenging tasks for the very first time. This, perhaps, is why reading experiences at home are so helpful to preschoolers. As parents read a book aloud to their children they provide the necessary support to engage them in a literary experience. We need to keep these ideas in mind as we seek to support all readers who are emerging in their development. Activities with books containing a repeated sentence pattern, as those shown in Figure 2-7, may be used to develop emergent literacy among very young readers.

scaffolding
Temporary support provided to students that enables them to perform a task they might not normally be able to do on their own.

WHICH COMPONENTS ARE MOST IMPORTANT DURING READING?

Because of extensive work conducted by researchers since the late 1800s, most people today agree that affective aspects, metacognitive knowledge, discourse knowledge, syntactic knowledge, vocabulary knowledge, decod-

FIGURE 2-8

Explanations about how a person reads

Reader-Based Explanations	Interactive Explanations	Text-Based Explanations
Prior knowledge components are most important.	All components are important.	Decoding is the most important component.

ing knowledge, automaticity, and emergent literacy are all a part of the reading process. There is, nevertheless, disagreement over how important each component is to reading comprehension and response. Some believe that background knowledge components such as metacognitive knowledge, discourse knowledge, syntactic knowledge, and vocabulary knowledge are the most important components in the reading process. As a result, these individuals spend most of their time teaching the background knowledge that readers use to help them comprehend and respond. Others believe that recognizing individual words is central to the reading process so decoding knowledge is thought to be most important. As a result, these individuals spend most of their time teaching decoding ability, especially in the early grades. Still others value all components of the reading process relatively equally. These individuals spend time helping children learn about all of the components of the reading process. Whatever your beliefs are, or come to be, about the most important components of reading, you can see how your beliefs will influence decisions about *what* you will teach about reading.

To a large extent, your beliefs about the most important components of reading reflect one of several theoretical explanations about how one reads. These theoretical explanations and their association with the various components of reading can be seen on the continuum in Figure 2-8. We have presented these beliefs on a continuum because a wide variety of beliefs exist at various points along this continuum. Where your beliefs fall on this continuum depends upon the emphasis that you assign to the components of background knowledge or to decoding knowledge. As you read more about each theoretical explanation, remember the five statements you selected at the beginning of this chapter in Figure 2-1 and try to determine your own beliefs about how a person reads and which components are most important to teach.

Reader-Based Explanations of How One Reads

Some individuals believe that the components of background knowledge are most important: metacognitive knowledge, discourse knowledge, syntactic knowledge, and vocabulary knowledge. These people adopt a **reader-based explanation** of how a person reads (Goodman, 1993, 1992; Smith, 1988). They believe that readers do not sound out every word they read; they believe, instead, that readers use background knowledge and the evolving meaning of a text to make predictions about upcoming words. According to this view, readers first make a prediction about the meaning of a word and only then perceive the word's letters. Thus, reader-based explanations assume that (1) meaning exists more in what a reader brings to a text than in the text itself; (2) reading is based more on predictions of upcoming words than on the translation of words into sounds; and (3) readers begin by using knowledge sources associated with background knowledge (metacognitive, discourse, syntax, and vocabulary) and only then apply decoding knowledge. According to reader-based explanations, readers continuously predict upcoming words and, when necessary, look at the letters in those words to see whether their predictions were correct.

One way to understand this type of explanation is to consider how we might read a popular romance novel. Before reading, we probably have clear expectations about the story structure. Our expectations of the plot are strong, and most of the words are familiar. We do not even notice the words, let alone the letters in those words, at the end of some sentences (e.g., "Courtney gracefully dove into the swimming ____"). We fly through the story, skimming the incidental portions to get to the more interesting sections. Indeed, we may finish the book in a single night.

Another way to understand this explanation for how one reads is to look at Figure 2-9, which shows how you might read the first sentence of a story according to a reader-based explanation. In this example you have started to read the beginning of a fairy tale—"Once upon a time, a princess kissed a . . ."—and you are now ready to read the word *frog.*

Initially, affective aspects are likely to determine your first response to this story. Perhaps the title or the cover illustration catches your attention and generates an interest in reading the story. While reading the opening sentence, strategic knowledge directs you to think about how this sentence might end and what the final word might be. Several expectations are then generated from discourse knowledge: first, this story is probably a fairy tale. Moreover, the beginnings of most fairy tales contain information about the main characters. And because a princess is about to kiss someone, you expect the second character to be mentioned next.

Expectations from discourse knowledge limit your expectations from syntactic knowledge: you expect a noun, the recipient of a kiss. These, in turn, limit expectations from vocabulary knowledge. The word must belong to a finite set of nouns that are potential main characters in a fairy tale and are likely to be kissed by princesses. This set includes kings, queens, and princes. It also includes frogs, if you are familiar with the princess-kisses-a-frog-and-finds-a-prince pattern of some fairy tales.

reader-based explanation
The belief that people read by using background knowledge to predict upcoming words and make meaning.

FIGURE 2-9

A reader-based model of comprehension and response

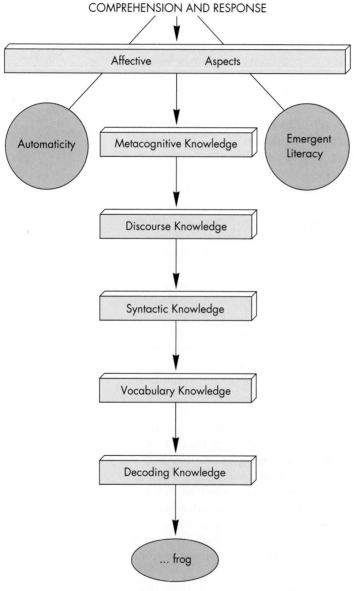

COMPREHENSION AND RESPONSE

Affective   Aspects

Automaticity

Metacognitive Knowledge

Emergent Literacy

Discourse Knowledge

Syntactic Knowledge

Vocabulary Knowledge

Decoding Knowledge

... frog

Step 1: Affective aspects determine a reader's initial response and interest in reading this passage.

Step 2: While reading the first sentence, strategic knowledge directs the reader to think about how this sentence might end and what the final word might be.

Step 3: After reading the beginning of this sentence, discourse knowledge leads to the expectation that this is a fairy tale.

Step 4: Given the syntactic structure of this sentence and the expectation that this is a fairy tale, you expect to find a noun and a recipient of a kiss, who will be a main character.

Step 5: Only a limited set of meanings fit previous discourse and syntactic constraints: king, queen, prince, frog. You expect to find *frog* as you know another version of this fairy tale.

Step 6: Because the meaning is likely to be "frog," decoding knowledge tells you to expect the sequence of letters: f r o g.

Step 7: You analyze the text and find the letters f r o g. You conclude that the meaning of the first sentence is, "Once upon a time, a princess kissed a frog."

Finally, vocabulary knowledge limits your expectations from decoding knowledge. You analyze the text for the graphic representation of one of the expected nouns, find the initial *f* in *frog,* and conclude that *frog* is the final word without even analyzing the other letters. Sometimes you may have such strong expectations that you do not even look at any letters in a word. Instead, you continue reading until some evidence in the story indicates that your prediction was wrong. In any event, you continue to read by using background knowledge and the evolving meaning of the text to make additional predictions about upcoming words.

People who believe that components such as affective aspects, metacognitive knowledge, discourse knowledge, syntactic knowledge, and vocabulary knowledge are most important tend to adopt more of a reader-based explanation for the process of reading. If you think that meaning is more in what the reader brings to a text than in the text itself, you think children need to develop useful sources of prior knowledge to bring to the reading experience. As a result, you spend instructional time helping students develop these components of prior knowledge.

Text-Based Explanations of How One Reads

Other people believe that decoding knowledge is more important than any other component. These people adopt a **text-based explanation** of how one reads (Gough, 1993). They suggest that a person reads by decoding, or sounding out, the words on a page. According to text-based explanations, readers translate print into sounds to uncover the meaning that exists in a text. Text-based explanations assume that (1) meaning exists more in the text than in what a reader brings to a text; (2) reading consists of translating printed words into sounds and sounds into meanings; and (3) readers begin by using the lowest knowledge source (decoding) and only then sequentially apply higher knowledge sources (vocabulary, syntactic, discourse, and then metacognitive knowledge).

text-based explanation
The belief that people read by translating print into sounds as they determine the meaning in a text.

One way to understand this type of explanation is to think about how many of us might read unfamiliar words in a Russian novel like *Roskolnikov, Ekaterinburg,* or *Fedorachovna.* Many of us would find ourselves attempting to sound out these difficult Russian names, hoping that hearing them would help us to remember them. Such an approach, translating the print into sounds, supports a text-based explanation.

Another way to understand a text-based explanation is to return to our earlier example of the fairy tale and look at Figure 2-10, which shows how a young child might read this story according to a text-based explanation.

According to a text-based explanation, a child first uses decoding knowledge to determine the oral equivalent of this word. Once the sound /frog/ has been determined, the child uses that sound to search vocabulary knowledge and locates two meanings: (1) "a small green amphibian" and (2) "of or pertaining to a frog" (e.g., frog legs). Both meanings are

FIGURE 2-10

A text-based model of comprehension and response

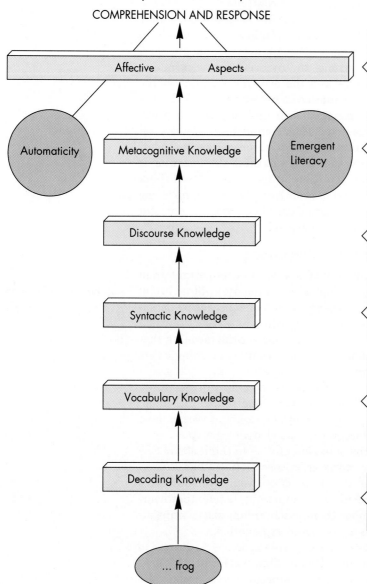

COMPREHENSION AND RESPONSE

Step 6: Affective aspects guide the initial response. Because this reader enjoys fairy tales, the reader begins to look forward to what will happen next.

Step 5: Monitoring comprehension from metacognitive knowledge, the reader decides the first sentence makes sense. Strategic knowledge directs the reader to the next sentence.

Step 4: Discourse knowledge informs the reader that this is the beginning of a fairy tale about a princess and a frog.

Step 3: Knowledge of syntax rules out the second meaning. The sound /frog/ is determined to represent a noun that means "a small green amphibian."

Step 2: The sound /frog/ is used to search vocabulary knowledge for an associated meaning. Two meanings are found: a) *noun* — a small green amphibian b) *adjective* — of or pertaining to a frog.

Step 1: Using decoding knowledge, the reader perceives the printed word *frog* and determines its oral equivalent: /frog/.

passed on to syntactic knowledge, which decides that the word *frog* is being used as a noun, not an adjective. Consequently, the first meaning of the word is chosen. At this point discourse knowledge concludes that the selection is a fairy tale because the beginning is consistent with that story type. Metacognitive knowledge is then activated: comprehension monitoring lets the child know that all this makes sense; and strategic knowledge directs attention to the first word of the next sentence, to see what is going to happen next. Finally, affective aspects will probably influence the initial type of response this child has to this story. If this child enjoys fairy tales and frogs, the child will probably become more engaged in the story to see how it ends. If this child thinks that fairy tales are uninteresting or is already familiar with the story, the child may become less engaged. Thus the reading process continues, moving always from lowest to highest knowledge source.

People who believe that decoding knowledge is the most important component of the reading process tend to adopt more of a text-based explanation for how one reads. If you think that children need to acquire proficiency in determining the oral equivalent of written words, you also think that meaning is more in the text than in the prior knowledge that readers bring to a text. The major task of a reader, according to these teachers, is to recognize the words in a passage. As a result, you spend much instructional time helping children develop extensive decoding knowledge.

Interactive Explanations

Some individuals think all components are important to reading. These people adopt an **interactive explanation** of how a person reads (Anderson, Hiebert, Scott, & Wilkinson, 1985; Rumelhart, 1976; Stanovich, 1980). They suggest that we read by simultaneously sounding out words at the same time we form expectations from vocabulary, syntactic, discourse, and metacognitive knowledge. An interactive explanation assumes that (1) meaning is located both in the text and in the meaning that readers bring to the text, (2) reading consists of both translation and expectation, and (3) reading proceeds as each knowledge source interacts simultaneously with the print on the page and with other knowledge sources. Thus, reading comprehension is a product of the interaction between text and reader.

One method of understanding an interactive explanation is to consider your own reading behavior. When your background knowledge is extensive about a topic, reading is easy and you are able to anticipate the words that come next. In this case, the meaning that you bring to the page closely matches the meaning that exists on the page. However, when your background knowledge is limited, reading is somewhat difficult and you may attempt to sound out unfamiliar words such as

interactive explanation
The belief that people read by simultaneously translating print into sounds and using background knowledge to predict upcoming words as they read.

> ┌───┐
> **OPPORTUNITIES TO CELEBRATE DIVERSITY**
> └───┘
>
> Each of us has a slightly different literacy framework that, together with our classroom experience, helps us to make instructional decisions. If teachers are diverse in terms of their beliefs, children are also very diverse as learners. After working with children most people are struck by how unique individual children are in the way they act, in the way they communicate, and in the way they learn. As you face issues about what to teach during reading, having an interactive explanation will allow you to adjust the content of your teaching to meet individual needs. It allows you to see how some children seem to benefit more when their prior knowledge components are supported and other children benefit more when decoding knowledge is supported. This is not always possible with the more extreme positions illustrated in Figure 2-8.

metacognitive to see whether their oral equivalent might help you recall their meaning. Readers who shift quickly back and forth between predicting words and decoding them are reading in an interactive fashion.

Consider once again, this time from an interactive perspective, how a young reader is apt to read the final word in the sentence, "Once upon a time, a princess kissed a. . . ." Readers who lack prior knowledge of the topic will read the word *frog* in a text-based fashion, as depicted in Figure 2-10. Children who are unfamiliar with fairy tales and who have never heard the princess-kisses-a-frog-and-finds-a-prince pattern must depend more on decoding knowledge to recognize this word. On the other hand, readers with an extensive prior knowledge of the topic will read the word *frog* in a reader-based fashion, as depicted in Figure 2-9. Children familiar with fairy tales and with the princess-kisses-a-frog-and-finds-a-prince pattern can generate accurate predictions. Consequently, they will depend more on metacognitive, discourse, syntactic, and vocabulary knowledge and will use decoding knowledge only to check predictions. For all readers the reading process is strongly influenced by the nature of their affective aspects. Their response and engagement in the story will depend largely upon their interest in the topic. As you can see, from an interactive perspective, the nature of the reading process varies from text to text and from word to word, depending on the extent of a reader's background knowledge.

Teachers who believe that all components of reading are equally important tend to adopt more of an interactive explanation for how one reads. The major task of a reader, according to these teachers, is to develop knowledge in a broad range of components that can assist the reading process. As a result, these teachers spend instructional time helping students develop all of the components of the reading process.

A Historical Perspective

The issue of how a person reads was very controversial during the 1970s. These three theories were developed to explain how people read and to explain which components were most important to teach. At the beginning of this period, people's beliefs tended to fall at either end of the continuum illustrated in Figure 2-8. Most had either strong text-based or strong reader-based explanations for the reading process. Over time the issue has become less divisive. People have concluded increasingly that neither a text-based nor a reader-based explanation is sufficient to explain how we read. At times, especially with unfamiliar or difficult texts, the evidence suggests that we read more by sounding out words; at other times, especially with familiar or easy texts, we read more by making predictions about upcoming words. Only an interactive explanation seems to account for both types of evidence. As a result, many people today believe that it is important to help students develop each component of reading.

HOW DO CHILDREN LEARN TO READ?

The second part of a literacy framework consists of your beliefs about how children learn to read. Such beliefs will largely determine how you will teach reading and which method frameworks you will use. Of the different explanations that exist concerning how children learn to read, the three most common are shown on the continuum in Figure 2-11. At one end of this continuum are explanations based on the idea that students best learn to read as they engage in purposeful, functional, and holistic reading tasks in authentic contexts. At the other end are explanations based on the idea that students best learn to read when they are taught specific reading skills. Somewhere in the middle are explanations based on the idea that students best learn to read through an appropriate combination of holistic reading tasks in authentic contexts and instruction in specific skills.

FIGURE 2-11

Explanations of how children learn to read

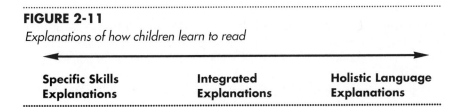

| Specific Skills Explanations | Integrated Explanations | Holistic Language Explanations |

Notice in Figure 2-11 that we again describe the three most common beliefs on a continuum. It is clear that a wide variety of beliefs exist at various points along this continuum. As you read about each theoretical

Teachers with a holistic language learning perspective believe that children should be presented with authentic reading experiences, a social context in which others are also engaged in literacy tasks, and a functional need to communicate in writing.

explanation, remember the five statements you selected at the beginning of this chapter in Figure 2-2 and try to determine your own beliefs about how children learn to read.

Holistic Language Learning Explanations

holistic language learning explanation
The belief that reading ability develops as students engage in holistic, purposeful, and functional reading tasks in authentic contexts and induce important literacy principles.

One theory about how students learn to read is a **holistic language learning explanation.** A holistic language learning explanation is based on two assumptions: (1) students learn best as they engage in holistic, purposeful, and functional reading tasks in authentic contexts; and (2) students learn best inductively. Reading comprehension and response are perceived to be holistic and unified entities that are difficult to break down into a fixed set of separate skills. Moreover, students are believed to induce most of the components required for reading during their self-directed learning experiences with print and their observations of others interacting with print in authentic reading contexts. Inductive learning is favored.

Supporters of a holistic language learning explanation contend that reading comprehension and response are not easily separated into a hierarchy of distinct skills (Clay, 1980; Goodman, 1993; Goodman & Goodman, 1979; Holdaway, 1979). They argue that comprehension and response are holistic processes and that separating them into isolated skills gives young children inappropriate information about the nature and purpose of reading.

Advocates of a holistic language learning explanation assume that written language skills (reading and writing) and oral language skills (speaking and listening) develop similarly (Weaver & Shonhoff, 1984). There is fairly clear evidence that oral language skills develop in an inductive fashion, as a result of meaningful and functional language interactions (Bruner, 1983; Vygotsky, 1978). Children induce the rules of oral language as they listen to it and speak it during social interactions, not as a result of direct instruction in specific skills.

Advocates of a holistic language learning explanation believe that written and oral language ability develop similarly as both are language processes. According to this explanation, children should be presented with authentic reading experiences, a social context in which others are also engaged in literacy tasks, and a functional need to communicate in writing. If these conditions exist, children will induce all the necessary generalizations they need to become proficient readers. Reading, like oral language, should develop in a natural manner.

Specific Skills Explanations

A **specific skills explanation** of how students learn to read is based on two assumptions: (1) reading ability develops to the extent that students master specific reading skills; and (2) reading ability develops to the extent that these skills are taught directly by the teacher in an explicit, frequently deductive, fashion. Thus, students are assumed to learn best when the development of reading skills is carefully directed by the classroom teacher.

specific skills explanation
The belief that reading ability develops as students master the specific skills taught directly and deductively by a teacher.

Teachers with a specific skills explanation of how children learn to read often organize instruction around an explicit set of reading skills, sometimes sequenced according to level of difficulty. Easier reading skills are usually taught first; harder reading skills are taught last. A teacher with a specific skills explanation might target skills such as these:

1. Students will develop familiarity with different forms of narratives including: fables, fairy tales, science fiction, contemporary realistic fiction, and fantasy.
2. Students will develop a wide range of response patterns in relation to both narrative and informational prose.
3. The student will develop effective strategies for learning the content of informational articles.

Such skills are often taught separately from the reading of stories and articles. Reading experiences are viewed either as opportunities to practice the specific skills that have been taught or as opportunities to develop a positive attitude toward and interest in reading.

In addition, a specific skills explanation assumes that reading ability develops best when students are taught in a direct, frequently deductive, manner. Thus, children are expected to learn best when teachers provide direct instruction on each separate skill.

Integrated Explanations

integrated explanation
The belief that reading ability develops as students engage in purposeful, functional, and holistic experiences with authentic texts and, acquire specific reading skills as a result of direct instruction.

Teachers who develop an **integrated explanation** believe that both holistic language learning and specific skills explanations are, alone, too limited to explain the nature of reading development among diverse students. These teachers believe that a specific skills perspective confines students too narrowly to the mastery of isolated reading skills, often in inauthentic reading contexts. Although some students benefit from this structure, others become bored and lose interest in reading. On the other hand, a holistic language learning perspective places too much responsibility on students for their own development. Although some students benefit from this freedom, others get lost in the opportunities for self-development.

An integrated explanation combines aspects of both of the previous explanations. It makes these assumptions: (1) reading ability develops to the extent that students engage in purposeful, functional, and holistic experiences with authentic texts and, at the same time, acquire specific reading skills; and (2) reading ability develops as a result of both teacher-directed, deductive experiences and student-generated, inductive experiences.

Teachers following an integrated explanation of reading development include elements from both holistic language learning and specific skills perspectives. They provide students a rich written-language environment, examples of others engaged in authentic literacy tasks in rich social contexts, and a functional need to communicate in writing. Moreover, they provide students direct instruction in reading skills as these appear necessary to support children's development.

A Historical Perspective

There is far less agreement about how children learn to read than there is about which components of reading are most important to teach. In fact, the question of how children learn to read is currently one of the more controversial issues in the field of reading instruction. Individual explanations can be found at nearly every point on the continuum. A specific skills perspective has long had a strong influence on the field of reading; traditionally, students have been thought to learn best when presented with a skill-based curriculum taught directly by a teacher. The composition of most published reading programs tends to reflect the assumptions of this perspective. It is also found in instructional recommendations that emphasize direct teaching in specific skill areas (Bauman & Schmitt, 1986).

During the past decade, however, evidence has demonstrated that children acquire literacy skills inductively through holistic, purposeful, and functional reading tasks in authentic contexts (Goodman, 1992; Harste, Woodward, & Burke, 1984). As a result, many teachers have associated themselves with what has come to be known as a **whole language** point of view, and this movement is powerfully influencing the development of new instructional materials and methods.

whole language
A philosophy about literacy learning favoring the use of authentic literacy contexts rich in social interactions to support students' literacy learning.

The term *whole language* is, however, quickly coming to represent many things to many people. Some (McKenna, Robinson, & Miller, 1993) have pointed out that the term suffers from a lack of clear and consistent definition. For some it represents an extreme position on the continuum illustrated in Figure 2-11, characterized by classrooms rich in literacy experiences and students who induce from these self-directed experiences the generalizations necessary to learn to read. The term *whole language* represents for others the middle of the continuum, characterized by classrooms that combine students' self-directed learning experiences with direct instructional experiences whenever students experience difficulty in a particular aspect of reading. Whole language appears to mean many things to many people. In each case, though, is the assumption that students will acquire important literacy insights from self-directed experiences with authentic reading and writing experiences that take place in rich social contexts. In some cases this will also include some teacher-directed learning experiences around specific skills or strategies. In others, it will not.

USING A LITERACY FRAMEWORK TO INFORM INSTRUCTIONAL DECISIONS

Developing a literacy framework is not easy; reading comprehension and response are abstract and complex concepts. You may have discovered this as you read this chapter, the most challenging one you will face in your book. Nevertheless, a literacy framework is a practical tool that can provide assistance with the instructional choices you will need to make as a teacher of reading. It also provides you with important insights about your students' development and the nature of the literacy tasks they face in your classroom.

Understanding the Components of Reading Comprehension and Response

Knowing how each component contributes to comprehension and response will help you understand the complexity of the reading process. It will also provide you insight about what your children know and what they need to know about reading. For example, knowing the nature of syntactic knowledge is useful when youngsters misunderstand the meaning of an appositive phrase. Your knowledge about this component will help you to understand why a student misunderstands a sentence like *Millie, Sandy's mom, went outside.* Knowing about the nature of discourse knowledge is useful when students encounter their first social studies textbook. Your knowledge about this component will help you to understand a student's confusion when this student asks you, "Is this a true story?" You will know that the student has confused the informational piece they have read with a narrative. Knowing about the nature of metacognitive knowledge is useful when students are able to decode words fluently but are unable to recall what they have read because they have failed to monitor their comprehension.

Consider, finally, the writing sample from a five-year-old child in Figure 2-12. Some would see little connection between the writing in this picture and the picture itself. Knowing the importance of decoding knowledge to young readers, however, and knowing that the child read this as, "The cat and the person" would provide you with many insights into what this child knows about reading. It is clear that this child already understands the left-to-right progression of print in English. Moreover, you would know that this child has a clearly developed sense of initial consonant sounds because the *C* represents the word "cat" and the 9 is a reversed *P* and represents the word "person." Finally, you would know that this child has acquired the important insight that written symbols represent concepts from our oral language.

You can see that understanding the components of the reading process provides teachers crucial insights into the nature of their instructional program, the nature of their students' knowledge, and the nature of their students' needs. Understanding the components of reading comprehension and response assists you in recognizing why you teach each component. We will be talking more about each of these components in the chapters to follow.

FIGURE 2-12

A writing sample from a five-year-old student who read her writing as "The cat and the person"

"The cat and the person."

Developing Insights About What to Teach

Your beliefs about the most important components of the reading process will inform decisions about what to teach and emphasize during reading instruction. Text-based, reader-based, and interactive beliefs lead to different conclusions about what to teach during reading. These relationships are summarized in Table 2-2.

Teachers with a reader-based explanation of how a person reads stress the acquisition of metacognitive, discourse, syntactic, and vocabulary

TABLE 2-2

Instructional consequences of different beliefs about how one reads

Beliefs	Instructional Consequences: What to Teach?
Reader-based	Metacognitive, discourse, syntactic, and vocabulary knowledge are thought to be most important and are emphasized. Prior knowledge components are taught most.
	Less time is spent developing decoding knowledge.
Interactive	Approximately equal attention is devoted to all knowledge sources: metacognitive, discourse, syntactic, vocabulary, and decoding knowledge.
Text-based	Decoding knowledge is emphasized, especially at younger levels.
	Less time is spent developing the elements of prior knowledge: metacognitive, discourse, syntactic, and vocabulary knowledge.

knowledge, believing that adequate higher-level knowledge leads to accurate expectations of upcoming meaning and richer response patterns. As a result, instruction emphasizes activities like those described earlier under metacognitive knowledge, discourse knowledge, syntactic knowledge, and vocabulary knowledge. Any activity designed to help students generate expectations is especially valued, such as the reading of predictable texts.

Teachers with a text-based explanation stress the acquisition of decoding knowledge more than any other type of knowledge, believing that strong decoding skills lead to successful translation of text meaning. Instruction, especially for younger readers, emphasizes activities that help students to recognize individual words.

Teachers with an interactive explanation of how a person reads devote relatively equal attention during instruction to the acquisition of metacognitive, discourse, syntactic, vocabulary, and decoding knowledge. These teachers believe that readers need to develop accurate expectations of upcoming meaning, richer response patterns, and automaticity with decoding processes. All activities described earlier in this chapter might be used by these teachers.

Developing Insights About How to Teach

Your beliefs about how children learn to read best will inform classroom decisions about how to teach reading. Holistic language learning, specific skills, and integrated explanations lead to quite different conclusions about how best to support students' development as literacy learners.

TABLE 2-3

Instructional consequences of different beliefs about how children learn to read

Beliefs	Instructional Consequences: How to Teach?
Holistic Language Learning	Student-directed reading experiences and inductive learning are emphasized.
	Reading experiences always take place in the context of authentic social contexts and always with authentic reading materials.
	Popular method frameworks include those that allow for inductive learning and much student direction.
Integrated	Both holistic language learning and specific skill perspectives are valued. Both inductive and deductive learning are used.
	Reading experiences take place in the context of authentic social contexts and with authentic reading materials. Specific skills are taught when needed, often in mini-lessons.
	Popular method frameworks include those that allow for inductive learning and much student direction and at the same time allow for specific skill instruction where needed.
Specific Skills	Teacher-directed instruction in specific skills and deductive learning are emphasized.
	Specific skills, often organized in terms of difficulty, are frequently taught and then practiced during reading activities.
	Popular method frameworks include those that allow for deductive learning and specific skill instruction.

These relationships are summarized in Table 2-3. Teachers with a holistic language learning explanation of how children learn to read provide opportunities for students to see literacy skills in action, always in the context of authentic social contexts and always with authentic reading materials. These would include literature selections chosen from the school or classroom libraries. Reading skills are not frequently taught in a direct fashion. Instead, teachers develop classroom experiences where self-generated, inductive learning is emphasized.

Teachers with a specific skills explanation provide students with direct instruction on progressively more difficult reading skills. These teachers will often use published reading series that provide for skill instruction. These teachers will also organize their classroom reading program around a set of reading skills that need to be mastered during the year.

Teachers with an integrated explanation of how children learn provide opportunities for students to direct their own reading and writing experiences. In addition, these teachers give direct instruction on specific skills as students require such support. These often take place in mini-lessons with individuals or small groups around a particular skill or strategy. These teachers tend to shift between teacher-directed and student-directed learning experiences as appropriate to meet particular student needs.

What Is My Literacy Framework?

A literacy framework can be extremely useful when you need to make instructional decisions. It provides insight into the reading process, helping you understand the different components of reading and supporting reasoned decisions about what to teach and how to teach it. Figure 2-13 shows how beliefs about the most important components of the comprehension and response process interact with beliefs about how children learn best about literacy. Because both issues are represented by a continuum, innumerable combinations are possible. What is important to remember is that each teacher of reading represents one of those combinations—reflecting a position on each continuum.

Let us now determine what your literacy framework is like at this point in your development. Look back at the statements you marked in

FIGURE 2-13

A matrix illustrating the range of different types of literacy frameworks that are possible in response to two major issues: How does one read? and How do children learn to read?

	How does one read?		
	Reader-Based Explanations	Interactive Explanations	Text-Based Explanations
Holistic Language Learning Explanations			
Integrated Explanations			
Specific Skills Explanations			

How do children learn to read?

Figures 2-1 and 2-2. Figure 2-1 contains statements reflecting different beliefs about which components of reading are most important. Some statements assume that prior knowledge components are most important. These are statements 2, 4, 9, 11, and 15. If the majority of your statements came from this category, your beliefs are most consistent with a *reader-based theory* of how one reads. You will probably be most interested in helping students develop the ability to bring prior knowledge to a passage and use this to comprehend and respond during reading.

Other statements assume that decoding knowledge is most important during reading. These are statements 1, 3, 5, 10, and 12. If the majority of your statements came from this category, your beliefs are most consistent with a *text-based theory* of how one reads. You will probably be most interested in helping students develop the ability to accurately recognize words and use this to comprehend and respond during reading.

A third set of statements assumes that both prior knowledge and decoding components are important during reading. These are statements 6, 7, 8, 13, and 14. If the majority of your statements came from this category or if you have a diverse set of statements, your beliefs are most consistent with an *interactive theory* of how one reads. You will probably be most interested in helping students develop proficiency with all components of reading. Your responses to Figure 2-1 should help you develop beginning insights about *what* you think is most important to teach about reading.

Now look at your responses to the statements in Figure 2-2. Figure 2-2 contains statements reflecting different beliefs about how children learn to read best. Some statements assume that children learn best in purposeful, functional, and holistic experiences in authentic reading contexts. These are statements 2, 4, 8, 9, and 14. If the majority of your statements came from this category, your beliefs are most consistent with a *holistic language learning theory* of how one learns to read. You probably believe that students learn best when they are engaged in meaningful and self-directed literacy experiences, and you will be most interested in creating purposeful and functional opportunities for students to read. You will probably find method frameworks most useful if they support students in directing their own literacy experiences in rich social contexts and with authentic reading experiences.

Other statements assume that children learn best when taught specific skills in a direct fashion. These are statements 1, 5, 6, 11, and 12. If the majority of your statements came from this category, your beliefs are most consistent with a *specific skills theory* of how one learns to read. You will probably be most interested in directing students' literacy experiences and teaching specific skills. You will find method frameworks most useful if they provide these types of teaching opportunities.

Some statements assume that children learn best in purposeful, functional, and holistic experiences in authentic reading contexts when

OPPORTUNITIES TO CELEBRATE DIVERSITY

It is important to recognize diversity in our students and take advantage of this for instruction. It is equally important, though, to recognize diversity in our colleagues, other teachers. Each of us has a slightly different literacy framework which, together with our classroom experiences, informs us about what we should teach and how we think that children will learn this information best. We need to respect other teachers' beliefs on these two fundamental issues that define the nature of reading instruction. To impose your own beliefs on other colleagues is to deny them the right to develop their own insights based on their own classroom experiences. Once we begin this process, we immediately communicate to colleagues that their insights are not valued, something that we find inconsistent with effective instruction and something that would be similar to requiring everyone to teach each day from the same page in the same book. Argue with colleagues about what is most important, challenge others to support their beliefs by describing effective instructional episodes, and question others about why they have their beliefs—but always respect others for the beliefs they have so long as they can articulate these beliefs clearly and support these beliefs with evidence and experience. Your own insight will increase as a result of these discussions.

taught specific skills at appropriate moments. These are statements 3, 7, 10, 13, and 15. If the majority of your statements came from this category or if you have a very diverse set of statements, your beliefs are most consistent with an *integrated theory* of how one learns to read. You will probably be most interested in helping students to direct their own literacy experiences in rich social contexts, using authentic reading experiences. You will also be interested in directly teaching some components of literacy when the need arises. You will find method frameworks most useful if they provide both types of opportunities.

Comments from the Classroom

Nikki Robinson, sixth grade teacher

When I first began teaching, I believed that there was a magic moment when most six- and seven-year olds were "ready to read." As I gained more experience, I never doubted the magical power of reading, but I discovered that children's individual differences required more of me than just waving the letter-sound relationships of the alphabet in front of the classroom like a magic wand.

My first year in the classroom, I taught second grade. Many of my decisions were based on keeping one step ahead of the children and surviving each day until 3 o'clock. Because the other teachers (many with years of experience) relied on basal readers and phonics workbooks, I decided I should too. Actually, looking back, it wasn't really a conscious decision—the books were there and my principal required me to use them. Was I an effective teacher? I wasn't sure. Most of my students could read and understand what they read during their reading groups. Some students still struggled with letter-sound relationships. A few actually seemed to read for pleasure during their limited free time. (Another decision: not much free time or I'd lose control!)

Through the years, I have come to realize how both my beliefs and experiences inform my teaching decisions every day. My personal experience has shown that children come to school with different backgrounds and strengths. I decided it was my responsibility to learn a variety of ways to teach, not just rely on the basal reading program. While having a complete and comprehensive program put together by experts worked for many students, it didn't work for everyone. Talking to the parents of the students who came to me as fluent readers, I discovered that the parents themselves really enjoyed reading, had lots of books available at home, and reported that their children loved to be read to from the time they were very young. By then I had my own daughter, and I knew these parents were on to something.

How did this new belief affect my teaching? I started to read aloud to my class every day. I encouraged them to read their favorite stories again and again during time I set aside for "reading for pleasure." My experience allowed me to be more comfortable with less structure to the school day without fear of losing "control"of the children. My belief that reading aloud was a key to motivating reading for pleasure informed my decision to allow children time to enjoy books. I no longer believed that marching together through the basal reading program was the only way children would learn to read fluently and with understanding. There's more than one path to the magic kingdom.

Source: Nikki Robinson has been teaching for twenty-three years in a variety of grade levels but is currently assigned to a sixth grade classroom in a large suburban elementary school in Columbus, Ohio. She explains that continually seeking formal education and practicing the strategies she learns had refined her teaching techniques. She feels that the longer she spends time in the classroom the more intuitive her decisions become.

Major Points

- A literacy framework is a personal perspective toward reading that helps you to develop insights about two important issues: 1) How does one read? and 2) How do children learn to read?

- The reading process involves a number of important components: affective aspects, metacognitive knowledge, discourse knowledge, syntactic knowledge, vocabulary knowledge, decoding knowledge, automaticity, and emergent literacy. Reading instruction promotes the development of these components through carefully designed learning activities.

- Beliefs about how one reads exist along a continuum ranging from reader-based to text-based, with interactive explanations somewhere near the middle.

- Beliefs about how children learn to read exist along a continuum ranging from holistic language learning to specific skills, with integrated explanations somewhere near the middle.

- Developing a perspective about how one reads will help you decide *what* to teach about reading. A perspective about how children learn to read will help you decide *how* to teach reading.

- Interactive and integrated beliefs allow you to accommodate diverse student needs in your classroom. Other types of belief require that all students receive similar types of literacy experiences.

Making Instructional Decisions

1. Identify your beliefs about how one reads on the continuum in Figure 2-8. Use the statements that you selected in Figure 2-1 to help you identify your beliefs. Describe the consequences of your beliefs for decisions about *what* you will teach during literacy lessons. Which activities described in this chapter would you use? Why?

2. Identify your beliefs about how children learn to read on the continuum in Figure 2-11. Use the statements that you selected in Figure 2-2 to help you identify your beliefs. Given your beliefs, how will you teach reading? What will characterize the nature of classroom reading experiences you develop?

3. If you believe that children have different reading needs and that it is important to individualize the nature of reading instruction, which set of beliefs will be most useful? Why?

Goodman, K. (1992). I didn't found whole language. *The Reading Teacher, 46*(3), 188–199.

A pioneer of whole language describes the theoretical, historical, and social context of his beliefs.

Goodman, K. (1986). *What's whole in whole language?* Portsmouth, NH: Heinemann.

Describes the nature of the whole language movement and the assumptions behind this perspective. Also provides examples of whole language programs in operation.

McKenna, M. C., Robinson, R. D., & Miller, J. W. (1993). Whole language and research: The case for caution. In D. J. Leu and C. K. Kinzer (Eds.), *Examining central issues in literacy research, theory, and practice:* Forty-second Yearbook of the National Reading Conference, pp. 141–152. Chicago: National Reading Conference.

Reviews the research supporting whole language *instructional practices. Points out that the term* whole language *has not yet been defined clearly enough to allow us to evaluate this point of view systematically.*

Spiegel, D. L. (1992). Blending whole language and systematic direct instruction. *The Reading Teacher, 46*(1), 38–47.

Describes ways to combine both holistic language learning approaches and specific skill approaches in an integrated classroom reading program. The article shows how this more integrated approach leads to gains in both students' and teachers' learning.

Swift, K. (1993). Try reading workshop in your classroom. *The Reading Teacher, 46*(5), 366–371.

Describes how a sixth-grade teacher used a holistic language learning approach developed by Nancy Atwell to support comprehension and response.

Further Reading

Adams, M. J. (1990). *Beginning to read:* Thinking and learning about print. Urbana-Champaign, IL: Center for the Study of Reading.

Anderson, R. C., Hiebert, E. H., Scott, J. A., & Wilkinson, I. A. G. (1985). *Becoming a nation of readers: The report of the commission on reading.* Washington, DC: National Institute of Education.

Baker, L., & Brown, A. (1984). Metacognitive skills and reading. In P. David Pearson (Ed.), *The handbook of reading research.* New York: Longman.

Bauman, J. F., & Schmitt, M. C. (1986). The what, why, how, and when of comprehension instruction. *The Reading Teacher, 39,* 640–645.

Bruner, J. (1983). *Child's talk: Learning to use language.* New York: Holt, Rinehart and Winston.

Chall, J. S. (1983). *Stages of reading development.* New York: McGraw-Hill.

Clay, M. M. (1980). *Reading: The patterning of complex behavior* (2nd ed.). London: Heinemann.

Cunningham, P. M., Hall, D. P., & Defee, M. (1991). Non-ability grouped multilevel instruction: A year in a first-grade classroom. *The Reading Teacher, 42,* 194–199.

Goodman, K. (1986). *What's whole in whole language?* Portsmouth, NH: Heinemann.

Goodman, K. (1992). I didn't found whole language. *The Reading Teacher, 46*(3), 188–199.

Goodman, K. S. (1993). Reading: A psycholinguistic guessing game. In H. Singer & R. Ruddell (Eds.), *Theoretical models and processes of reading* (4th ed.). Newark, DE: International Reading Association.

References

Goodman, K. S., & Goodman, Y. M. (1979). Learning to read is natural. In L. B. Resnick & P. A. Weaver (Eds.), *Theory and practice of early reading* (Vol. 1). Hillsdale, NJ: Erlbaum.

Gough, P. B. (1993). One second of reading. In H. Singer & R. Ruddell (Eds.), *Theoretical models and processes of reading* (4th ed.). Newark, DE: International Reading Association.

Harris, A. J., & Sipay, E. R. (1990). *How to increase reading ability* (9th ed.). New York: Longman.

Harste, J., Woodward, V., & Burke, C. (1984). *Language stories and literacy lessons.* Portsmouth, NH: Heinemann.

Holdaway, D. (1979). *The foundations of literacy.* Exeter, NH: Heinemann.

Irwin, J. W. (1986). *Teaching reading comprehension processes.* Englewood Cliffs, NJ: Prentice Hall.

Johnson, D. D., & Pearson, P. D. (1984). *Teaching reading vocabulary* (2nd ed.). New York: Holt, Rinehart & Winston.

Madden, L. (1988). Improve reading attitudes of poor readers through cooperative reading teams. *The Reading Teacher, 42,* 194–199.

McKenna, M. C., Robinson, R. D., & Miller, J. W. (1993). Whole language and research: The case for caution. In D. J. Leu and C. K. Kinzer (Eds.), *Examining central issues in literacy research, theory, and practice:* Forty-second Yearbook of the National Reading Conference, pp. 141–152. Chicago: National Reading Conference.

Meyer, D. K. (1993). What is scaffolded instruction? Definitions, distinguishing features, and misnomers. In D. J. Leu and C. K. Kinzer (Eds.) *Examining central issues in literacy research, theory, and practice:* Forty-second Yearbook of the National Reading Conference, pp. 41–54. Chicago: National Reading Conference.

Oldfather, P. (1993). What students say about motivating experiences in a whole language classroom. *The Reading Teacher, 46* (8), 672–681.

Palincsar, A. S., & Ransom, K. (1988). From the mystery spot to the thoughtful spot: The instruction of metacognitive strategies. *The Reading Teacher, 41,* 784–789.

Richardson, V., Anders, P., Tidwell, D., & Lloyd, C. (1991). The relationship between teachers' beliefs and practices in reading comprehension instruction. *American Educational Research Journal, 28* (3), 559–586.

Rumelhart, D. (1976). *Toward an interactive model of reading* (Report No. 56). La Jolla, CA: University of California, San Diego, Center for Human Information Processing.

Samuels, S. J. & Eisenberg, P. (1981). A framework for understanding the reading process. In F. J. Pirozzolo, M. C. Wittrock (Eds.), *Neuropsychological and cognitive processes in reading.* New York: Academic Press.

Smith, F. (1988). *Understanding reading: A psycholinguistic analysis of reading and learning to read* (4th ed.). Hillsdale, NJ: Erlbaum.

Stanovich, K. E. (1980). Toward an interactive-compensatory model of individual differences in the development of reading fluency. *Reading Research Quarterly, 16,* 32–71.

Teale, W. H., & Sulzby, E. (Eds.). (1986). *Emergent literacy: Writing and reading.* Norwood, NJ: Ablex.

Teale, W. H., & Sulzby, E. (1989). Emergent literacy: New perspectives. In D. S. Strickland & L. M. Morrow (Eds.), *Emerging literacy: Young children learn to read and write.* Newark, DE: International Reading Association.

Tierney, R. J., & Pearson, P. D. (1983). Toward a composing model of reading. *Language Arts, 60,* 568–580.

Vygotsky, L. S. (1978). *Mind in society.* Cambridge, MA: Harvard University Press.

Weaver, P., & Shonhoff, F. (1984). Subskill and holistic approaches to reading instruction. In A. J. Harris & E. R. Sipay (Eds.), *Readings on reading instruction* (3rd ed). New York: Longman.

CHAPTER 3

Material and Method Frameworks: Applying Initial Insights About Reading

"I will always recall my first day of teaching. It seemed like a hundred things were happening at once. The moment that I remember most clearly occurred as I was about to begin a literature experience with a small group of fourth graders. As we sat down at the table in the corner, Jeffrey's dad came into the class, asking about homework for his son, who had the flu. At the same moment, our principal began announcing over the classroom speaker that the "Welcome Back" assembly in the gym was being changed from 9:30 to 10:30, requiring me to change my schedule for the third time. Just as she finished, and before I could respond to Jeffrey's dad, Tama Forth came bouncing into the room, informing me that I had failed to send the milk money down to the school secretary. "Ms. Baines needs it right now," she stated in a firm and determined voice. As I turned to face her, I noticed Tommy Pierce, who had just picked up Mr. Mopps, our classroom bunny. Mr. Mopps, of course, managed to jump out of Tommy's hands and was now heading for the rug in the reading corner. He ran to that spot during times of great stress and was about to create major problems for both me and our janitor. At this point, I suddenly remembered the first words spoken by my reading professor, 'Teaching will require you to make many decisions.' Well, she was certainly right about that."

A teacher recalling her first day of teaching in a journal
entry about teaching experiences.

Reading instruction will require you to make many decisions as you work with children. Elementary classrooms are busy and complex places. Historically, teachers have relied on the lesson planning information in published reading programs to reduce the complexity of classroom decision making. The lesson plans in published reading programs have been widely used, especially by new teachers, perhaps because they provide such simple "recipes for teaching." Increasingly, however, teachers are replacing the material frameworks found in published reading programs with method and literacy frameworks as they seek to bring their own insights to instructional decisions and make learning to read more meaningful to youngsters. This chapter will show you how teachers use material and method frameworks during reading instruction. In addition, it will demonstrate how to use your developing insights from a literacy framework to make decisions about material and method frameworks. Most important, it will explain how to help your students become more proficient readers, prepared to enter the global and increasingly diverse society of the next century.

Chapter 2 includes information to help you think about questions such as:

1. If required to use a published reading program, how can I adapt it to assist my students?

2. Why are method frameworks often more useful than material frameworks?

3. How can I teach reading by using method frameworks such as: read aloud response journals, individualized reading, cooperative learning groups, language experience stories, directed reading activities, inductive instruction, and deductive instruction?

4. How can I use insights from my literacy framework to inform decisions about material and method frameworks?

KEY CONCEPTS

cooperative learning groups
deductive instruction
directed reading activity
individualized reading
inductive instruction

language experience stories
material frameworks
method frameworks
read aloud response journal activity

---

material framework
An instructional framework used to teach reading; includes a published set of materials and lesson planning information.

MATERIAL FRAMEWORKS

A **material framework** consists of a published set of instructional materials with lesson planning information in a teacher's manual. When teachers use material frameworks, decision making is reduced. Following the directions in a teacher's manual will tell you exactly which materials you need and how to use them. Clearly, this reduces the instructional decisions you have to make in your classroom.

A **published reading program** is the most common example of a material framework used to teach reading. A published reading program is a comprehensive, graded set of published materials used to teach reading in kindergarten through grades 6 or 8. It includes student books with reading selections, workbooks, teacher's manuals, and a host of other instructional materials. When you were in elementary school, it is likely that your teacher used a published reading program; most of our teachers did. Published reading programs are sometimes referred to as basal reading programs, basal readers, or simply basals. The use of published school reading programs is probably decreasing as some teachers turn toward more "authentic" types of reading experiences such as original works of children's literature and the reading of work written by students themselves. Still, as recently as 1986 some authors estimated that 98 percent of elementary school classrooms had at least one published reading program available (Flood & Lapp, 1986).

published reading program
A published reading program is a comprehensive, graded set of published materials used to teach reading in kindergarten through grades 6 or 8.

Published reading programs have been used to teach reading since 1836, when McGuffey's readers first appeared in the United States. Even though other materials had been used earlier, the McGuffey series was the first comprehensive, graded set of materials used to teach reading in grades 1 through 6. An example of a lesson from that early program can be seen in Figure 3-1.

Today reading programs are developed by several large publishers such as Silver Burdett and Ginn, Harcourt Brace, Houghton Mifflin, and Scott, Foresman. Developing a published reading program is a major undertaking, with the initial cost estimated at between $25 – $85 million. A major revision in each program usually occurs every five to six years, coinciding with state adoptions in Texas and California, the two largest states that regularly review published reading programs for their schools. Because published reading programs are altered during each revision, we usually refer to them by the publisher's name and the date of publication (e.g., Houghton Mifflin, 1996) to distinguish it from other series and other editions of the same series.

Published reading programs reduce the complexity of classroom decisions in at least three ways. First, they contain a wide variety of instructional materials used to teach reading, which reduces the time a teacher requires to select materials for reading instruction. Second, they systematically organize reading materials around well-defined grade levels, skill sequences, and thematic units, which reduces the time a teacher needs to spend planning integrated sequences of instruction. Finally, published reading programs contain a teacher's manual with step-by-step directions for teaching reading. This reduces the time a teacher needs to spend planning individual lessons. We will describe each of these aspects of published reading programs in the following sections.

FIGURE 3-1

A lesson from the first grade level of McGuffey's readers

LESSON XXVI.

| fạll | īçe | skātes | erȳ |
| wĭth | hăd | stōne | dĭd |

ạ   ç   sk

The boys are on the ice with their skates.

There is a stone on the ice. One boy did not see it, and has had a fall.

But he is a brave boy, and will not cry.

Source: From *McGuffey's Eclectic Primer, Revised Edition* (New York: American Book Company, 1909, p. 31.

Instructional Materials

Teachers often believe that a published reading program contains all of the materials necessary to teach reading in the elementary grades. While this is never the case, we should not be surprised at this perception. A published reading program contains many materials for teachers and

EXPLORING DIVERSE POINTS OF VIEW

A continuing controversy in reading instruction today is to what extent should teachers use a published reading program during reading instruction. Consider these statements from a group of teachers participating in a workshop on the use of different materials for reading instruction:

"Published reading programs spend too much time teaching isolated skills to students and provide too little time for students to select their own reading experiences."

"The predictable nature of lessons in basal reading programs quickly becomes boring. Students lose interest in reading and reading instruction."

"Following the lessons in a teacher's manual disempowers teachers, making it less likely for them to think creatively and productively about the unique needs of their students. It also gives students a false sense of all that real reading can and should be. Students and teachers both lose when we use basals."

"Basal reading programs don't contain real literature. I'd rather have my students read the complete and original works from children's literature. These are always more interesting."

Now consider another set of comments from the same workshop session:

"Basal reading programs help new teachers learn to teach reading. I learned more by using a basal manual during my first year than I ever learned in my reading methods course at the university."

"Published reading programs contain a complete set of reading skills. I know my students have been taught the essential aspects of reading."

"Basal reading programs save me a lot of time. They contain a complete set of stories, ideas for teaching, discussion questions, assessment activities, and answer keys. Time is my most valuable commodity these days and a basal program can free me to plan supplemental units."

"The reading selections in our new basal reading program are always well-known works from children's literature. This is great because the students are more excited and interested in reading these stories."

Clearly there is little agreement about the extent to which teachers should use a published reading program during reading instruction. As you begin to consider the use of published reading programs, what are your thoughts about this issue?

students: teacher's manuals, student's books, student workbooks, an assessment package, duplicating masters, and even multimedia software.

During the 1990s, two important changes have been made to the nature of materials included in published school reading programs. First, these programs now contain more original works of children's literature. Publishers are paying attention to evidence that children's literature selections are central to supporting reading development (Tunnell & Jacobs, 1989). While many of these selections are excerpts from a longer work and many of them have been reillustrated, published reading programs in the 1990s contain relatively few changes to the language of the original work (Leu & Ayre, 1992), changes that were common during the 1980s. Second, published reading programs are now beginning to include

The most recently published reading programs include extensive literature experiences for children and illustrate for teachers ways to incorporate writing opportunities as well. (Source: From *Macmillan/McGraw-Hill, A New View,* Teacher's Planning Guide for Grade 2/Level 6/Unit 3, pp. 283C and 284D. Copyright 1993 by Macmillan/McGraw-Hill Publishing Company.)

interactive multimedia selections as an optional part of their series. These computer programs contain engaging elements such as video, interactive graphics, and oral readings of the passage in several different languages.

To some teachers, one of the attractions of a published reading program is that it contains a variety of instructional materials. Having all of these materials at your fingertips clearly saves time and reduces the complexity of decision making as decisions have already been made about what children will read.

Organization

A second way in which published reading programs reduce decision making is by systematically organizing their materials. Published reading programs are designed around three organizational structures: grade levels, skill sequences, and thematic units. Systematically organizing materials around these three structures can save teachers time as they plan integrated reading experiences in busy classrooms.

Grade levels. Ever since the McGuffey readers, published reading programs have been organized according to levels of difficulty, traditionally designated by grade levels. In kindergarten most children receive early literacy materials with many listening and discussion experiences. First-grade students typically receive five different levels of materials: three preprimers (PP); a primer (P); and a first reader. In second and third grades most students use a first semester reader and a second semester reader, identified by a numbering system such as 2.1 or 3-1, and so on. Finally, students in fourth through eighth grades generally read from a single book. You can usually locate a table that defines the grade-level-to-book-title correspondence at the beginning of most teacher's manuals. Organizing materials for reading instruction by difficulty level reduces the amount of time teachers need to spend gathering materials that are appropriately challenging for their students.

Skills. Published reading programs are also organized around a set of reading skills developed in a particular sequence. The range of skills taught in any one program is referred to as the program's *scope;* the order in which skills are introduced is referred to as its *sequence*. Each published reading series will provide you with a scope and sequence table showing when each skill is introduced and when it is reviewed. This allows teachers to see which skills receive emphasis during each unit of instruction. It also makes it easier to plan instructional activities designed to support particular needs.

Thematic units. Published reading programs today are almost always organized by **thematic units** that serve to integrate reading, writing, and discussion experiences around a single topic or author such as: "Making Friends," "Celebrating Differences," "Fantastic Tales," or "Laura Ingalls Wilder." Organizing instruction around thematic topics permits teachers and students to engage in purposeful experiences as they find connections between reading selections, post-reading conversations, and writing experiences (Strickland & Morrow, 1990). Some programs have been criticized, though, for paying only minimal attention to substantive issues when defining their thematic structure. These programs organize instruction around thematic titles such as "Teddy Bears, Teddy Bears," "Wishes," or other thematic topics that fail to provide opportunities for reading, writing, and thinking about substantive issues.

thematic units
Instructional units organized around a single issue or theme that usually contain children's literature as well as integrated reading, writing, speaking, and listening experiences.

Organizing a thematic unit on your own requires considerable time (Staab, 1991). When thematic units are appropriately designed in published reading programs they reduce the amount of time that teachers must spend to develop these units themselves.

Teacher's Manuals

A third way in which published reading programs reduce the complexity of classroom instruction is by providing teachers detailed lesson plans.

Each teacher's manual contains elaborate lesson planning information, including copies of the students' reading selections, preparation experiences designed to provide supportive experiences before reading the selection, writing and discussion experiences to support students' responses after reading the selection, and supplemental experiences for students who need additional assistance. All published reading programs provide extensive lesson planning information in their teacher's manuals. This can save you time while planning instructional lessons.

If you compare lessons from several series, they will look very different; each will use different labels for the sections of their lesson plan. If you look closely, though, all series tend to follow an identical, underlying structure in lesson planning. You will notice that teaching plans in published reading programs are usually organized something like this:

I. Preview information for the teacher
   A. Summary of the selection
   B. New vocabulary for students
   C. Instructional objectives
   D. Instructional materials
II. Preparation activities
   A. Developing vocabulary
   B. Developing reading skills
   C. Defining a purpose for reading
III. Guided reading activities
   A. Reading the selection silently and then sometimes orally
   B. Discussing the selection
IV. Skill development and practice activities
V. Extension activities

preview information
The first section of most teaching plans in a traditional published reading program.

The first portion of most teaching plans contains **preview information** to help a teacher get a quick overview of the lesson before teaching. This section will include a summary of the story, a list of new vocabulary words that appear in the story, a list of instructional objectives, and a list of necessary instructional materials. Preview information allows teachers to understand the instructional purposes of a particular lesson and to decide whether and how a lesson should be taught. It also permits teachers to collect and prepare the necessary materials for each lesson.

preparation section
The second section of most teaching plans in a traditional published reading program; describes activities that prepare students to read the selection.

The second portion of most teaching plans is a **preparation section.** This is when your teaching activities usually begin. The preparation section of a lesson describes useful activities that prepare students to read the selection. New vocabulary words are listed, along with suggestions for how the new words should be taught. Often, specific reading skills are also developed during the preparation section. Such skills as developing useful reading strategies, monitoring comprehension, or recognizing common sight words in context may be taught because they will be important to reading and discussing the story selection. Finally, the preparation section defines a purpose for reading. You may be directed to have students read and think about connections with a previous selection, to read and see what they would have done in a situation related to the story, or to read and enjoy the way an author uses a stylistic feature such as humor.

The third section of most teaching plans suggests how to conduct a **guided reading** of the passage. Guided reading experiences usually take place in one of two ways. Often, students read the entire selection silently, and then the teacher initiates a discussion that may or may not include an oral reading of portions of the story. An alternative strategy has students read the story silently, a page or two at a time. After each portion is read, the teacher initiates a discussion that, again, may or may not include an oral reading. In both cases students have an opportunity to read stories silently before they are asked to read them aloud (Harris & Sipay, 1990).

After the guided reading section, many teaching plans provide suggestions for **skill development and practice.** These sections often consist of response journal or practice activities for students to complete independently at their desks. In a lesson designed to develop strategic reading skills, for example, students might be asked to describe in their response journals one strategy they used while reading the story. Later these might be shared. In another lesson where the meanings of new vocabulary words are developed, students might be asked to work together in small groups to complete a crossword puzzle containing these words.

Extension activities are often included in the lesson plan of a published reading program. Extension activities include functional and enjoyable activities related to the content or the skills associated with a selection. These may contain a variety of additional reading and writing experiences related to the thematic topic and the literature selection that was just read. After reading a selection from *The Voyage of the Dawn Treader,* for example, students might be asked to work in small groups to draw a map of this fantasy kingdom. Alternatively, they might be asked to create a map of their own fantasy kingdom or to read and discuss an excerpt from another fantasy. Or, after reading an excerpt from *Charlotte's Web,* students might be asked to create a spider's web on a piece of construction paper with cotton fiber and glue, weaving one word into the web that best describes their classroom. Afterwards these might be displayed in a prominent place in the room. Other similar experiences will be found at the end of each lesson.

guided reading
The third section of most teaching plans in a traditional published reading program; gives directions for guiding silent and sometimes oral reading.

skill development and practice
The fourth section of most teaching plans in a traditional published reading program; provides directions for specific skill instruction.

extension activities
The fifth section of most teaching plans in a traditional published reading program; contains review and enrichment activities.

MATERIAL FRAMEWORKS: THE CONTROVERSY

If published reading programs reduce the complexity of instructional decisions, why does a controversy surround their use? Isn't it helpful to reduce complexity in classrooms and be able to focus on the needs of individual students? Certainly. Reducing the complexity of classroom decisions by relying solely on a published reading program appears, however, to be a double-edged sword. At the same time a published reading program reduces the complexity of classroom decisions, it also appears to cause teachers to rely on judgments that have been made by others rather than valuing their own professional insights about individual students (Shannon, 1986). Thus, some believe that published reading programs make so many decisions that teachers will be subtly encouraged not to think about important instructional issues. Blindly following the directions in a teacher's manual may lead you to abdicate your developing ability as an insightful and skilled educator. One problem with published reading programs, then, is that they disempower teachers, resulting in teachers who fail to use their special insight about children and reading, an insight crucial to effective instruction.

A second criticism of published reading programs is associated with teachers' different literacy frameworks. Teachers who object to the use of a published reading program often have a holistic language learning explanation for how children learn to read. They believe that children learn best by reading authentic works to accomplish personal, purposeful, and practical tasks. They see published reading programs as teaching too many skills, providing too many drills, and isolating the teaching of reading from other subject areas. According to these teachers, published reading programs provide students too few opportunities to make personal and authentic reading choices. They prefer that children select their own works of children's literature from a school or classroom library and that teachers use these sources and a variety of method frameworks to develop proficiency in reading.

Some teachers, though, value the use of published reading programs. Such teachers often have a specific skills explanation for how children learn to read. Sometimes they will have an integrated explanation. Teachers who value the use of published reading programs believe in the importance of direct instruction in teaching reading skills or strategies. Moreover, these teachers argue that published reading programs provide important support and direction for new teachers. Such programs save new teachers from having to assemble all their own reading materials and activities. Also, these teachers note that published reading programs have recently changed and now include literature selections. Several programs, they point out, are actually anthologies of children's literature and include classroom libraries of children's books. These teachers argue, finally, that published reading programs have decreased instruction in isolated skills and increased the integration of reading with subject areas by organizing individual lessons within thematic units.

As you can see, the decision whether to use a published reading program is closely associated with your beliefs about reading. Teachers who believe that children learn best by reading authentic materials to accomplish significant and functional tasks do not value published reading programs; those who do believe that children learn to read best through more direct instruction value published reading programs. Teachers who believe that children learn best through a combination of these approaches value a published reading program used in conjunction with additional, self-selected reading and writing experiences.

Who decides whether to use a published reading program? In many situations that decision has been made by the local school district or the building principal. Increasingly, however, teachers are actively seeking a voice in the decision-making process. This trend is reflected in the recommendations made in the *Report Card on Basal Readers,* written by the Commission on Reading of the National Council of Teachers of English. These recommendations are listed in Figure 3-2. As a result, decisions about the use of published school reading programs are now more frequently made by building-level or district-level teams of teachers, parents, and administrators.

FIGURE 3-2

Recommendations from the National Council of Teachers of English

1. Teachers should develop, individually or with others, a clear position of their own on how reading is best taught.

   They should continually examine this position as they work with children.

   They should examine policies and instructional materials from this professional perspective.

   They should keep themselves well informed about developments in research and practice.

   They should communicate to administrators their own professional views.

2. Teachers individually and collectively need to take back the authority and responsibility to their classrooms for making basic decisions.

   They need to make their own decisions about how to use materials including, or not including, basals to meet the needs of their pupils.

   They need to be willing to take risks while asserting their professional judgments.

3. Teachers, through their organizations, should reject use of materials, including basals, that make them less than responsible professionals.

4. Teachers should communicate to administrators, publishers, and others their professional judgments about what they need in the way of resources.

   They should make clear to publishers the strengths and weaknesses of programs as they work with them.

   They should plan material purchases with administrators.

   They should demand a voice in text adoption decisions and policies.

Source: From K. S. Goodman, Y. Freeman, S. Murphy, and P. Shannon, *Report Card on Basal Readers* (Evanston, IL: National Council of Teachers of English, 1988).

TABLE 3-1

Advantages and disadvantages associated with the use of published reading programs

Advantages	Disadvantages
Published reading programs save time. Having a complete set of stories, instructional activities, assessment instruments, and answer keys means that teachers do not have to spend large amounts of time developing or acquiring each of these components (McCallum, 1988).	Selections in published reading programs often lack educational content. Stories and articles are often selected to teach a particular skill rather than to provide children with substantive knowledge about their environment (Schmidt, Caul, Byers, & Buchmann, 1984).
Published reading programs include a comprehensive set of reading skills (Osborn, 1984).	Selections in published reading programs are often uninteresting. They tend not to interest young readers to the same extent as unabridged children's literature (Goodman, Freeman, Murphy, & Shannon, 1988).
Published reading programs provide for regular and systematic review of skill development (Harris & Sipay, 1990).	Published reading programs direct teachers to assess children's performance more frequently than they teach children how to read (Durkin, 1981).
Published reading programs provide support for new teachers. They are thought by some to be more important than university courses in educating new teachers in reading instruction (McCallum, 1988).	Published reading programs are associated with an abdication of responsibility for classroom decisions. Teachers often believe that these materials must be correct because professionals prepared them (Shannon, 1986).

Whatever your beliefs are, or come to be, about reading instruction, it is likely that published reading programs will continue to be available in many schools. It may be useful, then, to consider both their advantages and disadvantages carefully as you decide about their role in your classroom. Some of the major conclusions about published reading programs that have appeared in the professional literature are presented in Table 3-1.

MODIFYING MATERIAL FRAMEWORKS TO MEET INDIVIDUAL NEEDS

Should you use a published reading program, it is essential to keep in mind this important point: *teachers should always modify published reading programs in order to best meet the unique needs of their students.* Lesson plans in teacher's manuals are intended to provide a range of suggestions and instructional ideas. They should never be followed slavishly from beginning to end. In fact, should you do so, you will quickly discover that there is insufficient time to complete any lesson.

In addition to modifying the lessons in a published reading program to meet your students' unique needs, there are other reasons to change these lessons: (1) to be more consistent with your beliefs about reading; (2) to increase students' interest in reading; (3) to integrate reading instruction with other subject areas; and (4) to include instructional activities known to be successful. How should you do this? Figure 3-3 summarizes a number of strategies teachers have used to modify published reading programs to meet their students' needs. We will describe others below. Then we will describe a number of more fundamental ways to modify published reading programs.

Modifying Preparation Activities

You will recall that preparation activities appear at the beginning of lessons in published reading programs and are designed to prepare students for the upcoming reading selection. There are several ways for you to adapt these activities. One approach is to substitute an activity from the extension section at the end of the lesson. Extension activities are excellent vehicles for developing the prior knowledge that is useful for reading a selection and is a common aspect of preparation activities (Reutzel, 1991). Most important, extension activities usually develop background knowledge in a more active and engaging fashion than those found in the preparation section. This will be important to you if you have a holistic language learning orientation or an integrated belief about how children learn to read.

Consider, for example, a lesson in one program using the story *Ira Sleeps Over* by Bernard Waber. This is a story about spending the night at a friend's house for the very first time and the anxieties this might generate. In the preparation section teachers are directed to present the meaning of several words from the story by writing them on the chalkboard in sentences. In the extension section at the end of the lesson, however, one activity suggests that you have students develop a letter together as a class. By transcribing the words from your class on the chalkboard, you are directed to help the class write an invitation to a friend to sleep overnight. If you moved this activity to the preparation section, you could develop important background knowledge before reading the story. Developing this letter together would lead to a discussion about important ideas that will soon appear in the story. You might, for example, engage students in a conversation about what to take on a sleepover or how people might feel on their very first sleepover. More important, students would see the important words in this story within a natural and meaningful context. Similar opportunities can be found in many lessons to develop vocabulary and background knowledge by using an extension activity in place of a preparation activity.

FIGURE 3-3

Strategies for modifying the teaching plans in published reading programs

 Reorganize the reading selections in your published reading program to create new combinations of thematic units related to your science and/or social studies programs. Integrate your reading experiences with these other content areas.

 Check to be certain that the skills taught in each lesson are actually useful for reading and understanding that selection. If they are not, skip them or look for other instructional experiences that *are* useful for reading the story. Teach these instead.

 Rather than having students complete skill experiences individually, consider ways of having them work together in small groups to accomplish these tasks and learn from each other.

 Skip or replace lessons when students are proficient at using the skills in those lessons. Use the reading selection for another reading, writing, listening, or speaking activity.

 Replace the reading of story selections in your published reading program with individual choices from children's literature. Visit your school library and assist your students in making these choices.

 Replace the preparation activity at the beginning of a lesson with an activity from the extension section at the end of a lesson. Preparation activities tend to emphasize a specific skill that is taught directly by the teacher. Extension activities can often be used to develop important prior knowledge about a story in a more engaging fashion.

 Divide students into several heterogeneous groups. Have each group read one story from a thematic unit and then plan a method for presenting it to the other groups. This might involve a dramatic reading of the story, a rewritten version of the story to be read by others, a dramatic pantomime of the story as one person reads it aloud, or a choral reading of the story. After all of the presentations, have each group discuss the common relationships between each of the selections. Share the results of these discussions in a large group and then engage students in a common experience requiring them to read each of the selections and then write something in response to their reading.

 Have students ask discussion questions of the teacher after reading the story. Explain your reasoning processes for each answer. Show students how you figured out each answer.

 Skip preparation activities that teach a reading strategy. Instead, have students read the passage and then describe in their journals the parts that were hard to understand. Share this information. Use it to begin a useful discussion on strategies to use when a story doesn't make sense.

There is a second way to modify vocabulary activities in the preparation section. As you have seen, lessons in published reading programs typically develop vocabulary knowledge *before* students read a story. You can change this, and develop important reading strategies, by having students develop vocabulary knowledge *as* they read a passage in the published reading program. Instead of teaching the meanings of new words

---

OPPORTUNITIES TO CELEBRATE DIVERSITY

Using extension activities in place of preparation activities in a published reading program is useful for all of your students. It may, however, be especially useful if you have students with different linguistic or cultural backgrounds. If you begin with your students' labels for concepts instead of the textbook's labels, your class can discover various means of experiencing the world and describing those experiences. Different cultural or linguistic groups may have very diverse ways of looking at the same experience and it is important for all of your students to observe these differences. Understanding and valuing diversity in language use does not always take place when you begin with the vocabulary words and definitions provided in the teacher's manual of a published reading program.

---

at the beginning of the lesson, encourage students to write down hard or unfamiliar words as they read. Then, engage students in a discussion about these words and the strategies that can be used to infer the meanings of unfamiliar words. Often, for example, there are many clues to the meanings of unfamiliar words in the surrounding portions of a passage. Show students where these clues are and how they can be used to infer word meanings.

Modifying Guided Reading Experiences

Guided reading experiences usually follow preparation activities in the lesson plans of published reading programs. During guided reading, children complete a silent reading of the story, then read the story together orally, and finally discuss the story with the teacher. This predictable lesson sequence becomes quite boring for students. Change this instructional sequence by using **response journals.** A response journal is an inexpensive spiral notebook where students can write down their feelings and ideas as they read a selection. As students read a selection, have them write an entry in their journal. These writing topics can be defined by you or the students themselves. Afterwards, assemble and encourage those who feel comfortable with sharing their work to read their entries aloud. Use these to engage students in a discussion of the story selection in place of the discussion questions listed in the teacher's manual.

Another way to modify guided reading experiences is to model your reading experience through a **think aloud.** It is not always easy for students to understand the strategies we use while we are reading. Reading strategies are invisible to an observer. Make strategies visible by reading aloud to your students; as you read, tell them what you are thinking and why you are rereading a section, why you are skipping back to see the title again, why you are looking at an illustration, and other things you do while you are reading. Think aloud activities like this are especially helpful for your less proficient readers who have not yet developed efficient reading strategies.

response journal
An inexpensive spiral notebook in which students can write down their feelings and ideas as they read a selection.

think aloud
A procedure during which a reader states aloud the thought processes and decisions that occur while reading.

Modifying Skill Development Experiences

The next section in most lesson plans contains skill development experiences. The most useful advice we can give you about this section is to be certain that the skill you seek to develop is necessary for reading the passage in a lesson. If it is not, spend your limited instructional time on something more important. For example, if you find that a lesson suggests you teach students about main ideas, an activity useful for informational writing, but the reading selection is a narrative or story, you should probably skip instruction in this skill until children are reading informational text.

A second suggestion may also be useful: skills should always be taught within the context of their use. Otherwise, it is difficult for students to see their usefulness and it is difficult for you to explain how a skill can help your students. From this perspective, it seems odd to find skill development experiences that appear in a lesson either after or before the reading of a story from a published reading program. It is much more reasonable to support skill development during the actual reading of a

Teachers may wish to supplement or replace specific skill lessons with more functional reading/writing activities.

passage. You may wish to change the timing for skill development experiences so that they take place as students read a passage.

Making More Substantial Changes to Published Reading Programs

Using your developing insights about reading to modify published reading programs can be useful for both you and your students. Thoughtful changes will allow you to adjust the program to fit your needs and the needs of individual students more closely. Still, you may wish to make more substantial changes than simply reordering the sequence of activities in a published reading program for students. This will be especially true if you have either a holistic language learning or an integrative explanation for how children learn to read but your school requires you to use a published reading program. If you wish to make more substantial changes, you have at least two options available to you.

One strategy involves using the reading selections in your program but reorganizing them around instructional units in at least one other content area, such as social studies or science. For example, a Native American folktale by Paul Goble like *The Girl Who Loved Horses* might appear in the thematic unit "Folktales" in a published reading program. Instead of using it here, though, you may wish to use it during a social studies unit on Native Americans. Similarly, a selection about a woman who decides to plant lupine flowers wherever she goes such as *Miss Rumphius* by Barbara Cooney might appear in the published reading program during a thematic unit on "Bringing Beauty to the World." Nevertheless, it could be used just as easily during a science unit you are planning on ecology. With this approach, you may choose to follow some of the instructional suggestions for each story or you may choose to create your own. Tightly linking reading and language arts experiences with content area study is often thought to be especially useful to growth in both areas (Herber & Herber, 1993).

A second strategy involves simply using the reading selections in your published reading program as a resource anthology. Some teachers, for instance, will not use the lesson planning information and all the ancillary materials from a published reading program. Instead, they will rely largely upon students' self-selected literature experiences from a school or classroom library. Sometimes, though, these teachers will use a few of the selections from the published reading program to supplement ongoing reading and writing activities. A story in a published reading program, for example, might be used as a read aloud experience. The teacher might read the selection aloud to initiate a discussion on a topic or to illustrate an author's writing style. Before a short lesson on the use of dialogue, for example, you may wish to read an excerpt aloud from *James and the Giant Peach* by Roald Dahl to show students how this master of dialogue handles his craft. At another time, you might have everyone read an excerpt to begin a discussion of an author. For instance, to introduce Jean

Craighead George to your students, you may have everyone read the excerpt in your published reading program from her book, *My Side of the Mountain.* Many other uses for the selections in a published reading program can be developed if you approach the stories in this program as a resource anthology. The advantage of this technique is that it permits each of your students to have a copy of the same selection, something that is at times hard to do when children are reading individual choices from the school library.

It is also possible that you may choose to drop the use of a published reading program entirely. You may feel that it is more important for students to read literature selections of their own choice. In fact, some have pointed out that it may be less expensive to devote the money that might be spent on a published reading program to purchasing children's literature for a classroom library (Jachym, Allington, & Broikou, 1989). If you decide not to use a published reading program, you will want to pay particular attention to the method frameworks presented in the next section and in each of the subsequent chapters. These will help you organize your instructional program in reading.

METHOD FRAMEWORKS: PROCEDURAL GUIDES

Material frameworks reduce the complexity of instructional decisions by telling you what to do at each step in a lesson. As you have seen, this can sometimes come at the expense of respecting your own insight about children and your own sense of effective instruction. It can also become repetitive and boring to students.

method framework
An instructional framework used to teach reading; contains procedural steps for teaching and options for completing each step.

A more engaging way to structure reading experiences is through the use of **method frameworks.** Method frameworks consist of two common elements: procedural steps for completing a learning activity and options for completing each of the procedural steps. Teachers employ many different method frameworks to guide instructional decisions. Listen to several teachers talking about the method frameworks they use in their classrooms, and see whether you can determine the procedural steps in each.

> "I really like to do Read Aloud Response Journals each day as we work in thematic units. I begin by reading a book or a chapter aloud to the whole class. It is always a book related in one way or another to the thematic topic. Then I give students a writing task to complete and we take about ten minutes to make an entry in our read aloud response journal. Afterwards, we share some of our entries. Later on, we will use some of these entries and work them up into larger pieces of writing." (A third-grade teacher talking to parents at "Back to School Night")

> "We're doing a language experience story today. We do one almost every day. It's easy. First we do a fun activity. Then we talk about it. As they tell me about it, I write their words down on the chalkboard. Then I

use their words to teach them something about reading. Watch me." (A first-grade teacher preparing her student teacher for the first day of class)

"We do the writing process in our class. First we prewrite. Then we write a draft. Next we revise. Then we proofread. And last we publish. The writing process helps the reading process because students are reading their own and each other's writing so much. I use it as often as possible." (A fourth-grade teacher overheard at a state reading conference)

Why are method frameworks so common during reading instruction? Method frameworks are popular because they help to reduce the complexity of instructional decisions while still permitting teachers to take advantage of their special insight about students. As method frameworks consist of clearly defined procedures that are easily learned, they reduce the complexity of instructional decisions and allow teachers to attend to the more important aspects of reading instruction. Knowing automatically what the next instructional step will be permits you to pay closer attention to your students' needs—one student's inability to understand a particular word, another student's failure to make an inference, or a third student's limited range of reading interests. Method frameworks free teachers to make appropriate instructional decisions for individual students in busy classrooms.

Moreover, because each procedural step may be accomplished with many different options, teachers are supported in using their special insights about literacy learning. Method frameworks differ from material frameworks as you have much more control over how you will use them to support literacy learning. With method frameworks, you decide when each will be used and which options you will select in any lesson. This allows you the opportunity to redefine method frameworks each time you use them around the unique needs of your students at that time. As a result, you can use the special insights you develop about your students as you use method frameworks. Method frameworks empower teachers much more than material frameworks.

COMMON METHOD FRAMEWORKS

This section presents seven common method frameworks used to help youngsters develop into avid and proficient readers and writers. In addition, it provides model lessons to demonstrate how each method framework can be used in your classroom. Many more method frameworks are presented throughout the rest of this book. Notice how becoming familiar with each of these method frameworks reduces the complexity of your instructional decisions yet simultaneously allows you to use your developing insights about individual students to meet their needs. You should also notice how each method framework is either more or less consistent with the different beliefs about how children best learn to read that were described in chapter 2.

Read Aloud Response Journal Activity

A **read aloud response journal activity** is a method framework used
to engage children in thinking and writing about a topic while listening
to a work of children's literature. Exploring responses to works of children's literature through journal writing is thought to provide important
support for literacy learners (Hancock, 1993). This method framework is
most consistent with a holistic language learning or an integrated belief
about how children best learn to read. A read aloud response journal
activity includes the following steps:

1. Read a selection aloud.
2. Engage students in a writing task related to the reading selection.
3. Have students write their response in their journals.
4. Share the responses.
5. At a later point, encourage students to go back to some of their
   earlier entries and expand these into larger writing projects.

The initial step in a read aloud response journal activity is to read a
selection aloud to your students. The selection may come from any
source: a newspaper article, a magazine article, a letter, or a book. Most
often, it comes from a children's literature selection, either a short picture
book or a chapter from a longer work. In either case, the selection is often
related thematically to a unit in reading or another subject area. Reading
aloud is widely recognized as having a powerful effect on children's interest in reading (Trelease, 1989).

The second step is to engage students in a writing task related to the
reading selection. Here, you need to plan a useful writing activity that
allows students to think about the reading selection they have just listened to and write a short response. These writing activities usually
allow students to connect their own thoughts or previous experiences
with something that took place in the read aloud passage. Teachers often
will develop several activities and encourage students to select the one
they wish to use in their response. Sometimes teachers will encourage
the students to brainstorm a list of possible response topics from which to
select. Table 3-2 shows how writing activities might be developed from
literature selections used in read aloud response journal activities.

During the third step, students make an entry in their read aloud
response journal. This is usually an inexpensive, spiral notebook that
each student uses to record responses to each selection that has been read
aloud. Sometimes teachers will encourage students to make their entries
in a common format with the title of the selection and the date at the top
followed by the writing prompt. This is followed, by the entry for that day.
An example of a response journal entry can be seen in Figure 3-4.

Students are next encouraged to share their responses with others.
This may take place in pairs, in small groups, or with the entire class.
Here, students may read their entry to others. If students feel that an

TABLE 3-2

Examples of children's literature and writing prompts for read aloud response journal activities in several different thematic units.

Thematic Unit	Title	Author	Writing Prompt
Courageous Acts	John Henry	Ezra Jack Keats	In this story, John Henry's courage was tested and he paid with his life. Can you think of a challenge that you would be willing to take on even if it cost you your life? Describe this challenge and describe why you believe it to be so important.
	Number the Stars	Lois Lowry	Define the meaning of the term "courage." Apply this definition to one of the many acts of courage you found in this story and explain why it was a courageous act. Or, describe an act in which you were courageous.
	Dear Mr. Henshaw	Beverly Cleary	Did Leigh Botts lead a courageous life? Did his mother? Did his father? Choose one of the main characters and explain your conclusion.
The Nature of Friendship	The Cat in the Hat	Dr. Seuss	Compare the *Cat in the Hat* to a friend you have. What makes them the same? What makes them different?
	The Giving Tree	Shel Silverstein	Can you think of anyone that is a friend to you the way the apple tree was a friend to the boy? Describe this person.
	Frog and Toad are Friends	Arnold Lobel	Who do you think was the better friend, Frog or Toad? Why?

entry is just too personal to share with others, they should be supported in their desire not to share their work. Other opportunities will come for them to share their responses. After students have shared their work, you may wish to encourage the listeners to make several positive comments about the entry. Sharing positive comments about entries helps students to feel more comfortable about sharing their writing and usually results in students wanting to write even better the next time.

FIGURE 3-4

An example of a response journal entry by a fifth grade student

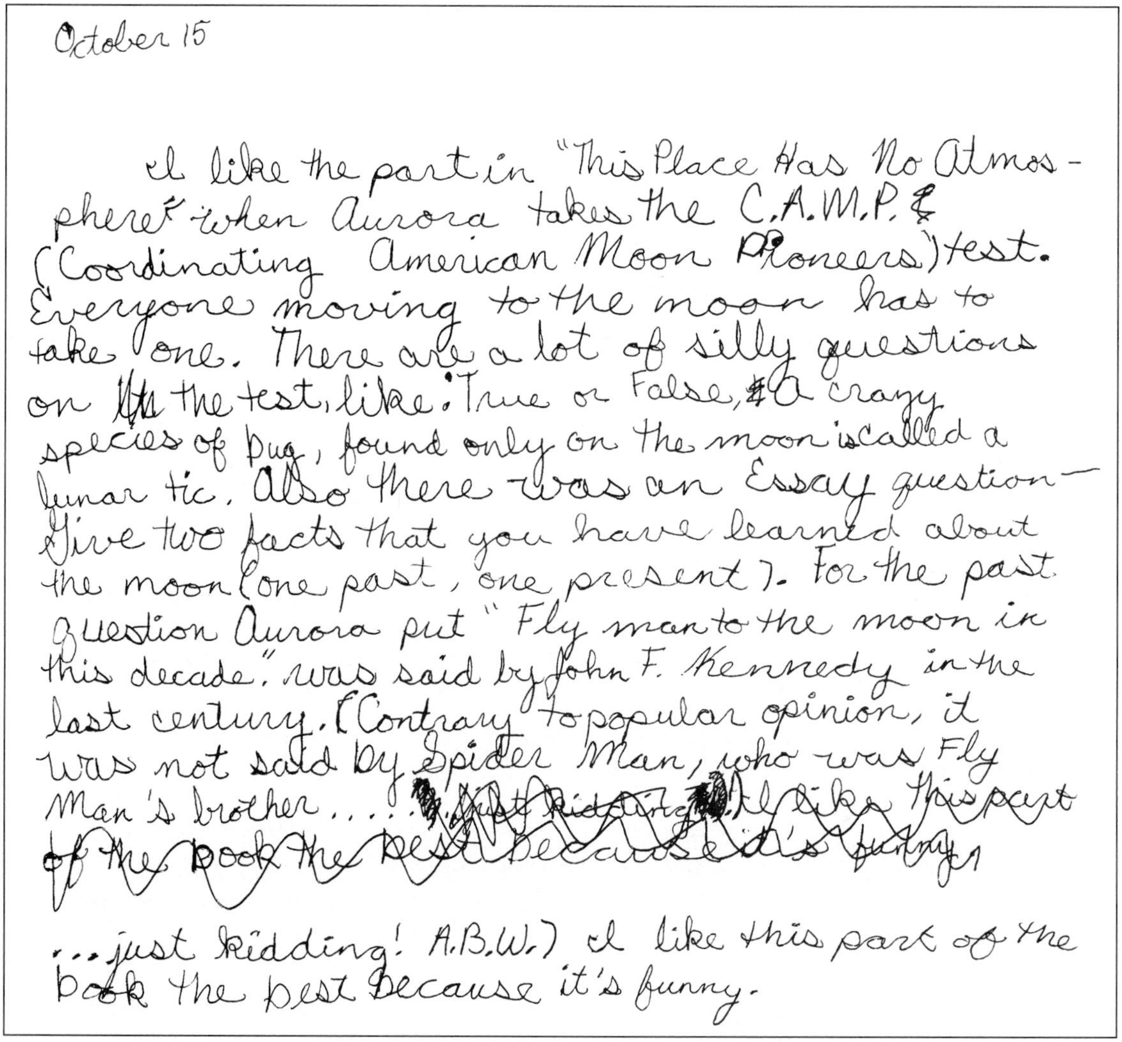

October 15

I like the part in "This Place Has No Atmosphere" when Aurora takes the C.A.M.P. (Coordinating American Moon Pioneers) test. Everyone moving to the moon has to take one. There are a lot of silly questions on the test, like: True or False, A crazy species of bug, found only on the moon is called a lunar tic. Also there was an Essay question— Give two facts that you have learned about the moon (one past, one present). For the past question Aurora put "Fly man to the moon in this decade." was said by John F. Kennedy in the last century. (Contrary to popular opinion, it was not said by Spider Man, who was Fly Man's brother.... ~~Just kidding! I like this part of the book the best because it's funny.~~

...just kidding! A.B.W.) I like this part of the book the best because it's funny.

At a later point you may encourage students to review some of their earlier entries and expand these into larger writing projects. Teachers who use a read aloud response journal activity to begin each day of a thematic unit will sometimes do this toward the end of the unit. The short entries in read aloud response journals should be seen as an artist's "sketch book" where the images of thoughts, feelings, and ideas are quickly jotted down. After students have made a number of short entries, you should show students how to reread their entries, looking for writing

MODEL LESSON
A Read Aloud Response Journal Activity in Ms. Esquevarra's Class

Read a Selection Aloud. Ms. Esquevarra's sixth-grade class is exploring a thematic unit in reading called "The Nature of Courage." She begins each day's experiences with a read aloud response journal activity. Today, she is reading a chapter from the book *Hatchet* by Gary Paulson, a story of wilderness survival. The chapter describes how, at one point, the main character, Brian, is very afraid of meeting a bear in a raspberry patch.

Engage students in a writing task related to the reading selection. After reading this chapter, Ms. Esquevarra encourages students to brainstorm several possible writing tasks about fear and courage. She writes these on the chalkboard: 1) Describe a time when you were afraid; 2) Write a definition of courage using examples to explain your definition; 3) How would you have handled being afraid in this situation?; 4) Does being courageous also mean that you are afraid? Explain how this applies or does not apply to this chapter. Then, students are encouraged to pick one of the prompts, and write an entry in their read aloud response journal.

Have students write their response in their journals. Students are given about 10 minutes to complete their entry. Towards the end, Ms. Esquevarra reminds them that writing time is drawing to a close and that they have 3 minutes remaining. This reminds students to wrap up their entry.

Share the responses. First, Ms. Esquevarra has students form groups with members who have each written on a different topic. She does this to allow each student the opportunity to hear ideas that were generated on each topic. As students read their entries, Ms. Esquevarra circles the classroom, reminding students to provide a positive comment to each student who reads an entry. When this first sharing session is completed, she has students form groups containing members who have written on the same topic. Again, students read their entries, providing each other with positive comments.

Encourage students to expand some of their earlier entries into larger writing projects. Three days before the end of the unit, Ms. Esquevarra begins to show students how to select one of their entries or to combine several of the entries into a larger writing project. She supports them as they develop an initial draft, as they revise this draft, as they edit the final draft, and as they share their "magnum opus" with the entire class.

---

ideas that can be elaborated upon and developed more thoroughly. Students then can work these up into larger units of writing and share them with the class. The model lesson above illustrates how one teacher used a read aloud response journal activity in her classroom.

Individualized Reading

Individualized reading is a method framework often used in place of a published reading program. It can also be used to supplement a published reading program. Individualized reading relies on self-selected literature to develop reading ability, a practice that has shown impressive results (Tunnell & Jacobs, 1989). Individualized reading is most often

individualized reading
A method framework consisting of these four steps: selecting a book, reading it independently, having a conference, and completing a project.

MODEL LESSON
Individualized Reading in Ms. Johnson's Class

The Student Selects a Book to Read. In this classroom, students may select their books from the classroom library, the school library, or the local library. Students choose selections based on their own interests. Ms. Johnson expects each student to complete at least three books each month. She has taught her second-grade students the five-finger guide to determining the difficulty level of a book. They are to read any page and put down one finger for each word they cannot read. If they have put down all five fingers before they get to the end of the page, the book is probably too difficult.

The Student Reads the Book Independently. In Ms. Johnson's classroom, students usually read at their desks or in one of the bean bag chairs in the reading corner. Every week or so, Ms. Johnson schedules a read-it-and-share-it day. On these days students read a favorite part of their books to a friend and explain why the books are good to read. Students also make predictions about how their stories will end. Then they reverse roles. Ms. Johnson knows that these activities provide students with rich oral language experiences and also expose them to possible reading selections for the future.

The Student Has a Conference with the Teacher. Ms. Johnson has each student sign up on a schedule located on her desk. Students must sign up at least one day before the conference, listing their name and the book they have read. This gives Ms. Johnson a chance to prepare herself for the conference. During conferences she asks students to read their favorite parts, while she checks for oral reading fluency. Then she asks several questions about the story and discusses a project that might be completed. She concludes by discussing possible reading selections to follow.

The Student Completes a Culminating Project. Students in Ms. Johnson's class complete one project for every two or three books they have read. The nature of the project is decided jointly by Ms. Johnson and each student, in keeping with each student's interests and needs. Around the room are several recent projects: a poster advertising the book I *Was a Second Grade Werewolf* by Daniel Pinkwater, a diorama of a scene from *Mufaro's Beautiful Daughters* by John Steptoe, and a crossword puzzle made by one student and completed by another after each had read *Patrick's Dinosaur* by Carol Carrick.

associated with a holistic language learning or an integrated belief about how children best learn to read. Individualized reading is described in a variety of ways but often includes the following steps:

1. The student selects a book to read from the classroom or school library.
2. The student reads the book independently, seeking assistance from the teacher or peers as required.
3. The student has a conference with the teacher about what was read.
4. The student has the option of completing a culminating project designed to share the book with others.

The first step in individualized reading is student selection of reading materials. Students determine what they will read, based on their own

interests and achievement levels. Teachers, however, help children identify interest areas and put students in touch with a range of books in each
area. Usually it is suggested that teachers have available four to five books
for each student in the class in order to effectively initiate an individualized reading program (Harris & Sipay, 1990). This number should provide
the necessary variety for your students' reading selections.

Teachers have many options in implementing this first step, especially
in terms of how much support they wish to provide as students make
their choices. For example, they might discuss possibilities with individual students, or they might ask that all students read a selection from a
particular genre: perhaps poetry, historical fiction, contemporary fiction,
or biography. When this method framework is used during a thematic
unit, students may be asked to select a book related to the topic of the
unit. It is most common, however, to leave the choice entirely up to the
student.

The second step in individualized reading takes place as students read
their selections independently, and again, many options are possible. For
example, teachers might provide instructional assistance whenever students request it, or they might ask students to meet with them every few
chapters in order to keep track of their reading and provide assistance if
necessary. Another possibility is to meet periodically only with students
who are thought to need additional support.

The third step in individualized reading is the conference, which usually takes place after students have finished reading their selections.
Sometimes teachers have an appointment chart so that students may
sign up in advance. In other cases teachers arrange for conferences as
students require them. During the conference session teachers informally
assess how well students have comprehended the selection through discussion questions. Individual progress can be recorded on a form similar
to the one in Figure 3-5. Teachers might also ask that a favorite section
be read aloud, and teachers and students might discuss what books will
be read next.

One option for the conferencing step is to have students conduct this
activity in small groups. Increasingly, teachers are being encouraged to
engage small groups of students in peer conferences about books that they
have read (Short, 1993). Encourage students who have each completed the
reading of a different book to share their reading experiences in a small
group. During this time, students themselves can direct the nature of the
presentation and discussion about each book. This often leads to wonderful connections that students make between different books; it also
exposes students to new books for future reading experiences.

In some cases the conference also includes a discussion of how students plan to share their books with the class—the optional fourth step in
an individualized reading activity. The project might be something as
simple as a short oral report or an illustration of a central scene. It might
be a crossword puzzle to be completed by the next student reading the

FIGURE 3-5

A sample conference record completed during individualized reading

Name Tonya Evertson   Date March 15
Title Lon Po Po   Author Ed Young

Response: Thoughtful comments about Chinese culture.
Made comparisons with Red Riding Hood.
Seems to focus on moral issues.

Comprehension: Able to make several important inferences.
Uses prior knowledge well. Some problems with
decoding, esp. words with multiple syllables.

Other Observations: Likes folk tales. Wants to read
"more books like this one."

Will the book be shared? How? Tonya will read this aloud
to the 1st grade class on Friday.
She will practice it this week. This
should help with decoding.

Ideas for additional support: _____

book. It could also be something as elaborate as a diorama with a written
synopsis of the book. Suggestions for projects are listed in Figure 3-6 and
in Table 3-3. In addition, the model lesson on page 94 describes how individualized reading is used in one classroom.

FIGURE 3-6

Sample activities/strategies that might be used to conclude any individualized reading experience

 Read aloud to the class an exciting episode from your selection. Do not tell the other students what the ending is but encourage them to check the book out and read it for themselves.

 Make an advertisement for your book that tries to sell others on reading it. Put your ad up with others on a bulletin board labeled "Great Buys on Great Books."

 Make a crossword puzzle using vocabulary words found in your reading selection. You may wish to use a computer program to help you. Have the next person reading this book attempt to complete the puzzle, with your help if possible.

 Come to school dressed as one of the major characters in your book. When people ask you about your character, be certain to describe what the person did and how he or she acted.

 Write a different ending to your reading selection. Make it the final chapter. Post it on the bulletin board.

 Create a shoebox diorama illustrating one of the scenes from your reading selection. Attach a page to it listing the author, title, and illustrator of the book, as well as a description of the scene you have created.

 Write a letter to the author of your reading selection; send it to the author in care of the publisher.

 Write a letter to one of the characters in your reading selection. Put this with letters from other students on a bulletin board labeled "Letters to Characters in Books We Have Read."

 Read several books on the same theme written by different authors. Then write one review, comparing all of the books. Post your review on a bulletin board labeled "Critics' Corner."

Cooperative Learning Groups

The use of *cooperative learning groups* is a third method framework often used to support students in developing reading proficiency. Group discussion about children's literature has been shown to have a powerful effect on learning (Leal, 1993). This method framework goes by many different names: cooperative learning, collaborative learning, cooperative learning strategies, cooperative integrated reading and composition, cooperative reading teams, or collaborative learning groups. Depending on the definition, cooperative learning may also have many different sets of procedural steps. Cooperative learning is most commonly associated with holistic language learning and integrated beliefs. This text uses the term **cooperative learning groups** to refer to a method framework with these procedural steps:

cooperative learning groups
A method framework containing these four steps: define the learning task, assign students to groups, have students complete the learning task in their groups, and allow the groups to share their results.

TABLE 3-3

Activities that might be used to conclude a specific book in an individualized reading experience.

Selection	Activity
Where the Wild Things Are by Maurice Sendak	Make a map describing the route Max took to get to the place of the "wild things."
Alexander and the Terrible, Horrible, No Good, Very Bad Day by Judith Viorst	Write a book about yourself that follows the predictable pattern in this story, entitled *(Your Name) and the Terrible, Horrible, No Good, Very Bad Day*
James and the Giant Peach by Roald Dahl	Make a papier-mâché model of the peach on which James flew away with all of his insect friends. Use a balloon to mold the basic shape. Then cut out an opening and show James and his friends inside their home.
The Very Hungry Caterpillar by Eric Carle	Make a "book caterpillar" around the walls of your classroom. Make a head for your caterpillar and post it on the wall. Then cut out a pattern for a segment of the caterpillar's body. Have students write the title and author of each book they read on one of these segments and post them on the wall in sequence behind the head. Your caterpillar can even go out into the hallway, announcing your reading to the rest of the school.
Frog and Toad Are Friends by Arnold Lobel	Draw a picture of your favorite story and write a sentence underneath the picture describing what happened. Post this and other illustrations on a bulletin board entitled "Friendship."
Little House in the Big Woods by Laura Ingalls Wilder	Write a book of pioneer recipes using the descriptions found in this book. Possible entries might include: head cheese, smoked ham, and sugar snow.
The Little Prince by Antoine de Saint-Exupéry	Make a papier-mâché model of the asteroid where the Little Prince lived. Use a balloon to mold the basic shape.

1. The teacher defines a learning task.
2. The teacher assigns students to groups.
3. Students complete the learning task together through cooperative group activity.
4. The results of the learning task are shared with the other groups.

The first procedural step is to define a learning task for students. Teacher options are nearly limitless but should be related to instructional goals. For example, cooperative learning groups might be used to complete the guided reading portion of a story in a published reading program, having each member of a group read one character's part. Or each group could be given a set of statements and asked to decide whether the story or article they had read supported—or did not support—each of the statements (Herber & Herber, 1993). In addition, the group might be required to record its answer and the evidence from the story that supports its decision. Figure 3-7 provides other examples of tasks that might be used within cooperative learning groups.

The second procedural step requires the teacher to assign students to groups, usually three to five students per group. Cooperative learning groups almost always consist of students with a range of reading abilities. Heterogeneous grouping such as this allows students to benefit from the unique insights of each group member. It also avoids the motivational problems that result when lower-achieving students are placed in a single group. Often cooperative learning groups change composition with every task; at other times more stable teams are formed.

During the third procedural step students complete the learning task together in their groups. Each group usually designates one person to serve as a recorder/reporter. This individual keeps a written account of the group's decisions. Recording this information is important because the results of the group's work are often shared in a brief oral report to the rest of the class.

The fourth step, sharing the results of the learning task with the entire class, provides students the opportunity to compare their thinking with the thinking that took place in other groups. During this step, the teacher often summarize's each group's report on the chalkboard, sometimes in a table.

FIGURE 3-7

Strategies that might be used in cooperative learning groups

 Before students read a story or an article, have small groups list all of the information they already know about this topic. Then get together as a class and compare notes.

 After students read a story, have them work in their groups to develop a short script from one portion of the selection. Let them practice reading this script several times before reading it to the class.

 Before they read an unfamiliar passage, give students a list of words from the story that may be unfamiliar. Have each group try to define the words and generate one sentence that uses each word correctly. Then get together as a class to compare definitions and sample sentences.

 After students read a chapter in a content area text, give them a list of statements about the topic. Have each group determine whether each statement is supported by the information in the chapter. Have them record the evidence from the chapter supporting their decisions.

 After students read a chapter in a content area text, give them a list of statements about the topic. Have each group determine whether each statement is explicitly supported by the information in the text or whether they must "read between the lines" to infer the statement.

MODEL LESSON

A Cooperative Learning Group in Ms. Gallagher's Class

The Teacher Defines a Learning Task. During the next three weeks, Ms. Gallagher has decided to have the class working in five different thematic groups, which will be organized around the three most popular reading interests her students have right now: mysteries, pets, and the upcoming Olympics. The students in one group, the Mysteries Group, will be required to read at least one mystery from the class or school library. During the final three days of the time period, members of this group will share the books they have read, select an exciting episode from one of the mysteries, practice acting it out, and then perform it for the entire class. A second group, the Hamster Group, will research the selection and care of hamsters. After reading everything they can find in the school library, these students will present a group report to the class. The third and fourth groups will do similar projects on mice and tropical fish. Then each of these animal groups will send one member to go with Ms. Gallagher on a lunchtime field trip to the local pet store to select the new pets for the class. These groups will then be responsible for feeding and caring for their respective pet. The fifth group, the Olympics Group, will read materials from the school library on the upcoming Olympics and then complete a fact sheet prepared by Ms. Gallagher. After collaborating on this fact sheet, each member will prepare a written report. This group will then organize a classroom Olympics to take place at the end of the three-week period.

The Teacher Assigns Students to Groups. Two days before the groups are assigned, Ms. Gallagher explains the group projects and puts out sign-up sheets for students. Because these are interest groups, students select the project on which they wish to work. However, Ms. Gallagher limits each group to five members.

Students Complete the Learning Task Together. During the three weeks Ms. Gallagher circulates through the classroom during reading time, assisting students with their particular needs. She does a short lesson for some students on the use of the library's card catalog. She helps others use the index in their books to find specific information. She helps others select an interesting mystery. Ms. Gallagher remains available to help as students near the completion of their group's project.

The Results of the Learning Task Are Shared with the Entire Class. At the end of the three-week period, time is set aside for each group to display the results of its work. The other fifth-grade class in the school is also invited to this session.

Language Experience Stories

language experience stories (LES)
A method framework consisting of these four steps: provide a vivid experience, elicit oral language, transcribe oral language, and help students read what was transcribed.

A **language experience story (LES)** is a method framework commonly found in lower elementary grade classrooms. These stories, created by the teacher and students, are often used to supplement or replace the selections in a published reading program. Language experience stories are most commonly used in kindergarten and first-grade classrooms to develop beginning concepts about reading. They may also be used among older students experiencing difficulty in reading (Heller, 1988). They are especially useful in conjunction with classroom writing activities (Coate & Castle, 1989; Karnowski, 1989). Language experience stories are most often associated with a holistic language learning or an integrated belief about how children best learn to read. When using language experience stories, teachers often follow these procedural steps:

MODEL LESSON

A Language Experience Story in Ms. Brown's Class

Provide Students with a Vivid Experience. It is the first day of school. Ms. Brown wants to start the year off right by providing her first-grade students with a positive reading experience. She has brought her pet rabbit, Fluffy, into the classroom, and she introduces Fluffy to the class. She explains how to feed and care for the rabbit. She gives each student a chance to pet Fluffy and feel her soft fur. Then Ms. Brown puts Fluffy back into her cage and explains that Fluffy will be visiting their room for one month. She concludes by answering each student's questions about this new member of the class.

Elicit Oral Language That Describes the Experience. Ms. Brown then has the students sit on the rug in front of a large piece of chart paper taped to the wall. She tells the students that they are going to tell a story together and that she will write down their words. She asks for a title for a story that will describe what they just did. Tomas suggests "Fluffy the Bunny." Other students contribute a sentence each until a story is formed, describing their experience.

Transcribe the Students' Oral Language. As each student contributes a sentence, Ms. Brown writes it down on the chart paper with a felt-tip pen. The completed story looks like this:

> ***Fluffy the Bunny***
> Ms. Brown brought her bunny to our class.
> Its name was Fluffy.
> Fluffy has pink eyes and white fur.
> Her fur is REALLY soft.
> Fluffy bit Alexandra.
> But Fluffy didn't mean to hurt her.
> She thought Alexandra's finger was a carrot.
> We get to keep Fluffy in our class.
> THE END

Help Students Read What Was Transcribed. Ms. Brown uses two strategies today. First, she reads the title aloud and points out the word *Fluffy*. Then she asks students to find this word at other points in the story. ("Who can find another word that looks just like this? What does it say? . . . My, you can read so well already. Did you read books over the summer? Now, can anyone else find another word that says 'Fluffy'? Read it for us. Very good.") Several students get to come up and point to the word *Fluffy* in the story. Ms. Brown's second strategy is to read each sentence aloud, running her finger under each word but stopping before the last word in each sentence. Then she asks for volunteers to read that word. Ms. Brown concludes the lesson by praising her students for getting off to such a good start in reading this year.

---

1. Provide students with a vivid experience.
2. Elicit oral language from students that describes the experience.
3. Transcribe the students' oral language.
4. Help students read what was transcribed.

To begin a language experience story, teachers must first provide students a vivid experience, which then provides the content for the story. Teacher options for this first step are limitless—a field trip; a leaf walk; a

OPPORTUNITIES TO CELEBRATE DIVERSITY

When we think of method frameworks that celebrate diversity in our classroom one should immediately think of cooperative learning groups. The use of cooperative learning groups allows students to see the benefits of bringing together people with diverse backgrounds for problem-solving tasks. As children work with many different types of students, they come to appreciate the advantages diverse communities create (Raphael & Brock, 1993). This is one of the reasons you should continually mix up members in cooperative learning groups; it is important that each student have the privilege of working with others who share different experiences. Working with a student who is learning English as a second language, a student who brings the rich traditions from a Hispanic or Asian family, a student who lives with an aunt, a student celebrating the fall festival of Kwanzaa, and a student whose family keeps kosher can lead to important insights about living and working in a multicultural society such as ours.

visit from a neighborhood helper (such as a firefighter or a mail carrier); a movie; a filmstrip; a classroom pet.

The second procedural step is to elicit oral language from the students as they describe the experience. Again, teachers have a wide variety of options. The entire class might orally compose a description of the experience. Or students might individually draw a picture of something that happened during the experience. As students are drawing, the teacher might circulate, asking students to talk about what they have drawn.

The third procedural step requires the teacher to transcribe the students' oral language. If the class dictated a story or a letter together, the teacher could transcribe each student's sentence on the chalkboard. Another option would be to transcribe the story on chart paper, to produce a more permanent record of events in the classroom. The teacher could also transcribe the story by means of a computer program designed for language experience activities. If students drew individual illustrations, the teacher could transcribe their comments on the illustration (e.g., "Here is the puddle Mike fell into").

The final step in a language experience story is to help students read what was transcribed. Even if youngsters have not learned to recognize any words, teachers can use this step to build important concepts about reading. With very young students, teachers can show how sentences are read from left to right. They can also read sentences aloud, stopping before each student name in the story and asking that individual to read his or her own name. Another option is to read all of a sentence except the last word and have a student complete it (e.g., "We went on a trip to an apple farm and picked _____"). Students will have enough background knowledge about the experience to fill in the final word in most sentences. The model lesson on page 101 illustrates the use of a language experience story.

OPPORTUNITIES TO CELEBRATE DIVERSITY

Language experience stories are especially useful for your class if you have students who are learning English as a second language. By transcribing the English that these students know you provide them with a reading opportunity that is both familiar and supportive. You also model positive attitudes toward members of our society who are learning English as a second language. In addition, however, other students will have an opportunity to discover the English forms that are familiar to your students who are learning English as a second language and should increase communication opportunities in your class.

Directed Reading Activity

A **directed reading activity (DRA)** is the method framework commonly used to structure reading lessons in published reading programs. However, it can also be transferred to other contexts such as the reading of a social studies textbook, for example. The steps of a DRA are:

1. preparation
2. guided reading
3. skill development and practice
4. enrichment

directed reading activity (DRA)
A method framework containing these four steps: preparation, guided reading, skill development and practice, and enrichment.

Directed reading activities are especially useful when you wish to teach skills directly to your students. Teachers who use a directed reading activity usually have a literacy framework that includes a specific skills or integrated explanation for how children learn to read. Teachers with a holistic language learning explanation for development do not often use a directed reading activity in their classroom.

During the preparation portion of a DRA, teachers introduce any new vocabulary that might be unfamiliar to students. In addition, the purpose for reading is set. Many options are available to teachers during this first procedural step. Teachers may introduce vocabulary words in a variety of ways. They may directly teach the meanings, or they may allow students to induce the meanings from sentences in which the words occur. In addition, teachers may wish to design a cooperative learning task to promote understanding of these new words. Teachers also have considerable freedom in defining the purpose for reading.

The second step of a DRA, guided reading, usually takes place silently first. Then selected portions of the passage may be read and discussed. Teachers may wish to focus discussion on certain types of questions, such as inferential or predictive questions. Cooperative learning groups can also be used to accomplish this procedural step.

After guided reading, the next procedural step is skill development and practice. Here, teachers may wish to create cooperative learning group tasks such as those described earlier. Alternatively, they may wish to teach a skill directly and have students practice using that skill as a whole class.

MODEL LESSON

A Directed Reading Activity in Ms. Simonetta's Class

Preparation. On Fridays Ms. Simonetta devotes one hour to reading and discussing the *News Explorer*, a newspaper containing articles on current events of interest to students in the fourth grade. This week the newspaper is focused on the upcoming elections. Yesterday, Ms. Simonetta read through the articles and selected the following words that she thought might not be clear to her students: *electoral college, popular vote, electoral vote, Senate, House of Representatives, Speaker of the House,* and *cabinet.* At the beginning of the lesson, she writes each word on the chalkboard, along with the sentence in which it appears. Volunteers read each sentence and attempt to define the targeted word. Ms. Simonetta clarifies meanings and then lets the class members decide their purpose in reading the newspaper. They decide to see whether there is information in the newspaper with which they are unfamiliar.

Guided Reading. Everyone reads the paper silently. Then Ms. Simonetta suggests that the students form cooperative learning groups and list the new information they learned from reading the articles. Ms. Simonetta forms five different groups and reminds each to appoint a recorder/reporter to keep a written account of the new information. Ms. Simonetta circulates through the classroom, observing each group's progress. After each group is finished, she calls the groups together and asks each recorder/reporter to report back to the class. These reports produce a number of interesting issues that get clarified as a result of the discussion.

Skill Development and Practice. Ms. Simonetta uses this opportunity to review the concept of a main idea and supporting details. She defines each term and uses the lead article to give examples. She then gives each cooperative learning group a new task: to pick one article in the newspaper and determine its main idea and three supporting details. The groups complete the task and then get back together again to report their results.

Enrichment. Ms. Simonetta's class just completed its own election of class officers last week. Students ran for different offices, made campaign posters, presented campaign speeches, and had an election. Ms. Simonetta has decided to have each student write a newspaper article about some aspect of the election. She reminds them that their article should contain a main idea and several supporting details. After brainstorming possible topics, students complete their rough drafts. Ms. Simonetta then announces that the articles are to be edited and revised. Final copies will be put into a class newspaper about the election, which will be circulated throughout the school. As this is the first issue, Ms. Simonetta announces that she will serve as editor but appoints an associate editor to assist. The associate editor will become the editor of the next issue and will pick an associate editor.

The final procedural step in a DRA consists of an enrichment or extension activity. The nature of the activity depends on the passage that students have read. If they have read a chapter in social studies about the first trip to the moon, the teacher might ask students to write a diary entry for different days of this voyage. These entries could then be put together to create a diary of the trip aboard the Apollo spaceship. If, instead, students have read a chapter in science about Madame Curie, the teacher might ask them to imagine that she is still alive and that they can ask her any question they want. Students might write their questions in letters addressed to Madame Curie, which could then be

Cooperative learning groups support students as they acquire insights about literacy.

posted for all to read and enjoy. There are many ways to create enrichment activities.

Deductive Instruction

Deductive instruction is a method framework commonly used to teach a specific reading skill to students. It is often used by teachers whose literacy framework includes a specific skills explanation for how children learn to read. Sometimes teachers will use this method framework if they have an integrated explanation for how children learn to read. Deductive instruction contains four procedural steps:

1. State the skill or rule.
2. Provide examples of the skill or rule.
3. Provide guided practice.
4. Provide independent practice.

The first procedural step is to state the skill or rule that students should learn. For instance, you may wish to teach strategic knowledge about how to use an index at the end of an informational text. In this case, you would

deductive instruction
A method framework containing these four steps: state the skill or rule, provide examples of the skill or rule, provide guided practice, provide independent practice.

MODEL LESSON

Using a Deductive Method Framework in Mr. Gordon's Class

Mr. Gordon wants his students to develop an awareness of the structural characteristics of a newspaper article. He is starting a unit where students will be asked to write articles for a class newspaper and wishes to help his students understand the characteristics of this form.

1. *State the rule.* Mr. Gordon explains to students that most newspaper articles are written to inform readers about important current events. He explains that this form of writing usually tells the reader information about who, what, when, where, and why.

2. *Provide examples.* Mr. Gordon has his class read two short newspaper articles. He helps his students to identify each of these elements (who, what, when, where, and why) by underlining and labeling them on the articles.

3. *Provide guided practice.* Mr. Gordon provides his students with another short article and asks them to find and underline information about who, what, when, where, and why. He writes these categories on the chalkboard. The class then discusses their selections. Mr. Gordon writes each piece of information on the chalkboard next to the appropriate category. He has his students check their work as he does this.

4. *Provide independent practice.* Mr. Gordon divides the class into cooperative learning groups and gives each group a different article. Then he has each group identify each type of information in the article. Afterwards, one person from each group shares their article and their decisions with another group.

begin the lesson by having students open to the index in their social studies textbook and saying something such as, "This is an index. The index of a book may be used to locate information. You do this by looking for a word that describes the topic you are interested in, finding the pages where this information is located, and then turning to those pages."

The second procedural step is to provide examples of the skill or rule you are teaching. If you were teaching students how to use the index to find information in a textbook, you might write several topics and their associated page numbers on the chalkboard. Then you might show students how to use this information to look up items in their textbook.

The third procedural step is to provide guided practice in using the skill or rule. Here you want to allow students the opportunity to practice what you have taught them but under your guidance so that you can assist them if they need help. In our example above, you might have students turn to the index in their social studies book and ask them to find the page where information about Frederick Douglass might be found. Once they have located this information you might have them turn to that page to find out why he was a famous American. After several practice opportunities like this, you might make it a bit more challenging by asking students to locate the answers to several questions with the help of their index. The questions might include items like: When did Hawaii become a state? Who was Thurgood Marshall? Whose rights did Cesar

Chavez demonstrate for? If students had trouble, you would provide the assistance necessary for them to acquire the skill.

The final step in a deductive method framework is to provide students independent practice opportunities. After you are certain students know how to use the skill or rule, you want them to practice it without your support. Continuing with our example of the index, you might provide your students with a page containing questions such as those above and ask them to locate the information by using the index. Note that this step could be done by individuals working alone or by using a cooperative learning group method framework as described earlier.

Inductive Instruction

Inductive instruction is a method framework commonly used to help students develop an important principle about literacy. Instead of teaching a skill directly to students as with deductive instruction, inductive instruction presents examples and supports students as they determine the principle that applies. Inductive instruction is often used by teachers whose literacy framework includes a holistic language learning explanation for how children learn to read. Sometimes teachers will use inductive instruction if they have an integrated explanation for how children learn to read. Inductive instruction contains four procedural steps:

1. Provide examples.
2. Help students discover the insight.
3. Provide guided practice.
4. Provide independent practice.

You may have noticed that the procedural steps in inductive instruction are identical to those in deductive instruction with one exception—the order of the first two steps is reversed. Inductive instruction begins with examples and then uses those examples to help students discover the rule or principle.

Thus, the first step in inductive instruction is to provide students illustrations of the rule they are about to discover. Using the earlier example about how to work with an index at the end of an informational text, you might begin by having students turn to a page in their book, identify the main topic on this page, and write both the topic and the page number on the chalkboard. You could repeat this several times with different topics and page numbers, listing each on the board.

The second step in an inductive framework is to use these examples to help students discover, or induce, the insight you want them to acquire. Continuing with our illustration, you might ask your students to turn to the index at the back and see what they find next to the first topic they listed on the chalkboard. Students will probably notice several numbers next to this topic, including the page number they had just been on. You might then ask them what these numbers are. Several students will probably reach the conclusion that they are page numbers

inductive instruction
A method framework containing these four steps: provide examples, help students discover the insight, provide guided practice, provide independent practice.

MODEL LESSON

Using an Inductive Method Framework in Ms. Johnson's Class

Ms. Johnson wants her students to develop an awareness of the structural characteristics of a fable. She has developed a unit on fables and this is one of the insights she wishes her students to acquire. She has decided to use an inductive method framework at the beginning of the unit to develop this insight.

1. *Provide examples.* At the beginning of the unit, Ms. Johnson reads one fable aloud each day for several consecutive days. After each listening experience, she has the class discuss the story and their responses to it.
2. *Help students discover the insight.* After several days, Ms. Johnson asks her students to help her list the characteristics that are common to all of the fables she read to them. They respond with the following observations: animals are the main characters, the animals talk and act like people, there is usually a lesson (moral) at the end of each story, the stories did not really happen. Ms. Johnson writes these observations on the board.
3. *Provide guided practice.* Ms. Johnson reads another fable to her class to see whether the same structural elements also appear in it. The students discuss the ones they noticed.
4. *Provide independent practice.* Now Ms. Johnson has her class dictate a fable in a language experience story. She writes it on large posterboard so the class will have a permanent record to read together at other times. They begin by brainstorming possible plot lines. As they develop this story together, Ms. Johnson has them check to be certain that each of the elements is in the story. Afterwards they read their story together.

where information about this topic is located. You could then have them check their predictions by turning to the other page numbers listed next to the topic in order to see if this topic is also discussed on these other pages. After doing this several times, you can help students formally state the insight they have just discovered, writing it on the chalkboard: "The index of a book may be used to locate information. You do this by looking for a word that describes the topic you are interested in, finding the pages where this information is located, and then turning to those pages."

The third procedural step is the same as that of deductive instruction—to provide guided practice with the insight students have just discovered. As in our example above, you want to allow students the opportunity to practice what they have discovered but doing so under your guidance so that you can assist them if they need help. Again, you might have students turn to the index in their social studies book and ask them to find the page where information about Frederick Douglass might be found. After they have located this information you might have them turn to that page to find out why he was a famous American. Again, after several practice opportunities like this, you might make it a bit more challenging by asking students to locate the answers to several questions with the help of their index. If students had trouble, you would provide the assistance necessary for them to develop the insight you wanted them to acquire.

The fourth procedural step is also identical to that of deductive instruction—to provide independent practice. Perhaps this time, though, you might wish to have students work cooperatively in groups to locate information to questions you provide by using their index to locate the appropriate information. Afterwards, each group could check their answers with the rest of the class.

USING INSIGHTS FROM YOUR LITERACY FRAMEWORK TO MAKE DECISIONS ABOUT MATERIAL AND METHOD FRAMEWORKS

You will recall from chapter 2 that a literacy framework is comprised of your beliefs about two issues: How does one read?, and, How do children learn to read? Your beliefs about how one reads inform decisions about *what* to teach. Your beliefs about how children learn to read informs decisions about *how* to teach.

Decisions about using material and method frameworks are largely decisions about *how* to teach reading. They say little about *what* you will teach. Thus, as you think about which material and method frameworks to use you should consider your beliefs about how children learn to read. Do you have more of a holistic language learning explanation, a specific skills explanation, or an integrated explanation?

Holistic language learning, specific skills, and integrated explanations lead to quite different conclusions about which material and method frameworks support literacy learners the best. These relationships are summarized in Table 3-4. Teachers with a holistic language learning explanation of how children learn to read provide opportunities for students to see literacy skills in action, always in the context of authentic social contexts and always with authentic reading materials. Reading skills are not often directly taught. Instead, teachers develop classroom experiences where inductive learning is emphasized.

Teachers with a holistic language learning belief about literacy learning would not choose, on their own, to use a published reading program for instruction. They find these programs contain instructional activities that focus too much on skill development taught directly by the teacher. While they might appreciate the literature selections that appear in newer programs, the instructional practices suggested in teacher's manuals are far too teacher-directed and skill-specific to be appealing. They would prefer that students have more choice in their reading experiences and that these experiences not be reduced to specific skill activities.

Which of the method frameworks described in this chapter would you prefer, if you believed that children learn to read best by engaging in meaningful, functional, and largely self-directed experiences in authentic literacy contexts? You would probably find five method frameworks most consistent with your beliefs: read aloud response journal activities, individualized reading, language experience stories, cooperative learning

TABLE 3-4

Instructional consequences of different beliefs about how children learn to read

Explanation for How Children Learn to Read	Beliefs	Instructional Consequences: How to Teach?
Holistic Language Learning	Students direct much of their own learning and inductive learning is emphasized. Reading experiences always take place in the context of authentic social contexts and always with authentic reading materials.	Common method frameworks include: read aloud response journal activities, individualized reading, language experience stories, cooperative learning groups, and inductive instruction. Published reading programs are not typically used.
Integrated	Both student-directed and teacher-directed experiences are used. Both inductive and deductive learning are used. Reading experiences take place in the context of authentic social contexts and with authentic reading materials. Specific skills are taught when needed, often in mini-lessons.	Common method frameworks include: read aloud response journal activities, individualized reading, language experience stories, cooperative learning groups, directed reading activities inductive instruction, and deductive instruction. Published reading programs may be used but not as the only instructional approach.
Specific Skills	Teacher-directed reading activities and deductive learning are emphasized. Specific skills, often organized in terms of difficulty, are frequently taught.	Common method frameworks include: directed reading activities and deductive instruction. Published reading programs are commonly used, often as the only instructional approach.

groups, and inductive instruction. Each provides purposeful and practical experiences with print. And each allows students to direct their own inductive learning as they interact in social contexts with authentic reading materials.

Teachers with more of a specific skills explanation provide students with direct instruction on progressively more difficult reading skills. Published reading programs are a popular material framework for these teachers because the programs are often organized around specific reading skills taught directly by the teacher. Which method frameworks would they use? Only two of the method frameworks described in chapter 2 are frequently used by teachers with more of a specific skills explanation: directed reading activities and deductive instruction. These method frameworks take more of a teacher-directed stance towards literacy learning, teaching specific reading skills in a direct fashion. Sometimes, though, cooperative learning groups are used to provide practice opportunities for skills that have been taught deductively.

Teachers with an integrated explanation of how children learn provide opportunities for students to direct their own reading and writing experiences. In addition, these teachers give direct instruction on specific skills as students require such support. These often take place in mini-lessons with individuals or small groups around a particular skill or strategy. These teachers might use a published reading program for skill instruction but would probably supplement it considerably with the use of many different method frameworks in order to provide more relevant and self-directed literacy experiences in authentic reading contexts. All of the method frameworks described in this chapter might be used by teachers with integrated beliefs about how children learn best. These teachers would shift between teacher-directed and student-directed learning experiences as appropriate to meet particular student needs.

Comments from the Classroom

Nikki Robinson, a sixth grade teacher

Our school decided not to purchase a new published reading program this adoption year. Instead, each teacher got to select and purchase children's literature for our classroom libraries. I will still use the published reading program from time to time, even though I'm not required to, because there are some skill lessons that I know will help my sixth graders such as learning to check predictions and creating mind maps.

Before I began using mostly children's literature this year instead of reading basals, I spent a few days at the college library looking for some ideas on how to use literature effectively. I read about several strategies in *The Reading Teacher*. One article described how to use reading response journal activities. I really liked this idea. It seems to be a very natural way to guide instruction. I have integrated all of my language arts (reading, speaking, listening, and writing) into the reading program, and I begin every day with a reading response activity. Today, I read another chapter from *On the Banks of Plum Creek* by Laura Ingalls Wilder. Then I asked students to write a response in their journals. Carrie, the student I have been most worried about this year, wrote that she admired Laura and her family "because they were happy even though there were many things they did not have." This is the first time Carrie has really involved herself in the story. That made my day.

In two weeks, we will be starting a unit on the American westward migration in social studies, and I chose the Laura Ingalls Wilder book to provide some useful background knowledge for my students. I know that the literature I use can help make connections to other subject areas as well!

After journal writing and sharing, most of my students move into individualized reading. As students complete their selections, I have them sign up for individual conferences with me. Sometimes, when several students have read the same books or books about the same subject, we set up a small group conference and talk for a bit about the similarities and differences among the books. This discussion often evolves into several students proposing an activity together during which they will work as a cooperative group. For example, after reading *The Illustrated World of Oceans* by Susan Wells and *The World Around the Sea* by Brian Williams, students worked together to create a colorful mural. Some students painted the background for an underwater scene. Others crafted ocean animals, plants, and a shipwrecked vessel out of construction paper. They put numbers near each animal and plant and made a key to reference the names of each one. Working on the mural led to numerous questions about the ocean and its life forms. Students went to the library to get more information. Now the whole class wants to learn even more about the ocean. I have a new science unit and will use student groups to make them responsible for deciding how to begin and how far to go.

Major Points

- Teachers use a material framework when they use a published reading program for instruction. Using such a program reduces the complexity of decision making but may sometimes result in teachers abdicating their responsibility as insightful, reflective professionals. There are several ways in which you can modify the nature of these lessons to meet the needs of individual students more effectively.

- Method frameworks consist of two common elements: procedural steps for completing an activity and options for completing each one of the procedural steps. Method frameworks, like material frameworks, are used to reduce the complexity of classroom decisions but they provide teachers with more of an opportunity to use their special insight about their students.

- Each of the following method frameworks is commonly used to teach reading: read aloud response journal activities, individualized reading activities, cooperative learning groups, language experience stories, directed reading activities, inductive instruction, and deductive instruction. You should be familiar with the procedural steps for each method framework and some of the options that are possible for each step.

- Your literacy framework can be used to inform decisions about the use of different method frameworks. Teachers with a holistic language learning belief about how children learn to read will favor the use of read aloud response journal activities, individualized reading, language experience stories, cooperative learning groups, and inductive instruction. Teachers with a specific skills belief about how children learn to read will favor the use of directed reading activities and deductive learning. Teachers with an integrated belief about how children learn to read will favor all of the method frameworks described in this chapter.

Making Instructional Decisions

1. As teachers read the description of a new method framework, they often respond very favorably or very unfavorably; there is seldom a neutral reaction. Teachers' responses are often related to their beliefs about appropriate reading instruction. If the method framework is consistent with these beliefs, teachers respond favorably. If it is not, teachers respond unfavorably. Which of the method frameworks described in this chapter did you like the most? What does your response to this method framework suggest about your beliefs about how children learn to read?

2. It is your first year of teaching. Your principal has required all teachers to use the Silver Burdett and Ginn reading program. You are allowed to replace, refine, supplement, or even skip lessons in the teacher's manual, but student growth will be regularly measured and monitored by the skill tests that accompany this program. Your evaluation is also somewhat related to your students'

performance on these tests. You believe, however, that basals teach too many skills and you feel uncomfortable with the decision that has been made about their use. This is a common situation for teachers who find that decisions about instructional materials run counter to their own beliefs. Mosenthal (1989) describes it as putting teachers between a rock and a hard place. How do you think teachers should handle this situation? Would you follow lesson plans in the program closely to be certain your students pass the tests? Would you adapt the lessons? If so, how would you do this? Would you replace basal lessons with method frameworks? What would these be? Why would you make these changes?

Further Reading

Au, K. H. (1993). *Literacy instruction in multicultural settings.* Fort Worth: Harcourt Brace Jovanovich.

This text describes ways to make changes to typical instruction to meet the needs of students with diverse backgrounds. Topics covered include the nature of literacy, cultural and linguistic variation, multiethnic literature, and writing experiences in multicultural classrooms.

Hancock, M. R. (1993). Exploring and extending personal response through literature journals. *The Reading Teacher, 46* (6), 466–475.

The author describes the importance of response opportunities for readers transacting with literature. She then describes a wide variety of prompts that may be used to support students' responses to works of literature. These may be used also to structure read aloud response journal experiences.

Karnowski, L. (1989). Using LEA with process writing. *The Reading Teacher, 42* (7), 463–465.

This article explains how the procedural steps of language experience activities (LEA) and language experience stories may be combined with a process approach to teaching writing. It presents many examples of young students' writing. This technique is especially appropriate for kindergarten and first-grade students who are just beginning to read and write.

Worthy, M. J. & Bloodgood, J. W. (1992). Enhancing reading instruction through Cinderella tales. *The Reading Teacher, 46* (4), 290–301.

The authors describe a thematic unit containing Cinderella tales from many different cultures: Africa, China, Germany, France, and the United States. In exploring these tales, students come to discover many important insights about literacy, other cultures, and themselves. The unit contains preparation activities, guided reading experiences, and post reading activities.

References

Coate, S. & Castle, M. (1989). Integrating LEA and invented spelling in kindergarten. *The Reading Teacher, 42* (7), 516–519.

Cox, S. & Galda, L. (1990). Multicultural literature: Mirrors and windows on a global community. *The Reading Teacher, 43* (7), 583–589.

Flood, J. & Lapp, D. (1986). Types of texts: The match between what students read in basals and what they encounter in tests. *Reading Research Quarterly, 21* (3), 284–297.

Hancock, M. R. (1993). Exploring and extending personal response through literature journals. *The Reading Teacher, 46* (6), 466–475.

Harris, A. J. & Sipay, E. R. (1990). *How to increase reading ability* (9th ed.). New York: Longman.

Heller, M. F. (1988). Comprehending and composing through language experience. *The Reading Teacher, 42* (2), 130–135.

Herber, H. L. & Herber, J. N. (1993). *Teaching in Content Areas.* Boston: Allyn & Bacon.

Jachym, N. K., Allington, R. L., & Broikou, K. A. (1989). Estimating the cost of seatwork. *The Reading Teacher, 43,* 30–35.

Karnowski, L. (1989). Using LEA with process writing. *The Reading Teacher, 42*(7), 463–465.

Leal, D. J. (1993). The power of literary peer-group discussions: How children collaboratively negotiate meaning. *The Reading Teacher, 47* (2), 114–121.

Leu, D. J. & Ayre, L. (1992). Changes to children's literature in the basals of the 1980's and the 1990's. Paper presented at the 42nd annual meeting of the National Reading Conference, San Antonio, Texas.

Mosenthal, P. B. (1989). The whole language approach: Teachers between a rock and a hard place. *The Reading Teacher, 42* (8), 628–629.

Norton, D. (1990). Teaching multicultural literature in the reading curriculum. *The Reading Teacher, 44* (1), 28–40.

Pang, V. O., Colvin, C., Tran, M., & Barba, R. (1992). Beyond chopsticks and dragons: Selecting Asian-American literature for children. *The Reading Teacher, 46* (3), 216–224.

Raphael, T. E. & Brock, C. H. (1993). Mei: Learning the literacy culture in an urban elementary school. In D. J. Leu & C. K. Kinzer (Eds.), *Examining central issues in literacy research, theory, and practice,* Forty-second Yearbook of The National Reading Conference. Chicago: National Reading Conference.

Reutzel, D. R. (1991). Understanding and using basal readers effectively. In B. L. Hayes (Ed.), *Effective strategies for teaching reading* (pp. 254–280). New York: Allyn & Bacon.

Shannon, P. (1986). The use of commercial reading materials in American elementary schools. *Reading Research Quarterly, 19,* 68–85.

Short, K. (1993). Intertextuality: Searching for patterns that connect. In D. J. Leu & C. K. Kinzer (Eds.), *Literacy research, theory, and practice: Views from many perspectives.* Forty-first Yearbook of the National Reading Conference. Chicago: National Reading Conference.

Staab, C. (1991). Classroom organization: Thematic centers revisited. *Language Arts, 68,* 108–113.

Strickland, D. S. & Morrow, L. M. (1990). Integrating the emergent literacy curriculum with themes. *The Reading Teacher, 44* (1), 604–605.

Trelease, J. (1989). Jim Trelease speaks on reading aloud to children. *The Reading Teacher, 43,* 200–206.

Tunnell, M. O. & Jacobs, J. S. (1989). Using "real" books: Research findings on literature based reading instruction. *The Reading Teacher, 42* (7), 470–477.

Walker-Dalhouse, D. (1992). Using African-American literature to increase ethnic understanding. *The Reading Teacher, 45* (6), 416–422.

Worthy, M. J. & Bloodgood, J. W. (1992). Enhancing reading instruction through Cinderella tales. *The Reading Teacher, 46* (4), 290–301.

PART 2

Developing a Knowledge Base

CHAPTER

The Central Role of Children's Literature

4

"When I was young, my dad would read to me every night. I remember him reading *Green Eggs and Ham* and other books. He always used different voices for each character. When my sister, Sarah, was about two he started reading each of us a separate story in our bedrooms. One night, after Dad had read us our stories and gone downstairs, Sarah whispered to me from her crib across the hall. She wanted me to come into her room and read my book to her. I grabbed my book, tip toed into her room, shut the door, turned the light on, and read the story to her as best I could. I made up most of the story from what I remembered and from the pictures. When I was done she said, 'You read good.' I felt so grown up!"

An undergraduate teacher-in-preparation, recalling an early reading memory.

If you are like many adults, you can still recall some of your favorite books from childhood, books such as *The Snowy Day, Babar, Green Eggs and Ham, Where the Wild Things Are, Stevie, Little House in the Big Woods, Charlotte's Web, The Velveteen Rabbit.* These titles usually bring back warm and pleasant memories about reading. And your ability to retain those memories when you have forgotten many other childhood experiences reflects the profound effect that literature exerts on young children. As teachers, we need to ensure that our students have similarly positive experiences with literature. This chapter will explain how to do this.

Chapter 4 includes information that will help you answer questions such as:

1. Why should literature be at the center of a classroom reading program?
2. How can I use literature to develop independent readers?
3. How can I use literature to help children understand the diversity of the human experience?
4. How can I use literature to increase the variety and depth of students' responses?
5. How can I support the development of narrative discourse knowledge?
6. How can I use my literacy framework to guide instructional decisions about the use of literature?

KEY CONCEPTS

aesthetic stance	narrative discourse structure
Caldecott Medal	Newbery Medal
culturally conscious literature	read-aloud session
directed reading-thinking activity	readers theater
efferent stance	sustained silent reading
grand conversations	text sets
independent readers	thematic units on diversity
literature discussion groups	

MAKING CHILDREN'S LITERATURE THE CENTER OF YOUR READING PROGRAM

literature
Often a story but comprises a variety of text types, including fiction, nonfiction, and poetry.

Experiences with **literature** should be at the center of every classroom reading program because it is such an important vehicle for learning (Anderson, Fielding, & Wilson, 1988; Tompkins & McGee, 1993; Tunnell & Jacobs, 1989). When we use the term *literature* we include many different types of writing: fiction, nonfiction, and poetry. At its core, though, literature often represents a powerful story: the story of individuals who celebrate life as they struggle with its challenges.

It is easy to learn many things from a good story. This is why literature is so helpful for teaching; stories transmit important information to the next generation. Using literature to educate the younger members of a society is not a new phenomenon: every culture has used stories to pass important information on to future generations. Clearly, a story is an important vehicle for learning that has been used as long as humans have had the power of language.

Another reason why literature is such a powerful vehicle for reading instruction is quite straightforward: literature's positive effects reach into every component of literacy you encountered in chapter 2. Literature is one of the few vehicles that helps children simultaneously develop all of the components important to reading comprehension and response: affective considerations, emergent literacy, automaticity, decoding knowledge, vocabulary knowledge, syntactic knowledge, discourse knowledge, and metacognitive knowledge. With the exception of writing experiences, no other tool at your disposal has such a profound and pervasive impact on literacy development. Knowing how literature contributes to each component will help you understand why it is so important to reading instruction and how you can use it in a classroom reading program.

Developing Affective Aspects through Literature

Literature has a powerful effect on interest, motivation, and emotional response, three important affective aspects. Good literature captures students' interest and motivates them to find out how a story ends. Interested readers invest more of themselves in reading experiences and thus take more away from those experiences. Interested readers are willing to work harder to recognize difficult words, guess the meaning of unfamiliar words, and think critically about what they have read. Interested readers are motivated readers who quickly learn many things from their reading experiences.

Literature is also useful for children who are struggling to understand the realities of life. Children often find emotional support in stories about an issue they are trying to understand—death, love, fear, personal relationships, self-respect. Literature shows children they are not alone in their emotions, and it often provides solutions to issues of personal concern (Harris & Sipay, 1990).

Developing Emergent Literacy through Literature

Literature is important for developing emergent literacy both at home and at school. Parents who read to their children are preparing them for later reading experiences at school (Taylor & Strickland, 1986). In fact, many suggest that reading aloud to children on a regular basis is the most important thing parents can do to support their children's literacy development. Young children develop important insights from having a parent read to them—reading is enjoyable, print progresses from left to right, written words are related to spoken language, stories have a predictable structure, letters are used to form words, words are used to form sentences, and many other important insights (Clay, 1989; Cochran-Smith, 1984; Trelease, 1989a, 1989b). Similar experiences with literature in preschool and elementary school classrooms continue this development (Tunnell & Jacobs, 1989). Teachers can assist the transition to literacy by encouraging parents to read frequently to their children and by making literature experiences the center of reading programs at school.

Developing Automaticity through Literature

It is common to hear teachers of reading say, "The more you read, the better you read." There are many important truths in this simple statement. Perhaps the most important is that as we read we are continually practicing all of the many aspects of the complex process we call reading. Reading exciting works of children's literature makes your students better readers as they learn to recognize words, make inferences, use efficient reading strategies, and anticipate outcomes—automatically. Good literature encourages the reading of more good literature. Clearly, "The more you read, the better you read."

Developing Decoding Knowledge through Literature

A major goal within decoding knowledge is to develop automatic decoding skills. Because automatic decoding permits readers to focus their attention on a text's meaning and on their response, both comprehension and response increase with the development of automatic decoding (Harris & Sipay, 1990). Literature provides opportunities for children to develop this automaticity (Rasinski, 1989). Good literature engages readers, drawing them into a book to discover how the story turns out and getting them "hooked on books" (Fader, 1976). One book by an author is just not enough for these children. Once hooked, they have greater opportunity to recognize words and, as a result, to develop automatic decoding skills more rapidly.

Developing Vocabulary Knowledge through Literature

Literature increases vocabulary knowledge as it captures, entertains, and enriches the lives of readers with vivid experiences that are impossible to replicate in a classroom. Literature lets you travel to the top of Mount Everest or to the bottom of the sea; to the edge of the galaxy or to the center of Earth; to the time of King Arthur or to the time of space traders—all without leaving a comfortable chair. And participating in these experiences, if only vicariously, enriches a child's vocabulary and conceptual knowledge. What better way is there to understand words such as *Nazi, Europe, terror,* and *diary* than to read *Number the Stars* or *The Diary of Anne Frank?* What better way to visualize *prairie, headcheese, journey, pioneer, hearth, covered wagon, fiddle, threshing,* or *harvest* than to discover the *Little House* series by Laura Ingalls Wilder?

────────────────────────── **EXPLORING DIVERSE POINTS OF VIEW** ──────────────────────────

Each elementary teacher seems to find children's literature useful for accomplishing whatever that person believes to be most important in the curriculum. As you have seen, some teachers find literature useful for developing the skills essential for reading. Others promote literature to increase a desire to read. Many teachers look to literature to lay a foundation for multicultural understanding. And others believe that it is through literature that students develop critical thinking and response. What are your beliefs about the role of literature in the elementary curriculum? Do some of these purposes seem more important to you than others? Which ones?

Developing Syntactic Knowledge through Literature

Literature also helps young readers enrich their syntactic knowledge. The work of the best writers provides excellent models of language use. Young children are already familiar with the syntactic patterns of oral language; reading frequently to them introduces the more complex syntactic patterns found in written language. This is one reason why reading to children before they come to school is so helpful. Familiarity with the more complex patterns of written language is important for older students, too, as they will encounter increasingly more complex sentence patterns in content areas such as social studies, science, and math.

Developing Discourse Knowledge through Literature

Literature helps children develop a clear sense of what a story is and how stories are structured. With literature, children learn that stories have certain types of beginnings. They come to recognize that stories usually contain problems faced by main characters, problems that often are resolved through a series of episodes. Children also discover that different types of stories have different types of structures; for example, the structure of a fable differs from that of a mystery or a work of science fiction. Knowing the structure of different forms of writing helps both reading and writing in many ways. Children develop an enriched sense of story by engaging in rich literature experiences.

Developing Metacognitive Knowledge through Literature

The rich contexts of literature also support the development of metacognitive knowledge, enabling readers to develop effective reading strategies and comprehension-monitoring abilities. When readers are entranced by a story, they often discover useful reading methods on their own as they seek to discover how a story ends. Interested readers look for new ways to decode a word, novel approaches to determining word meanings, and different methods of making inferences. These experiences lead to new types of reading strategies; literature is thus very useful in developing strategic knowledge.

Literature also helps students monitor their own comprehension of a story. Engaging literature selections, by definition, provide reading experiences that prompt students to check their understanding of a story, developing comprehension monitoring in a natural way.

USING LITERATURE TO DEVELOP INDEPENDENT READERS

You can see that literature is a powerful vehicle for learning, enabling students to develop each component important to reading and response. These instructional benefits are clearly essential to consider. Nevertheless, as important as it is to teach children how to read this is not the ultimate goal of any reading program.

independent readers
Readers who know how to read and actually choose to read for pleasure, information, and personal growth.

The ultimate goal of each of us who works to support reading is to develop **independent readers.** Independent readers are readers who not only know how to read but, in addition, *choose to read for pleasure, information, and personal growth.* Independent readers read at home, not just at school. They regularly visit a local library. Independent readers are children who sneak a flashlight under the covers at night to find out how a story comes out and those who are likely to read a book in the evening

It is important to create a reading corner in your classroom so that students can spend time with a favorite book in a pleasurable setting.

instead of just watching television. Because these children choose to read independently, they have additional opportunities to develop their reading ability beyond the limited time available at school. As a result, they become better readers (Anderson, Fielding, & Wilson, 1988). Independent readers are lifelong learners who know how to read and use this ability to improve their own lives as well as the society in which they live.

Teaching our students to read without also developing their desire to read independently is pointless (Fuhler, 1990). We do not want our students to read only while they are with us at school. We want them to seek out reading experiences after they have left us so that they continue to develop into thoughtful and informed citizens. We need to keep this point in mind as we plan learning experiences for our students.

All of us should make the development of independent readers the most important goal of our reading program. If we wish to cultivate independent readers in our classroom through children's literature, we must do three things: become familiar with popular children's literature, identify our students' reading interests, and put children and books together in pleasurable settings.

Becoming Familiar with Popular Children's Literature

There are so many ways to become familiar with popular children's literature. You can begin by looking at books that have won the Newbery or Caldecott medals. The **Newbery Medal** is awarded annually by the American Library Association and the Association for Library Service to Children to the author of the "most distinguished contribution to American literature for children published during the preceding year." The **Caldecott Medal** is awarded annually by the same organizations to the artist of the "most distinguished American picture book for children published in the United States during the preceding year." It is important to keep in mind that Newbery and Caldecott medal winners are selected by adults, using adult criteria. Although medal-winning books meet the highest standards of the two associations that select them, they do not always meet the unique needs of children. Newbery and Caldecott medal winners are listed in Appendixes A and B for your use. You may find some of your favorites from childhood in these lists.

A second way to become familiar with popular children's literature is to look at books that have been selected as either Children's Choices or Teacher's Choices by the International Reading Association and the Children's Book Council. Each year, a joint committee from these two organizations coordinates a selection process involving thousands of children who read new books and vote for their favorites. The results have appeared in the October issue of *The Reading Teacher* each year since 1974. A similar process has started recently for teacher's choices. A free copy of the most recent choices can be obtained by sending a self-addressed 9-by-12-inch envelope, stamped with first-class postage for a two-ounce weight, to the International Reading Association (P.O. Box

Newbery Medal
An annual award given to the author of the "most distinguished contribution to American literature for children."

Caldecott Medal
An annual award given to the artist of the "most distinguished American picture book published in the United States."

8139, Newark, DE 19714, Attn: Children's [or Teacher's] Choices). You might wish to purchase copies in bulk and enclose them in letters mailed out to parents at the beginning of the year.

A third way to become familiar with popular children's literature is to read journals devoted to children's literature: *Horn Book Magazine* or *The New Advocate*. The *Horn Book Magazine* is the major journal in the field of children's literature. *Horn Book Magazine* reviews new children's books and contains articles on children's literature. It appears six times each year and can usually be found in a school or local library. *The New Advocate* is a similar type of journal devoted to the use of children's literature in school settings.

Another way to become familiar with popular children's literature is simply to talk to different individuals at a school. A school librarian can identify the books that are popular at a particular grade level. In addition, grade-level colleagues can share their experiences with popular literature selections. You may wish to set aside one lunch hour each week for teachers at your school to talk about children's literature and share ideas for using literature in the classroom.

A final way to become familiar with popular children's literature is to consult a comprehensive annotated bibliography. The following contain general bibliographies of children's literature.

Association for Library Service to Children, *Notable Children's Books* (Chicago: American Library Association, annual)

The Horn Book Guide to Children's and Young Adult Books (Boston: Horn Book Inc., annual)

All of these methods can help you to become more familiar with children's literature. However, none take the place of actually reading children's literature regularly. Personal familiarity enables you to make appropriate choices as you work to build a classroom library and as you make suggestions to individual students.

As you begin to rediscover the world of children's literature, you should develop an easy-to-access filing system. It takes just a few minutes after reading each book to jot down bibliographic information, a synopsis of the story, and several questions you might use to begin a discussion. You should write this information in a consistent format on index cards or on disk, using data base management software. You will find your growing file a useful aid in selecting books. It will also be useful during discussions with students about the books they have read. A sample literature card is illustrated in Figure 4-1.

Becoming Familiar with Students' Interests

In addition to becoming familiar with children's literature, you must determine the unique interests of your students, especially those who are reluctant readers. Knowing your students' interests will help you recom-

FIGURE 4-1

A sample literature card

Steptoe, John   Mufaro's Beautiful Daughters   30 pages
                       New York: Lothrop, Lee & Shepard Books, 1987

Synopsis: An African folktale originally collected near the ruins of an
            ancient city in Zimbabwe, this story tells a tale of good and
            evil. Nyasha ("mercy") and Manyara ("ashamed") are two sis-
            ters who have been invited to appear before the king who will
            marry one of them. Manyara, true to her wicked ways, secretly
            leaves the village first so that she can become queen. Along
            the way, she ignores a starving boy and a wise woman. Nyasha
            follows in her footsteps but feeds the starving boy and helps
            the wise woman. Guess who becomes the queen? Beautiful
            illustrations! A wonderful tale!

Discussion Questions:

1. How did you feel when Manyara left the village ahead of her sister?
   Why?

2. Some individuals find Cinderella tales such as this to be insensitive to
   women today. Do you? Why or why not?

3. How is this tale similar to Cinderella? How is it different?

4. There is much useful information about this story that did not appear
   in the story itself. Where does this information appear and what did
   you learn from reading it?

---

mend exciting selections to them. It will also help you make insightful
decisions about the literature you wish to integrate into your classroom
reading program.

How can you best determine your students' interests? While many
methods are available, the most common is an **interest inventory.**
Interest inventories contain questions for students to answer about
things they enjoy. Teachers review each student's responses to develop a
better understanding of the topics in which each student is most interested. Interest inventories are especially useful in putting reluctant readers and interesting books together. An example of an interest inventory
can be seen in Figure 4-2.

Additional information can be collected informally as you interact with
students during the day. Information about favorite activities, hobbies,
games, or sports is often revealed during classroom discussions. During

interest inventory
A form used by teachers to
gather information about
student interests.

....

FIGURE 4-2

An interest inventory used in grades 3–8

WHAT ARE YOUR INTERESTS?

Name *Tomie*   Date *September 10*

Books

1. What are the titles of the last two books that you have read?
    Maniac McGee
    Lincoln : A Photobiography

2. Do you have a favorite author? Who is it?
    Katherine Paterson

3. If you were going on vacation tomorrow and could only bring one book with you, what would it be about?
    Bridge to Teribithia

4. Where do you get the books that you read?
    Manlius library , home , presents

5. Which book would you most like to read again?
    Number the Stars

6. What is your favorite type of book? fiction? nonfiction? science fiction? romance? adventure? biography?
    fantasy? folk tale? historical fiction?
    Fiction , History

After School

1. Do you have any hobbies? What are they?
    animals, I like them
    I have tetras and zebra fish and neons

2. What do you like to do in your spare time?
    Play with my friends. Ride bikes. Play baseball.

3. If you had a day in which you can do anything and go anywhere you wanted, what would
    you do, and where would you go?
    I'd go fishing with my dad.

4. Do you have any pets? What are they?
    I have fish

5. Which animal would you most like to have for a pet?
    A Dog !!!

6. Do you read any magazines at home? If yes, which ones?
    Ranger Rick

7. Do you like sports? Which ones do you like best?
    Baseball

8. What are your favorite TV programs?
    Home Improvment

....

the year, you can discover much about your students through these informal discussions.

Putting Children and Books Together in Pleasurable Settings

If you are familiar with popular children's literature and know your students' interests, you will be able to create a classroom environment rich in literature. Many children will take advantage of that environment to independently engage in reading. You will start them on the road to becoming independent readers, who are able to read and also choose to read on their own. Others, however, will still be reluctant to select and complete a book on their own, indicating that they find books boring and uninteresting. Despite your best intentions and concerted efforts, some students will read a book only if it is required for an assignment.

What can you do about these reluctant readers? You will need to actively seek out ways to put these children together with books in pleasurable settings. Fortunately, there are as many ways to combine children and books in pleasurable settings as a teacher has ideas (Hiebert & Colt, 1989; Zarrillo, 1989). Some methods such as read aloud response journals and individualized reading activities have already been described earlier; others will be described here.

Read-Aloud Sessions. One of the best ways to bring children and books together in a pleasurable setting is relatively simple—demonstrate the pleasure of reading a good book in a **read-aloud session** each day. A read-aloud session is a method framework often used by teachers to develop independent readers. Although teachers conduct read-alouds in a variety of ways, a common set of procedural steps includes these suggestions (Trelease, 1989a, 1989b).

read-aloud session
A method framework used to develop independent readers; involves choosing a book, practicing reading it, creating a comfortable atmosphere, reading the selection expressively, discussing unfamiliar words, and supporting students' response.

1. Choose a book with both your students and yourself in mind.
2. Practice reading the book.
3. Create a comfortable atmosphere for reading aloud.
4. Read the selection with feeling and expression.
5. Discuss the meanings of unfamiliar words.
6. Support students' response to what you have read.

It is especially important to select a book that both you and your students will enjoy. Your students will not listen for long if the story is not interesting, and you will not be able to be an effective model if you are not interested in what you are reading. A set of good books for read-aloud sessions is listed in Figure 4-3. You will discover many others as you explore the world of children's literature.

After you have selected an interesting book, you should practice reading it. Prepare for the intonation patterns in unusual or exciting scenes; perhaps try out different voices for each of the main characters. When

FIGURE 4-3

Good books to read aloud

Wordless books for very young readers

Amanda and the Mysterious Carpet by Fernando Krahn
The Creepy Thing by Fernando Krahn
Frog on His Own by Mercer Mayer
The Hunter and the Animals by Tomie dePaola
Shopping Trip by Helen Oxenbury
Shrewbetinna's Birthday by John Goodall
Up a Tree by Ed Young

For young readers

Alexander and the Terrible, Horrible, No Good, Very Bad Day by Judith Viorst
Anasi Finds a Fool by Verna Aardema
Brown Bear, Brown Bear, What Do You See? by Bill Martin, Jr.
The Giving Tree by Shel Silverstein
Hey, Al by Arthur Yorinks
Julian, Dream Doctor by Ann Cameron
Miss Nelson Is Missing by Harry Allard
Mufaro's Beautiful Daughters by John Steptoe
Oh, The Places You'll Go by Dr. Suess
The Ox-Cart Man by Donald Hall
The Polar Express by Chris Van Allsburg
The People Could Fly: American Black Folktales by Verna Aardema
Sky Dogs by Jane Yolen
The Velveteen Rabbit by Margery Williams
The Very Hungry Caterpillar by Eric Carle
The Year of the Panda by Miriam Schlein

For older readers

A White Romance by Virginia Hamilton
Bridge to Terabithia by Katherine Paterson
Journey of the Sparrows by Fran Leeper Bus
Dear Mr. Henshaw by Beverly Cleary
Dogsong by Gary Paulson
Faithful Elephants by Yukio Tsuchiya
Fast Sam, Cool Clyde and Stuff by Walter Dean Myers
Maniac Magee by Jerry Spinelli
My Life by Earvin Johnson
Nobody Nowhere: The Extraordinary Autobiography of an Autistic by Donna Williams
Number the Stars by Lois Lowry
Roll of Thunder, Hear My Cry by Mildred Taylor
Skin Deep by Toecky Jones
Taking Sides by Gary Soto
The Diary of Anne Frank by Anne Frank
The Lion, The Witch and the Wardrobe by C. S. Lewis

you are ready, create a comfortable atmosphere for reading aloud. If possible, gather the students in front of you in a cozy part of the room where they can get comfortable. Be sure that children can see the story's pictures. Many teachers bring in a rocking chair for themselves and a rug for the children to sit on.

When everyone is settled, read the selection with feeling and expression. Let your voice create the mood. If the story is scary, you might want to read slowly and carefully. If the story is humorous, stop and enjoy the humor with your students. If the story is sad, let your feelings show. If the story contains a predictable sentence or phrase that repeats itself, stop and have your students say it for you. Share the pleasure of the reading experience through your voice and intonation.

Read-aloud time is also a great time to develop an understanding of new word meanings. As you encounter words that may be unfamiliar to your students, briefly explain their meanings. However, do not disrupt the story excessively for this purpose.

Be sure to give students an opportunity to respond to what you have read. This step may be accomplished in a brief discussion of listeners' reactions or in a writing experience that follows the story. If students liked the book, be sure to mention other titles by the same author and let them know where those books can be found. You might even want to bring in a few to share at the end of your read-aloud session.

Many teachers have a read-aloud session each day after lunch. Having it at that time provides a transition from the relatively unstructured lunchtime activities to the more focused activities in the classroom. For younger students you might read a single short book each day. For older students you might read one or two chapters each day from a longer selection.

You can see how one teacher used a read-aloud session in the following model lesson. Ms. Brown is a first grade teacher who wanted to help her students develop greater confidence in their ability to read books. She had recently used language experience stories, developing her students' familiarity with high-frequency sight words such as *see, can, what, you, me,* and *I.* Her students are also becoming familiar with using context to predict upcoming words, yet many of them think they cannot read until they are able to read their first book, something many have not yet done by themselves.

Read-aloud sessions are a powerful way to bring children and books together in a pleasurable setting. They allow teachers to be effective advocates and role models for literature, and enthusiasm is contagious. If children see their teachers interested and enthusiastic about literature, they will be more interested in reading themselves. Chapter 3 described how Read Aloud Response Journals can be used with read aloud experiences. Read-aloud sessions can also be used as a springboard for other learning experiences, several of which are listed in Figure 4-4.

M O D E L   L E S S O N
A Read-Aloud Session in Ms. Brown's Class

Choose a Book with Both Your Students and Yourself in Mind. Ms. Brown spoke with Ms. Hamm, the school librarian, about her needs. Ms. Hamm suggested that she look at several predictable texts, stories with a repeated phrase, sentence, or episode. Ms. Brown selected *Brown Bear, Brown Bear* by Bill Martin, Jr. This story looked easy to read because it repeated a three-sentence pattern over and over, changing only the name and color of the animal that appeared in each picture: "Brown Bear, Brown Bear. What do you see? I can see a redbird looking at me. Redbird, redbird. What do you see? I can see a yellow duck looking at me. Yellow duck, yellow duck. What do you see? I can see a blue horse looking at me . . ." It also contained many common words that her students could recognize. And Ms. Brown liked the simple illustrations that went with each picture. She thought these would be useful to practice color names.

Practice Reading the Book. Ms. Brown read the book to herself that night. She decided to help her students read some of the predictable patterns on their own after she introduced the sentence pattern and showed them the picture for each new animal.

Create a Comfortable Atmosphere for Reading Aloud. After lunch, Ms. Brown had her students sit on the rug in front of her rocking chair and get comfortable.

Read the Selection with Feeling and Expression. Ms. Brown introduced the book by telling her class that she had found a book that they could each read by the end of the day. Ms. Brown started reading the book to her class. After several repetitions of the pattern, she encouraged her students to read the third sentence in the pattern aloud each time it appeared. Thus, Ms. Brown would read, "Yellow duck, yellow duck. What do you see?" Then she would turn the page so that her students could see the next animal (a blue horse) and note its color. The students would then read the next sentence on their own, "I can see a blue horse looking at me." The students really enjoyed reading their part of the pattern. When she reached the end of the story, where all of the animals were listed, Ms. Brown pointed to each word and had the class read the appropriate color and animal name that appeared under each picture (brown bear, redbird, yellow duck, etc.).

Discuss the Meanings of Unfamiliar Words. Because all of the words in this story were familiar, Ms. Brown did not discuss any new word meanings. However, she did encourage students to talk about the different animals in the story.

Support Students' Response. As the class talked about the different animals in the story, Ms. Brown encouraged the students to share what they knew about each one. She learned a lot about her students from what they said. Afterwards, the students wanted to read the book again. Ms. Brown showed them again how to use the predictable sentence pattern and the pictures to help figure out each sentence. Because nearly all of the sentences followed the same pattern, the students were able to read the entire story together without Ms. Brown's assistance. Ms. Brown told her students how impressed she was that they had read the book all by themselves. Then, Ms. Brown put the book on the table in the reading corner and she encouraged them to read it whenever they had a free moment. Many of her students were surprised to discover that they could read an entire book when it contained such predictable sentences. She could see an immediate difference in the way they approached other books, too. The experience was so positive that Ms. Brown decided to bring in more predictable texts for her class. She encouraged her students to take this book home at night to read to their parents and show them what good readers they were becoming.

FIGURE 4-4

Teaching strategies to use for read-aloud sessions

Counting Books and Alphabet Books. Use counting books to develop number concepts with preschool and kindergarten students. Use alphabet books to develop letter concepts. Consider using one of these:

Anno's Counting Book by Misumasa Anno
My First Counting Book by Lillian Moore
The Very Hungry Caterpillar by Eric Carle

A, B, C's: The American Indian Way by Richard Red Hawk
Anamalia by Graeme Base
Ashanti to Zulu: African Traditions by M. Musgrove

After reading a counting book aloud, encourage children to write their own. Provide blank pages and help students draw numbered sets of objects on each page (one pencil, two bikes, and so on). Then write students' words at the bottom as they dictate to you. Staple the pages together, and don't forget to have students number the pages in their books, too. Do a similar activity with alphabet books.

Recipe Reading. Use books related to food to provide an experience with recipe reading. Consider using one of these:

Kwanzaa: An African-American Celebration of Culture and Cooking
by E. Copage
Everybody Cooks Rice by Norah Doley
Cranberry Thanksgiving by Wende and Harry Devlin
The Gingerbread Man by Ed Arno
Stone Soup by Marcia Brown
Rain Makes Applesauce by Julian Scheer

After reading these books, have students read and follow a recipe to make the food described in the book. You may want to do this in the school kitchen with parent helpers. Duplicate the recipe and send it home with children to share with their parents. Note that recipes have a unique discourse structure with which students may not be familiar.

Readers Theater.   Another way to put children and books together in pleasurable settings is to use **readers theater.** Readers theater activities engage a group of students in a dramatic presentation of a short script they have adapted from a shared reading selection. As a method framework, readers theater follows four procedural steps.

1. Choose and read a literary selection.
2. Write a short script.
3. Practice reading the script.
4. Orally perform the script for the class.

readers theater
A method framework used to develop independent readers in four steps: reading, writing a short script, practicing, and performing.

OPPORTUNITIES TO CELEBRATE DIVERSITY

Readers theater is a wonderful method framework for all types of students. It is especially helpful for supporting students whose first language is not English (Wolf, 1993). During a readers theater experience, students have multiple opportunities to read and discuss the selection with their colleagues. This will take place, for example, as students prepare the script and practice reading it several times for their presentation. This is very supportive for Limited English Proficiency (LEP) students if they have an opportunity to work in a group with more proficient English speakers. The experience can be even more supportive if the work of literature comes from the same culture as an LEP student. This will broaden everyone's understanding of cultural differences as it connects reading and writing.

Readers theater is a useful method framework for supporting all types of readers, including students whose first language is not English.

In the first step, a small group of students chooses and reads a literary or nonfiction selection. It may be a piece that one member of the group has discovered or a selection that the teacher suggests. In either case the first step is to read the passage and become familiar with it. Then the group writes a short script, which usually comes from one of the more exciting episodes in the story. In this process the group turns the narrative into a script for a dramatic presentation.

MODEL LESSON

Readers Theater in Mr. Catney's Class

Choose and Read a Literary Selection. A group of students has been reading *Maniac McGee* by Jerry Spinelli in a literature discussion group. Mr. Catney suggests that the students prepare a readers theater presentation based on an episode in the book and then share it with the class. The students discuss different portions of the story and finally settle on an episode from one of the chapters near the end.

Write a Short Script. The group sets off to draft a script. One of the students writes a preliminary draft that night on her computer at home and brings it to school to share with the others. As the students read it together, they make suggestions for several changes. Another student then takes those ideas and revises the script on the disk and prints out copies for everyone. The next day the group makes a few final changes and agrees that the script is ready. The students edit and print out final copies for everyone in the computer lab.

Practice Reading the Script. The following day is spent reading the parts orally and practicing for the performance. Students try out different parts and different ways of reading each character's voice. Eventually, they settle on the way the piece should be read and practice several more times.

Orally Perform the Script for the Class. Every Friday morning Mr. Catney sets time aside for students to share the reading experiences they have had during the week. This group presents its oral reading of the script in front of the room; the performance is polished and entertaining. Afterwards, the group identifies the source of the script in case other students want to read the book. Mr. Catney notices several students jotting the title and author down, and later that day he sees them looking for the book when the class visits the school library.

The next step is to practice reading the various parts in the script with intonation, expression, and eye or hand movements. Students should try different ways of reading each line and should also try out different parts until agreement is reached about who will read each part and how it will be read. Practice should continue until the group feels ready to perform the script for the class.

Usually a readers theater performance is given without props and with readers sitting on chairs in the front of the room. Such a presentation differs from that of a play in that the message is usually communicated through the voices of the readers—their rhythm, intonation, and pace—rather than through the appearance and movement of actors. Some teachers and students, however, prefer to stage more elaborate readers theater in which props and moving actors are used.

Initially, readers theater may require teacher direction and guidance, perhaps even teacher-developed scripts to be used as examples. Commercially prepared scripts are available from Readers Theater Script Service (P.O. Box 178333, San Diego, CA 92117). However, after students have had several opportunities to participate in a readers theater presentation, they will be eager to select their own pieces, write their own scripts, and determine their own performances. In the model lesson on page 135, Mr. Catney's fifth graders have already completed several readers theater activities with prepared scripts. Now he wants them to read a literature selection and prepare their own script, which they will then practice and perform.

Reading Corners. If you are committed to putting children and books together in pleasurable settings, it is essential that you establish a **reading corner** in your classroom, where students can interact with books and other reading materials in a comfortable fashion. In addition to the reading materials, a reading corner often contains a bookshelf, magazine rack, newspaper rack, carpet, comfortable chairs, pillows, and display table. A reading corner should be designed to help students become independent readers.

With the cooperation of the school library or media center, you might establish a small classroom library in your reading corner. You could develop a rotating series of displays, highlighting particular authors or categories of books. And over time you could acquire your own classroom collection of books, which could then be used to implement individualized reading, a method framework described in chapter 3. Classroom libraries can be started without great expense, using paperback editions of children's literature, which publishers make available at reasonable prices. Several addresses are listed below:

Scholastic Book Services, 904 Sylvan Avenue,
Englewood Cliffs, NJ 07632

Troll Associates, 320 Route 17, Mahwah, NJ 07430

Xerox Educational Publishers, 245 Long Hill Road,
Middletown, CT 06457

In addition, publishers of paperback books for children often manage book clubs for classrooms. Once a month, classrooms receive a listing of available titles, and students may place orders through the teacher. Teachers and students are under no obligation to purchase books at any time, but teachers usually receive free books for their classroom libraries if a purchase is made.

You might also decide to have your class subscribe to one of several magazines devoted to children. If you do, be sure to announce each issue as it arrives and display it prominently in your reading corner. Popular children's magazines include the following:

Cricket (Cricket Magazine, P.O. Box 51144, Boulder, CO 80321-1144): stories, poetry, and informational articles

Ebony, Jr. (Johnson Publishing Company, 820 South Michigan Avenue, Chicago, IL 60605): articles, poetry, and stories about famous African Americans

Kids (Kids Publishing, Incorporated, 777 Third Avenue, New York, NY 10017): a magazine written by children for children

reading corner
Portion of a classroom devoted solely to reading and used to develop independent readers.

National Geographic World (National Geographic World, P.O. Box 2330, Washington, DC 20077-9955): material from *National Geographic* written for primary-grade students

Ranger Rick (National Wildlife Federation, Membership Services, 8925 Leesburg Pike, Vienna, VA 22180-0001): articles and stories on wildlife and conservation with color photographs

Sesame Street Magazine (Sesame Street Magazine, P.O. Box 52000, Boulder, CO 80321-2000): thematic issues with games, activities, and stories

A reading corner can become an important location for developing independent readers. You can develop many creative strategies to use in such a spot, some of which are described in Figure 4-5.

Sustained Silent Reading. Another way to bring students and books together is to provide regular **sustained silent reading (SSR).** Sustained silent reading, or uninterrupted sustained silent reading (USSR), is a method framework that provides uninterrupted time for both students and teachers to read self-selected materials (McCracken, 1971). Recently, sustained silent reading has also been referred to as a time to Drop Everything And Read or DEAR. Regardless of the label you use, this method framework consists of three procedural steps.

1. Introduce the purpose and procedures.
2. Be sure that everyone has something to read.
3. Everyone reads silently without interruptions.

sustained silent reading (SSR)
A method framework used to develop independent readers by providing time for them to read self-selected materials; involves introducing the process, ensuring that everyone has something to read, and reading silently without interruptions.

....

FIGURE 4-5
Teaching strategies to use with reading corners

Author of the Week. Make an author-of-the-week bulletin board for your reading corner, and have each student be responsible for the board for one week. Have the responsible student research a favorite author and create the display, which might contain a short biography, the titles of important books, and a photograph. If students select their authors early in the year, they could write to them, telling them about their selection for the display. The letters should be addressed to the authors' publishers. Some authors will respond, and the responses could be displayed.

Book Swapping. Set up a swap table in your reading corner, where each student who contributes a book to the table is entitled to take one. You might also consider requiring students to bring in two books for every one they take. You could then use the extra book in your classroom library.

Book Talks. Each week introduce new additions to your classroom library in a book talk. Tell your students a few things about each author and book, and then read a short paragraph from the book to interest students. When you are finished, place the books on the display table in your reading corner.

....

It is important that you introduce the purpose and procedures of this activity before beginning. Several days ahead you should explain what students will be expected to do during sustained silent reading. Tell them that this will be a time to read self-selected materials silently without interruption. It is especially important that students understand that they will need something to read each day there is sustained silent reading. It is best to schedule the activity on a regular basis so that students are always prepared with materials to read.

On the day that you begin, have students take out the materials they have chosen to read and start the reading session. Be sure to have several extra reading selections to share with students who may have forgotten to bring their own. It is very important that you, too, read something for pleasure during this period. Completing homework assignments, grading papers, and similar activities are not allowed. This is a time to read something for pleasure.

Initially you may wish to schedule SSR for short periods, but gradually the time can be increased. Interruptions are not allowed during sustained silent reading because they often result in a loss of comprehension and interest for readers. Questions, comments, and other conversation should be held until after the silent reading period has been concluded. In addition, no students should be asked to report on what they have read. Sustained silent reading must be truly free reading for pleasure if you hope to develop independent readers.

Although SSR is usually implemented within individual classrooms, an entire school can participate in the activity. When it does, children, teachers, and even the school secretary and custodian will be found reading at this time.

In the model lesson that follows, Ms. Pease has decided to use SSR in her eighth-grade class to provide more independent reading experiences for her students.

The School Library or Media Center. When considering pleasurable settings in which to bring children and books together, you should not be limited by the four walls of your classroom. The school library or media center should be at the center of each school's efforts to develop independent readers. Reserve time for a visit to this special place at least once a week, and coordinate the literature experiences that you and the school librarian can provide. Be sure to share what you are doing in the classroom and find out what the librarian is doing as well. In addition, ask about useful books on themes you are developing in class. These can be borrowed, introduced in a book talk, and placed in your reading corner.

Your school library is also the perfect place to obtain books for read-aloud sessions, sustained silent reading, or readers theater. And when students enjoy a particular story you have read aloud, remind them that it came from the library. Then, provide them with a list of related titles by the same author or on the same topic. Ask the librarian to assist you

MODEL LESSON
Sustained Silent Reading in Ms. Pease's Class

Introduce the Purpose and Procedures. On Monday, Ms. Pease announces to her students that they will begin SSR on Thursday. She explains that a 10-minute session each day will be devoted to reading whatever material anyone chooses to read. She tells her students that there are only two rules for this activity: (1) everybody must read, and (2) there will be no interruptions. Ms. Pease explains that the purpose of SSR is to encourage students to develop independent reading interests. She reminds them that they may read whatever they wish and that they will need to have something to read each day beginning on Thursday. One student asks whether he may read a comic book. Ms. Pease explains that students may read anything they wish, including comics, magazines, and newspapers. On Tuesday and Wednesday Ms. Pease again reminds students to bring something to read for Thursday's first SSR session.

Be Sure That Everyone Has Something to Read. Thursday afternoon Ms. Pease announces that it is now time to begin sustained silent reading. She reminds her students of the two basic rules: (1) everybody must read, and (2) there will be no interruptions. She tells students to take out what they brought to read and begin. Two students have forgotten to bring something. Ms. Pease takes out several magazines that she brought for this purpose and has the students choose something to read from these materials. Then, Ms. Pease begins reading the book she brought to read, JFK's *Profiles in Courage.*

Read Silently Without Interruptions. When several students begin whispering, Ms. Pease reminds them of the second rule for sustained silent reading. The remainder of the period goes quietly. After 10 minutes Ms. Pease announces that the time for sustained silent reading is over. She discusses the activity with her students; everyone seemed to enjoy it. Ms. Pease announces that the class will engage in sustained silent reading each day and that everyone should bring something to read. She mentions that she will increase the amount of time to 20 minutes as they become familiar with the activity.

with this task. Pass out the lists just before your regular class visit to the school library. Encourage students to locate books on the list and check them out.

If your school library is well-stocked, take full advantage of it. If you do not have a good library, advocate among your colleagues, principal, and students' parents to improve it. A good school library is important if students are to develop into independent readers.

The Home Environment. There is a well-known saying from Africa that "It takes an entire village to raise a child." This important insight could apply to the development of independent readers as well. As a teacher you need to enlist the support of all of the important people in the lives of your students. If you are committed to developing independent readers you must especially consider ways to extend pleasurable reading situations to children's homes. To do so you should actively seek the assistance of parents. Parents are almost always willing to help you in these efforts but sometimes do not know what to do. This will require you to regularly communicate the importance of a home environment that supports reading and provide clear examples of what parents can do to accomplish this. Enlist parents as an important part of your team at open houses, back-to-school nights, and report card conferences. Send home a letter listing specific ways in which they can help their children become better readers. Use a letter like the one in Figure 4-6. Feel free to copy or edit this letter if it will help you in your work.

Other Activities Promoting an Environment Rich in Literature. As you spend time in schools, you will encounter many new and exciting instructional activities, bulletin board ideas, reading-center tasks, and other means of developing a classroom environment that is rich in literature. Some ideas will come from colleagues, others will come from professional journals, and still others will come from your own thinking about and planning for tomorrow's lesson. It will be helpful for you to keep track of these ideas, regardless of their source.

You should begin now to collect and organize the ideas that you think are useful. Some teachers keep a notebook for literature ideas; others keep their ideas on separate 3×5-inch cards, organized in a file box. Still others organize this information on a computer, using data base management software. However you choose to record and organize your ideas, you might want to include some of the suggestions in Figure 4-7.

A Final Note

It is important that children leave your classroom at the end of the year as better readers. It is equally important, however, that they leave your room as independent readers. Becoming familiar with popular children's literature, identifying your students' reading interests, and putting children and books together in pleasurable settings are the tools of an effective independent reading program. As you acquire and refine your strategies for developing independent readers you will be rewarded by children taking books home to see how a story comes out. You will see children having a hard time putting a book down as your class goes off to lunch. And you will notice more and more of your students spending time in the enriching world of children's literature. These patterns will tell you that you have succeeded in helping the students in your class become independent readers.

USING LITERATURE TO HELP CHILDREN UNDERSTAND THE DIVERSITY OF THE HUMAN EXPERIENCE

There are other reasons, too, why literature should be at the center of your reading program. One of the most important is that literature is a tremendous tool for helping children understand the diversity of the

FIGURE 4-6

A sample letter sent home to parents at the beginning of the school year

September 4

Dear Parents,

The beginning of school is such an exciting time for everyone. It is a time of new beginnings, new friends, and wonderful new experiences. It is also the time when I receive many questions from parents. Most want to know what they can do to help their children in school.

The most important thing you can do is very simple—provide a home environment that supports reading. Reading independently at home will assist your child in each and every subject area, from reading to science, from math to social studies. Reading is central to everything your child does at school.

How can you create this environment? I have developed a list of six suggestions. Each is easy to do, each will make an important difference in your child's development.

1. Every day set aside a regular time to read with your child. Sharing a good book at bedtime is an enjoyable way to end the day. Reading together for 15 minutes each day is the single most important thing you can do to help your child at school.
2. If you have not already done so, take your child to the local library, and help him/her obtain a library card. Make a visit to the library a regular weekly event.
3. If you have not already done so, help your child establish a personal library. Both the necessary shelving and a beginning set of books can be acquired inexpensively. Shelving can be as simple as a freshly painted set of boards and bricks. Books can be acquired as birthday and holiday presents.
4. Create a quiet place in the home where your child can read without being interrupted—away from family traffic and television. Join your child in this place during a regular reading time.
5. Model your own reading habits for your child. When you come across something of interest as you read, show it to your child. Also, involve your child when you search for information in a phone book, TV guide, dictionary, or repair manual. Explain to your child what you are doing.
6. Encourage the members of your family to give books as holiday and birthday presents. Giving a book as a present tells your child how important reading is. If you need help selecting a good title I would be happy to help as would our school librarian.

If you have any further questions about how you can help your child, please call me. I welcome the opportunity to talk with you.

Cordially,

Emily Dodson

FIGURE 4-7

Opportunities to further encourage the use of children's literature

 Book Cover Doors. Turn your classroom door into a book cover each month, and use that opportunity to announce to the rest of the school what you are reading aloud to your class. In the lower grades let your students vote on their favorite read-aloud book from the past month. In the upper grades have your students design and construct the book cover for the chapter book you are reading aloud.

 Literature Motivators. Write to the Children's Book Council at 67 Irving Place, New York, NY 10003, for a catalog of bookmarks, posters, and other promotional material.

 RIF. Write to RIF (Reading Is FUNdamental) at the Smithsonian Institution, Department P, 600 Maryland Ave, SW, Washington, DC 20560. RIF coordinates a nationwide program to provide each child with three free books. RIF will provide 75 percent of the cost if local groups provide 25 percent. Inquire about current procedures for including your students in this program.

 Book Fairs. Encourage your school's parent-teacher organization to sponsor a book fair. Invite book dealers to display and sell their new books each year in the school auditorium or cafeteria.

---

human experience. As members of a democratic and increasingly multicultural society, each of us needs to understand the unique perspective of many different types of individuals, each with a special set of cultural, linguistic, and historical experiences. The nature of our democracy depends, ultimately, on our ability to understand and value these different experiences. Learning about other cultural experiences makes each of us a more sensitive, more knowledgeable, and more valuable member of society. Literature can be an important ally in accomplishing this goal.

Fortunately, we are able to draw upon an increasingly rich collection of what Harris (1992) refers to as **multicultural literature** and **multiethnic literature** to assist us in these important tasks. According to Harris, multicultural literature focuses on groups that have traditionally existed in a subordinate status relative to the dominant, mainstream culture of our country. This would include literature with people of color (such as African Americans, Hispanic Americans, Native Americans, and Asian Americans); regional cultural groups (such as Appalachian, Cajun, and French-Canadian); religious minorities (such as the Amish, Jewish, or Islamic members of society); the less abled; the aged; and literature that describes women and girls in non-stereotypical roles. Multiethnic literature, according to Harris (1992), includes literature that focuses on people of diverse ethnic groups such as African Americans, Hispanic Americans, Native Americans, and Asian Americans. Au (1993) and Yokota (1993) point out that the best literature in each category is literature that is culturally conscious. **Culturally conscious literature** accu-

multicultural literature
Literature focusing on groups that have traditionally existed in a subordinate status relative to the dominant, mainstream culture of our country.

multiethnic literature
Literature that focuses on people of diverse ethnic groups.

culturally conscious literature
Literature that accurately represents a group's values, culture, history, and language with characters who are complex and not stereotyped.

OPPORTUNITIES TO CELEBRATE DIVERSITY

Children's literature provides special opportunities to help everyone understand how people endeavor to fit into a society that wants to include all its citizens but struggles with how this should be done (Pang, Colvin, Tran, & Barba, 1992; Walker-Dalhouse, 1992). There simply is no other set of materials that are as rich in potential for celebrating diversity and for helping all of your students to understand what it is like to walk in someone else's shoes. Children's literature allows you to bring into the classroom a complete range of human experiences and cultural backgrounds, experiences that do not always exist in even the most diverse classroom (Norton, 1990; Worthy & Bloodgood, 1992). Bringing these works into your classroom sends an important message to your students about the respect and dignity each of us needs to accord every human experience (Cox & Galda, 1990). Your literature choices, your responses, and your approach to this issue are central to accomplishing this most important goal. Au (1993) has described several other important reasons for using literature that portrays a variety of cultural experiences. First, children feel pride in themselves and their culture when they see their backgrounds valued in classroom reading experiences. Second, students develop a richer appreciation of the historical forces that have shaped American society and the contributions made by different cultural groups. Finally, a literature of diversity enables all students to explore issues of social justice. Exploring issues of social justice is essential to preparing children for citizenship in a diverse society where these issues are fundamental to our collective well being.

rately represents a group's values, culture, history, and language with characters who are complex and not stereotyped. Examples of literature selections most would recognize as culturally conscious can be seen in Table 4-1.

Although these works inform us about some of the important cultural experiences in our country they are limited to cultural and ethnic groups within our own society. Understanding the diversity of the human experience should not be limited to our national borders. Our world is quickly shrinking in response to powerful social forces and technological innovations, bringing each of us into closer contact with people who have had cultural experiences different from our own. As citizens of our increasingly interdependent world, we have to rely upon one another for our survival and well being. Understanding the diversity of the global human experience is central to achieving the type of life that we all seek on this earth; sensitive works about the experience of people in other countries are important for this purpose. For example, *Sami and the Time of Troubles* by Florence Parry Heide and Judith Heide Guilliland concerns the struggle of people in Lebanon for peace in a time of strife; the French story *You Be Me, I'll Be You* by Pili Mandelbaum focuses on skin color in a mixed-race family; and *Faithful Elephants: A True Story of Animals, People, and War,* by Japanese author Yukio Tsuchiya, shares a touching story about the consequences of war.

TABLE 4-1

Examples of culturally conscious literature selections

Celebrating African American experiences

Anansi the Spider by Gerald McDermott
Ashanti to Zulu by Leo and Diane Dillon
Cornrows by Camille Yarbrough
The Dark Way by Virginia Hamilton
Fast Sam, Cool Clyde and Stuff by Walter Dean Myers
The Hundred Penny Box by S. B. Mathis
Jambo Means Hello: Swahili Alphabet Book by Muriel Feelings
John Henry by Ezra Jack Keats
Mufaro's Beautiful Daughters by John Steptoe
Moja Means One: Swahili Counting Book by Muriel Feelings
More Stories Julian Tells by Ann Cameron
Roll of Thunder, Hear My Cry by Mildred Taylor
Tailypo! by Jan Wahl
Tar Beach by Faith Ringgold
Shaka: King of the Zulus by Diane Stanley
Some of the Days of Everett Anderson by Lucille Clifton
A Story—A Story: An African Tale by Gail Haley
Traveling to Tondo: A Tale of the Nkundo of Zaire by Verna Aardema

Celebrating Hispanic experiences

...And Now Miguel by Joseph Krumgold
Baseball in April by Gary Soto
Benito by Clyde Bulla
The Black Pearl by Scott O'Dell
Dreams by Ezra Jack Keats
Flecha al Sol by Gerald McDermott
Friday Night Is Papa Night by Ruth Sonneborn
Gilberto and the Wind by Marie Hall Ets
The Girl from Puerto Rico by Hila Colman
Louie by Ezra Jack Keats
Mira! Mira! by Dawn Thomas
Nine Days to Christmas by Marie Hall Ets
Taking Sides by Gary Soto
Three Stalks of Corn by Leo Politi
Viva Chicano by Frank Bonham

Celebrating Asian experiences

Child of the Owl by Laurence Yep
Dragonwings by Laurence Yep

TABLE 4-1 *continued*

Dreamcatcher by Audrey Osofsky
Faithful Elephants by Yukio Tsuchiya
Farewell to Manzanar by Jeanne Wakatski Houston
First Snow by Helen Courant
Hello, My Name is Scrambled Eggs by Jamie Gilson
A Jar of Dreams by Yoshiko Uchida
Lon Po Po by Ed Young
The Journey: Japanese Americans, Racism, and Renewal by Sheila Hamanaka
The Star Fisher by Laurence Yep
Tales from the Gold Mountain by Paul Yee
Tet: The New Year by Kim-Lan Tran
Yeh-Shen: A Cinderella Story from China by Ai Ling Louie

Celebrating Native American experiences

Brother Eagle, Sister Sky by Susan Jeffers
High Elk's Treasure by Virginia Driving Hawk Sneve
Island of the Blue Dolphins by Scott O'Dell
Lone Bull's Horse Raid by Paul Gobel
Our Cup Is Broken by Florence Crannell Means
Pueblo Storyteller by Diane Hoyt-Goldsmith
Red Hawk's Account of Custer's Last Battle by Paul and Dorothy Gobel
The Desert Is Theirs by Byrd Baylor
The Girl Who Loved Wild Horses by Paul Gobel
The Sacred Path: Spells, Prayers, and Power Songs of the American Indians by
   John Bierhorst
The Sign of the Beaver by Elizabeth George Speare
Whirlwind Is a Ghost Dancing by Leo and Diane Dillon

Celebrating many additional cultural experiences

The Amish by Michael Erkel
Babushka's Doll by Paricia Polacco
Balancing Girl by Berniece Rabe
Stay Away from Simon! by Carol Carrick
Cowboy by Bernard Wolf
*Here I am! An Anthology of Poems Written by Young People in Some of
   America's Minority Groups* by Virginia Baron
Number the Stars by Lois Lowry
Dicey's Song by Cynthia Voight
How Could You Do It, Diane? by Stella Pevsner
Watch the Stars Come Out by Riki Levinson
Nadia the Willful by Sue Alexande

OPPORTUNITIES TO CELEBRATE DIVERSITY

To locate other children's literature that helps students understand the diversity of the human experience you may be interested in looking at reference volumes for multicultural, multiethnic, and international literature. The best we have found is:

> Miller-Lachmann, L (1992). *Our family. Our friends. Our world. An annotated guide to significant multicultural books for children and teenagers.* New Providence, NJ: R.R. Bowker.

This reference volume contains bibliographic information and summaries of children's literature reflecting the many different cultural experiences in our society and around the world. It is a tremendous resource for teachers but is sometimes hard to obtain. Most city libraries will have a copy of this work in their reference section or at the librarian's desk. If your school does not own a copy of this important resource, perhaps you can encourage them to purchase one.

Strategies for Using Literature to Celebrate Diversity

Rasinski and Padak (1990) describe four basic approaches to using multicultural and multiethnic literature in the classroom. Some teachers, they point out, use a **contributions approach.** With a contributions approach, lessons on diversity and related literature selections usually enter the classroom because of their relationship to the calendar. Cinco de Mayo, for example, might be a time when Hispanic literature is used to develop greater awareness of Hispanic Americans and their contributions to our country. Or, Black History Month might be a time to engage students in reading literature selections about the contributions of African Americans. Such an approach suffers from two important problems, however. First, it implicitly tells students that we should only think about issues of diversity when the calendar tells us it is important. More useful would be to engage students in thinking about the diversity of the human experience throughout the school year. Second, a contributions approach tends to limit the extent to which any single culture may be studied. As a result, we increase opportunities for developing a shallow, stereotypical understanding of cultural, ethnic, and national groups.

Other teachers take an **additive approach** to diversity. In this approach, content and concepts about diversity are added to the basic curriculum. Instead of being relegated to calendar celebrations, an additive approach includes multicultural and multiethnic literature within instructional units but these selections are more closely related to the core curriculum rather than to issues of diversity. So, alphabet books like *Ashanti to Zulu: African Traditions* by Margaret Musgrove and *A, B, C's: The American Indian Way* by Richard Red Hawk might be incorporated into a unit on alphabet books for young readers without a central focus

contributions approach
An approach to diversity where culturally conscious literature selections enter the classroom because of their relationship to the calendar.

additive approach
An approach to diversity where culturally conscious literature is used to add content and concepts about diversity within instructional units related to the core curriculum rather than to issues of diversity.

on their cultural or historical significance. Here, students are exposed to greater diversity in their literature experiences but relationships between dominant and subordinant groups are usually not addressed. In addition, the basic content of the curriculum does not change to address issues of diversity in the human experience.

Still other teachers take a **transformation approach.** In this approach, teachers transform the nature of the curriculum to include the perspective of subordinate cultures to concepts, historical events, and issues that are being studied. For example, a teacher planning a unit in social studies on the westward migration of European Americans might also include literature selections about this experience from the Native American perspective. In addition to historical information from a European American perspective, children might read selections such as dePaola's *The Legend of the Bluebonnet,* and learn how the Plains Indians valued living in harmony with nature. And they might also read Baker's *Where the Buffaloes Begin* and Gobel's *Buffalo Woman* to understand the close relationship that existed between the Plains Indians and the buffalo. Finally, they might read Culleton's *Spirit of the White Bison* to learn about the slaughter of the primary food supply of the Plains Indians by European Americans and how this disrupted much of their culture. One advantage of this type of approach is that it presents students with a culturally more diverse explanation of historical change. Moreover, students from different cultural groups find value from including their culture's perspective into the curriculum. There are also challenges with this approach: it requires substantial revision of the traditional curriculum, greater preparation on issues of diversity for teachers, and access to a wide body of children's literature.

A final approach described by Rasinski and Padak (1990) is a **decision-making and social action approach.** In this approach, children define an important social issue, gather the appropriate information related to the issue, use this information to clarify their assumptions, make decisions about the social issue, and then take action to address the issue. When teachers take a decision-making and social action approach, literature is used as the entry point into a social issue of importance. For example, *Martin Luther King, Jr. and the Freedom Movement* by Patterson might be used to begin a unit on human rights. This could be followed by reading related works such as *Frederick Douglass and the Fight for Freedom* by D. Miller, *Rosa Parks* by Eloise Greenfield, and *Anthony Burns: The Defeat and Triumph of a Fugitive Slave* by Virginia Hamilton. Reading experiences such as these could lead to discussions about equal rights that humans should guarantee to one another, which could be developed and listed by the class. This discussion could lead to gathering additional information about human rights as defined in the U.S. and Canadian constitutions, the Declaration of Human Rights from the United Nations, and other political documents, followed by collaborative writing and decision-making experiences in which students could define

transformation approach
An approach to diversity where culturally conscious literature is used to include the perspective of subordinate cultures to concepts, historical events, and issues.

decision-making and social action approach
An approach to diversity where children define an important social issue, gather the appropriate information related to the issue, use this information to clarify their assumptions, make decisions about the social issue, and then take action to address the issue.

their own list of human rights that are guaranteed to each member of the class by other members. A unit such as this could be especially useful at the beginning of the year to define the rights and responsibilities of citizenship in your classroom as well as citizenship in our larger society. Au (1993) points out that children learn an important lesson with this approach that transcends the literature itself: they can make a difference in the society in which they live. This type of approach, however, requires extensive planning and organization by teachers.

A different way of using literature to understand the diversity of the human experience has been proposed by Norton (1990). This approach uses **thematic units on diversity** that look intensively into a single cultural and/or ethnic experience as students explore different forms of literature within that experience. She suggests that units begin by broadly exploring a culture's themes through traditional literature such as folktales, myths, and legends. This first phase allows students to discover themes and issues that have traditionally been important to a culture. Next, teachers and students can explore this traditional literature in a second phase with a more focused lens, perhaps by looking at a single type of traditional tale within the culture or by looking at traditional tales from one subgroup within the larger cultural unit. During a third phase, factual accounts such as autobiographies, biographies, and historical nonfiction can be used to understand how individuals from this cultural group have responded to the historical challenges of life. During this phase, the beliefs, values, and themes discovered in the earlier exploration of the culture's traditional literature are employed to better understand the lives of historical figures. Historical fiction is then used in a fourth phase to explore how authors describe the response of fictional characters within this culture. Comparisons might be made between the works of authors who come from the culture and works by authors who do not come from the culture. Finally, the use of contemporary fiction, biography, and poetry can help students understand contemporary expressions of this cultural viewpoint during a fifth phase. At each phase, connections with the reading selections from previous phases become points of focus. In this way, children become aware of the major themes that emanate from any single culture and the sources of these themes in the literature of a culture. The five phases of Norton's (1990) sequence are described in Figure 4-8 along with literature selections that might be used in a thematic unit on the Native American experience. Similar units could be developed for other cultural groups.

A useful feature of Norton's approach is that students are encouraged to discover connections between their various reading experiences. As students read contemporary fiction about a particular cultural group, for example, they are encouraged to draw upon information gathered from earlier reading experiences with traditional tales, biographies, and historical fiction. These intertextual experiences are thought to be especially

thematic units on diversity
An approach to diversity that looks intensively into a single cultural and/or ethnic experience as students explore different forms of literature within that experience.

FIGURE 4-8

A unit on the Native American experience using Norton's Sequence for Multicultural Literature Study (Adapted from Norton, 1990)

Phase I: Traditional literature (generalizations and broad views)

Selections: *Raven's Light* by Susan and Robert Shetterly, *The Eye of the Needle* by Teri Sloat, *The Legend of the Bluebonnet* by dePaola, *Legend Days* by Highwater, *The Star Maiden* by Esbensen, *The Fire Bringer* by Baylor

A. Identify distinctions among folktale, fable, myth, and legend
B. Identify ancient stories that have commonalities and are found in many regions
C. Identify types of stories that dominate the subject
D. Summarize the nature of oral language, the role of traditional literature, the role of audience, and literary style

Phase II: Traditional tales from one or several areas (narrower views)

Selections from the Plains Indians: *The Ring in the Prairie: A Shawnee Legend* by Bierhorst, *Buffalo Woman* by Gobel, *The Girl Who Loved Horses* by Gobel, *Star Boy* by Gobel, *The Whistling Skeleton* by Grinnell, *Iktomi and the Boulder* by Gobel

A. Analyze traditional stories and compare with Phase I findings
B. Analyze and identify beliefs and themes in the traditional tales of one region.

Phase III: Autobiographies, biographies, and historical nonfiction

Selections: *Chief Sarah: Sarah Winnemucca's Fight for Indian Rights* by Morrison, *War Clouds in the West: Indians & Cavalrymen, 1800–1890,* by Marrin, *Buffalo Hunt* by Freedman.

A. Analyze for values, beliefs, and themes identified in traditional literature
B. Compare information in historical documents, biographies, and autobiographies

Phase IV: Historical fiction

Selections: *Sweetgrass* by Hudson, *Lost in the Barrens* by Mowat
A. Evaluate according to authenticity of setting, beliefs, values, and language
B. Search for the role of traditional literature in historical fiction
C. Compare with autobiographies, biographies, and historical nonfiction

Phase V: Contemporary fiction, biography, and poetry

Selections: *Moonsong Lullaby* by Highwater, *Thirteen Moons on Turtles Back* by Bruchac and London, *Hiawatha* by Susan Jeffers, *In My Mother's House* by Ann Nolan Clark, *High Elk's Treasure* by Sneve, *Jimmy Yellow Hawk* by Sneve, *When Thunder Spoke* by Sneve, *Ceremony—In the Circle of Life* by White Deer of Autumn.

A. Analyze appearance of beliefs found in preceding phases
B. Analyze characterizations and conflicts for authenticity
C. Analyze themes and look for similarities with other phases

useful to students. They allow students to discover additional meaning in a single selection by thinking about it in relation to other selections (Short, 1993).

SUPPORTING CHILDREN'S RESPONSES TO LITERATURE

As we think about the role of literature in our reading programs we also want to consider ways to increase the variety of responses children have to their reading experiences (Purves, 1993). Increasing children's response patterns increases their ability to think critically about what they have read and this, in turn, increases learning.

There are at least two ways of thinking about how students might read and respond to a work of literature. One way is to read a work for the factual information contained within it. Rosenblatt (1978, 1985) refers to this as reading from an **efferent stance.** When you read from an efferent stance you read to find out what each character did, why they did it, when they did it, and other factual aspects of a story.

Too often, children are asked to read and respond to works of literature from an efferent stance. This happens when a teacher asks factual questions about a story to determine how much everyone has understood. While sometimes useful, such an approach, used every day, really limits children's thinking. It leads students to believe that the only way to respond to a work of literature is by answering someone else's questions about narrow slices of information that are unconnected to their own lives. Such an approach to reading and response severely limits children's opportunities for critical thinking and learning.

A second way to read a work of literature is to enter the world created by the author, experience the events vicariously, and return to your own world with new knowledge and a new perspective on life. Rosenblatt (1978, 1985) refers to this as reading from an **aesthetic stance.** When you read a work from an aesthetic stance you vicariously live through the experiences in the world the author has created; you share in the feelings, problems, and thoughts of characters. Then, as a result of your "lived through" experience, you see your own world and yourself in a new and different way.

As you read a piece of literature, for example, you might visualize the situations in the story, worry about the imminent death of a character, wonder how an author develops such rich ideas, think about a similar experience in your past, or notice how an author's style includes a wonderful talent for dialogue. These are just some of the richer types of responses that are possible as you read a work of literature from an aesthetic stance. Clearly, each leads to a deeper and more thoughtful experience with the work of literature. We want to encourage the widest possible range of response patterns with our students so they gain from the many critical thinking experiences that are possible with literature. Supporting a variety of response patterns enables children to learn more from their reading experiences.

efferent stance
Reading a work for the factual information contained within it.

aesthetic stance
Reading a work to live vicariously through the experiences in the world the author has created.

One reason both reader-based and interactive teachers value literature is because it develops aesthetic responses from readers.

The best way to support children in developing a wide variety of response patterns is to keep the distinction between an efferent and aesthetic stance in mind. There will be times, of course, that you will want to focus children's attention on the factual elements of a story. This may occur, for example, as you discuss a culturally appropriate story and seek to develop insight about the diversity of the human experience. At the same time that we engage in these activities, though, we also want to think about expanding children's responses to what they have read. To do this we want to encourage their reading of a work of literature from an aesthetic stance—supporting their ability to have a "lived through" experience during the reading and then reflecting on this experience in relation to their own life. You will find many ways to accomplish this if you keep in mind the distinction between an efferent and an aesthetic stance. Several simple ideas are described in Figure 4-9.

In addition, three method frameworks may be especially useful as you seek to develop a wider range of response patterns among your students: read aloud response journals, "grand conversations," and literary study circles.

FIGURE 4-9

Examples of strategies designed to increase aesthetic responses.

 Diaries. As you read *The Diary of Anne Frank, A Hand Full of Stars* by Rafik Schami, or *Dear Mr. Henshaw* by Beverly Cleary to upper-grade students, have them make and keep their own diaries as one of the secondary characters in the story. Encourage students to make an entry each day. You may want to make the diaries private, or you may choose to collect students' diaries once a week and write a private response to each individual.

 Book Parties. Have a short book party several times during the year. Students can dress up as their favorite characters from books they have read in the previous month. Have students wear name tags showing their characters' names and the titles of their books. This activity is an excellent way to generate interest in and conversations about good books for future reading experiences.

 Literature Logs. Encourage students to keep and maintain literature logs by writing short reactions to each new book they read. Periodically collect, read, and react to students' comments in their logs. Help children design covers in the shape of a log.

 Taking Another Perspective. As you discuss issues in social studies, have students consider how some of the characters in literature selections they have read would look at the issue. Have students also explain why they think their characters would look at events in this way.

Read Aloud Response Journals

We encountered the use of read aloud response journals in chapter 3. This method framework contains five steps: read a selection aloud, engage students in a writing task related to the reading selection, have students write their response in their journals, share the responses, and encourage students to expand some of their earlier entries into larger writing projects.

The model lesson that follows shows how another teacher, Mr. Dunbar, uses a read aloud response journal activity to support aesthetic responses among his students. Mr. Dunbar is following Norton's outline to develop a better understanding of the African American experience among his fifth-grade students. They have read and discussed a number of traditional African tales to develop a broad understanding of traditional themes, beliefs, and values. They have also read and discussed a number of traditional tales from the African American experience on plantations in the southeastern United States. As they read, they compared how these stories compared to the traditional tales from Africa. Now, they are reading and studying several biographies of famous African Americans: Hamilton's *Anthony Burns: The Defeat and Triumph of a Fugitive Slave,* Ferris's *Go Free or Die: A Story of Harriet Tubman,* and Miller's *Frederick*

MODEL LESSON
Sweet Clara and the Freedom Quilt:
A Read Aloud Response Journal Activity in Mr. Dunbar's Class

Read a Selection Aloud. Mr. Dunbar's fifth-grade class is exploring a thematic unit on the African American experience. He has decided to read *Sweet Clara and the Freedom Quilt* to his class today. This is a story of how Sweet Clara is separated from her family and learns to make quilts for the master's family. Over time, Sweet Clara gathers information about her family's location and the route north across the Ohio River to freedom. Each new piece of information is added to a quilt that is actually a map of the way north. When all the information is recorded, Sweet Clara slips away, locates her family, and takes them to freedom. She leaves the quilt behind so that others may follow.

Engage students in a writing task related to the reading selection. After reading *Sweet Clara and the Freedom Quilt,* Mr. Dunbar has the class brainstorm possible writing topics. He writes these ideas on the chalk board as they are generated. Students are encouraged to use these ideas or to respond to the story in their own fashion in their read aloud response journal.

Have students write their responses in their journals. Students are given about 15 minutes to complete their entry. As Mr. Dunbar circulates around the room during this time, he notes the categories of responses students are making in their journals. Towards the end, Mr. Dunbar tells students that writing time is drawing to a close. This reminds students to wrap up their entry.

Share the responses. Mr. Dunbar writes several categories of responses on the board: Feelings, The Injustice of Slavery, Connections with My Own Life, and Other Types of Responses. He has students decide the category that best fits their responses and then forms groups around these categories. In their groups, students share their responses aloud. After a person has shared his or her entry, the other students are encouraged to respond with positive comments. Afterwards, Mr. Dunbar engages students in a discussion about their feelings as they listened to this story of freedom lovingly sought and found.

Encourage students to expand some of their earlier entries into larger writing projects. Mr. Dunbar requires that students develop two writing ideas during this four week unit into larger works of writing that are revised, edited, and polished. He reminds students that students may choose to develop one or several ideas from their read aloud response journal. He also reminds them that they are required to have a conference with him by the end of this week to plan their first writing project.

Douglass and the Fight for Freedom. The unit has been going well but Mr. Dunbar has found discussions and responses to focus on the factual aspects of the African American experience. He wants his students to engage in more of a "lived through" experience today, putting them in touch with the feelings, fears, hopes, and dreams of African American slaves on a plantation. To do this, he has decided to engage his students in a read aloud response journal experience with Deborah Hopkinson's *Sweet Clara and the Freedom Quilt,* a biographical story of how an African American woman used a quilt to record the route north to freedom.

Grand Conversations

Having **grand conversations** after reading a selection together is another way to help students develop wider response patterns to their reading. The term "grand conversations" was initially used by Mary Ann Eeds (cf. Eeds & Wells, 1989; Peterson & Eeds, 1990) to describe a special way of discussing a story that contrasted with what she called the more common "gentle inquisitions" that took place in many classrooms. During gentle inquisitions, teachers ask students to recall specific factual information after reading a story ("How did Sweet Clara record the information she gathered about the route north?"). This, of course, encourages narrower efferent responses instead of more diverse aesthetic responses. Grand conversations, by way of contrast, refers to talking about a book as adults might discuss a book in the evening after dinner. Here, everyone has the opportunity to contribute their different responses without one person calling upon others to answer factual questions about the story. Eeds and Wells (1989) have shown that a grand conversation approach to discussion increases the variety of response patterns. McGee (1992) has shown that children as young as first grade can benefit from engaging in grand conversation discussions. As a method framework, grand conversations usually contain four procedural steps:

1. Read a work of literature together with your students.
2. Remind students of the guidelines for grand conversations.
3. Engage students in a conversation about the work that the students themselves direct.
4. Ask one interpretive or literary question to further students' responses and thinking.

During the first step, you read a selection with your students. For younger students, this may mean that you read the work to them aloud. For older students, this might take place by each student individually reading the work silently.

During the second step, teachers take a moment to remind students of the guidelines for grand conversations. Over time, you will develop your own list but you might wish to begin with a list like the following:

Only one person talks at any one time.

Listen carefully so you can tell when someone has finished speaking.

Take turns speaking.

Everyone should share at least one idea.

No one should share more than two ideas until everyone has shared something.

Stay on topic.

During the third step, students share their own responses to the reading experience. This is the real heart of the grand conversation experience. Teachers often begin this step with a nondirective question in the same way an adult might begin this conversation with another adult, "So what did you think about this story?" Students are then encouraged to share their individual responses to the reading experience as long as they stay on topic. During a grand conversation, the teacher's role is to support the exchange of responses. Tompkins and McGee (1993) note that while students need to control this conversation, teachers should facilitate their efforts by encouraging students to elaborate on their responses when something is not clear ("I'm not quite clear about what you mean. Can you explain that again?").

The fourth step takes place after you sense that students have shared all of the responses they are likely to share. As this occurs, teachers sometimes ask a single literary or interpretive question to help students see the work of literature in an entirely different way. This question might help students discover a special literary technique or help them to interpret the work from a different perspective. To illustrate the use of a literary or interpretive question, consider the story *Sky Dogs*.

Sky Dogs by Jane Yolen is a wonderful legend from the Blackfeet of how horses became part of their culture. The author uses an elderly Piegan Indian, He-who-loves-horses, to relate the legend in a first person narrative. This, of course, is how oral legends were passed down from one generation to another. It also makes it easier for a reader to enter into the world of this story, sitting at the feet of the storyteller as he relates the legend. At the end of a grand conversation about this story, you might ask a literary or interpretive question like, "Why do you think the author had He-who-loves-horses tell this story?" Students might then discuss how this technique influenced their reading and response.

Literature Discussion Groups

Another way to encourage a wider pattern of responses is to engage students in **literature discussion groups.** In this method framework, small groups of students read a single work of literature on their own and then come together to have a grand conversation. Afterwards, they develop a project that allows them to share the work with the rest of the class. Teachers who use literature discussion groups often follow a six-step sequence:

1. The teacher introduces three to five different books to the class, each with multiple copies.
2. Students determine which book they want to read and form groups based on this book.
3. Students read the literature selection for their group independently.
4. The teacher and each group have a grand conversation about the work.

literature discussion groups
A method framework that helps students develop wider response patterns to their reading; small groups of students read a single work of literature on their own, come together to have a grand conversation, and then complete a project that is shared.

5. A project is developed to extend students' response and understanding of the work.
6. The results of the project are shared with the other groups.

To begin the use of literature discussion groups, you collect multiple
copies of several literature selections and introduce each work of literature to the class. During this introduction, you enthusiastically describe
information about the book and author in order to whet the reading
appetites of your students.

After all of the books have been introduced, you provide an opportunity
for students to pick the one book that each will read during the time you
have set aside for this experience. As a result of this self-selection process,
several different groups are formed, each with a different book to read.

During the third step, you allow students in each group to read their
work silently, without interruptions. Depending upon the age of your students and the amount of reading they need to complete, this time might
range from 15 minutes to as much as an hour each day.

After the students in a group have completed their reading, or sometimes after they have read only the first half of a longer book, you get
together with them to have a grand conversation. Here, you follow the
procedures described earlier in order to support a broad range of
responses. During this time, you allow children to direct the conversation
around their responses to the work.

When a group completes its discussion, it is time to think about a project that would be interesting to complete and useful for extending students' response and comprehension. Here it often helps to have a preliminary brainstorming session and list a number of different alternatives for
the project before having the group choose one to complete. The projects
might be related to a literary aspect of the work they have read
("Describe our feelings at one point in the story. Explain the techniques
this author used to make us feel this way. Share our results with the
class." "Find three different techniques the author uses for dialogue and
describe why we think each technique is used. Share our ideas with the
class in a bulletin board display."). Alternatively, the project might focus
on some content aspect of the work ("Conduct a readers theater presentation of an exciting episode in the book we have just read." "Collect and
read three more Anansi the Spider tales. Make a presentation of these
works for the rest of the class.").

The final step in the use of literature study circles is to share the
results of each group's reading activity with the rest of the class. Each
group's presentation will provide students with the opportunity to share
their ideas in public and inform other students about an exciting reading
experience.

Text Sets

There are many variations for conducting literature study circles. One
proposed by Short and her colleagues (Harste, Short, & Burke, 1988;

Short, 1993) is referred to as **text sets.** With this approach, members of each group do not read a single book. Instead, each group receives 5–15 conceptually related books, usually shorter selections or picture books. This approach is especially useful when you do not have multiple copies of books available for all of the members of a group.

Another difference when using text sets is that students do not always read every book in each text set before discussing their reading experience. Instead, individual students will read several books of their own choice from the set and then get together to share their responses, discussing similarities between the books, differences they have found, and discovering other books in the set to read next.

A third difference is that the use of text sets usually involves multiple discussions over a longer period of time. Students may get together three or four times after each student has a chance to read several more books in the set. Over time this provides each student with an opportunity to read and respond to many of the books in the set.

Text sets have been found to be especially useful for providing students opportunities to see connections between their reading experiences and to share those connections with others (Hartman & Hartman, 1993). Examples of several text sets can be seen in Figure 4-10.

text sets
A variation of literature discussion groups where members of each group do not read a single book but instead read multiple books that are related in some way.

DEVELOPING FAMILIARITY WITH NARRATIVE DISCOURSE STRUCTURE

A final aspect of children's literature should not be overlooked. Literature can help young children develop an important type of discourse knowledge—knowledge about **narrative discourse structure.** Narrative discourse structure refers to the structural organization that is common to all stories and narratives. The concept also includes the special structural characteristics common to particular types of narratives such as fairy tales, mysteries, science fiction, fables, and fantasies.

Knowledge of narrative discourse structure assists with comprehension in several ways (Spiegel & Fitzgerald, 1986). First, knowing the structure of narratives helps readers develop appropriate expectations for upcoming meaning. Do you remember the expectations you had in chapter 2 when you read the first sentence of a story that began, "Once upon a time. . ."? You immediately knew that the story was not true, and you knew that it took place in a kingdom long ago and far away. You also expected to see a prince and princess as characters, and you knew that a problem would appear that would require a solution. In addition, you expected a happy ending. You can see that knowing the structural characteristics of narratives makes reading easier because it helps readers develop appropriate expectations.

Second, knowing the structure of narratives is important because it allows a reader to infer structural information omitted by an author. Sometimes, for example, an episode in a narrative is left out because an

narrative discourse structure
The organizational structure common to all stories; includes setting information, a problem, and episodes that describe attempts to resolve the problem.

FIGURE 4-10

Examples of text sets used at different grade levels.

Text Sets for Third Graders

Award-winning picture books

Hey, Al by A. Yorinks
Song and Dance Man by K. Ackerman
Lon Po Po: A Chinese Red Riding Hood Tale by E. Young
The Polar Express by C. Van Allsburg
St. George and the Dragon by M. Hodges

Owl Moon by J. Yolen
Fables by A. Lobel
Shadow by B. Cendrars
Jumanji by C. Van Allsburg
Ox-Cart Man by D. Hall

The Cinderella cycle (Cinderella tales from different cultures and points of view)

The Egyptian Cinderella by S. Climo
Cinderella by A. Ehrlich
Yeh-Shen: A Cinderella Story from China by A. Louie
Cinderella: The Untold Story by R. Shorto

The Paper Bag Princess by R. Munsch
Prince Cinders by B. Cole
Moss Gown by W. H. Yeh-Hooks
Mufaro's Beautiful Daughters by J. Steptoe

Text Sets for Sixth Graders

Biography bonanza

The Many Lives of Benjamin Franklin by Aliki
Lincoln: A Photobiography by R. Freedman
Stonewall by J. Fritz
Can't You Make them Behave, King George? by J. Fritz

Deborah Sampson by H. Felton
The Wright Brothers by R. Freedman
The Double Life of Pocahontas by J. Fritz
Peter the Great by D. Stanley
Susanna of the Alamo by J. Jakes

Chris Van Allsburg: illustrator extraordinaire

The Garden of Abdul Gasazi by Chris Van Allsburg
Ben's Dream by Chris Van Allsburg
The Wreck of the Zephyr by Chris Van Allsburg
The Polar Express by Chris Van Allsburg

Jumanji by Chris Van Allsburg
The Mysteries of Harris Burdick by Chris Van Allsburg

author assumes that the reader will correctly infer what took place. The knowledge that narratives contain episodic structure makes it easier for a reader to infer the missing information.

Knowledge of the General Structure Common to All Narratives

Most researchers believe that narratives contain three basic structural elements: setting information, an initiating episode that establishes a problem to be resolved in the story, and succeeding episodes that explain how the problem gets resolved. Narratives typically contain a structure similar to the following:

 I. Setting information
    A. Time information
    B. Character information
    C. Location information

 II. Initiating episode (story problem)
    A. Initiating event
    B. Goal formation

III. Succeeding episodes (including the final resolution)
    A. Attempt
    B. Outcome
    C. Reaction

Setting information usually appears at the beginning of a narrative. It includes information about the time when the story takes place, the character(s) in the story, and the location where the action occurs. Setting information often appears in the first few sentences of a story.

Time:	Once upon a time,
Character:	there was a little girl with a red hood
Location:	who lived near the edge of a dark forest.

Not all stories contain all three elements at the beginning; one or more may be missing. Nevertheless, readers who know that character, location, and time information *should* be at the beginning of a narrative use available clues in the rest of the story to infer this information when it is missing.

An **initiating episode** is usually found in the first episode of a narrative. It specifies the problem that must be resolved in the story. Initiating episodes describe an initiating event and the formation of a goal by one or more characters.

Initiating event:	One day, Little Red Riding Hood's mother gave her a basket of bread and jam.
Goal formation:	She told Little Red Riding Hood to take the food to her grandmother's house in the woods.

Initiating events and goals are not always stated in a story. Again, however, readers who are familiar with narrative structure infer this information when it is missing by using surrounding clues in the rest of the story.

Succeeding episodes, including the final episode, describe how the character attempts to solve the problem established in the initiating episode. Succeeding episodes typically contain an attempt to solve the problem, the outcome of that attempt, and a reaction to that outcome. Succeeding episodes may also result in characters establishing new problems to be solved in the course of the story.

setting information
An element of narrative discourse structure found at the beginning of stories, Includes information about the character(s); location; and time.

initiating episode
One element of narrative discourse structure; usually the first organized sequence of actions that describe the problem to be resolved in the story.

succeeding episodes
The element of narrative discourse structure that tells how the character solves the problem established in the initiating episode.

Attempt:	Little Red Riding Hood walked all day on the trail to her grandmother's house.
Outcome:	When she arrived, they sat down immediately and feasted on the home-baked bread and strawberry jam.
Reaction:	They were so content that they didn't even think about the wolf that had bothered them the week before.

Readers use their knowledge of narrative discourse structure to infer missing structural elements in a story. When a structural element is not explicitly stated, knowledgeable readers will infer it by using clues provided in the rest of the story. But not all children are aware of narrative discourse structure, especially those who are quite young and those who have not listened to enough stories to become familiar with their structure. You can tell if children are familiar with story structure by listening to their own stories. If students are familiar with typical story structure their oral story will be well formed, containing all of the important structural features: setting information, a problem, and a series of episodes that attempt to resolve the problem. If a child is unfamiliar with the

Appropriate discussion questions are one tool for developing narrative discourse knowledge.

structure of stories, some of these elements will be missing. Figure 4-11 shows a story dictated by a child who was four and a half years old. Notice how the story contains some structural elements found in stories including a title and setting information. The story appears to wander, though, because the child did not include a problem in the story that gets resolved by the characters. This child appears to lack an understanding of the problem-resolution features that characterize a well-formed story. She is likely to miss these elements during a reading or listening experience, especially if the story requires her to infer them.

Knowledge of Specific Types of Narrative Structure

In addition to the common structural characteristics of all narratives, a variety of narrative forms have unique characteristics. Science fiction, for example, varies from contemporary fiction because of differences in the time information presented at the beginning of the story. Knowledge of those characteristics is important for effective comprehension of particular narrative types. For example, if we don't know that we are reading a fable, we may not infer an unstated moral or message. Table 4-2 lists the major narrative forms and their defining characteristics. These defining characteristics of different story forms are usually learned by children in the elementary grades.

Using a Directed Reading-Thinking Activity

It is possible to develop narrative discourse knowledge by using a method framework often referred to as a **directed reading-thinking activity**

directed reading-thinking activity (DRTA) A method framework used to assist students in predicting outcomes and drawing conclusions; includes predicting, reading, and proving.

....

FIGURE 4-11
An orally dictated story from a four-year-old that illustrates the consequences of not understanding the problem-resolution structure of stories

Time Goes

One bright sunny morning there were polar bears outside New York. And then Katie and Sarah went out to play in Sarah's new sled. And then they came in for a nice glass of hot chocolate. And then Katie had nice ten marshmallows. And then they went back outside. And then they went outside to come and make a snowman. And his name was Frosty the Snowman. And then they came down in the basement to play. And then on their new boats, Katie hopped on and Sarah hopped on one by one with their new animals. Then they went out to the part of the ghosts. And then they saw Count and Big Bird from Sesame. And then they saw themselves walking in the snow. And then they went to the ghost's house.

THE END

....

TABLE 4-2

Major narrative forms and their defining characteristics

Narrative Form	Setting Information	Episodes	Examples
Fiction			
Historical fiction	Characters: fictional and historical Time: in the past	Fictional characters enacting historically accurate episodes	Island of the Blue Dolphins The Courage of Sarah Noble
Modern realistic fiction	Characters: realistic Time: contemporary	Realistic episodes revolving around contemporary issues	Maniac Magee On My Honor
Folk tales	Characters: average citizens or animals Location: countryside Time: long ago	Fantastic actions with animals talking, witches casting spells, and so on.	The People Could Fly: Black American Folktales
Fairy tales	Characters: royalty Location: castle or kingdom Time: long ago	Magical or fantastic actions, with animals talking, witches casting spells, and so on.	Mufaro's Beautiful Daughters Yeh-Shen: A Cinderella Story from China
Fables	Characters: usually animals Location: countryside Time: long ago	Magical or fantastic actions with animals taking human characteristics and a moral often stated at the end.	Doctor Coyote: A Native American Fable Aesop's Fables Frederick's Fables

(DRTA). A DRTA includes three procedural steps—predicting, reading, proving—which are repeated as students read and discuss a selection. If you use a DRTA to develop knowledge of narrative discourse structure, you should guide students in the first step—making predictions about structural elements found in stories. At the beginning, this would mean that you would first ask students to make predictions about setting information. Here, you might guide predictions about the time, characters, or location by asking, for example, "Let's look at the title. When do you think this story took place? Who do you think might be the characters in this story? Where do you think this story takes place?"

After students make predictions about setting information, you invite them to read the beginning of the story where this information is likely to be found. This is the second step of a DRTA. After reading the beginning,

TABLE 4-2 *continued*

Narrative Form	Setting Information	Episodes	Examples
Fiction			
Myths	Characters: cultural hero(ine)	Hero(ine) demonstrates courage, bravery, and skill in resolving a serious challenge	John Henry: An American Legend. Iktomi and the Boulder
Modern fantasies	Characters: realistic Time: contemporary	Magical or fantastic actions	Jumanji
Science fiction	Characters: usually realistic Location: often outer space Time: future	Fantastic actions logically predicted when the story was written	A Wrinkle in Time Interstellar Pig
Nonfiction			
Biography	Character: historically important individuals	Factual account of an individual's life	Lincoln: A Photobiography
Autobiography	Character: historically important individual	Factual account of the author's life	The Land I Lost: Adventures of a Boy in Vietnam

you engage them in a discussion about the evidence they found that helps a reader become familiar with the time, characters, and location of the story. This is the third step of a DRTA.

The procedural steps of a DRTA can be used several times as you read a story together. For example, you might next repeat the first step and guide predictions about the problem in the story. This could be done by asking, for example, "Now, what do you think is going to be the main problem in this story? Who do you think is going to have this problem?"

After students make predictions about the problem in the story, you might invite them to read the next section of the story to discover if their guesses were correct. Then, after reading this section, you would again engage them in a discussion about the evidence they found that specifies the problem.

MODEL LESSON

Using Deductive Instruction to Teach the Structural Characteristics of a Fable

State the Skill or Rule. Mr. Burns begins by telling his students that they will be reading a special type of story called a fable. He tells them that a long time ago a man called Aesop told many fables to teach people how they should act. Mr. Burns writes the word *fable* on the chalkboard and asks whether anyone has ever read or heard a fable before. Several students respond, saying they think a fable has animals in it. One says that he has read a book of fables at home. After students respond, Mr. Burns lists the four characteristics on the chalkboard under the word *fable* and explains each one.

1. It is not true.
2. Animals are the main characters.
3. The animals act like humans.
4. A lesson, or moral, is often stated at the end of the story.

Provide Examples of the Skill or Rule. Mr. Burns has his students read *The Hare and the Tortoise* by Paul Galdone. He tells them to read the story to themselves and see whether they think it is a fable.

Provide Guided Practice. Everyone thinks that the story is a fable. Mr. Burns initiates a discussion about why students came to that conclusion. He directs their attention to the list of characteristics on the board, and students explain how each feature was contained in the story.

Provide Independent Practice. Each day that week, students read and discuss a different fable from the book *Fables* by Arnold Lobel. Toward the end of the week Mr. Burns has students write their own class fable, using a language experience story method framework. He duplicates the story to read in class and to send home with the students.

Finally, you might guide predictions about the resolution of the problem by asking, for example: "OK, how do you think this problem is going to be solved? Who do you think will solve the problem? How will they do this?" After reading the final section of the story, you again engage students in a discussion about the evidence in the story describing how the problem in the story is resolved.

Throughout this conversation you follow the three steps of a DRTA: Predict, read, and prove. At each point, your questions focus students' attention on the major elements of a story such as the setting, the story's problem, and the solution to the problem.

Deductive Instruction

deductive instruction
A method framework containing four steps: state the skill or rule, provide examples, provide guided practice, and provide independent practice.

Using a DRTA helps students discover the structural characteristics of narratives in an inductive manner; they gradually come to discover that stories have certain structural characteristics. You can also help students learn this information in a more direct fashion by using **deductive instruction,** a method framework described earlier in chapter 3. Do you remember the four procedural steps of a deductive method framework?

1. State the skill or rule.
2. Provide examples of the skill or rule.
3. Provide guided practice.
4. Provide independent practice.

When deductive instruction is used, the teacher defines the structural characteristics of a particular form for students, often listing these on the chalkboard. When teaching the structural characteristics of a fable, for example, the teacher might explain that a fable usually has four distinguishing features: (1) it is a story that is not true; (2) animals are usually main characters; (3) animals usually take on human characteristics; and (4) an explicit lesson, or moral, is often stated at the end.

During the second procedural step, the class reads an example of the form and discusses how the story reflects the defining characteristics of the form. During the next several days they might read and discuss other examples of that narrative form in guided and independent reading experiences. Often students conclude their study with a writing experience, perhaps producing their own fable and then sharing their work with others in the class.

In the model lesson on page 164, Mr. Burns has decided to introduce his students to fables and the structural characteristics of that narrative form.

USING A LITERACY FRAMEWORK TO INFORM INSTRUCTIONAL DECISIONS

You have seen the many ways in which literature can function in a classroom reading program. A literacy framework is useful as you consider the specific ways in which you integrate literature into reading instruction. It empowers you by informing two important types of decisions: *what* to teach with children's literature and *how* you will use literature to accomplish your goals.

Developing Insights about What to Teach

As you consider the use of children's literature in your classroom, you will need to decide *what* you will teach with children's literature. To help you with this aspect of decision making you should think for a moment about how you believe people read. Your belief will inform decisions about what you will teach with children's literature. Table 4-3 summarizes the relationship between this portion of your literacy framework and decisions about using children's literature.

Teachers who have a reader-based perspective emphasize the prior knowledge that readers bring to a text. Therefore, they value literature because it helps develop vocabulary, syntactic, discourse, and metacognitive knowledge, each of which is a prior knowledge component. In addition, these teachers find literature to be important for developing richer

TABLE 4-3

A summary of how a literacy framework can be used to inform decisions about what to teach with children's literature

Beliefs about How One Reads	Related Assumptions	Most Important Components	Probable Focus of Literature Use
Reader-based	Meaning exists more in what the reader brings to the text. Reading is a result of expectations. Reading begins with elements of prior knowledge.	Prior knowledge components: metacognitive, discourse, syntactic, and vocabulary knowledge.	Developing metacognitive, discourse, syntactic, and vocabulary knowledge. Developing aesthetic responses.
Interactive	Meaning exists in both the text and the reader. Reading is both translation and expectation. Reading uses each knowledge source simultaneously.	All knowledge sources: decoding, metacognitive, discourse, syntactic, and vocabulary knowledge.	Developing each of the knowledge sources is important for literacy. Developing both efferent and aesthetic responses.
Text-based	Meaning exists more in the text. Reading is translation. Reading begins with decoding.	Decoding knowledge.	Developing fluency and automaticity of decoding. Developing efferent responses.

aesthetic responses to their reading; they see literature as an important opportunity for their students to have a "lived through" experience with their reading. Literature is viewed as a means to travel to Africa to experience tribal life on the Serengeti, to visit King Arthur's court and live the code of honor among knights, or to see ancient China and feel the respect granted to elders. Teachers following a reader-based explanation of how a person reads, however, do not value the use of literature to develop decoding knowledge. Decoding knowledge is viewed as relatively unimportant. In addition, they do not see literature as an appropriate vehicle for developing efferent responses.

Teachers who follow a text-based explanation of how a person reads emphasize the importance of decoding knowledge. These teachers value literature because it helps develop fluency and automaticity in decoding. Predictable texts would be seen as useful for developing early decoding skills. Other literary selections would be viewed as important vehicles for practicing decoding skills and increasing fluency. In addition, these teachers also find literature crucial for developing efferent responses to their reading; they see literature as an important opportunity for their students to acquire factual information about cultures, people, and times. These teachers tend not to value the use of literature for developing those elements commonly associated with what readers bring to a text: vocabulary, syntactic, discourse, and metacognitive knowledge. Moreover, they are not too concerned about increasing the variety of aesthetic responses to literary works.

Teachers with an interactive perspective value the use of literature to develop both decoding components and prior knowledge components. These teachers use literature in classroom activities to develop decoding knowledge as well as vocabulary knowledge, syntactic knowledge, discourse knowledge, and metacognitive knowledge. Moreover, they find literature a powerful vehicle for developing both aesthetic and efferent responses.

There are also areas of agreement among all three types of teachers. Regardless of your beliefs about how one reads, it is likely that you will find literature to be a useful vehicle to develop affective aspects such as interest and motivation. All teachers want their students to be interested in reading. And, as a result, all teachers should support their students in becoming independent readers who not only can read but also choose to read on their own for pleasure, information, and personal growth. Most teachers, too, will find literature the most powerful tool for developing emergent reading abilities. Most would agree that reading aloud and other early literacy activities help young children develop important early insights about literacy; and all teachers probably would find literature very useful in helping children understand the diversity of the human experience.

Developing Insights about How to Teach

As you consider the use of literature in your classroom, you will also need to decide *how* to use children's literature to support literacy learning. Your conclusion about how children learn to read can be used to inform decision making in this area. Table 4-4 summarizes the relationship between this portion of your literacy framework and the method frameworks you would probably favor.

Teachers with holistic language learning beliefs do not often use deductive instruction with children's literature. They believe that reading is learned inductively as students engage in self-directed, functional, purposeful, holistic experiences with authentic literature. Thus, they use

TABLE 4-4

A summary of how a literacy framework can be used to inform decisions about how to teach with children's literature

Beliefs about How Children Learn to Read	Related Assumptions	Favored Method Frameworks and Instructional Activities
Holistic Language Learning	Students learn best in an inductive fashion as they direct their own learning and reading experiences. Students learn best during holistic, purposeful, and functional experiences with authentic literature.	Individualized Reading Cooperative Learning Groups Grand Conversations Literature Discussion Groups Text Sets Directed Reading-Thinking Activities Read Aloud Response Journal Activities
Integrated	Students learn best as a result of both student-directed, inductive experiences and teacher-directed, deductive experiences. Students learn best when they engage in purposeful, functional, and holistic experiences with authentic texts and when they acquire specific reading skills.	Individualized Reading Cooperative Learning Groups Grand Conversations Literature Discussion Groups Text Sets Directed Reading-Thinking Activities Read Aloud Response Journal Deductive Instruction Directed Reading Activities
Specific Skills	Students learn best when they are taught directly by the teacher in a deductive fashion. Students learn best when they master specific reading skills.	Deductive Instruction Directed Reading Activities

activities and method frameworks that provide greater ownership of the reading and learning experience. Individualized reading will be a popular method framework as will cooperative learning groups. In addition, grand conversations, literature discussion groups, and text sets will often be used. Note that literature discussion groups and text sets are really just variations of the generic method framework we have labeled "cooperative learning groups." Directed reading-thinking activities and read aloud response journal activities are also commonly found in classrooms with teachers who have student-directed beliefs. Each of these method frameworks allows students to direct much of their learning experience with literature.

Teachers with specific skill beliefs about how reading ability develops favor deductive instruction. They find this method framework to be more consistent with their concerns about directly teaching important aspects of children's literature. Deductive instruction is likely to be used, for example, to teach the structure of narrative forms. The other common method framework for this type of teacher is the directed reading activity. This was described in chapter 3. Other method frameworks might be used to teach aspects of literature but only infrequently.

Teachers with an integrated explanation of how reading develops believe that children learn best when they are exposed to authentic and holistic experiences with print and, at the same time, receive instruction in important skill areas. Thus, these teachers are likely to use all of the method frameworks described in this chapter.

There are also areas of agreement between all three types of teachers, largely because each type of teacher will value literature activities for developing independent readers. Read alouds, readers theater, reading corners, and sustained silent reading are popular method frameworks for developing independent readers and are likely to be used by all teachers. Similarly, because learning about the diversity of the human experience is valued by all teachers, the model presented in Figure 4-8 for developing units about this topic will probably be used by teachers regardless of their beliefs about how reading ability develops. Teachers with more of a holistic language learning belief, though, will probably use more inductive experiences throughout these units, while those with more of a specific skills view will tend to use more deductive teaching experiences. Teachers with integrated beliefs will use both inductive and deductive experiences to support their students as they learn about diversity through children's literature.

Comments from the Classroom

	Nikki Robinson, sixth grade teacher
	Each year, early in the spring, our school celebrates Right-to-Read Week. Classes abandon normally scheduled activities to participate in a variety of reading adventures using children's literature. Each day a new adventure begins and teachers and students get very creative! Last year the first grades celebrated Dr. Suess Day and made Cat-in-the-Hat hats and ate green eggs and ham. (I was personally thankful that I was teaching sixth grade.)

During Right-to-Read Week we try our best to involve the whole school community in some capacity. Parents, grandparents, neighborhood business people, the |

superintendent, and a host of others are invited to share a story or favorite chapter from a book with whole classes or small groups of students. Each class brainstorms several weeks ahead who they will invite. They mail out invitations and schedules are then coordinated around available times for our guest readers.

My students' favorite day of our Right-to-Read Week last year was READ-A-THON DAY. All the students and teachers in the school lugged cozy comforters or lumpy sleeping bags and fluffy pillows to school to take part in a reading marathon. It was on this day that we spent most of our time engrossed in good books. Late in the school day, however, everyone in the school put on a costume of their favorite book character and marched in an all-school READ-A-THON parade. Much to the delight of our students even the office and cafeteria personnel joined us in the parade. No prizes for costumes were awarded but everyone wrote a few lines about their favorite book telling why that book personally ranks as number one. These book testimonies were collected and compiled by PTO (Parent Teacher Organization) members in an all-school Book Review categorized by title, author, and subject. Every classroom and the library then got a copy of the review. After that, before students made a trip to the library or while they were in the library, they checked the recommendations for good books written by their friends.

The best part about our week to celebrate reading is that we walk our talk. We tell children how important reading is and how much fun it can be. We show them how reading plays a role in everyone's life no matter who they are or what they do. I am thankful that our school system now uses children's literature for our core reading instruction. It allows reading to play a more natural role in our curriculum. But I am equally glad that our school system makes an extra effort to highlight reading in such a special way as Right-to-Read Week. The spirit of unity—sharing in the value of literature and reading—permeates our hallways and surrounds our school and our students with a contagious desire to find a good book and curl up and read!

Major Points

- Experiences with literature should be at the center of every classroom reading program. Literature's effects on reading comprehension and response are all-encompassing; using literature develops every component of the process and supports the development of independent readers.

- To develop independent readers through children's literature, teachers must become familiar with popular children's literature, identify their students' reading interests, and put children and books together in pleasurable settings. Many method frameworks can help to develop independent readers: read-aloud sessions, sustained silent reading, and readers theater.

- Literature is a tremendous tool for helping children understand the diversity of the human experience. Culturally sensitive literature should be an important part of your reading program.

- Literature is useful to increase the variety of responses children have to their reading experiences. Developing aesthetic as well as efferent responses increases students' ability to think critically about what they have read and this, in turn, increases learning.

- Knowledge of narrative discourse structure is important for children to acquire. Teachers can develop knowledge of narrative structure by using directed reading-thinking activities and deductive instruction.

- A literacy framework can guide decisions about the use of children's literature. A conclusion about how a person reads can help determine what to teach and emphasize through children's literature. A conclusion about how reading ability develops can help determine which method frameworks you will find most useful.

Making Instructional Decisions

1. Briefly define your current literacy framework by identifying your beliefs about how one reads and how children learn to read. Then explain how you will use children's literature in your classroom reading program. Be sure to describe what you will teach and how you will teach it. Discuss the connection between your literacy framework and these two sets of instructional decisions.

2. This chapter described the importance of developing independent readers. Identify a grade level and then describe the ways in which you will go about helping your students achieve this.

3. Learning about the diversity of the human experience should be a goal for all teachers as they think about the role of literature. Explain how you will accomplish this important goal.

4. Select an interesting piece of children's literature for a read-aloud session. Practice reading it aloud until you have a clear sense of how you want it to sound. Then read your selection to a class of children or to your peers. Follow the procedural steps listed on page 129. Evaluate yourself after completing this experience. What pleased you about the experience? What decisions would you change next time?

Further Reading

Hartman, D. K. & Hartman, J. A. (1993). Reading across texts: Expanding the role of the reader. *The Reading Teacher, 47*(3), 202–211.

Describes ways in which teachers can expand the responses of students by reading several related literature selections. Discusses answers to four questions: (1) What types of texts can be used? (2) What are the ways to arrange texts? (3) What activities can students engage in? and (4) How can outcomes be represented?

Martinez, M. (1993). Motivating dramatic story reenactments. *The Reading Teacher, 46*(8), 682–688.

Describes how dramatic story reenactments can be used successfully in a kindergarten classroom to enhance students' responses and understanding of literature as well as develop knowledge of narrative discourse structure.

Norton, D. E. (1990). Teaching multicultural literature in the reading curriculum. *The Reading Teacher, 44*(1), 28–40.

Describes how to develop thematic literary units for studying the diversity of the human experience. By looking at a single cultural experience through a variety of discourse forms, students develop a better understanding of both the cultural perspective and the literary forms used in the unit.

Yokota, J. (1993). Issues in selecting multicultural literature. *Language Arts, 70*(3), 156–167.

The author describes trends in multicultural literature and criteria to keep in mind when selecting multicultural literature. Also in this article is a list of multicultural literature that is culturally conscious.

References

Anderson, R., Fielding, L., & Wilson, P. (1988). Growth in reading and how children spend their time outside of school. *Reading Research Quarterly, 23*, 285–303.

Au, K.H. (1993). *Literacy instruction in multicultural settings.* Fort Worth, TX: Holt, Rinehart and Winston.

Clay, M. M. (1989). Concepts about print in English and other languages. *The Reading Teacher, 42*(4), 268–277.

Cochran-Smith, M. (1984). *The making of a reader.* Norwood, NJ: Ablex.

Eeds, M. & Wells, D. (1989). Grand conversations: An exploration of meaning construction in literature study groups. *Research in the Teaching of English, 23*, 4–29.

Fader, D. N. (1976). *The new hooked on books.* New York: Putnam.

Fuhler, C. J. (1990). Commentary: Let's move toward literature-based reading instruction. *The Reading Teacher, 43*(4), 312–315.

Harris, A. J., & Sipay, E. R. (1990). *How to increase reading ability* (9th ed.). New York: Longman.

Harris, V. J. (1992). Multiethnic children's literature. In K. D. Wood and A. Moss (Eds.), *Exploring literature in the classroom: Content and Methods.* Norwood, MA: Christopher-Gordon, pp. 169-201.

Harste, J., Short, K., & Burke, C. (1988). *Creating classrooms for authors.* Portsmouth, NH: Heinemann

Hartman, D. K. & Hartman, J. A. (1993). Reading across texts: Expanding the role of the reader. *The Reading Teacher, 47*(3), 202–211.

Hiebert, E. H., & Colt, J. (1989). Patterns of literature-based reading instruction. *The Reading Teacher, 43*(1), 14–21.

McCracken, R. A. (1971). Initiating sustained silent reading. *Journal of Reading, 14,* 521–524, 582–583.

Norton, D. E. (1990). Teaching multicultural literature in the reading curriculum. *The Reading Teacher, 44*(1), 28–40.

Peterson, R. & Eeds, M. (1990). *Grand conversations: Literature groups in action.* Toronto, Ontario: Scholastic-TAB.

Purves, A. C. (1993). Toward a reevaluation of reader response and school literature. *Language Arts, 70*(5), 348–361

Rasinski, T. V. (1989). Fluency for everyone: Incorporating fluency instruction in the classroom. *The Reading Teacher, 42*(9), 690–693.

Rasinski, T. V. & Padak, N. V. (1990). Multicultural learning through children's literature. *Language Arts, 67*(6), 576–80.

Rosenblatt, L. (1985). Viewpoints: Transaction versus interaction—A terminological rescue operation. *Research in the Teaching of English, 19,* 98–107.

Rosenblatt, L. (1978). *The reader, the text, the poem: The transactional theory of literary work.* Carbondale, IL: Southern Illinois University Press.

Short, K. (1993). Intertextuality: Searching for patterns that connect. In D. J. Leu & C. K. Kinzer (Eds.), *Literacy research, theory, and practice: Views from many perspectives.* Forty-first Yearbook of the National Reading Conference. Chicago: National Reading Conference.

Spiegel, D. L., & Fitzgerald, J. (1986). Improving reading comprehension through instruction about story parts. *The Reading Teacher, 39*(7), 676–683.

Taylor, D., & Strickland, D. S. (1986). *Family storybook reading.* Portsmouth, NH: Heinemann.

Tompkins, G. E. & McGee, L. M. (1993). *Teaching reading with literature.* New York: Macmillan.

Trelease, J. (1989a). *The new read-aloud handbook.* New York: Penguin Books.

Trelease, J. (1989b). Jim Trelease speaks on reading aloud to children. *The Reading Teacher, 43*(3), 200–207.

Tunnell, M. O., & Jacobs, J. S. (1989). Using "real" books: Research findings on literature-based reading instruction. *The Reading Teacher, 42*(7), 470–477.

Wolf, S. A. (1993). What's in a name? Labels and literacy in readers theatre. *The Reading Teacher, 46*(7), 540–545.

Yokota, J. (1993). Issues in selecting multicultural literature. *Language Arts, 70*(3), 156–167.

Young, T. A. & Vardell, S. (1993). Weaving readers theatre and nonfiction into the curriculum. *The Reading Teacher, 46*(5), 396–406.

Zarrillo, J. (1989). Teachers' interpretations of literature-based reading. *The Reading Teacher, 42*(9), 22–29.

CHAPTER

Connecting Reading and Writing

"November 18

I remember us talking about the connection between reading and writing but I didn't really understand this idea until today in my field placement class. We were at the end of a cross-curricular thematic unit on the westward movement and students were taking turns in the author's chair, reading their final writing projects to the class. Each work was unique and so wonderfully done. One read a series of poems written by an imaginary pioneer family on the Oregon Trail. One read a diary she created for the explorer Jedediah Smith, recounting a trip to California and back. Another presented a story of the westward migration from a Native American perspective. Many of these writing projects came from ideas initially recorded in students' read aloud response journals after listening to me in a read aloud. As I thought about all the work that went into their projects, I saw what you meant about reading and writing supporting one another. These pieces all began with a reading experience that students wrote a response to. Later, they read their journals to find one entry to expand in writing. The project also required additional reading experiences to gather information that students wrote about. After they had written a draft, others read their work in a peer conference and gave them suggestions for improving their writing. Reading led to writing, which led to reading, which led to writing, and on and on. That's what you meant when you said that reading and writing should be connected, right?"

An entry from a student's reflective classroom journal, used to consolidate learning about reading instruction through writing.

The discovery made by this teacher is an important one. Effective teachers understand the benefits to be achieved by integrating reading and writing experiences. Consequently, they develop many method frameworks allowing them to integrate the two within their classrooms. This chapter will help you to make the reading-writing connection in your own classroom.

Chapter 5 includes information that will help you answer questions such as:

1. Why is writing important to the development of reading proficiency?
2. Which insights should guide the connection between reading and writing in my classroom?
3. Which method frameworks can help you to make the reading-writing connection?
4. How is a literacy framework associated with decisions about connecting reading and writing?

KEY CONCEPTS

author's chair
cross-curricular unit
dialogue journal
drafting
editing
integrated language arts unit
journal writing
pattern stories
predictable text
prewriting

process writing
publishing
reader response journal
reading/writing center
revising
story frame
style study
thematic units
writer's workshop

THE ROLE OF WRITING IN A CLASSROOM READING PROGRAM

In chapter 4 you discovered why literature is central to an effective classroom reading program. It is one of two vehicles that can be used to develop every aspect of reading comprehension and response. Writing is the other. Providing children with appropriate writing experiences should go hand in hand with using exceptional works of children's literature. The most effective classroom reading programs are those that regularly integrate the reading of children's literature with engaging writing experiences around important curricular goals.

But how, exactly, do writing experiences promote reading comprehension and response? Knowing the answer to that question will help us understand why writing is so important to reading and how we should make the reading-writing connection.

Using Writing to Develop Affective Aspects

Writers are interested and motivated readers (Shanahan, 1990; Smith, 1983). In fact, many teachers would argue that writing's greatest gift is the opportunity it provides for developing enthusiastic, interested, and sensitive readers. Writers are interested, of course, in rereading their own writing to be certain it says what they mean. They are also interested, however, in reading the writing of others. They read to gather information for their own writing. They also read to see how other authors present ideas. Thus, authentic writing experiences hold enormous potential for increasing interest in reading.

Writing can also be used to develop more thoughtful response patterns. Writing can help students think critically about their feelings, reactions, and beliefs. Students can learn about themselves and others as they write, discuss, and reflect on their reading and their writing (Hynds, 1989).

In addition, writing is a useful emotional outlet for dealing with life's crises. Writing about personal joys, pleasures, and difficulties can provide an important emotional outlet, especially in personal writing experiences such as a diary or a journal entry.

Using Writing to Develop Emergent Literacy Aspects

It used to be that people thought children could learn to write only after learning to read. As a result, writing opportunities were often delayed until children were able to read. Today we know that early writing experiences actually teach children important emergent literacy insights about reading (Chomsky, 1971; Clay, 1986; McGee & Richgels, 1990). In fact, some children learn to read by writing. Random scribbling, for example, changes to more organized left-to-right scribbling as youngsters discover the left-to-right nature of our writing system through their own early writing experiences. That discovery is an important developmental accomplishment.

Other aspects of emergent literacy also develop as youngsters compare their writing to the print around them. Letters start to appear in young children's writing as they begin to notice and replicate the symbols that we use in our writing system. This often happens before children can read individual words. Eventually, young children also begin to notice and use the spelling patterns that exist in our language as they explore the world of writing. Supporting these early attempts at writing helps very young children acquire insights important to emergent literacy.

Using Writing to Develop Decoding Knowledge

When young children write and attempt to spell words, they continually reflect on the relationships between sounds and letters (Read, 1971). This

Children develop important insights about emergent literacy through early opportunities to write.

leads to important insights about decoding knowledge. In early attempts, students invent their own spellings (for example, *pichr = picture*) because they have not yet learned conventional spellings. These inventions usually follow very logical insights about letter-sound relationships and help students to consider carefully what they know and need to know about letter-sound relationships. As young writers develop and compare their efforts with the print around them, they begin to understand readers' needs for more conventional spellings and eventually acquire them through their writing experiences. Thus, writing experiences contribute significantly to an understanding of the relationship between print and spoken language, a central component of decoding knowledge.

Using Writing to Develop Vocabulary Knowledge

Writing helps students develop vocabulary knowledge in at least two ways. First, writers learn the meanings of new words as they read and write about new ideas, new concepts, and new experiences. What better way to develop an understanding of the concepts associated with the Revolutionary War—the minutemen, Bunker Hill, Valley Forge, the stamp tax, the Constitution—than to read and then write about them? Writing allows us to try out new words in our language—to play with them in different sentences, practice using them, and see how they fit. Writers then come to own these new words and develop a richer, more powerful vocabulary because of their writing.

Writing also assists the development of vocabulary knowledge by helping us acquire a more precise understanding of word meanings. Have you

---

Writing instruction today is likely to be very different from the writing instruction you experienced in the elementary grades. The traditional model of writing instruction included substantial amounts of formal grammar instruction. Despite many studies, however, there is no compelling evidence that traditional grammar instruction improves students' writing ability. A report from the National Council of Teachers of English, for example, states that "The teaching of formal grammar was found to have a negligible or even harmful effect on the improvement of writing because it usually displaces some instruction and practice in actual composition" (NCTE, 1987). Today, many feel that children need more time to engage in authentic writing experiences and more opportunities to reflect about their writing. These are thought to be more valuable than learning definitions for parts of speech and diagramming sentences. The issue of how best to teach writing is closely related to your literacy framework, especially your beliefs about how one learns to read and write. Consider your beliefs about this issue. Which model of writing instruction do you favor?

---

ever found yourself trying to come up with the exact word for a particular idea in your writing? You probably ran through several similar words before deciding on the one that best fit the context. You may even have consulted a thesaurus or a dictionary. This type of experience results in a more precise understanding of word meanings, which is important to the development of vocabulary knowledge. Thus, writing not only expands our vocabulary knowledge but refines it as well.

Using Writing to Develop Syntactic Knowledge

Writing experiences also allow students to experiment with the consequences of different word combinations, thereby developing their syntactic knowledge. As we write, we try out different word patterns in order to communicate our exact meaning. We frequently write a sentence one way, read it, and decide that it does not quite say what we mean. Consequently, we modify the syntax of the sentence. We may change it from passive to active voice in order to be clearer; we may add a clause to modify one portion of the sentence, or we may even decide to make a complex sentence into several shorter sentences. As we experiment with these changes, we learn about the consequences of different syntactic patterns in our language. Thus, our writing experiences have helped develop our syntactic knowledge.

Using Writing to Develop Discourse Knowledge

Do you recall the first time you had to write an informational report at school? It was probably a report about a country or a state for a social studies assignment in third or fourth grade. Since we had never written a report before, many of us were confused by what a report should look like. And many of us solved the problem by going to an encyclopedia and using the headings and information we found there to organize our writing; headings like geography, industry, farming, the people, and major cities. This experience helped us to understand that reports are often structured around topical sections. This is a very different discourse structure from the episodic structure of narratives. Writing different types of discourse structures makes us keenly aware of the structural patterns each contains. Clearly, writing in an unfamiliar discourse form requires students to carefully attend to the structural characteristics of that form.

Using Writing to Develop Metacognitive Knowledge

Finally, writing experiences require students to consider how their audience will read their text, thus promoting the development of metacognitive knowledge. Will the audience skim a lengthy text? If so, it becomes important to provide clear topic sentences, a clear introduction, and a strong summary. Will the audience read the text carefully to acquire new information? If so, it becomes important to make connections between ideas as explicit as possible. Writers are forced to anticipate the strategic knowledge their readers will use, thereby developing their own metacognitive knowledge (Raphael & Englert, 1990).

PROVIDING APPROPRIATE WRITING EXPERIENCES

If writing is so important to reading proficiency, how should teachers go about providing appropriate writing experiences? During the past decade much research has focused on writing and has provided us with useful information on how writing should be used in classroom activities. The major insights from this research provide clear direction for structuring these writing experiences.

Writing is a process.

Writing experiences should serve an authentic communicative purpose.

Writing experiences are most valuable when they create complete, extended texts.

Reading and writing are similar types of processes.

Writing Is a Process

Traditionally, schools have simply assigned writing tasks to students and then evaluated their products (Applebee, 1981). By focusing on the outcome, traditional approaches treated writing as a product. In contrast, one of the most important conclusions from recent work is that writing should be viewed as a process, not a product (Calkins, 1983; Graves, 1983; Smith, 1982). **Process writing** is now rapidly replacing more traditional approaches to writing.

Teachers who take a process approach to writing do more than simply assign writing tasks and evaluate the results. Instead, they focus their

process writing
A view of writing instruction that allows you to support the elements of the writing process: prewriting, drafting, revising, editing, and publishing.

attention on the process of writing and look for ways to support students during each phase of this process:

prewriting

drafting

revising

editing

publishing

Recognizing writing as a process leads teachers to support each of these elements as they design appropriate writing experiences for their students.

Prewriting experiences are designed to generate potential topics and writing ideas by helping students explore personal knowledge related to their writing task. Everyone writes better if we take a moment to think about what we know before we begin. Examples of prewriting activities you may wish to use include: reading material related to a topic, brainstorming ideas, mapping relationships among ideas, listing sources of information, and even talking to a friend about various ideas. Appropriate prewriting experiences support students in this often-difficult beginning phase of the writing process.

At least three considerations should influence prewriting activities. First, students should explore a wide range of potential writing ideas during prewriting. Such exploration allows students to select their own topics from several possibilities and work on a writing task that is personally important and engaging. Second, it is important to provide sufficient time for this phase of the writing process. In a survey of U.S. classrooms, Applebee (1981) concluded that students have, on average, three minutes to think of a topic during a typical writing lesson. Much more time than this is needed if students are to have sufficient time to explore all possibilities. Finally, prewriting should be viewed as an opportunity for students to discover what it is they have to say about a topic. Prewriting gets ideas to flow; it is a time of beginnings. It is not a time when the final structure of a text must be decided. Examples of how prewriting activities might be used during writing instruction can be seen in Figure 5-1.

The second element of the writing process is **drafting,** which consists of initial attempts to capture ideas in writing. All of us write better if we know we don't have to worry about getting everything written perfectly in the first draft. Drafting is often messy, as writers erase, rewrite, or even start over. The goal is simply to get the writer's first attempt down on paper or computer disk. There will be plenty of time later for revising. Strategies that support the drafting phase of the writing process can be seen in Figure 5-2.

Revising is the third component of the writing process. As writers revise, they read their work, consider what they have written, and make changes in the content of their writing. Revising is an important but diffi-

prewriting
One element of the writing process during which writers generate potential topics and writing ideas.

drafting
One element of the writing process during which writers capture preliminary ideas.

revising
One element of the writing process during which writers consider what they have written and make changes in the content.

FIGURE 5-1
Strategies that support writers during the prewriting phase

 Diary Writing. Read together or conduct read-alouds of selections in which the main character keeps a diary. Consider these examples:

Anne Frank: Diary of a Young Girl

Diary of a Rabbit by Lilo Hess

Penny Pollard's Diary by Robin Klein

Tell your students that they, too, will have an opportunity to keep a diary. Brainstorm together (and list on chart paper) things that students might write about in a diary. Post this list permanently where students can refer to it when they are thinking about writing topics. After sufficient discussion give each student a small spiral notebook to use as a diary. Allow students to decorate their diaries in any way they wish before making their first entries.

 Reader Response Journals. Introduce the use of reader response journals. Explain that these are used to record ideas, feelings, and responses related to what has been read. Then have students generate a list of all the different types of responses writers might include in their response journals. Keep this list posted during the first few weeks so that students can use it to generate new types of responses in their journals. The list might include items such as these:

reactions to what you have read

evaluation of characters and their actions

predictions about what will happen next

ideas for writing projects that you get from your reading

ways you would have written (and improved) a text

feelings about events

Note that reader response journals themselves may be a useful prewriting experience because they are often a source of writing ideas for later projects.

cult part of the writing process. It is important because it holds great potential for developing insight into written language as students consider alternatives to their initial choices about words, sentence structures, discourse patterns, and other elements of writing. Revising is difficult for writers, though. Younger writers want to focus their attention on spelling and the appearance of their writing more than its content. They need to look carefully at word choices, sentence structure, and other elements from their reader's perspective. And writers of any age are often too close to their work to notice sections that are not clear.

To help students understand how to improve the content of their writing, teachers often use peer conferences, during which another student reads a writer's work and makes suggestions for improvement. It helps

FIGURE 5-2

Strategies that support the drafting phase of the writing process

 Co-authored Writing. Periodically, encourage pairs of students to work on a co-authored paper in a cooperative learning group activity. After a prewriting activity, they might want to work together on one draft, talking and making decisions as they go. Alternatively, after making preliminary decisions about topic and structure, they might want to write separate drafts and then compare and combine their ideas. Students often learn much from working with others and seeing how someone else writes. This is especially true when you match a more proficient with a less proficient writer.

 Writing Folders. Make separate writing folders for each of your students. Keep these folders in your reading/writing center (described later in this chapter). Encourage students to keep their drafts in their folders so that they will be available for use later during revision.

writers of all ages to have someone else read and react to their writing before they revise it. Readers can provide writers with the best suggestions for making writing clearer. Suggestions for conducting peer conferences are described in Figure 5-3.

The fourth aspect of the writing process is **editing.** During editing the writer should attend to the surface characteristics of writing, including spelling, capitalization, punctuation, and usage. Editing takes place near the end of the process so that attention has first been directed to the content of the piece during prewriting, drafting, and revising. Several strategies used to support the editing phase can be seen in Figure 5-4.

editing
One element of the writing process during which writers make changes in the surface characteristics of their work.

The final element in the writing process is **publishing,** when writers formally share their writing with a wider audience and receive recognition for their work. Sometimes publishing involves binding students' work and making it available for others to read. One method for binding books can be seen in Figure 5-5. This is not the only way to publish a work, though. Other strategies for formally sharing a finished work are described in Figure 5-6.

publishing
One element of the writing process during which writers formally share their work with a wider audience.

Using Process Writing in the Classroom

Focusing on writing as a process means that we provide support to students during each phase of the writing process. The writing project described in the model lesson below demonstrates how a teacher might provide support during each of these phases. However, two important points need to be made. First, it is important that teachers not require students to go through each phase of the writing process for every writing assignment. For example, some writing tasks, such as an entry in a journal or a diary, do not require careful editing and are rarely published or shared publicly. Teachers may want to allow their students to decide which of their many writing projects are developed all the way to publishing.

FIGURE 5-3

Using peer conferences to support the revision phase of the writing process

Peer conferences

Explain to students how to conduct a peer conference. First, a writer reads his or her work aloud to a listener so that both can hear it. Then the listener should provide three types of comments: things the listener liked about the paper (praise), things that were not clear in the paper (question), and suggestions to make the paper better (polish). After you give this explanation, model several peer conferences in front of the entire class so that students understand how to assist a writer. Then provide a written list of questions to guide each listener's responses.

What did you like? (praise)

What did you not understand? (question)

What will make the writing better? (polish)

Keeping track of peer conferences

As students use peer conferences to improve their writing, you may wish to have authors ask listeners to initial the draft in the upper right-hand corner. Some teachers require each draft to have at least two sets of initials before it is revised. They monitor this by requiring students to turn in rough drafts along with the final copy and checking the initials on each rough draft. Some teachers also encourage children to have parents be one of their listeners. This keeps parents informed about the work their children are doing at school.

FIGURE 5-4

Strategies that support the editing phase of the writing process.

Editorial Boards. Use an editorial board for large writing projects in the class. Appoint board members, and then have students with revised texts bring their work to a member of the editorial board for final editing. Regularly rotate the members of the board.

Editing Marks. Conduct a writer's workshop (see page 205) on the use of common editing marks, as illustrated below. Use either an inductive or a deductive method framework to teach the use of these conventions during editing. Show students how you use these marks when you edit your own work, and encourage them to use the same marks for their own editing.

≡	capitalize		delete something
⊙	use a period	⬭	check the spelling of this word
∧	insert something	¶	begin a new paragraph
∧	add a comma		transpose

FIGURE 5-5

One method for binding books to support the publishing phase of the writing process

Required materials

Ditto paper (8 1/2" x 11" 6–7 pieces)   Dental floss (20")
Cardboard or posterboard   Construction paper (9" x 12")
(6 1/4" x 9 1/2" 2 pieces)   Scissors
Rubber cement   Plastic letters (optional)
Wallpaper, adhesive-backed paper, or material (15" x 11")

Making the booklet

1. One at a time, fold 6 or 7 sheets of ditto paper in half to form book pages that are 5 1/2" x 8 1/2". Bring the sheets together, one inside the other. Fold the construction paper in half, forming a 6" x 9" rectangle. Place the ditto sheets inside the folded construction paper.
2. Open the booklet and lay it flat. Poke small holes through the center fold at about 1" intervals. Using the needle threaded with dental floss, sew the pages together along the fold. Begin sewing on the outside of the fold so that the knot at the end of the dental floss is not seen when the book is completely bound. Continue until the stitches cover the entire length of the fold.

Making the cover

1. Lay the wallpaper or other covering face down and place the two cardboard or posterboard pieces on top, leaving approximately equal overlap top to bottom and side to side and about 1/8" space in the center between the two pieces.
2. Use the rubber cement to glue the cardboard or posterboard pieces in place. Cut diagonally across each corner, and then glue down the overlap along the sides. Use the cut-off triangles to reinforce the inside corners if you wish.

Putting the booklet and cover together

1. Glue the construction paper of the booklet to the inside of the cover.
2. Use the plastic letters or some other material to add the title to the cover.

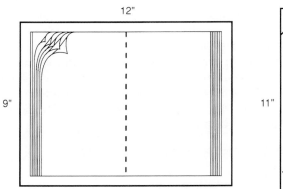
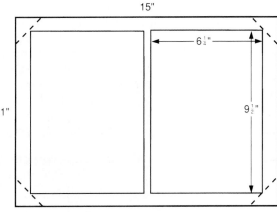

FIGURE 5-6

Strategies that support the publishing phase of the writing process

Author's Chair. Have a special author's chair, from which students read their works in progress or their finished works to the rest of the class. (Place this in a prominent place in your classroom.) Authors whose works are in progress can solicit ideas from their classmates to improve their work. Authors who read finished work should receive kudos of appreciation for their storylines, characters, illustrations, and the like. (Some teachers use a rocking chair or a used, over-stuffed chair for their authors.)

Author of the Week. Each week, designate one student as the author of the week in your class. Allow this student the opportunity to publish his or her favorite written works on a bulletin board display set aside for this purpose. Let the designated student introduce the display at the beginning of the week and read aloud his or her best piece of writing from the author's chair. Announce the next author of the week on Friday in order to allow this student time to put together the next display.

Class Newspapers. Publish stories and articles in a class or school newspaper. Send this home to parents to keep them informed of class activities. Be certain to send a copy to your principal, too.

Read-Aloud Variations. Have students' written work read regularly in the morning over the school communication system. You might also have students read their completed works to another class.

Author Parties. Every month set aside an hour for students to read their completed works to the rest of the class. Allow listeners to respond to the completed works. Celebrate with a small party for the authors.

Second, it is important to recognize that the writing process is more recursive than linear. In other words, writing does not always follow a strict sequential process of prewriting, followed by drafting, followed by revising, followed by editing, followed by publishing. When writers are drafting an article, they may also revise portions of it, or they may go back and edit word choices and spelling. They may even make plans to have their writing published. Writers appear to develop their own style during the writing process. Thus, Graves (1983) points out, writing is not easily packaged into a sequence of steps. And teachers who want to support their students throughout the writing process should not expect a neat linear sequence of procedural steps.

Writing Experiences Should Serve an Authentic Communicative Purpose

A second insight to guide instruction is that writing experiences are most appropriate when they serve an authentic communicative purpose. This seems like common sense, doesn't it? Who would want students to write

MODEL LESSON

A Process Writing Activity in Ms. Sanchez's Class

Prewriting. Ms. Sanchez's third-grade class has been reading a thematic unit on *pourquoi* tales, the "why" stories used by each culture to explain the origin of things. The students have listened to, read, and discussed *pourquoi* tales from several cultures.

How the Rhinoceros Got His Skin by Leonard Weisgard
The Fire Bringer by Margaret Hodges
Just So Stories by Rudyard Kipling

Ms. Sanchez tells her students that they will have a chance to create their own *pourquoi* tales and publish these in a book entitled *Just Our Stories (with apologies to Rudyard Kipling)*. This book will be placed in the local library for the community to enjoy before being returned to the class. Ms. Sanchez begins with a brainstorming activity. Students share possible titles for their *pourquoi* tales: "How the Snake Lost Its Legs," "How Ms. Sanchez Got Her Smile," "How San Francisco Got the Bay," "How the Eagle Got Its Wings." As each title is shared, Ms. Sanchez writes it on the board, and a few moments are spent brainstorming explanations that might be included in the story. Once a list of titles is developed, she encourages students to decide on their own titles and begin drafting their *pourquoi* tales.

Drafting. Ms. Sanchez circulates around the room, providing assistance and encouragement. When she notices interesting ideas that are being developed, she has students share them with the class. Nonetheless, several students are having difficulty getting started. She calls these students together for additional brainstorming and discussion about possible stories. As each possibility is brainstormed, Ms. Sanchez maps out the story's setting, problem, and resolution on the board. This support provides each student with the necessary structure to get started. At the end of each day's work, students return their drafts to their individual writing folders located in the writing center of the classroom.

Revising. As students finish their drafts, Ms. Sanchez assigns them to someone else in the room for peer conferencing. She has students share their work in two separate peer conferences so that they can obtain different reactions to their writing. She gives both writer and listener a paper with these procedures for peer conferencing.

1. Read the draft aloud.
2. Share your response to each of the following questions:
   What did you like?
   What did you not understand?
   What will make the writing better?

After receiving comments from two listeners, students begin to revise their work in a second draft.

Editing. Ms. Sanchez requires each tale to be read and edited by at least two people. The editors sign the front page of the second draft so that a list of their names can be compiled for inclusion in the final book. After two people have read and edited each story, students complete a third and final draft, taking into consideration their editors' suggestions.

Publishing. After each story is completed, Ms. Sanchez has the author sit in the author's chair and read it orally to the entire class. Then she prepares it for binding with the rest of the stories.

something with no purpose? Still, the only purpose of many classroom writing tasks appears to be simply to record that something was completed (Moffett, 1985). For example, writing a book report, which is turned in to the teacher and passed back with a grade, communicates only that the student has completed reading a book. On the other hand, a book review written to guide other students in making a reading selection would serve a more useful communicative purpose. The review might be read aloud to the class and then included in a collection of other reviews organized by title, topic, or author for later student reference.

Writing experiences that serve an authentic communicative purpose are both personal and meaningful for students. They are personal because students recognize that they are sharing a part of themselves with their readers. They are meaningful because the writing exists to communicate important information. When writing is both personal and meaningful, students invest considerable energy and attention. They are more careful because they realize they are sharing something important about themselves with their readers; and as a result, they gain more from the experience.

As teachers we need to create contexts in which students have authentic reasons for writing. A classroom should be viewed as a literacy community, where students use writing to communicate, satisfy needs, present information, express personal thoughts and opinions, record information, and interact with others. Examples of activities that use writing for authentic communication are described in Figure 5-7.

FIGURE 5-7

Strategies that promote student writing for authentic communication

 Get-Well Letters. Have students write get-well letters whenever a classmate is ill and absent from school for more than several days. Encourage students to describe what is taking place at school so that the absent student keeps posted on what is happening. Collect the letters at the end of the day, and ask a student who lives near the absent classmate to deliver them. Twenty or thirty letters from friends will always brighten someone's day.

 Suggestion Box. Create a classroom suggestion box. Encourage students to share their ideas for making the classroom a better place in which to learn. Regularly post suggestions on a bulletin board, and encourage students to write their reactions to the ideas. Post student responses as well.

 Letters to Visitors. Have students write letters to classroom visitors (e.g., fire fighters, police officers, doctors, librarians, authors, and others) *before* they arrive as well as after they have come. Encourage students to list questions in their letters that they would like to have answered when the person visits. Visitors appreciate knowing in advance what is on students' minds.

Writing Experiences Are Most Valuable When They Create Complete, Extended Texts

Writing experiences are most appropriate when they require students to create complete, extended texts such as letters, stories, or articles. Too often, the writing experiences in our schools only require students to fill in a blank or complete a sentence. In an analysis of language arts textbooks used in the elementary grades, DeGroff and Leu (1987) found that, on average, students were expected to write only one piece per week that was greater than a single sentence. That level of involvement in writing is simply not enough to develop proficient readers and writers.

Complete, extended texts offer numerous benefits. First, extended writing experiences promote the development of all components of the comprehension and response processes. More limited writing experiences make more limited contributions. For example, a task requiring students to write single-word answers demands attention only to spelling and vocabulary elements. Single sentences require only spelling, vocabulary, and syntactic knowledge. However, writing a letter, article, or story requires students to attend to all of the components associated with comprehension or composition. Thus, extended writing experiences hold greater potential for students to learn about written language.

In addition, writing a complete, extended text has much greater potential to develop critical thinking and reasoning abilities. We certainly cannot expect students to argue persuasively or explain their reasoning in a single word or sentence. And writing a complete, extended text also provides more reading opportunities at every phase of the process. Single words or sentences limit the rereading that students must do, especially during revision and editing. Finally, extended texts usually serve a greater communicative purpose than single words or sentences can. A single word or sentence typically reflects a student's understanding or completion of a reading assignment. Complete texts, on the other hand, permit purposeful communication. Strategies that describe extended writing experiences are described in Figure 5-8.

Reading and Writing Are Similar Types of Processes

It is important to keep in mind that reading and writing are similar types of processes. They have been compared by various authors as being two sides of the same coin, two wings of the same bird, or a mirror into which reader and writer peer from different sides. Each of these metaphors helps us understand how closely reading and writing are related.

In both reading and writing meaning is composed. Writers compose meaning as they construct a message for their readers. Readers then compose meaning as they reconstruct the author's message. Furthermore, Tierney and Pearson (1983) point out that both writers and readers plan, draft, align, revise, and monitor as they compose meaning.

FIGURE 5-8

Strategies that describe more extended writing experiences

 Pattern Writing. Read aloud a series of books containing a similar discourse structure, such as a set of fables, mysteries, or biographies. Then help students write their own stories following that same type of discourse structure. For younger students you may wish to use a single story with a predictable and repeated pattern, such as *Brown Bear, Brown Bear, What Can You See?* by Bill Martin. For older students you may wish to use an unfamiliar genre, such as science fiction. An interesting science fiction selection for older students is *This Place Has No Atmosphere* by Paula Danziger.

 Self-evaluations. Have students write descriptive self-evaluations of their work at the end of each marking period. Include these with their report cards to parents and use them during parent conference time.

 Social Studies Journals. Have students keep a social studies journal. Have them use it to ask questions, record interesting information, and summarize what they have read. Encourage students to use the journals to review information they have covered. Other writing activities related to social studies can also be recorded in these journals.

To begin, both writers and readers plan. Writers plan their messages, taking into account their goals and their audiences. Readers plan as they consider their purposes for reading, their knowledge about the topics, and the authors of the messages.

Similarly, both writers and readers engage in drafting. Writers create drafts as they initially craft the messages they wish to communicate. Readers create drafts as they acquire the meaning that they draw from the texts. They may create one draft before they start, a second as they read and refine their initial expectations, and yet another draft after they finish reading and have thought about the text more carefully. Readers continually draft new interpretations of what they are reading, just as authors develop new drafts of what they are writing.

The process of aligning refers to the stance that writers take toward their readers and that readers take toward writers. How each views the other influences how each performs the writing or reading task. Clearly, both readers and writers align themselves with the other.

In addition, both writers and readers revise their work. Writers revise as they attempt to make meaning clearer for their audiences. Readers revise as they attempt to reconstruct the meaning the authors intended. We probably notice this process most clearly when we finish a story with a surprise ending, and we are forced to revise our interpretations of the story.

Finally, both writers and readers monitor their work. Writers monitor their work as they create it, deciding when and where it needs to be revised, when and where it should be edited, and when it is complete.

Readers also monitor, deciding when something makes sense, what to do when something does not make sense, and when their comprehension of a text is complete. Both writers and readers use their metacognitive knowledge during this process.

Because reading and writing are such similar types of processes, it is important for teachers to make as many connections as possible between reading and writing experiences. Reading can assist the development of writing proficiency, and writing can assist the development of reading proficiency.

MAKING THE READING-WRITING CONNECTION

There is probably no limit to the ways in which creative teachers can make the reading-writing connection in their classrooms. Ideas range from something as simple as having very young students read their writing to you each day, to something as complex as integrating reading and writing activities within a thematically organized instructional unit. Creating new and productive learning experiences for children is one of the great satisfactions of teaching.

This section describes the more common ways that teachers make the reading-writing connection. You should consider modifying those procedures to meet individual students' needs and your evolving literacy framework. You should also think about creating your own activities to connect reading and writing.

Using Reader Response Journals

One of the best means of making the reading-writing connection is by encouraging journal writing activities. One type of journal often used for this purpose is a **reader response journal.** Reader response journals are used in a variety of ways to integrate reading and writing experiences. The most common procedural steps in this method framework, though, usually consist of these:

1. Read a section of a literary work.
2. Write a response to what was read.
3. Use some of your responses as beginning ideas for larger writing projects.

reader response journal
A type of journal and a method framework in which students record their ideas and feelings about what they have read.

Students use a reader response journal to record their ideas and feelings about what they have read. Reader response journals can be used in conjunction with independent reading selections as well as with teacher-selected reading assignments. A sample entry from a reader response journal is included in Figure 5-9.

Reader response journals allow students to assume control of their responses to reading assignments (Hancock, 1993; Kelley, 1990). They support readers in their aesthetic experiences with text, helping them to have a more complex "lived through" experience (Rosenblatt, 1985). And

FIGURE 5-9

A sample entry from a reader response journal

<u>Hatchet</u> by Gary Paulsen   Sarah   March 12

      Describe a time when you were afraid

    Dark! It was really dark! I had a hard time breathing the blankets were wrapped so tight over my head. There coming. I know there coming. Laser guns would shoot up through my mattress by the space invaders I knew were under my bed.

    I was five years old and I hadn't thought about how space invaders could of been anywhere outside of the theater or our TV. Still, I was sure they were there and it would happen. There coming!

    Suddenly it was morning and I had lasted another night in my new bedroom.

entries in reader response journals also find their way into more extended writing pieces. This happens when teachers encourage students to go back into their reader response journals and look for writing ideas that might be elaborated upon into larger written works.

One interesting variation of a reader response journal is to encourage students to write a character journal (Hancock, 1993). In a character journal, students assume the role of one of the main characters and make entries in the response journal as if they were this person. Character journals encourage a wider range of response patterns, help students develop more aesthetic or "lived through" experiences, and help them to better understand the perspective of a major character.

Teachers sometimes choose to devote a regular 10- or 15-minute period each day to writing in reader response journals. During this time all students in the class write about the selections they have been reading; they may write anything they wish, but they must write. In many ways this activity can be considered the writing equivalent of sustained silent reading, a method framework described in chapter 4.

Students should be supported in determining how they wish to respond to any reading experience. Sometimes, though, your students may need direction about how to make a response to their reading, especially when you begin this activity for the first time. Journal starters like those in the following list provide direction and guidance for students who may be uncertain about what to write in their journals.

The character I like best in this story is. . .because. . .

This character reminds me of somebody I know because. . .

This character reminds me of myself because. . .

This section makes me think about. . .because. . .

This episode reminds me of a situation in my own life. It happened when. . .

If I were. . .at this point I would. . .

(Youngblood, 1985)

Using Dialogue Journals

A **dialogue journal** gives teachers another method framework to connect reading and writing. Dialogue journals can be used in many ways, but the most common procedural steps in this method framework include these:

1. Students make entries in their individual dialogue journals.
2. The teacher collects the journals at the end of the day.
3. The teacher reads and writes responses in each of the journals, returning them to students the following day.

The first step in using dialogue journals is usually to have students make entries in their individual journals about any topic they choose. Students often write about what they are reading, events that have happened during the day, problems they are experiencing with other students, or important experiences they have had at home. It is important to allow students to select topics of personal importance in order to create authentic writing (and reading) experiences for them and to increase interest and motivation.

The second step is to collect the students' journals. Some teachers require students to make regular entries and turn in their journals each

dialogue journal
A type of journal and a method framework through which students engage in a written conversation with their teachers.

Many different types of journal experiences may be used to support literacy learning, especially if you have a holistic or integrated perspective about how children learn to read.

day. Other teachers have students turn in their journals only when they have made new entries, and still other teachers have students write in their journals whenever they choose but turn them in once a week. A useful strategy is to divide your class into five groups and then collect a different group's journals each evening. This reduces the number of responses you need to make during any single day so that you can thoughtfully respond to each student.

During the final step of the process the teacher reads through the students' entries and writes a response to each student. These responses include reactions to what students have written, answers to questions they ask, and process questions the teacher asks. Process questions require students to elaborate on their writing and extend the writing process; for example, "Tell me more about. . .," "Can you explain why. . .," "What are you going to do now?" and "How did that make you feel?"

Dialogue journals provide opportunities for students to solve personal difficulties, and give teachers useful insights into their students (Bode, 1989; Gambrell, 1985). In practice, dialogue journals prompt "written conversation between two persons on a functional, continued basis, about topics of. . .interest" (Staton, 1988, p. 312).

Fuhler (1994) has suggested that teachers encourage parents to become involved in both dialogue and reader response journals. By involving both parents and teachers in reading and responding to children's journals, important conversations take place that inevitably assist the literacy development of each child. These experiences also provide useful information to both teachers and parents as they read each other's responses.

An example of a dialogue journal entry between a second grade student and her teacher can be seen in Figure 5-10.

Using Buddy Journals

The use of **buddy journals** is a method framework quite similar to that of dialogue journals. Buddy journals are kept by pairs of students, writing back and forth and maintaining a written conversation about topics of mutual interest (D'Angelo Bromley, 1989). Buddy journals provide an authentic means of connecting reading and writing in the classroom. These journals involve three procedural steps:

buddy journal
A type of journal and a method framework through which pairs of students engage in written conversations.

1. Buddy journal partners are selected.
2. Students make entries in their journals.
3. Students exchange journals, read their partner's entry, and write a response.

The selection of partners for the buddy journal experience is important. Sometimes teachers assign buddy journal partners, accepting the possibility that some students may be uncomfortable with the partners selected for them. To minimize the discomfort, teachers might limit buddy journal teams to a period of only two weeks and then assign new partners. Other strategies are to assign partners randomly by selecting names out of a hat or to let students select their own partners. Letting students help determine the method used is often useful. But regardless of the method chosen, the teacher should be prepared to serve as a buddy journal partner if there are an uneven number of students in the class.

The second step in the process is to have students make entries in their own journals. Generally, students should be encouraged to write about topics of their own choosing in order to provide ownership and increase interest and motivation. At times, however, buddy journals can be used in conjunction with specific reading selections. Under those circumstances the teacher should encourage students to converse with each other about any topics related to their reading selections. This approach increases the connection between reading and writing and provides a unique means of discussing reading experiences.

The final step is to have students exchange their buddy journals, read their partner's entry, and write a response. This step gets the written conversation started. Several entries from a buddy journal are shown in Figure 5-11.

FIGURE 5-10

An example of a dialogue journal entry

> Oct. 4, 1989
> My whole class is working on a book, Cald Corduroy goes to hawaii. We are going to ilasterat it. Some are going to do it alone. Some ai are going to work with a parner. I am going to work with a parner. My parner is Ian.
>
> *I can't wait to see your illustrations and get our book published. It was such fun writing it.*

style study
A method framework where students develop insight about writing by looking closely at how authors use different language patterns and then try to emulate those patterns.

Conducting a Style Study

Another way in which to connect reading and writing is to conduct a **style study.** This method framework allows students to develop greater insight into an author's craft by looking closely at how authors use different language patterns. Afterwards, students are encouraged to try out

FIGURE 5-11

Several entries from a buddy journal

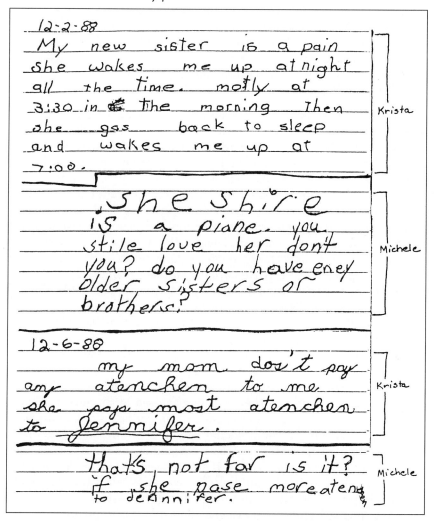

12-2-88

My new sister is a pain
she wakes me up at night
all the time. motly at
3:30 in the morning Then
she gos back to sleep
and wakes me up at
7:00 .   Krista

She Shire
is a piane. you
stile love her don't
you? do you have eney
older sisters or
brothers.   Michele

12-6-88
       my mom don't pay
any atenchen to me
she pays most atenchen
to Jennifer.   Krista

thats not far is it?
if she pase more ateng
to Jennifer.   Michele

Source: From K. D'Angelo Bromley, "Buddy Journals Make the Reading-Writing Connection," *The Reading Teacher, 43* (1989), p. 128. Reprinted by permission.

these techniques in their own writing. A style study is a wonderful way in which you can cultivate a deeper sensitivity to an author's craft through rich literary and writing experiences. And by carefully examining the writing of professionals students begin to read an author like a writer (Bearse, 1992). This is important because it means that students will begin to see new writing patterns on their own and then try out these patterns in their written work.

As a method framework, a style study contains the following procedural steps:

1. Read a passage from children's literature together.
2. Identify several stylistic patterns used by this author.
3. Discuss why the author probably chose to use these patterns.
4. Provide students with a writing task where they are asked to try out at least one of the patterns they have seen.
5. Share the results.

A style study can be used any time you are reading a common work of literature with your students. Because you will want students to look through the text for stylistic elements characteristic of a particular author, it is usually best when each student has his or her own copy of a work.

After you have read the passage together, draw students' attention to several stylistic features used by an author. You will want to have several examples identified in advance but with experienced students it is often useful to have them locate these features by themselves. These features might consist of a grammatical element like a sequence of participial phrases (He jogged along slowly, *singing a tune, thinking of his plan,* and *contemplating the marvelous catastrophe that was about to occur.)* Or, it might include a special technique during dialogue sequences like the use of very short sentences to communicate the desperation of a situation ("Now?" "Yes!" "Should I do it quickly?" "Yes. Just do it!"). After a while you will notice that each author excels at certain aspects of writing. Some are exceptional at dialogue, others at descriptions, and others at communicating mood.

After identifying each feature, it is often useful to engage children in a short discussion about why that feature was used by an author. This is important so that they might use the same technique for a similar purpose.

Next, you should provide students with a short writing task where they get to "try on" the author's stylistic technique and see if they can use it effectively in their own writing. If you noticed, for example, that the author uses short sentences in dialogue sequences when the characters are in a desperate situation you might brainstorm several similar situations and then ask students to write a short dialogue sequence with this technique.

Have students share their attempts at using this stylistic feature in their own writing. You will find that students can quickly adapt these techniques to their own writing. You will also begin to see these elements appear during other classroom writing activities as students pick up the tricks they find each author using. In addition, students often begin reading literary works very differently, noticing stylistic decisions and thinking about why the author chose a particular technique in a situation. A style study often leads to many new insights about reading and writing. The model lesson below shows how one teacher used a style study to connect reading and writing.

MODEL LESSON

Conducting a Style Study in Mr. Aaronson's Class

It is early in the school year and Mr. Aaronson wants to increase his students' awareness of stylistic conventions that authors use in their writing. He believes that introducing this idea to his fourth-grade class now will help them to see many other stylistic features in the course of the year. Mr. Aaronson has been reading aloud *James and the Giant Peach* by Roald Dahl to his class each day after lunch. Today he has brought in multiple copies of this work so that each pair of students has a copy to share.

Read a Passage from Children's Literature Together. Instead of reading the next chapter in *James and the Giant Peach* aloud to his class, Mr. Aaronson asks them to read this chapter, silently.

Identify Several Stylistic Features Used by This Author. After students complete their reading of the chapter, Mr. Aaronson asks them if they noticed any special aspects to this author's writing style. He points out that Roald Dahl is especially known for his use of dialogue. The students find two different stylistic features. One student notices that the author uses the word "and" a lot during dialogue but isn't certain why the author does this. Mr. Aaronson writes several examples that students found on the board:

"They will eat up the peach *and* then there'll be nothing left for us to stand on *and* they'll start on us." (p. 56)

"I'm going to take a long silk string," James went on, "*and* I'm going to loop one end of it around a seagull's neck. *And* then I'm going to tie the other end to the stem of the peach." (p. 61)

They also notice that Roald Dahl often uses a sequence of descriptive adjectives when he paints a word picture:

"Their eyes waited upon him, *tense, anxious, pathetically hopeful.*" (p. 56)

"Seagulls love worms, didn't you know that? And luckily for us, we have here the *biggest, fattest, pinkest, juiciest* Earthworm in the world." (p. 60)

Discuss Why the Author Probably Chose to Use These Features. Their discussion leads them to realize that the author uses the word *and* during dialogue because it makes the language sound more like the way we actually speak in an oral conversation. This is one of the tricks Dahl uses to make his writing more realistic. The students also notice that descriptive sequences of adjectives are a powerful way of describing feelings and appearances with a minimum number of words.

Provide Students with a Writing Task Where They Are Asked To Try Out at Least One of the Stylistic Features. Mr. Aaronson lets his students pick from one of two different writing tasks. They can write a dialogue between two individuals using *and* to connect ideas and make the dialogue sound more like oral language or they can describe something in the classroom using a sequence of descriptive adjectives.

Share the Results. Afterwards, Mr. Aaronson has his students share their results in small groups. As he circulates around the room, listening to their results he praises their work. He senses that his students have picked up new techniques that they will soon use in their own writing projects.

Developing Reading/Writing Centers

reading/writing center
A classroom location in which students participate in a series of independent activities that connect reading and writing.

A **reading/writing center** is a location in the classroom where children can participate in a series of independent, self-guided, teacher-designed activities that connect reading and writing. These centers take many forms but usually share several characteristics.

First, reading/writing centers contain all the reading and writing materials that students require to complete the activities. For example, the following materials were available for one reading/writing center activity at the third-grade level:

1. Ten articles about exotic animals from the nature magazine *Ranger Rick*. Each had been separated from the magazine and stapled into construction-paper covers.
2. Duplicated copies of a fact sheet, which was an outline with major headings such as name of animal, size, appearance, home, food, family, and unusual facts. Students had previously learned how to use this form for recording information about animals in a science project.
3. Writing paper and felt-tip pens.
4. Students' writing folders.

Second, reading/writing centers contain clear directions for completing particular learning activities. Usually, the directions are written in procedural steps that students should follow (see Figure 5-12). Third, these centers contain students' writing folders, in which they keep drafts of their writing projects. Students can take their folders as they need them and return them at the end of the day. Finally, reading/writing centers have a place to display completed work. Often this consists of a bulletin board where students may post their work and thus provide examples for other students.

Integrating Writing Activities within Thematic Units

thematic units
Multiple learning experiences that are integrated around a topic, an author, or a genre.

An increasingly common way of making the reading-writing connection is to integrate reading and writing experiences within **thematic units.** Thematic units consist of multiple learning experiences that are integrated around a single topic (for example, *Nature Is a Part of All Our Lives, The Time of the Dinosaurs, Making and Keeping Friends*), author (for example, Laura Ingalls Wilder, Katherine Paterson, Arnold Lobel), or genre (for example, biography, science fiction, mysteries). Thematic approaches to instruction have been prompted by a concern that school learning is too often fragmented, unconnected, and, as a result, not especially meaningful (Routman, 1991). By connecting learning in several areas around a thematic unit, teachers attempt to provide a meaningful focus for students' experiences. This makes both learning and teaching more of a meaningful enterprise (Lipson, Valencia, Wixson, & Peters, 1993). Thematic units have other advantages, too. They make it more

FIGURE 5-12

An example of a reading-writing center activity

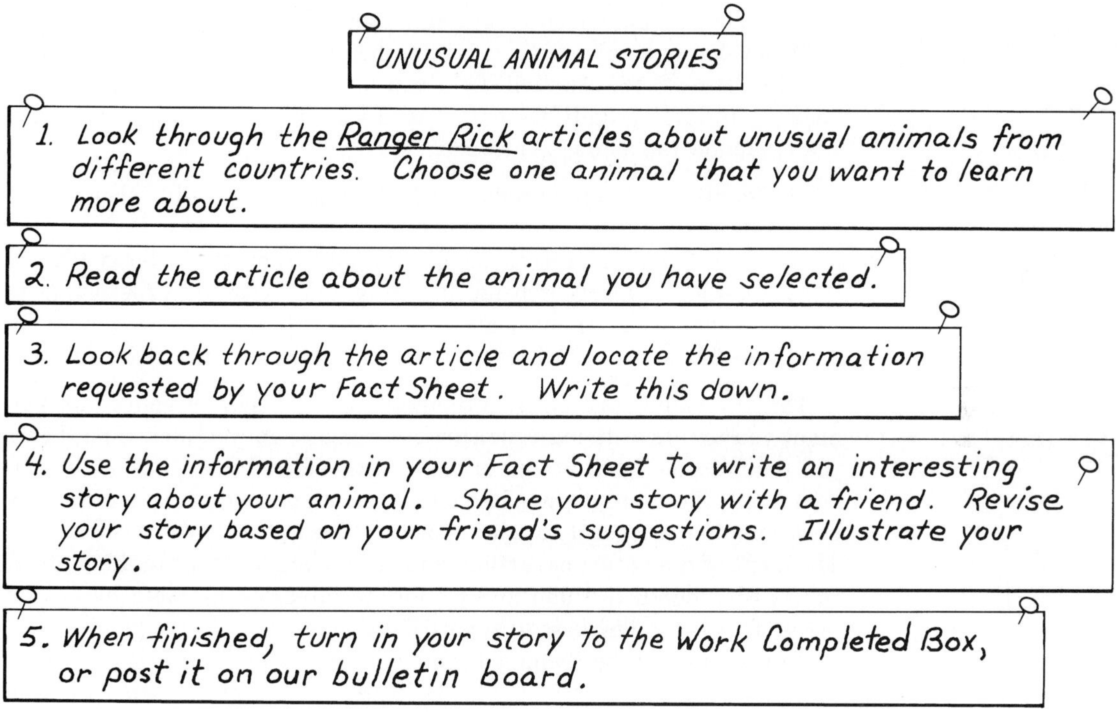

UNUSUAL ANIMAL STORIES

1. Look through the <u>Ranger Rick</u> articles about unusual animals from different countries. Choose one animal that you want to learn more about.

2. Read the article about the animal you have selected.

3. Look back through the article and locate the information requested by your Fact Sheet. Write this down.

4. Use the information in your Fact Sheet to write an interesting story about your animal. Share your story with a friend. Revise your story based on your friend's suggestions. Illustrate your story.

5. When finished, turn in your story to the Work Completed Box, or post it on our bulletin board.

likely that knowledge learned in one area will transfer to other areas. They allow students to read and think deeply about a single issue. Finally, thematic units appear to increase positive attitudes about reading and writing since these tasks always take place within authentic contexts.

There are two different ways in which teachers organize thematic units. Sometimes teachers will organize a thematic unit to integrate instruction in the language arts: reading, writing, speaking, and listening. This type of thematic unit is sometimes referred to as an **integrated language arts unit.** Here, reading, writing, speaking, and listening experiences are organized around a topic, author, or genre in an attempt to focus teaching and learning in the language arts. At other times teachers will organize a thematic unit in an attempt to integrate instruction in at least two different content areas, one of which is usually the language arts. This type of thematic unit is sometimes referred to as a **cross-curricular unit.** Here, a topic is used to focus teaching and learning on the language arts and at least one of the other traditional subject areas: math, science, social studies, art, physical education. An example of how

integrated language arts unit
A thematic unit where reading, writing, speaking, and listening experiences are organized around a topic, author, or genre to provide focus for teaching and learning in the language arts.

cross-curricular unit
A thematic unit that uses a topic to focus teaching and learning on the language arts and at least one of the other traditional subject areas: math, science, social studies, art, physical education.

a cross-curricular thematic unit was organized in one fourth grade class can be seen in an overview of this unit in Figure 5-13. Here, the unit theme of "Life in the Desert Southwest" is used to integrate the language arts with experiences in social studies, science, and art.

To develop a thematic unit it is often helpful to create an overview like that in Figure 5-13. This will help you keep the larger picture in mind before you develop daily lesson plans. To develop an overview you may wish to follow the following procedures:

1. Identify a thematic topic, author, or genre that will allow you to integrate multiple curricular goals.
2. Identify reading selections to accomplish your curricular goals.
3. Develop reading, writing, listening, and speaking experiences to meet your curricular goals.
4. Identify a major project to be completed by the end of the unit.

The first step is to identify a thematic topic, author, or genre that will allow you to integrate multiple curricular goals. As you identify a theme you should avoid what Routman (1991) has referred to as "themes of convenience." These are themes like circus, bears, or monsters that are easy to develop but do not deal with "powerful ideas" or issues of substance. The point of thematic instruction is to engage students in thinking about issues with depth to them in an effort to integrate learning in several areas. This is hard to do with superficial themes.

As you identify the theme for your unit you should also begin by looking closely at your curricular goals. Several authors (Lipson, Valencia, Wixson, & Peters, 1993; Routman, 1991) have pointed out that curricular goals are often sacrificed for entertaining thematic topics or activities that have little to do with the curriculum of a school. Since the purpose of thematic instruction is to increase learning across several areas we want to make certain what we wish students to gain from their experiences in the unit. Simply stated, curricular goals should determine themes and activities—themes and activities should not determine curricular goals.

If you are planning an integrated language arts unit you have three types of themes to consider: topical themes, author themes, or genre themes. On the other hand, if you are planning a cross-curricular unit you will probably want to consider only topical themes. Topical themes provide more opportunities to make connections with content in math, science, social studies or art.

The second step in planning an overview for a thematic unit is to identify reading selections that will allow you to accomplish your curricular goals. This is a challenging task, especially if you are not familiar with children's literature. One way to approach this phase is to seek assistance from your school or local librarian. You may also wish to consult some of the resources described in chapter 4. Or, you may wish to consult the extensive monthly reviews of children's literature that appear at the end of each issue of *The Reading Teacher*. As you review each work of lit-

FIGURE 5-13

A Thematic Unit Overview: Life in the Desert Southwest

Life in the desert southwest

Whole class reading experiences

The Skirt by Gary Soto
The Moon of the Wild Pigs by Jean Craighead George

Social studies	Science	Language arts	Art
Goals/concepts	**Goals/concepts**	**Goals/concepts**	**Goals/concepts**
• Develop an understanding of the cultures of the southwest	• Understand the weather cycles of the Sonoran Desert • Understand the major life forms in the desert • Understand the interrelationships between animals and plants in the desert	• Develop an understanding of Byrd Baylor's poetry • Write poetry about life in the desert • Maintain a reader response journal during whole class reading experiences • Develop report writing skills	• Develop an understanding of some of the art of the southwest
Read-aloud response journal activities	**Read-alouds**	**Read-aloud response journal activities**	**Read-alouds**
• *Dreamplace* by George Ella Layton • *The Great Change* by Carol Grigg • *Antelope Woman* by Michael Lacapa	• *Cactus* by Carol Lerner • *A Desert Year* by Carol Lerner • *Desert Animals* by Luise Woelflein • *Cactus* by Jason Cooper • *Cactus Hotel* by Brenda Guiberson	• *The Desert Is Theirs* by Byrd Baylor • *Desert Voices* by Byrd Baylor • *The Other Way to Listen* by Byrd Baylor	• *The Goat in the Rug* by Charles Blood and Martin Link • *Diego Rivera: Artist of the People* by Anne Neimark • *Children of Clay* by Rina Swentzell
Additional activities	**Additional activities**	**Additional activities**	**Additional activities**

• Reading and discussion from the chapter on "Cultures of the Southwest" in our social studies textbook
• Readers Theater presentation from one of the books in class where the story depicts a cultural group from the southwest (small groups)
	• Text set activities with informational books about animal and plant life in the south-west desert from the school library
	• Develop a report on one of the animals of the southwest desert
	• Create a shoebox diorama illustrating the environment of this animal
		• Style Study of Byrd Baylor
		• Literature Discussion Groups
		  • *Mystery of the Navaho Moon* by Timothy Green
		  • *A Brand Is Forever* by Ann Herbert Scott
		  • *Local News* by Gary Soto
		  • *Ten Mile Day* by Mary Ann Faser
			• Dyeing wool with natural dyes
			• Weaving with pocket looms
			• Make God's eyes
			• Make and decorate clay pots
			• Visit art exhibition

erature you should also do some preliminary thinking about how you wish to use it. Is it best used as a read aloud to prompt a journal response? Is it best used as a text set activity or a whole class reading experience? Or perhaps it is best used as a reference work for students as they develop their projects. Thinking about how it will be used as you review and collect materials will save you time later.

The third step in planning an overview for a thematic unit is to develop reading, writing, listening, and speaking experiences to meet your curricular goals. Here you should think about the different method frameworks described in this text and how they might be used in your unit: cooperative learning groups, deductive instruction, inductive instruction, read aloud response journals, reader response journals, literature discussion groups, grand conversations, readers theater, directed reading-thinking activities, sustained silent reading, and many others. You want to develop a plan for using these experiences to connect reading and writing as your students learn important concepts.

Finally, you may wish to have each student complete some type of project during the unit. For older students, this is likely to be some type of

A variety of method frameworks may be used during thematic units.

written project. For younger students it might be a dramatic presentation to another class or a sequence of smaller writing projects that are kept in a portfolio. Often it is useful to present several different projects to students and allow them to select the activity they wish to complete during the course of the unit. Older students who have worked in thematic units may wish to propose their own projects at the beginning of the unit. A brainstorming session is useful to generate a list of possibilities for students.

Developing Writing Activities for Published Reading Programs

If you use a published reading program it is also important to connect reading and writing in these experiences, too. Published reading programs usually contain descriptions of writing activities related to either the skill or the content of their reading lessons. These activities are most frequently found in the enrichment section of the individual lessons and should not be overlooked as a source of ideas to make the reading-writing connection. Such activities can be designed for either prereading or postreading experiences. When used before a selection is read, writing activities usually develop prior knowledge that will be useful to readers of the selection. When used after a selection is read, writing activities usually allow students to practice skills developed in the lesson or extend the reading experience in some fashion. When writing activities are not included in a published reading program, activities such as those listed in Figure 5-14 might be appropriate for individual lessons. The first three might be used before reading a selection. The final three might be used after reading a selection.

Conducting Writer's Workshops

A **writer's workshop** is a whole class session or a small group mini-lesson on a specific aspect of writing. It is usually directed by the teacher to assist students with their writing. Writer's workshops can be used for a variety of purposes. They can be used to introduce writing-process strategies, such as brainstorming or peer conferencing. They can also be used to explain strategies that writers use to solve common writing problems. For example, a writer's workshop might show students how to make meaning clearer in informational writing by using topic sentences in paragraphs. In addition, writer's workshops can provide a time during the day when students get together to read their work and help each other solve common writing problems. Examples of topics that might be covered during a writer's workshop session are listed in Figure 5-15.

Teachers organize writer's workshops in several different ways, depending on their literacy framework and their goal for the session. Some teachers rely on a deductive method framework to teach specific strategies. Others use an inductive method framework to organize the workshop lessons. Still others use a writer's workshop as a time to allow

writer's workshop
A mini-lesson for a whole class or a small group on a specific aspect of writing.

FIGURE 5-14

Strategies that might be used to integrate reading and writing within published school reading programs

Speculative Writing. Develop prior knowledge about a situation that students will meet in a reading selection by having them respond to the question "What would you do if. . .?" or "Have you ever. . .?" Have students write their responses the day before reading the particular selection. Then, before beginning the story, have students read their responses aloud to the group. Discuss the problem in the story that students will encounter.

Brainstorming. Before students read a story about a particular topic, have them spend five minutes writing down everything they know about that topic. Encourage them to write their information in a list and share it with the group. Use this information to begin a discussion about key concepts in the story. Work into your discussion the meanings of important vocabulary words listed in the teacher's manual.

Word Association. On the chalkboard write the vocabulary words listed in the teacher's manual. Have students copy the words and write next to each the first word that comes into their minds. Have students share their responses, and use those responses to initiate a discussion of each word's meaning. You might want to use your students' responses to draw semantic maps defining each word's meaning.

Rewriting a Story. After students have read a narrative, have them rewrite specific story elements. For example, students might rewrite the ending to a story or rewrite the same story in a different setting. If a story is told from the perspective of one character, suggest that students rewrite the story from a different character's perspective.

Guessing Biographies. After students have read several selections, have them write character biographies without naming their characters. Then have the students read their biographies and let other students guess their characters.

Writing Persuasive Essays. Have students write a persuasive essay defending or criticizing a story character's decision. Have them read their essays to a group of students who act as a jury. Let the jury decide the appropriateness of the character's action.

---

students to raise their own concerns and seek solutions for their individual writing problems.

In the model lesson on page 208, Ms. Dodson's third-grade class has been working in an integrated language arts unit called "The Time of the Dinosaurs." She created the unit by combining one selection in the published reading program with several additional reading and read-aloud experiences including :

Dinosaur Time by Peggy Parish

Patrick's Dinosaur by Carol Carrick

FIGURE 5-15

Examples of topics for writer's workshop lessons

Specific writing-process strategies

Brainstorming techniques
How to map writing ideas
How to outline writing ideas
How best to conduct a peer conference
Revision strategies that work
Using editing marks
How to prepare final copy for binding
How to use illustrations in the right locations

Strategies that writers use to overcome common problems

Using journal ideas as sources of writing topics
Working through writer's block
Writing patterns used by good writers
Making the message clear
Letting a draft sit to acquire "distance" before revising
Using headings and subheadings to organize informational articles
Using questions (and answers) to present information

Problems faced by individual writers

How should I end this story?
Something isn't right in this article—what is it?
Can you help me find a better title?
How can I organize my ideas better?

In the Days of the Dinosaurs by Roy Chapman Andrews

Digging up Dinosaurs by Aliki

Dinosaurs, Asteroids, and Superstars: Why the Dinosaurs Disappeared by Franklyn Branley

The Illustrated Dinosaur Dictionary by Helen Roney Sattler

Using Pattern Stories

Writing experiences can be especially helpful in developing an understanding of reading/writing patterns. As students think about what to write, they must reflect on the structural characteristics of a particular form. As a result, students acquire new insight into the structural characteristics of written language, which helps them with both reading and writing. One useful technique is to engage students in **pattern story activities.**

For younger children, pattern story activities often begin by reading a **predictable text,** a story containing a repeated pattern that makes reading the story easy because it is very predictable. This story is then

pattern story activities
A method framework where one story is used as a pattern for students to follow when writing their own, similar story.

predictable text
A story containing a repeated pattern that makes reading the story very predictable; may use repeated sentences, phrases, or structural elements.

MODEL LESSON

Inductive Instruction in a Writer's Workshop in Ms. Dodson's Class

To connect reading and writing, students are preparing written reports on their favorite type of dinosaur and, with the art teacher, are creating fired clay models, which the librarian wants to display in the school library to interest other readers on this topic. Students have collected their information on an outline fact sheet that Ms. Dodson prepared and are currently using that information to draft their reports. Ms. Dodson has noticed that students are having difficulty presenting and organizing their information. Consequently, she has scheduled a writer's workshop to show them two different approaches: topic headings (for example, size, appearance, favorite location) or question headings (for example, How Big Is a Brontosaurus? What Did a Brontosaurus Look Like? Where Did Brontosauruses Live?).

Provide Examples of the Skill or Rule. Ms. Dodson has duplicated two pages of text for her students to look at. The first comes from one of their reading selections on dinosaurs. It uses topical section headings to organize and present information: "Plant-Eaters," "Meat-Eaters," "Dinosaur Birds," and "The Dinosaurs Disappear." The other is from the book *Sharks* by Carl Green. It uses question headings to organize and present information: "How Long Do Sharks Live?" "Do Sharks Sleep?" "What Do Sharks Eat?" She reads both pages aloud and has her students follow along, paying attention to the way each author writes.

Help Students Discover the Skill or Rule. Ms. Dodson asks questions to help students notice the two writing styles: "What is the same about the way these two authors wrote their articles? Yes, they both wrote facts. But how did they organize those facts? Right—in parts or sections. Now, what is at the beginning of each section? Yes, a title. We call these little titles inside a book *headings*. They tell you what each section is about. Now look and see if you notice anything different about how these two authors wrote their headings. That's right—one author used what we call a topic heading and the other used a question heading." Then Ms. Dodson shares several other examples of these two organizational patterns in other books and has one student summarize the two ways writers can organize their facts.

Provide Guided Practice. Ms. Dodson writes these two organizational methods on the blackboard: topic headings and question headings. Then she asks students to brainstorm what they might choose for headings if they used the first method in their own papers. They quickly notice that each heading on their fact sheet ("Size," "Appearance," "Favorite Location," "Type of Food," and "Unusual Facts") could be used as a topic heading. Ms. Dodson writes those headings on the board under "Topic Headings." Then she asks students to brainstorm questions that might be used in place of those words and writes them on the board under "Question Headings": "What Size Was the Brontosaurus?" "What Did the Brontosaurus Look Like?" "What Was Its Favorite Location?" "What Type of Food Did It Eat?" "What Are Some Unusual Facts About the Brontosaurus?" Ms. Dodson and the class talk briefly about how students might use each type of section heading to organize their reports.

Provide Independent Practice. After the writer's workshop, students return to their work and use one of the two types of headings to organize their information. Ms. Dodson circulates through the class, helping students who need her assistance. She notices that one student has combined the two patterns by using a topic heading ("Size") and then beginning her paragraph with the related question ("How big was the tyrannosaurus?"). Ms. Dodson has this student read her draft aloud to the class so that they can see a third pattern to use.

OPPORTUNITIES TO CELEBRATE DIVERSITY

Pourquoi tales, or stories that explain natural phenomena such as the origin of fire, how the leopard got its spots, or why the sun always rises in the East, are excellent vehicles for pattern stories. The model lesson on page 187 shows how one teacher used pourquoi tales for this purpose. At the same time, pourquoi tales are wonderful vehicles for studying the similarities and differences between cultures. All cultures develop their own explanatory myths but each culture develops explanations for natural elements that are important to its own individual culture. Whenever you develop a thematic unit on diversity consider adding several pourquoi tales from this culture and using them to develop insight into the culture you study. Remember, too, to use these for pattern story activities. Or, develop a separate thematic unit on pourquoi tales from many different cultures and use these to study the similarities and differences between different cultural experiences.

used as a pattern for students to follow when writing their own, similar story. Pattern stories are especially useful with very young students, who often focus their attention on letters and sounds and not on higher-level aspects of written language organization. Pattern stories help these children understand that stories contain a regular structure, which is helpful to both readers and writers (Rhodes, 1981).

Beginning readers and writers enjoy writing pattern stories after reading counting books such as *One Is One* by Tasha Tudor, or alphabet books, such as *The Folks in the Valley: A Pennsylvania Dutch ABC* by John Aylesworth. They also enjoy writing pattern stories after reading narratives with a repeated sentence or episodic pattern, such as *Too Much Noise* by Ann McGovern.

With older students nearly any familiar story can be used as a pattern (Sipe, 1993). Variations can be created in many different ways—for example, by writing the same story told by another character, by changing the time in which the tale takes place, or by changing the solution to a problem. Recently, John Scieszka, a children's author, has published several marvelous examples that you may wish to share with students as examples of pattern stories including: *The True Story of the Three Little Pigs, The Frog Prince Continued,* and *The Stinky Cheese Man.* Other works of children's literature that you may wish to share with students as examples of pattern books are listed in Figure 5-16.

USING A LITERACY FRAMEWORK TO GUIDE THE CONNECTION OF READING AND WRITING

Your explanation for how one reads can be used as you consider what to teach and emphasize when connecting reading and writing. For example, a text-based explanation would lead you to connect reading and writing in order to develop decoding knowledge. Writing would be seen as a use-

FIGURE 5-16

Examples of pattern books published by children's authors

Jim and the Beanstalk by R. Briggs (1973). London: Puffin Books.
Instead of killing the giant, Jim helps him.

A Telling of Tales by W. Brooke (1990). New York: Harper & Row.
Five traditional tales including *Sleeping Beauty, Paul Bunyon,* and *Jack and the Beanstalk* are each transformed into a new version.

The Principal's New Clothes by S. Calmenson (1989). New York: Scholastic.
A variation of *The Emperor's New Clothes.* Here the principal is vain and ends up wearing only his underwear.

The Chocolate Touch by P. Catling (1981). New York: Bantam.
John Midas loves chocolate, not gold. In this story everything he touches turns to chocolate, even his mother, until he learns his lesson.

Prince Cinders by B. Cole (1989). London: Collins.
A variation of the Cinderella tale only here it is a boy who loses his suspenders at the ball.

Ruby by M. Emberly (1990). Boston: Little Brown.
A modern version of *Little Red Riding Hood* played by a mouse and a cat.

Pondlarker by F. Gwynne (1990). New York: Simon & Schuster.
A version of *The Frog Prince* only here the frog decides to remain a frog.

Chicken Little by Stephen Kellogg (1988). London: Beaver Books.
A modern day version of this classic tale.

The Paper Bag Princess by Robert Munsch (1980). Toronto: Annick Press.
In this version of the traditional "prince-rescues-a-princess" tale, the princess rescues the prince through her keen intelligence.

Sleeping Ugly by Jane Yolen (1981). New York: Coward-McCann.
A version of the classic *Sleeping Beauty.*

ful tool for developing spelling and automatic decoding skills. Practices like peer conferences would be seen as important because students can practice their decoding skills as they read their work aloud. If you have a reader-based explanation, however, writing would be seen as a useful tool for developing the prior knowledge important for reading, not decoding skills. Reading and writing would be connected to provide students with opportunities to learn about new concepts (vocabulary knowledge); try out different word order patterns (syntactic knowledge); learn about new discourse structures (discourse knowledge); and acquire effective reading and writing strategies (metacognitive knowledge). An interactive explanation would lead you to connect reading and writing in order to develop both decoding skills and the elements of prior knowledge.

Your explanation for how children learn to read can also be used to guide decisions as you make the reading-writing connection. Your explanation for this issue guides decisions about how to teach. If you have a specific skills perspective you will see writing as an opportunity to practice reading skills. In addition, you would favor the use of deductive instructional methods, especially during writing workshop sessions. And you would be more likely to make connections between reading and writing within a published school reading program where specific reading skills would be taught. If you have a holistic language view of how reading ability develops you see writing as the perfect opportunity to create functional, meaningful, and holistic experiences with print. You view writing as a means to learn insights important to reading, not as a means to practice specific reading skills. You will find several method frameworks to be useful: reader response journals, dialogue journals, buddy journals, pattern story writing, and thematic reading and writing experiences. Each uses writing in functional ways to develop important insights about reading. If you have an integrated perspective you see writing as both an opportunity to practice and to learn important insights about reading. All of the method frameworks described in this chapter would be used.

Comments from the Classroom

Judy Dill, first grade teacher

One of the best ways for first graders to understand the concept that words express meaning and that letters develop into words is to write language experience stories. Language experience stories are a big part of connecting reading and writing in the first grade.

Language experience stories are a whole class activity. I do one preliminary activity to prepare for each LES activity. Before my class embarks on any field trip, has a resource person visit the class, or gets involved in a big class project, we write the topic of the experience on a large sheet of chart paper. Then I make two columns—the first to list what we already know about that topic and the second to predict what we think we will learn. I feel I can help students make more sense of what they are about to see or do if I ascertain what they already know. And predicting the outcome of our learning makes a great directed reading-thinking activity.

After we return from our trip, say good-bye to our visitor, or complete our special class project, I ask a number of questions. "Did you see what you thought you would see? Did you learn (or do) what you thought you would? What happened that surprised you? In a third column of our chart we then fill in a "what did we learn" list. We add words we *learned and identify things that we did or saw. I find that if I write the children's names beside their responses they take ownership of that information. Then when we write our class story about our experience each child is apt to volunteer the same information again, reading it from our chart.*

One such language experience brought a community member to our class to demonstrate how to spin wool into yarn with her spinning wheel. She went through step-by-step the process of turning raw wool into yarn. Her visit was a big hit. (Of course the lamb that visited with her was as well!) Our language experience story then became a flow chart. I was still able to model proper capitalization, correct punctuation, and complete sentences.

After we write language experience stories as a class, the children then write thank-you letters or letters home to parents to tell about the experience. They have the words, thoughts, and ideas readily available that help them to be very successful in their writing. And they love reading their letters out loud before they send them.

Major Points

- Writing experiences are as important to the development of reading comprehension and response as the use of engaging literature selections. Writing experiences, like literature selections, can be used to develop all of the aspects of reading comprehension and response.

- Recent research has provided four major insights that should guide our attempts to connect reading and writing: (1) writing is a process; (2) writing experiences are most appropriate when they serve an authentic communicative purpose; (3) writing experiences are most appropriate when they require students to create complete, extended texts; and (4) reading and writing are similar types of processes.

- There are many ways to connect reading and writing in a classroom: reader response journals, dialogue journals, buddy journals, style studies, reading/writing centers, thematic units, writing activities for lessons in published reading programs, writer's workshops, and pattern story activities.

- A literacy framework assists teachers in making the reading-writing connection. An explanation of how a person reads guides decisions about what to teach and emphasize in these experiences. A text-based perspective is more consistent with an emphasis on decoding knowledge. A reader-based perspective emphasizes vocabulary, syntactic, discourse, and metacognitive knowledge. An interactive perspective gives equal emphasis to all components of the reading process. A teacher's explanation of how reading proficiency develops guides decisions about how to create the reading-writing connection. A specific skills perspective is more consistent with writing activities for lessons in published reading programs, deductive writer's workshops, and deductively taught pattern story activities. A holistic language perspective is more consistent with reader response journals, dialogue journals, buddy journals, reading/writing centers, writing activities related to thematic reading experiences, and inductively taught writer's workshops. An integrated perspective is consistent with all of the method frameworks and activities described in this chapter.

---

1. This chapter suggests that appropriate writing experiences can be used to develop each of the components of reading comprehension and response. If you were most interested in developing syntactic knowledge among your students, which of the method frameworks described in this chapter would you be most likely to use? Why?

2. Consider the learning experience described in the model lesson on process writing. Explain how this experience does or does not take into consideration each of the four major insights that should guide our attempts to connect reading and writing. Given your evaluation, do you think that this learning experience could be improved? If yes, how? If no, why not?

3. This chapter describes many different ways to make the reading-writing connection. These separate instructional practices can also be combined. Describe two combinations of instructional practices that you would consider using in your classroom, and explain in detail how you would implement them.

4. Define your own literacy framework. Then list the instructional practices described in this chapter that are consistent with your framework. Also, list any instructional practices described here that are inconsistent with your framework. Explain why you have identified each practice as you have.

**Making
Instructional
Decisions**

Further Reading

Baker, E. C. (1994). Writing and reading in a first-grade writer's workshop: A parent's perspective. *The Reading Teacher, 47,* 372–377.

The author, a parent volunteer, describes how writer's workshop functioned in a first-grade classroom to integrate reading and writing experiences with very young literacy learners.

Hancock, M. R. (1993). Exploring and extending personal response through literature journals. *The Reading Teacher, 46,* 466–474.

Describes the use of reader response journals for extending the nature of response patterns by students. Shows how many different types of response patterns can be supported by teachers and describes guidelines for increasing written transactions with literature.

Lewin, L. (1992). Integrating reading and writing strategies using an alternating teacher-led/student-selected instructional pattern. *The Reading Teacher, 45,* 586–591.

Explains how one can help students develop extensive strategic knowledge about reading and writing processes by connecting reading and writing experiences in the classroom.

Wollman-Bonilla, J. E. (1989). Reading journals: Invitations to participate in literature. *The Reading Teacher, 43,* 112–120.

Describes case studies of three fourth-grade students who used journals as they read Tucker's Countryside *by George Selden. Describes how each of these students developed as both a reader and a writer from their individual experiences in responding to literature.*

References

Applebee, A. N. (1981). Looking at writing. *Educational Leadership, 38,* 458–462.

Bearse, C. I. (1992). The fairy tale connection in children's stories: Cinderella meets Sleeping Beauty. *The Reading Teacher, 45,* 688–695.

Bode, B. A. (1989). Dialogue journal writing. *The Reading Teacher, 42,* 568–571.

Calkins, L. M. (1983). *Lessons from a child.* Exeter, NH: Heinemann.

Chaney, J. H. (1993). Alphabet books: Resources for learning. *The Reading Teacher, 47,* 96–104.

Chomsky, C. (1971). Write first, read later. *Childhood Education, 47,* 296–299.

Clay, M. (1986). Constructive processes: Talking, reading, writing, art, and craft. *The Reading Teacher, 39,* 764–770.

Crowhurst, M. (1979). The writing workshop: An experiment in peer response to writing. *Language Arts, 56,* 757–762.

D'Angelo Bromley, K. (1989). Buddy journals make the reading-writing connection. *The Reading Teacher, 43,* 122–129.

DeGroff, L. C., & Leu, D. J. (1987). An analysis of writing activities: A study of language arts textbooks. *Written Communication, 4,* 253–268.

Fowler, G. F. (1982). Developing comprehension skills in primary students through the use of story frames. *The Reading Teacher, 36,* 176–179.

Fuhler, C. J. (1994). Response journals: Just one more time with feeling. *Journal of Reading, 37,* 400–405.

Gambrell, L. B. (1985). Dialogue journals: Reading-writing interaction. *The Reading Teacher, 38,* 512–515.

Graves, D. (1983). *Writing: Teachers and children at work.* Exeter, NH: Heinemann.

Hancock, M. R. (1993). Exploring and extending personal response through literature journals. *The Reading Teacher, 46,* 466–474.

Hancock, M. R. (1993). Character journals: Initiating involvement and identification through literature. *The Journal of Reading, 37,* 42–50.

Hynds, S. (1989). Bringing life to literature and literature to life: Social constructs and context for adolescent readers. *Research in the Teaching of English, 23,* 30–61.

Kelly, P.R. (1990). Guiding young students' response to literature. *The Reading Teacher, 43,* 464–470.

McGee, L. M., & Richgels, D. J. (1990). *Literacy's beginnings: Supporting young readers and writers.* Boston: Allyn & Bacon.

Moffett, J. (1985). Hidden impediments to improving English teaching. *Phi Delta Kappan, 67,* 50–55.

Noyce, R. M., & Christie, J. F. (1989). *Integrating reading and writing instruction in grades K–8.* Boston: Allyn & Bacon.

Raphael, T. E. & Englert, C. S. (1990). Writing and reading: Partners in constructing meaning. *The Reading Teacher, 43,* 388–400.

Read, C. (1971). Preschool children's knowledge of English phonology. *Harvard Educational Review, 41,* 1–34.

Rhodes, L. K. (1981). I can read! Predictable books as resources for reading and writing instruction. *The Reading Teacher, 34,* 511–517.

Routman, R. (1991). *Invitations: Changing as teachers and learners K–12.* Portsmouth, NH: Heinemann.

Russell, C. (1983). Putting research into practice: Conferencing with young writers. *Language Arts, 60,* 333–340.

Sipe, L. R. (1993). Using transformations of traditional stories: Making the reading-writing connection. *The Reading Teacher, 47,* 18–26.

Smith, F. (1982). *Writing and the writer.* New York: Holt, Rinehart & Winston.

Smith, F. (1983). Reading like a writer. *Language Arts, 60,* 558–567.

Staton, J. (1988). Dialogue journals in the classroom context. In M. Farr (Ed.), *Interactive writing in dialogue journals: Practitioner, linguistic, social, and cognitive views.* Norwood, NJ: Ablex.

Tierney, R. J., & Pearson, P. D. (1983). Toward a composing model of reading. *Language Arts, 60,* 568–580.

Youngblood, E. (1985). Reading, thinking and writing using the reading journal. *English Journal, 74,* 46–48.

CHAPTER

Facilitating Beginning Readers' Emerging Literacy

6

"Just today a boy in my kindergarten class started to cry because 'he didn't know how to read.' But he cheered up after we sat down and looked at the signs that I had taped to various things in my room and he read them. We also looked in a newspaper that I had and he was able to read lots of words in the headings and in the advertisements. So I think he began to realize that he was able to read and that his reading would just be getting better and better. I sure hope that's what he felt, because I feel strongly that he is a normally developing reader. It just seems that I sometimes have to tell parents, and my students also, that sounding out letters from left to right isn't all there is to reading in kindergarten!"

A kindergarten teacher discussing her students' views
of what it means to be a reader.

Children have well-developed language abilities before they enter kinder-garten or first grade. Although many children, like the boy in the opening quo-tation, don't think that what they do counts as reading, teachers are increas-ingly viewing young children's literacy abilities as part of a continuum rather than as separate from "real" reading activities. In this chapter you will learn about programs based on emergent literacy and more traditional viewpoints. Chapter 6 includes information that will help you answer questions such as:

1. How do emergent literacy/whole language perspectives differ from tra-ditional views of reading readiness?
2. What literacy abilities do children have when they enter school, and how might a teacher of reading capitalize on those abilities?
3. How do teachers evaluate beginning readers, and how might that infor-mation be used?
4. How might instructional frameworks guide instruction in an emergent lit-eracy program?
5. How might a teacher deal with issues of diversity in an emergent liter-acy program?

KEY CONCEPTS

auditory perception/discrimination
auditory and visual discrimination
big books
cognition/cognitive factors
kidwatching
emergent literacy
functional reading/writing (literacy) tasks
holophrastic speech
invented spelling

language experience approach
morning message
observational (informal) data
prereading activities
reading readiness
shared book experience
telegraphic speech
think-alouds
visual perception/discrimination
whole language program

BUILDING ON CHILDREN'S STRENGTHS: WHAT BEGINNING READERS ALREADY KNOW

Although children learn a great deal about reading and writing in school, much has already been learned before they enter kindergarten or first grade. Before formal schooling begins, children have the perceptual abili-ties to discriminate among different letters, words, and sounds. They are already good users of their native language and are able to understand almost all basic types of sentences, including questions, statements, and exclamations. In addition, children in the early elementary grades have highly developed speaking vocabularies. Early studies indicated that a first grader's vocabulary averaged about 2,500 words; more recent studies have put that estimate as high as 8,000 words (Anderson & Freebody, 1985; Dale, 1965). Teachers use all of these language-related abilities to advance their students' reading development.

However, there are many things that mature readers do automatically that beginning readers must still discover. For example, beginning readers are developing **phonological awareness,** an awareness of the relationship between sounds and words. Examples of this awareness can be seen as young children repeat and make up rhyming words, as they notice and comment on the sounds or patterns of words, and as they play games that involve clapping as they say words or syllables. Beginning readers also must develop the convention that English text is read from left to right and top to bottom on a page, must be able to understand the relationships of punctuation to meaning, and are learning the concepts of "word" and "sentence." All of these are incorporated in the following general behavioral goals that are often targeted by reading programs for beginning readers (Durkin, 1987):

phonological awareness
The awareness of the relationship between sounds and print.

- to acquire an understanding of what reading and learning to read are all about
- to learn to want to be a reader
- to learn what is meant by *word*
- to understand the function of empty space in establishing word boundaries
- to learn about the left-to-right, top-to-bottom orientation of written English (pp. 110–111).

As this list implies, literacy programs for beginning readers do not wait for readiness to occur spontaneously in young children. Years ago, however—beginning in the early 1920s and continuing for 15 to 20 years—readiness was defined by mental age, largely because of the work of Morphett and Washburn (1931). It was thought that a child without a mental age of 6.0 to 6.5 was not ready to read and instruction would be wasted. Mental age was determined by this formula:

$$\text{mental age} = \text{intelligence quotient (IQ)} \times \text{chronological age (CA)} \div 100$$

Gradually, readiness for reading came to be viewed as something that could be developed rather than awaited, and measures of mental age stopped being used as a criterion for entry into kindergarten. Today, there is increasing emphasis on the idea that literacy develops continually and emerges from a child's ongoing exploration of the environment and of print, a concept known as **emergent literacy.**

emergent literacy
A view that literacy develops continually through children's interaction and exploration of writing and reading.

Although whole language instruction is making a significant impact on literacy education, some questions are being raised with regard to the whole language approach. For example, some say that there may be little difference between what are now being called whole language programs and what have been known as good teaching practices for the past two decades. Good teachers have usually incorporated writing with reading activities in meaningful contexts, often at the suggestion of basal reader programs, which McCallum (1988) cautions may be discarded prematurely. Others argue that there is little difference between whole language programs and language experience approaches if the LEA lesson is expanded to encompass more of the instructional program. Stahl & Miller (1989) are among those who have, at least to some extent, equated language experience and whole language. In addition, an increasing number of theorists believe that terminology such as *emergent literacy* and *whole language* is problematic since in fact *all* approaches hold that literacy acquisition is developmental or emergent (Bransford, 1988; Rowe, 1989; Rowe & Harste, 1990). An associated concern is the lack of consistent, comparative evidence regarding the value of whole language as opposed to that of other approaches. According to Catterson's (1989), Stahl & Miller's (1989), McKenna, Stahl, and Reinking's (1994), and McKenna, Robinson, & Miller's (1993) views of research evidence, whole language programs appear no more effective than traditional programs. Counterarguments appear in Smith (1994).

Another, related area of discussion focuses on whether reading and writing should be equally stressed in kindergarten programs or whether writing should receive greater emphasis. Durkin, for example, finds "particularly troublesome the assumption that *all* children should do a lot of writing right away. . . . what one child finds easy and meaningful and is successful with is not going to be the same for another child. . . . I think we're a little lopsided now about the way we look at some things. I think we need to be vigilant about unverified assumptions about reading and writing and the reading and writing connections" (Aaron, Chall, Durkin, Goodman, & Strickland, 1990, p. 305). Strickland responded to Durkin's comments by affirming the close relationship between reading and writing but agreed that to "place undue emphasis on one or the other is probably misplaced. . .offering opportunities for both reading and writing is very different from pressuring or requiring that children engage in writing early on." (Aaron et al., 1990, p. 305).

However, research and descriptions of children learning to read and write in whole language settings, both at home and in preschool and first-grade programs, support "whole language" approaches. These success stories cannot be ignored (for example, see Holdaway, 1979; DeFord, 1986; Harste, Woodward, & Burke, 1984; Wells, 1986; Mason, 1989; Rowe, 1994). Furthermore, these and other researchers have linked a whole language approach to theories of learning, classroom management, and functional, communicative uses of literacy. How might those theoretical links lead to further research into the relative effectiveness of the approach?

UNDERSTANDING EMERGENT LITERACY AND THE SHIFT FROM "READINESS" PERSPECTIVES

Traditional views often present reading readiness as a stage that children pass through before they become readers. In effect, proponents of this view look at nonreaders as not having required skills or abilities that are necessary for reading to occur. Consequently, traditional readiness programs attempt to provide activities that are aimed at developing those prereading skills and often do so with deductive methods.

The term **reading readiness** identifies that period of time in which students acquire the specific skills and abilities that allow reading to take place. *The Dictionary of Reading and Related Terms* (Harris & Hodges, 1981) defines *readiness* as "preparedness to cope with a learning task" and goes on to state that readiness for learning of any type at any level is determined by a complex pattern of intellectual, motivational, maturational, and experiential factors in each individual, which may vary from time to time and from situation to situation (p. 263). In the past, kindergarten reading programs focused on developing "readiness" for reading through **prereading activities,** which are activities designed to result in later, fluent reading.

In contrast, proponents of emergent literacy believe that *all* literacy-related activity is part of the reading and writing process. For example, scribbling is viewed as writing, especially if the child thinks that it is. Children's scribbles and descriptions of pictures in a book are seen as part of an evolution toward mature reading and are not separated from "real" literacy activities. Instruction from an emergent literacy perspective usually occurs in functional situations, without segmenting or isolating skills, and is usually based on inductive strategies and **functional literacy experiences.**

Some have argued that there is little theoretical difference between traditional and emergent literacy philosophies because both view children's literacy as moving from less mature to more mature forms of reading and writing (Harris & Sipay, 1990). Others disagree, citing the theoretical base of emergent literacy, which stresses the social nature of literacy acquisition (Luria, 1976; Vygotsky, 1978, 1986) and the emotional and psychological responses, included in reader-response theory, that are a part of reading and writing (Rosenblatt, 1988; Willinsky, 1988; Galda, 1988; see also Robeck & Wallace's 1990 presentation of the similarities and differences between Piaget's and Vygotsky's views). Indeed, emergent literacy views of reading development have brought into sharp focus the social, communicative nature of literacy (Rowe, 1989; 1994) and have made reading teachers look at the continuum of literacy activities, especially writing activities, as continually meaningful and evolving. Nonetheless, a major difference between traditional views of reading readiness and emergent literacy perspectives is in the instructional frameworks (deductive vs. inductive) that influence reading instruction.

reading readiness
Traditionally, the time when a beginning reader acquires the skills and knowledge needed for reading instruction.

prereading activities
Activities that aid comprehension and take place before a selection is read.

functional literacy experiences
Literacy tasks and activities that are meaningful, not artificial.

The fact that oral language evolves in clear stages, from babbling to mature speech, has been accepted by language and educational theorists for some time. Teachers and parents generally accept toddlers' halting and incorrect verbalizations as attempts at communication and call these attempts talking. Until recently, however, there was little formal recognition that reading and writing might also proceed through stages. Teachers and parents were often unwilling to call young children's scribbles writing. Few teachers were ready to acknowledge work such as that pictured in Figures 6-1 and 6-2 as meaningful attempts at writing.

FIGURE 6-1
Sample of preschool writing products.

FIGURE 6-2

Samples of emergent writing and invented spelling: (a) a preschooler's shopping list, (b) a kindergartner's note to a classmate ("I got a haircut"), and (c) the classmate's response ("I hope you had a good time—I hope I can come") [in response to an earlier question about a sleep-over].

(a) (b) (c)

More recently there has been increasing evidence that even very young children participate in and initiate literacy-related play in an environment that includes adults who model, answer questions, and encourage children's curiosity about reading and writing (J. Goodman, 1990; Harste, Woodward, & Burke, 1984; Teale & Sulzby, 1986, 1989). Such play can include writing activities that appear quite distant from what adults perceive as real writing yet are part of the experimentation and growth common to all learning.

Trial and error during literacy learning are especially visible in writing, which has many subcomponents. For example, mature writing is thought to consist of legible penmanship and attention to correct grammar and spelling, straight lines of text, consistent margins and indentation of paragraphs, punctuation, and capitalization. As children experiment with writing, many or all of these items may be missing or incomplete, yet one essential component is present—the products have meaning and are intentionally created as a form of expression and literary activity (Teale & Sulzby, 1986; Rowe, 1994). In other words, even young children are not randomly scribbling; they are intentionally writing products that have clear meaning to them.

Thus, an emergent literacy perspective implies that children's experiments with language are communicative acts that are evolving. Figure 6-1(a) shows a letter that Lauren (age: 3 years, 2 months) wrote to her grandmother. Lauren had just spent time watching her parents write a series of letters and Christmas cards. She took an envelope and went to her room. When she returned, she gave her parents her letter and addressed envelope, read her letter to them, and asked that it be mailed along with those her parents were writing. When asked to reread her letter about 30 minutes later, she did not deviate substantially from her earlier reading. Thus, even though adults would not be able to read Lauren's letter or addressed envelope, for her they were meaningful and had a purpose.

In the samples shown in Figure 6-1(b) and 6-1(c), Alexandra (age: 2 years, 8 months) has drawn an apple tree and signed her name. The drawing in 6-1(b) preceded the finished product in 6-1(c), and when questioned, Alexandra explained. She had rejected the "practice" tree in 6-1(b) for several reasons; when finally satisfied, she signed her name. The sample in Figure 6-1(d) also shows **intentionality.** Alexandra had stated that she was going to practice making a list using *As, Os,* and *Ps;* and although the letters are by no means perfectly formed, it is easy to see that she is practicing these letters and that her completed list fulfills her goal.

Figure 6-2 shows other examples of children's written work. The sample in 6-2(a) shows a shopping list (student age: 2 years, 6 months), whereas 6-2(b) and 6-2(c) show two kindergartners' correspondence with each other. Even though they could not read their friend's note, they read their own notes to each other and happily kept their friend's note. All these examples demonstrate that children express meaning in their written work, regardless of how unpolished it might seem to an adult. Clearly, these children have conceptualized and used certain literacy **conventions:** Lauren's letter and envelope in Figure 6-1(a) are in correct form (the envelope even has a stamp on it), the signature with the apple tree is in a suitable location, the shopping list is in list form, and so on. Such conventions will be refined through further practice.

Instructional Implications

The concept of emergent literacy has resulted in an instructional approach that is generally called **whole language** (see chapter 3). This term means to convey that instruction is based on all aspects of language—speaking, listening, reading and writing—and it implies that literacy instruction is holistic—that instruction does not break language

intentionality
The purposefulness of an activity, in contrast to random behavior or accidentally occurring responses that might be appropriate.

convention
A common way that language is used by a particular group of people.

whole language
The philosophy that all literacy and language processes interact and thus can be used to reinforce each other.

Providing early experiences with print, including reading to a child and sharing an interest in books, positively influences later success in reading and writing.

learning into isolated skill components. Instead, learning occurs in the context of meaningful literacy activities. For example, reading and writing skills are often taught within the context of complete stories. Thus, children's literature plays a large part in reading instruction in a whole language setting and traditional published reading programs, which are viewed as fragmenting skills, are deemphasized. However, as discussed in chapter 2, the recent emphasis on whole language instruction has resulted in published reading programs that incorporate children's literature, involve fewer worksheets and less teaching of isolated skills, and emphasize the shared reading model (Hoffman, et al., 1994).

The following list encompasses aspects of programs that are supportive of children's developing literacy.

1. Children should be allowed to control the focus and sequence of their literacy learning. This ensures that they are participating in activities they see as linked to their existing concepts about literacy.
2. Activities should be open-ended. Variation in learning outcomes should be expected.

OPPORTUNITIES TO CELEBRATE DIVERSITY

Consider how students' diverse backgrounds, abilities, interests, and cultures can enhance meaningful literacy activities. For example, if your class is creating books or big books, encourage children from diverse backgrounds to make books that will let the other students learn about their language, backgrounds, and interests.

Consider also that "meaningful" literacy activities may differ for students, depending on their interests and on the value their particular cultural group places on specific activities. Also, children whose literacy abilities are less well developed may view some activities as less meaningful or important than readers with more highly developed literacy abilities. That is, sending a letter to a children's literature author might be meaningful and motivating to some children, but sending a reminder note to a family member might be more relevant to many other readers or writers.

3. Children should be encouraged to form and test their own hypotheses about literacy, rather than to master preformed generalizations presented by the teacher.
4. Children should have opportunities to explore their hypotheses in many different types of literacy events over a long period of time.
5. Children should be encouraged to present their newest ideas, and to push beyond what they currently know to explore new ways of using literacy.
6. Rough draft thinking and communication should be valued.
7. Teachers should be familiar with children's current interests and hypotheses so they can present invitations and demonstrations related to that learning (Rowe, 1994, p. 203).

All of the literacy-related activities in whole language classrooms are intended to be relevant and meaning-based. Such activities need not always be shared, however. For example, a child might want to write a very private fantasy story that would not be shared even with friends or parents. For that child the writing activity would be meaningful and motivational even without sharing. On the other hand, literacy activities certainly can be shared, and children generally very much want to do so. Writing activities, especially, might lead to student conferences in which student writers share their "work in progress" with other students, eliciting comments, reactions, and suggestions from friendly but knowledgeable readers (Calkins, 1983; Graves, 1983). The resulting dialogue between writers and readers can lead to significant insights for each about both reading and writing. Meaningful activities can also be teacher-assigned tasks that are purposeful rather than purely artificial. For instance, if students are dictating a letter that the teacher transcribes, the letter should be delivered or mailed to a real person and the response shared and posted. In this way, students learn that writing is purposeful, and motivation for both writing and reading remains high.

The concept of emergent literacy also implies that students' written products are communicative acts in a state of evolution. Thus, students' written work should be considered meaningful and should be encouraged, shared, and highlighted. Teachers in whole language classrooms encourage children to ask questions as they work and to elaborate orally on what they are attempting to convey through their writing. According to an emergent literacy view, teachers should be tolerant of variations in form as children write and read their work. Nonstandard handwriting, spacing, margins, letter formation, and spelling are considered a part of the developmental process. Through teacher modeling, instruction, and ongoing attempts by the child, such variations will continue to more closely approximate traditional forms until the correct form appears. In short, variations in form are treated as normal stages of learning; and as in all learning, mistakes are made along the way toward expertise. Figure 6-3 shows some of the **invented spellings** that children use as their writing evolves.

invented spellings
Children's spellings that are meaningful to them but are inconsistent with the spellings accepted as correct by mature readers and writers.

Many of the method frameworks implied by a whole language perspective are immediately apparent in a whole language environment. Classroom walls are often covered with students' writing and illustrations, and students often have their own bulletin board. Students are busy with literacy-related play and reading/writing activities, including revision of previous work. In addition, the classroom probably has many things conducive to reading and writing in plain view and in use by the students: mobiles, reading corners, writing corners, and, in particular, much print everywhere—on the walls, in books on bookshelves, in magazines on tables, and in the artwork area.

Although the activities throughout this book can be modified for use with beginning readers, the activities in this section are especially appropriate for kindergarten classrooms that focus on meaningful literacy activities.

The Language Experience Approach. Many individuals have demonstrated the power of oral language and personal experiences in helping children learn to read (for example, Allen & Allen, 1976; Ashton-Warner, 1963, 1972; Nessel & Jones, 1981; Stauffer, 1980). The generic term **language experience approach (LEA)** has come to represent those efforts to teach reading that use children's language and experiences as a base. At beginning levels the language experience approach uses transcriptions of children's oral language to help them learn about reading. The most common language experience activity at this level is an experience story, which is detailed in chapter 3. Essentially, a language experience story begins with a memorable experience. Then the teacher elicits a description, or story, of the experience from the children and transcribes each student's contribution on paper or a chalkboard. When the story is completed, the teacher uses it to teach a variety of reading-related concepts.

language experience approach (LEA)
A method framework for teaching reading that is based on children's language and experiences.

FIGURE 6-3

Sample of two first-graders' writing products. These pieces of writing demonstrate the invented spellings present in many beginning readers' and writers' products.

(a) Little Kitten, by Alexa. She was a tabby gray and her name was Shea, and she slept by the fire. And my name is Alexa. My kitten is not full grown and I love my kitten and I got her for my birthday. My and she is fluffy and I do not have to share [her] with my family, and my kitten has white spots.

(b) I had great fun roller skating because it was my party. We had pizza for lunch and then we had cake and then we opened up the presents.

little Kitten
By: Alexa
She was taobee gray.
and hre name was Saer.
and She sleptby
the fired. and my
name is Alexa. my
kitten is not fool
groin. and I Love
my Kitten and
I got. hre for
my brthday my
and She is flofe
and I do not
hav to Sher
with my famle
and my Kitten
ha wire ptos

I had gaet fun rooler skating
bekus It was my paerty
we had pizza for luche
and then we had cake and
then we open up the preset

(a)   (b)

M O D E L   L E S S O N
A Language Experience Story in Ms. Platt's Class

Ms. Platt:	Boys and girls, let's write a story about our field trip today. We can use it to practice our reading, and then we can put it in the hall to tell the rest of the school where we went and what we did. What do you think we should call our story? What about a title?
Jaime:	I know. Let's call it "Apples, Apples, Everywhere!"
Ms. Platt:	[Writing.] Good, Jaime. I like that. Look at these capital letters. Titles always have capitals at the beginning of each word. Now, how shall we start our story?
Maggie:	I want to start: We had a special day. We had an apple day.
Ms. Platt:	[Writing.] Good. Now what shall we say?
Tom:	We went to Beak and Skiff Apple Farm. [Teacher writes.]
Pam:	And we got to ride on the tractor. [Teacher writes.]
Katie:	We got to pick apples. [Teacher writes.]
Jason:	And we got to eat apples. [Teacher writes.]
Sarah:	And Tom got his shoes wet. [Teacher writes.]
Kerrie:	We saw bees. [Teacher writes.]
Del:	When we got back, we were tired, and we got ready to go home. [Teacher writes.]

Ms. Platt explains to the students that they can sometimes use other words to help them read. She reads the first two sentences, stopping at the last word.

We had a special day. We had an apple _____.

Ms. Platt lets the students read the last word together. Then she gives them a chance to practice using context as she reads each sentence and lets the students supply the last word. Sometimes students say an entire sentence along with Ms. Platt or "read" a sentence on their own, especially if it is the sentence that they contributed to the story. At the end Ms. Platt restates the generalization about context use.

Ms. Platt then has each student draw a picture of the trip. As she walks around the room, she helps some students copy words or a short sentence from the experience story to serve as a caption for their picture. With other students Ms. Platt transcribes their dictated sentences or words on the bottom of their pictures. Finally, Ms. Platt places the experience story on the bulletin board in the hall and surrounds it with the students' pictures.

With beginning readers, a teacher might simply read back the language experience story, moving a hand under each word as it is read. The teacher might also comment about frequently occurring words or point out the left-to-right progression of the words. Another approach is to read a portion of the story and then stop before a word that is predictable and ask a child to read the word. Later on, a letter-sound pattern might be pointed out. Saving language experience stories over a period of time allows students and teacher to revisit, reread, and possibly to extend these enjoyable accounts of memorable experiences. An experience story is not the only language experience activity that can be used at beginning levels. Other examples are listed in Figure 6-4.

FIGURE 6-4
Teaching strategies that develop print-vocabulary through language experiences

 Student Name Cards. Make name labels for all the students in your class. Allow them to place the labels on their desks on the first day of school.

 Labeling. Have students give the names of important items in the classroom and watch you as you make labels for those objects. A similar activity is having students suggest labels for magazine pictures. Have them watch as you make the labels. Post the pictures and labels around the classroom or on a bulletin board.

 Word Walk. Take the students on a walk around the playground or around the block. Talk about what is around them. Later, make up word cards about some of the things they saw. Use the word cards as triggers for oral language. Let students randomly pick a card, think of the walk, and talk about the specific word on the card. Be ready to read the card for some students.

 Art-based Stories. When children come to school in the fall (or after winter vacation), have them draw a picture of an exciting summer (or winter) experience. Circulate and ask students to dictate a sentence or two about their pictures. Write their sentences on their pictures, ask students to read their sentences, and then bind the art stories into a book for the reading center.

 Class Diary. Keep a regular class diary, making entries each day. Include photos of class activities wherever you can. Keep the diary in the reading center for children to read and remember class events.

 Helper Chart. Construct helper charts with movable name tags. Rotate names regularly.

 Dictated Letter Writing. Write class-dictated letters to authors of books that you have read to your students.

The Morning Message. A favorite technique that uses literacy in a meaningful way is the morning message (for example, see Kawakami-Arakaki, Oshiro, & Farran, 1989). This is typically the first instructional activity of the school day and comes right after attendance is taken. Students watch the teacher write on the chalkboard or on chart paper the date and several short messages or announcements pertaining to the day's activities. At the beginning of the school year the messages are relatively short, increasing in length as the year goes on.

The morning message is often part of a daily **community meeting,** where the entire class comes together, usually in the morning, where announcements are made by both the teacher and students, where show-and-tell activities occur, where a new book being placed into the class-

community meeting
A gathering of all participants in a class (teachers, students, aides, parents, and others) to discuss upcoming events or to share general thoughts and information.

MODEL LESSON
The Morning Message in Mr. Titus's Class

Write a Message to the Class. After taking attendance, Mr. Titus writes the following message on chart paper, reading each word as he writes it.

November 4
Today is Thursday. Mr. Paolo will be here at story time. He will tell us a story about Brazil. You can take your art projects home today!

Read the Message to the Class. After the message is complete, Mr. Titus reads it to the class. The children are encouraged to read along if they are able. Mr. Titus runs his hand under the words as he reads them. Then the whole message is read in chorus (most of the children will be able to repeat it from memory at this point).

Discuss the Form and Content of the Message. Mr. Titus asks whether the children notice anything interesting about the written message itself. Tom says that the first letter is the same as the first letter of his name. Janie notices the exclamation mark and says that the message doesn't end "in a dot." Mr. Titus uses this input to draw the parallel between *Tom, Today,* and *Thursday*. He explains that these words begin with capital *T*s and also points out the lowercase *t*s in *storytime*. Then he explains why he used an exclamation mark instead of a period (the artwork is so good that he's excited about letting them take it home). Finally, the message itself is discussed. Mr. Paolo heard some interesting folktales while he was in Brazil recently, and he is coming to share those stories with the class.

room library might be discussed, where decisions are made about ordering more paper or other materials for the writing center, and so on. The community meeting is a time when students can share and help make decisions, and where the teacher can focus on significant, everyday literacy activities that are required to keep the classroom organized.

The Shared Book Experience. The shared book experience (Holdaway, 1979; Slaughter, 1993) has its roots in the bedtime story, where parents and children share a literacy activity in a supportive, secure, and pleasant way. In schools, the book used by individual parents with their children is usually replaced with a big book, discussed below, but the shared book experience still provides a model of reading and includes discussion in a nonthreatening and supportive way.

In kindergarten classrooms many reading activities center around **big books,** which usually reproduce in large format (sometimes as large as chart paper pads) children's literature selections. Big books are colorful and motivational and are found increasingly in traditional readiness programs as well. Even though big books are complete stories and are longer than language experience stories, teachers often read them to their students in much the same way that they read language experience stories—running their hands under the print as they read, commenting on a

big books
Children's literature selections reproduced in large format.

MODEL LESSON
A Shared Book Experience Using a Big Book

Choose a Big Book. Choose a big book appropriate for your students. This might be a book that has been read before and that students have enjoyed but have not tired of, a new book that relates to a theme that is of interest to the class, or a book that is on display in the classroom and that has captured the attention of one or more children.

Introduce the Story. Discuss the theme of the book, perhaps by allowing students to predict what might be in the story after you read the title, or as part of a discussion about the cover illustration. If the book has been read previously, have students remind each other about what the book is about, or have them tell which episode in the story is their favorite. As appropriate, talk about and write down on chart paper specific words that will (or might) be found in the story as it is read. During the discussion, be sure to credit the author and illustrator of the big book.

Read the Book. With the children sitting comfortably around you, hold the big book (or place it on a stand) so that the children can easily see the words and illustrations. Run your hand under the words and phrases as they are being read. Stop occasionally and state what you are thinking as you read, or comment on particular aspects of the story. Ask children to predict upcoming story episodes and to read along at appropriate points of the story. But be sure that the reading experience is enjoyable and that the story remains meaningful; that it is not too broken up with tangential discussions.

Discuss the Story. After reading, talk about the story. Model your approach to thinking about what was read, providing appropriate reasons for your opinions. Then ask the children what *they* thought about the story. Branch out into how they felt about the characters and their actions. Tie in the children's personal experiences by asking if they have experienced things similar to what went on. As appropriate, go back to certain words to point out interesting vocabulary, and perhaps how certain words have similar spelling patterns. End by asking if the story reminds them of any other book that they have read before, and whether they would like to read the book again.

particular word, or asking children to read a word or phrase if they can. Big books are available from most educational publishers but can also be created by teacher and students, with the teacher writing down on chart paper what children dictate (perhaps suggesting story lines that the children can refine).

In the shared book experience, children are encouraged to read along and to predict words or events as the story is read (this works especially well with repetitive texts). The model lesson above provides an example of a shared book experience with a big book.

Journal and Process Writing. As noted earlier and throughout this text, there is a close relationship between reading and writing, and beginning readers must be provided opportunities to do both. Partly for this reason, the physical classroom environment noted in Figure 6-5

Big books, which are often used in beginning reading instruction, can be purchased or created as a class project.

on page 237 includes space for a designated writing center. Each day, students should be given many opportunities to write new material and to extend what they have previously written.

Writing on a daily basis is often accomplished through journal writing. The journals should be kept in a designated area, where children can have access to them at any time. In fact, creating the covers for journals is a motivational activity that personalizes and provides a sense of ownership. Usually, five to 15 minutes each morning (often after the community meeting or morning message) are set aside for journaling. During this time, children can write on a topic of their own choosing, or might respond to a topic suggested by the teacher. They might write to extend something from the previous day's journal page, or might move to a new subject. In any case, this time should be used by *all* participants in the class, including the teacher and any visitors, for writing.

Initially, the children's writing will consist of drawings and/or a few letters. Later, the writing will include more letters, eventually clustered together in groups. Still later, more recognizable words with invented spellings will appear. All of these forms are meaningful and should be supported, as should copying, if children wish to do so. Often, especially for beginning readers and writers, illustrations predominate in their journals.

EXPLORING DIVERSE POINTS OF VIEW

An ongoing debate in early childhood education centers around the curricular content of kindergarten programs. Some educators believe that kindergarten should prepare children for later schooling by focusing on the social skills and curricular background necessary for instruction in first grade. According to this view, kindergarten should provide children with opportunities to scribble, draw, look at picture books, and explore literacy as their interests dictate. Others believe that kindergarten should more formally teach some basic decoding content, usually with regard to letter names, letter sounds, and discrimination of both upper- and lowercase letters. What do you think kindergarten instruction should accomplish? How does your literacy framework relate to this debate?

process writing
When focusing on writing, teaching that addresses stages of prewriting, drafting, revising, editing, and sharing as part of the writing episode.

Journal writing, as well as free writing of all types, are especially common in programs with emergent literacy perspectives. However, many teachers also use what has been called **process writing,** which includes prewriting, drafting, revising, editing, and sharing. These stages are applicable both to writers in kindergarten and to more mature writers. The products look different, but the process for kindergartners as well as adult writers moves through the steps noted above. In particular, teachers must be supportive during the drafting, revising and editing stages. Young writers should know that they can revisit earlier work—that a piece of writing is never truly "finished."

Writing should begin when children first arrive in the kindergarten classroom, and teachers should model writing early and often. Modeling can include how a topic is chosen, and can precede each of the steps in the writing process. Choose one of the steps (perhaps drafting or editing) and show how you work through this step. Model the process on chart paper, talking through your thoughts as you write. Show the children that writing is valuable to an author, even if others cannot read everything on the page. That is, writing is still writing, even if the children can't read it! But do encourage, especially during sharing time, each author to share and read what was written to the rest of a group or to the whole class. Then, allow time for constructive discussion about the writing, as well as time for authors to edit their work.

Many different writing activities can be used to create excitement in the kindergarten classroom. Several are listed in Table 6-1.

Broader Applications. Even though emergent literacy/readiness concepts are most often applied to beginning readers, they can also relate to proficient readers. For example, even mature readers are apt to have difficulty understandinng the following passage:

> Comprehensive allocation is more consistent with the accounting for liabilities than roll over, such as accounts payable. New accounts payable continually replace accounts being paid, much the same as originating

TABLE 6-1

Examples of types and categories of writing

advertisements	labels
agendas	letters
announcements	lists
banners	maps
books	menus
bumper stickers	messages
captions	notes
cards	poems
cartoons	postcards
certificates	posters
coupons	questions
descriptions	reminders
diaries	requests
directions	riddles
envelopes	rules
fact sheets	signs
fortune cookie inserts	stories
invitations	telegrams
jokes	tickets

timing differences replace timing differences that reverse. Each credi-tor's account is accounted for separately, even though aggregate accounts payable continue to roll over. Consistency requires that timing differences related to a particular asset or liability likewise be accounted for separately (Davidson, Stickney, & Weil, 1980, pp. 20–26).

How well did you comprehend the concepts in the above passage? Try to answer the following questions:

1. Why is comprehensive allocation more consistent with liabilities than roll over?
2. What is the concept of timing differences, and what is their importance to accounts payable?
3. What is the paragraph about? Explain it in your own words.

You are a fluent reader, yet you may not be "ready" to read such a passage from an accounting text (an accountant would have had no difficulty with it). You could probably have used some prereading activities—perhaps some additional background knowledge, definitions of new vocabulary, and maybe discussion of overall meaning. The point is that emergent literacy/readiness does not stop with the acquisition of decoding knowledge. A broader view acknowledges that we all may encounter text that we are unprepared to read, given our current level of knowledge.

....

CREATING SUPPORTIVE LITERACY ENVIRONMENTS

Teachers begin to make instructional decisions well before their students arrive at school. One of the first decisions that you will have to make is how to set up your classroom so that literacy learning will occur in supportive, meaningful environments. Thus, although classroom organization is discussed more fully in chapter 13, this section deals specifically with environments for supporting literacy in kindergarten classrooms.

Creating a learning environment that will facilitate your students' emerging literacy processes has to do with organizing materials and physical room layout to support desired activities and instruction. The room arrangement is important, because it can facilitate or deemphasize social interaction and exploration of literacy by students.

A Typical Kindergarten Classroom

Although teachers are always constrained by the physical space provided to them, there are some common features of kindergarten classrooms that facilitate literacy learning. For example, it seems intuitive that young children need room to move, explore, and play; desks that are fixed in rows would be inappropriate. Also, the kindergarten curriculum includes art, music, and other aspects that can be incorporated into literacy development, assuming that the room is structured in a way that allows this to occur.

Figure 6-5 shows a room layout that is fairly typical of a kindergarten classroom. As you see, the room is divided into areas that serve as holding space for materials that are needed for specific activities. The art area is where art supplies are kept, and where students have tables and work areas where they can explore and be messy, as appropriate, while painting, working with clay, making collages and using glue, and so on. Similarly, the room has centers for science and mathematics, where materials and work space are allocated to facilitate these activities. In addition, you see that there are areas where the whole class can come together, where the teacher can read to the class, and where show-and-tell and other sharing activities can easily occur. The dramatic play area includes space for dress-up clothes and props as necessary. The reading and listening center has been placed next to the author's corner. These areas include tape recorders and tapes to be used for listening activities with headphones; chart paper on a stand; lots of writing materials (paper, pencils, markers, crayons); and many, many books. Books and other reading material might include wordless picture books, caption books, big books, minibooks, predictable-text books, magazines, brochures, reference books, tactile books, pocket-chart stories, flannel boards where words and stories can be read, and so on.

Missing from the drawing in Figure 6-5 are the touches that make the room feel cozy and inviting. For example, most kindergarten rooms have a rug, overstuffed pillows, and an armchair where students can read. A

FIGURE 6-5

Drawing of a typical kindergarten classroom.

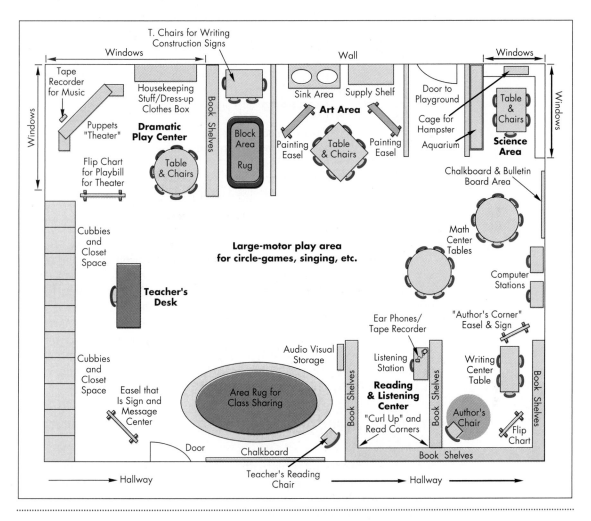

rocking chair is also often seen in kindergarten classrooms—one large enough for the teacher to sit with a student and read together. Stuffed animals, donated by parents or older students, often provide a warm feeling, as do appropriate bulletin boards, good use of color, and personalizing touches, such as photographs of each student in the class. Of course, a major part of the kindergarten room will include books and reading material of all types. When setting up the room look for items that will impart a cozy, supportive feeling. Keep in mind that the room is there for the students, and they should feel that it is *their* room. They should not feel like visitors.

TABLE 6-2
Sample daily time-plan

8:00	Morning sign-in (perhaps a snack, if needed)
8:15	Circle/community meeting time (whole group activities; sharing; daily calendar; morning message)
8:35	"Center" time (art area, dramatic/creative play area, science area, math area, writing/authors' area, reading/listening area)
10:45	Music/singing/story time (large group)
11:15	Lunch
11:45	Outdoor/indoor active play
12:15	Journal writing/silent reading time
12:45	Nap/rest time
1:00	Center time (as above, but includes time for reporting to others or to the whole group, as needed)
2:30 or 3:00	Home

Also important, of course, is the general organization of the day. Below is a typical daily structure for a kindergarten room. However, many school districts provide instruction on a "half day" basis; others require that teachers provide more time for rest periods. The decision about specific time allotments will depend, in some sense, on your particular school district and the needs of your students. Although the activities and time breakdown shown in Table 6-2 are consistent with most programs, teachers will vary the order of the items. For example, journal writing might occur in the morning rather than after lunch.

FACTORS AFFECTING EMERGENT LITERACY/READING READINESS

A number of factors interact to affect literacy development. Some, such as cognitive factors, are internal; others, such as home environment, are external. All, however, influence prereaders and continue to influence their reading throughout life. These interacting factors are presented separately here for ease of discussion.

Cognitive Factors

Two psychologists, Jean Piaget and Lev Vygotsky, have been instrumental in shaping educators' views about the relationship between thought and language. While Vygotsky has enjoyed a greater influence more recently, Piaget's work indicated that all human beings have the capability of progressing through four levels of **cognition:** sensorimotor, preoperational, concrete operational, and formal operational (Inhelder & Piaget, 1964; Piaget, 1963), and among the cognitive operations related to reading are these : **seriation,** ordering, **temporal relations, conserva-**

cognition
Knowing; thought processes.

seriation
The ability to order a set of objects logically.

temporal relations
A relationship based on either the passage of time or a particular interval of time.

conservation
The ability to keep an unchanging property of something in mind when perceptual conditions are changed.

tion, one-to-one correspondence, spatial relations, classification, and number relations (Almy, Chittenden, & Miller, 1966; Bybee & Sund, 1982; Waller, 1977). Seriation and ordering, for example, play a part in learning left-to-right progression and in realizing that letters and words go together in sequence.

In order to understand the importance of these cognitive operations, first consider the following sentences:

> The boy was hungry. He stole some food. When the lady came in, he hid under a table that had a large pot of flowers on it.

Now, answer these related questions, for which Bybee and Sund (1982) have identified the required cognitive operations.

What happened first—the boy's being hungry or his stealing the food? (seriation, ordering, and temporal relations)

What do you think the boy will do next? (ordering)

Where was the boy at the end of the story? (spatial relations)

Questions like these are often asked by teachers without adequate attention being given to the cognitive demands involved. Although questions that extend and appropriately challenge students are necessary for learning, questions that are too difficult can frustrate and prompt students to give up prematurely. Thus, teachers must be careful not to use concepts that are beyond the level of beginning readers. Many kindergarten programs, especially those that are more traditional, try to provide activities to build many of the concepts that adults take for granted—such as *before, in front of,* or *under.* Teachers can demonstrate such concepts in everyday teaching routines. For example, there are ample opportunities for students to stand *beside* one student but *in front of* another. Students can also be asked to manipulate objects, placing them on, under, and around other objects. Or they might perform a sequence of activities, allowing other students to describe the order of events. These activities often occur normally in the classroom, and simply drawing students' attention to this terminology during such activities provides a basis for learning in context. Teachers have found activities such as those listed in Figure 6-6 to help students learn sequencing and following directions.

Following directions is another potentially difficult cognitive task. However, teachers frequently ask students to do several things at once—for example, "Put your pencils down, close your books, and pass your journals forward before you line up for recess"—forgetting that some young children may have difficulty grasping multiple directions. Again, many kindergarten programs provide specific activities targeting listening skills and following directions. Simple games such as Simon Says, or a classroom treasure hunt that requires students to follow instructions, can help students to sequence and follow directions. Keep in mind, however, that activities that are tied to literacy are most valuable.

FIGURE 6-6

Sample activities/strategies designed to draw students' attention to left-to-right sequencing and following directions.

Left-to-right sequencing

Observing Writing. Ask students to point to the places on a page of chart paper where you should start and stop writing. Then ask them to watch as you write— perhaps transcribing a simple story or sentence they dictate to you. Draw their conscious attention to where you start and stop each line.

Picture-story Sequencing. Cut simple cartoon strips into individual frames. Then, have the children arrange the frames from left to right so that the story is told. After the frames are arranged, have students tell the story in their own words, frame by frame, pointing to each frame as appropriate.

Meaning Match. Have the children draw lines from left to right between two pictures that, when joined, make sense. For example, pictures on the left might show a squirrel, a car, and a boat; pictures on the right, a nut, a garage, and a lakeshore. Say to the children, "Help the squirrel [car, boat] get to the nut [garage, water] by drawing a line from left to right between the two."

Sequencing and following directions games

Supply students with pictures that are labeled, and ask them to follow specific, sequential instructions (for example, "Put an *X* below the house and then circle the dog").

Provide motor activities such as drawing pictures to certain specifications (for example, "Draw a man in one corner, two dogs in the middle, and a car between the man and the dogs"). Then help students label their pictures.

Have students give directions to you or another student to perform a simple task.

Present a simple board game and explain the directions. Have students repeat the directions to check for understanding. After they have played the game, change the directions, and discuss the effect on the game. Write down the directions and post them for future use.

Bring a simple recipe to class (for example, popcorn or Jell-O). Make the item by reading and following the directions step by step. Discuss how important the directions were.

Although Piaget was instrumental in our understanding that language and thought are closely related, Vygotsky (1978, 1986) showed us that language learning is a social process. Specifically, Vygotsky believed that **cognitive development,** including the development of language, is greatly affected by an individual's social interaction with others. In other

cognitive development
Growth in mental abilities and thought processes.

words, mediators, such as teachers and parents, influence a child's cognitive and language skills. Thus, emergent literacy/readiness is viewed as an evolving stage, or phase, that is influenced by teachers, rather than a static stage that a learner progresses through independently.

One of Vygotsky's major contributions is the **zone of proximal development,** which represents the difference between what learners can do on their own and what they can accomplish with guidance. Within that zone concepts are maturing; that is, they are being refined through social interaction, but they are not yet sufficiently developed to be applied without help. Vygotsky believed that learners can do more with appropriate mediation than by themselves. Thus, a teacher's actions are viewed as critical in a child's cognitive development. The instructional implications of Vygotsky's concepts include these suggested behaviors:

1. Identify the learner's zone of proximal development. This area lies immediately beyond the area in which the learner can function without help.
2. Present tasks that the child can do with the help of others who are able to complete the tasks on their own. The tasks should be completed through social interaction and participation. The child should not simply watch others complete the task but should actively collaborate in completing it.
3. Monitor the learner's ability to complete tasks. The zone of proximal development shifts to a higher level whenever the child is able to complete tasks previously performed only with help.

Another of the implications of Vygotsky's work is the use of modeling within social situations. The social, sharing nature of reading activity makes this an excellent time for modeling to occur, especially through a procedure known as a **think-aloud** (Davey, 1983; Fitzgerald, 1983). A think-aloud is a method framework (detailed in Chapter 10) in which the teacher reads a passage aloud and talks through the processes used to make sense of what is being read, thereby modeling the thought processes and application of background knowledge necessary to understand the text. Think-alouds should be an occasional part of oral reading activities, and can be incorporated into any shared book activity.

Oral Language Factors

The language base of beginning readers is critically important to their learning to read. A solid oral language foundation allows them to generalize from what they already do well, and children who do not have well-developed aural and oral language skills have more difficulty learning to read.

Early oral language progresses through three basic stages: babbling, holophrastic speech, and telegraphic speech. In the initial babbling stage, the infant generates random sounds. Although these sounds may not be an attempt to actively communicate, the infant does appear to be experimenting with the vocal system. The sounds that are generated include,

zone of proximal development
According to Vygotsky, the zone where learners can achieve success with guidance.

think-aloud
A procedure whereby a reader states aloud the thought processes and decisions that occur while reading.

MODEL LESSON
A Think-Aloud Procedure in Ms. Jerrald's Class

Ms. Jerrald wants to use a modified think-aloud procedure with the book *Ten Little Caterpillars* (Martin, 1967), which includes the following lines of text on four different pages:

The first little caterpillar crawled into a bower.
The second little caterpillar wriggled up a flower.
The third little caterpillar climbed a cabbage head.
The fourth little caterpillar found a melon bed. (pp. 3, 5, 7, 9)

First, she reads the title and says, "I wonder what this will tell me about the ten caterpillars. It could tell about how they live together or about what they do." After the first line she says, "*Bower*. Now that's a word I haven't seen before. I wonder what it means. Maybe I can find out by looking at the picture on this page or by reading farther. If not, I might have to ask someone or look in the dictionary." After the second line she says, "This sentence tells me about the second caterpillar. I wonder if the rest of the sentences will tell me about what the other caterpillars do."

After the third line she says, "It sure looks like each sentence is going to tell about a different caterpillar. How many of you think so? Thumbs up if you do, down if you don't. I have a picture in my mind of a caterpillar climbing into a cabbage head. It's easy to think of a cabbage head because I sometimes buy them in the grocery store and because they grow in my neighbor's garden. I wonder if she has caterpillars in her garden." After the fourth line she says, "The first part of each sentence is pretty much the same. That makes it easier to read. I wonder what a melon bed looks like. The bed I sleep in is a place to lie down. A melon bed is probably a place where the melon sits in the garden."

Ms. Jerrald continues in a similar fashion. At the end of the story she wraps it up by saying, "Well, after the title I predicted that we might find out about how the caterpillars live or what they might be doing. It looks like the book is mostly about what they are doing. I never did find out the meaning of *bower*. I think I'll go look it up in case I see it again."

---

but go beyond, the sounds that will eventually make up the infant's native language. Only later, when children learn which sounds make up the language of the communicating group to which they belong, are unnecessary sounds dropped. Perhaps because of lack of need and practice, adult speakers have great difficulty pronouncing and even hearing sounds that are not used in their native language.

After the babbling stage the infant appears to apply words to events, apparently using single words logically and consistently to label complete thoughts. For example, a single word such as *milk* or *doll* might be used to communicate thoughts like "I want more milk" or "Give me the doll." This stage, beginning midway to late in the first year of the infant's life, features what is called **holophrastic speech.** Early in this stage parents might hear the child say *papa* or *mama,* even when the adult is not the father or the mother. At a certain stage of cognitive development, children do overgeneralize. In addition, it appears that early sound combinations are the ones that are farthest apart in the **vocal tract.** Thus, it seems easy

holophrastic speech
A stage of early language acquisition when a child uses a single word to express a thought.

vocal tract
Speech organs used to make sounds.

to rock back and forth between the two sounds of *mama* or *papa:* both the "m" and the "p" are formed at the front of the vocal tract with the mouth closed, whereas the "a" sound is formed at the back with the tract open.

Soon after the holophrastic stage, the child begins to string two or three words together in **telegraphic speech.** Examples of such utterances are "Milk here," "All gone milk," or "Baby milk." The child's speech is not yet in the form of complete sentences, yet thoughts seem to be grouped in sentence form. One problem with interpreting an expression like "Milk here" is that we really have no way of knowing whether the child means "Bring the milk here," "The milk has spilled over here," "Here is the milk," or something quite different. In many instances what adults think a child means is not, in fact, the intended meaning. This problem also applies to the speech of kindergarten and first-grade students, and teachers must be careful not to impose their adult interpretation on what their young students say. Figure 6-7 includes strategies that support children's development of oral expression.

telegraphic speech
A stage of oral language development when all but essential words are omitted.

FIGURE 6-7
Teaching strategies that support the development of oral expression

 Picture/Sequence Story. Show a picture or a sequence of two or three pictures, and have students tell a story about what is shown.

 Expressing Emotions. Have students pretend that they are certain animals or objects in a given situation and talk about their feelings.

 Activity Sequence. Have students think of a specific sequential activity, such as getting ready for school in the morning, going home from school, or getting from the classroom to the library. Then have students tell a partner or a group the specific directions to follow to perform the activity. If the activity has not been stated, other students can try to guess it from the set of directions.

 Relating Intonation and Mood. Tell a story to your students. Then tell it again, varying your tone of voice and general expression. Discuss how the different readings made the story seem scarier, happier, and so on. Have students try to vary their own expression on sentences that they repeat after you. Other students can guess the moods that are being expressed.

 Build a Story. Have students sit in a circle. Begin a story with one sentence and have each student add another sentence until the story gets back around to the teacher. If the session is tape-recorded, transcribe the whole story while the students watch. Later, let students illustrate the story and post it on the classroom bulletin board.

 Show and Tell. Ask students to bring something special with them from home. Let them show the item and talk about it (that is, show and tell).

Parents and teachers should provide many opportunities for oral expression. Storytelling by children is a beneficial activity, as is the recapping or retelling of a story that has been told to them. Structured oral language activities should form an ongoing part of an emergent literacy/readiness instructional program. Such activities can range from dictating a story to the teacher, to explaining or describing an event, to planning a class play. Teachers should also provide opportunities for students to build conversational skills, such as turn-taking, listening, and **intonation.**

Perceptual Factors

intonation
The rise, fall, and stress in a voice and the pauses in speaking.

Perception deals with the senses and is divided into visual (seeing), auditory (hearing), tactile (touching), olfactory (smelling), and tasting categories. In traditional readiness programs emphasis was placed on **visual and auditory discrimination** because the normal reader depends on vision to differentiate between letters (Braille readers depend on tactile perception instead), and because hearing is instrumental in differentiating the sounds associated with different letters. In whole language programs perceptual and discrimination activities are deemphasized in favor of more integrated reading and writing activities.

visual and auditory discrimination
The ability to see (visual) and hear (auditory) likenesses and differences.

Four terms are important to remember in a discussion of perceptual factors.

- *Acuity.* The "strength of the signal." Related questions include, How well does the child hear? and How good are the child's eyes?
- *Discrimination.* The ability to notice similarities and differences.
- *Recognition.* Awareness that something being experienced is the same as something previously experienced. Visually recognizing a word signals an awareness that the word has been seen before.
- *Identification.* Deals specifically with identifying, or grasping, meaning.

These definitions are consistent with those found in the *Dictionary of Reading and Related Terms* (Harris & Hodges, 1981).

Visual and Auditory Discrimination. While the ability to discriminate letters and sounds is important for reading, discrimination is often confused with perception. Basically, **visual perception** is the ability to notice that there are lines and squiggles on a page. Normal reading is impossible in total darkness because visual perception is impossible, but light intensity can vary widely without affecting reading. Can you think of the variety of lighting conditions under which you have managed to read over the years? The more important aspect of the visual factor is discrimination, which allows readers to recognize differences between printed letters, words, and so on.

visual perception
In reading, the ability to see the characteristics of such things as letters, words, or lines of print.

Some kindergarten programs attempt to enhance students' concepts of "same" and "different" by using discrimination activities that are closely linked to stories that children are reading or writing, while more tradi-

Although concepts of "same" and "different" can be taught in many ways, they are *best* taught within print-based activities.

tional programs might attempt to do so by having children match words, letters, or combinations of words and letters in different sizes, shapes, and colors. However, because the goal of early literacy programs is to facilitate later fluent reading, it is best to provide activities that bridge to more authentic, realistic texts.

For example, if you wish to reinforce the importance of noticing that even small differences in letters are significant, you might point out that the letters *m* and *n* both appear in a recently completed language experience story. Then, carefully clarify the similarities and differences, as demonstrated in this short exercise with *m* and *n*.

Look at [or trace] *m* and *n*. Are they the same?

Do both have straight lines? Where? How many?

Do both have curved lines? Where? How many?

Such specific questioning can help students differentiate between particular features of letters and allows them to examine the details that make up overall configurations.

Similarly, auditory perception is basically the ability to notice the presence of sound. More important for reading, however, is the ability to discriminate between the sounds of various letters, syllables, and words. Controversy continues to surround what should be taught in the auditory discrimination component of emergent literacy/readiness reading programs. For example, according to Gibson and Levin (1980):

> Auditory perceptual analysis of words is an important skill for learning to read, and training in it helps and does show transfer, at least in the initial stages of learning to read. . . . Clapping for each unit, marking (with dashes), deleting sounds, producing omitted sounds, and substituting sounds are successive stages of training, with apparently successful results in kindergarten and first grade (p. 260).

However, Aulls (1982) is less definite about the value of such activities, citing a number of studies that support his conclusion that

> Emphasizing reading tasks such as sounding out words or emphasizing phonics may be a waste of time for many kindergartners. . . .[although] there does appear to be justification for teaching auditory segmentation to those children who have naturally begun to sound out words and who have already begun to read (p. 99).

One benefit of auditory discrimination activities is that they provide a common terminology for both teacher and student, as has been clearly demonstrated in teacher's guides for some time:

> The purpose of giving practice in listening for beginning sounds is not to teach children to "hear" sounds or to distinguish sounds from one another. Children who understand and reproduce their language do this automatically. However, many pupils in kindergarten or first grade have trouble with the concept that a word has a beginning because they think of a word as one undifferentiated sound. Since children will be taught in a later lesson that one sound to use in decoding is the sound "at the beginning of a word," they need to know exactly what this expression means (*Getting Ready to Read*, p. 21).

As in visual discrimination, later transfer to print is better when auditory discrimination tasks center around reading-related materials. Figures 6-8 and 6-9 include print-based auditory and visual discrimination activities that can also refine emerging concepts of "same" and "different."

Auditory/Visual Integration. Beginning readers are learning that oral language can be represented in symbolic form, that sounds and symbols are linked, and that the purpose of reading is to acquire meaning. Activities that build these concepts relate to **auditory/visual integration.** In traditional readiness programs, children are presented with both the visual text and the sound(s) represented. They must see and hear both at the same time, perhaps naming an item aloud, in chorus with the teacher, while they look at it.

auditory/visual integration
The linking or association of sound and sight.

FIGURE 6-8

Sample activities/strategies to help develop concepts of same *and* different.

Word-matching Games. Divide a piece of poster paper into large rectangles. Print a word in each rectangle. Make a matching set of rectangular word cards. Then have students cover the words on the paper with the appropriate word cards. You can turn this activity into a bingo game by having students, perhaps in pairs, cover the words that you point to on your "bingo card." You might also make labels for objects around the classroom and attach an envelope below the label on each item. Then give children a set of word cards that include the labeled items and have them place their word cards in the envelopes under the appropriate labels. If children's names are on their word cards, you will have a quick check of who is having difficulty matching cards to labels.

Letter-matching Games. Using plastic or paper letters, arrange groups of letters that are the same except for one that is obviously different.

C C X C C   F S F F F

Ask children to replace the one that is different so that all the letters are the same. Gradually increase the similarity of the letters.

C C O C C   F F E F F

Discriminating Letter Features. Help children perceive the differences among letters by discussing and pointing out the features of letters—curved lines, straight lines, and height. Present two letters with color on the parts that make them different.

Discriminating Word Features. Ask children to discriminate between similar words, drawing a circle around the part(s) that are different (e.g., *near/rear, rat/rut, window/widow*). Also, discuss similarities and differences between words of clearly different shapes and lengths. For example, write *mow* and *motorcycle* on the board or on chart paper. Discuss how they are the same and different (e.g., one is longer, two of the letters in *mow* are in *motorcycle,* one word has a letter with a "tail," and so on).

Thus, activities to promote auditory/visual integration differ somewhat from those that target visual and auditory discrimination. For example, whereas a purely auditory activity might ask students to repeat the beginning sound in *baby,* a corresponding auditory/visual integration activity would present the visual image of the word while the teacher pronounced it. Students might be asked to repeat the beginning sound or point to the part of the word that has the /b/ sound *as they say the letter sound with the teacher.* Traditionally, such activities focus on the association between specific sounds and specific parts of a word and are used with sounds in beginning, medial, and ending positions, as well as with whole words and phrases.

Although some kindergarten programs will implement specific auditory/visual integration activities in their curriculum, such activities are deemphasized in whole language programs. Within a whole language

FIGURE 6-9

Sample activities/strategies to help develop recognition and discrimination of beginning and ending sounds of words.

Picture-sound Match. Provide magazines and blunt scissors. Have students find and cut out pictures of objects that have names beginning with the same sounds that the students' own names begin with. Then have them say the names of the pictures they have cut out, and let the other students determine whether the beginning sounds are the same.

Key-word Banks. Take cut-out pictures, and place them in a box. Also, provide containers that are labeled, each with a single word. Have students take the pictures out of the box and place each in a container that has a label beginning with the same sound as that particular picture.

Tongue Twister Sounds. Find or make up simple tongue twisters (for example, "Six silly sheep saw a slippery snake"). Have students repeat the twisters after you, first slowly, then slightly faster. Put several twisters into a box, and have students choose ones for you to say. Then have them suggest other words that might make each tongue twister longer (for example, "Saw a slippery snake sliding").

Key-word Spaceship. On a large piece of posterboard draw a spaceship on Earth, aimed toward the Moon. Present a target word, and have children provide words or pictures with a sound similar to that of the target word. For every three correct words, move the ship closer to the Moon. Dividing students into teams makes this a motivational game.

Key-word Match. Present key words that begin or end with a specified sound. Provide students with other words and ask them to decide whether the sounds are the same.

environment, children learn to integrate the auditory and visual aspects of reading within real reading acts—for example, as teachers use big books and run their hands under the words being read while children watch or read along, or by reading predictable, repetitive books.

Affective Factors

We have all experienced tasks that seemed to be completed in record time, whereas others dragged on and on. Think back to tasks of both types. Did you discover that the tasks you found pleasant flew by, whereas those you did not enjoy moved slowly? Your affective set—the way you felt about the tasks—influenced your motivation and performance. This principle also applies to the reading task.

Most children come to school eager to learn to read. They view reading as potentially exciting (Downing et al., 1979). Much of that feeling comes from having had interesting and exciting stories read to them at home, which leads, in turn, to the dual realization that their pleasure originated in books and that learning to read would be a real mark of independence. Hopefully, parents will continue to read to their children after they come to school. But teachers should read to their pupils also. Reading to students is a vital part of any kindergarten literacy program that intends to foster a desire to read.

Teachers should read to beginning readers often—sometimes individually, sometimes in small groups or in whole-class situations. In addition, it is important to allow time for discussion of what was read, pointing out pictures and interesting drawings and thereby fostering positive attitudes as well as story comprehension. Encouraging students to talk about personal experiences that relate to the reading selection is also highly motivational, especially with beginning readers, who are often **egocentric.**

Issues of motivation are closely tied to feelings. Is a specific activity liked or disliked? Our response is called **attitude.** A closely related term is **interest,** which indicates the importance we place on pursuing a given topic or activity. To illustrate how these two affective factors interact, consider that you might dislike something yet be interested in finding out more about it. For example, someone might have an intensely negative *attitude* toward snakes but have a strong *interest* in finding out more about them—perhaps where they are most likely to be found in order to avoid them! Conversely, it is possible to feel very positive about something but have no interest in studying it further. Someone might find Gothic architecture visually pleasing but at the same time have no interest in studying its history or specific characteristics.

In literacy instruction, teachers need to be aware of both the interests and the attitudes of their students. Often students' attitudes toward learning to read may be positive, but their interest in performing specific instructional tasks may be quite low. To generate interest in required assignments, teachers must foster a positive attitude toward the task being performed. And for young children, long-term goals do not provide strong motivation. Telling students that they need to complete a task so that they will eventually become good readers is not conceptually relevant for them. The immediate task must, in itself, be motivational.

A short attitude survey can help teachers choose instructional tasks and materials to motivate their students. Heathington (1976) has developed attitude scales for use in both primary and intermediate grades. The answer sheets for the Heathington primary scale ask students to show how they feel about various things by marking a set of faces that range from smiles to frowns. The scales provide a variety of pertinent questions—for example, "How do you feel. . .when you go to the library?"—but teachers sometimes supplement with their own questions about students' attitudes and interests. "What do you like to do most? What are your favorite TV shows? Do you have (want) any pets? Your favorite story is. . .? The best day of the week is. . .? When you grow up, you'd like to be. . .?" (Further discussion and more examples of attitude and interest assessment are included in Chapter 11.)

egocentric
Describing the self-centeredness of children, who are unable to take another's point of view.

attitude
The way a person feels about something.

interest
Intentional focusing of attention on something as a result of motivation.

Beginning readers often enjoy the repetitive patterns found in predictable texts and later imitate these patterns in oral and written activities.

Even though an attitude/interest inventory can be a valuable tool, teachers must recognize that young children have short attention spans and their interests can change fairly quickly. Consequently, it is important to talk to young students often to keep abreast of their current interests. Furthermore, with students who have somewhat poor attitudes toward reading, teachers should make a special effort to identify motivational materials. They should pick stories likely to be of high interest to such students and should spend extra time reading to them and discussing their interest in the stories.

The Home Environment

internalized
Made a part of one's existing knowledge.

Before students come to school, they have had vast learning experiences. They have learned how to communicate and have **internalized** a set of language rules, in addition to acquiring a sophisticated awareness of the behaviors necessary for effective communication (for example, turn taking, intonation, gestures, and facial expressions). During those formative

years several home environment factors are highly **correlated** to reading achievement. Through interviews with parents of early readers,
Durkin (1966, 1974-1975) has identified these common elements:

correlated
Showing a relationship to
something else.

- Parents of early readers spend much time in conversation with
  their children.
- Early readers ask many questions, and their parents take the
  time to answer those questions.
- A frequent question asked by early readers is, "What's that
  word?"

The importance of home environment and parental involvement has also
been noted by the Commission on Reading (Anderson, Hiebert, Scott, &
Wilkinson, 1985; see also Mason, 1980):

> Parents play a role of inestimable importance in laying the foundations
> for learning to read. Parents should informally teach preschool children
> about reading and writing by reading aloud to them, discussing stories
> and events, encouraging them to learn letters and words and teaching
> them about the world around them. These practices help prepare chil-
> dren for success in reading (p. 57).

Other factors related to children's later reading success include:

- the value that adults in the home place on literacy
- the amount of reading done by adults in the home (modeling)
- the amount of reading material available in the home
- the number of language-based games and activities in the home
- the availability of personal reading materials for the child

There are literally thousands of books available for the preschool child,
ranging from colorful picture books, with and without story lines, to fairly
complex stories. One type of book that is popular with young children contains highly predictable patterns of language—perhaps rhyming patterns,
repeated words and phrases, or predictable concepts. Such books are
highly motivational because they allow children to begin quickly to read
along with a parent or teacher, using prior knowledge to predict and thus
aid understanding, just as mature readers do. An example of a predictable
text is *Ten Little Caterpillars,* which was cited and excerpted in the model
lesson on page 242. Other predictable texts are included in the more
extensive discussion of such books in chapter 4.

Reading to children from an early age plays such an important role in
establishing later success in reading that parents often ask their children's kindergarten or first-grade teacher to suggest appropriate reading
materials. Numerous reference sources provide titles, critiques, or suggestions for parents about reading to their children at home. Here are
several.

M O D E L   L E S S O N
Fostering Discourse Knowledge and Predicting Outcomes in Ms. Kim's Class

To help beginning readers get an initial sense of the role of prediction in understanding what they read, Ms. Kim uses the following simple strategy.

Choose an interesting story to read, and divide it into two parts. Have paper or a chalkboard available.

Read the first part of the story, and discuss it. Ask for suggestions about what might come next, that is, what might happen in the rest of the story. Record responses. Ask for reasons to support the predictions. Be ready to help clarify the information in the text that provides the bases for the predictions.

Read the next section of the story.

Go back to the predictions. Discuss them. Talk about why some predictions may not have appeared in the story.

Cullinan, B. E., & Galda, L. (1994). *Literature and the child.* New York: Harcourt Brace College Publishers.

Stoll, D. R. (Ed.). (1994). *Magazines for kids and teens.* Newark, DE: International Reading Association.

Trelease, J. (Ed.). (1992). *Hey! Listen to this. Stories to read aloud.* Newark, DE: International Reading Association.

Trelease, J. (1989). *The new read-aloud handbook.* New York: Penguin.

Additionally, the International Reading Association (800 Barksdale Road, Newark, DE 19711) publishes informational material for parents, including *Children's Choices* and *Teacher's Choices,* which are annual compilations of children's and teachers' favorite books.

Good reading habits are built when children are read to with appropriate intonation and evident pleasure and when their attention is drawn to the reading material. Reading a wide variety of materials to children helps to build their discourse knowledge, use of syntax, and use of context. As parents use specialized reading vocabulary (for example, "Let's turn the page." or "Isn't that a funny title?"), children learn terms that will serve them well in school reading.

The activity described in the model lesson above is appropriate for use with young children. Nevertheless, parents should be cautioned not to force their children but to wait until they exhibit an interest in such an activity. Teachers, too, might want to use this kind of interaction with their young students.

Beyond actual reading, many games and activities allow young children to classify ("Let's put all the blocks with the big letters together"); to match items ("Let's see if this puzzle piece will fit into this slot"); to discriminate ("Let's see if we can find what's wrong in this picture"); or to build concepts of *same* and *different* ("Let's see if we can find a word that looks the same"). A guessing game like I Spy allows children to play with language ("I spy something with a color that rhymes with *bed*"). All of these activities can be done at home, and all aid in the successful completion of future reading tasks.

EVALUATING BEGINNING READERS

Teachers are decision makers who continually make instructional choices based on the information around them. For beginning readers that information is gathered in three ways: formal and informal tests, observations of student behavior and abilities, and information from parents and students. The characteristics of formal and informal tests are discussed in Chapter 11, as are assessment procedures appropriate across grade levels. The discussion here looks at testing specifically within the context of emergent literacy/readiness classrooms and includes special considerations for teachers who are assessing literacy development in young children.

Formal Tests

Four areas appear to predict success in reading: knowledge of letter names, general oral vocabulary knowledge, recognition of whole words, and visual discrimination ability (Barrett, 1965; Bond & Dykstra, 1967; Loban, 1963; Richek, 1977-1978; Silvaroli, 1965). Although some studies have failed to show that these four areas are predictive of later reading ability (Calfee, Chapman, & Venezky, 1972; Olson & Johnson, 1970; Samuels, 1972), they are generally included in formal emergent literacy/readiness tests. Such tests usually measure the following abilities:

auditory perception	awareness of left-right sequence
auditory discrimination	letter identification and recognition
visual perception	oral sentence or short passage comprehension
visual discrimination	
auditory/visual integration	word identification and recognition
concepts of *same, different, over,* and *under*	motor skills

Formal tests at this level range from paper-and-pencil tests given to groups of students, to tests administered individually. Traditional, formal reading readiness tests often require that students match pictures, words, letters, or shapes to either visual or auditory stimuli. For exam-

"Kidwatching" students during games and other activities is part of informal assessment and can provide valuable information.

ple, children might be asked to listen to or look at an item and then find that item in a series of choices, or they might complete an item to match a stimulus. There have been several criticisms and cautions raised with regard to these traditional tests.

One caution has to do with children understanding clearly what they are expected to do, and whether or not they view the task as important. Even with seemingly simple tasks, teachers must be careful that young students clearly understand test directions, for beginning readers easily confuse some test items and may be unable to grasp certain types of instructions (for example, "From the pictures on the right, mark the one that is the same as the one on the left"). In addition, teachers should be sure that a test clearly relates to what is being measured. For example, it should not evaluate a student's ability to follow directions unless that is the specific objective of the test.

Another caution regarding the testing of young children relates to their attention spans. Teachers must be sure that testing tasks are within a child's attention span. A kindergarten or first-grade student is often a bundle of energy, unused to sitting still and focusing attention for extended periods. Most formal tests contain time lines, beyond which rest periods or other activities are suggested. Teachers should never ignore such instructions.

Before deciding on a formal test, teachers should answer the following questions:

- What exactly do I want to measure, and why?
- What exactly does this test measure, and how?
- Does the test measure what it says it is measuring?
- Is there a close relationship between what I want to measure and what the test measures?

To answer these questions, you will need to become familiar with a particular test, taking the time to examine it carefully and to read the test manual completely. A test manual contains valuable information on administration procedures and the intent of the test. With that information you should decide whether to spend potential instructional time on testing. If the test is mandated, requiring its administration, you should follow the test's directions and consider its results carefully, keeping in mind what you know about the children and their literacy behavior in more authentic situations.

Formal reading readiness tests were developed mainly from the 1920s to the 1950s, with periodic revisions and updates through the present date. They have become less popular in recent times, partly because studies have shown that the predictive power of such tests is fairly low. In other words, a good score on a formal emergent literacy/readiness test does not always predict with a high degree of certainty how well a student will learn to read. For this reason many now advocate using more informal and observational measures at this level (Durkin, 1987; Goodman, Goodman, & Hood, 1989; Sulzby, 1990).

Teachers in whole language programs may have special difficulty assessing students with traditional, formal tests (Valencia, Hiebert, & Afflerbach, 1994; see also Stallman & Pearson, 1990, for a discussion of formal readiness tests and their incompatibility with shifting views of literacy development). Because whole language programs generally do not structure teaching within skill units, formal assessment instruments (which usually measure independent or isolated skills) are often viewed as less appropriate. In keeping with beliefs that literacy develops through interaction with more authentic reading and writing tasks, students in whole language programs may be better assessed through observational and informal measures during more genuine literacy tasks, and through an ongoing compilation of student work. Such compilations, or portfolios,

FIGURE 6-10

Sample page from Clay's Stones: The Concepts About Print *test. Instructions for administration are found in Clay's (1979)* The Early Detection of Reading Difficulties *(3rd ed.). Auckland, New Zealand: Heinemann. Notice that the test pages shown below come from a real book. Children are asked to make decisions and choices within this real-book context.*

Stones

Marie Clay

I saw a bird in the tree
and stones
on the ground.

can be extremely useful in documenting students' progress. In addition, tests such as *Sand: The Concepts About Print Test* and *Stones: The Concepts About Print Test* (Clay, 1972, 1979, see Figure 6-10) measure more global aspects of literacy—aspects that are learned through interaction with print rather than through direct teaching of isolated skills (Clay, 1980a, 1980b). Thus, such tools may be more compatible with whole language programs than traditional tests, and more closely match the instructional situation and environment.

Observational and Informal Data

A school environment provides a wealth of opportunity for the observant teacher to informally assess student abilities, interests, attitudes, and social skills. Assignments, oral responses to questions, student-initiated questions, attention span, speed of task completion, and patterns of responses all provide data on which to base instructional decisions. In addition to specific, individual reading- and writing-related tasks, group activities and observation of playground behavior can also provide valuable information. Is the child an active participant in games? Does the child take leadership or passive roles? In what kinds of activities? Is the child shy or more of a bully? How do other students react to the child? Does the child participate in group or individual play that includes activities such as labeling, naming, and so on? Answers to such questions provide valuable insights. Informal observations should be recorded along with formal test data, for together these pieces of information enable teachers to plan instructional activities according to student needs. The structured observation of students to make instructional decisions has been called "kidwatching," a term often attributed to Ken and Yetta Goodman (see Pike, Compain & Mumper, 1994).

If observation is to play a significant role in instructional decision-making, it is important to be systematic in your observations. All children will need to be observed. You will need to guard against focusing on certain children over others—something that is easy to do. Thus, before beginning systematic observations, plan to set aside a portion of the day to watching your students. Ensure that each day has a certain set of students designated as "targets" for observation. Also, be aware that observation is an informal procedure. It need not require that you stay away from student activities and merely listen and observe in a "hands off" manner. Although this might occur at times, the teacher is certainly a part of the class, and observations will often take place while the teacher participates in classroom activates. Such actitivies can include discussions, shared reading and writing experiences, conferences, and question-answer dialogues. When these occur during designated observational time feel free to participate, but be sure to record your observations in an organized record-keeping system.

Observations can be recorded on checklists, in notebooks, on file cards, or in any way that allows easy access and a consistent way to summarize data. Many publishers offer commercial checklists, and schools or school districts often have suggested checklists for teachers' use. One simple checklist is presented in Figure 6-11, and can help draw attention to specific behaviors and abilities. Some of the items can be deduced by observation; others require input from parents or students. Such a checklist can suggest activities or items that might be motivational and can identify students who might need a little special consideration. As with any informal evaluation instrument, teachers should modify checklist items to fit particular instructional situations.

Parental Input

Informal discussions with parents can prove to be very productive, providing valuable information about students. Through parent conferences; parent-teacher association (PTA) meetings; and notes or questionnaires sent to parents, teachers can learn about students' siblings, motivating factors, attitudes toward school, and home reading environments. Parents can also be a tremendous help in more direct instructional aspects of an emergent literacy/readiness program. Usually, parents are aware of the value and importance of good reading abilities and are willing to help in whatever way they can. Having parents function as storytellers, give demonstrations, or help with class activities can provide valuable assistance and can extend regular classroom learning, especially when that parental involvement is used as a base for oral, written, or art experiences. In addition, young children are typically proud when their parents visit their classes and thus try hard to do their best. Parental involvement often helps foster positive student attitude and motivation.

Working parents who are unable to come to class during school hours might be able to arrange an interesting field trip to their business or place of work. Or perhaps they have a hobby that can be brought to school and left for the teacher and students to discuss whenever it is appropriate. These types of parental involvement can form the basis for highly motivating lessons that build experiential background, oral language, and vocabulary. They can also serve as background for language experience lessons and tasks such as brainstorming what to write in a journal, a letter of invitation, or a thank-you note.

USING A LITERACY FRAMEWORK TO GUIDE EMERGENT LITERACY

The way that you implement emergent literacy/readiness instruction will depend on your literacy framework. If you believe that reading takes place through exact pronunciation of what is written, you may stress perceptual, discrimination activities in your program. Such an approach has as its goal the direct teaching of sound-symbol relationships, and you

FIGURE 6-11

Informal checklist of behaviors and abilities.

Student's name: _____   Date: _____

Age: Years _____ Months _____

Use the following scale in the decision column: 1 = yes, 2 = somewhat, 3 = no.
Comments should be added whenever possible, especially if the decision is "somewhat."

	Decision	Comments
1. Knows the alphabet (can say it with little or no help)	_____	
2. Can write alphabet	_____	
3. Can distinguish between upper- and lowercase letters	_____	
4. Recognizes written letters by name	_____	
5. Can rhyme words	_____	
6. Can count to 20	_____	
7. Can state numbers from written form	_____	
8. Can write numbers	_____	
9. Recognizes and matches items that are the same	_____	
10. Knows relational words (*before, after, back, front, under, above, until*)	_____	
11. Can describe (tell) a picture-based story	_____	
12. Can appropriately order a simple picture-story (i.e., a cartoon strip)	_____	
13. Can read common words (*stop, dog, run*)	_____	
14. Can read own name when written by teacher	_____	
15. Can write own name	_____	
16. Knows own age	_____	
17. Can repeat sequence of events in a simple story	_____	
18. Speaks in sentences rather than in words or phrases	_____	
19. Knows simple reading terms (*page, word, story*)	_____	

General comments (e.g., attentiveness, concentration, ability to follow directions, shyness, pronunciation of words/sounds, general verbal fluency):

_____

_____

_____

┌───┐

OPPORTUNITIES TO CELEBRATE DIVERSITY

Assessment, whether formal or informal, provides much information that allows teachers to learn about the diverse nature of their students. Although assessment information, in terms of student diversity, is usually linked to their relative abilities or scores on a test, other information about the diversity found in a class also becomes readily apparent. As a teacher, you will be able to use assessment to learn about your students and to use what you learn to create appropriate learning opportunities for them.

In kindergarten as well as in other elementary grades, observations of students are especially helpful in learning about students. For example, observations can tell you whether or not students of similar backgrounds or cultures are extending their circle of influence beyond children of their own background or culture. If not, try, through flexible grouping or through show and tell activities that allow other students to learn about a particular students' culture or interest, to provide opportunities for these students to interact meaningfully with all students in the class. Similarly, assessment of interests and attitudes often indicates that these are grounded within a particular student's cultural background, and you can use this information to choose particularly appropriate materials for given students.

Finally, home environments will also differ widely with students in any class. These different environments will be more and less supportive of school, of literacy, and of you as a child's teacher. You will need to consider and plan for how different home environments and values will influence your teaching of literacy.

└───┘

would provide many activities aimed at helping students understand that letters and sounds are related. If you believe, instead, that reading takes place as readers sample text to confirm or reject their predictions, then you may stress more meaning-based activities, such as language experience activities or functional writing tasks.

Although few would argue that emergent literacy/readiness programs should teach exclusively either sound-symbol relations or extraction of meaning from print, there is disagreement about the degree of emphasis of either component. Some advocate a focus on sound-symbol relationships and decoding processes (Chall, 1979, 1989; Liberman & Shankwiler, 1980). Others think that decoding is not central to reading and imply that emergent literacy/readiness programs should focus on meaning (Goodman & Goodman, 1979; Smith, 1980; Carbo, 1988). A third argument holds that reading is an interactive process between text and reader and that a reader's initial focus therefore depends on factors such as overall reading ability, the reader's purpose for reading, and the difficulty of the text. (Danks & Fears, 1979; Fredericksen, 1982). Table 6-3 shows some of the instructional consequences of these different beliefs.

TABLE 6-3

Instructional consequences of different beliefs about how children learn to read.

Explanations for how children learn to read	Beliefs	Instructional consequences: How to teach
Holistic Language Learning	Students direct much of their own learning and inductive learning is emphasized. Reading experiences always take place in the context of authentic social contexts and with authentic reading materials.	Common method frameworks include the language experience approach, shared book experience, morning message, journal writing, and think-alouds. Published reading programs and skill sheets are not typically used. Big books, much children's literature and other print material, and children's oral and written language form the basis for most instruction. Informal assessment, with an emphasis on observation and "kidwatching," is typically used to evaluate students' progress.
Integrated	Both student-directed and teacher-directed experiences are used. Both inductive and deductive learning are used. Reading experiences take place in authentic social contexts and with authentic reading materials. Specific skills are taught when needed, often in mini-lessons.	Common method frameworks include the language experience approach, shared book experience, morning message, journal writing, think-alouds and, as needed, inductive and deductive instruction in skills such as left-to-right sequencing, concepts of "same" and "different," letter and sound discrimination, and auditory/visual integration. Evaluation includes both formal as well as informal and observational practices.
Specific Skills	Teacher-directed reading activities and deductive learning are emphasized. Specific skills, often organized in terms of difficulty, are frequently taught.	Common method frameworks include deductive instruction that targets specific skills, such as left-to-right sequencing, concepts of "same" and "different," letter and sound discrimination, and auditory/visual integration, often based on a scope and sequence suggested in a published program. Evaluation is generally formal; when informal it focuses on specific skills.

Comments from the Classroom

Judy Dill, first grade teacher

When my children come to me in the fall their reading levels are divergent. Some children arrive not being able to name more than a few letters of the alphabet. Some children know all of the alphabet letters, the sounds associated with them, and are eager and ready to "begin" reading in first grade. A few children have been exposed to good literature and even have favorite authors; others have not had the opportunity to enjoy many books at all.

Because of this diversity I think the most important strategy I can do is to spend a lot of time reading to the class as a whole, to small groups, and one-on-one as time allows. Listening to the printed word helps them get a "sense of story." When I read out loud I can model for them what I am thinking about the story. I predict what might happen and wonder what certain characters might do. I also ask my students lots of questions about what they are thinking about the story as I read.

When I finish reading a book, I always put it in the reading center where students can read it again. I listen to hear students retelling the story to each other as they remember it. I praise each child for accomplishing whatever success I observe—their decoding of predictable text or the way they interpret the pictures to tell the story in their own words.

One other strategy I used to promote emergent literacy is to place labels or labels and pictures around the room to expose children to environmental print. I label items such as the flag, the door, my desk, the sink, and the learning centers as well as provide pictures and labels for certain well-placed posters, bulletin board items, animal pictures, science collections, math manipulatives, and so on. It is surprising how students learn to read these words and use them in their writing and reading.

Parents play a big role in the emergent literacy picture as well. If they are not already reading to their children I encourage them to do so through letters I send home with suggested readings and through parent meetings. It is during the first parent conference *of the year that I take time to identify what I believe are three developmental reading levels for children, the beginning reader, the developing reader, and the independent reader. I explain how learning to read is a process not unlike learning to walk or talk and that the process takes time. I emphasize that children pass from one level to another at an individual pace. I also emphasize how a parent's praise and encouragement can make a difference in a child's success.*

Major Points

- Beginning readers should be read to often; allowed to use their oral language skills; and provided with many chances to experiment with print.

- Kindergarten programs based on emergent literacy or whole language viewpoints teach traditional readiness aspects in a more integrated manner, using inductive methods and functional reading and writing experiences.

- Traditional readiness programs for beginning readers stress auditory and visual discrimination, emphasize the relationship of sounds and symbols, and build an understanding of reading-related concepts. Deductive methods are most common, as is teaching of specific skills.

- A number of factors interact to affect literacy development: cognitive development, oral language, perceptual factors, affective factors, and home environment.

- Emergent literacy/readiness activities for beginning readers are most effective when they deal specifically with print-related items (for example, letters, letter groups, words, sentences, stories, and concepts such as *page*).

- Informal measures and observational data, in addition to more formal emergent literacy/readiness tests, are used to assess beginning readers' literacy development.

Making Instructional Decisions	1. Make a list of what you think a child entering first grade might already know that would help in learning to read. Tell how the things you have identified relate to reading. How would you capitalize on what the child already knows in your emergent literacy/readiness program?
	2. Differentiate between attitude and interest. How do you think the terms are related? How do they differ? How might aspects of both affect your emergent literacy/readiness instruction?
	3. If possible, visit two kindergarten classrooms to observe what is taking place. Try to visit one "traditional" class and one whole language class. Discuss with each teacher how activities are planned, which seem to be most appropriate for the students, and why. Then write down your impressions of each classroom and how you might modify what you see in each situation to more closely reflect your own beliefs.
	4. Examine a formal and an informal readiness test (these are probably available in your curriculum library). What similarities and differences do you see, both in terms of structure and focus of evaluation? How would you use the information from each in an emergent literacy/readiness program?

Further Readings

Lass, B. (1982). Portrait of my son as an early reader. *The Reading Teacher, 36,* 20–28.

Provides a brief overview of research on characteristics of early readers and provides a timeline of emerging reading behaviors.

McGee, L. M., & Richgels, D. J. (1989). "K is Kristen's": Learning the alphabet from a child's perspective. *The Reading Teacher, 43,* 216–225.

Discusses case studies of children's and parent's dialogues and games that lead to development of children's alphabet knowledge. Provides guidelines for classroom adaptations.

McKenna, M. C., Stahl, S. A., & Reinking, D. (1994). Critical issues: A critical commentary on research, politics, and whole language. *Journal of Reading Behavior, 26,* 211–233.

A synopsis of the style of debate surrounding issues of whole language, and a call for professionalizing the rhetoric in literacy education.

Morrow, L. M., Burks, S. P., & Rand, M. K. (Eds.). (1992). *Resources in early literacy development: An annotated bibliography.* Newark, DE: International Reading Association.

An annotated bibliography that provides reference sources on topics such as the home environment, oral language, writing and drawing, children's literature, developing comprehension, learning about print, play, television, computers, assessment.

Sampson, M. R. (Ed.). (1986). *The pursuit of literacy: Early reading and writing.* Dubuque, IA: Kendall-Hunt.

A short volume containing representative articles from a variety of experts familiar with emergent literacy and whole language. A good introduction for teachers wanting information in this area. Very readable articles.

Slaughter, J. P. (1993). *Beyond storybooks: The shared book experience.* Newark, DE: International Reading Association.

A very readable paperback that describes the shared book experience and is filled with a wealth of ideas for using this experience to address specific reading tasks within meaningful book experiences.

Strickland, D. (1988). Some tips for using big books. *The Reading Teacher, 41,* 966–968.

A chart presenting an overview of what the teacher does, what the child does, and what the objectives are for big book activities.

Strickland, D. S., & Morrow, L. M. (1989). *Emerging literacy: Young children learn to read and write.* Newark, DE: International Reading Association.

A series of short articles on emergent literacy, from theory to classroom implementation.

Vukelich, C. (1984). Parents' role in the reading process: A review of practical suggestions and ways to communicate with parents. *The Reading Teacher, 37,* 472–477.

Points out the most frequent suggestions made to parents and provides suggestions, methods, and activities to involve parents.

References

Aaron, I. E., Chall, J. S., Durkin, D., Goodman, K., & Strickland, D. S. (1990). The past, present, and future of literacy education: Comments from a panel of distinguished educators, Part I. *The Reading Teacher, 43,* 302–311.

Allen, R. V., & Allen, C. (1976). *Language experience activities.* Boston: Houghton Mifflin.

Almy, M., Chittenden, E., & Miller, P. (1966). *Young children's thinking: Studies of some aspects of Piaget's theory.* New York: Teachers College Press.

Anderson, R. C., & Freebody, P. (1985). Vocabulary knowledge. In H. Singer & R. B. Ruddell (Eds.), *Theoretical models and processes of reading* (3rd ed., pp. 343–371). Newark, DE: International Reading Association.

Anderson, R. C., Hiebert, E. H., Scott, J. A., & Wilkinson, I. A. G. (1985). *Becoming a nation of readers: The report of the commission on reading.* Washington, DC: National Institute of Education.

Ashton-Warner, S. (1963). *Teacher.* New York: Simon & Schuster.

Ashton-Warner, S. (1972). *Spearpoint.* New York: Knopf.

Aulls, M. W. (1982). *Developing readers in today's elementary schools.* Boston: Allyn & Bacon.

Barrett, T. C. (1965). Visual discrimination tasks as predictors of first grade reading achievement. *The Reading Teacher, 18,* 276–282.

Bond, G. L., & Dykstra, R. (1967). The cooperative research program in first grade reading instruction. *Reading Research Quarterly, 2,* 5–142.

Bransford, J. D. (1988, August). Personal communication.

Bybee, R. W., & Sund, R. B. (1982). *Piaget for educators.* Columbus, OH: Merrill.

Calfee, R., Chapman, R., & Venezky, R. (1972). How a child needs to think to learn to read. In L. Gregg (Ed.), *Cognition in learning and memory* (pp. 139–182). New York: John Wiley & Sons.

Carbo, M. (1988). Debunking the great phonics myth. *Phi Delta Kappan, 70,* 226–237.

Catterson, J. (1989). Reflections: An interview with Jane Catterson. *Reading-Canada-Lecture, 7,* 40–49.

Chall, J. S. (1979). The great debate: Ten years later, with a modest proposal for reading stages. In L. B. Resnick & P. A. Weaver (Eds.), *Theory and practice of early reading* (Vol. 1, pp. 29–55). Hillsdale, NJ: Lawrence Erlbaum.

Chall, J. S. (1989). Learning to read: The great debate 20 years later—A response to "Debunking the great phonics myth." *Phi Delta Kappan, 70,* 521–538.

Clay, M. M. (1972). *Sand: The concepts about print test.* Exeter, NH: Heinemann Educational Books.

Clay, M. M. (1979). *Stones: The concepts about print test.* Exeter, NH: Heinemann Educational Books.

Clay, M. M. (1980a). *The early detection of reading difficulties: A diagnostic survey* (2nd ed.). New York: Heinemann Educational Books.

Clay, M. M. (1980b). *Reading: The patterning of complex behavior* (2nd ed.). New York: Heinemann Educational Books.

Dale, E. (1965). Vocabulary measurement: Techniques and major findings. *Elementary English, 42,* 895–901, 948.

Danks, J., & Fears, R. (1979). In L. B. Resnick & P. A. Weaver (Eds.), *Theory and practice of early reading* (Vol. 3). Hillsdale, NJ: Erlbaum.

Davey, B. (1983). Think-aloud—Modeling the cognitive processes of reading comprehension. *Journal of Reading, 27,* 44–47.

Davidson, S., Stickney, C. P., & Weil, R. (1980). *Intermediate accounting concepts: Methods and uses.* Hinsdale, IL: Dryden Press.

DeFord, D. E. (1986). Classroom contexts for literacy learning. In T. E. Raphael & R. E. Reynolds (Eds.), *The contexts of school-based learning* (pp. 163–190). New York: Random House.

Downing, J., Dwyer, C. A., Feitelson, D., Jansen, M., Kemppainen, R., Matihaldi, H., Reggi, D. R., Sakamoto, T., Taylor, H., Thakary, D. V., & Thomson, D. (1979). A cross-national survey of cultural expectations and sex-role standards in reading. *Journal of Research in Reading, 2,* 8–23.

Durkin, D. (1966). *Children who read early: Two longitudinal studies.* New York: Columbia University, Teachers College Press.

Durkin, D. (1974-1975). A six-year study of children who learned to read in school at the age of four. *Reading Research Quarterly, 10,* 9–61.

Durkin, D. (1987). *Teaching young children to read* (4th ed.). Boston: Allyn & Bacon.

Durkin, D. (1989). *Teaching them to read* (5th ed.). Boston: Allyn & Bacon.

Fitzgerald, J. (1983). Helping readers gain self-control. *The Reading Teacher, 37,* 249–253.

Fredericksen, J. R. (1982). *A componential theory of reading skills and their interaction* (Tech. Rep. No. 242). Champaign, IL: University of Illinois, Center for the Study of Reading.

Galda, L. (1988) Readers, texts, and contexts: A response-based view of literature in the classroom. *New Advocate, 1,* 92–102.

Getting Ready to Read (teacher's ed.). (1979). Boston: Houghton Mifflin.

Gibson, E. J., & Levin, H. (1980). *The psychology of reading* (3rd ed.). Cambridge, MA: MIT Press.

Goodman, J. R. (1990). *A naturalistic study of the relationship between literacy development and sociodramatic play in five-year-old children.* Unpublished doctoral dissertation, Peabody College of Vanderbilt University, Nashville, TN.

Goodman, K. S., & Goodman, Y. M. (1979). Learning to read is natural. In L. B. Resnick & P. A. Weaver (Eds.), *Theory and practice of early reading* (Vol. 1, pp. 137–154). Hillsdale, NJ: Erlbaum.

Goodman, K. S., Goodman, Y. M., & Hood, W. J. (Eds.). (1989). *The whole language evaluation book.* Portsmouth, NH: Heinemann.

Graves, D. H. (1983). *Writing: Teachers and children at work.* Exeter, NH: Heinemann.

Harris, A. J., & Sipay, E. R. (1990). *How to increase reading ability* (9th ed.). White Plains, NY: Longman.

Harris, T. L., & Hodges, R. E. (Eds.). (1981). *A dictionary of reading and related terms.* Newark, DE: International Reading Association.

Harste, J. C., Woodward, V. A., & Burke, C. L. (1984). *Language stories and literacy lessons.* Portsmouth, NH: Heinemann.

Heathington, B. S. (1976). Scales for measuring attitudes. In J. E. Alexander & R. C. Filler (Eds.), *Attitudes and reading* (pp. 27–32). Newark, DE: International Reading Association.

Hoffman, J. V., McCarthy, S. J., Abbott, J., Christian, C., Corman, L., Curry, C., Dressman, M., Elliott, B., Matherne, D., & Stahle, D. (1994). So what's new in the new basals? A focus on first grade. *Journal of Reading Behavior, 26,* 47–73.

Holdaway, D. (1979). *The foundations of literacy.* Exeter, NH: Heinemann.

Inhelder, B., & Piaget, J. (1964). *The early growth of logic in the child.* New York: Norton.

Kawakami-Arakaki, A. J., Oshiro, M. E., & Farran, D. C. (1989). Research into practice: Integrating reading and writing in a kindergarten curriculum. In J. M. Mason (Ed.), *Reading and writing connections* (pp. 199–218). Needham Heights, MA: Allyn & Bacon.

Liberman, I. Y., & Shankwiler, D. (1980). Speech, the alphabet, and teaching to read. In L. B. Resnick & P. A. Weaver (Eds.), *Theory and practice of early reading* (Vol. 2). Hillsdale, NJ: Erlbaum.

Loban, W. D. (1963). *The language of elementary school children.* Urbana, IL: National Council of Teachers of English.

Luria, A. R. (1976). *Cognitive development: Its cultural and social foundations.* Cambridge, MA: Harvard University Press.

Martin, J. B., Jr. (1967). *Ten Little Caterpillars.* New York: Holt Rinehart & Winston.

Mason, J. M. (1980). When do children learn to read: An exploration of four-year-old children's letter and word reading competencies. *Reading Research Quarterly, 15,* 203–223.

Mason, J. M. (Ed.). (1989). *Reading and writing connections.* Needham Heights, MA: Allyn & Bacon.

McCallum, R. D. (1988). Don't throw out the basal with the bathwater. *The Reading Teacher, 42,* 204–209.

McGee, L. M., & Richgels, D. J. (1990). *Literacy's beginnings: Supporting young readers and writers.* Boston: Allyn & Bacon.

McKenna, M. C., Robinson, R. D., & Miller, J. W. (1993). Whole language and research: The case for caution. In D. J. Leu & C. K. Kinzer (Eds.), *Examining central issues in literacy research, theory, and practice* (pp. 141–152). Chicago, IL: National Reading Conference.

Morphett, M. V., & Washburn, C. (1931). When should children begin to read? *Elementary School Journal, 31,* 496–503.

Nessel, D., & Jones, M. (1981). *The language experience approach to reading.* New York: Teachers College Press.

Olson, A. V., & Johnson, C. (1970). Structure and predictive validity of the Frostig Development Test of Visual Perception in grades one and three. *Journal of Special Education, 4,* 49–52.

Piaget, J. (1963). *The origins of intelligence in children.* New York: Norton (Original edition by International Universities Press, 1952).

Pike, K., Compain, R., & Mumper, J. (1994). *New connections: An integrated approach to literacy.* New York: Harper Collins College Publishers.

Richek, M. A. (1977-1978). Readiness skills that predict initial word learning using two different methods of instruction. *Reading Research Quarterly, 13,* 209–221.

Robeck, M. C., & Wallace, R. R. (1990). *The psychology of reading: An interdisciplinary approach* (2nd ed.). Hillsdale, NJ: Erlbaum.

Rosenblatt, L. M. (1988). *Writing and reading: The transactional theory.* (Tech. Rep. No. 416). Urbana, IL: Center for the Study of Reading.

Rowe, D. W. (1989). Author/audience interaction in the preschool: The role of social interaction in literacy learning. *Journal of Reading Behavior, 21,* 311–350.

Rowe, D. W. (1994). *Preschoolers as authors: Literacy learning in the social world of the classroom.* Cresskill, NJ: Hampton Press.

Rowe, D. W., & Harste, J. C. (1990). Learning how to write. In R. Tierney, S. Greene, & N. Spivey (Eds.), *Writing, learning and knowing: Social-cognitive perspectives.* Unpublished manuscript.

Samuels, S. J. (1972). The effect of letter-name knowledge on learning to read. *American Educational Research Journal, 9,* 65–74.

Shanahan, T. (Ed.). (1990). *Reading and writing together: New perspectives for the classroom.* Norwood, MA: Christopher-Gordon.

Silvaroli, N. J. (1965). Factors in predicting children's success in first grade reading. In J. A. Figure (Ed.), *Reading inquiry international* (Vol. 10, pp. 296–298). Newark, DE: International Reading Association.

Slaughter, J. P. (1993). *Beyond storybooks: The shared book experience.* Newark, DE: International Reading Association.

Smith, C. B. (Moderator). (1994). *Whole language: The debate.* Bloomington, IN: ERIC Clearinghouse on Reading, English and Communication.

Stahl, S. A., & Miller, P. D. (1989). Whole language and language experience approaches for beginning reading: A quantitative research synthesis. *Review of Educational Research, 59,* 87–116.

Stallman, A. C., & Pearson, P. D. (1990). Formal measures of early literacy. In L. M. Morrow & J. K. Smith (Eds.), *Assessment for instruction in early literacy* (pp. 7–44). Englewood Cliffs, NJ: Prentice Hall.

Stauffer, R. (1980). *The language experience approach to the teaching of reading* (2nd ed.). New York: Harper & Row.

Sulzby, E. (1990). Assessment of emergent writing and children's language while writing. In L. M. Morrow & J. K. Smith (Eds.), *Assessment for instruction in early literacy* (pp. 83–109). Englewood Cliffs, NJ: Prentice Hall.

Teale, W. H., & Sulzby, E. (Eds.). (1986). *Emergent literacy: Writing and reading.* Norwood, NJ: Ablex.

Teale, W. H., & Sulzby, E. (1989). Emergent literacy: New perspectives. In D. S. Strickland & L. M. Morrow (Eds.), *Emerging literacy: Young children learn to read and write* (pp. 1–15). Newark, DE: International Reading Association.

Valencia, S. W., Hiebert, E. H., & Afflerbach, P. P. (1994). Definitions and perspectives. In S. W. Valencia, E. H. Hiebert, & P. P. Afflerbach (Eds.), *Authentic reading assessment: Practices and possibilities* (pp. 6–21). Newark, DE: International Reading Association.

Vygotsky, L. S. (1978). *Mind in society.* Cambridge, MA: Harvard University Press.

Vygotsky, L. S. (1986). *Thought and language.* (A. Kozulin, Ed. & Trans.). Cambridge, MA: MIT Press (Originally published 1962).

Waller, G. T. (1977). *Think first, read later! Piagetian prerequisites for reading.* Newark, DE: International Reading Association.

Wells, G. (1986). *The meaning makers: Children learning language and using language to learn.* Portsmouth, NH: Heinemann.

Willinsky, J. (1988). Recalling the moral force of literature in education. *Journal of Educational Thought, 22,* 118–132.

CHAPTER

Decoding and Literacy

7

"I didn't pay much attention to decoding because I didn't think we spent much time on it in our program. It also didn't seem too important during my first placement in the sixth grade where we spent a lot of time on reader response, writing, and comprehension. In my second placement (first grade) I am learning just how important decoding knowledge is for very young children. A lot of our time is spent helping children develop fluency with decoding. And it is very clear that the children who are not doing as well as others in reading and writing are almost always weaker in decoding knowledge. We are using big books, reading predictable texts together, engaging in daily writing experiences, developing language experience stories, and conducting reader workshop sessions to help these children. I worry that if they fall behind now it will be harder for them to catch up later."

A reflective journal entry from a teacher in preparation, teaching in a first grade classroom.

Knowing how to determine the oral equivalent of written words is often helpful during reading. We refer to this component of the reading process as decoding knowledge. As the opening quotation indicates, decoding knowledge is especially important in the younger grades. Being able to determine the oral equivalent of words means that children have discovered the written symbol system we use to represent language. This is an important step on the road to literacy. This chapter discusses three different types of decoding knowledge and describes instructional practices to develop each type.

Chapter 7 includes information that will help you answer questions such as:

1. What is decoding knowledge and how does it contribute to literacy?
2. What instruction is appropriate to develop context knowledge?
3. What instruction is appropriate to develop phonic knowledge?
4. What instruction is appropriate to develop sight word knowledge?
5. How can a literacy framework be used to guide instructional decisions about decoding?

KEY CONCEPTS

cloze tasks	invented spelling
context knowledge	making words
decoding knowledge	phonic knowledge
deficit explanation	sight word knowledge
dialect	sight word learning routine
difference explanation	traditional whole word method
individualized word banks	

WHAT IS DECODING KNOWLEDGE?

decoding knowledge
The knowledge that a reader uses to determine the oral equivalent of a word; includes context knowledge, sight word knowledge, and phonic knowledge.

Decoding knowledge is the knowledge a reader uses to determine the oral equivalent (i.e., pronunciation) of a written word. We use decoding knowledge when we read aloud. We also use it at various other times during reading, such as when we encounter an unfamiliar word and attempt to determine its pronunciation. Decoding knowledge contributes to reading when a printed word is within the listening vocabulary of the reader. Decoding knowledge does not contribute to reading when the meaning of a word is unfamiliar to the reader. All reading programs for young children develop decoding knowledge, including whole language, though each goes about it in a different fashion (Stahl, 1992).

Decoding knowledge is especially important to beginning readers (Adams, 1990; Chall, 1983). Because beginning readers know the meanings of many words they encounter in print, determining the oral equivalent of a printed word gives them a reasonable opportunity to determine its meaning. Consequently, instruction in decoding knowledge receives the greatest attention in the primary grades (kindergarten through third). Helping young readers develop decoding knowledge will enable them to meet with early success as they begin the road to literacy.

Readers use three different types of decoding knowledge to determine the oral equivalent of a written word: context knowledge, phonic knowledge, and sight word knowledge. Decoding instruction helps children develop each of these types of knowledge.

DEVELOPING CONTEXT KNOWLEDGE

Context knowledge refers to a reader's ability to use information from the text in conjunction with background knowledge to assist the reading process. Readers often use context knowledge to determine the oral equivalent and meaning of a word.

context knowledge
One element of decoding knowledge; the reader's ability to use information in the text along with background knowledge to assist the reading process.

For example, notice how you decode the italicized words in the following sentence:

Alexandra will *read* the book after you have *read* it.

Even though the same word appears twice, you decoded it differently. You first decoded the word as /reed/ and later as /red/. In each case you relied on the information from the text in conjunction with your background knowledge to determine the appropriate oral equivalent and meaning. In other words, you used context knowledge. For the first use of the word the information in the text suggests a future tense verb. Your background knowledge told you that the word *read* is pronounced /reed/ in the future tense. For the second use of the word the text suggests a past tense verb. Your background knowledge told you that the word *read* is pronounced /red/ in the past tense. Readers frequently use context knowledge like this to determine the oral equivalent and meaning of words.

Sometimes readers use context knowledge so proficiently that they do not even perceive certain words. Consider this sentence with a missing word.

Sarah, an only child, had always wanted a brother or a
_____.

In this example you could again rely on the information from the text along with your own background knowledge to determine that the missing word is *sister*. The text indicates that the word is something that an only child wants. It is also a noun and must fit with *brother*. Your own background knowledge tells you that the word *sister* fits all these conditions and is therefore a likely candidate. Thus, readers are able to use context knowledge to predict upcoming words when they possess sufficient background knowledge and when text information is sufficiently rich.

Instructional Methods

Even before children learn how to read, they have developed context knowledge from their oral language experiences. Children have learned how to use the information in spoken messages along with background knowledge to help them recognize speech sounds. Thus, helping children use context knowledge during reading builds on a skill they already have. Several instructional practices can help students see the utility of using context knowledge during reading: cloze tasks, inductive instruction, and deductive instruction.

cloze tasks
Used to develop context knowledge; the reader is asked to determine a missing word by using text information and background knowledge.

Cloze tasks present a reader with writing that contains at least one missing word. The reader's task is to use the information in the text along with background knowledge to determine the word that is missing. The following sentence gives just one example.

My mother comes home late at _____.

A cloze task is probably the most common technique used to develop context knowledge. It requires students to rely on contextual knowledge, just as they must when they are unable to recognize a word from its spelling.

Many teachers will use cloze tasks during the reading of a story with children to get them used to predicting upcoming words. With this approach, sometimes called an oral cloze task, all you have to do is to periodically stop reading just before you come to the last word in a sentence and ask children to predict the missing word. This approach is especially useful during the reading of a predictable text, containing repeated sentence patterns. Periodically predicting missing words actively engages children in the reading of the story and gives them greater confidence in their own reading ability.

Other teachers will prepare a lesson with written materials for students. To prepare a lesson with written cloze tasks, teachers can select commercial materials or make their own. For instructional purposes any one of several elements associated with the task can be varied: the length of the passage, the location of the target word, the information available at the target word location, or the nature of the available contextual information.

By varying the length of the cloze passage, teachers can use single sentences to provide instruction in syntactic and vocabulary context. Longer selections may be used to provide instruction in discourse context. Longer passages are easier to complete than single sentences because more information is provided in the text, as illustrated in the following examples from *Curious George* (Rey, 1952).

> He knew how to ride a _____, but he had never had one of his own. (p. 6)

> He took George out to the yard, where a big box was standing. George was very curious. Out of the box came a bicycle. George was delighted; that's what he had always wanted. He knew how to ride a _____, but he had never had one of his own. (p. 6)

A second element that can be varied is the target word location. Putting the target word at the end provides practice in using preceding context to recognize a word; putting it near the beginning helps teach students to read past an unknown word and use the contextual information that appears after it. Notice the different reading strategies that are required in these two examples:

> A _____ is a person who delivers mail.

> A person who delivers mail is a _____.

A third element that can be varied is the information available at target word locations. Traditionally, only a blank space is provided. However, the task can be made easier by providing the first letter or two of the target word. It can be made easier still by placing two or more words underneath the blank and having students choose the correct word. Notice that the task becomes progressively easier in each of the following examples:

> We went to the _____.

> We went to the st_____.

> We went to the _____.
> (run, store)

When only a blank space is provided, students receive practice using context knowledge alone to recognize words. If the first letter or two are provided, students can practice using context knowledge while also

Context knowledge, which allows readers to use what they know together with information in the text, is often used during decoding.

attending to letter-sound information. When several words are available, students must pick the best letter-sound combination to fit the context.

A fourth element that can be varied is the nature of available contextual information. Certain sentence patterns provide useful clues to readers attempting to identify a word: patterns of definition, comparison, contrast, and example. Definition patterns define the meaning of a word within the sentence. Often the meaning is provided in a clause or appositive phrase that follows the troublesome word. However, students must know enough to read beyond the troublesome word to find the clue. The following examples illustrate this pattern:

＿＿＿＿＿＿ is a force that keeps you from floating out into space.

The plane was ＿＿＿＿＿＿, or made late, by the weather.

The ＿＿＿＿＿＿ (a person who flies airplanes) enjoyed his job.

Comparison patterns compare one word or phrase with another. Such patterns feature two locations with important and related information.

Often, students can use the information in one location to identify a troublesome word in the other. Comparison patterns may also require readers to read past a troublesome word.

My ancient car is as _____ as the earth.

I _____ going to bed. In fact, I hate it.

Contrast patterns also feature two locations with important and related information. However, with contrast patterns one word or phrase is contrasted with another. Again, students can use the information in one location to identify a troublesome word in the other.

My sister is _____, unlike my rude brother.

It is _____ during our winters, unlike the warm weather that you enjoy.

Example patterns provide examples after the troublesome word. Students must learn to read past the troublesome word and use the examples to identify it.

We went into several _____ in New York, but the World Trade Towers were the tallest.

There are seven _____: Europe, Asia, North America, South America, Africa, Australia, and Antarctica.

Inductive instruction is often used with written cloze tasks to develop context strategies during a readers' workshop session. As presented in chapter 3, inductive instruction follows four procedural steps. Initially, the teacher provides students with several examples of the skill that is to be learned. Second, the teacher guides students to discover and articulate the skill or rule. Third, students receive guided practice experiences. And fourth, students receive independent practice experiences. Table 7-1 illustrates how inductive instruction can help students learn to read past a troublesome word and search for useful context clues.

Deductive instruction can also be used with cloze tasks to develop context strategies during a readers' workshop session. As presented in chapter 3, deductive instruction contains four procedural steps. First, the teacher states a rule. Second, the teacher shows students several examples of how that rule operates. Third, students receive guided practice. Fourth, students receive independent practice. Table 7-2 shows how deductive instruction can help students learn to identify an unknown word when it appears in an example pattern.

Often the best way to provide instruction on context use is to incorporate this aspect of decoding knowledge into ongoing reading experiences, thus encouraging students to make context use a habit. Several examples of this approach are included in Figure 7-1.

inductive instruction
A method framework containing these four steps: provide examples, help students discover the insight, provide guided practice, provide independent practice.

deductive instruction
A method framework containing these four steps: state the skill or rule, provide examples of the skill or rule, provide guided practice, provide independent practice.

TABLE 7-1

Inductive instruction used to teach students how to use context clues

Procedural step	Activity
Provide examples.	Show students several cloze sentences, taken from their literature selections, in which important contextual information follows the blank. Definition, comparison, contrast or example patterns might be used.
Help students discover the skill.	Ask whether any students can determine the missing words in the cloze tasks. If so, ask them to explain how they solved the tasks. Write their solutions on the board and point out how reading past an unfamiliar word is often a useful strategy.
Provide guided practice.	Have individuals practice the new strategy with several different sentences. Encourage students to share their reasoning aloud as they read past the target word to find the clues.
Provide independent practice.	Give students a practice page containing cloze sentences from literature selections in which the useful information follows the missing words. Divide students into cooperative learning groups to complete the page.

TABLE 7-2

Deductive instruction used to teach students how to use context clues

Procedural step	Activity
State the skill you want students to learn.	Show students several sentences containing example patterns. Tell them that these are example patterns, which require reading past the target word to find useful clues in the examples. Write this strategy on the board.
Provide examples.	Show students several new sentences containing example patterns and target words that are difficult to recognize. Demonstrate how to read past the target words and use the examples as clues. Explain your thinking aloud to students.
Provide guided practice.	Have individuals practice this strategy with several new example patterns. Encourage students to share their reasoning aloud.
Provide independent practice.	Provide students with a practice page containing cloze tasks within example patterns. Have students complete the page in cooperative learning groups.

FIGURE 7-1

Strategies that integrate context use into ongoing reading experiences.

Oral Cloze Tasks. Use oral cloze tasks during read-aloud experiences. While reading children's literature aloud to your class, periodically omit the last word in a sentence. Then ask students to complete the sentence for you. This experience is especially enjoyable with younger readers and predictable texts. Try using any of these selections with first-grade students:

The Very Hungry Caterpillar by Eric Carle
Polar Bear, Polar Bear, What Do You Hear? by Bill Martin
Brown Bear, Brown Bear, What Do You See? by Bill Martin
Chicka Chicka Boom Boom by Bill Martin
The House That Jack Built by Janet Stevens
Too Much Noise by Ann McGovern

Cloze Tasks with New Vocabulary Words. Present each new vocabulary word in a cloze task, and see whether students can guess its meaning from the context.

Pirates often carry a long sharp _____ .
The pirates had to pull up the _____ before the ship could leave.

Encourage students to describe their own successful strategies. You may wish to keep a running list of these strategies posted in your room.

Oral Reading Strategies. Help students use context strategies during oral reading. When children have difficulty recognizing a word, suggest that they read the sentence over from the beginning, looking for clues as to what the troublesome word might be. Then encourage them to make a guess, consistent with their clues and with the initial letter of the troublesome word.

DEVELOPING PHONIC KNOWLEDGE

A second type of decoding knowledge is **phonic knowledge.** Phonic knowledge consists of two elements: (1) knowledge of the relationship between letters and sounds and (2) the ability to put together, or blend, the sounds represented by letters. Letters in English do not always represent a single sound; nevertheless, knowledge of the more regular letter-sound relationships helps us recognize many of the words we encounter. Understanding the basic elements of phonic knowledge is especially important for teachers of beginning readers (Stahl, 1992).

No other topic in reading inspires more controversy and less agreement than that of phonics instruction (Adams, 1990; Chall, 1983). Some have argued against the utility of extensive phonics instruction because English does not contain a perfect one-to-one relationship between letters and sounds (Hittleman, 1988; Smith, 1988). These individuals tend to

phonic knowledge
Knowledge of letter-sound relationships and the ability to blend the sounds represented by letters.

have reader-based beliefs about how a person reads. On the other hand, there is enough regularity in the relationship between English letters and sounds that other individuals support phonics instruction (Adams, 1990; Harris & Sipay, 1990). These individuals tend to have a text-based or interactive belief about how a person reads.

Even the experts who advocate phonics instruction, however, have different ideas about which letter-sound relationships need to be taught. This text describes those relationships that are most consistently included in instructional programs. Consonant generalizations are presented first, followed by vowel generalizations.

Consonants

In English, single consonants contain the most consistent relationship between letters and sounds. As a result, those relationships are usually taught to beginning readers. Figure 7-2 presents the single consonant relationships that are included in most instructional programs. The letters *c* and *g* are unique single consonants; the sound for each is dependent on the vowel that follows. When the letter *c* is followed by the letters *e, i,* or *y* it usually represents the "soft" *c* sound, /s/, as in the words cent, city, or cymbal. When the letter *c* is followed by the letters *a, o,* or *u* it usually represents the "hard" *c* sound, /k/, as in the words cat, coat, or cut.

The same pattern follows for the letter *g*. When the letter *g* is followed by the letters *e, i,* or *y* it usually represents the "soft" *g* sound, /j/, as in the words gem, ginger, or gym. When the letter *g* is followed by the letters *a, o,* or *u* it usually represents the "hard" *g* sound, /g/, as in the words game, go, or gun. The patterns of *g*, however, have a number of exceptions such as finger, get, forget, give, forgive, and girl.

FIGURE 7-2

Letter-sound relationships for the single consonants included in most instructional programs.

b as in *boy*	*c* as in *cent, cat*	*d* as in *did*
f as in *feet*	*g* as in *gem, go*	*h* as in *home*
j as in *job*	*k* as in *king*	*l* as in *like*
m as in *make*	*n* as in *no*	*p* as in *pan*
q as in *queen*	*r* as in *rat*	*s* as in *sat, has*
t as in *time*	*v* as in *very*	*w* as in *we*
x as in *six*	*y* as in *yes*	*z* as in *zoo*

In addition to single consonants, there are **consonant clusters,** which consist of two or three consonant letters that often appear together. Three different types of consonant clusters are consonant digraphs, silent letter combinations, and consonant blends. **Consonant digraphs** are two different consonant letters that together represent a single sound. Some consonant digraphs represent sounds not usually associated with either letter—for example, *ch (child), ng (sing), ph (phone), sh (fish),* and *th (thin).* Other consonant digraphs represent sounds associated with one of the letters—for example, *kn (knit), wr (write), ck (check), gn (sign), mb (comb),* or *gh (ghost).* Because the other letter is silent, these digraphs are often called **silent letter combinations.**

A third type of consonant cluster is called a **consonant blend.** It contains two or more consonant letters, each with a separate sound that is blended together. Consonant blends include combinations such as the following: *bl (blue); br (brick); sc (scare); scr (scream); sk (skip); sm (smile); str (street); thr (three).*

Vowels

Vowels include the letters *a, e, i, o, u,* and sometimes *y* and *w.* Like consonants, vowels are divided into single vowels and vowel clusters. Single vowels include long vowels, short vowels, and *y* when it functions as a vowel. A **long vowel sound** is identical to the vowel names of the five traditional vowel letters—*a, e, i, o,* and *u.* Long vowel sounds occur most frequently in two positions: (1) when a vowel occurs at the end of a syllable, as in me, no, pa-per, ce-dar, and ci-der; and (2) when a vowel is followed by a consonant and the letter *e,* as in mane, theme, time, rope, and cute. The final *e* in this pattern is usually silent.

Each of the five traditional vowel letters also has a **short vowel sound.** These sounds are usually learned with a set of key words, each with a short vowel sound at the beginning:

a as in apple

e as in elephant

i as in ink

o as in octopus

u as in umbrella

Short vowel sounds occur most frequently in syllables that end in a consonant or consonant cluster, such as *hap-py, let, win, ot-ter,* or *fun.*

Y functions as both a consonant and a vowel. It functions as a consonant in words like *yes, yellow,* and *yet.* There are two positions, however, when *y* functions as a vowel: (1) when *y* appears at the end of a word with more than one syllable, it usually represents a long *e* sound, as in *sandy, baby,* or *sixty;* and (2) when *y* appears at the end of a word with only one syllable, it usually represents the long *i* sound, as in *try, my,* or *cry.*

---

consonant clusters
Two or three consonant letters that often appear together.

consonant digraphs
A type of consonant cluster in which two different consonants together represent a single sound.

silent letter combinations
A type of consonant cluster in which two consonants express the sound of only one of the letters.

consonant blend
A type of consonant cluster in which two or more consonants blend together their separate sounds.

long vowel sound
A sound identical to the name of each of the five traditional vowels: *a, e, i, o,* and *u.*

short vowel sound
One of the five vowel sounds found at the beginning of each of these words: *apple, egg, ink, octopus,* and *umbrella.*

-------- **EXPLORING DIVERSE POINTS OF VIEW** --------

Phonics instruction has probably generated more debate over the years than any other area of reading. In 1965, a classic work *Beginning to Read: The Great Debate* by Jeanne Chall concluded that early and systematic decoding instruction, including attention to letter sound relationships, was superior to later and less systematic decoding instruction. The debate continues to this day. Some teachers believe phonics skills are central to early reading success and teach many of them. Other teachers believe phonics skills are not necessary. How do you see the role of phonics in a primary grade classroom? What should be taught? How should it be taught? Why? As you think about these issues consider the nature of your literacy framework, especially your beliefs about how one reads.

vowel clusters
Two or three vowels that often appear together.

vowel digraphs
A type of vowel cluster in which two different vowels together represent a single sound.

diphthongs
A type of vowel cluster in which two or more vowels blend together their separate sounds.

Like consonants, vowels also appear in clusters. **Vowel clusters** consist of two or three vowel letters that often appear together, such as *ou, ee, ai, ew,* and *oy.* Notice that both *w* and *y* can function as vowels when they appear in a vowel cluster. **Vowel digraphs** are two different vowel letters that together represent a single sound—for example, *oo (boot); au (caught); ea (each);* and *oa (boat).* Some vowel digraphs represent sounds not usually associated with either vowel letter: *oo (shoot); ew (new); aw (saw); au (auto).* Other vowel digraphs represent sounds usually associated with one of the letters: *ay (say); ea (beach); ee (see); oa (coat); ai (bait);* or *ei (sleigh).* Vowel blends, or **diphthongs,** are two vowel letters that represent a blending of the sounds often associated with each letter: *oi (soil); oy (toy); ou (mouse);* and *ow (cow).*

Instruction

When considering ways to support the development of phonic knowledge among young children it is important to remember that phonic knowledge is merely a means to an end. Phonic knowledge is only useful when it contributes to either comprehension or response. Phonic instruction should never become an end in itself.

In addition, certain principles of instruction apply, regardless of framework or approach. These include the following:

- *Provide many opportunities for students to apply phonic generalizations in functional reading experiences.* Make sure students have opportunities to read widely and often outside regular instructional materials.

- *Be consistent.* Students benefit from consistency in the selection of instructional terms and in the expression of phonic generalizations.

- *Encourage students to be flexible in their application of phonic strategies.* Students need to know that exceptions exist to every rule. They should also try alternative letter-sound relationships when the application of one generalization fails to yield a familiar word.

- *Spend more time on consonants than on vowels.* Consonants have more consistent letter-sound relationships than vowels do. Consonants also carry more information about words, as can be seen in the examples that follow. The same sentence is shown first with only its vowels and then with only its consonants. Notice which one is easier to decode.

  ```
  _ _ e _ _   _ o _ e   _ i _ e   o _   _ o _ _ o _ a _ _ _ !
  S p _ n d   m _ r _   t _ m _   _ n   c _ n s _ n _ n t s !
  ```

- *Be sure that students can actually use a phonic generalization.* Do not assume that they can use a generalization when they are able to verbalize it. The point of learning any phonic generalization is not to parrot back a verbal rule, but to have a strategy for determining the pronunciation of a difficult word.

Several instructional practices are often used to develop phonic knowledge: inductive instruction, deductive instruction, making words, and invented spelling.

We have encountered the method frameworks known as inductive instruction and deductive instruction earlier in this chapter and in chapter 3. Each is a useful instructional practice for helping students acquire insight about a particular aspect of literacy. The model lessons that follow describe how two teachers helped students acquire an understanding about one aspect of phonic knowledge, each in a different way. Ms. Dodson, because she has more of an integrated belief about how children learn to read, used inductive instruction. Mr. Burns, because he has more of a specific skills belief about how children learn to read, used deductive instruction.

Making words is another method framework, developed by Cunningham and her colleagues (1991), used to support phonic knowledge. This method provides students with a limited number of letters and then guides their manipulation of these letters to make words. The method contains several procedural steps:

making words
A method framework for developing decoding knowledge; provides students with a limited number of letters and then guides their manipulation of these letters to make words.

1. Identify a central word from a recent or future reading experience with literature.
2. Create letter sets for students and yourself using the letters in this central word.
3. Call out a two-letter word from the letter set.
4. Have each student attempt to make that word with their letter set.
5. Have one student make the word with the teacher's letter set so that others can check their work.
6. Repeat for all two-, three-, four-, five-, etc. words in the letter set.
7. Help the students to make words according to meaning and sound patterns.

M O D E L   L E S S O N

Inductive Instruction in Ms. Dodson's Class

Several of Ms. Dodson's second-grade students had been confused about the two sounds of *y* at the ends of words. Consequently, she decided to bring them together for a short lesson to help them develop insight about these letter-sound relationships.

Provide Examples of the Skill or Rule. Ms. Dodson began by writing the following words on the chalkboard for her students to analyze. She read each word aloud as she wrote it.

try	baby
my	rapidly
cry	sticky

Help Students Discover the Skill or Rule. Ms. Dodson asked questions to help students notice the two sounds of *y* at the ends of words. "Which letter is at the end of all these words? That's right! *Y* is at the end, isn't it? Now, which sounds do you hear at the ends of these words? Yes, we hear the sound /ī/ at the end of the word *try* and the sound /ē/ at the end of the word *baby*. Can anyone state a rule that would apply to these words?" Ms. Dodson helped the students state the rule and then wrote it on the board: "When *y* is at the end of a word, it can have two sounds: /ī/ as in *try* or /ē/ as in *baby*." Then Ms. Dodson asked questions to help the students notice where each of those sounds occurred. "What is the same about all these words in the first column, where *y* has the long *i* sound? That's right! They are all short words, aren't they? How many syllables does each word have? Right, only one syllable. Now look at the second column, where *y* has the long *e* sound. What is the same about all of these words? That's right! They all have more than one syllable. Can anyone help us change our rule to include this new information?" Ms. Dodson helped the students state the new rule and then wrote it on the board: "*Y* has the /ī/ sound at the end of a word with one syllable. *Y* has the /ē/ sound at the end of a word with more than one syllable."

Provide Guided Practice. Ms. Dodson then presented a new set of words to see whether students had acquired the rule and to show them how the rule applied to other words: *pry, why, fry, quickly, rainy,* and *sunny.* She asked individuals to read each new word aloud, tell the group which column it should go in, and explain why. Ms. Dodson helped when students had difficulty.

Provide Independent Practice. Ms. Dodson then provided her students with a short cooperative learning group task, using a worksheet she had made and duplicated. She gave each student a copy of the page but explained that it should be completed by the group together and then shared with her. The page she gave them looked like this:

Directions: Put each of the following words into the correct column according to the sound of *y* at the end of each word.

happily	dry	shy	silly	spy
cry	runny	Christy	sly	windy

Words like MY	Words like BABY
_____	_____
_____	_____
_____	_____
_____	_____
_____	_____

MODEL LESSON
Deductive Instruction in Mr. Burn's Class

Next door to Ms. Dodson's room, Mr. Burns also had several second-grade students who were confused about the two sounds of *y* at the ends of words. He also decided to bring them together for a short lesson to help them develop insight about these letter-sound relationships but, having a different belief about how children learn to read, used a deductive method framework to teach this concept.

State the Skill or Rule. Mr. Burns began by stating the phonic generalization: "Sometimes you will find words ending with the letter *y*. *Y* has the /ī/ sound at the end of a word with one syllable. *Y* has the /ē/ sound at the end of a word with more than one syllable. Look at these examples."

Provide Examples of the Skill or Rule. Mr. Burns wrote the following words on the board:

try	baby
my	rapidly
cry	sticky
sky	pretty

He read some of the words aloud and asked students to read others. As they read the words, Mr. Burns pointed out that the one-syllable words ending in *y* had the /ī/ sound, whereas the words with more than one syllable had the /ē/ sound.

Provide Guided Practice. Mr. Burns then presented a new set of words to his students: *pry, why, fry, quickly, rainy,* and *sunny.* He wanted to be sure that his students had acquired the rule, and he also wanted to show them how the rule applied to other words. He asked individual students to read each new word aloud, tell the group which column it should go in, and explain why. Mr. Burns helped when students had difficulty.

Provide Independent Practice. Mr. Burns then gave his students the same cooperative learning group task that Ms. Dodson gave her students (see previous model lesson). Mr. Burns gave each student a copy of the page but explained that it should be completed by the group. He appointed one student to serve as the leader of the discussion and asked that they let him know when they were finished so they could go over the page together.

During the first step, you should identify a word that is central to a previous or future reading experience for students. This word should have five or six letters so that many words can be created from combinations of the individual letters. For example, if students recently read *Anansi the Spider* by Gerald McDermott you might select a word like *spider*.

Next, you create letter sets for each of the students and one for yourself. For students you can quickly make a master with each of the letters in the word and duplicate sufficient copies for students. In the example above, this would include the letters *s, p, i, d, e,* and *r*. Then, you or the students can cut out the individual letters to make one set for each student. The teacher's letter set should consist of larger letters on individual index cards so that all students can see the words you will form with your letter set.

Third, call out a two-letter word that can be created from the letter set. In the example above, this might be the word *is.*

Next, have each student try to create this word from their letter set as one student comes to the front and makes the word using your letter set. After the student has made the correct word at the front, encourage your students to check their own work.

Then, continue with three-, four-, five-, and six-letter words that are possible using this letter set. Three-letter words might include the words *red, rid, dip,* and *sip.* Four-letter words might include *ride, side, rise,* and *drip.* Five-letter words might include *drips* and *pride.* And finally, the six-letter word would include, of course, *spider.*

After all of the words had been created and checked, you can provide students with meaning clues or sound pattern clues and see if they can create the appropriate word. For example, "Make the word that tells us the color of Benito's shirt" (red); or, "Make a word that has the silent *e* at the end" (ride, side, or rise); or, "Make the word that tells us what you do when you drink a hot cup of cocoa" (sip).

Making words is a useful way to get all students involved in thinking about individual letters and their function in representing sounds in our language. It is used in groups containing students with a range of abilities so that more proficient students can help the less proficient ones. It is also a wonderful way to integrate decoding instruction with the use of children's literature.

invented spelling
A method framework containing these procedural steps: encourage students to draw a picture, have students write something about their picture, and have students share their work.

Invented spelling is also another method for developing phonic knowledge among very young literacy learners. You will recall the discussion of invented spelling in chapter 6 where it was defined as a developmental process that characterizes the acquisition of letter-sound and spelling patterns. Invented spelling can also be defined as a method framework. As a method framework, invented spelling usually contains three procedural steps:

1. Encourage students to draw a picture.
2. Have students write something about their picture.
3. Have students share their work.

During the first step in an invented spelling method framework children are encouraged to draw a picture about something they have recently experienced. Sometimes teachers will use invented spelling as a follow-up activity to a shared reading experience with a big book. In this case, students might be encouraged to draw a picture about something that happened in the story. At other times, students may be encouraged to draw a picture about a classroom visitor, an experience at home, or an activity completed in class.

Next, students are encouraged to write something about their picture. Here, the important point is not to worry about correct spelling but, rather, to support children as they attempt to create a written represen-

Encouraging emergent writers to use invented spellings can help young students develop decoding knowledge, especially if you have a holistic or integrated perspective about how children learn to read.

tation of their ideas. As students attempt to spell unfamiliar words they naturally consider relationships between letters and sounds. This is why invented spelling experiences are so useful for developing phonic knowledge in a natural way.

Finally, you will want children to share their work. Here, you can encourage them to read their writing to you, to a friend, to a small group, or to the entire class. When students read their work to you, you may wish to transcribe what they read on the back of their page so that you have a record of what they read. This is useful as you compare early writing at the beginning of the year with students' writing at the end of the year. Figure 7-3 shows one example of how a kindergarten youngster completed an invented spelling activity after one year of completing this activity on a daily basis.

FIGURE 7-3

An example of a kindergarten student's writing completed during an invented spelling activity at the end of the school year. He read his work as "I love Dad and Mom and my Taurus, that was a car, and me and Mom and Dad watch TV."

DEVELOPING SIGHT WORD KNOWLEDGE

sight word knowledge
One aspect of decoding knowledge; the ability to recognize the pronunciation of words automatically, without conscious use of other decoding strategies.

Sight word knowledge refers to the ability to recognize the pronunciation of words automatically, without conscious application of other decoding strategies. It is a third type of decoding knowledge.

Mature readers recognize most words by relying on their extensive sight word knowledge. Beginning readers have far less sight word knowledge, and some readers have none at all. If beginning readers knew that they had to recognize so many different words by sight, they might give up. Memorizing the pronunciation of thousands of separate items would be a tremendous challenge.

Fortunately, however, two considerations reduce the difficulty of developing extensive sight word knowledge. First, a small set of words appears frequently in writing. By knowing how to recognize these 200 to 400 words by sight, readers can immediately recognize 50 to 65 percent of the words in nearly any reading selection (Harris & Sipay, 1990). Second, most of the other words that become part of sight word knowledge are acquired experientially over a period of time. Initially, readers attempt to recognize each new word by using either a context or phonic strategy. However, after a number of such experiences with a particular word, a reader becomes able to recognize it automatically, without using a conscious strategy to determine its pronunciation (Stahl, 1992). Many more sight words are acquired from reading experience and use than from deliberate instruction. With beginning readers, then, it is not our goal to teach automatic recognition of all of the words in our language. The sight word knowledge necessary for beginning readers consists of a limited set of words that share several characteristics.

- *High frequency.* Words taught as initial sight words should appear frequently in print. Thus, words like *is, a, the, to,* and *she* should be taught, but not words like *excavation.*

- *Familiar meanings.* The meanings of initial sight words should be familiar to beginning readers; that is, they should know the words from their oral language. Thus, words like *car, come, good,* and *school* are better candidates than words like *turbine* or *nucleus.*

- *Phonic irregularity.* Words taught as initial sight words often cannot be recognized by applying phonic generalizations. Words like *one, said, where,* and *some* are thus more appropriate for early instruction than words that can be identified by applying common phonic generalizations.

Which specific words, then, should be familiar to beginning readers? Published reading programs usually have their own list of words that students are expected to know as sight words. In addition, there are several different lists of sight words that are based on a wider range of reading material. The list in Figure 7-4 includes words that appear frequently in the oral language of kindergarten and first-grade students and in a variety of published materials.

Instruction

Whenever possible, sight word instruction should take place within meaningful reading experiences. Children are more certain about a word's meaning when it appears in a sentence or phrase. Confusion about meaning can be great among words that look or sound alike, and it is important to establish the habit of using context to identify words. These examples illustrate the potential for confusion.

The book was *red.* The book was *read.*

That play was *close.* That play will not *close.*

....

FIGURE 7-4

Sight words that should be familar to first graders at the end of the school year.

a	day	had	let	off	table	want
above	days	hand	like	old	than	wanted
across	did	hard	little	one	that	was
after	didn't	has	look	open	the	way
again	do	have	love	or	then	we
air	don't	he		out	there	well
all	door	help	make	over	these	went
am	down	her	making		they	what
American		here	man	past	think	when
and	end	high	may	play	this	where
are		him	me	point	those	which
art	feet	home	men	put	three	who
as	find	house	miss		time	why
ask	first	how	money	really	to	will
at	five		more	red	today	with
	for	I	most	right	too	work
back	four	if	mother	room	took	
be		I'm	Mr.	run	top	year
before	gave	in	must		two	years
behind	get	into	my	said		yet
big	girl	is		saw	under	you
black	give	it	name	school	up	your
book	go	its	never	see		
boy	God	it's	new	seen	very	
but	going		night	she		
	gone	just	no	short		
came	good		not	six		
can	got	keep	now	so		
car		kind		some		
children				something		
come				soon		
could				still		

....

Source: From *Teaching Reading Vocabulary*, second edition by Dale D. Johnson and P. David Pearson. Copyright 1984 by CBS College Publishing. Reprinted by permission of Holt, Rinehart and Winston, CBS College Publishing.

sight word learning routine
A method framework for developing sight words by using familiar stories, poems, songs, or chants.

A second reason for teaching sight words in context is to more closely approximate the reading task. Presenting words in isolation sometimes leads children to think that reading is simply a process of recognizing the pronunciations of separate words. Slow, inefficient, word-by-word reading without attention to meaning is often the result.

A very useful way for younger readers to develop sight word knowledge in context is to follow a **sight word learning routine** developed by

Johnson and Louis (1987). This method framework contains seven procedural steps:

1. Help students to learn an engaging story, poem, song, or chant.
2. Help students to prepare a chart or book version.
3. Help students recognize familiar lines of text.
4. Help students recognize familiar words of text.
5. Help students identify familiar lines of text.
6. Help students identify words.
7. Encourage individuals to read portions of the text by themselves.

The first step is for you to help your students learn an engaging story, poem, song, or chant. Often this step is completed by reading a predictable text together that has been published in a **big book.** The predictability of repeated sentence patterns makes learning the story easier for young children. Other material could be used, though, such as a poem, a song, or a chant.

big book
A children's literature selection reproduced in large format often used with younger readers.

Big book activities can be useful for developing important insights about decoding knowledge.

If students did not learn the material in a big book, you will next want to make a chart or big book version of the text. This can be something as simple as writing the text on a large sheet of chart paper. It could also be something as elaborate as helping your class to make its own big book from the story. Here, you will need to write the text on large sheets of construction paper and encourage groups of children to illustrate each page. Then use yarn or metal rings to bind the big book together and display it in a prominent place.

Next, assist students to recognize familiar lines of text. As you read the big book version of your text together, point to the words. As you encounter familiar or repeated lines help your students to recognize them by pointing them out or providing verbal clues. As you have repeated reading experiences with this text over several days continue to point to familiar lines and encourage children to identify them.

After several lines are familiar to students, frame one of the words in the line with your hands and help students to read it. Their familiarity with the line will help them to quickly spot the individual words within that line. Continue with other words in that line and then move on to other familiar lines.

As students engage in rereading experiences help them to identify some of the familiar lines by asking questions such as, "Now where does it say, 'Yellow duck, yellow duck, what do you see?'" Encourage individuals to locate the lines of text you call out.

After each line is located, ask students to identify individual words within that line. Let all of the children have an opportunity to do this, saving the last word in a line for the student who is weakest at recognizing words. This should be the easiest to recognize in most contexts.

Finally, encourage individuals to read the words in entire lines by themselves. By rereading favorite stories this will become a popular activity, one that you will have many volunteers for.

individualized word banks
One means of developing sight word knowledge; uses words written on index cards and filed in index card boxes.

Sight word knowledge can also be developed by using **individualized word banks.** Such banks consist of index card boxes (shoe boxes make an inexpensive substitute) with cards inside. Words that children have not yet learned completely are written on those cards; on one side the words may be written in isolation, and on the other side, in a sentence context. The words can be practiced individually or with a partner. In addition, cooperative learning group activities can be designed using these boxes. When a sufficient number of words are accumulated, the cards can be organized alphabetically, to develop familiarity with alphabetical order in a functional learning experience. Figure 7-5 shows an example of a word bank.

Often individualized word banks are used in student-centered programs in which the students themselves decide which words they need to practice and learn (Ashton-Warner, 1963). In conjunction with writing activities, a teacher might write a new word on a card whenever a stu-

FIGURE 7-5
A word bank for sight words.

dent asks for its spelling. That word card could then go into that student's word bank after it was used in the writing activity.

In some first- or second-grade classrooms initial sight word instruction follows a **traditional whole-word method.** This method framework presents new words to beginning readers as whole units. According to Durkin (1983), whole-word methods follow several procedural steps:

1. Present the new word in sentence context for children to see.
2. Help children read the entire sentence. Have several individuals read the new word.
3. Point to the new word. Have students read, spell, and reread it.
4. Check to be sure the meaning is understood.
5. List words that appear similar. Discuss the similarities and differences.
6. Erase everything but the new word. Have students read, spell, and reread it.

It is important with this approach to be sure that students actually look at each complete word as it is presented. Calling their attention to the spelling of the word helps focus their attention on it. Usually no more than three or four words are presented in a single session, and some type of independent practice or cooperative learning group activity should be provided.

There are many ways to develop sight word knowledge. An aphorism known to most teachers of reading is that "the best way to learn to read is to read." This advice is sound because the more opportunities students have to read real texts, the more they encounter the high-frequency words in our language. It is important, therefore, for them to have many opportunities to read during daily classroom activities. Reading promotes

traditional whole-word method
A method framework used to develop sight word knowledge.

FIGURE 7-6

Teaching strategies that can be used to integrate sight word development in classrooms.

 The Naming Game. Play the naming game with kindergarten or first-grade students. Each day label three new objects in your classroom before your students arrive. At the end of each day see whether anyone has found and can read all three new labels. In the beginning this task will be easy. Quickly, though, as labels begin to cover the room, it will be difficult to find the three new objects. The real benefit of this activity is that students are continually reading the names of objects in the room as they search for the three new labels each day.

 Predictable Texts. Have your beginning readers read many predictable texts with repeated sentence patterns. High-frequency words are repeated in such patterns, and exposure to those high-frequency words in predictable texts has been demonstrated to significantly increase sight word knowledge. Predictable texts that are especially useful for developing sight word knowledge include these:

Drummer Hoff by Barbara Emberly
Brown Bear, Brown Bear, What Do You See? by Bill Martin
The House That Jack Built by Janet Stevens
The Very Busy Spider by Eric Carle
The Three Billy Goats Gruff (several versions)

the development of sight word knowledge, and sight word knowledge, in turn, promotes the development of reading.

Creating a literacy environment in the classroom can do much to develop sight word knowledge. Labeling objects, pictures of objects, and art work provides excellent exposure to the sight words students should know. Teachers might also consider prominently displaying weather charts, calendars, and job charts. In addition, writing activities such as those described in chapter 5 are particularly useful for providing exposure to high-frequency words. The teaching strategies in Figure 7-6 offer further suggestions.

SUPPORTING THE DECODING NEEDS OF LINGUISTICALLY DIVERSE CHILDREN

It is increasingly likely that you will have the opportunity to work in a classroom where several different dialects of English are spoken. This creates many useful opportunities for instruction. It also creates the potential for inappropriate instructional responses to nonstandard dialects, especially during oral reading and decoding instruction. Thus, it becomes important to understand several important principles of language variation.

What is a **dialect?** Dialects are alternative language forms commonly used by regional, social, or cultural groups. Dialects can be understood by speakers of the same language group, but they feature important differ-

dialect
An alternative language form used by a regional, social, or cultural group and understood by speakers of the same major language.

ences in sounds (for example, *this* or *dis*), vocabulary (for example, *soda* or *pop*), and syntax (for example, "He is tired" or "He tired"). Nearly every major language has evolved a number of different dialects. All are equally logical, precise, and rule-governed; no dialect is inherently superior to another. Usually, however, one dialect becomes the standard language form in a society because it is used by the socially, economically, and politically advantaged members of that society.

In the United States the standard language form has sometimes been called Standard American English (SAE). Although it is difficult to define precisely, Standard American English is commonly identified as the form of English spoken by newscasters in most parts of the United States. It is thought to be most similar to the main dialect found in the midwestern states.

There are many nonstandard dialects spoken in the United States. One is common to the southern United States. Another is common to the Appalachian region. And one is commonly found in New England. Speakers of these dialects share certain language conventions, but there remains some degree of variation within each dialect.

One of the more popular dialect variations has traditionally been referred to as Black Standard English by linguists. This dialect variation is spoken among some, not all, African Americans and is also found among some European Americans, Hispanics, as well as Asian Americans. As with other dialects, while the label Black Standard English refers to a set of common linguistic patterns, there is much variability in this dialect. Thus, when we speak of a Black Standard English dialect, we must recognize that speakers of Black Standard English in one region may differ slightly from speakers of Black Standard English in another region. Black Standard English is the dialect considered in the following discussion, but all that is said about it also applies to other dialects.

Dialect Differences

When students who speak a dialect read aloud, they often alter the sounds, words, and syntax of the writing to be consistent with their own dialect. A speaker of Black Standard English, for example, might read the sentence "He is playing" as "He playing." Although it may appear that the child has not decoded the sentence correctly, there is no evidence that this behavior interferes with comprehension (Eller, 1989; Simons, 1979). Indeed, this behavior reflects an attempt to understand the text in the dialect of the reader and should not be discouraged. To do so would force the student to attend to the surface conventions of writing at the expense of comprehension.

At the same time it is important to encourage students to self-correct any decoding mistakes that interfere with comprehension and are unrelated to a dialect (for example, "He painting" instead of "He is playing"). Thus, teachers need to be aware of the dialects of their students and distinguish between oral reading patterns reflecting dialect differences and oral reading patterns reflecting comprehension difficulties.

To become familiar with some of the more common dialect differences between Standard American English and Black Standard English, you should study Table 7-3. Every dialect contains similar differences that are regular and predictable. By listening to your students speak, you should be able to discover those regularities and then let your knowledge of dialect differences guide decisions during oral reading and decoding instruction.

TABLE 7-3

A partial summary of common differences between Standard American English and Black Standard English

Language trait	Standard American English	Black Standard English
Phonological Differences		
Initial		
th (becomes d)	this	dis
th (becomes t)	thin	tin
str (becomes skr)	stream	scream
thr (becomes tr)	three	tree
Final		
sks (becomes ses)	tasks	tasses
sk (becomes ks)	ask	aks
th (becomes f)	teeth	teef
l (has no sound)	tool	too
r (has no sound)	four	foe
General		
Final consonant clusters simplified	best	bess
	walked	walk
	books	book
	talks	talk
i (becomes e before nasals)	pin	pen
Syntactic Differences		
Omission of to be verbs	He is playing.	He playing.
Use of be for extended time	He is always here.	He be here.
Use of third-person singular verbs	There were two girls.	There was two girls.
Change in irregular verb forms	She rode her bike.	She rided her bike.
Omission of indefinite article	Give him a book.	Give him book.
Use of more for comparatives	He is bigger than you.	He is more bigger than you.
Use of double negatives	I don't want any.	I don't want none.

Instruction

Because reading is a language process and because some speakers of dialects may attain lower reading levels, it may seem reasonable to assume that nonstandard dialects interfere with reading comprehension. That assumption, which was common before 1970, is referred to as a **deficit explanation** (Eller, 1989). According to that line of thinking, nonstandard dialects are not only different from the standard dialect, but are also illogical, imprecise, and unsystematic. In an attempt to overcome the perceived deficit that nonstandard speakers faced in their use of dialect, several instructional practices were recommended.

deficit explanation
A view of nonstandard dialects as less logical, less precise, and less rule-governed when compared to standard dialects.

Teach the students with reading materials that match their dialect.

Use dialect-neutral stories, that is, reading materials that do not conflict with the nonstandard dialect.

Teach the students to speak Standard American English before teaching them to read.

None of these approaches were particularly effective in increasing the students' reading ability (Simons, 1979). In addition, because each proposal assumed that the children had deficits, they were being told implicitly that their language was inferior. The result was a negative impact on self-image and motivation.

Research during the 1970s led most educators to accept a **difference explanation** of dialect differences. In other words, nonstandard dialects are now recognized as different but equally logical, precise, and rule-governed. Moreover, we recognize that speakers of nonstandard dialects can understand Standard American English very well, even if they do not speak it. Dialect differences, by themselves, are not the cause of reading failure.

difference explanation
A view of nonstandard dialects as being different from the standard dialect but equally logical, precise, and rule-governed.

Today, five instructional practices are usually encouraged in classrooms with nonstandard dialect speakers.

1. Language experience approaches are used in the beginning stages of reading to help children see the close connection between their language and printed words.

2. Culturally relevant materials are used to provide a supportive environment for reading and to increase interest and motivation. Such materials also ensure that students' background knowledge is consistent with the background knowledge required to comprehend a text. In addition, they provide multicultural reading experiences for all of the students in a class. Literature selections portraying different cultural and ethnic groups are described in chapter 4.

3. Children's background knowledge is carefully considered in relation to the texts they read (Maria, 1989). During vocabulary instruction, students' understanding of key concepts is probed to

M O D E L   L E S S O N

Responding to Dialect Errors During Oral Reading in Mr. Stanton's Class

Mr. Stanton is reading and discussing a story with a small group of his sixth-grade students. Darleen, who speaks a variation of Black Standard English, reads the following sentences:

Text: They won't ask for the two books. They are afraid.
Darleen: Dey woan aks for duh two book. Dey [pause] after?

As Darleen reads, Mr. Stanton must quickly decide how to respond. He does not want to correct a word that simply reflects a pattern in Darleen's dialect and does not interfere with comprehension. On the other hand, if a word changes the meaning of the story, Mr. Stanton needs to point that out to her.

Mr. Stanton ignores Darleen each time she reads *they* as *Dey*. Darleen's dialect uses /d/ to represent the /th/ sound in Standard American English. He also ignores Darleen's reading of *the* as *duh* and *ask* as *aks*. None of these deviations interfere with comprehension, and each reflects the pronunciation patterns of Darleen's dialect.

Mr. Stanton also ignores the reading of *won't* as *woan* because Darleen's dialect simplifies final consonant clusters such as /nt/. The same basic principle applies to her reading of *books* as *book*; the final consonant cluster /ks/ was simplified to /k/. Mr. Stanton is confident that this change did not alter Darleen's comprehension because she correctly read the word *two* just before she read *book*. Mr. Stanton also ignores Darleen's omission of the word *are*: *to be* verbs are sometimes dropped in her dialect.

However, Mr. Stanton is concerned about the last word. Darleen reads *afraid* as *after*, and the question intonation gives Mr. Stanton a clue that Darleen is uncertain of that word. He also notices that this error is not based on a pronunciation rule in her dialect. And most importantly, this error changes the meaning of the sentence. Consequently, he asks Darleen to look at the ending sound of the word, especially the last four letters. When she notices the word *raid*, he asks her to read the sentence again. Darleen reads the final sentence correctly in her dialect: "Dey afraid."

determine what they need to know about key terms. Instruction then helps students understand word meanings with which they are unfamiliar (appropriate techniques are described in chapter 8). Semantic mapping activities are especially useful, also.

4. Cooperative learning group activities are frequently used, again to provide a supportive environment in which students can accomplish tasks that they might be unable to complete alone (techniques are described in chapter 3). Discussion and debate often serve to clarify understanding.

5. During oral reading, teachers ignore reading errors when they do not alter the underlying meaning of a text but merely reflect a student's dialect.

This last point is an especially important one when it comes to oral reading experiences with children who speak a variety of Black Standard English. Often teachers will attempt to correct the oral reading of past tense verbs where two consonant sounds appear at the end of the word such as skipped, picked, hopped, or turned. A very common rule within Black Standard English is sometimes referred to as "consonant simplification." This rule requires speakers of this dialect to simplify multiple consonant sounds at the ends of words to a single consonant sound. Thus, words like "skipped" /SKIPT/ are pronounced as "skip" /SKIP/. Similarly, "picked" becomes "pick," "hopped" becomes "hop," and "turned" becomes "turn." Children who pronounce words like this during oral reading understand the correct tense of the word and the correct meaning of the sentence; they are simply following the phonological rules of their dialect. These oral reading behaviors should not be corrected. To correct them during oral reading interferes with the comprehension process. And, if you do try to correct them, children will follow the logical rules of their dialect and begin pronouncing words like "skipped" /SKIPT/ as "skip-ed" /SKIP-ED/. This will happen because their dialect simply does not permit two consonant sounds to appear at the end of a word without putting a vowel sound between them.

Does all of this mean that teachers should never try to develop oral competency in the standard dialect? On the contrary, teachers should provide learning experiences that promote such competency because the standard dialect provides access to power and influence in any society. However, the appropriate time for such efforts is not when students are demonstrating competence in decoding and comprehension during oral reading. Activities such as those described in Figure 7-7 can be used to direct students' attention to the conventions of the standard dialect.

FIGURE 7-7

Teaching strategies that can be used to support dialect speakers.

 Writing Conferences. Use writing conferences, as suggested in chapter 5, to direct students' attention to the conventions of the standard dialect. Because writing makes language permanent and concrete, it is easier to discuss differences between standard and nonstandard dialects during writing experiences.

 Read-aloud Sessions. Incorporate culturally appropriate materials into read-aloud sessions. Use these to generate discussions of dialect differences. You might want to write down examples of how each dialect communicates the same message.

 Two-sided Stories. Have students write stories in dialect, putting a few sentences and an illustration on one side of each page. Then help them rewrite the story in standard dialect on the reverse side of each page. This activity could also be carried out as a language experience story, for which you write down sentences as the students dictate them.

USING A LITERACY FRAMEWORK TO INFORM INSTRUCTIONAL DECISIONS ABOUT DECODING

You will face two basic decisions as you consider decoding instruction. First, you will need to decide what to teach about decoding knowledge. In addition, you will also need to decide how to teach decoding knowledge to your students. Your literacy framework will guide you in both these decisions.

What to Teach and Emphasize

To guide decisions regarding what to teach about decoding, you should consider the portion of your literacy framework that identifies your beliefs about how one reads. Table 7-4 summarizes how these beliefs can be used to guide instructional decisions.

TABLE 7-4

A summary of how a literacy framework can be used to inform decisions about what to teach in decoding.

Beliefs about how one reads	Related assumptions	Probable time spent on decoding instruction	What is taught?
Reader-based	Meaning exists more in what the reader brings to the text. Reading is a result of expectations. Reading begins with elements of prior knowledge.	Little	Context knowledge
Interactive	Meaning exists in both the text and the reader. Reading is both translation and expectation. Reading uses each knowledge source simultaneously.	Average	Context knowledge Sight word knowledge Phonic knowledge
Text-based	Meaning exists more in the text. Reading is translation. Reading begins with decoding.	Much	Phonic knowledge Sight word knowledge

If you follow a reader-based explanation of how a person reads, you believe that reading consists largely of expectations for upcoming words. Thus, you believe that extensive prior knowledge leads to successful reading because readers are able to accurately predict upcoming words. As a result, you will probably spend little time on the development of decoding knowledge. The limited time that you do spend will be devoted to developing context knowledge, and you will encourage children to use contextual analysis strategies to decode words. Context knowledge, of course, helps students develop more accurate expectations for upcoming words.

If you follow a text-based explanation of how a person reads, you believe that reading consists largely of translating words into sounds, for which task readers use decoding knowledge before any other knowledge sources. As a result, you will probably decide to spend much time on the development of decoding knowledge, especially with beginning readers. And you will probably emphasize phonic and sight word instruction, rather than the development of context knowledge. Instruction in both phonic and sight word knowledge facilitates the translation of printed words into sounds.

If you follow an interactive explanation of how a person reads, you believe that reading consists of both expectations for upcoming words and the translation of words into sounds. Thus, you believe that extensive prior knowledge and strong decoding skills both contribute to successful reading. As a result, you will probably spend an average amount of time on decoding instruction, about as much as you will spend developing the other knowledge sources associated with comprehension and response: vocabulary, syntactic, discourse, and metacognitive knowledge. In addition, you will probably teach all three aspects of decoding knowledge—context, phonics, and sight words—with a balanced emphasis.

How to Develop Decoding Knowledge

To guide your decisions about how to teach decoding knowledge, you should consider the portion of your literacy framework that identifies your beliefs about how children learn to read. Table 7-5 summarizes how these beliefs can be used to guide instructional decisions about which method frameworks to use.

If you follow a holistic language learning explanation of development, you favor learning experiences that are inductive in nature. As a result, you will probably use inductive methods to teach context or phonic knowledge and will integrate sight word development into daily classroom activities, perhaps by using individualized word banks and letting your students determine the words to enter into the banks. You will also favor the use of invented spelling to develop phonic knowledge. You may also provide functional literacy activities to encourage your students to read widely and interact with print, again to develop extensive sight word knowledge.

TABLE 7-5

A summary of how a literacy framework can be used to inform decisions about how to teach decoding knowledge

Beliefs about how children learn to read	Related assumptions	Favored method frameworks and instructional activities
Holistic Language Learning	Students learn best in an inductive fashion as they direct their own learning and reading experiences. Students learn best during holistic, meaningful, and functional experiences with authentic literature.	Inductive instruction to develop context and phonic knowledge. Invented spelling to develop phonic knowledge. Individualized word banks to develop sight word knowledge
Integrated	Students learn best as a result of both student-directed, inductive experiences and teacher-directed, deductive experiences. Students learn best when they engage in purposeful, functional, and holistic experiences with authentic texts and when they acquire specific reading skills.	Both inductive and deductive instruction to teach context and phonic knowledge Invented spelling and making words used to develop phonic knowledge Sight word learning routine, individualized word banks, and traditional whole-word method to develop sight word knowledge
Specific Skills	Students learn best when they are taught directly by the teacher in a deductive fashion. Students learn best when they master specific reading skills.	Deductive instruction to teach context and phonic knowledge Traditional whole-word method to teach sight word knowledge

If a specific skills explanation of development is your orientation, you favor learning experiences that are deductive in nature and that focus on specific skills. As a result, you will probably use deductive methods to teach context and phonic knowledge and a traditional whole-word method to develop sight word knowledge. In general, you will organize your direct instruction around a set of specific decoding skills.

When an integrated explanation of development is your preference, you will use both deductive and inductive methods to develop context or phonic knowledge. You will also find invented spelling and making words useful to develop phonic knowledge. To develop sight word knowledge, you will probably use some combination of individualized word banks, making words, a sight word learning routine, and a traditional whole-word method.

Comments from the Classroom

Judy Dill, first grade teacher

Because reading and writing are so closely connected, I have often had students learn certain decoding strategies from their emergent writings and inventive spellings.

Two years ago I was having a difficult time getting one child to do any independent reading. But he did love writing in his journal. He actually used inventive spellings quite effectively and was able to decode what he had written to me and to his mom. As the year progressed and he felt even more successful at decoding what he had written, he gained enough confidence to try reading on his own. He really liked several of the Eric Carle books that had predictable storylines.

Another exciting experience I had in using an effective decoding strategy was while working with an older child during a summer reading clinic. Previous teachers had worked with Sam using short paragraphs to avoid overwhelming her with text. But I decided that Sam needed longer amounts of copy to get a better sense of what she was reading. I encouraged her to read whole sentences before she tried to decode a word she stumbled upon. She had a habit of skipping words altogether that she could not easily figure out. I let her get away with it for a little while, trying to get a sense of what she could really do. What I discovered is she often figured out some of the words she had previously skipped, not even hesitating over them the second time. I am sure this was because she was now reading enough text to infer from the context what the story was about. I discussed with her what was happening. She became much less tentative about decoding words and was more confident to read more frequently.

- Decoding is the process that readers use to determine the oral equivalent of written words. Decoding knowledge includes context knowledge, phonic knowledge, and sight word knowledge. Decoding contributes to the reading process when a word's pronunciation helps a reader determine its meaning. Decoding knowledge is especially important for beginning readers.

Major Points

- Several instructional practices can be used to develop context knowledge: cloze tasks, inductive instruction, and deductive instruction.

- Several instructional approaches are used to develop phonic knowledge: inductive instruction, deductive instruction, making words, and invented spelling.

- Sight word knowledge can be developed by using a sight word learning routine, individualized word banks, or employing a traditional whole-word method framework.

- It is important to consider issues of language diversity as you plan decoding instruction.

- A literacy framework can be used to guide decisions about the content and manner of decoding instruction. An explanation of how one reads can help determine what to teach. An explanation of how children develop reading ability can help determine how to teach.

Making Instructional Decisions

1. Consider the following list of decoding skills that are taught in one particular reading program. Identify the type of decoding knowledge represented by each listed skill: context knowledge, phonic knowledge, or sight word knowledge.
   a. Recognizes mastery words in isolation and in context.
   b. Decodes the appropriate sound for *f.*
   c. Uses picture context.
   d. Uses meaning and syntax to recognize words.
   e. Knows that one sound is represented by different letters.
   f. Recognizes these common words: *the, a, one, he, she, here, we, run,* and *goes.*

2. Develop a lesson to teach some aspect of context use, such as reading past a troublesome word. Use an inductive method framework. Then develop another lesson using a deductive method framework to teach that same aspect.

3. Define your own literacy framework. Then specify the range of phonic skills you will include in your instructional program. Will you teach letter-sound relationships for consonants? Which ones? Will you teach letter-sound relationships for vowels? Which ones? Explain how your literacy framework determines the phonic instruction you will include.

4. Specify how you will develop sight word knowledge in your instructional program. Which methods and activities will you use? Explain how your literacy framework has guided your decision making.

5. Describe the literacy framework of a second-grade teacher who makes these decisions about decoding instruction:
   a. Decoding will receive far less attention than the development of vocabulary, syntactic, discourse, or metacognitive knowledge.
   b. Context knowledge will receive greater emphasis than the development of phonic or sight word knowledge.
   c. Inductive methods will be used to develop context knowledge.
   d. Sight word knowledge will be developed through writing experiences and the use of individualized word banks.

   Explain how this teacher's literacy framework has guided these instructional decisions.

Further Reading

Cunningham, P. M., Hall, D. P., & Defee, M. (1991). Non-ability grouped, multilevel instruction: A year in a first-grade classroom. *The Reading Teacher, 44,* 566–571.

Describes an instructional program for first grade that incorporates writing activities, basal reader instruction, children's literature, and decoding instruction and explains why children seemed to make much progress in this type of learning environment.

Dowhower, S. L. (1989). Repeated reading: Research into practice. *The Reading Teacher, 42,* 502–507.

Describes a useful technique for developing fluency in decoding processes. Summarizes research showing how repeated reading contributes to both automatic decoding and improvements in comprehension.

Jacobson, J. M. (1990). Group vs. individual completion of a cloze passage. *Journal of Reading, 33,* 244–250.

Describes a study in which students completed cloze tasks individually and in cooperative learning groups. Results favored the use of cooperative learning groups for completing cloze passages.

Stahl, S. A. (1992). Saying the "p" word: Nine guidelines for exemplary phonics instruction. *The Reading Teacher, 45,* 618–625.

Discusses the principles that should guide phonics instruction in the primary grades. Illustrates each principal with an episode from classroom practice.

References

Adams, M. J. (1990). *Beginning to read: Thinking and learning about print.* Champaign, IL: Center for the Study of Reading.

Ashton-Warner, S. (1963). *Teacher.* New York: Simon & Schuster.

Burmeister, L. E. (1983). *Foundations and strategies for teaching children to read.* Reading, MA: Addison-Wesley.

Chall, J. S. (1983). *Stages of reading development.* New York: McGraw-Hill.

Cleary, B. (1968). *Ramona the pest.* New York: Scholastic Book Services.

Clymer, T. (1963). The utility of phonic generalizations in the primary grades. *The Reading Teacher, 16,* 252–258.

Cunningham, P. M., Hall, D. P., & Defee, M. (1991). Non-ability grouped, multilevel instruction: A year in a first-grade classroom. *The Reading Teacher, 44,* 566–571.

Dolch, E. W. (1960). *Teaching primary grade reading.* Champaign, IL: Garrard Press.

Durkin, D. (1983). *Teaching them to read* (4th ed.). Boston: Allyn & Bacon.

Fry, E. (1980). The new instant word list. *The Reading Teacher, 34,* 284–289.

Harris, A. J., & Sipay, E. R. (1990). *How to increase reading ability* (9th ed.). New York: Longman.

Hittleman, D. R. (1988). *Developmental reading* (3rd ed.). Columbus, OH: Merrill.

Johnson, T., & Louis, D. (1987). *Literacy through literature.* Portsmouth, NH: Heinemann.

Lesiak, J. (1984). There is a need for word attack generalizations. In A. J. Harris & E. R. Sipay (Eds.), *Readings on reading instruction* (3rd ed.). New York: Longman.

Leu, Donald J., Jr., DeGroff, Linda-Jo C., & Simons, Herbert D. (1986). Predictable texts and interactive compensatory hypotheses: Evaluating differences in reading ability, context use, and comprehension. *Journal of Educational Psychology, 78,* 347–52.

Resnick, L. B., & Beck, I. L. (1984). Designing instruction in reading: Initial reading. In A. J. Harris & E. R. Sipay (Eds.), *Readings on reading instruction* (3rd ed.). New York: Longman.

Rey, H. A. (1952). *Curious George rides a bike.* Boston: Houghton Mifflin.

Samuels, S. J., & Eisenberg, P. (1981). A framework for understanding the reading process. In F. J. Pirozzolo & M. C. Wittrock (Eds.), *Neuropsychological and cognitive processes in reading.* New York: Academic Press.

Smith, F. (1988). *Understanding reading* (4th ed.). Hillsdale, NJ: Erlbaum.

Stahl, S. A. (1992). Saying the "p" word: Nine guidelines for exemplary phonics instruction. *The Reading Teacher, 45,* 618–625.

CHAPTER

Vocabulary and Literacy

I always tell my student teachers to listen carefully to children's speech. The words they use say a lot about how they feel, where they come from, and what they think. I once heard on a radio commercial: "We think about people based on the words they use." I also remember reading that vocabulary knowledge is highly related to success in reading. Of course, that makes sense, because knowing what the words mean helps understand what's being read. And I like playing with language and learning new words myself. My student teachers are usually fascinated with the wide variety of language and vocabulary used by my students. And teaching vocabulary, which is really concept development, always seems to end up among their favorite lessons.

A teacher reflecting on the diversity of language found in her classroom.

Vocabulary knowledge is one of the most important factors in reading comprehension and response. Not knowing the concept represented by a particular word makes it difficult, if not impossible, to understand the author's intended meaning. This chapter examines the importance of vocabulary in reading comprehension and response. It also looks at the complexity of meaning acquisition and a variety of effective instructional strategies.

Chapter 8 includes information that will help you answer questions such as:

1. What is the role of concept development in teaching and learning new vocabulary?
2. How are pronunciation and meaning determined in reading?
3. How does vocabulary teaching differ across primary and intermediate grades?
4. What are effective techniques to teach new meanings for already-known words?

KEY CONCEPTS

content-specific vocabulary	instantiation
content vocabulary	learning center
environmental print	morphemes
feature analysis	multiple response card
function vocabulary	schema
homonyms/homophones/homographs	semantic map/web

THE MEANINGS OF WORDS

Good speakers and readers of English almost unconsciously select the appropriate meanings of words from a large number of possibilities. Even the simplest words often have more than one meaning, and many shades or gradations of meaning. Look at these examples:

Copper is a good *conductor* of electricity.
Give your ticket to the *conductor*.
The orchestra *conductor* was quite young.

She wanted to *staple* the three pages together.
Corn was a *staple* in some Native Americans' diet.

The *frog* jumped into the pool.
He started coughing because he had a *frog* in his throat.

The sunset was fiery *red*.
She has *red* hair.
The fire engine was bright *red*.

The first three sets of examples show that words can have more than one meaning; the last set demonstrates that a word can have multiple shades of meaning, too. Did you not visualize a different color in each of the last three sentences? Almost all words in our language have multiple meanings, yet we use most of them appropriately from a very young age. In fact, we are usually not even aware of our own skill in distinguishing among the possible variations. Think of the common word *up*.

Look *up* at the moon.
Look *up* the word in the dictionary.
Lock *up* the car.
The drain is stopped *up*.
Sam said he's tied *up* and can't come.

In order to help students develop and expand their vocabularies, teachers must understand how words and their meanings are learned. In addition, they must understand how concepts are stored in memory and how they are accessed for use in appropriate situations.

The Relationship of Words and Concepts

Chapter 1 noted that words themselves have no meanings—words are simply labels for concepts. When we read, we attempt to match a printed label to a concept in memory. The word-label can be thought of as a trigger to access the concept. Thus, a concept must be present before a word for that concept should be taught.

This line of reasoning raises several questions. Can we know something without a language label? For example, can we have a concept for a *chair* and can we access it without using a language label? Is it possible to have an internalized concept in memory without thinking of it in language-related terms? Such questions are important and have led to perspectives that advocate teaching word-labels and concepts together, as opposed to learning the concept first and later attaching a label to it.

Have you ever had the experience of trying to say something and not being able to, even though you knew clearly what you were trying to say? Often we say that something is on the tip of our tongue even though we are unable to verbalize it at that moment. This **tip of-the-tongue phenomenon** supports the belief that we do have internalized representations of concepts that can be accessed, or triggered, by language (Brown & McNeill, 1966). Thus, the implication is that we can and do know things without a labeling term's being accessible at all times.

tip-of-the-tongue phenomenon
Having a concept and a word in memory, but being unable to access that knowledge at that time.

Primary and Intermediate Grade Level Concerns. Vocabulary knowledge changes throughout our lives, with new concepts being learned and others being increasingly refined. Teachers need to be sure that the concept for a new word is known when they attempt to link the word and its concept. In the primary grades students usually have a concept in their speaking vocabulary before they are taught its printed form.

Because beginning readers have not yet learned to use decoding strategies, they are still attempting to understand what the "squiggles" on the page represent, and oral vocabulary can be a bridge between written words and concepts. For this reason, vocabulary in traditional published reading programs was controlled to focus on the speaking vocabulary of young children, although recently published programs tend not to focus on controlling the vocabulary found in reading selections (Hoffman et al., 1994). Thus, vocabulary lessons in the primary grades generally teach the written forms of known concepts. Teachers need to be sure that those words are actually in the children's speaking vocabulary before introducing them in print, but it's not usually necessary to teach the underlying concepts. Although some would argue that such lessons are an exercise in word recognition (as teaching concepts isn't the stated goal), most teachers and published reading programs call them "vocabulary lessons," especially if decoding or word analysis strategies are not included in the instruction.

In later grades children are relatively competent decoders and are confronted with new concepts as well as new word-labels for those concepts, especially in subject areas such as social studies, mathematics, and science. In the intermediate grades and beyond, therefore, teachers must more often teach the new concept in addition to forging the link between the written word and its concept. Figure 8-1 illustrates the difference

FIGURE 8-1

A representation of the basic difference in vocabulary instruction in primary (concept known) and intermediate (concept unknown) grades

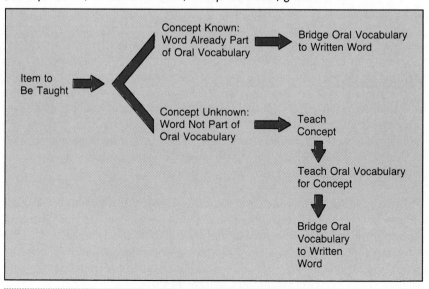

between vocabulary lessons in primary and higher grades. For clarity the figure represents concepts as being either known or unknown, even though in reality students may have a partial idea about what something means. It is really the degree to which something is known that determines whether the concept needs to be taught.

Factors in the Communication of Meaning

What is it that allows people within a culture to communicate with each other? It is the commonality of shared experiences within a culture or a social group that allows communication to take place (Carroll, 1964a, 1964b). In other words, individuals communicate by referring to their overlapping, common experiences. When society, or a group, accepts a word-label to refer to a particular experience or concept, everyone familiar with that word is then able to access that concept. However, if society has not agreed on a word-label, then communication about that concept is difficult or impossible. In addition, if the continuing experiences of different groups cause an underlying concept to be differently perceived, then

When reading, students encounter function words, content words, and content-specific words.

OPPORTUNITIES TO CELEBRATE DIVERSITY

Cultural and social groups have common vocabularies and communication occurs without difficulty between members of a given group. Communication across these groups might be difficult, however, partly because of differences in word-labels for common concepts. In your class, such groups may include students who speak a language other than English, or who live in close communities that have developed their own word-labels. For example, African-American or Hispanic students may have different labels for the same concepts, and these labels might differ from those used by other students, or the teacher.

In general, students are fascinated with how others speak. Use the children's language as a way to broaden students' understanding and vocabulary knowledge. The vocabulary differences between the students in your class will prove a rich place to start. Ask students to provide different word-labels for pictures of items and post these around your classroom. After completing language experience stories, allow students to restate the story in their own, unique words and post both. Have a child or a group of children perform a brief skit, using their "everyday" language, and allow other students to interpret what certain words mean. Allow the performing group to explain the vocabulary. Have fun using these and other activities to celebrate differences while drawing the classroom community closer together!

even a shared word-label may cause confusion! Listen to children talk to each other on the playground, your school's hallway and in class—even in school, children develop their own shared labels, or jargon, which is often difficult for teachers to understand.

Thus, when communication fails, any of several factors may be responsible. For example, someone from France and someone from the United States attempting to communicate about a furry domestic animal that meows may not understand each other for one or more of these reasons:

- There may be no shared experience with such an animal.
- The two societies or cultures may have evolved a different word-label for such an animal.
- The same word-label may represent different concepts in the different societies.

In this case the second reason is the most likely explanation, for we know that people in France also keep cats as pets, and people in the two countries do speak different languages. In France such a creature is called *le chat*. Thus, because the two individuals do not share the same word-label for the same concept, communication is difficult if not impossible.

In your classroom, you may find students who have difficulty with vocabulary for any of these three reasons: they may not have the relevant concept as part of their knowledge base; they may have a different label for the targeted concept; or they may have a somewhat different meaning for the label. Effective teachers must be aware of the diversity in their students' backgrounds and must ensure that vocabulary lessons are related to students' prior knowledge and shared experiences.

··

BUILDING CONCEPTS
The Importance of Examples

Examples, which can take many forms, allow students to experience and clarify meaning and integrate it into existing knowledge (Duffelmeyer, 1985). Concrete examples should be used whenever possible and appropriate, providing the opportunity for students to see, touch, smell, and otherwise experience concrete examples during concept development. For abstract concepts, such as truth or beauty, concrete examples are difficult to provide. In such cases teachers often let character actions from literature serve as examples. A discussion about how a character felt or acted in certain situations, or about how other characters felt about the main character, can clarify concepts such as heroism or other abstract notions that do not lend themselves to concrete examples.

Experience. Experience is the most concrete way of teaching a new concept. Often, teachers take their classes on field trips and point out things that will form the basis of a vocabulary lesson when the class returns to school. A field trip need not be an expensive outing; it can be a walk around the block. Direct experience can also be provided by bringing an object into the classroom. It is critical, however, to focus the students' attention. They must actively perceive the object, not simply look at it. As appropriate, the students should have opportunities to touch, see, smell, and otherwise experience the object, and they should be helped to identify features that link the new concept to a familiar one.

Facsimile. Often, it is not possible to provide hands-on experience when developing a new concept. In such cases providing a facsimile can be nearly as effective. Common facsimiles are drawings, photographs, filmstrips, videotapes, audiotapes and computer simulations related to the object or concept under discussion. Teachers must remember, however, to build the concept actively and not to allow students to be passive observers.

Discussion. Although less concrete than experience or a facsimile, a purposeful discussion can lead to understanding and acquisition of a new concept. The discussion must relate to things already a part of students' knowledge, while focusing on the unique features of the new concept. For example, a teacher needing to teach the concept "gorilla" might begin by asking whether anyone knew of an animal that lived in trees in the jungle. If students suggested a monkey, the teacher might build on that knowledge in further questions: What is a monkey like? What makes a monkey a monkey and not an elephant? The class could then discuss the similarities between monkeys and gorillas and could conclude by establishing similarities and differences between gorillas and other animals.

Feature Analysis

As infants interact with the world, they encounter many new things, and each new experience adds to conceptual understanding and memory. Initially, however, such concepts may be overgeneralized. If you have had experience with a young child, you may have noticed that for a little while all furry, four-legged animals were called "doggie." The child may have seen a particular furry, four-legged animal that was called doggie and may have generalized that set of features to include *any* furry, four-legged animal. Later, as the child gained experience with different kinds of animals and focused on finer discriminations, features such as barking, having a cold nose, and chewing bones may have been added, and "doggies" may have come to include only the appropriate animals.

To see how we use features to discriminate among related items, let's work through a sample exercise. In the blank to the right of each feature, write *all possible* choices from the word list.

		dog	cat	horse	poodle	toy dog

1. Has four legs: _____
2. Is alive: _____
3. Eats meat: _____
4. Barks: _____
5. Has a long
   nose and is
   often trimmed
   to have a ball
   of fur at the
   end of its tail: _____

This example is not intended as a completely accurate representation of how we identify perceived items, but it illustrates that internalized features can provide a basis for classification. As more features of an item are identified, classes of objects become more narrowly defined. This same process is what enables infants to make fewer overgeneralization errors as they recognize more features.

What you did in the preceding example is a type of **feature analysis.** When linguists analyze words to determine differences in meaning, they often use feature analysis, employing plus and minus signs to indicate the presence or absence of a given feature (Katz, 1972; Leech, 1974; Lyons, 1977).

feature analysis
A linguistic method that specifies differences between concepts; can aid understanding of new vocabulary concepts.

Boy	**Man**	**Girl**
+ alive	+ alive	+ alive
+ male	+ male	− male
− adult	+ adult	− adult

A feature analysis chart, developed in a class discussion, often aids students' understanding of a new concept by relating it to concepts they already know. Anders and Bos (1986) point out that feature analysis can be very effectively used in content-area reading with content-specific concepts. Using this approach at various stages (before, during, and after reading) allows students to relate their already-acquired knowledge to new concepts and increases their interest in the selection.

To use feature analysis effectively, teachers need to provide clear examples that focus on important features of the concept to be acquired. Activities should include both positive and negative examples of the concept, to help define its boundaries and show how it is both similar to and different from already-known concepts. For example, if the concept "goblet" is to be learned, a teacher might show and discuss several kinds of drinking vessels and might also show things similar to but different from goblets—perhaps drinking glasses and bowls. A discussion of common and different features of goblets, drinking glasses, and bowls will help to build knowledge about goblets as well as to place that concept within already-known items related to "containers that hold liquid and that you can drink from." In addition, teachers should be aware that concepts are continually refined as features are identified and clarified; they are not learned on a one-shot basis.

Use of Context

If we keep in mind that the goal of reading instruction is the comprehension of text, then to-be-learned words and concepts should always be linked to larger contexts, either through their use in texts and conversations, or through links to already-known concepts such as in the model lesson below. Children need to see that vocabulary is useful; moreover, using new vocabulary in meaningful contexts teaches students that words have particular shades of meaning and play different roles in sentences.

Context can also be a powerful tool to help readers derive meanings for unfamiliar words. Nevertheless, we must not assume that all students will understand new concepts simply because they have been used in written context. Contextual interpretations require good language facility and appropriate background knowledge, both of which allow students to relate new, unknown terms to what they already know. Thus, an effective teacher provides or makes explicit appropriate background information before students are expected to use the context clues embedded in a sentence or story.

The three following examples illustrate the limitations of context in clarifying meaning.

1. A common practice, especially when the salvage value is assumed to be zero, is to apply an appropriate percentage, known as the depreciation rate, to the acquisition cost in order to calculate the annual charge (Davidson, Stickney, & Weil, 1980).

MODEL LESSON

Discussion of Features in Ms. Amato's Class

In this lesson Ms. Amato is trying to relate her students' prior knowledge about different kinds of boats to the new word *canoe*. The word to be learned was chosen because it appears in a story to be read after the vocabulary lesson.

1. Ms. Amato shows the class a picture of a rowboat. Pointing to the rowboat, she asks, "Who can tell me what this is?" She writes the students' response on the chalkboard: "boat."
2. Pointing to a picture of a canoe, Ms. Amato says, "Raise your hands if you know what this is called." Three of the eight students in the instructional group raise their hands.
3. Ms. Amato asks one of the students to name the item and receives the response "canoe." She writes *canoe* on the chalkboard beside the word *boat*.
4. Ms. Amato shows the students a picture of a sailboat and asks whether this is also a boat. With a little guidance the students decide that the original word *boat* is not specific enough. They should have called the first boat a rowboat; this one a sailboat. Ms. Amato erases the word *boat* from the chalkboard and replaces it with *rowboat*.
5. Ms. Amato says, "Let's list how a rowboat and a canoe are the same and how they're different. Tell me how they're the same."
6. As the students provide responses, Ms. Amato writes them on the chalkboard in the appropriate columns.

Near the end of the discussion, Ms. Amato may write the word *sailboat* to the right of the other two words and ask which of the features already identified apply to the sailboat.

7. The students generate sentences using the word *canoe*. The sentences must reflect the word's meaning and be specific enough that a reader would not confuse it with another kind of boat.

---

2. The giraffe, a tall animal with a long neck, lives in Africa.
3. John, the basketball player, is really quite skinny and has red hair and a fair complexion. His friend Sam, however, is corpulent.

If the concepts of salvage value and depreciation rate are not already a part of your background knowledge, it is unlikely that the context clues embedded in the first example will help you with the concept of annual charge. Furthermore, if you know what a giraffe is and have the word in your speaking vocabulary, then the context clues in the second example will probably help. But if you know nothing about giraffes, you will probably need a picture to acquire the concept. Finally, in the third example there are simply too many possible meanings for *corpulent*. The contrast might be implying that Sam is dark complexioned, does not have red hair, or is not a basketball player, in addition to the correct implication that Sam is overweight.

Despite these limitations, context is a valuable aid in developing concepts. Also, context teaches something beyond a word's basic meaning—it shows the way a particular meaning is used in a sentence, thus refining a word's meaning even if a common meaning is already known. Much vocabulary is acquired "in context" simply by reading, and encouraging reading in your classroom will help students develop their vocabulary knowledge. For example, Sustained Silent Reading (SSR), discussed in chapter 4, is an activity that will positively influence children's vocabularies. In addition, context helps the reader to understand how a word is used in a sentence; that is, its part of speech. Figure 8-2 presents several common activities to help students internalize a word's function in a sentence.

FIGURE 8-2

Examples of group activities that might be used to teach the part of speech of clock

1. Modified cloze (fill-in-the-blank) procedure:

   Instructions to students: A clock is something used to tell time. It is used in sentences in the same way that the word *boy* is used. Write the word *clock* wherever it appropriately completes the sentence.

   a. Don't touch the _____ .

   b. My house is _____ .

   c. Bring me the _____ .

   d. Where is the _____ ?

2. Categorization excercises:

   Instructions to students: Circle all the words that can be used in sentences (a) and (b). Underline all the words that can be used in sentences (c) and (d).

       sit   eat   clock   jump   dog   table   go   spoon

   a. She is looking at the _____ .

   b. The _____ is in the kitchen.

   c. He will _____ soon.

   d. Don't _____ in the bedroom.

3. Correcting excercises:

   Instructions to students: Put a check mark in front of each sentence in which *clock* is used properly. If *clock* is not used properly, cross it out, choose a word from the following list, and write it on the blank in front of the sentence.

           sit   jump   eat   go

   _____ a. He will <u>clock</u> on the chair.

   _____ b. The <u>clock</u> was on the table.

   _____ c. Look at the <u>clock</u>!

   _____ d. She wants to <u>clock</u> the candy.

FIGURE 8-3

Sample activities to promote the use of concrete examples and context

 Experiencing New Concepts. Have students see, touch, smell, taste, and use an item as appropriate, and then discuss the name and the features of the item being experienced.

Have students walk around the school yard with you. Stop periodically to write a word on a notepad, and discuss it before moving on. Follow up by using these words in language-related classroom activities. (This activity can be done as part of any field trip.)

 Using Facsimiles. Using a picture, videotape, movie, audiotape, or other secondary source, have students focus closely on the features of the item in the facsimile. Discuss the item's size, looks, possible uses, relationship to similar items, and so on.

 Using Context. During discussion of a new vocabulary item, have students close their eyes. Present a detailed, verbal picture of the concept. Then, after students open their eyes, link the concept to the written form of the word. Finally, give sentences with the target word omitted, and let students supply it to see how the word is used in context.

Provide for free reading time. Ask students to write down three words that they feel are particularly interesting, or that they would like to know more about. The activity not only allows students to choose words of interest, but facilitates reading in longer, more appropriate and authentic contexts.

Such activities are best used with a group of children where discussion can occur, rather than within individually provided worksheets.

Note that the instructions in Figure 8-2 never actually state that *clock* is a noun. Memorizing a word's part of speech does little to facilitate proper use of a word and may be confusing and faulty if the word is later used in a different context. If the goal of instruction is students' proper use of new vocabulary in good sentences, then practice in context will be of far more value than memorized parts-of-speech definitions. The activities in Figure 8-3 promote the use of both concrete examples and context. Memorizing parts-of-speech definitions will not transfer easily into students' use of new vocabulary in real-world situations. Use of new words in context will aid such transfer.

DECIDING WHAT TO TEACH
Types of Words

Vocabulary can be divided into two general types: function words and content words. Figure 8-4 illustrates these two categories and a subcategory called content-specific words and provides examples of each.

function words
Words that facilitate comprehension by connecting other words and phrases.

Function Words. **Function words** are often called the glue that holds a sentence together. Frequently occurring words such as articles (for example, *a, an, the*); conjunctions (for example, *and, but, or*); prepositions (for example, *at, into, over,*); and auxiliary verbs (for example, *could* run, *had* snowed) are function words. They make a sentence cohesive, linking words and phrases so that understanding can occur. Function words are often irregular in spelling and/or pronunciation. And if taught out of con-

FIGURE 8-4

Different categories of vocabulary

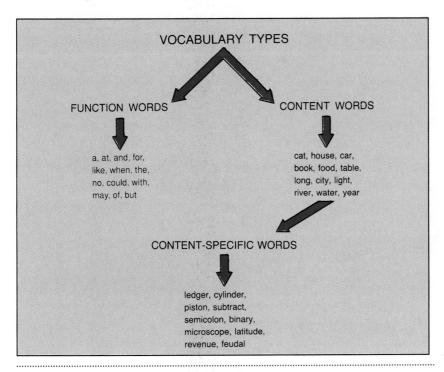

text, they can be difficult for young children to conceptualize, because the concepts they represent are not concrete. Although there are times when it is appropriate to present words in isolation (for example, when discussing the "context" of a prefix), this text advocates teaching all vocabulary in context. Context generally serves to clarify meaning.

Content Words **Content words** such as nouns (for example, *house, car*); pronouns (for example, *I, his, they*); verbs (for example, *run, swim*); adjectives (for example, *hot, sticky*); and adverbs (for example, *then, neatly, suddenly*) have concrete meanings. Everyday content words, such as *dog* or *car,* are sometimes called general vocabulary words. Nevertheless, the same word can have both general and specific meanings, depending on the context in which it is used.

The *race* was run yesterday.

The Asian *race* has a long and fascinating history.

Again, vocabulary requires context to clarify meaning, and teachers cannot assume that students know any meanings other than those they appropriately demonstrate in context.

content words
Words with definitions in general use in everyday language.

Cooperative word games and word puzzles often ask children to spell and use thematically-linked words. Such games can refine concepts that children may be familiar with and can link related ideas.

content-specific words
Words with definitions specific to a content area; words that are not used in everyday language.

Content-Specific Words. Content-specific words always have specialized meanings within a particular subject area and must be learned within the context of that area. For example, *beaker* and *isotherm* do not have general-meaning counterparts; their meanings are embedded in a subject area, such as science. Especially in the middle grades, teachers should spend time teaching their students the meanings of words that are apt to be encountered in their reading material. In subject areas such as science, social studies, and mathematics, words often have content-specific meanings, and not knowing those meanings can make comprehension impossible. Chapter 10 deals with this issue in more depth.

Selection of Vocabulary Items

In general, teachers select the vocabulary they will teach from three sources:

1. words used by students in their natural, oral language
2. words that students will encounter in current reading materials
3. graded word lists

Although teachers may use all three sources, they generally draw from one most heavily.

The first vocabulary source centers around the students' use of oral language and is closely related to the language experience approach discussed in chapter 3. A teacher might have a student dictate a story, which the teacher writes down. That story then forms the basis of vocabulary instruction. The teacher can point out synonyms that might be appropriate substitutions for some of the student's words. In addition, having the child attempt to read the dictated story may show that certain words are in the student's speaking but not reading vocabulary and should therefore be targeted for instruction. This approach is highly motivational and helps forge a link between already-known concepts and print. Nonetheless, using a child's oral language as a base for vocabulary lessons is sometimes criticized because only known concepts are used. The sample activities in Figure 8-5 are intended to expand a child's vocabulary while using oral language as a foundation.

The second source of vocabulary items is based on the philosophy that vocabulary is best learned and retained when the items to be learned occur in real, meaningful situations. Consequently, vocabulary identified as critical to students' understanding of an upcoming passage or story are taught before a selection is read, and revisited using context from the selection after reading. With this approach someone must determine which words in the text are important for overall understanding of the passage. Sometimes this task is accomplished for the teacher; for example, teacher's guides often present a list of words introduced in each unit or each story, with the expectation that teachers will focus on those new and important words.

One possible disadvantage of teaching vocabulary based on words suggested within a published reading program is that not all reading materials introduce the same vocabulary at identical grade levels. In fact, Harris and Jacobson (1982) showed that words introduced in different basal

FIGURE 8-5

Sample activities to expand a child's vocabulary through oral language

Logical Cloze. Transcribe a story provided by a student(s). Then present logical replacements for some of the original words, teach and discuss the new words and ask the children to place them in the appropriate blanks. For example, the words to be taught might be *morning, cape, previous,* and *annoyed.*

    The girl was on her way to school. It was a rainy day _____, and she had her raincoat _____ and her umbrella with her. She hoped that she wouldn't forget her umbrella at school like she did the last _____ time. Her mother was upset _____ with her when she didn't bring her umbrella home.

Thesaurus Detective. After students have mastered the skills necessary to use a thesaurus, cut pages out of a newspaper and have students work in pairs. Within each pair have one student circle five familiar words that the other student is to replace with words found in a thesaurus. Then have students read the words to each other one at a time, with the listener attempting to provide the meaning of the synonym and the original word.

readers can vary by as much as five grade levels. Because the vocabulary in published reading programs is becoming less controlled and is increasingly being based on selections of children's literature, the variance in vocabulary across published reading programs is increasing. In our highly mobile society, where a significant number of children change school districts and instructional materials from one year to the next, differences in vocabulary acquisition can easily occur. Thus, teachers must always remember that students will have been taught using a variety of materials, and will not have been exposed to a similar or core set of vocabulary.

The third way teachers might select vocabulary to teach is from graded word lists. There are many published word lists available that indicate the frequency of words encountered by students at specific grade levels. These lists are usually developed from an analysis of reading materials, including textbooks, that children are expected to read in each grade. Teachers who systematically use such a list generally construct pretests and then teach the specific words that students do not know. Some common lists are identified here:

Dale, E., & O'Rourke, J. (1976). *Living word vocabulary: The words we know.* Elgin, IL: Dome.

Fry, E. B., Kress, J. E., & Fountoukidis, D. L. (1993). *The reading teacher's book of lists* (3rd ed.). Englewood Cliffs, NJ: Prentice Hall.

Harris, A. J., & Jacobson, M. D. (1982). *Basic reading vocabularies.* New York: Macmillan.

Marzano, R. J. & Marzano, J. S. (1988). *A cluster approach to elementary vocabulary instruction.* Newark, DE: International Reading Association.

Word lists can provide useful information, such as the number of students at a given grade level who do not know a specific word or a frequency ordering of words encountered by students in elementary reading materials. There are also lists of roots, prefixes, suffixes, synonyms, antonyms, homophones, commonly misspelled words, and so on. Such lists can provide words that are conceptually or semantically related (for example, Marzano & Marzano's list) as well as words that might be specific to regional or cultural areas (for example, Gunderson, 1984). Systematic teaching from a list, however, means that the words taught may not match the words students find in their reading.

Pretesting

As students do not have identical needs when it comes to vocabulary instruction, a quick and informal pretest of new or necessary terms may help identify those students who will benefit from instruction. Although it is good practice to revisit, reinforce, and use previously taught vocabulary in real text, it is not a good use of time or resources to teach already known words. Thus, pretesting makes teaching more effective, interesting, and relevant, and it also helps to prevent student boredom or frustration. Figure 8-6 shows several ways to test students' vocabulary knowledge quickly.

After pretest results are known, it may be difficult to decide how to group students for instruction. One student may not know any of the words to be taught, another may know all but three, and still another may know all but a different three. Logistically, it is impossible to teach individual vocabulary lessons to each student, but groups can be formed to minimize the ratio of known to unknown words. For example, let's imagine that five words are to be taught (1, 2, 3, 4, 5) to a group of five students (A, B, C, D, E). The teacher performs a brief pretest and decides on this arrangement.

Student	Unknown words	Group placement
A	1, 2	1
B	3, 4, 5	2
C	1, 2, 3	1
D	1, 3, 5	2
E	4	1

With this grouping, students in Group 1 are exposed to a maximum of two already-known words; those in Group 2, only one. Teaching the five

FIGURE 8-6

Sample activities to test students' definitional vocabulary knowledge quickly

Oral Question. Who knows what _____ means? (This is perhaps the most common, yet least effective, approach because not all students respond.)

Oral (or Written) Expression. Say (or write) in a sentence.

Matching Activity. Match the word with the meaning.

      a. house _____   1. grows in the garden
      b. flower _____   2. a place to live

Fill in the Blank. Using the choices provided, write the appropriate word in each sentence.

          house   flower
    a. The _____ grows in the garden.
    b. The _____ has three bedrooms.

Multiple Choice. Choose the best meaning for each word.

        house
        a. a place to live
        b. something to eat
        c. a large animal

students as one group would have resulted in exposure to as many as four already-known words (for student E).

This example shows that pretesting does not result in perfect matches but can help target vocabulary instruction. The example may seem unrealistic because of the relatively low number of already-known words included in the grouping arrangements. But in reality, when more words are presented to a greater number of students, grouping does substantially reduce the number of already-known words that are taught. And teaching specific words to a targeted group occurs easily during the day if a teacher uses a flexible grouping arrangement, allowing time for small group activities as appropriate.

DECIDING HOW TO TEACH
General Principles

There are some general principles that apply to all vocabulary instruction, regardless of grade level. Nagy (1988) points out that effective vocabulary instruction has three components.

1. *Integration.* Teaching strategies must use methods that integrate the concept to be learned with existing knowledge.
2. *Repetition.* Teaching strategies should provide sufficient practice so that meaning is accessed automatically, without the need to decode the word during reading. This level of familiarity requires many encounters with a new word—certainly far more than the number of repetitions necessary just to learn a definition.
3. *Meaningful use.* Teaching strategies should provide opportunities for students to use a new concept and word in context rather than in isolation. This approach facilitates inferencing and allows for repetitive practice that is interesting and motivational.

Other common strategies include revisiting words that are learned over a period of time. Although words receive the greatest attention during the initial teaching phase, students need to revisit them periodically. This task is simplified if students collect vocabulary words in some form as they are learned. For example, students might maintain a **word bank** or a special section of a notebook. Periodically, then, teachers could remind students to use words from their word banks or notebooks in their writing or in other meaningful activities.

Beck, McKeown and Omanson (1987) also point out that vocabulary should be specifically taught, and describe a vocabulary program that is rich and has the following features:

1. Students should manipulate words in varied ways, perhaps by describing how they relate to other words and to students' experiences.
2. Activities should involve a great deal of discussion and students should justify the associations and relationships that they make.

word bank
A place to organize word cards and a means to help develop decoding and vocabulary knowledge.

3. Words should be encountered many times.
4. Students should be encouraged and supported in their efforts to use new vocabulary words outside of the vocabulary lesson.
5. Children should make their thinking explicit and teachers should model this process.

The authors also note that extensive reading and exposure to environments where oral presentations use unfamiliar words help to develop students' vocabulary. Anderson & Nagy (1993) also note that systematic instruction that promotes curiosity about words and their meanings, independence in word analysis, and wide, ongoing reading will result in vocabulary growth. They point out that even a slight amount of ongoing, daily reading can lead to gains of several thousand words per year, especially when multiple meanings and nuances of meanings are considered.

Environmental Print and Vocabulary Development

Children learn a great deal about reading from the print they see around them. Partly because of this, chapter 6 pointed out the importance and benefits of labeling known items in kindergarten classrooms. And, even at higher grade levels, teachers with emergent literacy/whole language perspectives often present vocabulary instruction as an **incidental learning** experience, consciously using new vocabulary during morning message and story reading, conversations, or functional writing activities. Within these activities, students' attention is drawn to the new words and follow-up activities—writing tasks, dictation, and other literacy activities—allow students to practice writing, seeing, and hearing the words in context (see Noyce & Christie, 1989, for a discussion of the value of copying and dictation activities). Such activities—which result in discussion and examination of a word and its use, and which focus on letters and parts of words—are important and valuable. It is the discussion, not merely the exposure to print, that is important to word use and acquisition.

incidental learning
Learning that takes place without direct instruction, often as part of everyday routines.

In fact, there is evidence that simple exposure to print in the child's environment is not the critical factor in word recognition and print-vocabulary development. Among others, Stahl & Murray (1993); Gough, Juel, & Griffith (1992); and Masonheimer, Drum, & Ehri (1984) have found that children do not seem to develop word-recognition knowledge from exposure to environmental print. In studies that examined children's ability to read print that is embedded in logos used by fast-food companies, cereals, sneakers, and so on, children who did not already have some knowledge about print focused on the logo as a whole, rather than the print, and the exposure to environmental print embedded within a logo accounted for little word learning. In fact, Stahl & Nagy (1993, p. 232) state that "Children seem not to attend to the words in logos unless they are already reading words. The print in the logos. . .seems not to be salient for emergent readers and does not seem to be a significant source of word meaning." What appears most impor-

········· **EXPLORING DIVERSE POINTS OF VIEW** ·········

Some people believe strongly that incidental learning is very effective, especially as practiced in whole language classrooms. Although it is not yet possible to say whether vocabulary instruction is more or less effective in whole language classrooms, there is some evidence that first-grade children in such classrooms generate vocabulary at least comparable to that used in published reading programs (Shapiro & Gunderson, 1988) and that listening to stories contributes significantly to vocabulary acquisition (Elley, 1989). However, there is also evidence suggesting that direct instruction in word meanings should be combined with such approaches (Jenkins, Matlock, & Slocum, 1989). Will you merge these two findings to teach vocabulary in your classroom? How?

tant is to develop children's knowledge about print through interactions with print, through interactions with adults about and around print, and through subsequent discussions of new words in context.

Conceptual Links

Research indicates that certain concepts are closely linked with each other (Adams & Collins, 1979; Anderson, Reynolds, Schallert, & Goetz, 1977). For example, if people are asked to say the first word that comes to mind when they are presented with List A, most will respond with the words in List B.

A	B
mother	father
boy	girl
man	woman
dog	cat
day	night

schema theory
A theory about knowledge that says objects and their relationships form a network in memory.

Moreover, research in **schema theory** implies that there are sets, or networks, of concepts that appear to help trigger each other (Anderson & Pearson, 1984; Anderson, 1994). For instance, a person given the stimulus word *restaurant* is more apt to respond with *menu, food,* or *waiter* than with *car* or *television.*

Notice that although the words in the lists are opposites, they are in the same domain—that is, each pair deals with parents, children, pets, and so on. This supports the notion that associated concepts might be stored in memory as being related, and that accessing one concept in a linked network helps to access others that are associated with it. Nagy and Scott's (1990) research also implies that schemas for words in general are applied to learning new words and their parts of speech. These research findings support instructional practices that attempt to link words into meaningful networks rather than teach each word separately. This can be done in a variety of ways, but one common option is teaching in thematic units, as discussed below.

MODEL LESSON
Linking Vocabulary in Thematic Contexts in Ms. Dill's Class

Ms. Dill wanted her first-grade students to see how words could be linked together to create a meaninngful narrative passage. As students brainstormed together they began to get a sense of how the relationship of one word to another can develop an appropriate context.

1. Discuss the following words with students—what they mean, how they might be related to each other, and so on.

   barn   difficult   handle   horse   cheerful   beautiful

2. Have students write a brief story, as a class or individually, that uses the target words. The example included here was suggested by a group of four first-grade students. As each student presented the teacher with an oral sentence, the teacher wrote it on the chalkboard, and the students copied it in their notebooks. The last sentence was provided by the teacher; a title was determined after the story was completed.

   There was a cheerful horse who lived in a barn. The horse was cheerful because he got to live in a big barn and had lots to eat. There was a big handle on the door of the barn. It was difficult to turn. The horse was cheerful because his barn was beautiful.

3. Have students underline the vocabulary words. Discuss the words' appropriate contextual use, and how they help the story "fit" together and make sense.

Thematic Units. The fact that concepts seem to cluster—that is, that one concept seems to facilitate access to related concepts—implies that vocabulary might be effectively presented in **thematic units.** Figure 8-7 presents a thematic practice activity that is common in commercially available materials.

thematic units
Instruction organized around a common idea.

This activity is intended for children in kindergarten or beginning first grade; their task is to match the picture to the appropriate word and then write that word in the puzzle. Such activities allow children to match word-labels and picture clues, and also provide an opportunity for students to write the words. Young children often enjoy such crossword and find-a-word puzzles, but teachers will need to add contextual activities to such puzzle-sheets. It is important to relate words to each other within sentences and stories. The model lesson that follows presents one popular and effective way of teaching vocabulary by linking meanings within a coherent context.

Concept Webs. Webs of related concepts can also be used to present vocabulary. For example, restaurant terms might be diagrammed as a web, with the central component being the most general or generic concept and outlying components representing increasing detail or specificity. The amount of detail in such a concept, or semantic, web varies according to the age and level of students. The semantic web shown on page 331 is reasonably complex.

FIGURE 8-7

A sample practice activity with conceptually linked words

IN THE CLASSROOM

Humpty Dumpty likes to go to school.
Help him do the classroom puzzle.

RULER   PENCIL   CRAYON   ERASER   INK
BOOK   PEN   CHAIR   DESK

3-ACROSS
5-ACROSS
2-DOWN
1-DOWN
6-ACROSS
4-DOWN

82

83

Source: From Gilda Waldman, *The Big Book of Puzzles* (New York: Playmore, 1976), pp. 82–83. Reprinted by permission.

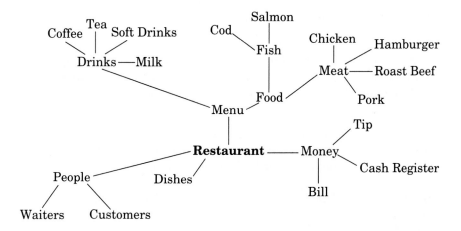

Semantic webs are most effective when discussion specifically relates to students' background knowledge, explains the concepts behind the words used, and corrects students' misunderstandings (Stahl & Vancil, 1986). In addition, a concept web can contain both known and new concepts, allowing connections to be highlighted between the two (Johnson, Pittleman, & Heimlich, 1986). Teachers interested in concept webs should find Marzano and Marzano's (1988) cluster approach helpful; these authors have organized more than 7,000 words into semantically related clusters, and they present a number of webbing approaches to the teaching of those words. Additional approaches to semantic webbing have been provided by Heimlich and Pittleman (1986).

Synonyms. We know that individuals use their interpretive abilities to remember things that were not specifically stated in what they read. For example, look at the following sentence:

The woman was outstanding in the theater.

Readers who are presented with such a sentence often believe that the word *actress* was used in the sentence. Their response suggests that readers remember the essence of what they have read, not the particulars. The process of remembering the key idea as it fits the context has been called **instantiation** (Anderson, Pichert, Goetz, Schallert, Stevens, & Trollip, 1976). Related research has provided a rationale for using synonyms—in addition to appropriate, logically related examples—in vocabulary instruction. If you were teaching the word *hammer,* for instance, you might say something like this:

He hit the nail with a _____

What word fits in the blank? What other words could be used? Which is most appropriate? Why? What do all the words have in common?

instantiation
Remembering what the reader perceives to be the most important information in the material that was read.

You might also approach it this way:

> He hit the nail with a hammer.
> What other words could be used instead of *hammer* (for example, *rock, wrench,* and so on)? Why could we use those other words? Why might *hammer* be the best choice? Where might a hammer be found?

Such discussion methods use children's prior knowledge and help them place the new concept into a network of similar items (for example, tools, or items used to hammer), thus facilitating learning.

Analogies and Continuums. Analogies and continuums use known concepts to build new ones, implying that knowledge is organized in a series of related, linked concepts. Using analogies to teach students new words and their uses is appropriate at all grade levels. For example, if students are learning *conductor* and *foal,* students can be presented with items such as these:

> *Pipe* is to *water* as *conductor* is to *electricity.*

> *Dog* is to *puppy* as *horse* is to *foal.*

Used with discussion, analogies foster concept development because they show the relationship between known items and incorporate one unknown item in a way that helps students to infer the unknown meaning. Teachers must be sure that all other words in the analogy are known and should focus discussion on the relationship within the familiar half of the analogy. Questions about the relationship on the other side of the analogy should then follow naturally.

Continuums, which include meanings that are known as well as one or more to be taught, also facilitate vocabulary development by using prior knowledge. For example, students might be shown the following:

scream   shout   speak   murmur   whisper

Discussion of the change in gradation of meaning from left to right presents a scheme in which students can fit the new, to-be-learned term—in this case, *murmur.*

Use of Word Parts

Although knowledge of word parts aids word recognition, it also helps readers discover the meanings of words and thus expand their vocabularies. Nagy et al. (1992) point out that implicit instruction of structural analysis can help students with word meanings and vocabulary acquisition. They note, too, that instruction in such strategies should take place in sentence context and include discussion about when structural analysis works and does not work; and that structural analysis should be used together with other strategies.

When readers use word parts as clues to meaning, they are using their knowledge about affixes (prefixes and suffixes) and root words. **Morphemes,** the smallest meaningful parts of language, include prefixes, suffixes, and root words. For example, these words each contain one morpheme:

play   run   cow

These words contain two morphemes each:

playful   rerun   cows

Knowing the meanings of common prefixes and suffixes can help determine word meanings. For instance, knowing that the prefix *non-* means "not" or "no" helps a reader understand words like *nonprofit, nonsense,* and *nonstop.*

Prefixes, suffixes, and roots are often taught as vocabulary items in reading instruction. Although teaching all affixes and roots is impossible, teaching the most common ones is worthwhile. There are many published lists that contain the most useful morphemes—for example, Fry, Polk,

morphemes
Prefixes, suffixes, and roots.

Discussion based on a concept web, which visually links concepts, is an effective vocabulary teaching technique.

and Fountoukidis's *The Reading Teacher's Book of Lists,* 3rd ed. (Englewood Cliffs, NJ: Prentice Hall, 1993). In addition, you will be able to use activities such as those shown in Figure 8-8 to teach affixes and roots.

Dictionaries

Although dictionary definitions are of relatively minor importance in teaching word meanings, dictionaries can be used to create vocabulary

---

FIGURE 8-8

Sample activities to help teach affixes and roots

 Affix Deletion. Write several sentences containing words with the same affix.

1. He had to <u>reheat</u> the food because it had cooled down.
2. After she used the towel, Mary had to <u>refold</u> it.
3. Because the color came out of his shirt when it was washed, Sam had to <u>redye</u> it.

Have students state the meaning of each underlined word. Then cross out the affix and discuss how the meaning of the word has changed. Finally, agree on the meaning of the affix.

 Affix Addition. Change the previous activity by using the key words without affixes and requiring the students to add them. Present the activity like this:

Re- is a prefix that means again. Use it to change the meaning of the sentences. (You will have to add it to one of the underlined words, and take out the other.)

1. He had to <u>heat</u> the food <u>again</u> because it had cooled down.
2. After she used the towel, Mary had to <u>fold</u> it <u>again.</u>
3. Because the color came out of his shirt when it was washed, Sam had to <u>dye</u> it <u>again.</u>

Discuss with students that the prefix *un-* means "not" and can have a strong influence on meaning. Present this example:

> They were welcome at the picnic.

Then tell students to add *un-* to "welcome" in the sentence, and discuss what happens to the meaning of the entire sentence.

 Root Word Addition. Write affixes on the chalkboard, and have students supply root words.

-less (without)	**-en (like)**
care(less)	wool(en)
thought(less)	gold(en)
hope(less)	wood(en)

 Affix and Root Word Hunt. Have students look through a reading selection and circle certain prefixes, suffixes, and/or roots. Then have students present their findings, explaining how the meanings of the words would have been different if the prefix or suffix had not been used.

learning experiences. They are also reference sources for students during independent reading activities. Dictionaries can be used at all grade levels: there are many attractive and useful dictionaries for elementary-aged students, beginning with picture dictionaries. Such dictionaries make effective use of color, drawings, photos, and other visual aids to explain and define concepts. Popular primary dictionaries include these three:

Halsey, W. D. (1987). *First Dictionary*. New York: Macmillan.

Jenkins, W. A. (1987). *My first picture dictionary*. Glenview, IL: Scott, Foresman.

Root, B. (1993). *My first picture dictionary*. Richmond Hill, Ontario, Canada: Scholastic.

Nonetheless, we need to remember that using a dictionary to look up an unknown word's meaning requires a number of skills. For example, a child must (1) be able to alphabetize by at least the first letter of a word; (2) be able to locate a word without turning every page of the dictionary; (3) be able to associate word and meaning; (4) be aware that a word often has more than one meaning; and (5) use context to select one meaning from alternatives. If these skills are present, the dictionary can be a useful tool, especially as students encounter unfamiliar words in content-area subjects. However, dictionary definitions generally need to be discussed, used in meaningful examples, and related to students' prior knowledge.

To teach your students the value of using a dictionary, you can model its use and draw students' attention to the reason the dictionary is being consulted (see Figure 8-9). Modeling the use of a thesaurus and a glossary is also effective. Modeling can result in students using these tools independently when they find new words in reading assignments. Certainly, a dictionary and other reference sources, written at an appropriate level, should be available for student use in every classroom.

Learning Centers

A **learning center** is an area in a classroom that contains a variety of instructional materials dealing with a specific goal or objective. Because it is often used independently by students, provisions are usually made for

learning center
A classroom location where instructional materials are used independently by students.

FIGURE 8-9
Sample activities for facilitating dictionary use in acquiring word meanings

 Modeling. Pick an interesting, unknown word and use it incidentally during the day. Say something like this: "Yesterday I heard someone say that he really doesn't like canines. I'd like you to help me look that up in the dictionary and see what *canine* means." Then have students help you find the word in the dictionary, read the meaning, and relate it to previous knowledge.

 Finding Correct Meanings. Present sentences like "He put the fish on the *scale* to find out how heavy it was" and "Her wedding dress had a long *train*." Have students find the words in the dictionary and decide which of the listed meanings make sense in the sentence context.

self-evaluation. Such a center lends itself to vocabulary instruction, whether in thematic units or not. Included in a vocabulary-learning center can be activities related to any of the methods outlined in this chapter. Students can work in pairs or small groups to complete analogy or continuum exercises, can create and discuss webs, can self-select vocabulary to be learned, can revisit (or add to) words in their word banks, and so on.

A learning center, sometimes called an activity center or a learning station, contains a set of activities to support students' learning. Because students work independently, they must be aware of acceptable behavior at the center and must also be aware of the goal of the activities. Careful planning is required to create an effective learning center. Huff (1983) and Sherfey and Huff (1976) suggest that the following steps be considered in planning a learning center:

1. Clearly define the center's purposes.
2. Consider the characteristics and the needs of students who will be using the center.
3. Define the concepts and skills to be developed in the center.
4. Outline expected learning outcomes.
5. Select appropriate activities and materials.
6. Evaluate the center.
7. Implement needed changes.

Children can use learning centers individually or in small groups and should spend about 15 minutes there at one time. The center should be sturdy enough to withstand classroom use and should include a variety of activities focused on the targeted concept. A learning center can be many things, ranging from teacher-made posterboard items to a microcomputer and software. The critical component is how the center is related to overall instructional goals. When well-planned and carefully implemented, learning centers represent an efficient use of a teacher's time.

Response Cards

response cards
Cards that provide a teacher with immediate information about a child's response.

Another useful and efficient activity in vocabulary instruction and evaluation uses true-false and A-B-C **response cards** to replace papers and pencils. For this activity teachers should print one to three vocabulary words on cards, along with a response choice. The single-word cards are used with true-false responses; the multiple-word cards prompt a response of A, B, or C. The single-word card can also be used as a vocabulary flash card. Students can also perform response-card activities in pairs, using words from their word banks. Figure 8-10 shows both types of cards; the model lesson that follows outlines the procedure.

This simple procedure can be modified easily, yet it remains valuable for several reasons.

- Children are not self-conscious about responding. As the response is not oral and all students face the teacher, other students cannot see an incorrect response.

- Teachers do not spend time grading papers or worksheets but gain an overview of student comprehension. With a class list of names handy, teachers can quickly note the students who show problems with certain words and need individual help.

- The cards are inexpensive, easy to make, and simple for students to copy for their word banks.

- The activity provides a quick way to review and reinforce previously presented vocabulary.

FIGURE 8-10

Response cards for use in a vocabulary lesson

MODEL LESSON

Response Cards

1. Ask students to tear a piece of paper into either two (for true-false activities) or three (for A-B-C activities) parts and write either *true* and *false* or *A, B,* and *C* on their papers.

2. Check your vocabulary cards to be sure that the statements or clues appear on the backs of the cards. The process needs to flow smoothly.

3. For the true-false activity, hold up a single-word vocabulary card, and provide a statement or phrase about the word that is either true or false. For example, for the word *smoke* you might say, "Something that is usually present with a fire" or "Something we eat." Have children hold up their *true* or *false* paper in response.

4. For the word-choice activity hold up a multiword vocabulary card, and provide context clues to help students choose the appropriate word from the card. Have students hold up their A, B, or C paper to match the letter under the word that they think is correct.

....

TWO SPECIAL CASES
Homonyms

Often there is confusion in terminology about what to call words that sound the same. Because there is a difference between words that are identical in sound and spelling and words that sound the same but are spelled differently, you should learn the following precise terms. Calling them all homonyms is inaccurate and can lead to instructional confusion. Learning the precise terms will help you when you encounter them in teacher's guides and in professional reading.

homophones
Words with the same pronunciation but different spellings and meanings.

homographs
Words with the same spellings but different pronunciation and meanings.

homonyms
Words with the same pronunciation and spelling but different meanings.

Homophones	Words that sound alike, are spelled differently, and mean different things (for example, "He *led* his horse." "It looked like *lead*.")
Homographs	Words that do not sound alike, are spelled alike, and mean different things (for example, "He *read* the book." "He will *read* the book.")
Homonyms	Words that sound alike, are spelled alike, and mean different things (for example, "the bathroom *scale*"; "the fish *scale*")

Homonyms present an interesting methodological challenge to the teacher. As neither the written (graphemic) nor the oral (phonological) form of a homonym changes between meanings, young children sometimes become confused when the two meanings are presented together, especially when a teacher focuses attention on the known meaning and then tells students to learn the new meaning (Kinzer, 1982). In fact, research has shown that children who are unable to perform cognitive tasks associated with multiple class membership do better when not asked to focus on the meaning they already know (Kinzer, 1981).

As students mature, it is appropriate to teach new meanings for homonyms by relating each new meaning to both its word-label and an already-known meaning. But with children in the primary grades, teachers must tread carefully. If the goal is to teach a new meaning for a homonym, then learning the meaning is more important than realizing that the word is a homonym. Thus, teachers in the lower grades should teach new meanings of homonyms in the same way that they teach normal words with single meanings.

The suggestion here is not that young students cannot use words in more than one way or with more than one meaning. Children know at an early age that an airplane can fly and that a fly is a sometimes-bothersome insect. The confusion results when young children are asked to become consciously aware that the label for two separate concepts is the same. Young students seem to believe instead that the two words are separate items even though they sound the same. This ability to see similarity and difference across several dimensions at the same time appears to be unavailable until children can comprehend membership in multiple classes. In time, the ability to perceive multiple meanings with similar labels develops naturally.

Referential Terms

Certain vocabulary terms have **referential properties** and can be fully understood only through experiential knowledge (Murphy, 1986). In other words, experiences with language clarify certain references that are not explicitly stated. Consider the following examples, and try to decide where Steve is physically located.

referential properties
Word characteristics requiring readers or listeners to use background to determine what item is being mentioned.

1. On the telephone, Steve says, "Come to my house tonight."
2. On the telephone, Steve says, "Go to my house tonight."

Now try to decide where the food is physically located.

Many vocabulary activities are available in computer formats. The best of these present concepts in context, often within children's literature selections or in content-area simulations.

3. Sally, Bill, and Tom are sitting at a table. Sally says to Tom, "He has the food."
4. Sally, Bill, and Tom are sitting at a table. Sally says to Tom, "The food is over here."
5. Sally, Bill, and Tom are sitting at a table. Sally says to Tom, "The food is over there."

You probably decided correctly that Steve was at home while on the telephone in the first example and not at home in the second. In example 3 Bill had the food, in 4 it was near Sally, and in 5 it was not near Sally. Your ability to specify the locations in these examples indicates your facility with one kind of reference—place reference. Other forms of reference and their effects on comprehension of text are discussed in chapter 9.

For our purposes here it is important to note that referential terms can cause great difficulty for young children, and teachers must be aware that vocabulary items often have referential meanings that go beyond the words' literal use. With such terms it is not enough to explain word meanings. Discussion must develop the students' understanding of the referential nature of the terms and should include several examples of their use. Examples of such activities are shown in Figure 8-11.

Part of the difficulty children have in understanding referential terms is related to their cognitive level and to the differences between oral and

---

FIGURE 8-11

Sample activities to teach the referential nature of pronouns

Pronoun Examples. Use examples to teach pronoun reference in a number of sentence structures. Use sentence pairs similar to these:

1. a. The teacher gave both Sue and Joyce *erasers,* even though the girls didn't need *them.*
   b. Even though the girls didn't need *them,* the teacher gave both Sue and Joyce *erasers.*
2. a. *Chris* wanted a drink of water because *she* was thirsty.
   b. Because *she* was thirsty, *Chris* wanted a drink of water.
3. a. Bill said *the bike was new,* but Tipp did not believe *it.*
   b. Tipp did not believe *it,* but Bill said *the bike was new.*

Discuss with the students that some referential terms can refer to items in front of them or behind them. Also, draw attention to the fact that referential terms can refer to one or more words, a phrase, a clause, or a sentence.

Extending Sentences. Present a gradual sentence expansion, leading ultimately to the replacement of one or more parts of the sentence with a referential term(s).

> Susie eats.
> Susie eats lunch.
> Willy eats lunch.
> Susie and Willy eat lunch.
> *They* eat lunch.
> Susie and Willy eat *it.*
> *They* eat *it.*

written language. We know that children's understanding of time and place does not develop fully until about the third grade (Bybee & Sund, 1982; Lowery, 1981). In addition, written language loses the physical clarifiers of oral communication. For example, in speech the sentence "The food is over there" or "He has the food" is usually accompanied by some form of head motion or gesture, such as pointing, which clarifies meaning and makes it more concrete. Saying that print is speech written down is an inaccurate simplification. In text, for instance, quotation marks are intended to aid meaning but can also cause confusion. Try to locate the food in this example:

> Sally said, "Tom said, 'The food is here.'"

Thus, cognitive development and differences between oral and written language combine to produce confusion when children are asked to comprehend referential vocabulary terms in text.

USING A LITERACY FRAMEWORK TO INFORM DECISIONS ABOUT VOCABULARY INSTRUCTION

Your literacy framework will serve as a guide as you decide both what to teach and how to teach vocabulary knowledge to your students. Table 8-1 summarizes the part of your literacy framework that identifies your beliefs about how one reads, and shows how these beliefs can be used to guide instructional decisions.

What to Teach and Emphasize

If you follow a reader-based explanation of how one reads, you believe that reading consists largely of predicting; of expectations for upcoming words. Thus, you believe that prior knowledge is important to successful reading because readers are able to use this knowledge to accurately predict the meanings of words. As a result, you would probably spend little time on teaching isolated words, and little time on structural analysis that examines the components of words. Instead, you would encourage children to use contextual strategies, such as thematic units, concept webs, analogies and so on.

If you follow a text-based explanation of how one reads, you believe that reading consists largely of translating words and word parts into sounds and blending these sounds together to form words. Thus, you would probably spend time analyzing how word parts (prefixes, roots, and suffixes) join together to form meanings, rather than spending time developing contextual strategies. You might also use the dictionary as a basis for your lessons, as it includes word meanings as well as aids to decoding and structural analysis.

If you follow an interactive explanation of how one reads, you believe that reading consists of both expectations for upcoming word-meanings

TABLE 8-1

Instructional consequences of different beliefs about how one reads

Explanations for how one reads	Related assumptions	Probable focus of vocabulary instruction
Reader-based Explanations	Meaning exists more in what the reader brings to the text.	Developing strategic use of context and contextual strategies.
	Reading is a result of expectations.	Vocabulary as a knowledge source and as part of predicting meanings and relating new vocabulary to already-known concepts would be stressed.
	Reading begins with elements of prior knowledge.	
Interactive Explanations	Meaning exists in both the text and the reader.	Developing each of the knowledge sources is given equal time.
	Reading is both translation and expectation.	Relating new meanings to old, the importance of prior knowledge, and teaching vocabulary within decoding lessons would take place.
	Reading uses each knowledge source simultaneously.	
Text-based Explanations	Meaning exists more in the text.	Developing structural analysis skills.
	Reading is translation.	Vocabulary would receive emphasis largely as it relates to decoding.
	Reading begins with decoding.	

and strong decoding and structural analysis skills, which combine to help discover and learn word meanings. As a result, you would probably spend an average amount of time on vocabulary instruction (about the same amount of time as you would spend on the other knowledge sources associated with reading comprehension) and would likely use both context and structural analysis to teach vocabulary.

How to Develop Vocabulary Knowledge

Table 8-2 summarizes beliefs about how children learn to read, and how these beliefs can be used to guide instructional decisions about which method framework to use in vocabulary instruction.

If you follow a holistic language learning explanation, you favor learning experiences that are inductive in nature. Thus, you would probably use inductive methods to teach context and would integrate vocabulary development into daily classroom activities such as language experience activities and content lessons in mathematics, science, social studies, and so on. You would almost certainly use word banks and encourage your students to read widely and interact with print to extend their vocabularies.

If you follow a specific skills explanation, you favor learning experiences that are deductive and that focus on specific skills. Thus, you would

TABLE 8-2

Instructional consequences of different beliefs about how children learn to read

Explanations for how children learn to read	Beliefs	Instructional consequences: How to teach
Holistic Language Learning	Students direct much of their own learning and inductive learning is emphasized. Reading experiences always take place in the context of authentic social contexts and with authentic reading materials.	Common method frameworks include contextualized approaches, usually within the language experience approach, shared book experience, morning message, and writing activities. Word lists and skill sheets are not typically used. Big books, children's literature, other print material, and children's oral and written language form the basis for most vocabulary instruction. Students are allowed to self-select or indicate which words should be a part of the vocabulary lesson.
Integrated	Both student-directed and teacher-directed experiences are used. Both inductive and deductive learning are used. Reading experiences take place in the contexts of authentic social contexts and with authentic reading materials. Specific skills are taught when needed, often in mini-lessons.	Common method frameworks include inductive and deductive instruction in skills such as structural analysis and dictionary use, as well as contextualized activities such as webs and wide reading. Words to be taught are both teacher-provided and student-selected.
Specific Skills	Teacher-directed reading activities and deductive learning are emphasized. Specific skills, often organized in terms of difficulty, are frequently taught.	Common method frameworks include deductive instruction that target specific skills, such as structural analysis and dictionary knowledge. Instruction is often based on word lists or suggested vocabulary lists from published reading programs.

likely use deductive methods and organize your direct instruction around a set of specific skills such as structural knowledge of words, dictionary use, and so on.

If you follow an integrated explanation, you would use both deductive and inductive methods to develop vocabulary knowledge. You would probably combine all of the approaches discussed in this chapter, and would select the words you think should be taught, as well as allow your students to self-select words they feel they need to learn.

Comments from the Classroom

Nikki Robinson, sixth grade teacher

Because older students have had more life experiences—read more books, visited more places, and yes, watched more television—I try to build on these experiences and create opportunities for students to attach new words and concepts to their existing knowledge. Ms. Davis, the fifth grade teacher, says she imagines students wearing a velcro suit that represents what they already know. In my reading methods book, the velcro suit is called "existing schema." Ms. Davis and I try to get new words to "stick" to those "suits," to expand students' exising schema by adding more layers. We use a variety of strategies to get new words to "stick" in students' minds.

We try to use more meaning-centered variations of the "look the new words up in the dictionary or glossary" study strategy. While sometimes the dictionary seems the most efficient way to find out what a list of words mean, merely writing down the meaning often doesn't allow the word to "stick."

My students like to work in pairs. The partners read the word in context, create a new sentence using the word, write their definition, draw a picture of the word (nouns, pronouns, adjectives) or perform a demonstration of the word (verbs, adverbs), find a rhyming word, find a word that means the opposite, and create an analogy using the word or describe the situation in which they may have heard the word before or could use the word in the future. At that point, the partners compare their work with the dictionary definition. The partners share their new understanding orally with the rest of the class, or sometimes if the vocabulary is basic to a thematic unit, the partners place their vocabulary work on a bulletin board—a variation on a word wall. That way the words are accessible for future writing assignments.

We don't always take time to do each of those things, but if the vocabulary is key to understanding a story or theme, then taking the time to build the foundation is worth it. I have discovered that because the meanings are attached to what the students already know, they seem to have a deeper understanding. Anytime a student has drawn a picture or demonstrated the meaning of the word, it really "sticks;" they don't forget it. An interesting by-product is that students seem to also absorb the correct spelling of a word learned in a more meaning-based way.

- In the primary grades teachers generally teach the words for already-known concepts. In intermediate grades and beyond, teachers generally teach both concepts and their word-labels.

- Before presenting an unknown word, teachers should teach the concept represented by the word.

- Vocabulary should be explicitly taught. Lessons can be based on word lists, reading materials, children's oral language, or any combination of these three sources.

- When teaching vocabulary, teachers should, whenever possible, give concrete examples that are grounded in rich contexts. It is also helpful to compare the features of the unknown items to those of similar, known items.

- Vocabulary activities should include many varied examples of the unknown concept in context. Vocabulary words should be revisited often.

- Homonyms and referential terms can be difficult for children in lower elementary grades to learn.

- Vocabulary growth continues throughout life, as known terms are refined and new terms are added.

Major Points

1. The following words can be categorized as function (List A); content (List B); and content-specific (List C) words.

is	car	cat	at
shelf	that	cumulus	molecule
beaker	table	microchip	and

Two examples in each list have already been provided, one of which comes from the words presented here. Place each of the remaining words into one of the three lists. Then explain how you might teach the words from each list differently and why.

A	B	C
on	door	ledger
is	shelf	beaker
_____	_____	_____
_____	_____	_____
_____	_____	_____

Making Instructional Decisions

2. Imagine that you need to teach the following new terms to first-grade students, who already know the meanings given in the second column. Describe your lesson.

To Be Learned	**Already Known**
Fish *scale*	weighing *scale*
human *race*	run a *race*
pig *pen*	*pen* to write with

3. Why would a teacher use both positive and negative examples when teaching vocabulary?

4. How might vocabulary teaching differ in primary and intermediate grades? Why? The words in Item 2 above reflect one source of difference, but there are others.

5. Look at two different levels of a published reading program. Examine the introductory material to see how new vocabulary is identified and introduced. How are instructional strategies presented in the teacher's guide? Which strategies would you use? Which would you modify or reject? Why?

Further Reading

Beck, I., & McKeown, M. G. (1983). Learning words well—A program to enhance vocabulary and comprehension. *The Reading Teacher, 36,* 622–625.

Describes a program of varied methods to teach vocabulary to fourth-grade students. Involves cognitive, physical, and affective elements.

Fry, E., & Sakiey, E. (1986). Common words not taught in basal reading series. *The Reading Teacher, 39,* 395–398.

Points out that basal series generally teach about 50 percent of the 3,000 most common English words. Suggests that teachers may want to supplement basal lists with lists provided in the article.

Johnson, D. D., & Pearson, P. D. (1984). *Teaching reading vocabulary* (2nd ed.). New York: Holt, Rinehart & Winston.

A readable paperback including many ideas and suggestions for teaching vocabulary and providing a good conceptual background.

Koskinen, P. S., Wilson, R. M., Gambrell, L. B., & Neuman, S. B. (1994). Captioned video and vocabulary learning: An innovative practice in literacy instruction. *The Reading Teacher, 47,* 36–43.

Presents strategies for using captioned video to increase vocabulary learning, especially of lower-ability students.

Marzano, R. J., & Marzano, J. S. (1988). *A cluster approach to elementary vocabulary instruction.* Newark, DE: International Reading Association.

Discusses teaching vocabulary in clusters of concepts, and presents an extensive list of word clusters.

Nagy, W. E. (1988). *Teaching vocabulary to improve reading comprehension.* Newark, DE: International Reading Association.

A short monograph that presents the reasons for the failure of certain types of vocabulary instruction as well as practical suggestions for improving that instruction.

Stallman, A. C., Commeyras, M., Kerr, B., Reimer, K., Jiminez, R., Hartman, D. D., & Pearson, P. D. (1990). Are "new" words really new? *Reading Research and Instruction, 29,* 12–29.

A research-based article that examines whether second- and fifth-grade children already know the meanings of vocabulary to be taught in basal readers. Points out that there are various reasons for including vocabulary lessons in published reading programs and that direct instruction can account for only a small part of the words children learn.

References

Adams, M. J., & Collins, A. M. (1979). A schema-theoretic view of reading. In R. O. Freedle (Ed.), *Discourse processing: Multidisciplinary perspectives.* Norwood, NJ: Ablex.

Anders, P. L., & Bos, C. S. (1986). Semantic feature analysis: An interactive strategy for vocabulary development and text comprehension. *Journal of Reading, 29,* 610–616.

Anderson, R. C. (1994). Role of the reader's schema in comprehension, learning, and memory. In R. B. Ruddell, M. R. Ruddell, & H. Singer (Eds.), *Theoretical models and processes of reading* (4th ed., pp. 469–482). Newark, DE: International Reading Association.

Anderson, R. C., & Freebody, P. (1981). Vocabulary knowledge. In J. T. Guthrie (Ed.), *Comprehension and teaching: Research reviews* (pp. 77–117). Newark, DE: International Reading Association.

Anderson, R. C., & Nagy, W. E. (1993). *The vocabulary conundrun.* (Report No. 570). Urbana, IL: University of Illinois, Center for the Study of Reading (ERIC Document Reproduction Service No. ED 354 489).

Anderson, R. C. & Ortony, A. (1975). On putting apples into bottles—A problem of polysemy. *Cognitive Psychology, 7,* 176–180.

Anderson, R. C., & Pearson, P. D. (1984). [A schema-theoretic view of basic processes in reading. In P. D. Pearson (Ed.),] *Handbook of reading research* (pp. 255–317). New York: Longman.

Anderson, R. C., Pichert, J. W., Goetz, E. T., Schallert, D. L., Stevens, K. V., & Trollip, S. R. (1976). Instantiation of general terms. *Journal of Verbal Learning and Verbal Behavior, 15,* 667–679.

Anderson, R. C., Reynolds, R. E., Schallert, D. L., & Goetz, E. T. (1977). Frameworks for comprehending discourse. *American Educational Research Journal, 14,* 367–381.

Anderson, R. C., Spiro, R. J., & Anderson, M. C. (1978). Schemata as scaffolding for the representation of information in discourse. *American Educational Research Journal, 15,* 433–440.

Beck, I. L., McKeown, M. G., & Omanson, R. C. (1987). The effects and uses of diverse vocabulary instructional techniques. In M. C. McKeown & M. E. Curtis (Eds.), *The nature of vocabulary acquisition* (pp. 147–164). Hillsdale, NJ: Lawrence Erlbaum Associates.

Bolinger, D. L. (1961). Verbal evocation. *Lingua, 10,* 113–127.

Brown, R., & McNeill, D. (1966). The tip-of-the-tongue phenomenon. *Journal of Verbal Learning and Verbal Behavior, 5,* 325–337.

Bybee, R. W., & Sund, R. B. (1982). *Piaget for educators.* Columbus, OH: Merrill.

Carroll, J. B. (1964a). Words, meanings and concepts: Part I. Their nature. *Harvard Educational Review, 34,* 178–190.

Carroll, J. B. (1964b). Words, meanings and concepts: Part II. Concept teaching and learning. *Harvard Educational Review, 34,* 191–202.

Dale, E., O'Rourke, J., & Bamman, H. A. (1971). *Techniques of teaching vocabulary.* Palo Alto, CA: Field Enterprises.

Davidson, S., Stickney, C. P., & Weil, R. L. (1980). *Intermediate accounting concepts, methods and uses.* Hinsdale, IL: Dryden Press.

Duffelmeyer, F. A. (1985). Teaching word meanings from an experience base. *The Reading Teacher, 39,* 6–9.

Eeds, M. (1985). Bookwords: Using a beginning word list of high frequency words from children's literature K–3. *The Reading Teacher, 38,* 418–423.

Elley, W. B. (1989). Vocabulary acquisition from listening to stories. *Reading Research Quarterly, 24,* 174–187.

Fry, E., & Sakiey, E. (1986). Common words not taught in basal reading series. *The Reading Teacher, 39,* 395–398.

Gipe, J. (1978-1979). Investigating techniques for teaching word meanings. *Reading Research Quarterly, 14,* 624–644.

Gold, Y. (1981). Helping students discover the origins of words. *The Reading Teacher, 35,* 350–351.

Gough, P. B., Juel, C. & Griffith, P. L. (1992). Reading, spelling, and the orthographic cipher. In P. B. Gough, L. C. Ehri, & R. Treiman (Eds.), *Reading acquisition* (pp. 35–48). Hillsdale, NJ: Erlbaum.

Gunderson, L. (1984). One last word list. *Alberta Journal of Educational Research, 30,* 259–269.

Halff, H. M., Ortony, A., & Anderson, R. C. (1976). A context-sensitive representation of word meaning. *Memory and Cognition, 4,* 378–383.

Harris, A. J., & Jacobson, M. D. (1982). *Basic reading vocabularies.* New York: Macmillan.

Heimlich, J. E., & Pittleman, S. D. (1986). *Semantic mapping: Classroom applications.* Newark, DE: International Reading Association.

Hirsch, E. D., Jr. (1989). *First dictionary of cultural literacy.* Boston: Houghton Mifflin.

Hoffman, J. V., McCarthy, S. J., Abbott, J., Christian, C., Corman, L., Curry, C., Dressman, M., Elliott, B., Matherne, D., & Stahle, D. (1994). So what's new in the new basals? A focus on first grade. *Journal of Reading Behavior, 26,* 47–73.

Huff, P. (1983). Classroom organization. In E. Alexander (Ed.), *Teaching reading* (2nd ed., pp. 450–468). Boston: Little, Brown.

Jenkins, J. R., Matlock, B., & Slocum, T. A. (1989). Two approaches to vocabulary instruction: The teaching of individual word meanings and practice in deriving word meanings. *Reading Research Quarterly, 24,* 215–235.

Johnson, D. D., & Pearson, P. D. (1984). *Teaching reading vocabulary* (2nd ed.). New York: Holt, Rinehart & Winston.

Johnson, D. E., Pittleman, S. D., & Heimlich, J. E. (1986). Semantic mapping. *The Reading Teacher, 39,* 778–783.

Katz, J. J. (1972). *Semantic theory.* New York: Harper & Row.

Kinzer, C. K. (1981). *Regular vs. mixed meanings effects on second and sixth graders' learning of multiple meaning words.* Unpublished doctoral dissertation, University of California, Berkeley.

Kinzer, C. K. (1982). *Interference effects of known meanings on vocabulary learning: Encountering the unexpected during the reading process.* Paper presented at the annual meeting of the International Reading Association, Chicago, IL.

Kurth, R. (1980). Building a conceptual base for vocabulary development. *Reading Psychology, 1,* 115–120.

Labov, W. (1973). The boundaries of words and their meanings. In J. N. Bailey & R. W. Shuy (Eds.), *New ways of analyzing variations in English*. Washington, DC: Georgetown University Press.

Leech, G. (1974). *Semantics*. New York: Penguin.

Lenneberg, E. H. (1967). *Biological foundations of language*. New York: John Wiley & Sons.

Lowery, L. (1981). *Learning about learning: Classification abilities*. Berkeley: University of California, Berkeley, PDARC Department of Education Publication.

Lyons, J. (1977). *Semantics* (2 vols.). Cambridge, MA: Cambridge University Press.

Marzano, R. J., & Marzano, J. S. (1988). *A cluster approach to vocabulary acquisition*. Newark, DE: International Reading Association.

Mason, J., Kniseley, E., & Kendall, J. (1979). Effects of polysemous words on sentence comprehension. *Reading Research Quarterly, 15*, 49–65.

Masonheimer, P. E., Drum, P. A., & Ehri, L. C. (1984). Does environmental print identification lead children into word reading? *Journal of Reading Behavior, 16*, 257–271.

Murphy, S. (1986). Children's comprehension of deictic categories in oral and written language. *Reading Research Quarterly, 21*, 118–131.

Nagy, W. E. (1988). *Teaching vocabulary to improve reading comprehension*. Newark, DE: International Reading Association.

Nagy, W. E., et al. (1992). *Guidelines for instruction in structural analysis*. (Report No. 554). Urbana, IL: University of Illinois, Center for the Study of Reading (ERIC Document Reproduction Service No. ED 345 207).

Nagy, W. E., & Scott, J. A. (1990). Word schemas: Expectations about the form and meaning of new words. *Cognition and Instruction, 7*, 105–127.

Noyce, R. M., & Christie, J. F. (1989). *Integrating reading and writing instruction*. Needham Heights, MA: Allyn & Bacon.

Rosch, E. H. (1978). Principles of categorization. In E. H. Rosch & B. B. Lloyd (Eds.), *Cognition and categorization* (pp. 27–48). New York: Erlbaum.

Shapiro, J., & Gunderson, L. (1988). A comparison of vocabulary generated by grade 1 students in whole language classrooms and basal reader vocabulary. *Reading Research and Instruction, 27,* 40–46.

Sherfey, G. & Huff, P. (1976). Designing the science learning center. *Science and Children, 14*, 11–12.

Stahl, S. A., & Murray, B. A. (1993). Environmental print, phonemic awareness, letter recognition, and word recognition. In D. J. Leu & C. K. Kinzer (Eds.), *Examining central issues in literacy research, theory, and practice* (pp. 227–233). Chicago, IL: National Reading Conference.

Stahl, S. A., & Vancil, S. J. (1986). Discussion is what makes semantic maps work in reading instruction. *The Reading Teacher, 40*, 62–67.

Vygotsky, L. S. (1962). *Thought and language*. (E. Haufman & G. Vokow, Trans.). Cambridge, MA: MIT Press.

Woodson, M. I. C. E. (1974). Seven aspects of teaching concepts. *Journal of Educational Psychology, 66*, 184–188.

CHAPTER

Comprehension of Extended Text

9

"'You mean that sometimes the words on the page don't mean what they say, Ms. Allen?' Julian asked me this question today and it led to a wonderful discussion about reading between the lines. I was surprised at how many of my students didn't know that they often contributed their own meaning to a story. Many of them thought that the meaning of a story came only from the words themselves. I am going to have to pick up on this discussion each day as we read our big books together and as they listen during read alouds. It is important, I think, for my first graders to understand that they contribute to the meaning of a story and that, often, individuals have different interpretations of the same story."

A reflective journal entry from a first-year teacher.

Units of writing that are at least a sentence in length are called extended text. When readers encounter extended text, three new types of knowledge become important: syntactic, discourse, and metacognitive knowledge. This chapter describes instruction that is designed to help students comprehend these elements of extended text. It also considers the special situation of students attempting to comprehend extended text with limited English proficiency. Our discussion of comprehension issues will continue in chapter 10 where we will look at the use of content-area reading selections.

One important concept in this chapter is the role that inferences play in our understanding of language. We use syntactic, discourse, and metacognitive knowledge to make inferences as we read. A second important concept is that differences between oral and written language make reading comprehension a challenge for young children. Both of these concepts will be discussed at the beginning of the chapter since they provide important insights about the nature of comprehension processes.

Chapter 9 includes information that will help you answer questions such as:

1. How do inferences contribute to comprehension and response?
2. How is syntactic knowledge developed?
3. How is discourse knowledge developed?
4. How is metacognitive knowledge developed?
5. How can we support the comprehension needs of students with limited English proficiency?
6. In what ways can questioning strategies be used to develop reading comprehension?
7. How can a literacy framework guide the use of extended text?

KEY CONCEPTS

author-and-you QARs
cause-and-effect relationships
drawing conclusions
DRTA
inference
in-my-head QARs
in-the-book QARs
language experience sentences
metacognitive knowledge
on-your-own QARs

predicting outcomes
putting-it-together QARs
reciprocal questioning
reciprocal teaching
right-there QARs
sequence relationship
slot-filling inference
syntactic knowledge
text-connecting inference

HOW DO INFERENCES CONTRIBUTE TO COMPREHENSION AND RESPONSE?

Before considering instructional practices that support comprehension, let's take a look at two important concepts that are at the center of any discussion about comprehension: inferential reasoning and the differences between oral and written language.

Some people refer to inferential reasoning as reading between the lines (Beck, 1989). Strictly speaking, an **inference** is a reasoned assumption about meaning that is not directly stated in the text. Readers make inferences whenever they add meaning to the explicit, or stated, meaning of a text. They do this with nearly every sentence they read. There are two basic types of inferences: text-connecting and slot-filling. A **text-connecting inference** occurs when a reader connects two different pieces of information in a text. For example, most readers would make a text-connecting inference if they read the following sentences:

> The Marshall Islands consist of low coral atolls. Majuro is the capital of the Marshall Islands.

These sentences do not explicitly specify that Majuro lies on a low coral atoll. Nevertheless, a proficient reader is likely to make that inference since the Marshall Islands are low coral atolls and Majuro is in the Marshall Islands.

A second type of inference is a **slot-filling inference,** which occurs when a reader adds background knowledge to a text, thereby filling in missing "slots" of meaning. For example, if you happen to have the appropriate background knowledge, you can correctly infer the activity in this sentence:

> Dr. Christiansen made the cast quickly with his Orvis graphite and double-taper.

With background knowledge about fly-fishing, you may have correctly inferred that Dr. Christiansen was fishing with his Orvis graphite fly rod and his double-taper fly line. Without that knowledge you may have incorrectly inferred that Dr. Christiansen was repairing a broken bone. In either case you made a slot-filling inference; you added background knowledge to the text to fill in missing information. Reading is very much an inferential process.

DIFFERENCES BETWEEN ORAL AND WRITTEN LANGUAGE

Reading is also a process that requires young children to become familiar with the differences between oral and written language. Beginning readers are already effective users of oral language (McGee & Richgels, 1990). With fairly sophisticated skill they orally communicate their needs, share

inference
A reasoned assumption about meaning that is not explicitly stated in the text.

text-connecting inference
An inference that occurs when a reader connects two pieces of textual information to make a reasoned assumption about meaning.

slot-filling inference
An inference that occurs when a reader uses background knowledge to add meaning to a text.

their joys, and articulate their disappointments. What they have yet to acquire on the road to literacy consists primarily of those aspects of written language that are different from oral language (Leu, 1982; Purcell-Gates, 1989).

These differences exist within each knowledge source important to the reading process, and teachers must understand them if they hope to meet their students' needs in becoming proficient readers and writers.

Differences Associated with Decoding Knowledge

There is one obvious difference between oral and written language in the area of decoding knowledge: separate symbol systems are used to represent meaning. In oral language, sounds are used; in written language, letters represent meaning. Beginning readers are already familiar with how sounds are used, but they are relatively unfamiliar with how letters are used. In order to access meaning in written language, young readers must become familiar with the relationships among letters, words, and sounds. This difference between oral and written language and many instructional practices are described in chapter 7.

Differences Associated with Vocabulary Knowledge

All words can be used in either oral or written language. Nevertheless, some words appear more frequently in written language, and young readers need to learn those meanings and labels that they may not yet have acquired from their oral language experiences. For example, children are familiar with the word *car* in oral language but are not so familiar with the words *auto* or *automobile,* which are more common in written language. Such words usually occur in content-specific writing, which is discussed in chapter 8.

Differences Associated with Syntactic Knowledge

There are at least two important syntactic differences between oral and written language. First, children must become familiar with how punctuation is used in written language to represent the stress and intonation patterns of oral language. Punctuation is important in conveying appropriate meaning, as the following examples demonstrate:

1. Now! I need your help! (Not: Now I need your help.)
2. Bob talked to the teacher with Bill and Becky. Lou wanted to talk to him, too. (Not: Bob talked to the teacher with Bill and Becky Lou wanted to talk to him too.)

Second, children must become familiar with the syntactic patterns that are common in written language. The oral language that they already know uses many coordinated patterns, often linked by the word *and.* If you listen to the oral language of children during Sharing Time (sometimes called Show and Tell) you will notice this coordinated oral style:

Activities that allow a child to role-play using background knowledge in ways that links writing and reading can enhance comprehension and build links between oral and written language.

> I saw José *and then* I went to Bill's house *and then* I played ball *and then* I rode my bike *and* I went home.

Beginning readers use this coordinated pattern frequently in their oral language (Michaels & Cook-Gumperz, 1979). Written language contains more integrated patterns, especially to express sequence and cause-and-effect relationships, which use words like *because, consequently, before,* and *after:*

> I saw José *before* I went to Bill's house. *After* seeing him, I played baseball. *After* the game, I rode my bike home.

Beginning readers need to develop an understanding of these written language patterns. Often this is done by reading aloud to children so they have a chance to hear these patterns. Familiarity with these written language patterns is also developed from their reading and writing experiences.

EXPLORING DIVERSE POINTS OF VIEW

Some individuals believe that one can not teach children how to comprehend. They argue that it is something that one develops on one's own as a result of extensive reading, thinking, and discussion opportunities. These teachers attempt to maximize reading experiences and opportunities for students to think and discuss what they have read. They believe that each child will acquire insights about comprehension that are uniquely appropriate for that child as a result of these experiences. Others believe that comprehension processes can be taught. These teachers teach specific comprehension skills and strategies to their students. They believe that too many children are missing basic comprehension strategies and need direct instruction in this area. Still other teachers believe that children learn best when they have extensive reading, thinking, and discussion opportunities combined with specific instruction in comprehension strategies where they see it to be necessary. How do you feel about this issue? As you consider your response, think about your beliefs about how children learn to read. Can you find a connection between this aspect of your literacy framework and your initial thoughts about comprehension instruction?

Differences Associated with Discourse Knowledge

Two important differences between oral and written language exist in discourse knowledge. First, young children are used to seeing the meaning of pronoun and adverbial references (for example, *he, she, this, here, there, now*) in oral language contexts. Written language, however, often requires that readers infer the meanings of implicit pronoun and abverbial references without a visible context (Rubin, 1980). Consequently, the text-connecting and slot-filling inferences demanded by pronouns and adverbs in written language represent an important learning task for beginning readers since they often must imagine the references to these words (Murphy, 1985).

Second, the difference in the discourse structure of oral and written language also presents difficulties for young children learning to read (Teale & Sulzby, 1986). Through oral language experiences children develop knowledge about how oral conversations are organized. However, they have few opportunities to develop an understanding of how different narrative forms are organized (Sulzby, 1982). And they have even fewer opportunities to understand how different types of informational writing are organized. This is why reading a social studies or science textbook is such a challenging task for children in the elementary grades. Nonetheless, knowledge of these discourse forms is important to a proficient reader.

Differences Associated with Metacognitive Knowledge

Different types of metacognitive, or strategic, knowledge are also required for oral and written language tasks. Oral language is temporary, whereas written language is permanent. And that permanence allows special strategies to assist decoding, vocabulary, syntactic, and discourse processes. Consider decoding, for example. Students need to acquire strategies that help them determine the oral equivalent of a word. Rereading a sentence to better understand the surrounding context is a strategy unique to written language. With oral language the message occurs in a single stream of sounds that disappears quickly.

This same situation exists within other knowledge sources important for reading. Within discourse knowledge, for instance, young readers need to know that reading the summary at the end of an informational article can give them a preview of the major points in the article before they read it. They also need to know how to skim a piece quickly to see whether it contains the general information they are seeking. And they need to know how to scan a piece to find the specific information they want. All of these strategies are examples of the unique metacognitive knowledge that young readers need to acquire in order to understand written language.

It is clear, then, that children who are familiar with oral language patterns need to become familiar with the different patterns that exist in written language. Much of comprehension instruction is based on this principle.

DEVELOPING SYNTACTIC KNOWLEDGE

Syntactic knowledge includes an understanding of the word order rules that determine grammatical function, meaning, and pronunciation. For example, it helps us distinguish the difference in meaning between *Tom saw Maria* and *Maria saw Tom,* two sentences with identical words but different word order. Syntactic knowledge contributes to a reader's comprehension of extended text, and children's literature can be especially helpful in developing this knowledge.

syntactic knowledge
The knowledge that readers have of the word order rules that determine the meaning of sentences.

Developing Syntactic Knowledge with Children's Literature

Children's literature can be an especially supportive environment for increasing children's knowledge of syntactic structures that occur in written language. Studying the sentence patterns used by some of our best authors allows students to closely observe the ways in which word order patterns contribute to meaning. A useful method framework for developing syntactic knowledge, especially among older students, is a **style study.** This method framework was described earlier in chapter 5 as a means to connect reading and writing experiences. It consists of the following procedural steps:

style study
A method framework where students develop insight about writing by looking closely at how authors use different language patterns and then try to emulate those patterns.

1. Read a passage from children's literature together.
2. Identify several stylistic patterns used by this author.
3. Discuss why the author probably chose to use these patterns.
4. Provide students with a writing task where they are asked to try out at least one of the patterns they have seen.
5. Share the results.

Often, teachers will incorporate a style study with the reading of chapter books, periodically looking at a chapter carefully for syntactic patterns used by a particular author and then having students try using these patterns in their writing. This is an excellent chance to expose students to patterns that do not often occur in their oral language experiences such as participial phrases at the beginning of sentences (*Having noticed the dark clouds,* Louise pulled her collar up tight around her neck.) or the use of related independent clauses separated by a semicolon (The sky was dark; it would rain before she got home.). Many other syntactic structures will appear as you read exceptional works of children's literature together. As you encounter them, consider the use of a style study to help students discover their meaning and to help students incorporate them into their own writing patterns.

A style study is effective in helping young readers develop familiarity with three important aspects of syntactic knowledge: punctuation, sequence relationships, and cause-and-effect relationships. Each is related to the inferences readers must make and to the differences between oral and written language.

Punctuation

A reader's ability to determine stress and intonation in written language contributes to the comprehension process (Cook-Gumperz & Gumperz, 1981). Knowledge of punctuation assists a reader in determining the correct stress, intonation, and meaning of a sentence.

Instruction in using punctuation takes place early in a reading program, usually by the end of third grade. Teachers often teach punctuation concepts by linking children's oral language to its written representation. They sometimes use a method framework referred to as **language experience sentences,** a variation of the language experience story described earlier (see chapter 3). Language experience sentences include these four procedural steps:

1. Elicit oral language containing the target punctuation.
2. Transcribe the language containing the target punctuation.
3. Read the transcribed language, modeling the use of punctuation.
4. Practice reading similar sentences.

During the first step the teacher elicits an oral sentence containing the desired stress and intonation pattern. This task is often accomplished by asking students about something they have done or said. In step two the teacher transcribes that sentence, usually on the chalkboard. For a more permanent copy the sentence could be transcribed on a large sheet of card stock or other heavy paper. Step three requires the teacher to model the use of punctuation while reading the transcribed sentence aloud. The stress and intonation pattern represented by the punctuation mark should be clearly expressed, the punctuation mark should be identified,

language experience sentences
A method framework used to develop an understanding of punctuation.

MODEL LESSON
....
Teaching Punctuation Using Language Experience Sentences in Ms. Brown's Class

Elicit Oral Language Containing the Target Punctuation
Ms. Brown: Daria, tell us three things that you do before you come to school in the morning.
Daria: Let's see. I wake up, I eat breakfast, and I brush my teeth. That's three things.

Transcribe the Language Containing the Target Punctuation.
Ms. Brown writes the following sentence on the blackboard:
  Daria wakes up, eats breakfast, and brushes her teeth in the morning.

Read the Transcribed Language, Modeling the Use of Punctuation
Ms. Brown: Listen while I read this sentence. [Ms. Brown reads.] Do you see that I wrote this little mark between each of the things Daria does in the morning? This mark is called a comma. Can you say that word? Comma. What happens when I'm reading and I come to a comma? Listen again. [Ms. Brown reads.]
Sam: You kind of stop for a bit but not like at the end.
Ms. Brown: Right. With a comma you should stop reading for just a little bit, but not as long as you do at the end of a sentence.

Practice Reading Similar Sentences
Ms. Brown: Let's read some more sentences like this. Michael, what do you do when you get home after school? Tell us three or four things so we can write them down and put commas between them.
Michael: I go home. I change my clothes and have a snack, and I ride my dirt bike, and I have dinner.
[Ms. Brown transcribes this series with commas and has children read it orally: Michael goes home, changes his clothes, has a snack, and rides his dirt bike until dinner. Then she repeats this activity with other students and other sentences containing commas to separate items in a series.]

and its function discussed. Finally, the teacher should elicit other sentences containing the desired stress and intonation pattern, transcribe them, and have students practice reading them. In the model lesson, Ms. Brown is teaching her first-grade students the stress and intonation pattern associated with a comma separating items in a list. She is using language experience sentences to teach this concept.

In addition to the use of language experience sentences, other strategies may be used to support students' understanding of punctuation. Several are described in Figure 9-1.

Sequence Relationships

Sequence relationships are often expressed in syntactic patterns. This structure is sometimes difficult for younger children to grasp. A sequence relationship expresses the time relationship between two or more events. Often these events are mentioned in the same or adjacent sentences,

sequence relationship
A relationship of time between two or more events, explicitly or implicitly stated.

FIGURE 9-1

Strategies used to develop an understanding of how punctuation serves to determine meaningful relationships within sentences

 Dramatic Reading. Encourage cooperative learning groups to choose a short selection (one or two paragraphs) for dramatic reading to the class. Be sure the selection contains a variety of punctuation marks. Allow each group a short period to practice and agree on the exact intonation to use as they talk about the meaning of each sentence. Use this activity to introduce new books to your students, both the students doing the oral reading and the students who will be listening.

 Same Sentence, Different Meaning. Give students sentence pairs that are identical except for punctuation.

> "Linda!" said Peter. "I need that paper now."
> Linda said, "Peter, I need that paper now."

Have students work in cooperative learning groups to read each sentence with the correct intonation and identify the correct meanings.

 Style Studies. Style studies can be expecially useful with younger students to develop their understanding of punctuation as they read works of chidren's literature together. Think about using this method framework to help them see patterns with quotation marks, exclamation points, colons, parentheses, and ellipses.

---

sometimes in separate paragraphs. Sequence relationships can be either explicitly or implicitly stated, as shown in the following examples:

Explicit

Events appearing in the order in which they happened	Tom finished his work *before* he went home.
Events appearing in the opposite order from that in which they happened	Tom went home *after* he finished his work.

Implicit

Events appearing in the order in which they happened (separate sentences)	Tom finished his work. He went home.
Events appearing in the order in which they happened (linked by a coordinating conjunction)	Tom finished his work, and he went home.

Explicit sequence relationships contain signal words, such as *before, after, then, later, following, first, initially, earlier, afterwards, next,* or *finally.* These signal words state the time relationship between the two events and thus should make such relationships easy to comprehend. Unfortunately, however, two elements of explicit sequence relationships are difficult for young children. First, the signal words for sequence relationships are not common in the oral language of young children. Consequently, they are often unfamiliar with the meanings of signal words and must learn both their meanings and their function in explicit sequence relationships.

A second difficulty is that relationships may appear in the opposite order from that in which they happened. In oral language, children are accustomed to events being stated in the order in which they occur, and they assume that a similar situation exists in written language. As a result, children often interpret sentences such as "Tom went home after he finished his work" as "Tom went home, and then he finished his work." Children have the greatest difficulty comprehending explicit sequence relationships when the events appear in the opposite order from that in which they happened (Pearson & Camperell, 1981; Pearson & Johnson, 1978).

Sequence relationships can also be implicitly stated, requiring readers to make an inference, usually a text-connecting inference. Implicit sequence relationships may be indicated by sequentially ordered events in separate sentences or by the coordinating conjunction *and* within a single sentence. Such relationships require readers to infer the temporal relationship between events. This type of inference presents little difficulty for young readers because sequence relationships are expressed in the same way in oral language.

With younger readers sequence relationships are often taught within a language experience story, which typically contains these steps:

1. Provide students with a vivid experience.
2. Elicit oral language that describes the experience.
3. Transcribe the students' oral language.
4. Help students read what was transcribed.

Throughout a language experience story, discussion should help students identify the various events and their sequence relationships. Special attention should be devoted to helping students understand the meanings of signal words and the ways in which they identify sequence relationships. Ms. Sanchez demonstrates in the model lesson how this method framework can be used to develop an understanding of sequence relationships.

Among older readers, instruction in understanding sequence relationships often takes place during the discussion of a story. Questions that can be used to initiate a discussion about sequence relationships include these:

When did X take place?

What happened before X?

What happened before Y?

Did X happen before or after Y?

An important distinction must be made here, though, between using questions to test and to teach reading comprehension (Durkin, 1981,

M O D E L   L E S S O N

Teaching Sequence Relationships in a Language Experience Story in Ms. Sanchez's Class

Provide Students with a Vivid Experience. Today, Ms. Sanchez is taking her first-grade class to the library. She decides to build on this experience when they return to the classroom.

Elicit Oral Language That Describes the Experience. When they return, Ms. Sanchez has her class sit on the carpeted floor in front of the chalkboard. She elicits several sentences from the students, one for each event they experienced in the library.

Transcribe the Students' Oral Language. Ms. Sanchez writes down each sentence on the chalkboard as the student says it.
> We went to the library.
> Ms. Hamm showed us the new bookshelves.
> We sat in a circle.
> Ms. Hamm read us a story about the ox-cart man.
> We got to check out a new book.
> We came back to our room.

Help Students Read What Was Transcribed. Ms. Sanchez has her students read the entire sequence of sentences. Then she carries out three activities to assist her students' understanding of sequence relationships.

First, Ms. Sanchez initiates a discussion, asking sequence questions such as "What happened before we sat in a circle? What happened before Ms. Hamm read us a story? What happened before we came back to our room?" She writes the students' responses next to the story they had dictated earlier.
> Ms. Hamm showed us the new bookshelves *before* we sat in a circle.
> We sat in a circle *before* Ms. Hamm read us a story.
> We got to check out a new book *before* we came back to our room.

Second, Ms. Sanchez discusses the meaning of the signal word *before* and then has students read this second set of sentences. Together they discuss the sequence of the different events and the way in which certain words like *before* are used to show that order.

Third, Ms. Sanchez has her students draw pictures of two events, one happening before the other. She walks around the classroom, helping students write a sentence containing the word *before* to describe their pictures. Afterwards, students read their sentences and show their pictures in a short cooperative learning group activity.

1986). If you accept correct responses and reject incorrect responses and do nothing else, you are testing reading comprehension. You are simply determining whether students can answer the questions. If you follow sequence questions with a request for students to model their reasoning processes, you are teaching reading comprehension. After each sequence question, for example, you might ask, "How did you figure that out?" In order to answer, students would have to model the reasoning processes that they used. The suggestions below will help you teach, not test, understanding of sequence relationships during the discussion of a story.

- Avoid playing the can-you-guess-the-answer-I-have-in-mind game. Ask a sequence question to direct students' attention to particular events in a story and then initiate a discussion about the sequence relationships that exist there. Do not ask a question merely to obtain a correct response.

- Follow a sequence question with a brief discussion. For example, ask students how they determined their answer to your question. What information did they use from the text? What information did they figure out by themselves because it was missing from the text? Have they ever used such a strategy before? Is it a good one to remember? After students model their reasoning processes, model your own, and explain how you arrived at your answer. Your explanation should help students who were unable to determine the sequence relationship.

- Pay particular attention to sequence relationships that present events in the opposite order from that in which they occurred. Those will be most difficult for young readers to understand.

- Before reading a story with difficult sequence relationships, use a prereading question to direct students' attention to the important information. For example, say to students, "Read and see whether you can find out which happened first—*X* or *Y*."

In addition to language experience sentences, language experience stories, and discussion techniques, the strategies in Figure 9-2 can also be used to teach sequence relationships.

Cause-and-Effect Relationships

A **cause-and-effect relationship** expresses the relationship between two events in which one event is the consequence of the other. Often the two events appear in the same or adjacent sentences; sometimes they appear in separate paragraphs. Cause-and-effect relationships can also be either explicitly or implicitly stated.

Explicit cause-and-effect relationships contain signal words such as *because* and *therefore,* which clearly indicate the causal relationship between the two events. Again, we might think that such words would make these explicit relationships easy to comprehend, but unfortunately, young children are often unfamiliar with the meanings of those words. Consequently, both the meanings of signal words and their function in explicit cause-and-effect relationships are frequently taught to young children. The cause-and-effect signal words usually taught are listed in Table 9-1.

Implicit cause-and-effect relationships require readers to infer the correct relationship between two ideas in the absence of signal words. The two events are stated in separate sentences or are connected by the

cause-and-effect relationship
A causal relationship between two or more events, explicitly or implicitly stated.

FIGURE 9-2

Strategies for supporting students' understanding of sequence relationships

 Time Lines. Use time lines like the one below to help children understand the sequence relationships in a story. Time lines are especially helpful when event sequences are complicated or lengthy. They are most commonly used after a story has been read but can also be used as a prereading activity to develop expectations and guide students as they read a story.

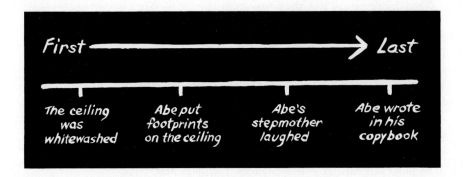

 Cloze Tasks. Use sentence pairs like the following to initiate discussions of why certain words were selected and whether the sentences express the same meaning. Cooperative learning groups could provide the forum for these discussions.

_____ putting on his shoe, Jim tied the laces.
(Before, After)

Jim put on his shoe _____ he tied the laces.
(before, after)

TABLE 9-1

Signal words for cause-and-effect relationships.

Signal words	Examples
because	He went home *because* he was ill.
so	He was ill, and *so* he went home.
therefore	He was ill and *therefore* went home.
hence	He was ill. *Hence* he went home.
thus	He was ill and *thus* went home.
since	*Since* he was ill, he went home.
as a result	He was ill and *as a result* went home.
consequently	He was ill and *consequently* went home.
for this reason	He was ill. *For this reason* he went home.
that being the case	He looked ill. *That being the case,* he went home.
on account of	*On account of* his illness, he went home.
accordingly	He looked ill and *accordingly* went home.

M O D E L   L E S S O N
Teaching Cause-and-Effect in Ms. Clancy's Class

Ms. Clancy's students understand the concepts *cause, effect,* and *signal word.* They have been reading the book *The Secret Soldier* (McGovern, 1975) and have just finished a page that began with the following paragraph.

> The trouble was getting worse. In many villages, people were getting ready for war. Groups of men and young boys began training to be soldiers. They were called minutemen because they were ready to fight at a minute's notice. (p. 19)

Ms. Clancy:	Look up at the first paragraph. Why were these soldiers called minutemen?
Marcus:	Because they could fight at a minute's notice.
Ms. Clancy:	Tell us how you know that, Marcus.
Marcus:	It says *because.*
Ms. Clancy:	Right! *Because* is a signal word that signals a special relationship between two ideas. It tells us why something happened. Can you find the two ideas in this sentence?
Linda:	"They were called minutemen" and "they were ready to fight at a minute's notice."
Ms. Clancy:	Good! Can anyone find the cause and the effect statements in this sentence?
Bonnie:	I can. "They were ready to fight at a minute's notice" is the cause, and "They were called minutemen" must be the effect. Being ready to fight at a minute's notice causes them to be called minutemen.
Ms. Clancy:	Good! Now look at the first two sentences in this paragraph, and read them again to yourself. Sometimes signal words are missing, yet we still have a special relationship between the two ideas. One sentence can be the cause and another sentence the effect, even without a signal word. Does one of the first two sentences describe a cause?
Joan:	I think people were getting ready for war, so the trouble was getting worse. "People were getting ready for war" is the cause.
Marcus:	But the people didn't cause the trouble. The trouble caused the people to get ready for war. I think "The trouble was getting worse" is the cause.
Ms. Clancy:	One way to test your idea is to put these two sentences together with a signal word like *because* at the beginning of each sentence. That usually tells you which one is the cause and which one is the effect.
Joan:	Because the trouble was getting worse, the people were getting ready for war. Yeah. That's what I mean. "The trouble was getting worse" must be the cause.

coordinating conjunction *and* in the same sentence. The following examples show both explicit and implicit cause-and-effect relationships.

Explicit

The hatch had just started, and *therefore* the fish began to feed.
    (cause)   (signal word)   (effect)

Implicit

The hatch had just started. The fish began to feed.
    (cause)   (effect)

The hatch had just started, and the fish began to feed.
    (cause)   (effect)

With implicit cause-and-effect relationships readers must have the appropriate background knowledge in order to infer the correct meaning. Without that knowledge readers may interpret the two events as being temporally, but not causally, ordered. For example, the implicit sentences just presented might be interpreted as "First, something unrelated to the fish (maybe a bird's egg) hatched. Then the fish began to feed." In that case the two events would not be thought to be causally related. However, appropriate background knowledge would lead to the correct inference, that the mayflies are hatching, and this causes the fish to begin feeding.

Instruction in cause-and-effect relationships often takes place during the discussion of a story. Questions that might be used to direct students' attention to cause-and-effect relationships include these:

Why did Z take place?

What happened as a result of X?

How are Z and X connected?

Which words tell us that Z happened because of X?

As with sequence relationships, it is important to initiate discussions that teach, not test, comprehension. It is also important to direct student attention to the text so that concrete examples of causes, effects, and signal words can be seen. The model lesson above shows how Ms. Clancy taught cause-and-effect to her sixth graders.

Discussions in either oral or written contexts can be used to develop an understanding of cause-and-effect relationships. In addition, there are many other strategies, several of which are described in Figure 9-3.

FIGURE 9-3

Strategies for developing an understanding of cause-and-effect relationships

 Marking Cause-and-Effect Relationships. Present cause-and-effect statements, and show students how to identify each component in the relationship, marking each with an appropriate letter or symbol.

      ⓒ   ⓔ
The school bell rang for recess, <u>so</u> the children went outside.

 Signal Word Cloze Tasks. Teach the meanings of new signal words according to methods outlined in chapter 8. Then have students practice using the new words in cloze sentences.

Debbie was ill _____ she went home
(and thus, previously, earlier)

_____ the test, Bill was nervous and irritable.
(On the other hand, On account of, On my own time)

DEVELOPING DISCOURSE KNOWLEDGE

Discourse knowledge also contributes to comprehension (Beck, McKeown, Omanson, & Pople, 1984). It includes the knowledge of language organization that helps us understand entire texts. Whereas syntactic knowledge allows us to determine meaningful relationships among words, discourse knowledge allows us to determine meaningful relationships among sentences. At least three aspects of discourse knowledge are important for young readers to acquire: pronoun and adverbial references, drawing conclusions, and predicting outcomes. Each is related to oral and written language differences and to the inferences that readers are required to make as they comprehend a text.

> **discourse knowledge**
> The knowledge that readers have of the language organization that determines meaning beyond the single-sentence level; includes knowledge of different types of writing.

Pronoun and Adverbial References

Pronoun references are words that are substituted for nouns or noun phrases; they include words like *I, you,* and *she.* **Adverbial references** are words that are substituted for specific designations of time or location; they include words such as *here, today, now, last week,* and *last month.* Both pronoun and adverbial references are very common, as we can see in the following example:

> **pronoun references**
> Words that are substituted for nouns or noun phrases.
>
> **adverbial references**
> Words that are substituted for specific time or location designations.

> Heather and *her* friend were determined to see the solar eclipse in *their* viewing box. *They* struggled with the box to get *it* right. First the hole was not big enough. Then *it* was too big. Finally, by putting tape across the hole and then poking a tiny hole in *it* with a toothpick, Heather was able to get the light to shine. *"We* can see *it here now," she* said.

Readers must infer the meanings of pronoun and adverbial references by imagining a situation they cannot see. This task is easy for mature readers, familiar with the demands of written texts. It is much more difficult for young readers (Anderson & Shifrin, 1980; Rubin, 1980), who are accustomed to seeing, not imagining, the meanings of such words in oral language contexts.

Pronoun and adverbial references require either a text-connecting or a slot-filling inference. For example, the word *they* in the preceding paragraph requires a text-connecting inference. It requires readers to understand its logical connection to its referent in the passage—the words *Heather and her friend.* Other examples in this paragraph of references that require a text-connecting inference include *her (Heather); their (Heather and her friend); it (the box); it (the hole); it (the tape); We (Heather and her friend); it (the eclipse);* and *she (Heather).*

When pronoun or adverbial references do not have an explicit referent in the text, they require readers to make a slot-filling inference. The word *here* in the example paragraph requires a slot-filling inference, in which readers must understand the logical connection between *here* and its unstated referent—the inside wall of the box. When pronoun or adverbial

Discourse knowledge, including knowledge of organizational patterns, helps readers understand entire texts.

references require a slot-filling inference, readers must have the appropriate background knowledge to fill in the missing meaning. Slot-filling inferences with pronoun or adverbial references are especially difficult for young readers to make.

The ability to infer the meanings of pronoun and adverbial references is developed early in most instructional programs, usually during the first two grades, for two reasons. First, pronoun and adverbial references are among the most common words in our language. Second, imagining the referents for pronoun and adverbial references in written language is a new task for young children.

Instruction in making text-connecting inferences for pronoun and adverbial references usually precedes instruction in making slot-filling inferences. It is easier to show students in a concrete way the connections between references and their referents. Those connections are often demonstrated by circling the references and drawing lines back to their referents. Both text-connecting and slot-filling inferences can be taught inductively but are more often taught deductively, as in the model lesson by Mr. Burns.

M O D E L   L E S S O N

Using Deductive Instruction to Teach Text-Connecting Inferences with Pronoun and Adverbial References in Mr. Burns' Class

Before beginning the lesson, Mr. Burns writes the following sentences on the chalkboard.

> Peter was talking to Joan on the phone. He said, "I don't know if Hal is at work today. Maybe he stayed at home. Is he there with you, Joan?"
> Joan said, "No. He isn't here. And Mark isn't here either. Do you know where he is? Maybe they are together somewhere."

State the Skill or Rule. Mr. Burns begins by pointing to the sentences on the blackboard and saying, "Sometimes when you read, one word will take the place of another word or phrase. Both will mean the same thing. Look at these sentences on the board. Can you read them for us, Matt?" Matt reads the sentences aloud.

Provide Examples of the Skill or Rule. Mr. Burns shows that pronoun and adverbial references are logically connected to their referents. He circles the first *He* on the board and draws an arrow back to its referent, *Peter.* Mr. Burns does the same thing with *I* and draws the arrow back to *Peter.* Then he circles the second *he* and draws an arrow back to *Hal.* While he does all of this, Mr. Burns explains that certain words often mean the same thing as other words in a story.

Provide Guided Practice. Then Mr. Burns asks the students to look at the second paragraph on the board and find similar kinds of words that mean the same thing as other words. He asks individuals to come to the board and circle each pronoun or adverb and then draw arrows back to its referent. Students follow this procedure for *he* (Hal); *here* (at work); and *they* (Hal, Mark). Mr. Burns has the students explain their decisions to the group.

Provide Independent Practice. Mr. Burns gives each student a copy of a page from *James and the Giant Peach* by Roald Dahl. He directs them to read the page looking for pronouns and their referents. Each student is to circle the pronoun and draw an arrow back to its referent. Then they are to get together in three cooperative learning groups to check their answers. When they are finished, the three groups get together with Mr. Burns and compare their answers.

Predicting Outcomes and Drawing Conclusions

Both of these processes rely on the same type of schema knowledge—**procedural knowledge**—which consists of knowledge of common event sequences. Your own procedural knowledge is probably extensive. For example, you have procedural knowledge about the first day of class in a university course, and you use that knowledge to make inferences, either when you experience that first day yourself or when you read about the experiences of someone else. The first event sequence in your procedural knowledge includes your arrival. Within that sequence you probably have a location where you prefer to sit, based on previous experiences. Some students look to the front row, others to the back row, and still others to

procedural knowledge
Knowledge of common event sequences.

an aisle seat. Your knowledge probably includes the meanings associated with sitting in each of those locations. People often sit in the front to make an impression, sit in the back to avoid making an impression, and sit next to the aisle to make a quick exit. All of this knowledge is a part of the initial event sequence in your procedural knowledge of the first day of class.

Your second event sequence probably includes your professor's arrival. It may include the fact that professors are likely to be carrying a stack of syllabi, which they set down on the table or lectern at the front of the room. It may also include your professor's writing the title of the course and his or her name on the chalkboard. Your procedural knowledge for the first day of class probably contains a number of other event sequences that define your expectations for the remainder of that first period: passing out the syllabus, going over the syllabus, finding out where the text may be purchased, and hearing why this course is the most important course in your college career.

You possess thousands of procedural schemata such as this in your background knowledge, each containing procedural steps and event sequences. You have, no doubt, a procedural schema for eating at a restaurant, driving home, eating dinner at home, flying on an airplane, and many other events. Throughout the day you use this knowledge to make inferences about what is happening or what you are reading.

The following passage and related question show how procedural knowledge is used to make inferences during reading.

> The two boys were across the street from José's house when they saw the ominous line of clouds approaching and heard the thunder. They were playing under a tall eucalyptus tree at the time and could see the lightning flash all along the storm front as it came closer. "Hurry," said José.
>
> What do you think the two boys will do?

If you have a procedural schema for what to do in a lightning storm, you are familiar with the common event sequences that accompany such a storm: getting away from trees, staying away from metal objects, heading for cover, and so on. Based on the information in the passage and your own procedural knowledge, you probably inferred that the two boys would head for shelter inside José's house.

Your inference illustrates a comprehension task referred to as **predicting outcomes,** which requires the reader to infer future effects from a stated cause. The inference in such a task is always projected into the future; it is usually a slot-filling inference about a future effect.

A related comprehension task, **drawing conclusions,** requires the reader to infer an unstated cause from a stated effect. In this case the inference is always backward to what has been read in the text. Drawing a conclusion usually requires readers to use their procedural knowledge to make a slot-filling inference about a previous cause. Let's look at the

predicting outcomes
A comprehension task requiring the reader to use appropriate procedural knowledge to infer a future effect from a stated cause; a forward inference.

drawing conclusions
A comprehension task requiring a reader to infer an unstated cause from a stated effect; a backward inference.

following passage and related question to see how this process takes place.

> The team raced to the far end of the court to cut the net down. The captain climbed up to the hoop, cut the net, put it around his neck, and let out a yell. The crowd was going crazy with excitement!
>
>   Why was everyone so excited?

Were you able to infer backwards from the stated effects in the passage to determine the unstated cause—that a basketball team had just won a tournament? If so, you relied on the information in the text and your procedural knowledge of the events commonly associated with winning a basketball tournament to make a slot-filling inference and draw a conclusion.

One of the most common method frameworks used to help children predict outcomes and draw conclusions is a **directed reading-thinking activity (DRTA).** A DRTA is an instructional procedure first developed by Stauffer (1976). It consists of three procedural steps, which are repeated as students read and discuss a selection:

1. predicting
2. reading
3. proving

During the predicting step the teacher asks students to predict the outcome and explain their inferential reasoning. At the beginning of a story, a teacher might use questions like these to initiate responses:

What will a story with this title be about? Why do you think so?

Who do you think will be in a story with a title like this? Why?

Where do you think this story will take place? Why?

Each student is expected to make a prediction and support it with a reasonable explanation. Teachers should encourage different predictions as long as students can justify them logically.

The second procedural step in a DRTA is to have students read. Teachers should ask students to read silently up to a predetermined point, at which students' earlier predictions should be checked. Directions like these might be given:

> Now that you have all told me what you think this story is going to be about, who will be in it, and where it will take place, I want you to read and see if you were correct. Read up to the end of page 2, please.

The third procedural step is proving. During this step students are asked to draw conclusions and explain their reasoning process. In discussion, students are asked to evaluate the evidence in relation to their pre-

directed reading-thinking activity (DRTA) A method framework used to assist students in predicting outcomes and drawing conclusions; involves predicting, reading, and proving.

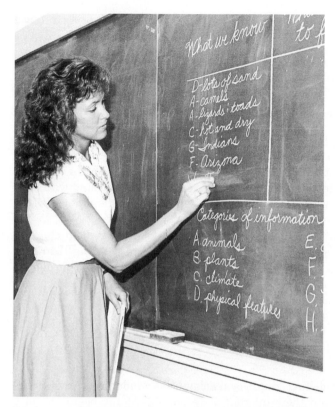

Teachers need to consider what prior knowledge is required to comprehend extended text and also how that knowledge should be integrated into reading new information.

dictions. They see whether they were correct or incorrect and, most importantly, *why* they were correct or incorrect. Questions like the following can be used to begin the discussion:

Was your guess correct? Why or why not?

What do you think now? Why?

Why do you think X happened?

Why did A (a character) do X (an event)?

What do you think will happen next?

At the end of this discussion the three-step procedure is repeated, beginning with making predictions about the next outcome.

This type of method framework can be used whenever children read a story together. It encourages them to continually think about what they have read and what is likely to happen next. Other instructional strategies can also be used, however, to develop the ability to predict outcomes and draw conclusions. Several are described in Figure 9-4.

FIGURE 9-4

Strategies that might be used to support children's ability to predict outcomes and draw conclusions

 Riddle Reading and Riddle Writing. Reading riddles provides opportunities to practice drawing conclusions in an enjoyable fashion. You may want to write a riddle on the board each day and then at the end of the day see who has figured out the answer. Older students might enjoy writing and sharing their own riddles. You could then develop a class riddle book to share with other classes in your school.

 Thematic Units. New experiences develop procedural knowledge for students, especially when they are integrated into other subject areas. For this reason thematic units across subject areas are very helpful. Organize reading experiences around specific themes. Plan experiences in other subject areas around those themes. Chapter 4 describes how thematic units can be developed.

 Reading Mysteries. Mysteries are especially valuable for providing practice in predicting outcomes and drawing conclusions. Be sure to select mysteries for read-aloud sessions. Have students predict outcomes, draw conclusions, and then explain their reasoning at various points in the story. You may wish to provide experiences with the following books:

The Case of the Cat's Meow by Crosby Bonsall

Encyclopedia Brown Saves the Day by Donald Sobol

Encyclopedia Brown: Boy Detective by Donald Sobol

Mystery at the Edge of Two Worlds by Christie Harris

Something Queer Is Going On by Elizabeth Levy

The House of Dies Drear by Virginia Hamilton

DEVELOPING METACOGNITIVE KNOWLEDGE

Metacognitive knowledge—which includes the strategies we use during reading, as well as our monitoring of comprehension—also contributes to the comprehension of extended text. As texts become more complex, metacognitive knowledge is increasingly required to facilitate comprehension. Questioning strategies are often used to develop this knowledge, but in this case teachers show students how to ask questions themselves as they read an extended text. Two method frameworks are most commonly used: reciprocal questioning and reciprocal teaching.

metacognitive knowledge
A type of knowledge important for reading that includes the strategies used during reading and comprehension monitoring.

Reciprocal Questioning

Reciprocal questioning, or **ReQuest,** is a method framework first developed by Manzo (1969). It was initially designed for remedial reading instruction but works equally well for developmental reading instruction. The following procedural steps are recommended to implement reciprocal questioning.

1. Teacher and students read.
2. Students question teacher.

reciprocal questioning (ReQuest)
A method framework designed to improve metacognition and comprehension; involves reading and questioning by both teacher and students, predicting, and checking predictions.

MODEL LESSON

Reciprocal Questioning in Ms. Dodson's Class

Ms. Dodson is using *Nate the Great and the Snowy Trail* by Marjorie Weinman Sharmat. The story tells how Nate the Great discovers his lost birthday present by following several clues.

Teacher and Students Read. Ms. Dodson passes out a copy of the book to each student. Together they talk briefly about the author and look at the cover illustration. Ms. Dodson asks students to speculate and tell what they think the story might be about. Several possibilities are identified. In the course of the discussion, several important concepts in the story also emerge and are explained. Then Ms. Dodson tells her students that good readers act like detectives and look for clues to the meaning of a story. She asks her students to read the first page silently.

Students Question Teacher

Ms. Dodson: Now, what questions do you want to ask me about what we've read? Let's try to ask questions with answers that aren't right in the story. Let's see whether I can use the clues in the story well.

Tomas: OK, how about this one: how did Nate the Great and Sludge feel?

Ms. Dodson: That's a good one. I think they were cold and wet. The story talks about the snow dog and snow detective that Nate was making and says, "They were cold, and white, and wet." That's a clue that helped me. Then Nate says, "And so were we." That's another clue. I put those two sentences together and figured out that Nate and Sludge were cold and wet.

Dominic: What was Nate the Great?

Ms. Dodson: Oh, that's easy. He was a detective. It says right there in the book, "I, Nate the Great, am a detective." Can you ask me a question with an answer that isn't right there in the book?

Dominic: What time of year was it?

3. Teacher questions students.
4. Students predict the story's outcome.
5. Teacher and students finish reading to check predictions.

During the first step both teacher and students read a portion of the selection silently. Manzo originally suggested that this be a single sentence when working with remedial readers, and that practice may be appropriate with beginning readers. With other readers, however, longer portions of a story should be used—perhaps a paragraph, a page, or even several pages.

The second procedural step has students ask the teacher questions about what they have read. In answering these questions, the teacher explains the reasoning process involved and shares with students the evidence from the text and from personal background knowledge that went into the various answers. During this phase, teachers often encourage students to ask questions that are challenging and require some degree of inferencing.

Then the teacher asks questions of the students about the same story portion. The teacher may wish to require that students explain the evi-

MODEL LESSON— *continued*

Ms. Dodson: Good. I think it was winter. It doesn't say that anywhere, does it? But they were making a snow detective and a snow dog. That's the clue that made me think it was winter.

Teacher Questions Students
Ms. Dodson: OK, my turn. I've got one that will really make you think. What kind of stories do you think Nate likes to read?
Mike: I know. I think he likes mysteries. It says he's a detective, and detectives like to solve cases, like in *Encyclopedia Brown*.
Ms. Dodson: Well done. That was hard, but the author did give you a clue. Now let's read by ourselves to page 21. Try to find out what you think the problem in this story is.

Ms. Dodson repeats these three steps several times as she and the students read the story. She always allows her students to ask her several more questions than she asks them because she wants them to develop the habit of asking themselves good questions as they read a story.

Students Predict the Story's Outcome. Just before the solution is revealed, Ms. Dodson asks her students what they think the birthday present will be. Answers range from a sled, to a book, to a cat.

Teacher and Students Finish Reading to Check Predictions. Ms. Dodson has her students read the rest of the story. She asks them to find out what the present is and how Nate discovers it. Afterwards they discuss all the clues in the story that should tell a good detective what the present is. Ms. Dodson concludes by pointing out that readers need to be detectives, too. Just like Nate the Great, they need to look for clues as they are reading and figure out what each one means.

dence they used to determine each answer because that process—making explicit the strategies used to determine an inference—helps develop metacognitive knowledge. These first three steps may then be repeated several times with succeeding portions of the reading selection.

Whenever an important event in the story is about to occur, the teacher should ask students to predict what will happen next. This fourth step is similar to the predicting step of a DRTA. The teacher should ask students what they think will take place or how they think the story will end. As a part of their answers, students should explain their reasoning processes. The teacher might also share his or her own prediction and give an explanation of the reasoning involved.

Finally, teacher and students should read to the end of the selection and check their predictions. A short discussion of the story's conclusion might be appropriate to end this step.

Reciprocal questioning is a method framework that may be used to guide the reading of a story with a group of students. It allows the discussion to focus on comprehending the story and the metacognitive strategies that

MODEL LESSON

Reciprocal Teaching in Ms. Clancy's Class

Ms. Clancy has a chart on the board listing the steps for reciprocal teaching and the questions to be asked at each step. She has already introduced the informational selection called *The History of Chocolate* by James Reder and has developed an understanding of the important vocabulary concepts. Ms. Clancy and her students have read the first two pages of the selection and are now reading the following portion of the passage.

> The people of Spain didn't want other people to find out about their special drink that came from Mexico. They kept it a secret for more than a hundred years.
>
> Finally, though, other people found out about the secret. They learned where the special beans came from. Then they started growing the kakahuatl tree, or cacao tree, in other parts of the world so they could get more of the special beans. Still, only the very rich people could afford the special chocolate drink because the cacao beans were so expensive.
>
> Today, cacao beans grow around the world and chocolate is not so expensive. We can all eat chocolate because so many cacao trees produce the chocolate bean.

Summarize

Ms. Clancy: Let's see. Let me look on our chart here. First, I need to summarize and ask myself, "What did I read?" Well, I read that Spain kept the secret of chocolate, but now it's not a secret, and we can all eat chocolate. I'm glad about that. I really like chocolate.

Clarify

Ms. Clancy: Now let's see. I need to ask, "Are there any parts that are not clear to me?" Yes. I'm not really clear about why there are so many cacao trees now and chocolate is not so expensive. I'd better read that part again. [Ms. Clancy reads the passage aloud.] Here it is. It says, "They learned where the special beans came from. Then they started growing the kakahuatl tree, or cacao tree, in other parts of the world

---

contribute to comprehension. Reciprocal questioning can be used at all grade levels. In the model lesson on pages 374–375 Ms. Dodson is using this method framework to help a small group of her students develop greater strategic knowledge and increase their understanding of inferences.

Reciprocal Teaching

reciprocal teaching
A method framework designed to improve metacognition and comprehension with these steps: summarize, clarify, question, and predict.

Reciprocal teaching is a second method framework often used to develop metacognition. It is especially useful in helping students develop their ability to monitor comprehension. Reciprocal teaching consists of four steps that teacher and students repeat as they read a passage:

Summarize

Clarify

Question

Predict

so they could get more of the special beans." More and more people must have kept learning about the beans because it also says, "Today, cacao beans grow around the world and chocolate is not so expensive."

Question

Ms. Clancy: Now I need to ask a question that a teacher would ask about this portion of the passage. Let's see. I know. Are there more cacao trees now or when the Spanish were keeping their secret?

Toni: I know. There are more now.

Ms. Clancy: Good. How did you figure that out?

Toni: I read two things in the story and put them together. First it says everyone is growing them around the world, and it also says that chocolate is not so expensive now. If we had fewer trees today, it would be more expensive, not less.

Predict

Ms. Clancy: Great! Now I need to ask, "What will probably happen next in this passage?"

Raghib: I think we're going to read about all the different kinds of chocolate they make. At the end of this section it talks about how we all can eat chocolate. It sounds like the author will tell us next about all the different ways we use chocolate.

Ms. Clancy: Let's read the next two pages to ourselves and find out what the author does talk about next.

Ms. Clancy and her students read the next two pages silently. They discover that Raghib's guess was correct. Then Ms. Clancy guides one of her students to follow the same steps that she has just modeled. When the student finishes by making a prediction about the next portion, teacher and students read several more pages silently. Then another student becomes the teacher and completes each of the four steps. This process is repeated until the informational selection is completed.

The goal of reciprocal teaching is to help readers internalize these steps so that they use them independently during their own silent reading. The instructional approach is to have the teacher model the use of the procedural steps first and then have students follow the teacher's lead, all while reading a story together. Students are expected to follow the steps on their own after a number of practice sessions in the group setting.

During the first step readers ask, "What did I read?" They are expected to summarize the main point(s) of what they have just read. At the second step readers ask, "Are there any parts that are not clear to me?" Then they reread portions that are not clear and attempt to clarify the meaning.

When they reach the third step readers ask, "What question would a teacher ask about this portion of the passage?" They should ask (and answer) a comprehension question related to the main point(s) of what they have just read. At the fourth step readers ask, "What will probably happen next in this passage?" They then predict what they will read in the next portion. These four steps are repeated at regular intervals as readers work their way through a passage. Teachers usually model the steps first, as Ms. Clancy does in the model lesson. They then have students take turns modeling the steps aloud. Ms. Clancy is using reciprocal teaching to help her seventh-grade students practice monitoring what they are reading.

Reciprocal questioning and reciprocal teaching are useful method frameworks for developing metacognitive knowledge. Both give students models of how proficient readers interact with texts. In addition, the strategies in Figure 9-5 can be used to develop metacognitive knowledge.

SUPPORTING THE COMPREHENSION NEEDS OF STUDENTS WITH LIMITED ENGLISH PROFICIENCY

limited English proficiency (LEP) students
Students whose first language is not English and who have not yet developed fluency in English.

It has been estimated that at least 7½ million school-aged children in the United States are nonnative speakers of English (Gonzales, 1981). Many of these are **limited English proficiency (LEP) students,** whose first language is not English and who have not yet developed fluency in the English language. LEP students come from a variety of linguistic backgrounds: Spanish, Cajun, Vietnamese, Cambodian, Haitian, Korean, Cantonese, Mandarin, or one of several Native American languages. At least one public school district on the West Coast has students who speak more than 80 different primary languages (McNeil, Donant, & Alkin, 1980).

It is important for teachers to understand the comprehension needs of these students. It is also important for teachers to develop instructional practices to meet their special needs. Although many of these students are provided with outside educational services, many LEP students still receive most of their instruction from the regular classroom teacher (Feely, 1983; Gonzales, 1981).

FIGURE 9-5
Other strategies that may be used to develop metacognitive knowledge

 Think-Alouds. Try reading aloud to your students a portion of text. As you read, articulate the reading and reasoning strategies that you are employing, including any prediction you make, any questions you pose to yourself, and any inferences you make about what you are reading. Then ask students to do the same. Such explicit modeling of the reading comprehension process has been shown to contribute significantly to improved metacognitive skill (Baker & Brown, 1984; Wade, 1990).

 Cooperative Learning Groups. After students have developed an understanding of the steps in reciprocal questioning and reciprocal teaching, try using either of these methods in cooperative learning groups. Such groups can provide a useful variation for conducting the reading of a story.

┌───┐
│ **OPPORTUNITIES TO CELEBRATE DIVERSITY** │
└───┘

Raphael and Brock (1993) studied the literacy development of a Vietnamese LEP student, Mei, as she engaged in literature discussion group activities. (See Chapter 4 for a description of this method framework.) In addition to substantial gains in comprehension, they found Mei increased the amount of her participation in discussions and gained substantially in self-confidence. These differences were especially noticeable when the discussion group read and discussed a book about life in Vietnam. The book allowed Mei to take advantage of her background knowledge during reading and discussions. It also allowed her to help other students understand the story about life in Vietnam. This study suggests that it is important to include culturally sensitive works of literature in your classroom to support the literacy learning of LEP students. Including culturally sensitive works of literature also allows your other students to develop a wider appreciation of different cultural experiences. Everyone gains when we include culturally sensitive works of literature in our classrooms.

Challenges Faced by LEP Students

Two important challenges are faced by LEP students. First, LEP students lack the knowledge of spoken English that is necessary to comprehend what they read. Acquiring the ability to speak English, therefore, is crucial to their developing reading proficiency. Time must be devoted to helping these students learn to communicate orally in English.

The second challenge faced by these students is that differences between English and another language often impede comprehension. Thus, it is important to become familiar with the differences between English and a student's native language. The major differences between English and Spanish, one of the more common languages of LEP students, are listed in Table 9-2.

To understand the differences between other languages and English, you might seek information from three sources—(1) a speaker of the other language who also speaks English, (2) your local or state coordinator of bilingual education services, and (3) either of the following organizations:

Center for Applied Linguistics
1611 North Kent Street
Arlington, VA 22209

Dissemination Center for Bilingual Bicultural Education
6504 Tracor Lane
Austin, TX 78721

Instruction

Research into reading instruction with LEP students is still in its infancy, and consistent findings are limited. Nevertheless, several

TABLE 9-2

A partial listing of differences between Standard American English and Spanish

Language trait	Standard American English	Spanish
Phonological differences		
i (becomes e)	bit	beet
a (becomes e)	pat	pet
a (becomes e)	late	let
b (becomes p)	bar	par
z (becomes s)	buzz	bus
j (becomes ch or y)	jam	cham or yam
th (becomes s)	thank	sank
th (becomes d)	this	dis
Syntactic differences		
Negatives	Bill is not here.	Bill is no here.
	They do not go to school.	They no go school.
	Don't go.	No go.
Use of be	I am eight.	I have eight years.
	I am hungry.	I have hunger.
Tense	I will see you later.	I see you later.
	I needed help yesterday.	I need help yesterday.
Omission of determiner	He is a teacher.	He is teacher.
Omission of pronoun	Is it time to go?	Is time to go?
	It is time.	Is time.

immersion approaches
An instructional practice that challenges LEP students to learn English as rapidly as they can without special intervention.

ESL approaches
An instructional practice that teaches LEP students oral English in structured lessons before they learn how to read and write in English.

instructional approaches are commonly found in schools: immersion; English as a Second Language (ESL); and bilingual approaches. **Immersion approaches** make no special provision for LEP students. Students are expected to pick up as much as they can, as fast as they can, during regular classroom lessons. This practice assumes that immersion in English will contribute to learning. Although this has been the traditional form of instruction for LEP students in the United States, it is not necessarily the most effective.

ESL approaches teach LEP students oral English skills before their reading instruction begins. Special ESL teachers work with students, usually in structured oral drills and usually outside the regular classroom, to develop fluency in oral English. Reading instruction in the regular classroom begins only after students have established an understanding of oral English.

Bilingual approaches teach reading and writing skills in a student's native language at the same time that they teach oral language skills in English. Reading instruction in English begins only after students have learned to read and write in their own language and have acquired fluency in oral English. Bilingual approaches often involve teachers who are fluent in the native language of their students.

Regardless of approach, you should keep the following suggestions in mind as you work with students who are just learning to speak English.

bilingual approaches
An instructional practice through which LEP students learn reading and writing in their native language concurrently with instruction in oral English.

1. Encourage discussion among all your students, but especially between LEP students and others. Speaking and listening experiences develop important prerequisites for reading and writing. Thus, LEP children need a language-rich environment in order to develop greater proficiency in English (Krashen & Terrell, 1983).

2. Make frequent use of cooperative learning group activities. This method framework provides a supportive environment for LEP students—a group learning situation with extensive use of oral English. LEP students are able to participate successfully in cooperative learning groups, thereby increasing their self-perceptions.

3. Try to reduce the anxiety level of LEP students as much as possible. These students appear to learn best in classrooms in which anxiety levels are reduced (Dulay, Burt, & Krashen, 1982).

4. Pay less attention at the beginning to your students' pronunciation and accent. Concentrate on meaning and communication.

5. Understand the difficulty that your students face in learning a second language, and help your other students to appreciate this challenge also. LEP students may require as many as five to seven years of instruction in English before they can read English textbooks effectively (Cummins, 1981).

6. Select books for read-aloud sessions that are culturally appropriate for your LEP students. Use those opportunities to encourage their participation in oral discussions.

7. Respect your students' linguistic and cultural heritage. Work those aspects of diversity into classroom activities (Au, 1993).

8. Use language experience activities as much as possible to teach beginning reading skills. Language experience activities allow LEP students to simultaneously improve their oral and written English language skills. They also allow students to use their background knowledge to maximum advantage.

Several additional strategies are described in Figure 9-6.

USING QUESTIONING STRATEGIES TO DEVELOP READING COMPREHENSION AND RESPONSE

It is important for both readers and teachers to ask questions about what they are reading. For readers, questions serve to monitor comprehension,

FIGURE 9-6

Two strategies for supporting LEP students

 Picture Dictionaries. Have your LEP students write and publish a picture dictionary. Include common school objects and activities. Have other students help them in this task.

 Peer Tutoring. Have one student regularly work with each LEP student in your classroom. They can complete many enjoyable and productive tasks together:

- reading a storybook together and talking about the pictures
- writing and illustrating a story together
- writing buddy journals together (see chapter 5)
- playing Simon Says together

focus attention on puzzling aspects of the text, and guide the search for answers. Questions are an essential part of the comprehension process. For teachers also, questions serve a variety of functions.

- *Modeling the reasoning process.* Questions, along with answers and explanations of how answers were derived, can be used to model reasoning processes that are important for comprehension.
- *Initiating a discussion.* Questions can be used to trigger discussion of central information before a passage is read, thus increasing the background knowledge that readers bring to the text. Questions can also be used to initiate a discussion about what has happened or is likely to take place in the text.
- *Guiding students' reasoning.* Questions can be used to guide students' thinking. Teachers can use questions to help students replicate the reasoning strategies of proficient readers.
- *Focusing attention.* Questions can be used to focus attention on a specific portion of text for subsequent instructional purposes.
- *Providing practice in specific comprehension tasks.* Questions can be used to engage students in specific types of inferential tasks, such as cause-and-effect, sequence, pronoun and adverbial references, predicting outcomes, or drawing conclusions.
- *Assessment.* Questions can be used to monitor students' understanding of a passage they have read.

Comprehension Questions

There are a variety of ways to organize the questions that teachers use during reading instruction. The traditional approach identifies the levels of comprehension addressed by the questions.

When used appropriately, questions can motivate students and are a useful instructional tool.

A levels approach organizes comprehension questions according to the type of information a reader must contribute to the answer. Three levels are specified: literal, inferential, and evaluative. **Literal-level questions** ask for information directly from the text. Readers can answer literal-level questions by relying on the literal, word-for-word meaning of a passage; they must contribute little, if any, information to respond to literal-level questions because the answer is explicitly stated in the text.

Inferential-level questions ask for information not explicitly stated in the text. Readers must use their background knowledge in conjunction with text information and read between the lines. Inferential-level questions require readers to make either text-connecting or slot-filling inferences.

Evaluative-level questions ask readers to make a critical judgment about information in the text. In order to answer such questions, readers must evaluate textual information in relation to their own values and experiences. Examples of each type of question can be seen in Figure 9-7.

literal-level questions
Questions asking for information explicitly stated in the text.

inferential-level questions
Questions asking for information that requires a reader to use background knowledge in conjunction with information explicitly stated in the text.

evaluative-level questions
Questions asking readers to make critical judgments about information in the text, using previous experiences or values.

FIGURE 9-7

Examples of literal, inferential, and evaluative questions

Text

Bob and Claire wanted to go out to eat, so Bob called to make a reservation. They drove to the restaurant, but when they arrived, no one was there. The door was locked, and a sign said "Closed on Mondays."

"What's going on?" Bob asked. "I just reserved a table over the phone."

Claire answered, "Are you sure you called the Steak House?"

"Oh, oh," said Bob apologetically. "I think I may have called the Steak Place."

Literal questions

1. Who wanted to go out to eat? (Bob and Claire)
2. Why did Bob call? (to make a reservation)

Inferential questions

1. When did Bob and Claire drive to the restaurant? (after Bob made the reservation)
2. On what day did this story take place? (Monday)
3. At what restaurant did Bob make a reservation? (the Steak Place)
4. Where did Bob and Claire go? (the Steak House)

Evaluative questions

1. What would you have done next in this situation? (All logical answers are acceptable.)
2. What do you think Bob and Claire should have done differently? (All logical answers are acceptable.)

---

question-answer relations (QAR)
A taxonomy of relationships between questions and answers.

right-there QARs
One type of in-the-book QAR; questions with answers that are explicitly stated in the text.

putting-it-together QARs
One type of in-the-book QAR requiring readers to make a text-connecting inference.

A second way of organizing questions used during discussion is referred to as **question-answer relations,** or **(QAR).** Raphael (1982, 1986) has suggested that it is appropriate to consider questions and their answers together. By doing so, we can be more precise in our use of questions and our understanding of why students have difficulty with certain questions. Based on an initial taxonomy developed by Pearson and Johnson (1978), Raphael has developed a system referred to as question-answer relations, or QAR.

A QAR approach organizes questions into two basic groups: questions that are "in the book" and questions that are "in my head." In-the-book questions have answers that can be found in the text. These questions come in two types: "right there" and "putting it together." **Right-there QARs** are similar to literal-level questions. They require literal recall of explicitly stated information. In other words, the answer is right there in the text. **Putting-it-together QARs** require readers to connect information stated in two or more locations; thus, they require a text-connecting inference.

FIGURE 9-8

Examples of in-the-book and in-my-head questions

Text

Bob and Claire wanted to go out to eat, so Bob called to make a reservation. They drove to the restaurant, but when they arrived, no one was there. The door was locked, and a sign said "Closed on Mondays."

"What's going on?" Bob asked. "I just reserved a table over the phone."

Claire answered, "Are you sure you called the Steak House?"

"Oh, oh," said Bob apologetically. "I think I may have called the Steak Place."

In-the-book questions

Right There
1. Who wanted to go out to eat? (Bob and Claire)
2. Why did Bob call? (to make a reservation)

Putting It Together
1. When did Bob and Claire drive to the restaurant? (after Bob made the reservation)
2. At what restaurant did Bob make a reservation? (the Steak Place)

In-my-head questions

Author and You
1. At what restaurant were Bob and Claire? (the Steak House)
2. On what day did this story take place? (Monday)

On Your Own
1. How would you feel if you took a friend to dinner and the restaurant was closed? (All logical answers are acceptable.)

The second major category includes in-my-head question-answer relationships. These questions also come in two types: "author and you" and "on your own." **Author-and-you QARs** require readers to connect information in the text with information they bring to it. The answer is not explicitly stated but requires readers to make a slot-filling inference. **On-your-own QARs** feature answers that are not in the text. Readers rely entirely on their own experiences and can even answer on-your-own QARs without reading the text. Examples of each type of question-answer relationship can be seen in Figure 9-8.

author-and-you QARs
One type of in-my-head QAR requiring readers to connect background knowledge to information in the text.

on-your-own QARs
One type of in-my-head QAR calling for answers that are not in the text but that depend on the reader's own experiences.

Guidelines for Using Questions

Questioning occurs frequently during classroom reading lessons. Therefore, it is important for you to think about how you will use questions in your own classroom. The following suggestions should help.

- Do not use questions solely to test comprehension. Durkin (1979, 1981) found that teachers use questions largely to test, not teach, reading comprehension. As mentioned earlier, when teachers play the guess-the-answer-I-have-in-my-head game with students, they are testing, not teaching. To teach reading comprehension, you should model your own reasoning processes aloud to students and ask them to explain their reasoning processes as well. This procedure is sometimes referred to as "think aloud" (Davey, 1983; Fitzgerald, 1983). For example, you might follow up each comprehension question with "Can you tell us how you figured out that answer?" Making reasoning processes explicit is especially helpful for less proficient students and provides important insights to teachers about their students' comprehension processes (Wade, 1990).

- Help students understand that answers may come from the text or from the knowledge about the world that they have in their heads. Students are not always aware of this distinction. Some research suggests that knowing the distinction between in-the-book and in-my-head QARs facilitates comprehension (Raphael, 1982, 1986).

- Ask higher-level questions. If you take a levels approach to questions, higher-level questions are more appropriate than lower-level questions because the former provide more reasoning opportunities for readers. For example, to answer an evaluative-level question, readers must consider information at the literal, inferential, and evaluative levels. To answer an inferential-level question, readers must consider information at both literal and inferential levels. However, to answer a literal-level question, readers need to consider only information at the literal level. Higher-level questions also provide greater opportunities to model reasoning processes.

- If students are unable to answer a higher-level question, ask a related lower-level question. Breaking down the reasoning task into easier elements provides a supporting scaffold, or foundation, on which students can make an inference.

- Accept greater variation in responses as you ask higher-level questions. Answers to literal-level questions or in-the-book QARs are either correct or incorrect: the answers are explicitly stated in the text. However, answers to inferential-level questions, evaluative-level questions, or in-my-head QARs rely on background knowledge, which differs among individuals. As a result, higher-level questions usually have more than one acceptable answer.

- Ask questions before students read a story. This approach helps students attend to important background knowledge that is required to comprehend a passage. For example, ask students whether they have ever experienced a problem like the one in the story they are about to read. Then have a short discussion about how they solved their problem. Hansen and Pearson (1980) found this strategy to be especially helpful for students because it builds an instructional scaffold that supports students' comprehension. Evaluative-level questions and on-my-own QARs are especially appropriate for prereading activities.

- Plan discussion questions in advance. Devising questions as you discuss a story with students will result in many literal-level questions or in-the-book QARs. It is nearly impossible to generate more complex questions without advance planning. Thus, before discussing a story, you should be sure that you have thought about the types of questions you will ask.

USING A LITERACY FRAMEWORK TO GUIDE INSTRUCTION IN THE COMPREHENSION OF EXTENDED TEXT

There are two basic decisions that you will face as you consider instruction related to extended text, and your literacy framework can assist you with both. First, you will need to decide what to teach and emphasize. Should you try to develop syntactic, discourse, and metacognitive knowledge? How much should you emphasize these types of knowledge? Your conclusion about how a person reads will guide you in these decisions.

Second, you will need to decide how you will teach the knowledge sources associated with extended text. Should you favor deductive or inductive learning experiences? Should you follow a hierarchical sequence of comprehension skills, or should you teach comprehension within reading experiences as the need arises? Should questions be used to practice and assess comprehension, or should they be used more to develop comprehension through modeling experiences? Which method frameworks should you use to teach comprehension? Your conclusion about how reading ability develops will assist you in these decisions.

What Should I Teach and Emphasize?

To guide you in deciding what you will teach and emphasize, you need to consider your beliefs about how a person reads. Table 9-3 summarizes how that portion of your framework can be used to guide decision making about comprehension instruction.

Reader-Based Explanation. Teachers who follow a reader-based explanation of how a person reads spend the most time developing syntactic, discourse, and metacognitive knowledge because they believe that meaning exists more in what a reader brings to a text than in the text itself. Inferences are especially important to these teachers; therefore,

TABLE 9-3

A summary of how a literacy framework can be used to inform decisions about what to teach regarding extended text

Beliefs about how one reads	Related assumptions	Probable time spent on extended text	What is taught?
Reader-Based	Meaning exists more in what the reader brings to the text.	Much	Predicting outcomes
			Implicitly signaled relationships
	Reading is a result of expectations for upcoming words.		Inferential or evaluative questions
	Reading begins with elements of prior knowledge.		In-my-head QARs
			Metacognitive knowledge
Interactive	Meaning exists in both the text and the reader.	Moderate amount	All aspects
	Reading is both translation and expectation.		
	Reading uses each knowledge source simultaneously.		
Text-Based	Meaning exists more in the text.	Little	Punctuation
			Explicitly signaled relationships
	Reading is translation.		Signal words
	Reading begins with decoding knowledge.		Literal questions

predicting outcomes and drawing conclusions are encouraged since they involve inferences, either looking forward toward upcoming information or looking backward toward previous information. Implicit cause-and-effect and sequence relationships requiring readers to make inferences are also emphasized. This is true because teachers with reader-based beliefs are most concerned with developing readers' abilities to bring prior knowledge to a text and this is especially true of implicit relationships. In addition, inferential- and evaluative-level questions and in-my-head QARs are used more than other types of questions.

Text-Based Explanation. Teachers who follow a text-based explanation of how a person reads spend the least amount of time developing syntactic, discourse, and metacognitive knowledge. Because they believe that meaning exists more in the text than in the prior knowledge a reader brings to that text, they spend more time developing decoding knowledge. When these teachers do teach elements related to the comprehension of extended text, they focus instructional time on elements that help readers comprehend the meaning that exists in the text: punctuation, explicitly signaled sequence relationships, explicitly signaled cause-and-effect relationships, signal words, literal-level questions, and in-the-book QARs. These teachers spend less time teaching elements that help readers bring meaning to a text, such as predicting outcomes or drawing conclusions.

Punctuation, explicitly signaled cause-and-effect relationships, explicitly signaled sequence relationships, and signal words are all taught because they are elements of meaning in a text. Implicit relationships that require readers to make an inference and contribute meaning to a text are not emphasized. Literal-level questions and in-the-book QARs are used more than other types of questions, again, because they help a reader comprehend the meaning that already exists in a text.

Interactive Explanation. Teachers who follow an interactive explanation of how a person reads spend a moderate amount of time developing syntactic, discourse, and metacognitive knowledge. But even as they develop those elements associated with what a reader brings to a text, they are also developing decoding and vocabulary knowledge wherever necessary, elements associated with the meaning that is already in a text. These teachers help youngsters draw conclusions and predict outcomes. They help students with punctuation, key words and explicit cause-and-effect and sequence relationships, as well as with the inferences required in implicit cause-and-effect and sequence relationships. These teachers use the complete range of questions to develop reading comprehension: literal, inferential, and evaluative questions, in addition to in-the-book and in-my-head QARs.

How Should I Teach?

You will also need to make decisions about how to teach the comprehension of extended text. Your conclusion about how reading ability develops should guide you in those decisions. Table 9-4 summarizes how that portion of your framework can be used in decision making.

Holistic Language Explanation. Teachers who follow a holistic language explanation believe that reading ability develops as students engage in holistic, meaningful, and functional experiences with print. As a result, inductive experiences are favored, and comprehension instruction always takes place, as needed, within the context of functional read-

TABLE 9-4

A summary of how a literacy framework can be used to inform decisions about how to teach elements of extended text

Beliefs about how children learn to read	Related assumptions	Favored method frameworks and instructional activities
Holistic Language Learning	Students learn best in an inductive fashion as they direct their own learning and reading experiences	Inductive experiences
		Instruction during reading experiences
	Students learn best during holistic, meaningful, and functional experiences with authentic literature	Questions used to develop comprehension through modeling experiences
		Most common method frameworks: style studies language experience sentences inductive instruction language experience stories DRTA cooperative learning groups reciprocal questioning reciprocal teaching think-alouds
		Most common method frameworks: deductive instruction and directed reading activities
Integrated	Students learn best as a result of both student-directed, inductive experiences and teacher-directed, deductive experiences	Both inductive and deductive experiences as appropriate

ing experiences. Questions are used more for modeling than for practice and assessment, and the most common method frameworks include these: style studies, language experience sentences, language experience stories, inductive instruction, DRTA, cooperative learning groups, reciprocal questioning, reciprocal teaching, and think-alouds. In addition, method frameworks from other chapters that are also based on inductive learning are often used such as text sets and literature discussion groups (see chapter 4).

Specific Skills Explanation. Teachers who follow a specific-skills explanation believe that reading ability develops as students learn specific reading skills, which should be taught in teacher-directed, deductive lessons. As a result, deductive experiences are favored, and a hierarchy of

TABLE 9-4   *continued*

Beliefs about how children learn to read	Related assumptions	Favored method frameworks and instructional activities
	Students learn best when they engage in purposeful, functional, and holistic experiences with authentic texts and when they acquire specific reading skills	Some comprehension skills targeted and taught during reading experiences
		Questions used to both assess and develop comprehension through modeling experiences
		Most common method frameworks: style studies language experience sentences deductive instruction directed reading activities language experience stories inductive instruction DRTA cooperative learning groups reciprocal questioning reciprocal teaching think-alouds
Specific Skills	Students learn best when they are taught directly by the teacher in a deductive fashion	Deductive experiences
		Hierarchy of comprehension skills taught to mastery
	Students learn best when they master specific reading skills	Questions used to practice and assess comprehension

specific comprehension skills are apt to guide instruction. Questions are used mainly to practice and assess students' developing skills, and the most common method frameworks include deductive instruction and directed reading activities (DRAs).

Integrated Explanation. Teachers who follow an integrated explanation of development share both specific-skills and holistic perspectives. Inductive as well as deductive experiences are used. And even though a hierarchy of specific comprehension skills may not determine instruction, comprehension skills are developed during reading experiences. Questions are used both to assess and to develop comprehension through modeling experiences. In addition, all of the method frameworks described in this chapter are used.

Comments from the Classroom

Nikki Robinson, Sixth Grade Teacher

I recently noticed that teaching using thematic units sometimes has a hidden benefit—students become involved in reading entire articles, magazines, and books as they attempt to broaden and deepen their understanding of a topic. The textbook was just a place to start. Concrete, hands-on experiences stimulated further study in reference materials, novels, and informational books.

For example, the initial chapter in social studies on the industrial revolution held little meaning for my students. In order to give them a taste of that era, we set up a factory assembly line cutting out and decorating construction paper bookmarks to sell to other classes. Each child was hired (assigned) for a specific part of the process, given a specific place on the assembly line, and the materials to do only that job. The teachers "hired" quality controllers, transportation runners, suppliers, managers, and sales people.

At first, it was fun for everyone. The assembly line was going smoothly at the front because all of those workers were busy. However, the end of the line had nothing to do but wait for the product to reach them, and boredom set in. Managers to the rescue! Quality controllers threw out the bookmarks that didn't pass class standards. The managers had the people at the end of the line research and create new designs as well as write a list of characteristics determining the acceptable bookmark standards while they were waiting.

The grumbling started during the early afternoon. "I'm tired of sitting in the same spot." "My hands hurt from cutting." Paste was everywhere, and the more fastidious students hated the mess. By the second day, when told they couldn't change jobs with a friend, many didn't want to work. More research. What did workers do when they were frustrated? A strike was discussed. Suppliers ran out of inventory. What happens then? Suppliers and managers met for a fifteen-minute debate. The result? A classroom of purchasers was offered a choice of two "new" colors and designs to replace their first choice, which was no longer available. As workers in the front of the assembly line were "laid off," many became interested in the way workers throughout history had improved their conditions.

I really knew the unit was a success when I looked around the room and saw that while the line was temporarily shut down, some students were working out the math for "overtime" and "vacation" pay, some were adding up the cost of supplies, one group was looking up profit and loss and debating how to tell if we would make a profit, and yet another group was trying to use a software manual to learn how they could use the classroom computer to keep financial records. The middle of the second day the principal stopped by and asked how this whole thing got started. I couldn't help but smile when Leroy looked up from his task and said, "What? You don't know about the industrial revolution?"

Major Points

- An inference is a reasoned assumption about meaning that is not explicitly stated in the text. Readers make inferences by using their background knowledge to connect different pieces of information in a text and to fill in missing information. Inferential reasoning is sometimes referred to as reading between the lines.

- Young children have extensive knowledge of oral language but far more limited knowledge of written language. Understanding the differences between oral and written language can give teachers important insights into what their students must acquire in order to become proficient readers and writers.

- There are many ways to develop syntactic knowledge. The most common method frameworks include style studies, language experience sentences, and language experience stories. In addition, discussion and instruction in the meaning and function of signal words are often used.

- There are also many ways to develop discourse knowledge. The most common method frameworks include deductive instruction, inductive instruction, and directed reading-thinking activities.

- There are many ways to develop metacognitive knowledge. The most common method frameworks include reciprocal questioning and reciprocal teaching.

- Students with limited English proficiency often need to develop proficiency with oral English to support their ability to comprehend written texts in English. Cooperative group learning activities are particularly supportive environments for these students as are culturally appropriate thematic units.

- Questioning strategies can be used to teach many aspects of reading comprehension. Traditional approaches use different levels of questions. More recent approaches use a taxonomy based on question-answer relationships.

- A literacy framework assists with decisions about what to teach and emphasize and how to teach it.

Making Instructional Decisions

1. Identify at least four inferences a reader must make to comprehend the following passage. Specify whether each is a text-connecting or a slot-filling inference.

   It was raining, and they went inside the old barn. They unloaded their rifles and climbed the ladder to the loft. The hay was warm and dry. Craig and Bill sat swapping tales of their adventures with grouse and waiting for a chance to get back outside. They both enjoyed the chance to stretch the truth a bit. Finally the rain stopped, and Bill said, "Let's get going. We have to bring something home for dinner." Craig noticed, though, that it was already dark outside.

2. We can informally assess young children's knowledge of written language conventions by listening to their speech. Look at how two first-grade students told the story contained in the wordless picture book *Frog, Where Are You?* by Mercer Mayer.

   ### Tama

   You see . . . there's a little frog, and he . . . and a little boy had him for a pet. And he had a little dog, and the frog was in the little bucket. And then they were walking, to do something, and the frog jumped out of . . . out of the bucket . . . and the frog just started looking at the flowers. And then they saw someone at a picnic, and they were having a picnic. And he got into their picnic basket, and then . . . the lady was gonna get . . . something out of her picnic basket . . . and the frog jumped on her hand . . . and . . . and then the lady got really mad.

   ### Jessica

   Um . . . once upon a time, there was a little boy . . . who had a little frog for a pet. After they were walking for a while . . . the little frog jumped . . . out of the bucket and hopped away. The frog . . . saw two people who were having a picnic . . . Because he was a naughty frog . . .

he hopped into their picnic basket. After the lady put her hand . . . into the picnic basket, the frog jumped out . . . because he thought . . . that she was gonna get him. The lady was scared . . . since she didn't like frogs.

What can you tell about each student's familiarity with written language conventions?

a. Which student is more familiar with the conventions of written language? How can you tell?

b. Which types of written language knowledge do you see in these oral language samples? decoding? vocabulary? syntactic? discourse? metacognitive? Explain.

c. Do you think sequence and cause-and-effect relationships might be difficult for one of these students to understand during reading? Why?

3. Plan a lesson using a language experience story to teach either sequence or cause-and-effect relationships. Identify which experience you will provide, how you will elicit oral language, and what you will do to teach sequence or cause-and-effect relationships.

4. Define one question each that you might use to assess comprehension of the passage in Item 1 on a literal, inferential, and evaluative level. Then develop right-there, putting-it-together, author-and-you, and on-your-own QARs for the same passage.

Further Reading

Baumann, J. F., Jones, L. A., & Seifert-Kessell, N. (1993). Using think alouds to enhance children's comprehension monitoring abilities. *The Reading Teacher, 47,* 184–193.

Describes how the use of think alouds can be used to support children's comprehension by helping them to monitor their own comprehension processes. Describes many useful classroom activities that can be used with think alouds to support comprehension.

Commeyras, M. (1993). Promoting critical thinking through dialogical-thinking reading lessons. *The Reading Teacher, 46,* 486–494.

Describes a method framework called Dialogical-Thinking Reading Lessons (D-TTRL) that engages students in discussion and thinking about a story-specific issue. The process helps students to understand strategies and reasoning processes that are central to reading comprehension from their discussions about how they interpreted a story.

Goldenberg, C. (1992). Instructional conversations: Promoting comprehension through discussion. *The Reading Teacher, 46,* 316–326.

The author explains how instructional conversations may be used to help children comprehend reading selections more deeply and to develop useful strategies for reading. He argues that this approach is especially important with minority children who often receive instruction only in lower level skills.

Swift, K. (1993). Try reading workshop in your classroom. *The Reading Teacher, 46,* 366–371.

Describes a year-long project conducted by a teacher to study the effects of a reading workshop approach. The approach uses many writing and journal experiences along with discussion and group instruction to support reading comprehension and response.

References

Anderson, R. C., & Shifrin, Z. (1980). The meaning of words in context. In R. J. Spiro, B. C. Bruce, and W. F. Brewer (Eds.), *Theoretical issues in reading comprehension.* Hillsdale, NJ: Erlbaum.

Au, K. H. (1993). *Literacy instruction in multicultural settings.* Fort Worth: Harcourt Brace Jovanovich.

Baker, L., & Brown, A. L. (1984). Cognitive monitoring in reading. In J. Flood (Ed.), *Understanding reading comprehension,* Newark, DE: International Reading Association.

Beck, I. (1989). Reading and reasoning. *The Reading Teacher, 42,* 676–682.

Beck, I. L., McKeown, M. G., Omanson, R. C., & Pople, M. T. (1984). Improving the comprehensibility of stories: The effects of revisions that improve coherence. *Reading Research Quarterly, 19*(3), 263–277.

Cook-Gumperz, J., & Gumperz, J. (1981). From oral to written culture: The transition to literacy. In M. F. Whiteman (Ed.), *Writing: The nature, development, and teaching of written communication.* Hillsdale, NJ: Erlbaum.

Davey, B. (1983). Think-aloud: Modeling the cognitive processes of reading comprehension. *Journal of Reading, 27,* 44–47.

Durkin, D. (1979). Reading comprehension instruction in five basal reading series. *Reading Research Quarterly, 14,* 481–533.

Durkin, D. (1981). Reading methodology textbooks: Are they helping teachers teach comprehension? *The Reading Teacher, 39*(5), 410–417.

Fitzgerald, J. (1983). Helping readers gain self-control. *The Reading Teacher, 37,* 249–253.

Hansen, J., & Pearson, P. D. (1980). *The effects of inference training and practice on young children's comprehension* (Tech. Rep. No. 166). Urbana: University of Illinois, Center for the Study of Reading.

Leu, D. J., Jr. (1982). Differences between oral and written discourse and the acquisition of reading proficiency. *Journal of Reading Behavior, 14*(2), 111–125.

Manzo, A. V. (1969). The request procedure. *Journal of Reading, 11,* 123–126.

McGee, L. M., & Richgels, D. J. (1990). *Literacy Beginnings.* Boston: Allyn & Bacon.

McGovern, A. (1975). *The secret soldier.* New York: Scholastic Books.

Michaels, S., & Cook-Gumperz, J. (1979). A study of sharing time with first grade students: Discourse narratives in the classroom. *Proceedings of the Berkeley Linguistic Society, 5,* 87–103.

Murphy, S. (1985). Children's comprehension of deictic categories in oral and written language. *Reading Research Quarterly, 21,* 118–131.

Pearson, P. D., & Camperell, K. (1981). Comprehension of text structures. In J. T. Guthrie (Ed.), *Comprehension and teaching.* Newark, DE: International Reading Association.

Pearson, P. D., & Johnson, D. D. (1978). *Teaching reading comprehension.* New York: Holt, Rinehart & Winston.

Purcell-Gates, V. (1989). What oral/written language differences can tell us about beginning instruction. *The Reading Teacher, 42*(4), 290–295.

Raphael, T. E. (1982). Teaching children question-answering strategies. *The Reading Teacher, 36,* 186–191.

Raphael, T. E. (1986). Teaching question-answer relationships, revisited. *The Reading Teacher, 39,* 516–522.

Raphael, T. E., & Brock, C. H. Mei. Learning the literacy culture in an urban elementary school. In D. J. Leu and C. K. Kinzer (Eds.), *Examining central issues in literacy research, theory, and practice: The forty-second yearbook of the National Reading Conference.* Chicago: National Reading Conference.

Rubin, A. (1980). A theoretical taxonomy of the differences between oral and written language. In R. J. Spiro, B. C. Bruce, and W. F. Brewer (Eds.), *Theoretical issues in reading comprehension.* Hillsdale, NJ: Erlbaum.

Stauffer, R. G. (1976). *Teaching reading as a thinking process.* New York: Harper & Row.

Sulzby, E. (1982). Oral and written mode adaptations in stories by kindergarten children. *Journal of Reading Behavior, 14*(2), 51–60.

Teale, W. H., & Sulzby, E. (Eds.). (1986). *Emergent literacy: Writing and reading.* Norwood, NJ: Ablex.

Wade, S. E. (1990). Using think alouds to assess comprehension. *The Reading Teacher, 43,* 442–451.

CHAPTER

Content-Area Reading and Study Skills

When I think back, it seems that school didn't really teach me to read the kinds of books that I read most often. What I mean is, I learned how to read stories, and I loved reading them. But right after third grade, I had to read more and more textbooks, and now, in college, I have to read articles and other things that don't have anything to do with stories. And when I ask my parents and others what they read most, it's business-related and job-related material— memos, letters, instruction manuals, maps, and so on. It really seems like we are taught to read stories, but in real life we read other things. I can't help wondering if I'd be a better reader today, in college, if my reading teachers would have spent a bit more time on how to read things in addition to stories. I'm not suggesting that we get rid of good children's literature, but I would like to see more informational materials that would help children learn to read other things also. The literature I read as a young child helped me a lot. It kept me wanting to read, and it taught me lots of important things. And it made me look forward to reading. But I'm not sure that it helped me figure out how to learn things by reading books that were not children's literature or stories. I do have to say, though, that I still look forward to reading when I get tired or just want to relax!

An undergraduate student talking about her recollections about the value of reading instruction in primary grades.

Previous chapters have noted that not all reading is alike and that even good readers have difficulty reading specialized texts such as books in law or business. This chapter shows that the materials that students are expected to read in different school subjects are also specialized, with varying structures that make different demands on a reader. As textbooks are still the predominant tool used in educating children, instruction in content-area reading skills cannot be ignored. Students who are not able to read well in content areas are at a great disadvantage throughout their educational careers.

Chapter 10 includes information that will help you answer questions such as:

1. What are the major differences between the kinds of reading material children encounter while learning to read and the kinds they must read in various academic subject areas?
2. What are the different reading demands required in different subject areas?
3. How are textbooks structured differently in social studies, mathematics, and science and how do these characteristics affect comprehension?
4. Which techniques can help students better read and study required reading material in content-area subjects?

KEY CONCEPTS

advance organizer	semantic mapping
DRA	skimming
expository text	SQRQCQ
jigsaw grouping	SQ3R
K-W-L strategy	structured concept outline
marginal gloss	study guide
PQRST	text structure
scanning	think-aloud

CHANGES IN READING THROUGHOUT THE GRADES

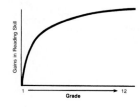

Let's think back to our own elementary school days and the changes in both reading ability and reading instruction as our grade level increased. If we look at how much we learned (or improved), related to reading in each grade, we might end up with a graph something like the one pictured in the margin note. Clearly, the largest increase in reading ability takes place in the earliest stages of schooling. Examples are easy to imagine. Think of the difference between an average reader in the middle of first grade and an average reader in the middle of third grade. Then try to specify the difference between an average 10th-grade reader and an average 12th-grade reader. Differences in both curriculum and performance become more difficult to identify at higher grade levels.

As you might have guessed, most reading instruction takes place in the early school years. By about the third grade, instruction specifically related to reading tapers off, and more emphasis is placed on learning content in academic subject areas. In fact, the whole school experience is often restructured as a child moves from primary to intermediate grades. Where there was only one classroom and one teacher, there now may be different teachers and different classrooms for various subjects. And where there was previously a great deal of stability, there now may be a continually changing instructional environment, which will continue to change throughout the intermediate grades and become even more pronounced in secondary grades.

Along with different subject areas come varied demands on readers. In science, students are required to understand and manipulate various formulas and to learn many new, content-specific terms. In mathematics they must read many self-contained units, such as word problems, and comprehend many numerical examples and rules in the form of theorems and laws. In addition, different types of texts demand different strategies from the reader, in terms of approach and interpretation as well as background knowledge and recognition of text structure. For example, readers unaware that a text is designed to persuade may interpret it as fact and use it incorrectly.

Differences in text styles seem fairly easy for people to recognize within narrative writing. After all, poetry is clearly different from dramatic scripts and both differ from stories even in visible ways. It also seems easy to note the different ways in which people read different narrative **genres.** The fact that readers read poems differently from the way in which they read plays causes no great controversy. However, the general differences between **expository** texts and narratives and the concept that expository texts in different subject areas make different demands on readers seem somewhat more difficult to recognize. Nonetheless, knowing these differences and understanding how readers comprehend different text types will make you a more effective teacher, better able to prepare your students to read the wide range of materials ahead of them.

genres
Categories of literary compositions, each having a special style, form, or content.

expository
Designed to explain or present.

Identifying Book Parts

Textbooks are often composed of similar sections—usually a title, copyright page, preface, table of contents, reference list, index, and glossary. Likewise, a chapter within a book usually contains a title, introduction, headings, subheadings, conclusion, and perhaps questions and activities. Although not all books and chapters have each of these parts, most books do that are not narratives (for example, novels, plays, and so on).

Knowing about each of a book's parts helps a reader comprehend what is presented. For example, the copyright page can tell us whether the

Normally, content-area texts are read for information, whereas narratives are read for pleasure. Content-area textbooks and expository texts in general, which permit the reader to discover new ideas or perhaps to reinforce and extend already-known concepts, form the bulk of the reading that students are required to do beyond the primary grades. Thus, it might be argued that expository material should be an early focus, allowing children to learn to read using materials like those they will encounter later. Do you agree with this argument? Would it present any difficulty for a teacher who believes strongly in using children's literature to teach reading?

information contained in the book is out of date or whether the book was published by a special-interest group and might be biased. The preface can point out the purposes for which the book was written. And the table of contents presents an outline of what the book covers and helps set up expectations. Each book part contains important information that can help the reader.

Lessons that teach the parts of books and show how they can help the reader should be included in reading instruction. Students need to be aware of the various parts, the information each contains, and the uses of each. The following strategies in Figure 10-1 include suggestions for teaching this aspect of reading.

Recognizing Differences in Text Organization

Text structure is also an important factor in the reading process. The major structural difference between narrative and expository text is that narratives are usually written along a time sequence, whereas exposition is organized according to **superordinate** and **subordinate concepts.** This difference is easy to see, even in the partial tables of contents shown here. The example on the left comes from a mathematics textbook (Bassler, Kolb, Craighead, & Gray, 1981); the example on the right, from a fictional narrative (Defoe, 1967).

superordinate concept
Part of the organizational pattern in expository text; a major unit supported by subunits.

subordinate concept
Part of the organizational pattern in expository text; a subunit that supports a larger unit.

Table of contents	Table of contents
Addition and subtraction—whole numbers	I Go to Sea
Rounding numbers through hundred thousands	On the Island
Finding sums and differences through 6 digits	We Plan to Leave the Island
Estimating sums and differences by rounding	The English Ship
Checking addition and subtraction	Home!
Multiplication and division—whole numbers	
Multiplying by 1- and 2-digit factors	
Estimating products by rounding	
Solving multiple-step problems	

FIGURE 10-1

Strategies that help students understand the role of various parts of books

 Table of Contents. Using a book's table of contents, have students predict what specific information might be found in various chapters and in various sections and subsections. Write their predictions on the chalkboard. Then have students go to the appropriate pages to check their predictions.

Provide a list of specific items or information found in a book's various chapters, sections, and subsections. Allow students to match the items on the list with the titles in the table of contents. Have them explain and discuss the reasons for their matches, and check to see whether the matchups are correct.

 Copyright Differences. Examine several copyright pages and tables of contents from books in one subject area but with copyright dates spanning 15 years (for example, science books). Have students use the tables of contents to compare the topics. Then have them use the copyright pages and attempt to match copyright pages to tables of contents. Be ready to provide some guidance with this activity, pointing out which topics are relatively recent and thus would not have been included in earlier books.

 Glossary and Index Activities. Discuss the difference between a glossary and a dictionary: a glossary contains definitions only for words that appear in that particular book, whereas a dictionary includes many other words. Find sentences that contain content-specific vocabulary in a book with a glossary, and have students look up the meanings of the specialized words in the glossary. Then read the paragraphs that contain the terms to see whether the definitions are appropriate.

Compare the pages of an index and a glossary of a book. Have students identify the differences, and write their suggestions on the chalkboard (for example, glossary contains definitions, index contains page numbers, and so on). Discuss the purposes of each and the ways in which the differences help to meet those purposes.

These examples show clearly the conceptual organization of exposition and the sequential arrangement of narratives.

Several organizational patterns are found in content-area texts, with certain patterns more common in certain subject areas. For example, the following passage demonstrates the time-order sequence usually found in the narrative materials of language arts. See whether you can find the cues that tell the reader that the organizational pattern here is a time sequence.

> Tracy knew she would not be able to sleep. But her mother had told her to brush her teeth and put on her nightgown anyway, and Tracy did as she was told.
>
> Just as she got into her nightgown, a loud crack of thunder filled the air! Tracy jumped into bed and pulled the covers over her head. When Meg peeked into the room, Tracy wailed, "The last time we had a storm like this, I stayed awake all night!"
>
> Meg sat beside Tracy and tucked her little sister in. Then she started to hum softly. It was one of Tracy's favorite songs.
>
> As the song went on, Meg noticed that Tracy's eyes had closed. Meg turned off the bedroom light as she tiptoed out of the room. Tracy didn't

Reading in the content areas can require specialized skills that are used increasingly as students move thoughout the grades. Content-area reading, however, should be a part of the curriculum at all grade levels.

hear the next clap of thunder as the storm continued into the night. (Carson, 1990)

Background knowledge tells children that brushing teeth happens before getting into bed, getting tucked in, and going to sleep. In addition, conjunctions such as *and* can indicate sequential order, as can specific references such as *last time, then,* and *next.* Students have less difficulty with this type of text than with other organizational patterns.

The following passage, taken from a social studies textbook, demonstrates how number order is used as an organizational pattern. In this case the structure of the passage outlines its content. The organizational cues lie in the enumeration of points—*first, second*—and in the two-part activity that relates to and balances the two factual statements that precede it.

Look at the map above. It shows you two things. First, it tells you the periods in which early Islam spread. Second, it shows the areas into which Islam spread. Islam began in the cities of Mecca and Medina. Use the map key to find the name of the area in which these two cities are found. Use the map key to find the territory that Muslims had conquered by Muhammed's death in 632. (Myers & Wilk, 1983, p. 272)

Can you pick out the cues indicating that the next passage, taken from a science textbook, is organized in a comparison/contrast pattern? Notice the comparisons between radio and television and the implicit assumption that the reader's background knowledge will incorporate this new information.

Television is the most popular form of communication in the world today. Television is very similar to radio. In radio, sound energy is changed to radio wave energy. Radio wave energy is sent through space. In television, both sound and light are changed to invisible waves. Television sets change the invisible waves back to light and sound. (Sund, Adams, & Hacket, 1980, p. 275)

The last organizational pattern presented here is one of cause and effect. Often, events happen because of other events. This can be noticed especially in history textbooks, for example, where the causal relationships between historical events are a primary focus. Cause-and-effect relationships can also be subtle, as in the following example from an elementary mathematics textbook (Bassler, Kolb, Craighead, & Gray, 1981). Notice that the passage implies that a plane boundary is dependent on a plane region; therefore, the plane region can be considered the cause of the plane boundary.

A closed plane figure together with its inside is called a plane region. The figure around the plane region is called its boundary. Plane regions are named for their boundaries.

Teachers must not assume that students who can read one kind of text structure can read another with similar ease. To build student awareness of the different structures, teachers might discuss how authors use language to signal the type of organization they are using (see Figure 10-2 for representative activities). Vacca and Vacca (1986, p. 33) provide a representative list of signal words for the four organizational patterns discussed here. Obviously, not all of the words are found at all elementary grade levels. Teachers should preview the material that their students will be reading and then discuss the signal words that they will encounter.

FIGURE 10-2

Sample activities to facilitate students' understanding of various text structures

 Signal Word Search. Choose a paragraph or page in a future reading assignment that demonstrates the overall structure of the selection. Tell students about the structure being used, including the signal words appropriate to such a structure. On a copy of the chosen paragraph or page, have students mark any signal words that they find. Then discuss how each of the marked words specifically indicates the pattern in the passage.

 Sequence Completion. Create an ordered list of the steps in a selection with a time-sequenced or a numbered, step-by-step organization. Then delete some of the steps in the sequence, give the list to students before they read the selection, and discuss the concept of a sequenced organizational pattern. Have students check the steps on the list as they meet them in their reading and add those that are missing.

 Sequence Reorder. For a similar activity, create an out-of-order list of the steps in a sequence. Before students read the selection, discuss the concept of an ordered sequence and have students decide how to reorder the list so that it makes logical, sequential sense. Then have students read to see whether their reordered sequence holds true, and discuss again the concept of sequence.

 Predicting in Categories. For a superordinate/subordinate structure, discuss the pattern, and list the major categories found within a given selection. Have students predict what might be found under each category. Then have students read to see whether their predictions were accurate. In a postreading discussion, examine which of the predictions were on target, and discuss why some were not.

Time	Enumeration	Comparison/contrast	Cause-effect
on (date)	to begin with	however	because
not long after	first	but	since
now	second	as well as	therefore
as	next	on the other hand	consequently
before	then	not only/but also	as a result
after	finally	either . . . or	this led to
when	most important	while	so that
	also	although	nevertheless
	in fact	unless	accordingly
	for instance	similarly	if . . . then
	for example	yet	thus

Adapting Reading Rates

Reading rate depends on a number of factors, among them the reader's purpose for reading. For instance, a mathematics word problem requires a different reading rate from that required by a story read for entertainment. Within some content-area texts it is vital not to miss even one word; the directions for a science experiment are just one example. Many suggest that reading rates be consciously changed to meet the demands of each reading task (Farr & Roser, 1979; Shepherd, 1982). To build the idea that reading speed does vary and that reading materials need not

FIGURE 10-3

Teaching strategies to help students acquire skimming abilities

Newspaper Page Skim. Provide students with the front page of a newspaper, and allow only enough time for students to skim the page. Then, from a list of topics, have students identify those that were on the page. Follow up with a discussion of which topics are of most interest to them.

Skim for Sequence. Provide a passage that has a sequenced organizational pattern. As a prereading activity, discuss which words signal sequence. Then have students skim the passage to determine the sequence.

Skim for Main Idea. Provide a paragraph or passage, and direct students to find the main idea. Set a time limit that allows only rapid skimming, not careful reading. After they have skimmed, have students write down the main idea and then go back and read the selection carefully, writing down supporting details.

always be read from beginning to end, teachers can use activities designed to enhance skimming and scanning abilities.

Skimming. Many content-area reading techniques discussed in this chapter require that a student first preview the reading material. Usually this step entails **skimming,** which is quick movement through a text to discover key concepts and main ideas. Skimming gives the reader an idea of what to expect on more detailed reading; the process is aided by an awareness of headings and subheadings.

    There are many reasons for skimming. We may skim a newspaper to decide what to read in depth. We may skim an encyclopedia entry to decide whether any or all of it needs careful attention. Or we may skim a journal article to determine whether it contains information relevant to a particular assignment. Skimming can save valuable time, and teachers need to help students develop that ability (see Figure 10-3).

skimming
Reading rapidly to get a general idea of material that will be reread in detail.

Scanning. **Scanning** is rapid movement through a reading selection to find specific information. It is another skill that mature readers use daily. Looking through a telephone directory to find a specific telephone number is just one example. Teachers need to foster this skill by giving their students the opportunity to practice it (see Figure 10-4).

scanning
Reading rapidly to find specific information.

FIGURE 10-4

Specific strategies to help students develop their scanning abilities

Scanning for Information. Ask students to scan to find the following:

1. a particular date in a history selection
2. the murderer's name in a short mystery story
3. a specific heading in a science chapter
4. a specific ingredient in a recipe
5. answers to questions like "Who wrote _____?" [to be found in a list of titles and authors.]

Using Research Materials

Especially in higher grades, students are required to study more informational material and are expected to use the library to find background or supplementary material. To perform effectively, they must use card catalogs, encyclopedias, almanacs, newspapers, books on related topics, atlases, and abstracts. Research abilities are important in content-area subjects and require skills such as organizing, alphabetizing, and summarizing, in addition to knowing about reference tools and sources, their contents, and their proper use.

The use of reference materials such as encyclopedias and tools such as the card catalog is usually included in a language arts program before specific content-area textbooks are encountered. Trips to the library and a discussion of what the library contains should begin early in the primary grades. In addition, picture encyclopedias specifically designed for young

---

FIGURE 10-5

Sample activities to help develop reference-use abilities

 Library Hunts. Each week, post a question that requires students to use reference skills in the school library. Ask older students questions like "What is one book written by Judy Blume after 1979?" or "Who illustrated *Where the Sidewalk Ends?*" For younger students ask questions like "Where would you find a book by Ezra Jack Keats?" or "What are the titles of one fiction book and one nonfiction book?" Put the question up on the chalkboard just before library period, and see who can return with the answer. Place a box below the question, in which children are to submit their answers. Before the end of the day, write one or more of the correct responses below the question, and discuss how the answers were found.

 Reference Match. After a discussion and demonstration of various types of reference materials, provide a list of reference materials and a separate list of information found in those materials. Have students match the information to the source, for example:

Atlas	_____	a. Map
Encyclopedia	_____	b. Information about famous people
Thesaurus	_____	c. Use to find out which rivers flow through California
		d. Use to find out how the telephone was invented and how it works
		e. Use to find synonyms

 Topic Sort. Place a number of topics in a box. On the chalkboard have an illustration of the spines of an encyclopedia set. Have students choose a topic and state which volume they would use to find information on that topic.

1	2	3	4	5	6	7	8	9	10	11	12	13	14	15	16	17	18	19	20	21
A	B	C–Ch	Ci–Cz	D	E	F	G	H	I	J–K	L	M	N–O	P	Q–R	S–Sn	So–Sz	T	U–V	WX YZ

children should be used early to teach young readers that there are information sources available for numerous topics. The sample activities in Figure 10-5 show some ways that children can be taught needed reference skills.

TEACHING APPROACHES FOR CONTENT-AREA READING

Although the general teaching strategies discussed throughout this text apply to both narrative and expository materials, the method frameworks discussed in this chapter are specifically appropriate to content-area reading instruction. And even though all teachers of reading should use both narrative and expository materials, the particular approaches described here are especially important for middle-school teachers, whose students will encounter predominantly expository texts. Ideally, a sepa-

---

FIGURE 10-5 *continued*

Newspaper Fact Hunt. After a discussion of the general purpose of an index, provide newspapers to familiarize students with newspaper parts and a newspaper index. Have students use the index to find answers to questions like these: Where would you look for information about football scores? Where would you find out which movies are in town and when they are being shown? What page are the comics on? On what page would you find the weather forecast and the highest and lowest temperatures in the United States yesterday?

Dictionary Keys. Discuss the concept of key words in dictionaries, asking students how they know which words are on any given page of a dictionary. Write on the chalkboard the key words for a dictionary page, as well as words that would and would not appear on that page. Have students place the words in alphabetical order, stating whether or not they would be found on the page indicated by the key words.

Atlas Information. Have students use an atlas to find information; for example, which state borders another, which is the longest river in a particular area, which two cities are farther apart than another two, which of two European countries is farther north, and so on.

Card Catalog Search. Visit the library and discuss the card catalog with students: its function and the three types of cards it contains (author cards, subject cards, and title cards). Then present one list with information desired and another with the three types of cards. Have students match the two columns. Also, have students use the card catalog to find out how many books by a particular author are owned by the library, how many books written on a given subject in the past two years are in the library, and so on.

As more and more school libraries are also placing card catalogs on computer databases, students will also have to be taught how to find library information on the library's computer as well as in its card catalog. Notice, however, that the research and search strategies will not change—computerized card catalogs still use author, title and subject (keyboard) categories to categorize information.

rate course in content-area reading should be a part of your teacher preparation. However, as an introduction some representative, readable texts in this area are listed at the end of this chapter.

Modeling

Other chapters have pointed out the benefit of having teachers model reading behavior and processes. In particular, the modeling of question-ing strategies and metacognitive aspects of reading can result in students transferring those behaviors to their own reading practices. Modeling is especially valuable in content-area reading, where different strategies are required because of the different text structures and the demands of subject-specific reading material. Modeling the reading process in differ-ent subject-area texts highlights the fact that reading strategies need to be adapted to the material being read. Modeling also helps students acquire appropriate strategies to use with specific kinds of text.

think-aloud
A method to show students the thoughts that occur as people read; requires that teachers read a text and tell students what they are thinking as they read.

An effective modeling technique is the **think-aloud** method (Davey, 1983), in which the teacher reads a passage and talks through the thought processes that occur. Specifically, the teacher focuses on the use of predictions, imagery (creating a picture of what is being read), links between background knowledge and the text (that is, creating analogies to something already known), monitoring to see whether understanding is taking place, and fix-up strategies to address problem areas. Teachers should model not only how to read, but also when and why to use certain strategies. After students become familiar with the approach, they can practice it with partners and then try to apply the think-aloud strategies in their silent reading. To keep them conscious of think-aloud strategies, Davey suggests that students complete a check sheet similar to the one shown in Table 10-1 after reading a passage. The model lesson that fol-lows shows a teacher demonstrating the use of a think-aloud approach with a social studies passage (Myers & Wilk, 1983).

Other modeling method frameworks are discussed in chapter 9. Partic-ularly applicable here is the ReQuest procedure (Manzo, 1969; 1985), which allows teachers to model questions at all comprehension levels and allows students to acquire needed background knowledge in a supportive way.

TABLE 10-1

A check sheet to monitor use of think-aloud strategies.

| What I did | How often I did it | | | |
	Not very often	A little bit	Much of the time	All of the time
Making predictions				
Forming pictures				
Using *like* (analogies)				
Finding problems				
Using fix-ups				

Directed Reading Activity

Directed reading activity (DRA) is commonly associated with a formal reading program but is also applicable to content-area reading. Of the four basic steps in a traditional DRA, Steps 1, 2, and 4 are emphasized slightly more in expository texts than they are in narrative texts.

1. *Preparation.* This step involves providing needed background; preteaching necessary vocabulary (especially important in content-area reading); and providing motivation for reading.
2. *Guided reading.* With questions or outlines the readers' attention is directed as they proceed through the material. This step aids retention and comprehension of what is read.
3. *Skill development and practice.* Direct instruction in comprehension or other areas is provided, as are opportunities to practice what is taught.
4. *Enrichment.* Activities based on the reading selection often allow children to pursue topics more specifically related to their own interests.

We know that background knowledge influences the comprehension process, and that interaction is especially important with content-area material. The preparation stage, therefore, is critical. Shortly before assigning reading material, teachers must carefully read the selection with their students in mind. Prereading discussion can then center around the concepts that are covered in the reading, with background knowledge provided as needed. Teachers should also deal with unknown vocabulary and should provide students with a clear and definite purpose for reading the assigned text.

With content-area material the second DRA step requires an awareness that textbooks are to be used as instructional tools, and teacher guidance is expected. A study guide or outline, periodic help with vocabu-

directed reading activity (DRA)
A method framework containing the following steps: preparation, guided reading, skill development and practice, and enrichment.

M O D E L L E S S O N

Think-Aloud with Content-Area Material in Mr. Eckert's Class

Herders and Nomads of the Steppe

Thousands of years ago nomads traveled the grasslands of Europe and Asia. Skilled at riding horses, they became warriors feared for their raids on settled communities. During the time of the Romans, some rode out of the north and east to attack cities of the empire. (p. 237)

Introduction. Mr. Eckert tells the students that they will soon be reading a selection in their social studies book—"Herders and Nomads of the Steppe." First, however, he wants them to listen as he thinks aloud about his own reading of the first part of the selection.

The Think-Aloud. Mr. Eckert reads the title, "Herders and Nomads of the Steppe." He says, "I know about herders. They're like shepherds—people who take care of animals. And I know that a nomad is a wanderer, but I'm not sure about *steppe*. I can probably use context to find out. The words *of the* probably mean that the *steppe* is where the herders do their wandering. But that doesn't really tell me what the steppe is. I'll have to look for clues as I read on, but I might need to use a dictionary or ask someone about this word. Based on the title, I predict that the passage will tell me about what kind of animals the herders kept, where they wandered, and what a steppe is."

After reading "Thousands of years ago," Mr. Eckert says, "This tells me that the passage is not about what is going on now. But maybe there are things going on now that relate to what happened thousands of years ago. I'll probably have to make these connections myself, based on what I know." After reading the rest of the second sentence, Mr. Eckert notes, "Now I know where this takes place— in Europe and Asia. I went to Italy last summer (that's in Europe!) and saw lots of grassland. I wonder if that's where these nomads roamed thousands of years ago."

After reading "During the time of the Romans, some rode out," he says, "This is confusing me. Does the 'some' who rode out refer to the Romans or the nomads? I'll look back and see. Since it says that the nomads were good at riding horses, I'll guess *some* refers to the nomads—but I'll have to change my prediction if other things don't fit."

Purpose Setting. After the first paragraph, Mr. Eckert reminds students that they should try to think aloud as they read silently and that they should complete their check sheets every half page.

Reading and Follow-up. Students read and complete their check sheets. Mr. Eckert then discusses the passage and allows students to share their check sheets. He also allows some students to practice thinking aloud on some other paragraphs in the selection they have just read.

lary and concepts, and other support must be available as students read. As readability and other analyses have consistently shown, most content-area textbooks are more difficult for students than narrative materials intended for comparable grade levels.

In content-area reading the skill-development and practice step of a DRA can provide practice with vocabulary terms and concepts that are difficult for students. Each student might keep an informal list of difficult or unknown items encountered while reading. Class discussion can then

MODEL LESSON
Directed Reading Activity in Ms. Alejandro's Class

Preparation. Ms. Alejandro states that students will be reading about different ways of growing food. She notes that the popular belief is that food can best (or perhaps can only) be grown in soil, and asks why that belief is popular. Ms. Alejandro also asks students if they know of any methods of growing food, other than in soil, and if they would like to share any experiences they have about farming. In addition, Ms. Alejandro sets a purpose for reading: to find out why alternative ways of growing food are becoming more important.

Guided Reading. Ms. Alejandro provides a study guide (see p. 415) for the students to use while reading. Then, during the reading she walks around and provides help to students who need it, asking individual questions periodically. When the reading and study guide activity have been completed, Ms. Alejandro leads a class discussion that addresses student understanding of the selection and reviews main ideas, as well as their relationship to students' general knowledge.

Skill Development and Practice. Ms. Alejandro decides to combine a lesson on scanning with additional attention to the vocabulary and concepts introduced earlier. Students are directed to scan certain pages to find vocabulary items. Then they discuss how each word is used and what it means in this specific social studies selection. The class also discusses the potential benefits of scanning and the different types of materials in which scanning might be useful. Thereafter, students practice using the vocabulary items and concepts, and they use telephone books and newspapers for further scanning activities.

Enrichment. Ms. Alejandro provides a list of three items and asks students which they are most interested in: (1) finding out about more ways to feed the world's increasing population, (2) finding out about how foods grown by hydroponics are being received by consumers, or (3) finding out about the effects of fertilizer on the soil. The students divide into groups and go to the library to research their interest. Each group prepares a brief report and later presents it to the rest of the class.

teach the needed vocabulary, as well as review main ideas and supporting details. Teachers should check students' understanding of the selection and point out relationships to previous work and knowledge, thereby setting up the enrichment step of the DRA. As in other types of reading lessons, the enrichment stage in a content-area DRA should provide activities that allow students to apply new knowledge and go beyond the text.

Several authors have addressed the application of DRA to content areas (Rubin, 1983; Thomas & Alexander, 1982). They note that, as in all teaching, the activity must take into account the special demands of the appropriate subject area and individual differences among students. A model of a content-area DRA appears above.

Vocabulary and Concept Development

One of the major barriers to comprehension in content-area reading is the high number of new concepts presented. When reading in science, mathematics, or social studies, students encounter words that are familiar in everyday use but that have unfamiliar meanings within the particular subject area. They are also confronted with new words and concepts that are subject specific. Consequently, content-area teachers must identify and teach the vocabulary and concepts that are required for their subject areas. Because students learn vocabulary best when it occurs in meaningful situations, content-specific vocabulary should be presented as part of a reading assignment. Both content-specific vocabulary and concept development are discussed further in chapter 8.

vocabulary self-selection strategy (VSS)
An instructional procedure that uses words selected by students as its base.

The **vocabulary self-selection strategy (VSS)** is appropriate to aid in students' acquiring and retaining content-area vocabulary (M. Ruddell, 1993). In this approach, students are asked to nominate one or more words from a selection or passage that they have read. Words nominated for discussion are written on the board, and the student, or group, that has nominated the word explains the context in which the word was found (perhaps reading the sentence as part of this explanation). The students then explain what they think the word means in that context, and why it might be important for the class to learn the word. The teacher also nominates a word. The entire class then discusses the words chosen for study, which is done always with a focus on each word's meaning within the context in which it was found. Words studied by the class are then defined, discussed and related to students' backgrounds, and placed in vocabulary journals or word banks.

Jigsaw Grouping

Jigsaw grouping is a method framework that was developed to encourage active participation in cooperative group learning situations. Originally developed by Aaronson et al. (1975, 1978) it has been modified by Slavin (1986) into Jigsaw II and is especially valuable in facilitating participation by students of diverse cultural and ethnic backgrounds. Both Jigsaw and Jigsaw II are based on features of a jigsaw puzzle, where pieces fit together and form a whole. Students are divided into groups, with the number of groups equal to the number of students in each group. Before reading an assigned text, each student in a group is assigned a topic on which to become "expert," with the topics related to the main idea of the reading so that understanding each topic enhances understanding of the central issue or concept.

After reading, each student does appropriate research and additional reading activities to explore the assigned topic. Then, the students with common topics from all groups meet in "expert groups" to discuss and further refine their answers, after which students go back to their originally assigned groups to teach each other their topics. Finally, a culminating group project or product is developed, in which knowledge of all of the topics is useful. The Jigsaw and Jigsaw II procedures are beneficial in facilitating discussion and can be incorporated into any subject area.

MODEL LESSON

Study Guides in Ms. Lee's class

Students will be reading "Food for the Future" (Buggey, 1983), which is a social studies passage discussing how food might be grown to feed the world's increasing population. Ms. Lee wants students to learn about different ways of growing food and has constructed the following three-level guide. The parenthetical information was included because she felt that the students needed additional help in some areas.

Level I *[literal level]*

Why will we need more food in the future?
Why will we not be able to use more land? (p. 213, par. 1)
What three methods of growing food other than using farmland are discussed? (Look at subheadings.)
Why are conditions inside greenhouses "perfect for growing crops"? (p. 232, par. 2)
What does *hydroponics* mean? (p. 233, par. 2)
Will plants grow closer together in water or in soil? (p. 233, par. 2)

Level II [inferential level]

Why does the author say that greenhouses can be used in many places where crops usually cannot grow? (p. 232, par. 2)
How does irrigation in deserts allow crops to grow? (p. 232, par. 1)
How are insects and weeds kept from getting inside a greenhouse?
What is the major difference between greenhousing and hydroponics?

Level III [evaluative level]

Why do you think plants grown in water don't need as many roots as plants grown in soil?
How might greenhouses control growing conditions?
Do you think it would be better to irrigate in deserts instead of using greenhouses? Explain. (p. 232, par. 1 & 2)

Study Guides

Study guides help students comprehend and remember what they have read. Some guides are referred to during reading; others are used after the selection has been read. A teacher should incorporate into a guide the important content of a reading selection and the organizational structure of the material. As noted by Herber (1978); Herber and Herber (1993); and Tierney, Readence, and Dishner (1990), a study or "levels" guide should have three levels, each corresponding to one of the three general levels of comprehension questions—literal, inferential, and evaluative. Also, the study guide must be easy to read. The guide may include specific page and paragraph references or other aids, depending on the teacher's assessment of student abilities. Study guides are not intended to stand alone but should be used as part of an overall lesson, for example, within a directed reading activity.

study guides
Teacher-designed aids that assist students in reading text.

Marginal Glosses

Another technique that is applicable to reading in all content areas is called glossing. It provides a system of marginal notes designed to explain concepts, point out relationships, and otherwise clarify the text as the student reads. **Marginal glosses** are constructed by the teacher and are provided for the student when a passage is assigned. In effect, the marginal glosses reflect the presence of the teacher, providing a guide for the reader while demonstrating the kinds of questions to be asked during reading. Just as questioning strategies provide a model for students to follow when reading independently, glosses also model what should take place when students read on their own.

marginal glosses
Teacher-constructed margin notes that aid students' comprehension by emphasizing and clarifying concepts, noting relationships, and modeling questions.

Singer and Donlan (1989) suggest the following steps for teachers to use in preparing a relevant and useful gloss. As an alternative, it may be desirable to have more able readers prepare the glosses for (or together with) less able readers.

1. *Preview.* The teacher identifies vocabulary or other material to emphasize or clarify.
2. *Create the gloss.* The teacher writes the marginal notes on copies of the original passage, which appears in Figure 10-6. Glosses can be used for all or part of a selection.
3. *Hand out the gloss.* The teacher gives copies of the passage with glosses to students to insert in the appropriate places in their texts and refer to as they read.

Figure 10-6 shows how glosses can clarify vocabulary, point out relationships, direct attention, and emphasize important points.

Advance Organizers

advance organizers
Aids that enhance comprehension by explaining concepts, encouraging prediction, or establishing background knowledge.

independent reading level
The level at which students can read by themselves with few word recognition problems and excellent comprehension.

Although **advance organizers** are, technically, any prereading guide or aid that clarifies concepts, sets up expectations, or builds background, they are usually thought of as specific, brief selections or outlines that are read before a main reading assignment is attempted. Advance organizers require that teachers present a brief outline related to the assigned reading and written at the students' **independent reading level.** Organizers should always foster comprehension and thus should never be difficult to read. An advance organizer appropriate to a science textbook passage on the measurement of electricity is shown in Figure 10-7. Advance organizers do not always appear in written form (although that is usual)—specific prediscussion or visuals that begin a reading selection can also be considered advance organizers.

Mapping and Other Schematic Overviews

A number of techniques visually relate important concepts in the reading selection, thereby enhancing retention and also providing a study guide. Most often, these techniques expect the reader to identify main ideas and

FIGURE 10-6
Text with marginal glosses

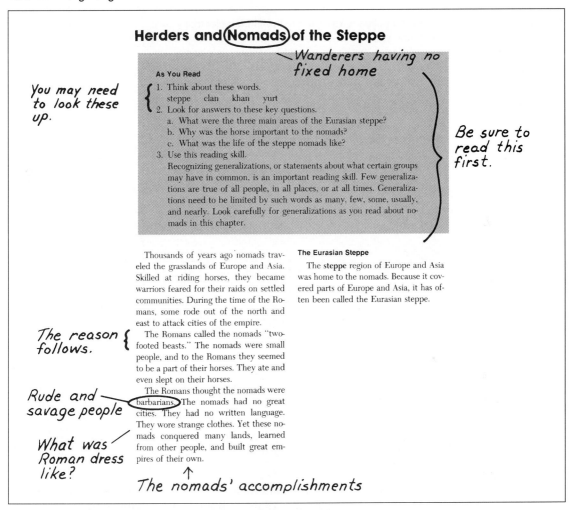

Herders and Nomads of the Steppe

Wanderers having no fixed home

You may need to look these up.

As You Read

1. Think about these words.
   steppe   clan   khan   yurt
2. Look for answers to these key questions.
   a. What were the three main areas of the Eurasian steppe?
   b. Why was the horse important to the nomads?
   c. What was the life of the steppe nomads like?
3. Use this reading skill.
   Recognizing generalizations, or statements about what certain groups may have in common, is an important reading skill. Few generalizations are true of all people, in all places, or at all times. Generalizations need to be limited by such words as many, few, some, usually, and nearly. Look carefully for generalizations as you read about nomads in this chapter.

Be sure to read this first.

Thousands of years ago nomads traveled the grasslands of Europe and Asia. Skilled at riding horses, they became warriors feared for their raids on settled communities. During the time of the Romans, some rode out of the north and east to attack cities of the empire.

The reason follows.

The Romans called the nomads "two-footed beasts." The nomads were small people, and to the Romans they seemed to be a part of their horses. They ate and even slept on their horses.

Rude and savage people

The Romans thought the nomads were barbarians. The nomads had no great cities. They had no written language. They wore strange clothes. Yet these nomads conquered many lands, learned from other people, and built great empires of their own.

What was Roman dress like?

The Eurasian Steppe

The **steppe** region of Europe and Asia was home to the nomads. Because it covered parts of Europe and Asia, it has often been called the Eurasian steppe.

↑ The nomads' accomplishments

Source: From C. B. Myers and G. Wilk, *People, Time, and Change* (Chicago: Follett, 1983). Reprinted by permission.

important concepts, together with their supporting details. Because poorer readers have difficulty identifying main ideas and relationships, teachers must not only teach the techniques but must also discuss why certain concepts are identified as important and why a particular item is related to another, perhaps in a subordinate way. Students then need to practice the techniques, at the same time identifying main ideas and supporting details.

FIGURE 10-7

An advance organizer

You will be reading about measuring electricity. The unit you will read has three parts. The first part will tell you about one way of measuring electricity, using a unit of measurement called VOLTS. The other two parts in the reading will tell you about measuring electricity with units called AMPERES and WATTS.

When you read, try to find out why there are three different units to measure electricity. What is the purpose of each unit of measurement? Do you think we need three ways, or units, to measure electricity?

Before you start reading, write down a sentence or two about what you think you might find out by reading the unit on measuring electricity.

_____

_____

_____

Semantic Mapping. Hanf (1971; see also Johnson and Pearson, 1984) has suggested semantic mapping as a method of organizing ideas to enhance note-taking and as a recall and study technique (see R. Ruddell & Boyle, 1989, for research with older students; also Garner, 1987). The strategy consists of identifying and recording main ideas and related supporting details in visual, graphic form. Semantic mapping requires these two steps:

1. Record the title or main idea anywhere on a piece of paper, leaving enough room so that additional information (the supporting details) can be added around the central idea.
2. Place the secondary, related ideas around the main idea in an organized pattern. Plan the placement of the secondary ideas so that their proximity to the main idea reflects the strength of the relationship.

A semantic map can be a small-group, whole-class, or individual activity. As a prereading activity, teachers might provide a list of the main ideas and supporting details. Through guided discussion, students should then decide which item is the main, or superordinate, idea and rank order the supporting details by importance. Based on the discussion, create the map on the chalkboard or chart paper and have students copy it to use as an aid for study, discussion, or recall. Then reading takes place. It is also possible for students to generate the map during reading, noting ideas as they arise, or to create the map as a postreading activity. Figure 10-8 on page 420 presents a sample semantic map. Novak and Gowan (1984) present and discuss a concept map, which differs slightly from a semantic map in its stronger emphasis on linking the chosen words to concepts.

Structured Concept Outlines. A structured outline represents schematically the relationships among concepts in reading material. This technique requires that concepts be ordered into superordinate, coordinate, and subordinate categories. For example, the following outline might apply to a selection about growing tomatoes.

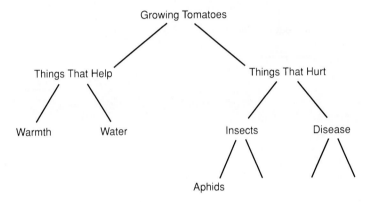

Such an outline may serve the function of an advance organizer or may be used as an aid for postreading activities. In either case, it is important for teachers to point out what relationships exist and also to discuss with students how and why the various concepts are related. A structured outline is similar to the herringbone technique (Tierney, Readence, & Dishner, 1990), which tells who, what, where, when, why, and how in a schematic format that provides structure for recall and study. Figures 10-9 and 10-10 on page 421 suggest how structured concept outlines can be used.

SQ3R

Originally developed by Robinson (1961) as a study strategy for college students, SQ3R is also taught as a study tool for secondary and upper elementary-grade students. SQ3R stands for these actions:

Survey   Quickly skim through the material. Focus on headings and titles to get a general feel for what the material covers.

Question   Based on the survey just completed, identify questions that the material will probably answer.

Read   Read the material to answer the questions previously identified.

FIGURE 10-8

An example of a semantic map

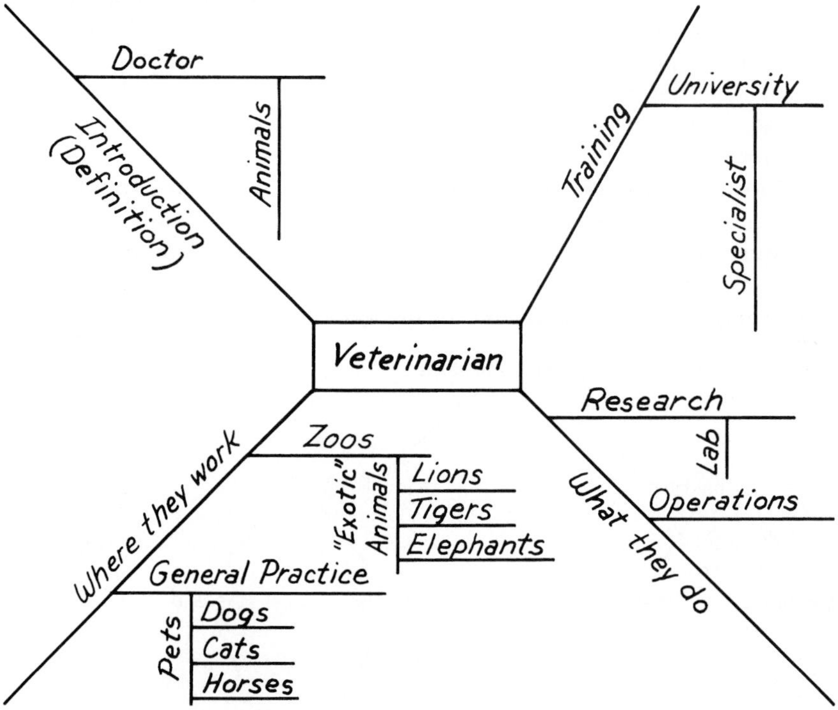

Recite	Orally or in writing attempt to answer the identified questions.
Review	Reread portions of the material to verify the answers previously given.

Although SQ3R has been shown to be an effective study strategy when used as described, it is rarely used spontaneously by students (Cheek & Cheek, 1983) and needs to be taught and reinforced. Some (Vacca, 1981) believe that students need more structure than is provided by SQ3R. Pauk (1984), for example, suggests a more structured method of presenting the technique and stresses setting purposes at each step. In addition, he has added *record* after *reading,* thus making his technique SQ4R. Pauk believes that students should record succinct margin notes of ideas, facts, and details from their reading, thus establishing cues for immediate and future reviews.

CONNECTING WRITING AND CONTENT-AREA READING

Writing activities should be used in all types of classrooms, ranging from more traditional to whole language, to help build students' comprehen-

FIGURE 10-9

Marginal gloss combined with a structured concept outline

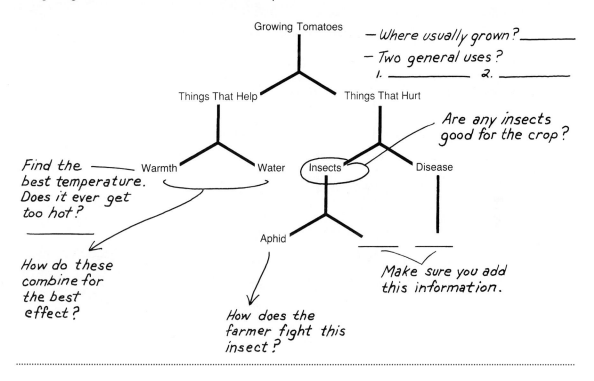

FIGURE 10-10

Strategies that illustrate the use of structured concept outlines

 Concept Outline Discussion. Prepare, duplicate, and distribute a structured concept outline. Use it as the basis for discussion with students prior to their reading the selection.

 Concept Outline Completion. Omit certain parts of an outline, and tell students to complete it as they read. This activity provides a purpose for reading, and allows students to make active choices while they read.

 Combined Glosses and Structured Concept Outlines. Combine a structured concept outline with marginal glosses, leaving adequate space for students to write their responses. Instruct students to make notes or otherwise complete the outline as requested by the gloss (see Figure 10-9).

sion of content-area, or expository, texts. Teachers should provide practice with different text structures and should ensure that the classroom environment includes books of many types—children's literature as well as expository materials. Teachers should also ensure that writing activities move beyond stories.

MODEL LESSON

SQ3R in Ms. Dodds' Class

Ms. Dodds begins with a discussion of SQ3R, reminding students of the steps involved.

Survey. Students are asked to survey a science passage about the invention of the telephone, quickly skimming the headings and overall content. A short period of time is allowed, and then students are asked to identify the title of the passage and the three subheadings.

Question. Ms. Dodds lists on the board the title and subheadings that students provide and asks what questions might be answered in each subsection. Students generate these questions:

The Telephone: A Useful Invention
    Q: Why is the telephone useful?
    Q: What makes the telephone useful?
    Q: How was it invented?
Before the Telephone
    Q: How did people talk to each other before the telephone?
The Invention
    Q: Who invented the telephone?
    Q: When was it invented?
    Q: How was it invented?
After the Invention
    Q: What happened after the invention?
    Q: How did the telephone change people's lives?

Read. Students are asked to read the selection, keeping the questions in mind.

Recite. Students actively but silently recite or write down the answers to the questions as the information is learned.

Review. When finished reading, students review their answers—in a large group with Ms. Dodds, in pairs or small groups, or individually. The parts of the passage that provide answers are reread, and the passage as a whole is discussed.

Flood, Lapp, and Farnan (1986) suggest a three-step procedure that links reading and writing.

1. *Prewriting.* Students choose a topic and brainstorm what they already know about it, listing what is generated. Students are then directed to gather additional information about the topic—from reference sources, interviews, or a targeted expository selection. After they have gathered the information, students list the facts that they learned about the topic.
2. *Writing.* Students select the most important topic (the most all-encompassing) from the two lists created during the prewriting

Connecting reading and writing allows teachers to provide opportunities for students to incorporate many research skills such as use of the card catalog (whether in traditional or computerized form), which requires alphabetizing and indexing knowledge.

stage and list supporting details or subtopics under that main idea. Following their main topic-subtopic outline, students then write a short expository paragraph.

3. *Feedback and editing.* Partners or groups can read each other's paragraphs to determine whether a main idea and supporting details are included. Feedback or further information can be provided, which the original author can use to rewrite and strengthen the paragraph.

The language experience approach (LEA) can also be used to build familiarity with expository text structures (Kinney, 1985). The language experience is provided by the teacher, who might use a feature analysis to compare ideas or vocabulary terms or might list headings and subheadings from a text and allow students to brainstorm what might be found in the selection. Students then dictate a story or description to the teacher, based on the brainstorming or information session. The teacher can guide the students, perhaps asking for information that might fit under a specific heading or asking for a contrast or comparison sentence at some point. After the dictation is completed, students can read and discuss their writing, copy it into their notebooks, and read the target selection. An interesting follow-up to reading is a discussion that compares the dictated story to the actual selection from which the headings came.

Summarizing, Notetaking, and Organizing

Many of the strategies and techniques discussed in this chapter require that information be summarized or organized, often in written form. These skills can be developed from the earliest stages of schooling. When students are asked to restate or paraphrase a story, their summarizing ability is enhanced, as are their notetaking skills when summary statements or main points are compiled in written form. When children are asked to categorize similar items, they are developing categorizing skills that help in organizing information.

Brown, Campione, and Day (1981; see also Brown & Day, 1983) identify the following actions as helpful in summarizing:

- deleting nonessential information
- deleting repetitive information
- using blanket terms to replace lists of simpler items (for example, *pets* to replace "dogs, cats, hamsters, and goldfish")
- selecting topic sentences or, if there are none, creating topic sentences

Tei and Stewart (1985) suggest that the first two of these actions are the most appropriate for middle school students. However, with teacher guidance and modeling, students can use all of them to write summary paragraphs. Figure 10-11 on page 426 includes strategies that help develop summarizing and note-taking abilities.

K-W-L
A method framework with three steps: know, want to know, and learn.

The K-W-L Strategy. The **K-W-L** method framework (Ogle, 1989) includes both writing and reading, and requires brainstorming, categorizing, and information-gathering/notetaking activities. K-W-L stands for *k*now, *w*ant to know, and *l*earn. The procedure begins with discussion about what students already know about the topic. That information is then organized into categories, after which students raise questions that might need to be answered. During and after reading, students record what they are learning and what they still want to know. The K-W-L procedure recognizes the importance of prior knowledge, group learning, writing, and a personalized learning experience. When extended to use semantic mapping, as discussed in chapter 8, the process is called K-W-L Plus (Carr & Ogle, 1987).

M O D E L   L E S S O N
K-W-L in Ms. Percy's Class

Before Reading (Know). Ms. Percy models and then facilitates discussion and activity in four areas.

1. *Brainstorming.* Ms. Percy asks students to brainstorm what they know about a topic and writes their responses on the chalkboard or chart paper. As conflicts or uncertainty about the appropriateness of a response arise, questions are also noted (for example, Is _____ a part of the topic?). The questions become part of what needs to be found out.
2. *Categorizing.* Ms. Percy encourages students to categorize items generated during brainstorming. If students have trouble with this task, she models the categorizing process, using a think-aloud procedure. Another strategy is to write similar items closer together in the beginning, as they are generated.
3. *Anticipating.* Ms. Percy facilitates discussion about what readers may discover when they read about the categorized topics.
4. *Questioning.* Ms. Percy helps students specify certain questions to be answered during and after reading. It is important that such questions be specific.

During Reading (Want to Know). Students are asked to read and actively look for new information and ideas, which are noted on a worksheet/table like the one shown here. Longer or more difficult reading assignments should be broken into manageable chunks.

What We Know	What We Want to Find Out	What We Learned

After Reading (Learn). As a class activity, Ms. Percy compiles the information that the students learned and helps them relate it to what they previously knew and what they needed to find out. During discussion both Ms. Percy and students add additional information to the worksheet/table, which can then be used to generate a written summary.

READING IN SPECIFIC CONTENT AREAS

The techniques presented earlier in this chapter can be used in any subject area. In addition, there are method frameworks appropriate for use with texts in specific subject areas. The discussion that follows presents some of the specific demands faced by readers in social studies, science, mathematics, and language arts and describes method frameworks that

---

FIGURE 10-11

Strategies that help develop summarizing and notetaking abilities

 Summary Statements. Have students listen to a story or an expository reading. Then ask them to restate or paraphrase the main idea of the selection. At another time students might be asked to provide a one- or two-sentence written statement.

 Notetaking Contrasts. Model and then allow students to practice taking notes in various forms—listing points, summarizing paragraphs, and outlining. Use a short reading selection, film, or audiotape as the basis for the notetaking activity. Be sure to discuss the students' work, focusing on their reasons for including and not including certain information.

 Outline Completion. Provide headings and subheadings in outline form, but leave the outline incomplete. Then read a selection that pertains to the outline, and have students complete the outline. This activity enhances both notetaking and summarizing skills.

 Picture Categories. For young students, compile a set of pictures that includes items in two categories. Mix up the pictures and have students tell which belong together. Alternately, identify a category and have students tell which pictures do not belong.

---

specifically address reading in those subjects. Those areas are not in any way superior to others, but all four use reading material as a major instructional component.

Social Studies

Organizational Differences. Often students who have difficulty reading mathematics and science texts have less difficulty reading language arts and social studies materials (Muhtadi, 1977). This distinction may result from patterns of text organization. The majority of reading materials within language arts are narrative texts, organized along a time sequence. Science and mathematics texts, on the other hand, are usually organized hierarchically. Social studies texts can be organized along either of these patterns, although history, one particular component of social studies, is usually presented in a time-sequenced format.

We can usually determine a book's general organization from its title and the headings included in the table of contents. Can you see the hierarchical organization in the following example?

Climates of the World

Arid Climatic Regions
   Arid Climate Defined
   Arid Regions
      African Continent
      European Continent
      American Continents

Desert Climatic Regions
  Desert Climate Defined
  Desert Regions
    African Continent
    Asian Continent
    American Continents

On the other hand, a title such as *Decline of the Dinosaurs* would imply a time-sequenced organization, moving from the evolution of dinosaurs through their most prolific period to their decline and eventual extinction. Organizational structures can also have a mixed organization, like the time sequence within a hierarchical pattern illustrated here.

Government in the United States

Government at the Federal Level
  Evolution of Federal Government
    The Prerevolutionary Period
    The Postrevolutionary Period
Government at the State Level
  Evolution of State Legislatures

Thus, in social studies material, students are often required to contend with different organizational structures within one reading selection, and students need to be aware of that possibility.

Graphic Elements. Social studies readers also see graphic elements—maps, charts, and graphs—that are not normally used in narrative texts. Although other content areas include such material, the graphs and charts in social studies can incorporate fairly unique symbols. The examples in Figure 10-12 typify the graphics that students encounter in their social studies textbooks, in addition to more normal photographs, graphs, and charts. Even good readers may have difficulty interpreting graphic information and may be unable to move back and forth between textual material and graphics without losing their place. Interpretation of maps and graphs is rarely taught as a specific skill, even though the complexity of such reading has been noted (Summers, 1965; Vacca, 1981).

Fry (1981) presents a taxonomy of graphs with six main subdivisions, although combinations across these types are often used.

1. *Lineal graphs,* showing sequential data (for example, simple time lines, parallel time lines, and flow charts).
2. *Quantitative graphs,* used for numerical data (for example, growth curves, bar graphs, pie graphs, and multiple variable graphs).
3. *Spatial graphs,* representing area and location (for example, two-dimensional road maps and three-dimensional contour maps).
4. *Pictorial graphs,* depicting visual concepts (for example, realistic drawings, schematic drawings, and abstracted representations).

FIGURE 10-12

Graphic material from a representative third-grade social studies text

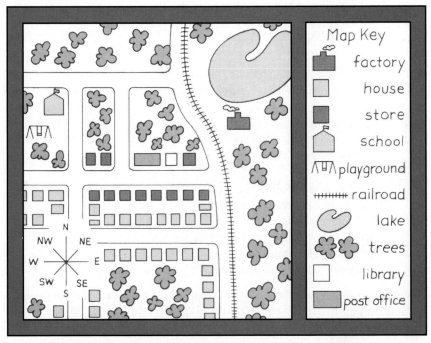

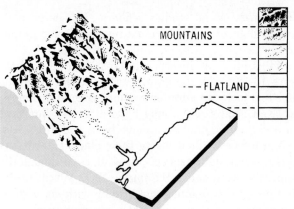

Source: From J. Buggey, *Our Communities* (Chicago: Follett, 1983), pp. 18, 94. Reprinted by permission.

5. *Hypothetical graphs,* demonstrating an interrelationship of ideas (for example, sentence diagrams or semantic maps).

6. *Intentional omissions from the taxonomy of graphs: high verbal figures* (for example, posters and advertisements); *high numerical tables* (for example, statistical tables); *symbols* (for example, word equivalents like the outline of a man on a restroom door); *decorative designs* (for example, designs whose main purpose is decorative rather than conceptual or informative).

Summers (1965) has pointed out differences between what he calls map readers and **map thinkers.** A map reader can locate information but cannot interpret the presented information, much as a student might be able to locate literal information in text yet be unable to assimilate that information into existing knowledge structures or interpret it in the general context of the text as a whole. Obviously, a teacher's goal is to move students beyond being map readers and mold them into map thinkers. According to Summers, a map thinker must be aware of these six elements:

map thinkers
Students who are able to locate information on a map and interpret it.

1. *Map title.* Similar to a book title, this tells what the map depicts; it provides an introduction to the map and its features. Discussion of

Learning to read and interpret information on maps, charts, and graphs is important to fully understand certain types of information.

the title and other activities similar to those associated with a book or story title are appropriate.

2. *Legend.* Often compared to the table of contents in a book, the legend indicates what map symbols stand for and provides other information, such as the map scale. The legend usually appears in a box within the map or graph. Students should try to focus on each item in the legend and visualize whatever it represents. For example, a map thinker should try to imagine the vast oceans that a legend might equate with the color blue.

3. *Direction.* The top of a map usually, but not always, indicates north. Students must be taught to realize that north is not just a direction; it is also a concept with related understandings of true and magnetic north, intermediate distances, and polar regions.

4. *Distance scale.* Three types of scales are common: graphic, statement, and fractional scales. The scale must be kept in mind because it enables a reader to tell how far or how big something is. A small-scale map depicts a large area made smaller, whereas a large-scale map depicts a small area made larger.

5. *Location.* This is usually depicted by a grid system that segments maps, most often with horizontal and vertical lines. Township range lines and marginal letters and numbers are common grid systems, as are parallels and meridians, which locate places by latitude and longitude.

6. *Types of maps.* Major map types include land, elevation, climate, vegetation and water features, political, economic, and population. Combinations of these types are often found on one map.

Miscellaneous Concerns. In addition to changes in structure and different kinds of graphic information that must be actively incorporated into the text, social studies readers face other challenges.

- Vocabulary terms involve a larger-than-normal proportion of words with Latin and Greek roots, prefixes, or suffixes.

- Social studies vocabulary and concepts reflect a variety of disciplines: anthropology, sociology, economics, political science, and more.

- Many social studies textbooks focus on details to such an extent that important major issues may be difficult to grasp. History segments often stress many details without drawing clear relationships to the larger picture.

- In our world of rapid change, the material in social studies textbooks can become rapidly dated. Sometimes, it is obsolete or even false. As a result, children who have seen more recent or correct information in newspapers or on news broadcasts may be confused.

OPPORTUNITIES TO CELEBRATE DIVERSITY

The areas traditionally part of social studies—history, geography, civics, culture, and so on—provide many opportunities to study aspects related to multiculturalism, segregation, the economic conditions and other topics that can relate directly to students in your class, and are vital for all students to know. Aspects of social studies can also provide opportunities for all students, and their parents, to provide their expertise in everything from show-and-tell sessions to oral (or written) histories of their families. Studying maps and charts can be used to find information in activities that address issues of diversity, and to summarize and present students' research findings to the class. In short, students can use the strategies that enhance reading in social studies, including map-reading and map-thinking skills, to contexts that celebrate diversity.

- Differentiating fact, opinion, and propaganda can be difficult.
- Some younger children may have trouble grasping time-dependent concepts. Students at certain lower **cognitive levels** have problems understanding concepts involving time, space, and distance relationships, all of which are important to social studies and appear in various kinds of maps.

cognitive levels
Stages of intellectual development.

Instructional Strategies. The teaching procedures noted earlier in this chapter apply to social studies material as well as to other content areas. Building student background, providing prereading activities, and implementing other techniques discussed throughout this text are certainly important activities for teaching social material. Students will benefit from cloze and **maze procedures,** both of which emphasize context clues to aid comprehension. Cause-and-effect activities should also be emphasized, along with activities to build concepts and vocabulary. All of these techniques have been discussed in previous chapters. Figure 10-13 presents several strategies that relate to teaching map-thinking, fact/opinion, and cause/effect within social studies material.

maze procedure
A fill-in-the-blank activity to measure comprehension.

Mathematics

Differences in Content and Approach. The exercises in Figure 10-14 are representative of reading demands in mathematics. We can see that mathematics passages contain numerous items not generally found in narrative texts. Perhaps the most obvious are the numeric symbols that must be read. Just as a set of letters represents a concept, numbers and other symbols also represent meaning. For example, the number 50 represents a quantity of items totaling a certain amount, which could be expressed as "2 more than 48" or in innumerable other ways. Thus, just as readers must learn the specific concepts represented by letter combinations, so must they also learn the concepts for other symbol sets. Look

FIGURE 10-13

Examples of strategies that foster the development of map-thinking, fact/opinion and cause/effect skills

 Map Information Hunt. After a discussion of the information that can be found in various parts of a map, provide a list of questions that students should answer while referring to a specific map.

 Map Drawing. Provide a summary of information in paragraph or list form. Then have students use that information to draw a map or create a graph. Discuss the advantages of the information in graphic form (for example, better overview, visual summary, ease of seeing relationships).

 Fact and Opinion Statements. Find statements of fact and opinion in newspapers, or create statements that would fit into those categories. Present the statements in pairs, and have students discuss and explain which is fact and which is opinion.

Factual statement	Opinion statement
1. American Airlines and Northwest Airlines both reported losses [in income] during the first quarter.	The airlines will close down if they lose money in the next quarter.
2. All land and buildings in Davidson County will be reassessed before the next taxation year.	All taxes on real estate in Davidson County will go up next year.

 Cause-and-Effect Statements. Follow the same initial procedure as that in the previous activity. Then delete either a cause or an effect, and direct students to supply the deleted item. Have students present and explain their answers.

Cause	Effect
1. There have been several airplane accidents recently.	Fewer people want to travel by airplane nowadays.
2. Fewer people want to travel by airplane nowadays.	The airlines are making less money.
3. All land and buildings in Davidson County will be reassessed before the next taxation year.	The county clerk needs to hire more staff to update Davidson County's tax records.
4. The county clerk needs to hire more staff to update Davidson County's tax records.	_____ _____ _____

These examples show that causes and effects can be transposed; that is, the effect of one cause may, in turn, be the cause of a different effect. Such transpositions serve to focus attention on the differences between causes and effects.

FIGURE 10-14

A sample mathematics page from an elementary text

PRACTICE

Add or subtract. Write each answer in lowest terms.

1. $3\frac{2}{5}$ $\quad -2\frac{1}{5}$

2. $6\frac{2}{6}$ $\quad +3\frac{2}{6}$

3. $5\frac{2}{3}$ $\quad -1\frac{1}{3}$

4. $6\frac{1}{4}$ $\quad +2\frac{1}{4}$

5. $8\frac{7}{8}$ $\quad -\frac{2}{8}$

6. $5\frac{1}{6}$ $\quad +3\frac{1}{6}$

7. $9\frac{3}{4}$ $\quad -1\frac{3}{4}$

8. $3\frac{3}{8}$ $\quad +3\frac{1}{8}$

9. $8\frac{5}{12}$ $\quad +\frac{3}{12}$

10. $3\frac{4}{9}$ $\quad +1\frac{2}{9}$

11. $6\frac{5}{7}$ $\quad -\frac{2}{7}$

12. $4\frac{2}{5}$ $\quad -2\frac{1}{5}$

13. $7\frac{5}{9} + 3\frac{2}{9} = \square$

14. $5\frac{1}{2} - 2\frac{1}{2} = \square$

★ 15. $(3 + 2\frac{1}{2}) - 1\frac{1}{2} = \square$

Follow the rule to complete.

Rule: Add $1\frac{2}{7}$.

	Input	Output
16.	$3\frac{4}{7}$	
17.	$1\frac{1}{7}$	
18.	$2\frac{3}{7}$	

Rule: Subtract $1\frac{1}{8}$.

	Input	Output
19.	$1\frac{2}{8}$	
20.	$2\frac{3}{8}$	
21.	$5\frac{5}{8}$	

APPLICATION

22. Ralph filled $7\frac{3}{4}$ bags with leaves. Rudy filled $5\frac{1}{4}$ bags with leaves. How many more bags of leaves did Ralph fill?

★ 23. Rosa wants to knit 2 scarves. She needs $4\frac{1}{2}$ packages of yarn for one, and $3\frac{1}{2}$ packages for the other. She has $9\frac{1}{2}$ packages. After making the scarves, how much yarn will she have left?

Mixed Practice

1. $5.1 + 6.5 = \square$

2. $4.64 + 3.81 = \square$

3. $82.1 - 49.6 = \square$

4. $3.6 - 2.9 = \square$

5. 99.62 $\quad +48.43$

6. 137.72 $\quad - 48.36$

7. 362 $\quad \times 38$

8. $17 - 2.58 = \square$

9. $48 \times 97 = \square$

10. $386 \div 25 = \square$

11. $42\overline{)847}$

12. $\$6.38$ $\quad \times 81$

13. $52.4 + 3.73 = \square$

14. $178.6 - 5.2 = \square$

15. $50 \times \$6.71 = \square$

16. $36\overline{)\$7.20}$

17. $32\overline{)946}$

18. $4.26 - 3.8 = \square$

Source: From L. J. Orfan and B. R. Vogeli, *Mathematics* (Morristown, NJ: Silver Burdett, 1987), p. 331. Reprinted by permission.

again at Figure 10-14, and notice the other numeric arrangements and process symbols that are generally not used in narrative texts: decimals (for example, 5.1, 6.5), fractions (for example, ⅜, ¼), mathematical symbols (for example, +, −, =).

In addition to different symbol sets, other differences are also associated with reading mathematics materials.

- Specialized vocabulary that is content specific—for example, *division, quotient, digit, multiplication, product, numeral,* and so on.

- Specific shapes and diagrams—for example, triangle, rectangle, parallelogram, and so on.

- A slower rate of reading than is necessary in narrative texts and in some other expository texts, such as history books. Word problems and theorems must be carefully read and read more than once.

- Eye movements that deviate from the expected left-to-right sequence, as in this problem:

$$3 + 2 (6 + 1) = 17$$

  Mathematical rules require that $6 + 1$ be computed and the sum multiplied by 2 before that product is added to 3. Eye movements also go from up to down and from down to up in addition and division problems, as well as diagonally in the multiplication of fractions.

- A different approach to comprehension. For example, word problems such as the following require attention to parts of the text not normally thought important.

  > John was going to the store. On the way, he stopped at Mary's house. Mary lived 2 blocks from John. John and Mary went to the store together. The store was 2 blocks past Mary's house. How far did John go to get to the store?

  Normally, children would read to find out who the people in the story were or what the action was. However, for this problem such information is unimportant. With mathematics problems students who focus on the types of questions asked with narrative materials may attend to inappropriate items. In fact, reading difficulties may account for as much as 35 percent of student errors on mathematics achievement tests (O'Mara, 1981).

Instructional Strategies. Fay (1965) suggests that a strategy called **SQRQCQ** be used to solve word problems.

Survey   Read the problem rapidly, skimming to determine its nature.

SQRQCQ
A study strategy for reading math word problems: survey, question, read, question, compute, and question.

M O D E L   L E S S O N
SQRQCQ in Ms. Jackson's Class

Ms. Jackson knows that there are really only three things that prevent a student from correctly completing a word problem: (1) reading the problem incorrectly and thus not finding the appropriate information; (2) not performing the appropriate computation (for example, subtracting when addition is needed); and (3) not performing the computation correctly (for example, multiplying incorrectly). Ms. Jackson has decided to address the first point by teaching her students SQRQCQ. She first explains that SQRQCQ will help them better understand their mathematics problems. She then explains what the letters stand for and demonstrates how to read a mathematics problem (written on the chalkboard) using the SQRQCQ technique.

After Ms. Jackson is sure that her students know what SQRQCQ requires a reader to do, she tells them that they will practice the technique together. She hands out a sheet of simple word problems and instructs students not to begin reading until she says to. After all students have sheets, she asks several students to describe the first step in SQRQCQ. Then she directs students to skim the first problem rapidly and to turn their papers over when they have finished skimming.

When the students are finished, Ms. Jackson discusses with them what the problem is generally about. She then reminds them what the next step in the procedure is, suggests that they write down what is being asked, and again instructs them to turn over their papers when they are finished.

Ms. Jackson continues this process, discussing each step of the SQRQCQ procedure, both before and after it is attempted. She has students practice several of the problems on the sheet in this way and reinforces the technique several times during the next week and periodically thereafter.

Question	Decide what is being asked—in other words, what the problem is.
Read	Read for details and interrelationships.
Question	Decide which processes and strategies should be used to address the problem.
Compute	Carry out the necessary computations.
Question	Ask whether the answer seems correct. Check computations against the facts presented in the problem and against basic arithmetic facts.

Kane, Byrne, and Hater (1974) suggest a modification of the traditional cloze technique for mathematics. Their **modified cloze procedure** first specifies areas of student difficulty in textual aspects of mathematics material and in comprehension of mathematical concepts. The modification is then completed as a joint activity among students or among teacher and students. The exercise should be accompanied by discussion that focuses student attention on pertinent information that helps fill in the blanks. As the teacher models the thought processes nec-

modified cloze procedure
A comprehension assessment procedure that departs from the traditional routine of deleting every fifth word.

essary to replace the deletions, students can learn the reasoning specific to mathematics. An example of a mathematics cloze passage is shown in Figure 10-15.

It is also necessary to teach students the specialized symbolic vocabulary of mathematics. All of the process symbols have the same properties as letter- and word-based vocabulary. For example, the various multiplication and division signs shown below represent the same concept and can be considered synonyms.

$$3 \times 2 \qquad 3 \bullet 2 \qquad 3(2)$$
$$2\,\overline{)3} \qquad 3 \div 2 \qquad \tfrac{3}{2}$$

These symbols can be taught with the same procedures used to teach synonyms that are words. Any symbols that stand for concepts can be considered vocabulary items and can be taught with the techniques presented in chapter 8.

FIGURE 10-15

Adaptation of the cloze procedure for mathematics

Following is a brief passage that could occur in a mathematics book written for upper elementary or middle school students. To the right is a cloze test constructed for the passage on the left. In actual practice, longer passages are used so that many more blanks are obtained.

Divide 20 by 5. Now, multiply 20 by $\frac{1}{5}$. Is dividing by 5 the same as multiplying by $\frac{1}{5}$? Are these sentences true?	Divide 20 by ___. Now multiply 20 ___$\frac{1}{5}$. Is _____ by 5 the same ___ multiplying by $\frac{1}{}$___? Are these sentences true?
$36 \div 18 = 36 \times \frac{1}{18}$	___$6 \div 18$ ___ $36 \times \frac{1}{18}$
$72 \div 8 = 72 \times \frac{1}{8}$	72 ___ $8 = 72$ ___ $\frac{1}{8}$

Here are some observations you should note concerning the cloze test:

1. Both word tokens (i.e., words) and math tokens (i.e., numerical digits or process symbols) are counted in this procedure.
2. Every fifth token is deleted, starting with the fifth token.
3. Deleted tokens are replaced by blanks of two sizes. The shorter blanks are used for math tokens.
4. Tokens are ordered according to the words used to read them. For example, $\frac{1}{5}$ can be thought of as one, process symbol, five. Therefore, these tokens would be ordered as 1, /, 5. What is important is that the translation to words be consistent within a passage.

Source: From R. B. Kane, M. A. Byrne, and M. A. Hater, *Helping Children Read Mathematics* (New York: American Book, 1974), pp. 18–19. Adapted by permission.

Science

Technical Reading. The following passage from an elementary science textbook (Sund, Adams, & Hackett, 1980) illustrates some of the reading demands in this content area.

> The chart below shows several common compounds. It also shows the chemical formula and the phase of the compound.

Compound	Formula	Phase of matter
carbon dioxide	CO_2	gas
water	H_2O	liquid
ammonia	NH_3	gas
salt	$NaCL$	solid

> There are simple rules for writing chemical formulas. The formula for water is H_2O. The small number 2 means that a water molecule has two hydrogen atoms. The O has no number after it. No number means there is only one atom of oxygen. The number 1 is not written in chemical formulas. A molecule of water has 2 atoms of hydrogen and 1 atom of oxygen. CO_2 is the formula for carbon dioxide. What elements make up carbon dioxide? How many atoms of each element are in a molecule of carbon dioxide? (p. 90)

Science texts often seem more technical than other content-area texts. For example, the above explanation of the rules for writing formulas is specific and reflects technical writing. It must be carefully read, or the concept may not be grasped. The passage also includes several terms specific to science: element, molecule, compound, atom, dioxide, and formula. And, like mathematics and social studies, science uses several symbol sets. The chemical symbols and the numerical subscripts in the formulas must all be mastered in order to understand this science passage correctly.

Like social studies, science draws on several disciplines for its knowledge base. In fact, science materials show some overlap with social studies materials; units on space exploration and on weather and climate are two examples. Thus, the previous discussion of maps and charts applies to science as well. And science, too, has a great many words with Latin and Greek **morphemes.**

morphemes
The smallest meaningful linguistic units.

A further distinction in the vocabulary found in science materials is the high number of words with a meaning specific to science—that is, words that are not found in everyday speech. Whereas social studies and mathematics include many words with both general and content-specific meanings, science has a large number of words with only content-specific meanings. Thus, teachers may need to preteach specific science concepts before students see the terms in text. Even though context often helps, we cannot assume that unknown words will become clear through reading alone.

All content-area materials, including textbooks, journals, and newspapers make specialized demands on readers.

A key component in understanding science material is reading to follow directions, particularly in laboratory exercises, where even the slightest departure can result in a failed experiment. In addition, science experiments follow a structure that is different from that of other textual materials.

1. Problem   4. Observation
2. Hypothesis   5. Collection of data (results)
3. Procedure   6. Conclusions

If students are unfamiliar with this structure, it must be taught.

PQRST
A science study technique that stresses previewing, questioning, reading, summarizing, and testing.

Instructional Strategies. **PQRST** is an effective study technique specific to science (Spache, 1963; Spache & Berg, 1966). It recommends that students reading science materials follow a five-step sequence.

Preview   Rapidly skim the selection to be read. The reader should not move on until the generalization or theory of the passage has been identified.

Question   Raise questions for study purposes.

MODEL LESSON

PQRST in Mr. Hernadez' Room

Mr. Hernandez, a fourth-grade teacher, has decided to teach his science class the PQRST study technique. He explains that science textbooks are often structured so that a generalization or theory is stated near the beginning of a selection, the generalization is expanded and supported throughout the rest of the selection, and a summary statement of the generalization or theory is usually presented at the end. He has his students look at a section in their science textbooks that demonstrates this structure.

Mr. Hernandez then explains that a technique called PQRST helps readers consciously identify the generalization or theory and become more aware of the supporting details. He reminds his students that they should be active readers who anticipate what may come next, based on what has come before. He then presents each of the steps in PQRST, demonstrates what a reader might do at each step, and verbally tests a number of students to make sure that they know what should be done at each step.

Preview. Mr. Hernandez asks his students to open their books to a specific selection that has not been read before. He tells them to preview the selection, jotting down a note about the generalization or theory. When all are finished, he asks what they think the generalization is and has several students supply the reasons for their decision.

Question. Mr. Hernandez tells students to write down questions they might have about the generalization or theory and questions that they think might be answered as they read through the selection. He tells students not to refer to their books at this stage.

Read. Mr. Hernandez knows that a different class might need to continue this lesson on another day, but he thinks that this class can go ahead. He tells students to keep their questions in mind and to read the selection, writing down brief notes that might help them answer their questions.

Summarize. Mr. Hernandez reminds his students about the need to summarize. He suggests that they group relevant facts and also attempt to specifically answer their own questions, using their notes as a place to start.

Test. Because Mr. Hernandez wants to do this final step as a group activity, he has five or six students read their summaries aloud while the other students silently compare their own to those that are read. Students then discuss the accuracy of the summary statements and the answers to the questions identified earlier. During this process, students are encouraged to use the selection as a reference to justify their conclusions. Mr. Hernandez reinforces the use of PQRST on a continuing basis.

Read	With questions in mind, read the selection and answer the questions. Sometimes experiments need to be done before the questions can be answered.
Summarize	Organize and summarize the information gathered through reading. Group relevant facts and summarize answers to each question. This step is best done in writing.

Test   Go back to the reading selection and check the summary
                    statement for accuracy. Can the generalization or theory
                    identified in the first step be supported through the
                    answers and summaries?

Forgan and Mangrum (1985) note that the difference between SQ3R and
PQRST is "more than semantic" and agree with Fay (1965) that PQRST,
rather than SQ3R, should be used with science material.

Language Arts

In some ways the reading task in a language arts or English classroom
can be the most demanding of all. Although the various subject areas
make specific demands on a reader, a language arts reading assignment
can include any or all of the demands and text structures previously discussed. Although the general reading requirements in language arts
revolve around narrative text structures, once students are able to read
on their own, they are required to read everything from autobiographies
to historical fiction. As a result, the reading requirements are varied and
complex.

Part of the structure of a mathematics text may appear within the context of a biography of a mathematician, or that of a history text may
appear in a historically based novel. In language arts reading materials,
students must cope with different structures in different genre forms and
also with specialized concepts, such as mood, setting, imagery, characteri-
zation, plot, foreshadowing, and other literary techniques. In addition, a
literary selection may combine vocabulary from other content areas with
its own, unique vocabulary demands. Thus, a wide range of vocabulary concepts can be encountered in literature, including vocabulary and language
structures that are archaic or unfamiliar, as in the following passage:

> "Say, Tom, let me whitewash a little."
>
> Tom considered, was about to consent; but he altered his mind.
>
> "No—no—I reckon it wouldn't hardly do, Ben. You see, Aunt Polly's
> awful particular about this fence—right here on the street, you know—
> but if it was the back fence I wouldn't mind and she wouldn't. Yes, she's
> awful particular about this fence; it's got to be done very careful; I reckon
> there ain't one boy in a thousand, maybe two thousand, that can do it the
> way it's got to be done."
>
> "No—is that so? Oh come, now—lemme just try. Only just a little—I'd
> let you, if you was me, Tom." (Twain, 1982, p. 25).

The various demands of language arts materials require prereading
attention to concepts and textual organization. Teachers should give particular care to literary techniques, as well as to visual imagery. The
specific teaching suggestions presented in chapter 4 are appropriate for
the various genres found in language arts reading.

THE RELATIONSHIP OF A LITERACY FRAMEWORK TO CONTENT-AREA INSTRUCTION

The method frameworks discussed in this chapter are most compatible with an interactive explanation of how a person reads. From that perspective, meaning is not thought to reside in either text or reader but is seen as the result of their interaction. Similarly, the method frameworks presented here require readers to bring their own knowledge to bear on the text, while at the same time using the information in the text. For example, these method frameworks commonly expect readers to identify main ideas and supporting details. Thus, readers must have some knowledge about the text and must bring to bear existing world knowledge about the topic.

Another aspect of this interaction is that many of the method frameworks used in content-area reading also require readers to monitor comprehension (Baker & Brown, 1983; Markam, 1981). For example, during the reading step in SQ3R, students keep questions in mind and monitor to see when answers are found. **Comprehension monitoring** means that readers must actively attend to content, be aware of key ideas, separate important information from unimportant, and know when something has not been properly understood. In essence, all of the method frameworks discussed in this chapter are an attempt to foster internal comprehension monitoring and metacognitive abilities.

comprehension monitoring
The ongoing process through which readers check their understanding as they read.

Thus, the teaching suggestions in this chapter are based on interactive explanations of how people read. Nonetheless, teachers in content-area classrooms may have literacy frameworks involving text-based or reader-based explanations of reading. Some teachers may say that students need to read a content-area selection again in order for the meaning to become clear, thus implying that meaning resides in the text. Other teachers may talk around a subject, rarely referring to the textual material actually read by students. Regardless of personal framework, however, all teachers recognize the importance of teaching appropriate reading and study strategies, even as they emphasize different procedural steps within those strategies.

Comments from the Classroom

Judy Dill, first grade teacher

Because my first graders live in a rural community, it is a challenge to help them develop literacy because of their age and somewhat limited experiences. These children therefore have little prior knowledge to understand what is being described in their textbooks and other reading materials. I feel it is my responsibility to fill in some of the gaps. Creating a thematic unit that integrates as many language experiences as possible is one of the things I do to try to balance their experiences and expose them to new knowledge.

Although we live in Maine, many children live at least 200 miles from the ocean so one of the themes I like teaching is "All About the Ocean." It is difficult for my children to envision what the ocean is like from a picture. So we study sea creatures, do activities which involve ocean projects, and incorporate reading a number of related "information" books. I integrate as many subject areas as possible to help children make important connections between them.

I usually start my ocean unit by having the children listen to a tape of ocean sounds. Then I play it again and have them draw what they think might be making the sounds. Next, after sharing *There's a Sea in My Bedroom* by Margaret Wild, I put a large conch shell on the writing center table. I include paper with a story starter that says "There's a sea in my classroom." Children pick up the shell and "listen" for the sound of the ocean. They really get excited writing their stories and sharing them with the rest of the class.

We also do research on the creatures that would live in the ocean as opposed to those who live in our nearby lakes and streams. In the art center, children read and follow directions to create ocean creatures which we hang around our room. In our math center, we have a box of seashells for counting and sorting. After handling these smooth and rough shells, children write about the differences and describe how it feels to touch them.

The children also think of various ways to classify the shells into groups. After sorting them, they invite other class members to try to guess what their classification technique is. This is my favorite way to connect math and science.

After a culminating activity, we take a field trip to the southeastern part of the state. There, we spend part of a day at a marine museum and the remainder of the day at the *shore. Both the children and parents who have not had the opportunity to visit the ocean love it. Before we go to the ocean we brainstorm a list of things we expect to see there. And, after returning from our trip, we go over our list. We write a language experience story adding or deleting whatever information we gained in our study. Finally, I replay the tape of ocean sounds. It is amazing to see their new knowledge show up in their drawings as they make more detailed and accurate pictures.*

On one recent ocean visit, one of my six-year-old students made me realize how important my efforts were in opening doors for children's learning. He stood by me, looked out over the waves, and watched the surf as it rolled in and out. He stood for several minutes and then looked up at me and said, "How's it do it, Mrs. Dill, how's it do it?"

Major Points

- Reading and content-area teachers who expect children to read texts in specific subjects must provide students with reading instruction connected to specific reading-related skills associated with that subject area.

- Knowledge of book parts and general research skills helps children's comprehension and should be a part of reading instruction.

- The organization of narrative texts, which are generally used to teach reading, and expository texts, which students are required to read in subject areas, differs greatly. Textual organization also differs among subject areas.

- Reading rate depends largely on the purpose for reading. Flexibility in reading rate needs to be taught.

- Method frameworks used in content-area reading include frameworks that can be used in any subject, as well as frameworks specific to one subject.

- Most effective reading and study strategies are based on an interactive explanation of how a person reads.

**Making
Instructional
Decisions**

1. List and discuss the specific reading demands of social studies, mathematics, science, and language arts materials. Identify general differences in organizational patterns and reading requirements. Find an elementary school textbook for each subject area, provide specific examples of the items on your list, and devise a lesson using at least two of the method frameworks in this chapter.

2. Find a reading unit in any content-area subject, and construct a directed reading activity for a reading selection. Then construct a three-level study guide and a set of marginal glosses for the same material.

3. If possible, practice using the SQ3R technique with an elementary school student. Otherwise, practice guiding a classmate through SQ3R, or use it yourself in your own reading.

4. How does a map reader differ from a map thinker? How might your instructional practices foster the development of map thinkers?

Further Reading

Dillner, M. (1994). Using hypermedia to enhance content-area instruction. *Journal of Reading, 37,* 260–270.

   Discusses the procedures and decisions a teacher made to create a hypermedia lesson, and gives some examples of how students used that lesson. Incorporates interesting ideas for developing lessons using hypermedia.

Duffelmeyer, F. A. (1994). Effective Anticipation Guide statements for learning from expository prose. *Journal of Reading, 37,* 452–457.

   Provides guidelines for writing anticipation guides, as well as examples of effective and ineffective statements with respect to such guides.

Egan, M. (1994). Capitalizing on the reader's strengths: An activity using schema. *Journal of Reading, 37,* 636–641.

   Provides techniques that allow readers to use their prior knowledge to interact with print.

Glasglow, J. (1994). Teaching visual literacy for the 21st century. *Journal of Reading, 37,* 494–500.

   Discusses the need for visual literacy instruction and uses advertisements in instruction to help students move toward understanding the messages encoded in visual images.

Hadaway, N. L. & Young, T. A. (1994). Content literacy and language learning: Instructional decisions. *The Reading Teacher, 47,* 522–527.

   Discusses the use of teacher modeling and interaction with textbooks in ways that help students integrate literacy processes and help diverse learners. Part of a themed issue dealing with literacy in the content areas.

Horowitz, R. (Ed.). (1994). A themed issue about classroom talk about text: What teenagers and teachers come to know about the world through talk about text. *Journal of Reading, 37,* 628–714.

A themed issue that includes articles about facilitating student-to-student discussion, authentic discussion about texts, learning in science, inviting multiple perspectives, the role of student-led discussions, and the role of discourse diversity.

Monahan, J. & Hinson, B. (1988). *New directions in reading instruction.* Newark, DE: International Reading Association.

A flip-chart format that provides a summary of research-based ideas for teaching content-area reading. Includes more than 20 topics.

Moore, D. W., Readence, J. E., & Rickelman, R. J. (1989). *Prereading activities for content area reading and learning.* Newark, DE: International Reading Association.

Describes activities useful for pre- and post-content-area reading at all grade levels.

Ruddell, M. R. (1993). *Teaching content reading and writing.* Needham Heights, MA: Allyn & Bacon.

A readable textbook that deals with content-area reading. Although its focus is on middle and secondary grades, the strategies discussed can be easily adapted for younger children.

Slater, W. H., & Graves, M. F. (1989). Research on expository texts: Implications for teachers. In K. D. Muth (Ed.), *Children's comprehension of text* (pp. 140–166). Newark, DE: International Reading Association.

Provides a synthesis of research findings focusing on comprehension of expository texts, as well as a classification system that allows teachers to categorize texts in ways that aid teaching. Also discusses a model and strategies for teaching expository texts.

Smith, C. B. (1990). Vocabulary development in content area reading. *The Reading Teacher, 43,* 508–509.

A brief discussion of several approaches to vocabulary development in content-area reading.

References

Baker, L., & Brown, A. C. (1983). Metacognition and the reading process. In P. D. Pearson (Ed.), *Handbook of reading research.* New York: Plenum Press.

Bassler, O. C., Kolb, J. R., Craighead, M. S. & Gray, W. L. (1981). *Succeeding in mathematics* (revised). Austin, TX: SteckVaughn.

Brown, A. L., Campione, J. C., & Day, J. D. (1981). Learning to learn: On training students to learn from texts. *Educational Researcher, 10,* 14–21.

Brown, A. L., & Day, J. D. (1983). Macorules for summarizing texts: The development of expertise. *Journal of Verbal Learning and Verbal Behavior, 22,* 1–8.

Buggey, J. (1983). *Our communities.* Chicago: Follett.

Carr, E., & Ogle, D. M. (1987). K-W-L Plus: A strategy for comprehension and summarization. *Journal of Reading, 30,* 626–631.

Carson, J. (1990). Unpublished manuscript.

Cheek, E. J., Jr., & Cheek, M. C. (1983). *Reading instruction through content teaching.* Columbus, OH: Merrill.

Davey, B. (1983). Think-aloud—Modeling the cognitive processes of reading comprehension. *Journal of Reading, 27,* 44–47.

Defoe, D. (1967). *Robinson Crusoe* (abridged and adapted by Ron King). Belmont, CA: Fearon.

Dupuis, M. M. (Ed.). (1984). *Reading in the content areas: Research for teachers.* Newark, DE: International Reading Association.

Farr, R., & Roser, N. (1979). *Teaching a child to read.* New York: Harcourt Brace Jovanovich.

Fay, L. (1965). Reading study skills: Math and science. In J. A. Figurel (Ed.), *Reading and inquiry* (pp. 93–94). Newark, DE: International Reading Association.

Flood, J., Lapp, D., & Farnan, N. (1986). A reading-writing procedure that teaches expository paragraph structure. *The Reading Teacher, 29,* 556–562.

Forgan, H. W., & Mangrum II, C. T. (1985). *Teaching content area reading skills* (3rd ed.). Columbus, OH: Merrill.

Fry, E. (1981). Graphical literacy. *Journal of Reading, 24,* 383–389.

Garner, R. (1987). Strategies for reading and studying expository text. *Educational Psychologist, 22,* 299–312.

Hanf, M. B. (1971). Mapping: A technique for translating reading into thinking. *Journal of Reading, 13,* 225–230.

Herber, H. (1978). *Teaching reading in content areas* (2nd ed.). Englewood Cliffs, NJ: Prentice Hall.

Herber, H. L., & Herber, J. N. (1993). *Teaching in content areas with reading, writing, and reasoning.* Needham Heights, MA: Allyn & Bacon.

Kane, R. B., Byrne, M. A., & Hater, M. A. (1974). *Helping children read mathematics.* New York: American Book.

Kinney, M. A. (1985). A language experience approach to teaching expository text structure. *The Reading Teacher, 38,* 854–856.

Manzo, A. V. (1969). The ReQuest procedure. *Journal of Reading, 11,* 123–126.

Manzo, A. V. (1985). Expansion modules for the ReQuest, CAT, GRP, and REAP reading/study procedures. *Journal of Reading, 28,* 498–503.

Markham, E. M. (1981). *Comprehension monitoring in children's oral communication skills.* New York: Academic Press.

Muhtadi, N. A. (1977). Personal communication.

Myers, C. B., & Wilk, G. (1983). *People, time, and change.* Chicago: Follett.

Novak, J. D., & Gowan, D. B. (1984). *Learning how to learn.* Cambridge: Cambridge University Press.

Ogle, D. M. (1989). The know, want to know, learn strategy. In K. D. Muth (Ed.), *Children's comprehension of text* (pp. 205–223). Newark, DE: International Reading Association.

O'Mara, D. A. (1981). The process of reading mathematics. *Journal of Reading, 25,* 22–30.

Pauk, W. (1984). The new SQ4R. *Reading World, 23,* 274–275.

Robinson, F. P. (1961). *Effective study.* New York: Harper & Row.

Rubin, D. (1983). *Teaching reading and study skills in content areas.* New York: Holt, Rinehart & Winston.

Ruddell, M. R. (1993). *Teaching content reading and writing.* Needham Heights, MA: Allyn & Bacon.

Ruddell, M. R. (1992). Integrated content and long-term vocabulary learning with the Vocabulary Self-Collection Strategy (VSS). In E. K. Dishner, T. W. Bean, J. E. Readence, & D. W. Moore (Eds.), *Reading in the content areas: Improving classroom instruction* (3rd. ed., pp. 190–196). Dubuque, IA: Kendall Hunt.

Ruddell, R. B., & Boyle, O. F. (1989). A study of cognitive mapping as a means to improve summarization and comprehension of expository text. *Reading Research and Instruction, 29,* 12–22.

Shepherd, D. L. (1982). *Comprehensive high school reading methods.* Columbus, OH: Merrill.

Singer, H., & Donlan, D. (1989). *Reading and learning from text* (2nd ed.). Hillsdale, NJ: Erlbaum.

Spache, G. D. (1963). *Toward better reading.* Champaign, IL: Garrard Press.

Spache, G. D., & Berg, P. C. (1966). *The art of efficient reading.* New York: Macmillan.

Summers, E. G. (1965). Utilizing visual aids in reading materials for effective reading. In H. L. Herber (Ed.), *Developing study skills in secondary schools.* Newark, DE: International Reading Association.

Sund, R. B., Adams, D. K., & Hackett, J. K. (1980). *Accent on science* (Level 6). Columbus, OH: Merrill.

Tei, E., & Stewart, O. (1985). Effective studying from text: Applying metacognitive strategies. *Forum for Reading, 27,* 36–43.

Thomas, E. L., & Alexander, H. A. (1982). *Improving reading in every class* (abridged 3rd ed.). Boston: Allyn & Bacon.

Tierney, R. J., Readence, J. E., & Dishner, E. K. (1990). *Reading strategies and practices: A compendium* (3rd ed.). Boston: Allyn & Bacon.

Twain, M. (1982). *The adventures of Tom Sawyer.* New York: Wanderer Books.

Vacca, R. (1981). *Content area reading.* Boston: Little, Brown.

Vacca, R. T., & Vacca, J. L. (1986). *Content area reading* (2nd ed.). Boston: Little, Brown.

PART 3

Assessment and Instructional Needs

C H A P T E R

Supporting Literacy Through Assessment

Often, when I think of when I was in school, I think of tests. There were written tests, oral tests, spelling tests, tests with answer sheets, and homework that sure seemed a lot like more tests! I know that tests are needed to show that children are learning, but there just seemed to be so many of them. In some of my reading I've come across things like "portfolios," and "alternative assessment." I don't know exactly what those are yet, but maybe they'll help teachers see how much children are learning without testing so often. I think a lot about different kinds of tests and ways of testing, and wonder which will be the most appropriate for me as a reading teacher.

Undergraduate student's comments in an interview about her memory about tests as a child.

As a teacher, you will use a variety of data to make instructional decisions. These data will range from informal observations of students to formal, standardized tests. This chapter presents different strategies and techniques that you will be able to use to evaluate students, reading materials, and their interaction.

Chapter 11 includes information that will help you answer questions such as:

1. What are the general issues in assessment that should concern you as a teacher of reading?
2. What are the differences among formal, informal, and teacher-made tests, and how are these instruments used in instructional decision making?
3. What do assessment tools measure when assessing readers and reading materials?
4. How will assessment tools help you to consider diversity in your classroom?
5. How does a literacy framework guide the use of assessment tools and the interpretation of test results?

KEY CONCEPTS

alternative assessment	norm group
assessment program	passage independent question
authentic assessment	percentage score
cloze test	percentile score
criterion-referenced test	portfolio assessment
diagnostic test	process vs. product assessment
formal test	raw score
frustration reading level	readability formula
grade equivalent score	relative standing
idea unit	reliability
independent reading level	running record
informal reading inventory (IRI)	self-assessment
informal test	standard error of measurement
instructional reading level	standardized testing
kidwatching	stanine score
listening comprehension level	survey test
management system	think-aloud
miscue	validity

....
GENERAL ISSUES IN ASSESSMENT

Tests and testing are topics that are under much discussion. You will find that some teachers and administrators feel that far too much time is spent in testing, and that they are dissatisfied with the tests that have been traditionally used in schools. Other teachers, administrators and parents feel that traditional, formal tests are needed to ensure a continuous evaluation of students' performance.

Often, the debate about testing includes terms like "alternative assessment," with the implication that there are alternatives to traditional measures and that these are better than tests used in the past. Nevertheless, although many school districts are moving toward alternative assessment, you will be required to administer traditional measures as well. Thus, this chapter discusses both forms of assessment and presents the benefits and potential difficulties of each.

Instructional Decision-Making: Clarifying the Goals of Assessment

In chapter 1 we discussed the modification of instructional frameworks and instructional decisions (see Figure 1-3). Teachers generally modify their instruction based on the outcomes of their instructional decisions, as seen through observations of childrens' classroom performance, or their performance on a more formal measure. Assessment, whether formal or informal, plays a very large role in teachers' decision-making, and knowledge about assessment tools will make you better able to modify instruction to suit your students' needs. The International Reading Association, together with the National Council for Teachers of English (1994), provide the following goals and implementation procedures regarding assessment of literacy:

GOALS

1. The interests of the students are paramount in assessment.
2. The primary purpose of assessment is to improve teaching and learning.
3. Assessment must reflect and allow for critical inquiry into curriculum and instruction.
4. Assessments must recognize and reflect the intellectually and socially complex nature of reading and writing and the important roles of school, home, and society in literacy development.
5. Assessment must be fair and equitable.
6. The consequences of an assessment procedure are the first, and most important, consideration in establishing the validity of the assessment.

IMPLEMENTATION

7. The teacher is the most important agent of assessment.
8. The assessment process should involve multiple perspectives and sources of data.

9. Assessments must be based in the school community.
10. All members of the educational community—students, parents, teachers, administrators, policy makers, and the public—must have a voice in the development, interpretation, and reporting of assessment.
11. Parents must be involved as active, essential participants in the assessment process.

IRA/NCTE Joint Task Force on Assessment. (1994). *Standards for the assessment of reading and writing.* Newark, DE: International Reading Association.

As you read the above guidelines, you probably noticed the emphasis on the teacher's role, and on the goal of assessment to improve learning. Indeed, the role of the teacher as a decision-maker who uses multiple sources of data to make instructional choices cannot be overemphasized.

Assessment can demand substantial amounts of a teacher's time, whether traditional or alternative approaches are used. Traditional assessment tools require time not only for test administration, but also for preparation, scoring, and interpretation of completed tests. Alternative assessment procedures require time for close examination of individual students' work, for record-keeping procedures, and for individual conferencing and interviews. Some time for assessment will be used for yearly **standardized testing** required by nearly all school districts to compare their students' progress to the progress of students in other districts or previous years, and detailed record keeping by their teachers as part of a management system. A management system specifies what students should learn and requires a continual **assessment program** to document progress. Although emergent literacy perspectives are causing some rethinking of such an approach to reading instruction, it still predominates; assessment is a large part of published reading programs.

standardized testing
Evaluation using standardized materials and standardized procedures for administration and scoring.

assessment program
Systematic evaluation of students' progress by various testing methods consistent with a teacher's or school district's goals.

Choosing an Assessment Strategy

Because it is important to use instructional time in the best possible way to maximize learning, choosing assessment instruments to match specific measurement objectives is critical. The choice of an assessment tool is largely determined by reasons for testing, and there are many purposes for administering various kinds of measures in school (Ruddell & Kinzer, 1982). Assessment results are used by many people in addition to teachers: district staff, superintendents, school board members, curriculum committees, principals, and others. Each has slightly different goals and purposes, all of which influence instructional decisions and the selection of measurement tools. Certain measures assess specific skills and are closely tied to individual students' instructional situations, while others assess students' progress as seen in their actual reading or writing. Some measures provide only group or survey data, which cannot easily be used for specific diagnostic purposes; other measures are specific to children's individual portfolios. There are also measures appropriate for comparing different sets of instructional materials—perhaps before purchasing decisions are made.

As a teacher of reading, you will commonly use assessment tools for a variety of reasons:

1. to find a student's general reading competency (and strategies and processes used)
2. to see whether one book is more difficult than another
3. to identify motivational material for a student or class (that is, to find out students' interests and attitudes)
4. to match a student with appropriate materials
5. to find out whether a student has mastered a desired goal
6. to see if a student is making progress over time

Can you see that these **targets of assessment** differ? For example, Goals 1, 3, 5, and 6 are student centered; that is, the student is the target and the assessment relates directly to the student. Goal 3 differs slightly from 1, 5 and 6 in that it measures an affective response rather than reading ability, but it still deals with the reader. Goal 2 does not relate specifically to a student. Instead, it assesses the difficulty of reading material, perhaps through an analysis of factors such as print size or density of ideas. Goal 4 combines two categories: it measures both the materials and the student in combination. Thus, assessment can focus on the student, the materials, or the student and the materials together. The target and goal of assessment jointly determine the type of measurement tool needed.

targets of assessment
Who or what is being assessed; may include the student, the text, or the student and the text together.

Several additional considerations can help you to further define the choice of an assessment tool:

1. *Do I want or need to assess more than one student at a time?* **Group tests** are administered to several students at the same time. Such tests result in overall time savings when a class or an entire school of students needs to be evaluated. Traditional measures include standardized tests that are designed for this purpose; alternative assessments include informal measures such as cloze tests, discussed later in this chapter.

group tests
Assessment instruments that are administered to more than one person at the same time.

2. *Do I want or need to assess one student at a time?* **Individual tests** are administered in one-on-one situations. Such tests allow more controlled conditions and permit closer observation of student behavior. Traditional measures include standardized tests that are designed for this purpose; alternative assessments include interviews, observations, or examining a student's portfolio.

individual tests
Assessment instruments that are administered to one person at a time.

3. *Do I want to assess general reading (or writing) ability?* **Survey tests** provide indications of general ability. Reading tests that indicate general reading level but not specific strengths and weaknesses fall into this category. Traditional measures include stan-

survey tests
Assessment instruments that evaluate general ability in a certain area.

Making appropriate instructional decisions is a major goal in an assessment program.

dardized tests that are designed for this purpose; alternative assessments include portfolios and think-alouds.

diagnostic tests
Assessment instruments that evaluate specific product and process characteristics so that instructional decisions can be made.

4. *Do I want to diagnose a specific reading deficiency?* **Diagnostic tests** assess specific abilities and can provide information leading to specific instructional practices. Traditional measures include standardized tests and can be group tests (for example, *Stanford Diagnostic Reading Test*) or individual tests (for example, *Durrell Analysis of Reading Difficulty*) but not survey tests. Alternative assessments include retellings, running records, informal reading inventories, and miscue analyses.

5. *Do I want to focus more on formal assessment or do I want to see how a child or a group of children perform in realistic reading situations?* This question interacts with the others, above. The answer to this question will help you decide whether your purposes can be served through one or more of the above tools, or whether less formal observation of students' behavior while reading and writing are the most appropriate.

product assessment
Assessment that evaluates primarily the outcomes of student performance.

Process vs. Product Assessment. Assessment that looks mainly at the outcomes of student performance is called **product assessment.** Assess-

EXPLORING DIVERSE POINTS OF VIEW

As our knowledge of the reading process has increased, testing has changed little. Consequently, Valencia and Pearson (1987) note that reading tests and testing procedures often do not match what we know about reading. Not surprisingly, an increasing number of voices are being raised in favor of alternatives to traditional tests and testing methods, especially in favor of process assessment. Process measures are valuable, however, only to the extent that individual teachers understand the reading process and are able to infer students' processes based on their overt behavior.

Unfortunately, not all teachers understand the reading process equally or similarly, and disagreement in interpreting process measures could lead to problems of accountability with parents and others. Whereas, then, some argue that process measures can provide important knowledge about how students do what they do, others point to the difficulty of process analysis and the inconsistency of interpretation. Will you favor product measures, process measures, or a combination of both in your classroom?

ment that attempts to interpret performance in an effort to evaluate underlying strategies, actions, or behaviors is called **process assessment.** Wittrock (1987) points out that most formal assessment instruments can answer questions about how well students do but cannot answer questions such as, "What strategies does this student use to construct main ideas?" or, "How does this student relate prior knowledge and experiences to the text?" (p. 734). Despite the fact that process measures might be more important to teachers in making individual instructional decisions, however, all types of tests can be useful if they are closely tied to the purposes of testing. Nevertheless, standardized tests, especially multiple-choice tests, have been increasingly criticized as being harmful to minorities, as contributing to an overreliance on testing, and as hindering educational reforms (Gifford, 1990). If this is true, why are traditional product measures still so heavily used?

Assessment of products is easier to conduct than assessment of processes. To assess products, a teacher needs only to follow the specific guidelines that come with a formal, published test, or to grade a student's work only on its observable, surface features. Process assessments, however, require reasoned decisions about a reader's underlying reading processes. For example, in a product assessment a student might be asked to read a passage and answer a question. The result—the answer—is assumed to indicate whether the passage was understood. In process assessment, on the other hand, a teacher must attempt to find out how the answer was arrived at and what strategies were used and/or rejected by the reader.

Process assessment has received increasing attention because of an emphasis on higher-order thought processes, such as critical thinking and problem solving (for example, see Nickerson, 1989; Siegler, 1989; CTGV, 1993). One difficulty associated with process assessment is that there are usually multiple paths to solving a problem, and individuals

process assessment
Assessment that evaluates primarily the strategies, actions, or behaviors underlying the products of student performance.

may process information differently. This flexibility makes it inappropriate to interpret the results of process measures in terms of a single strategy (Gardner & Hatch, 1989; Siegler, 1989). Consequently, teachers who use process-based assessments must consider multiple paths to an answer, thereby making assessment and interpretation more difficult. Such assessment is more student-centered, however, as students are not automatically penalized for answers that differ from an expected response. Thus, with a process measure a teacher must determine whether the test can accurately infer a reader's processes and whether that inference is reflected in scoring and interpretation. The assessment tools and procedures discussed throughout this chapter include both process and product measures.

Traditional vs. Alternative Assessment. Traditional measures include a wide variety of tools, from formal, multiple-choice tests with computer-scored answer sheets to teacher-made comprehension questions asked of students at the end of a reading selection. As perspectives about the value of these measures have shifted, alternatives have become more prevalent, and include portfolio assessment, performance assessment, and outcome-based assessment. Herman, Aschbacher and Williams (1992) present several characteristics as common to alternative assessments. Table 11-1 presents these characteristics and juxtaposes them with characteristics of traditional measurement.

One aspect of alternative assessment that is attractive to people is wrapped up in what is often called "authentic assessment." This term

TABLE 11-1

Characteristics common to alternative and traditional assessment procedures

Alternative assessment procedures usually	Traditional assessment procedures usually
• require students to perform, create, or produce something	• require students to respond to fairly narrow, specific tasks or questions
• focus on higher-level thinking and problem-solving	• focus on lower-level, literal knowledge
• require tasks that are based on meaningful instructional activities	• require tasks that are out of context and are often unrelated to specific instruction
• have close linkages to real-world applications	• include activities created specifically for the assessment and that may not be grounded in real-world applications
• require people to do scoring, using human judgement	• require people or machines to do the scoring, often with answer keys that minimize human judgement
• suggest new assessment roles for teachers	• imply a continuation of past assessment role

means that the tasks and procedures used in evaluation are closely related to (a) tasks found in the real world; (b) tasks found in instructional situations; and (c) tasks that are as similar as possible to real literacy tasks. The following items are often thought of when alternative assessment is discussed:

- portfolios
- interviews
- informal measures
- performance, including presentations
- journals and self-reports
- think-alouds
- documented observations
- demonstration projects

In contrast, the following are often thought of as more traditional measures:

- standardized, machine-scored tests
- low-level, literal questions
- assessment of specific skills
- multiple choice tests

What Makes a Good Assessment Tool?

Assessment instruments range from formal, standardized tests purchased from test publishers, to questions constructed by individual teachers, to samples of students' ongoing work. Nonetheless, there are certain factors common to all assessment that determine whether a measurement tool is good or bad. Understanding these factors will help you choose a test or an overall assessment program to best meet your measurement objectives. Many people define a good assessment tool like this:

- It is **valid.** It measures what it is supposed to measure—what it says it measures. Sometimes a test claims to measure a particular skill or ability, but an examination of the actual test items, procedures, or testing tasks may show that it does not. At other times a valid test might be used in a manner not intended by its authors. For example, a survey test providing information about general reading ability might be inappropriately used to infer areas of specific reading disability, or a portfolio containing only samples of a student's writing might be claimed to reflect a student's reading progress.

validity
The ability of a test to measure what it claims to measure.

- It is **reliable.** It gives consistent results, not random or changing over time. If a test is given to a student over and over again and yields the same score each time, then it is extremely reliable. In fact, if the scores are identical each time, the test is 100 percent reliable. In reality, tests are not 100 percent reliable; differences in student learning and in affective, physical, or environmental factors all influence the test/retest results of any given student. A test's instructor's or technical manual will pro-

reliability
The ability of a test to provide consistent information.

vide information about a test's reliability, stated in terms of a reliability coefficient. In education, a reliability coefficient above 0.80 is considered acceptable.

standard error of measurement
A statistic that indicates how much a score must increase or decrease before the difference is attributed to something other than chance.

- It has a low **standard error of measurement**. Because tests are not 100 percent reliable, teachers must know how widely students' scores can vary by chance. The standard error of measurement specifies exactly how much a score must increase or decrease before the difference is attributed to something other than chance. Such information can be viewed in plus and minus terms. For example, if a student scored 17 on a 20 item test and the test had a standard error of measurement of 2, then that student's score would really be 17 plus or minus 2. In other words, it would fall between 15 and 19. Thus, if the student was tested again and received a score of 19, it would not be appropriate to assume that improvement had been shown, because the two scores are both within the range of the standard error of measurement. That is, they are within two points of each other, and the difference could be due to chance. Standard error of measurement applies more to traditional, formal tests than to alternative or informal assessment, although a student's performance on an informal assessment tool will also differ even in back-to-back administrations and thus may be thought of as including a standard error of measurement.

- It is manageable in terms of administration time. There is always a trade-off between time that is taken away from instruction for assessment. If you have a choice, consider carefully the benefits to your instructional program that will result from the assessment information, and try to balance the value of the information you will receive with the instructional time lost.

- It is easy to score and interpret. This is related to reporting procedures and teacher knowledge. Formal, standardized tests will often report results in a variety of ways, and you will have to decide if the type(s) of scores are appropriate for your needs. Similarly, the types of information placed in a portfolio and the teacher's knowledge of the reading process are critical to interpreting the information that a portfolio can provide.

content validity
One of several types of validity; assesses whether a test measures skills appropriate to the subject area being tested.

curricular validity
One of several types of validity; assesses whether a test measures what children have been taught.

All of the above aspects should be considered when choosing an assessment strategy, and all depend heavily on your knowledge of the reading process. For example, when considering validity you should examine test items and procedures carefully to determine whether a test does what it claims to do, and also whether it measures appropriate reading skills and therefore has **content validity.** In addition, classroom teachers are in the best position to determine whether an assessment tool has **curricular validity;** that is, whether it measures what children have been

Many people feel that alternative assessment tools, especially those that analyze performance or outcomes on tasks that are a part of the normal instructional routine, have much higher curricular validity than do traditional measures. However, others criticize alternative assessment procedures because it is difficult to determine traditional validity and reliability estimates for such assessment tools. Because alternative assessments do not have standard requirements for administration and scoring, it is not surprising that different items in a portfolio can yield different information; nor is it surprising that two readers who are similar in ability might read and react to informal measures differently. When discussing alternative assessments, it is more appropriate to think of validity as very high because tasks are authentic reading and writing tasks that take place as part of the normal classroom routine, and to think of reliability in terms of the degree of agreement between two professionals, such as two teachers, who independently interpret a student's performance.

taught. Other aspects, such as a test's reliability, are also important because teachers need to be able to assume that any assessment provides consistent information. Then, if differences across time are found, teachers can more confidently attribute changes in student performance to learning rather than to chance.

TESTS AND TEST SCORES
Types and Uses of Tests

Teachers can choose from three general categories of traditional measures: informal, teacher-made, and formal tests. Because all can be useful, you should know the strengths and weaknesses of each type and the circumstances of their appropriate use.

Informal Tests. These tests allow for teacher judgment in administration, scoring, and interpretation. They may be purchased as stand-alone items, may be included as part of a larger set of materials, or may be based on regular instructional material in use by a teacher. Although tests in this category have general procedures to be followed, a teacher's judgment is critical within those procedures. For example, an informal test might indicate that testing should stop when a student becomes frustrated, or require the teacher to look for patterns within a student's work or performance to make decisions about that student's abilities and needs. Clearly, the teacher's judgment would play a major part in determining when frustration occurred or in deciding on the occurrence of a pattern. When people talk about "alternative" assessment, they are generally talking about informal tests.

Teacher-Made Tests. These tests are made and used by teachers to assess their students' knowledge or performance, usually within a particular instructional unit or lesson. For this category of test the teacher alone determines administration and scoring procedures. Teacher-made tests are often a part of alternative assessment tools such as portfolios.

Formal Tests. These tests have strict guidelines for administration, scoring, and interpretation. They are purchased from test publishers and are often called standardized tests. When people talk about "traditional" assessment, they are generally talking about formal tests.

The types of tests and the targets of assessment together provide a framework (see Figure 11-1) within which assessment tools can be analyzed and chosen.

Whichever types of tests are used, they must not be used indiscriminately. Teachers should observe students in the classroom situation and proceed with formal and/or informal assessments to discover or confirm areas of need so that instructional decisions can be made more reliably.

Types and Uses of Scores

Students' scores on traditional reading tests are commonly reported in five ways:

1. raw scores
2. percentage scores
3. percentile scores
4. stanine scores
5. grade-equivalent scores

Each of these reporting methods yields different information and can be misleading if not used properly. While percentile and stanine scores are applicable only to traditional, formal measures, raw scores, percentage

FIGURE 11-1

A framework of test types and targets of assessment

Targets of Assessment / Test Types	Informal Tests	Teacher-Made Tests	Formal Tests
Readers			
Materials			

scores and grade-equivalent scores are also used in informal assessments such as cloze procedures, think-alouds, running records, or informal reading inventories.

Raw scores are determined by simply adding up the number of correct responses, regardless of the total number of items on a test. A student who gets eight items right has a raw score of 8. When a single test is given to a student or group of students, the scores can be valuable because all students are taking the same test and there are no variations in how long the test is or what the test is assessing. Nevertheless, many formal, published tests consist of a series of subtests, which usually measure different reading components and have different numbers of items. For example, a comprehension subtest might include 25 items, whereas a vocabulary subtest might include 40 items. Thus, a raw score of 20 on each of the subtests would not indicate relative ability in the subtest areas.

Percentage scores are one way to deal with some of the shortcomings of raw scores. Percentages are calculated by dividing the number of correct responses by the total possible and then multiplying the result by 100. This process yields a theoretical score out of 100 regardless of the length of the test, thus allowing more representative comparisons. In the earlier example a raw score of 20 on both the 25-item comprehension subtest and the 40-item vocabulary subtest would produce percentage scores of 80 and 50, respectively. Thus, percentage scores allow clearer comparisons.

Percentile scores indicate the percent of the norm population scoring below individual students' scores, thereby reflecting the relative standing of those students within the norm group. In other words, a percentile score of 80 says that 80 percent of the norm group scored below that student's raw score. In our example the raw score of 20 (or 80 percent) on the 25-item comprehension subtest probably seems fairly good. However, if the student's peer group averaged 24 (or 95 percent), then the 20 was below average when compared to students of similar ability. Unlike percentage scores, which mask an individual's rank within the peer group, percentile scores provide information about relative standing.

Normal curve equivalents (NCEs) are sometimes confused with percentiles because they are constructed so that only values of 1 through 99 are assigned as scores, and because percentile and NCE scores of 1 and 99 are equivalent. NCE scores are often used in Chapter 1 evaluation reports, and some school districts are moving toward their use. A discussion of NCEs is beyond the scope of this text, and you should pursue this topic in an assessment course or in a measurement text if necessary.

Stanine scores also allow a comparison of relative standing. Stanines indicate where in the overall distribution of scores the score in question lies, assuming that the total distribution of scores falls into a **normal curve.** The curve is then divided into nine bands, numbered 1 through 9, which correspond to predetermined percentages of scores falling into each

raw scores
The number of correct responses on a test.

percentage scores
The percentage of correct responses on a test.

percentile scores
Ratings that indicate the percent of the norm population scoring below a student's score.

stanine scores
Scores related to consistent bands on a normal curve, ranging from 1 to 9.

normal curve
A bell-shaped curve that if based on enough cases, represents a naturally occurring distribution.

band. A score in the fifth stanine would fall in the middle of the normal curve; scores of 4, 5, or 6 are considered average. Thus, in addition to relative standing, stanine scores indicate the relation of a student's score to the overall distribution of scores.

grade-equivalent scores
A measure of relative standing that compares a student's raw score to average scores across grade levels.

Grade-equivalent scores are also commonly used to provide information about relative standing. For example, if a student receives a grade-equivalent score of 7.0, that student's raw score is equivalent to the average score of beginning seventh graders in the norm population. Unfortunately, grade-equivalent scores can be deceptive and can inadvertently label students. Consequently, the International Reading Association is opposed to grade-equivalent scores, and test publishers have moved away from providing them.

EVALUATING READERS AND WRITERS
The Portfolio

Teachers in both whole language and traditional classrooms are turning increasingly toward portfolios to supplement or replace traditional measures. Portfolio assessment involves collecting students' work on an ongoing basis and examining it for evidence of growth in literacy. Rather than an evaluation based on norms or externally imposed criteria, portfolio assessment allows a teacher to see—and to show children, parents, and administrators—what students have done over time.

Lapp and Flood (1989) point out the difficulty of making parents understand that a student who achieves at the 50th percentile every year is making average and expected progress from grade to grade. They suggest that teachers place in student portfolios a variety of items that can be shared with parents and others as appropriate. Their suggestions are similar to the recommendations of others (for example, see Farris, 1989; Jongsma, 1989; Pikulski, 1989; Glazer & Brown, 1993) and are included in the following list:

- formal norm- and criterion-referenced test scores
- informal measures such as informal reading inventories, think-alouds, running records, and retellings in response to reading
- dated writing samples
- dated titles of books read voluntarily (for example, during free reading time)
- dated samples of what students have read (photocopied pages)
- dated self-evaluations of reading ability and comments on feelings toward reading and writing
- dated photographs, audiotapes, and videotapes of reading, writing and other classroom activities

There is increasing recognition that teachers are the experts with regard to their students and are in the best position to judge progress on a day-to-day basis (Harp, 1989; Johnston, 1987). Several checklists and specific forms have been suggested that can be used to summarize students' progress and then can be inserted into their portfolios. For example, Eeds (1988) has adapted suggestions by Gentry (1982) to aid teachers in documenting development in early writing (see Figure 11-2). Such forms can facilitate formal reporting to parents and the transfer of specific information to management forms, as required by many school districts.

Although it is not necessary to use any particular form, and teachers are encouraged to create their own evaluation summaries, it *is* important to document and summarize students' work periodically. To be effective, portfolios require student samples or teacher comments every two to three weeks across all areas of literacy. Figure 11-3 illustrates the considerable growth in Tanisha's writing in only 4½ months. Note the longer sentences, more complete punctuation, improvement in capitalization, greater number of words, and better-formed letters. All of these features should be noted on a summary form that is inserted regularly into Tanisha's portfolio. Summary forms for students at various grade levels and for different assessment procedures across reading, writing, speaking, and listening may be found in many publications, including those by Farr & Tone (1994); Traill (1993); Johnston (1992); Glazer & Brown (1993); Tierney, Carter, and Desai (1991); and Barrs, Ellis, Hester, and Thomas (1989).

In addition to writing samples and summary sheets, portfolios should include photocopied pages from materials that students are reading fluently. Growth in reading can be easily shown when material read at the beginning of first grade (characterized by short sentences, single-syllable words, large print, many pictures, and short selections) is compared to material being read in the middle of first grade. Students like to be able to look back at their progress, and parents enjoy seeing how far their children have come.

Self-reports by students—either through interviews or, in higher grades, through writing—should also be part of a portfolio. Wixson, Bosky, Yochum, and Alvermann (1984) have noted that self-assessment interviews can provide much valuable information. Such reports can indicate what is being read, what reactions students have toward reading and writing, what strategies they use when they come to a hard word, how they select reading materials, what they think they are learning, how well they think they are doing, where help might be appreciated, and so on. Self-reports should be completed on a regular schedule, either in oral form and noted by the teacher or in writing by the students. To facilitate self-reporting, summary forms that ask students to comment on the items noted above should be made available.

Self-assessment and self-reports can be done in a number of ways. Perhaps the most common is during a portfolio conference, where students can be asked about their perceptions of progress and needs. In fact, along

....

FIGURE 11-2

Checklist for developmental stages in early writing

Name _____ Age _____ Grade _____

			I	II	III	IV

Precommunicative Stage   Date

1. Produces letters or letter like forms to represent a message.
3. Demonstrates left-to-right concept.
4. Demonstrates top-bottom concept.
5. Repeats known letters and numbers.
6. Uses many letters and/or numbers.
7. Mixes upper and lowercase letters.
8. Indicates preference for uppercase forms.

The Semiphonetic Stage   Date

1. Realizes letters represent sounds.
2. Represents whole words with one or more letters.
3. Evidence of letter name strategy.
4. Demonstrates left-to-right sequence of letters.
5. Puts spaces between words.

The Phonetic Stage   Date

1. Represents every sound heard.
2. Assigns letters based on sounds as child hears them (invented spellings).
3. Puts spaces between words.
4. Masters letter formation.

The Transitional Stage   Date

1. Utilizes conventional spellings.
2. Vowels appear in every syllable.
3. Evidence of visual as opposed to phonetic strategy.
4. Reverses some letters in words.

Comments _____

_____

_____

_____

....

Source: From M. Eeds, "Holistic assessment of coding ability," in S. M. Glazer, L. W. Searfass, and L. M. Gentile (Eds.), *Reexamining reading diagnosis: New trends and procedures* (Newark, DE: International Reading Association, 1988), p. 56. Reprinted by permission.

FIGURE 11-3

Writing samples from Tanisha's first-grade portfolio: (a) September 9th ("I like to help my daddy, Leon. He's building! I like Nintendos!"); (b) January 31st

(a)

Tanisha

ILIKEToHELPmYdadeLEon

HisBuilcLing!

ILiKEninTEndoc

(b)

My   Favorite   Animal

By Tanisha   Jan. 31

I   like   monkeys because

they   are   good   at   tricks.

I   mean tricks! They   are

better   then   a   poodle.

with many others, we feel that portfolio conferences should be cyclical in nature, with the beginning of the conference focusing initially on what has occurred since the last conference, and the end of the conference allowing the student to articulate and/or write down goals to be a focus during the time before the next conference.

Self-assessment also takes place when:

- students are asked to select pieces of their work that they think show their growth, and to state why they have made their selections;

- students keep a "learning log" and update their thoughts on progress and needs on an ongoing basis;

- students work in cooperative groups and discuss their thoughts about their needs in relation to their assignments;

- students are asked to talk about what they are reading and writing, with a focus on their thoughts and interests with regard to the respective selection;

- students have the opportunity to revise their work, discuss their revision process, and talk about how the revision makes their work better; and

- students are asked to "think aloud" as they read or write.

Many of the above can be done in writing or you, as teacher, can make notes during discussion. These notes should be included in each student's portfolio and on cumulative checklists or summary sheets as appropriate.

Portfolios should not be viewed as a teacher's property. They change over time because of all that goes into them, and student access needs to be encouraged, especially to revise work or to add information about reading and writing. Furthermore, students should develop pride in their

Games and other materials not specifically intended for assessment can be used to discover students' needs and abilities.

portfolios and be encouraged to share them with others. Peer input, in turn, may prompt effective writing revision and book selection. Teachers must be careful, however, to structure sharing experiences so that they are purposeful and helpful.

Students must always know how their portfolios will be used—especially if teachers plan to use them in grading decisions at the end of a formal reporting period. In such cases students should be given the opportunity to revise or add to their work. Portfolios can also serve an important function during student-teacher conferences and can, in addition, be a place through which teachers and students can communicate with each other. For example, a teacher's comments in a portfolio might include any or all of these:

- the names of students who are reading or writing about similar topics and suggestions for a sharing session;

- book titles with themes similar to a book that is currently being read;

- information that might be included in a piece of writing;

- a television show that might relate to an area of interest;

- supportive comments about progress; and

- expression of personal interest in a particular topic, piece of writing, or book read by the student

Thus, a portfolio is not simply a repository of work waiting to be graded: it is a dynamic entity that is continually modified and clearly reflects ongoing progress. Although some argue that, strictly speaking, portfolios "are a means of communicating about student growth and development—not a form of assessment" (Stiggins, in press), portfolio assessment has, through general usage in the literacy field, become a significant term within alternative assessment. This usage is seen, for example, in highly regarded books about literacy assessment—books with titles such as *Portfolio Assessment in the Reading-Writing Classroom* (Tierney, Carter, & Desai, 1991). Such publications point out that any assessment tool or procedure, including those described in this text, can provide data for inclusion in a student's portfolio. Through inclusion of multiple pieces of data, portfolios can be viewed as a whole to indicate student growth and progress as well as student needs at a point in time.

Many of the items that are considered in portfolio assessment (particularly those that do not rely only on children's written products) may be considered as part of "kidwatching" (see chapter 6 for a discussion of this aspect of assessment in emergent literacy programs). Noticing what children do in real reading and writing tasks and using this observational data on summary sheets that lead to instructional decision-making are critical aspects of informal assessment. In its broader usage, most of the informal and alternative assessment procedures discussed in this chapter, including the use of think-alouds, retellings, informal reading inventories, and so on, depend on the teacher's observations and interpretation of reading and writing behavior.

The Informal Reading Inventory

**informal reading
inventories (IRIs)**
Individualized tests that use
a graded word list and
passages to determine a
student's reading ability and
provide diagnostic
information.

Informal reading inventories (IRIs) allow a teacher to match students and materials. They provide information that will help you place students at appropriate instructional levels within a set of graded materials. The information is obtained by having students read increasingly difficult passages and stop reading when they come to a passage that is too difficult. The students' patterns of errors indicate materials that could be used appropriately with a particular student. IRIs are included as a part of most published reading programs, can be purchased as stand-alone items, or can be teacher-developed.

An informal reading inventory must be administered individually to students and requires some expertise to score and interpret. It thus requires somewhat more time to administer than some other measures, but it provides information that can be of great value in instructional decision making. Teachers typically use IRIs near the beginning of a school year as one information source to help determine instructional groupings and appropriate levels of materials for students. IRIs are also used when a teacher desires more information about some observed reading behavior. IRIs describe the functioning level of a reader, indicating that student's independent, instructional, and frustration reading levels. These are important concepts that you will often encounter.

Independent reading level. At this level students can read on their own without teacher assistance. Their reading is fluent and free of undue hesitations. Intonation is appropriate for the punctuation and phrasing of the material.

Instructional reading level. At this level students can read if support and instruction are provided. Material at this level is challenging but not frustrating to read.

Frustration reading level. At this level students have great difficulty, even with teacher guidance and instruction. In effect, they are unable to read the selection even with support.

Typically, an IRI provides three scores, each corresponding to one of these three general levels of reading. For example, an IRI might determine that a student's independent reading level is at approximately the third-grade level, whereas that student's instructional and frustration levels might be at about the fourth and fifth grades, respectively. These scores indicate the difficulty of materials appropriate for instruction, practice, and free-reading.

miscues
Oral reading responses that
deviate from the text being
read.

Published informal reading inventories usually include two copies of each reading selection so that the teacher can note any **miscues** and make other comments on one copy while the student reads from the other. The teacher's copy is usually double spaced to allow written comments and includes suggested comprehension questions with space to record student responses. After each IRI passage is read, different kinds of comprehension questions are asked—for example, questions that deal with vocabulary, details, inferences, and main ideas.

Although IRIs have generally been praised for including a range of questions, Duffelmeyer and Duffelmeyer (1989) have noted that approximately 50 percent of the main idea questions in IRIs might be inappropriate because the IRI passages may not have had an explicitly stated main idea or a unified passage focus. This condition was especially prevalent among narrative passages. Thus Duffelmeyer and Duffelmeyer (1989) note that a student's poor performance on main idea questions is "as likely to be a reflection of ill suited passages as of the student's inability to comprehend main ideas" (p. 363). As a result, teachers should be cautious when scoring student responses to main idea questions in IRIs, and the questions should be examined carefully.

Deciding Where to Start Testing. An IRI includes passages with varying difficulty levels. Thus, teachers must decide at what level to begin the test. Passages that are either too difficult or too easy should be avoided. Published IRIs usually provide entry to the oral reading passages through a set of graded word lists. Beginning with the list suggested by the IRI being used, a student reads successive lists until a certain number of errors occur within a given list. Most IRIs suggest that the student begin reading the passage that corresponds to the highest level list that was read perfectly, or perhaps the passage one level below that list. The word lists come in two forms: one for the teacher and one for the student. Student responses must be noted by the teacher, since miscue patterns can provide valuable information.

Noting Student Miscues on an IRI. The marking system in Figure 11-4 can be used to indicate reading behavior on the word lists as well as on subsequently administered passages. Different IRIs use different symbols or methods to mark reading miscues and other behaviors. Nevertheless, because the miscue types are well accepted, the particular marking system is not important. It is important, though, to choose one system and use it consistently.

The scoring system in Figure 11-4 can be used to mark all reading behaviors, and noting all miscues allows patterns to be more easily observed. Nevertheless, when counting miscues to decide whether a student's frustration level has been reached, a teacher must decide whether a miscue is significant. IRIs such as the *Classroom Reading Inventory* (Silvaroli, 1994) suggest that "insignificant" miscues be noted but not necessarily counted.

Significant miscues are those that interfere with fluency or change the meaning of what was written. The following examples illustrate the difference between significant and insignificant miscues:

FIGURE 11-4

Informal reading inventory marking system

Miscue/Behavior	Mark	Example
Miscues That Are Usually Significant (always counted)		
Omission Not reading something in the text (e.g., part or whole word, phrase, punctuation)	Circle the omission.	He likes the big (yellow) car.
Insertion Adding something not originally present in the text	Use caret (^) and add insertion.	*and blue* He likes the big ^ yellow car.
Substitution Replacing something in the text with something else (e.g., *this* for *the*)	Cross out original and add substitution.	*takes* He ~~likes~~ the big yellow car.
No response Substantial pause indicating inability to read the word, resulting in the teacher's pronouncing the word	Write *P* over teacher-pronounced items.	*P* He likes the big yellow car.
Miscues That Are Usually Not Significant (always marked, sometimes counted)		
Repetition Repeated reading of a word or group of words	Put dome over repeated items.	He likes the big yellow car.
Hesitation Pause that interrupts the flow or pattern of reading	Put checkmark at point of hesitation.	✓ He likes the big yellow car.
Transposition Reversing order of letters in words or words in sentences	Put reverse *S* around transposed items.	He likes the big yellow car.
Mispronunciation Pronunciation clearly different from normal (e.g., *k* in *knife* or *w* in *sword*)	Write phonetic pronunciation or use diacritical marks.	*līkĕs* He likes the big yellow car.
Self-correction Corrected by the student without teacher help	Write *C* above the miscue.	*C* *large* He likes the big yellow car.

Text:	The boy likes the kitten. Ask him where it is.
Student 1:	The boy likes the cat. Ask him where it is.
Student 2:	The boy likes the kitchen. Ask him where it is.
Student 3:	The boy like da kitt'n. Ax him where it is.
Student 4:	The boy likes the kitten let's ask where she is.
Student 5:	The boy likes the kitten. Ask him to go where it is.

You may have noticed that some of the miscues preserved the essential meaning of the text, whereas others did not. For example, substituting *cat* for *kitten* (Student 1) or combining the two sentences (Student 4) did not substantially alter the original meaning of the text, although neither student read exactly what was presented. Do you think it would be appropriate to consider those inconsistencies mistakes? If such reading occurred in your classroom, would you stop it and correct the mistakes immediately or allow the reader to go on? Although the students did not read exactly what was written, they did comprehend the text. Such occurrences should be noted for later analysis; but as the miscues were semantically correct, they should not be scored as significant.

What does Student 2's miscue tell us? Does the substitution of *kitchen* for *kitten* indicate anything more than the fact that comprehension has not taken place? Notice that the substitution is an appropriate part of speech, even though the sentence now means something different from the original. Thus, the student has used syntactic cues effectively, correctly placing a noun where it belongs in the sentence, that is, after an article. Notice also that the student has used many of the letters in the original word in the substitution. Indeed, the only difference between the two words is the replacement of the second *t* in *kitten* with a *ch*. Thus, the student is not making wild guesses about what is to be read; active and logical processing is taking place. The same may be said of Student 5. Although the meaning of the original sentences has been altered, the student's miscue is not arbitrary. The **pattern of miscues** that emerges from several such instances, never from just one, permits a teacher to draw generalizations about the reader.

But what about Student 3's reading? How did you categorize that student's miscues? Did you think that the student read incorrectly or simply reflected a normal dialect pattern? Some believe that there are times when dialect differences should be focused on to make a student aware of more-accepted standards. Nevertheless, in the IRI scoring situation dialect variations do not usually impact comprehension and are not typically counted as miscues (Goodman & Buck, 1973; Harris & Sipay, 1990).

In recent years, there has been increasing recognition that IRIs focused on a subskills model of reading, categorizing children's word recognition and comprehension abilities, whereas instruction has moved

pattern of miscues
A group of similar miscues from which a teacher may draw generalizations about the reading process or strategies used by a reader.

It is important to realize that dialect patterns within cultural groups are complex and that no dialect is more logical than or superior to any other.

to incorporate more holistic models of reading. Thus, several IRIs, including the *Classroom Reading Inventory* (Silvaroli, 1994), present forms of the IRI that include both the traditional, subskill format as well as what is called a literature format (Silvaroli, 1994, p. 3), where students are not asked questions after reading, but rather are asked to predict, retell, and discuss the selections with the teacher.

Administering an Informal Reading Inventory

Although every IRI may have its own guidelines for administration, there are certain aspects to administering an IRI that are quite consistent across the various tests that can be purchased. The checklist that follows should help you administer any IRI effectively.

1. Have all materials ready. Type word lists on separate sheets of paper or cards, as needed. Avoid having to shuffle papers during the session with the student. Be familiar with a marking system and the passages.

OPPORTUNITIES TO CELEBRATE DIVERSITY

Listening to children read, particularly as part of an Informal Reading Inventory, will clearly point out the diversity in your classroom. This diversity will manifest itself in differences on comprehension questions that are inferential in nature, because inferential questions require students to use their background knowledge and experiences to answer these questions. Because your students will come from different backgrounds, this will result in different responses to such questions. Similarly, as the preceding discussion notes, students from different cultural or socioeconomic groups may have speech patterns and dialects that differ from each other, leading to differences in pronunciation that will become apparent during oral reading.

These differences can form the basis for interesting classroom discussions about language and language variation, with the dialect speakers becoming the "experts" who can teach others about their own, dialect appropriate pronunciations and vocabulary. Similarly, differences in background knowledge (consider how a new South American or European student might interpret "football" differently from other students) provide opportunities for all students to learn from each other the similarities and differences in different countries' interpretation of words that are common to us in the United States. Thus, while recognizing that differences in background, culture and language will be found through testing, you should look for opportunities to use test results to celebrate children's differences in knowledge, and as a basis for providing needed instruction.

2. Have a tape recorder ready. It is sometimes difficult to keep up with the reader, and most students don't mind if a tape recorder is used unobtrusively. However, don't turn the recorder on and off throughout the session, drawing undue attention to the machine.

3. Begin with a word list one or two grade levels below the student's actual grade. This selection may vary, depending on your knowledge of a student or the specific instructions of a given IRI.

4. Continue with word lists until the criterion level for miscues has been reached. Record all discrepancies between the student's reading and the words on the list.

5. Begin the IRI passages at a level one or two grades below that of the word list on which the criterion error level was reached. Use your knowledge of the student and your observation during administration of the word lists to modify the level of the initial passage as necessary. Also, consult the IRI manual guidelines regarding the entry level of the test being used.

6. Be sure to read the focusing statement to the student before allowing the student to begin reading the passage. A brief discussion can take place to activate the student's prior knowledge, but the teacher should not provide any information or clues about the passage.

MODEL LESSON

Informal Reading Inventory in Ms. Chen's Class

Joann and her parents have just moved to a new neighborhood, where school has been in session for just over one month. On Joann's first day Ms. Chen welcomes her to her third-grade class and introduces Joann to her new classmates. To help determine Joann's reading ability and to match her ability with books from the classroom library, Ms. Chen decides to administer an informal reading inventory. The IRI takes place while the other students are involved in art activities under the supervision of Ms. Chen's parent-volunteer aide.

Ms. Chen uses an IRI she has created using passages from several books used in her classroom. The books varied in difficulty, based on Ms. Chen's experiences with children, and on reading grade levels provided by the book's publishers. After administering the appropriate word lists and passages, Ms. Chen decides that Joann can probably read material just a little more difficult than that being read by the average readers in her class. However, Ms. Chen wants to confirm her assessment through some regular classroom work and also wants Joann to experience success in her new situation, so Ms. Chen places her with a group of average readers for the next group-learning activity. She makes a note on her class record sheet, though, to review Joann's work after a short period of time to see whether she should be moved to more difficult material, and encourages her to self-select books from the classroom library.

7. Note any miscues during oral reading of the passages. Record any discrepancies between the student's reading and the original text.

8. Ask the student the comprehension questions for each passage, noting errors and recording the student's responses. Do not allow the student to refer to the passage. It is appropriate to give partial credit for answers.

9. Discontinue the student's oral reading of the IRI passages when the frustration level has been reached. Again, use your own judgment. Some students reach frustration level earlier on word recognition errors than they do on comprehension questions. Other students reverse that pattern, and still others reach frustration level simultaneously in both aspects. Discontinue if both word recognition and comprehension aspects test at frustration level; use your judgment about continuing the test if only one aspect is at this level. In any case, let your observation of the student in the testing situation guide your decision about when to stop.

10. To determine listening capacity (or listening comprehension level), begin reading the next passage beyond the one on which you discontinued the student's oral reading. Ask comprehension questions as before. Listening capacity indicates the level at which students can comprehend information presented orally, rather than in written form. Discontinue testing after the frustration level has been reached, as indicated by the score on the comprehension questions. Theoretically, the difference between a student's listening compre-

hension and reading comprehension indicates whether that student is reading to potential (Harris & Sipay, 1990).

11. After completing the inventory, fill out a summary sheet. Published IRIs usually include summary pages as part of the inventory, like the example shown in Figure 11-5. This particular summary includes information about word recognition (WR) miscues

FIGURE 11-5
Summary sheet for an IRI

Form A Inventory Record ───────────────────────

Summary Sheet

Student's Name _Debbie_   Grade _2_ Age (Chronological) _7-2_
                                                              yrs. mos.
Date _9/8_   School _____   Administered by _____

Part 1 Word Lists			Part 2 Graded Paragraphs			
Grade Level	Percent of Words Correct	Word Recognition Errors		SIG WR	Comp	L.C.
		Consonants	PP			
PP	_____	___ consonants	P			
1 P		___ blends	1	INST/FRUST	IND	
1	100	✓ digraphs	2	INST	INST	
		___ endings	3			90
		___ compounds	4			90
		___ contractions	5			75
		Vowels	6			
		✓ long	7			
		___ short	8			
2	90-95	___ long/short oo				
		___ vowel + r	Estimated Levels			
		___ diphthong				
		✓ vowel comb.			Grade	
		___ a + 1 or w	Independent		1	
		Syllable	Instructional		2 (range)	
3	80-85	___ visual patterns	Frustration		3	
4	60-65	✓ prefix	Listening Capacity		5	
		___ suffix				
5	_____	Word Recognition reinforcement and Vocabulary development				
6	_____					

Comp Errors	Summary of Specific Needs:
3 Factual (F)	MINIMAL INFORMATION ON WHICH TO
0 Inference (I)	BASE WORD RECOGNITION ERROR
0 Vocabulary (V)	PATTERNS. SUGGEST DIAGNOSTIC
N/A "Word Caller" (A student who reads without associating meaning)	TEST IF CLASSROOM OBSERVATIONS CONFIRM THE PATTERNS NOTED HERE.
N/A Poor Memory	

From Silvaroli, N. J. (1994). Classroom Reading Inventory (7th ed.). Dubuque, IA: Brown & Benchmark, p. 59.

from the word lists as well as comprehension (COMP) errors on the IRI passages. Additionally, a **listening capacity (LC) level** is indicated. The summary sheet also notes any trends or patterns found in the IRI.

Creating an Informal Reading Inventory. There are many published IRIs readily available, and most published reading programs also include one or more. Nonetheless, you may sometime wish to create your own. For example, you might want IRI passages to come from a specific set of materials that will be used in class: such passages would have more curricular validity than a generic IRI. In order to create your own IRI, you will need to choose passages at various levels and will also need to know scoring guidelines to establish independent, instructional, and frustration reading levels. With published IRIs the specific number of miscues corresponding to each of the reading levels for a given passage is generally determined by the percentage of miscues within the total words read (for word recognition) or the percentage of wrong answers within the number of comprehension questions (for comprehension). However, there has been some disagreement regarding the scoring criteria for IRIs (Aulls, 1982; Betts, 1946; Cooper, 1952; Powell, 1970). We agree with Burns, Roe, and Ross (1988), who suggest combining the criteria proposed by Johnson, Kress, and Pikulski (1987) with those of Powell (1970). You can use the result, shown here, to determine reading levels on an IRI, but you should remember that these percentages are only approximate guidelines.

Reading level	Word recognition accuracy		Comprehension accuracy
independent	99% or higher	(and)	90% or higher
instructional	85% or higher (Grades 1–2)	(and)	75% or higher
	95% or higher (Grades 3 and above)	(and)	75% or higher
frustration	below 90%	(or)	below 50%
listening capacity			75% or higher

The Running Record

The **running record,** initially developed by Marie Clay (1985), allows a teacher to record a student's oral reading in much the same way that is done during the oral reading phase of the IRI. Also similarly to the IRI, the running record provides an indication of a reader's strategies while reading as well as areas of difficulty; nevertheless it differs from the IRI in that it does not require any specific passage for administration, does not require graded word lists, and does not yield a reading level score. The running record is also less formal than the IRI, as the teacher does not tape record the reading; nor is the administration procedure as specific. In fact, teachers need only a paper and pencil to conduct a running record (the passage being read is not required). It can be done at any time that a child is reading and with any material that is being read. Johnston (1992) feels that these are advantages over the IRI and result in teachers being more willing and able to use running records on an ongoing basis with their students.

The scoring system resembles the IRI notation provided on page 472. Omissions, insertions, substitutions, repetitions, self-corrections, attempts, and teacher-provided pronunciations are recorded during reading. Nevertheless, because the teacher does not have a copy of the student's text, words read correctly are indicated by a check mark. On a piece of paper, you would place a check mark for each word read exactly as it appears in the text, with each line of check marks corresponding to each printed line being read. If there were five words on a line being read, then there would be a maximum of five check marks on that line of the running record.

It is important that only the student's oral reading behavior be recorded at the time of reading. At some point after reading, you will need to go back and add to the running record sheet the specific words that were omitted, substituted, and so on, from the original text. The one-to-one correspondence between check marks and words per line will allow you to do so accurately. The scoring system for a running record is shown below.

Text: ## Tracy knew she would not be able to sleep.

Student 1: (Correct)   Tracy knew she would not be able to sleep.

Record: √ √ √ √ √ √ √ √ √

Note: the nine checks indicate that all nine words were read correctly.

Student 2: (Omission)   Tracy knew she would be able to sleep.

Record: √ √ √ √ $\overline{}$ √ √ √ √
                              NOT

Note: the dash above the line indicates that the 5th word ("not") was omitted; the omitted word is written below the line after the reading session.

Student 3: (Insertion)   Tracy knew that she would not be able to sleep.

Record: √ √ THAT √ √ √ √ √ √ √

Note: the inserted word ("that") is written above the line; a dash is written below the line to show that this is not a substitution.

Student 4:   Tracy felt she would not be able to sleep.
(Substitution)

Record: √   <u>FELT</u>   √   √   √   √   √   √   √
               KNEW

Note: the substituted word ("felt") is written above the line; the original word ("knew") is written below the line after the reading session.

Student 5:   Tracy knew she would . . . she would . . . not be able to
(Repetition)   . . . to . . . to sleep.

Record:
                                    R   R^3
           √   √   √   √| √   √   √   √   √

Note: an "R" is written at the right-hand end of the repetition ("would"), and a line is drawn back along the number of check marks that correspond to the words repeated. If something is repeated more than once, the number of repetitions is indicated beside the "R" notation.

Student 6:   Tracy k . . . now . . . knew she would not be able to
(Attempt)   sleep.

Record: √   <u>K| NOW |</u> √   √   √   √   √   √   √   √
               KNEW

Note: Above the line, write each attempt, including a check mark showing that the word was ultimately correctly read; write the original word below the line after the reading session.

Student 7:   Tracy knew she wants . . . would not be able to sleep.
(Self-Correction)

Record: √   √   √   <u>WANTS |SC</u>   √   √   √   √   √
                        WOULD

Note: Write the miscue ("wants") above the line, the notation for self-correction (SC) to the right of the line division, and the original word below the line (after the reading session).

Student 8:   Tracy knew she [pause, teacher pronounces "would"] not
(Teacher   be able to sleep.
Pronounced)

Record: √   √   √   <u>—</u>   √   √   √   √   √
                        WOULD |T

Note: The dash indicates the student omitted the word, the notation for teacher pronunciation (T) is written below the line to the right of the line division, and the original word is written below the line (after the reading session).

Following the running record, a summary sheet is completed in much the same way as is done for an IRI. This summary sheet can then be added to the student's portfolio. Traill (1993) has stated that a running record should be done with each child at least once every six weeks, and that comparisons of summary sheets be used to indicate progress in both skill and strategic aspects of reading. Summary sheets can be fairly simple and typically include the items indicated on the form in Figure 11-6. Although the six-week cycle recommended by Traill may be optimal, the time between running records will vary depending on the age and reading ability of your students, with older students and more able readers being evaluated through a running record less often than younger or less able readers. Also, when counting errors for summary purposes, Johnston's (1992) modification of Clay's (1985) categories is often used:

- Omissions, insertions, and multiple repetitions that are not proper nouns count as one error each time; proper nouns are counted only the first time.

FIGURE 11-6
Sample running record summary sheet

Reader: _____ Date: _____

Book title, page: _____

Read before? (If "yes," how often?) _____

Error Rate (number of errors divided by number of words, times 100): _____%

Accuracy Rate (Error rate minus 100%): _____%

Number of Errors: _____   Total Self Corrections: _____

Print-Based Self Corrections: _____

Meaning-Based Self Corrections: _____

Rereads often: _____   occasionally: _____   never: _____

Uses phonic analysis (provide examples): _____

Uses context (provide examples): _____

Talks about the text, background or personal experiences, etc. (explain):

_____

_____

_____

_____

- An omitted line counts only as one error; do not count each omitted word on the line as an error.

- A teacher intervention (such as "try again" or a pronunciation) counts as one error and other errors are counted in the rereading.

- When in doubt about scoring, choose that which fits your interpretation of error patterns. If still in doubt, choose the lowest error count.

- You might end up with more errors on a line than there are words (because of insertions, and so on), but do not score more errors than there are words on a page. If this occurs, you may want to discontinue the running record and simply note how the child is creating the story (perhaps from related pictures on the page, from prior knowledge, and so on).

The Cloze Procedure

cloze procedure
A fill-in-the-blank task used to estimate the level at which a child can read with assistance.

The **cloze procedure** is often used to match readers with specific reading materials. For this purpose, it is sometimes preferred to the IRI because it allows group rather than individual administration. A cloze task also involves a student directly with the text, without the intervening teacher questions. Table 11-2 outlines the major differences between cloze and IRI. As described earlier, a cloze procedure presents students with a passage that has blanks in place of some of the words. Students attempt to fill in the blanks with the words that were deleted from the original passage. The teacher uses the scoring procedure described later in this section to indicate whether the passage is at independent, instructional, or frustration level for the student and, thus, whether the material from which the passage came is appropriate.

Cloze gained widespread use after its modification by Taylor (1953). With its roots in Gestalt psychology, cloze makes use of the human drive to add closure to incomplete items. In the reading cloze procedure, this inclination has been translated into the reader's use of context to complete passages from which words have been systematically deleted. It is essentially a fill-in-the-blank task (see Warwick, 1978; Rankin, 1974, 1978; Jongsma, 1980).

Constructing a Cloze Test. In order to match students and materials, cloze passages can be constructed from the material that students will be reading. The passages should be representative of that material and should not be broken up by illustrations or other potentially distractive features. Within the chosen passages, words are systematically deleted, and blanks are substituted for the deleted words. The following steps describe the construction of a cloze test in detail, and Figure 11-7 illustrates a cloze test ready for use.

1. Choose a representative passage from the beginning, middle, and end of material (usually a book) that you wish to use with your

TABLE 11-2

General differences between cloze and IRIs

	Cloze	IRI
Administration	Group or individual Written (or oral) Passages	Individual Oral Word lists, passages, oral questions
Uses	Match student and materials Find a student's general reading level Provide general readability measure	Match student and materials Find a student's general reading level Provide general readability measure Permit inferences about student's reading process
Type of information	Ability to use context Comprehension score Independent, instructional, frustration reading levels	Word recognition score Comprehension score Listening capacity score Independent, instructional, frustration reading levels

student(s). For high reliability, each passage should contain approximately 250 words, although that length may not be possible in primary grade materials. Using a number of representative passages is strongly recommended so that the results can be averaged, thereby increasing the validity and reliability of the procedure.

2. Leave the first sentence of the passage intact to provide a contextual base.

3. Beginning with the second sentence, replace every fifth word with a blank. Be sure that your blanks are the same size so that their length does not give a clue to the length of the deleted words. Continue until 50 words have been deleted, if possible. However, do not delete the following: proper names, dates, abbreviations, or acronyms. When such words are encountered, the next word is deleted, and the every-fifth-word rule proceeds from that point.

4. Conclude with a complete, intact sentence without deletions.

Scoring and Interpreting a Cloze Test. A cloze test is similar to an informal reading inventory in that it provides an indication of a reader's independent, instructional, and frustration reading levels. Cloze tests determine that level by calculating the percentage of exact replacements of

FIGURE 11-7

Sample cloze passage

That evening they all had dinner together in the enchanter's cozy kitchen. Then Albion took Petronella _____ to a stone building _____ unbolted its door. Inside _____ seven huge black dogs.

"_____ must watch my hounds _____ night," said he.

Petronella _____ in, and Albion closed _____ locked the door.

At _____ the hounds began to _____ and bark. They showed _____ teeth at her. But Petronella _____ a real princess. She _____ up her courage. Instead _____ backing away, she went _____ the dogs. She began _____ speak to them in _____ quiet voice. They stopped _____ and sniffed at her. _____ patted their heads.

"I _____ what it is," she _____ . "You are lonely here. _____ will keep you company."

_____ so all night long, _____ sat on the floor _____ talked to the hounds _____ stroked them. They lay _____ to her.

In the _____ , Albion came and let _____ out. "Ah," said he, " _____ see that you are _____ . If you had run _____ the dogs, they would _____ torn you to pieces. _____ you may ask for _____ you want."

"I want _____ comb for my hair," _____ Petronella.

The enchanter gave _____ a comb carved from _____ piece of black wood.

Prince Ferdinand _____ sunning himself and working _____ a crossword puzzle. Petronella _____ to him in a _____ voice, "I am doing _____ for you."

"That's nice," _____ the prince. "What's 'selfish' _____ nine letters?"

"You are," _____ Petronella. She went to _____ enchanter. "I will work _____ you once more," she _____ . That night Albion led _____ to a stable. Inside were seven huge horses.

Source: From J. Williams, *Petronella* (New York: Scholastic, 1973). Reprinted by permission.

deleted words. Synonyms are not usually counted as correct in scoring a cloze test. For the cloze test shown in Figure 11-7, the following replacements were provided by Lee, a third-grade student. Underlined numbers indicate correct replacements, making Lee's score 24 out of 50 or 48 percent.

	Original deletion	Lee's replacement		Original deletion	Lee's replacement
1.	out	away	**26.**	close	beside
2.	and	and	**27.**	morning	morning
3.	were	sat	**28.**	her	her
4.	you	we	**29.**	I	I
5.	all	all	30.	brave	alive
6.	went	went	31.	from	No response
7.	and	and	**32.**	have	have
8.	once	No response	33.	now	so
9.	snarl	growl	34.	what	anything
10.	their	their	**35.**	a	a
11.	was	No response	**36.**	said	said
12.	plucked	No response	**37.**	her	her
13.	of	of	**38.**	a	a
14.	toward	toward	39.	was	lay
15.	to	to	40.	at	No response
16.	a	her	**41.**	said	said
17.	snarling	No response	42.	low	nice
18.	she	she	**43.**	this	this
19.	see	know	**44.**	said	said
20.	said	said	45.	in	about
21.	I	No response	46.	snapped	said
22.	and	then	**47.**	the	the
23.	she	she	48.	for	with
24.	and	and	49.	said	cried
25.	and	then	50.	her	Petronella

Several researchers have attempted to specify the scoring criteria for interpreting cloze results (Bormuth, 1968; Rankin, 1971; Rankin & Culhane, 1969). Although this text suggests the percentage bands noted by Rankin and Culhane, Bormuth's percentages are also noted here. Both scales are widely accepted.

Reading level	Percentage of exact replacements (Rankin & Culhane)	Percentage of exact replacements (Bormuth)
independent	above 60%	above 57%
instructional	40% to 59%	44% to 57%
frustration	below 40%	below 44%

In our example, Lee's percentage of replacements was 48, placing his reading of the passage at the instructional level.

Common Questions about Cloze. *Why are only exact replacements counted and not synonyms?* The **exact replacement criterion** allows more accurate scoring and resolves the potential problem of different interpretations by different people. Some might argue, for example, that *home* and *house* are not the same—that a house is only a building, whereas a home implies much more. Because of the exact replacement criterion, however, the percentages corresponding to the various reading levels are set quite low. Thus, a student can correctly replace as few as 4 out of 10 deletions (40 percent) yet still be placed at the instructional reading level. In addition, the percentage bands for the various reading levels are quite wide—20 percent for the instructional level—so that students are not penalized. Some people do score synonyms as correct; but they must then use higher scoring percentages, and the test becomes more difficult to score, thus taking more teacher time.

How accurate is the cloze procedure? The cloze procedure is quick and easy to use and provides approximate measurements consistently. Because teacher judgment plays a significant part in cloze interpretation, students should be given the benefit of the doubt if their percentage scores border the bands separating the different reading levels. The test is most accurate when at least three passages are used from the material under consideration.

Should there be a time limit when administering a cloze test? No. Generally, students are given as much time as they wish to complete the cloze passage, and they are certainly allowed to go through a passage more than once.

Does spelling count when scoring a student's replacements? No. This is not a spelling test.

exact replacement criterion

A scoring procedure that counts as correct only responses that match the precise words deleted from the text.

Other Uses of the Cloze Procedure.   The cloze test has traditionally been used to examine the match between readers and specific reading material. However, there are other ways in which the cloze procedure can benefit the teacher of reading. First, the cloze test can be used with a graded set of materials to determine a student's general reading level; this approach allows the teacher to generalize the student's score beyond the material from which the cloze test was constructed. With this application a set of graded passages should be used to construct a series of cloze tests. Scoring should then provide a rough guide to the student's reading level (corresponding to the grade level of the passage) at which frustration reading level is reached. Instead of a leveled set of passages taken from a published reading program, readability formulas (discussed later in this chapter) can also be used to determine the reading grade level of the selected passages.

The other common use for cloze is as a teaching technique with several variations. For instance, teachers might delete specific parts of speech (for example, nouns, adjectives, or verbs) or might provide choices above the blanks. As an instructional aid, however, cloze requires time for significant discussion of replacements. It is not enough simply to grade a student's effort; instead, students must be led to understand why given replacements are appropriate, what other options might fit, and why some replacements are not very good choices.

Retellings

Retelling scores are derived when students are asked to read a passage and then retell in their own words what was read. Retellings are useful measures of comprehension. They have been used in informal reading inventories to supplement or, at times, replace the comprehension questions generally asked at the end of an IRI passage. Some believe that retellings are more accurate than answers to questions, because questions can sometimes be answered from general knowledge without even reading the passage. In fact, Allington, Chodos, Domaracki, and Truex (1977) have shown that approximately 30 percent of the questions asked in informal reading inventories are **passage independent.** That is, they can be answered without first reading the passage to which they refer (see also Tuinman, 1974, for a discussion of passage dependent/passage independent questions).

To use retelling as an assessment procedure, the teacher should first divide the original passage into units, often called **idea units,** or thought units. The following example would be categorized as two idea units.

The boy ran / although his leg was hurt.

To increase the reliability of this procedure, two people should work together to segment the passage. Thereafter, the following procedure and scoring system can be used (Clark, 1982; Morrow, 1988):

retelling scores
A measure of comprehension obtained by having readers tell in their own words what they have just read.

passage independent
Describes questions that can be answered from general knowledge rather than from a reading of the text.

idea units
Thought units used to determine comprehension.

1. Assign each unit a number from 1 through 3 in terms of its importance (1 being very important, perhaps a main idea, and 3 being of relatively little importance, perhaps an insignificant detail).
2. Make a three-columned scoring sheet with the importance ratings on the left, the units in the middle, and recording space on the right (see Figure 11-8).
3. As the child retells the passage, use the right-hand column to number the units in the order in which they are recalled.
4. Score the recall by first comparing the sequence of the recalled units with that of the original, then totaling the number of units recalled in each category of importance, and finally dividing that number by the total possible in each category.

Comparing the three categories allows inferences about how well the reader has understood and remembered the various levels in the passage.

Figure 11-8 shows a completed retelling measure for a passage introduced in chapter 6 (Carson, 1990). An instructional reading level was determined by the degree of consistency between the retelling and the segmented passage. Generally, a 60 to 70 percent match is used as the criterion for the instructional reading level. However, that determination is influenced by teacher judgment, especially as it relates to the amount and specificity of the ideas recalled and the order and fluency of the retelling. In addition, it is important that students have an opportunity to practice the retelling procedure before it is used in evaluation. Morrow (1988) points out that students who are unfamiliar with the procedure do not know what is being asked of them and are at a disadvantage.

Think-Alouds

Think-alouds are similar to retellings in that they are individually administered and can be used with material that is chosen by the teacher or by the student. It differs, though, in that retellings occur after reading, while think-alouds occur during reading. Thus, Glazer and Brown (1993) point out that retellings are influenced by memory factors and are more closely related to the product of reading, while think-alouds are more closely related to "on line" thinking and the in-process activity that occurs during reading. Many have recently suggested that oral think-alouds are excellent windows into the comprehension process, and the think-aloud procedure has been used widely in classroom assessment as well as in research (for example, see Wade, 1990; Johnston, 1992).

When performing a think-aloud, choose a passage that is not too easy or too difficult for the reader. A passage that is too difficult will result in frustration and may yield frustration responses rather than insights into the reading process. Conversely, a selection that is too easy often results in the reader's simply making comments like "that's interesting," or "that's neat!" A final consideration when using think-alouds is that readers are not typically used to stating their process or thoughts as they

FIGURE 11-8

Completed retelling score form

Importance	Unit	Retelling Sequence
1	Tracy	1
1	knew she would not	2
1	be able to sleep.	3
3	But her mother	
3	had told her	
2	to brush her teeth	
2	and put on her nightgown anyway,	
3	and Tracy did as she was told.	
3	Just as she	4
3	got into her nightgown,	5
1	a loud crack of thunder	6
3	filled the air!	
1	Tracy jumped into bed	7
2	and pulled the covers	
3	over her head.	
3	When Meg	12
3	peeked into the room,	13
3	Tracy wailed,	
2	"The last time	8
2	we had a storm like this,	9
2	I stayed awake	10
2	all night!"	11
2	Meg sat	14
2	beside Tracy	15
3	and tucked her little sister in.	
2	Then she started to hum softly.	16
2	It was one of Tracy's	17
2	favorite songs.	18
2	As the song went on,	
2	Meg noticed that Tracy's eyes	20
3	had closed.	21
2	Meg turned off the bedroom light	19
2	as she tiptoed	
2	out of the room,	
1	Tracy didn't hear	23
1	the next clap of thunder	
2	as the storm continued	22
3	into the night.	

	Units Recalled	Possible Units	Score (%)
Category 1:	6	6	100%
Category 2:	12	18	67%
Category 3:	5	13	38%
Total:	23	37	62%

Comments: OVER 60% MATCH IN UNITS RECALLED. FAIRLY CLOSE MATCH IN SEQUENCE ORDER. HAS A GOOD SENSE OF IMPORTANT INFORMATION. INSTRUCTIONAL LEVEL.

read. Thus, you will have to model the procedure for students, and be prepared to gently prompt the reader for comments during reading. Johnston (1992) reminds us that such prompts may be necessary, as might be simple reminders that comments are expected. These reminders can be gentle statements to comment while reading, or subtle reminders such as clearing your throat or shifting your position to make the reader aware of you and the task at hand.

During the think-aloud you should have a copy of the selection being read, spaced so that you can write down student's comments and behaviors. Figure 11-9 shows such a text, together with a second-grade student's

---

FIGURE 11-9
Sample think-aloud responses

Text	Response
Tracy knew she would not be able to sleep. But her mother had told her to brush her teeth and put on her nightgown anyway, and Tracy did as she was told. Just as she got into her nightgown, a loud crack of thunder filled the air! Tracy jumped into bed and pulled the covers over her head. When Meg peeked into the room, Tracy wailed, "The last time we had a storm like this, I stayed awake all night!" Meg sat beside Tracy and tucked her little sister in. Then she started to hum softly. It was one of Tracy's favorite songs. As the song went on, Meg noticed that Tracy's eyes had closed. Meg turned off the bedroom light as she tiptoed out of the room. Tracy didn't hear the next clap of thunder as the storm continued into the night.	*I wonder why?* *"Did as she was told"— I bet not always!* *Who's Meg?* *"Whiled?" – oh, well!* *So! Meg's her sister!* *I wonder what the song was?* *Thunder usually wakes me up!*

(Handwritten annotations within text: "What's this word?" pointing to "wailed"; "Meg or Tracy?" pointing to "her")

comments. After the think-aloud, take the time to complete a summary form such as that illustrated in Figure 11-10. Notice that the summary form includes patterns of responses found during the think-aloud. Both the think-aloud and the summary form can be included as part of the reader's portfolio. Looking at the summary forms over time can indicate categories that appear and become stable, as well as movement of responses from the "occasionally" to the "often" column. These patterns, when seen over time, can provide important evidence of a reader's progress as well as information for instruction of comprehension strategies.

Assessing Attitudes and Interests

One of the most powerful pieces of information available to a teacher is an awareness of student attitudes and interests. Informal measures can be used to discover motivational topics that can enhance instruction. Published reading programs provide assessment inventories, and other published inventories are also available. Nevertheless, teacher-made assessments in this area are often more valuable than those commercially available.

Unfortunately, it is easy to get so involved in teaching students how to read that enhancing reading ability becomes an end in itself. This situation can result in students who are able to read but do not want to. On the other hand, when students develop a love of reading it becomes a lifelong activity. Thus, the most effective teachers go beyond simply teaching students how to read; they show students that reading is relevant and interesting. And materials that students find interesting lead to increased time on task and enhanced learning.

Dulin and Chester (1984) have published interest and attitude surveys (see also Dulin, 1984), and their scales imply that children's interests and attitudes be tested across a number of areas, such as the following:

1. Comparing literacy activities to other activities; for example, by asking students to show which activity, perhaps reading a book or playing outside, they would rather do.
2. Finding out about the purposes of literacy activities; for example, by asking students the degree to which they agree with statements such as "Reading is for learning but not for enjoyment."
3. Finding out the relative desirability of various literacy activities in relation to each other; for example, by asking students to divide up 100 points across activities such as reading books, reading magazines, reading comics, writing stories, writing letters, and so on.
4. Finding out about the students' self perception with regard to literacy tasks; for example, by asking students to rate how well, compared to other students in the class or of the student's age, they think they read.
5. Finding out how students feel about the rewards of literacy activities; for example, by asking students to rate their feelings about

FIGURE 11-10
Sample of a completed think-aloud summary sheet

Reader's Name: _Jill_   Date: _11/5_   Age _7·6_

Title and page of passage read: _Tracy — teacher created story._

Summarize reader and reading characteristics during reading (e.g., tentative, willing, appropriate

intonation, etc.): _good pace, fluency, and intonation._

SPECIFIC ASPECTS OF THE THINK-ALOUD:	Often	Occasionally
Evidence of Text Comprehension		
Restates text in own words		X
Restates text with words from passage		X
Adds (appropriate) own ideas to text	X	
Evidence of Comprehension Monitoring		
Comments on lack of word comprehension		X
Comments on lack of sentence comprehension		
Comments on lack of paragraph or larger-unit comprehension		
Evidence of Metalinguistic Knowledge		
Comments about personal, related experiences or background knowledge	X	
Notices and comments on text features and writing style		
Predicts, reasons, and/or evaluates ideas in the text	X	
Other summary comments		
Rereads		
Makes "backward" references to what has been read		

the value of rewards such as a grade for reading, extra credit for reading, and so on.

6. Finding out the value of things teachers can do to motivate reading; for example, by having students rate their interest in things such as having the teacher read a chapter or excerpt from a book to the class each day, or having the teacher read and discuss the first few pages of a book that students then can choose to finish.

7. Finding out how valuable students feel various post-reading activities are; for example, by asking them to rate the value of activities such as taking an oral or written test on what they read, writing a book report, making a diorama, and so on.

These categories of items demonstrate that attitude/interest measures can examine various important aspects related to reading instruction:

- how students feel about reading
- how they feel about various instructional methods and reward systems
- how they feel about different types of materials
- how they feel about themselves in relationship to literacy and literacy activities

The affective information gathered through interest/attitude inventories should be added to the informal classroom records previously discussed. In addition, as children's interests and attitudes change fairly quickly, both should be assessed several times during a year, and ongoing anecdotal records of current trends, fads, and interests should be maintained.

Assessing Stress Factors in Reading

A poor attitude toward reading can indicate that a student is experiencing stress resulting from poor reading skills or from a teacher's demands to read. Gentile and McMillan (1987, 1988) point out that stress is often related to reading difficulty and present a scale for assessing stress reactions to reading. They categorize students' stress reactions as fight or flight responses. Fight responses manifest themselves in confrontations with the teacher and with reading material; they can be summarized as "I won't read, and you can't make me." With this response students condemn reading, books, school, and teachers; anxiety is directed outward, and the students are confrontational. The flight reaction can be characterized as "I can't read and no one can teach me." These students condemn themselves; anxiety is directed inward, and they retreat from teachers (Gentile & McMillan, 1988, p. 21).

Their stress reaction scale is a simple, fifteen-item instrument that provides information about how a child deals with stress related to reading. In addition, it highlights for teachers student behaviors that might

There are a wide variety of published instruments available to use for assessment. Matching updated editions of these instruments to your comprehension framework, together with informal measures and "kidwatching" during literacy tasks, will provide information that will appropriately guide instructional decisions.

be seen during classroom observations during daily routines. Gentile and McMillan recommend a number of specific strategies to deal with fight and flight reactions to reading. Their strategies focus on goal setting, personal incentives, and self-monitoring. In general, teachers working with fight-response students need to channel the students away from confrontation and into reading. Flight-response students must be drawn out and interested in successful completion of reading tasks. Normally, fight reactions are more easily dealt with because they have a force behind them that can be redirected into reading. Flight reactions are generally passive, and teachers must intervene more directly to involve students and provide them with feelings of success. This might involve one-on-one intervention with reciprocal reading activities, or other activities that allow the child to achieve success in easily observable ways.

Teacher-Made Tests

Perhaps the most common assessment instruments used in reading classrooms are teacher made. Such measures have the advantage of being closely tied to the curriculum and program being taught; they can be written to apply specifically to one student or a whole class. Length, type and number of items, testing duration, and format all vary in teacher-made tests.

Effective teachers must be aware of the wealth of information available to them and use it in an informed manner to make their daily instructional decisions. Assignments are more than simple practice pieces for students; they are part of an overall data-gathering and decision-making process. Thus, in this context teacher-made tests go beyond quizzes or other graded items and include all the things that a teacher might ask a student to do as a part of the learning process, whether in the classroom, at home, or elsewhere. All such activities reveal student needs and capabilities.

Effective use of incidental and teacher-initiated information requires, first of all, keen observation of student behavior in all learning situations. Moreover, assessment is greatly facilitated by careful planning. For example, if a comprehension assignment is carefully constructed to include all levels of comprehension, then a teacher can determine whether a student is having difficulty within a particular level(s) and can adjust instruction accordingly.

Monitoring all aspects of student performance requires a clear, up-to-date record-keeping system. Maintaining such a record of student strengths and weaknesses allows teachers to be much more focused in their instruction and to target specific students' individual needs. A record-keeping system for a vocabulary assignment might look like the one in Figure 11-11.

Formal, Norm-Referenced Tests

Norm-referenced tests compare an individual or a group to a **norm group** of similar individuals. These tests form the stereotype of traditional assessment. A norm-referenced test usually contains several subtests. For example, a survey reading test might include subtests in vocabulary, reading rate, comprehension, and study skills. A diagnostic reading test might include subtests in knowledge of word parts; blending ability; inferential and literal comprehension; identification of relationships (for example, cause and effect); oral vocabulary; and so on. Before you choose a norm-referenced test, you should carefully examine the test manual(s) to find out about the group to which your students would be compared. You need to determine whether your students are similar enough to the norm group for valid comparison. A manual should provide norm-group information such as the following:

- number of males and females
- range of ages
- distribution across geographic regions
- representation of rural and urban areas
- number of bicultural, minority, and ethnic students

It is also important to realize that norm group scores are presented as an average or norm, making individual student comparisons less reliable

norm-referenced tests
Tests that compare an individual or a group to a group of other, similar individuals.

norm group
The group whose test performance is used to establish levels of performance for a standardized test.

FIGURE 11-11

Sample class record sheet

ASSIGNMENT: *Vocabulary — write words in sentence, then use all words in story or paragraph. Words: observe, suspect, strut, elegant, modest.*

NAME	COMMENTS	DATE: *10/12*
Allison	*Used words correctly. Misspelled elegant both times used "elegent"*	
Bobby	*Left out strut, modest.*	
Julio	*No problems.*	
Kathleen	*Words used correctly. Neatness and hand-writing still a problem.*	
Latisha	*modest, elegant used incorrectly*	
Wanda	*modest used incorrectly.*	

GENERAL COMMENTS: *Reteach modest. Have Kathleen recopy grade only on neatness. See Bobby individually about this assignment. Add elegant, modest to spelling list*

than comparisons of groups to the norm. For example, comparing a class average to the norm would be more accurate than comparing the scores of an individual student. The model lesson that follows relates the experiences of one third-grade teacher with a norm-referenced test.

Formal, Criterion-Referenced Tests

criterion-referenced test
A test that compares a student's performance to a predetermined measure of success.

A **criterion-referenced test** (CRT) does not compare a student to a norm group. Its intent is simply to provide a picture of student performance by comparing it to an established criterion (Popham, 1978). Nevertheless, because criterion assessment is usually performed to judge mas-

M O D E L   L E S S O N

Experience with a Norm-Referenced Test at Ms. Henshaw's School

All students in the third grade at Ms. Henshaw's school are to be given a norm-referenced test. The goal of the assessment is to compare students' achievement over several years and to see how these third graders perform relative to other third graders across the nation. The teachers and principal have determined that the test is both reliable and valid and that the school's third-grade population adequately reflects the norm group for comparative purposes.

A faculty meeting is called to discuss test administration. Everyone realizes that the test instructions need to be followed to the letter. Instructions are to be read to students as stated in the test manual, a stopwatch is to be used to make sure that timed sections are accurate, subtests are to be done in order, and so on. Test booklets and answer sheets are to be collected at the end of the testing session and will be scored electronically, with the results returned to the teachers.

Several months later, Ms. Henshaw receives those results. She notices that there are several parts to the report: a section listing overall scores for her class; a section comparing her class to a norm group; a section that notes how many students missed particular items; and a section that lists her students' names along with the items each student missed. This information is clustered within question types that appeared on the test.

Because the test was given late in the school year, the results will not greatly influence Ms. Henshaw's instruction for the students that were tested. However, her third graders compared favorably to their peers. Ms. Henshaw does record individual students' deficiencies on her class record sheet and on the students' official cumulative record cards. She knows that her students' next teachers will be looking at these records and will thus have an indication of general areas that might need some attention. Ms. Henshaw will use other, informal assessments to corroborate the findings of this test. She will also share the information the following year, when teachers tell each other about their classes from the previous year.

tery on a specific set of isolated skills such as letter sounds, letter names, blends, main ideas, and so on, criterion assessment is usually valued by teachers who believe in more specific-skill explanations for learning. Because criterion tests are relatively skill-specific in their makeup, they are generally not placed in the alternative assessment category. In contrast to norm-referenced assessment where a student's score is compared to those of a norm group of peers, in criterion-referenced assessment a student's score is compared to a predetermined criterion of success. As Mehrens and Lehman (1984) have stated, "To polarize the distinction, we could say that the focus of a normative score is on how many of Johnny's peers do not perform (score) as well as he does; the focus of a criterion-referenced score is on what it is that Johnny can do" (p. 18).

In part, the popularity of criterion-referenced assessment lies in its ability to determine whether a student has mastered a specific lesson and can be moved on to the next level of instruction. This approach has been criticized, however, because it implies that all necessary reading subskills have been correctly sequenced and identified and that a strict sequence of instruction is known to be best for all students. Unfortunately, even though much is known about reading, there is still much to learn. And even though certain skills are generally thought to be necessary in reading, they are interrelated and are difficult to separate. A difficult issue to resolve in criterion-referenced measurement is the fact that the absence of any one subskill presented in a criterion reading test does not usually reflect an inability to read. A similar situation exists for most skill areas, leaving individually tested skills on a CRT open to question (see Johnston, 1983, for a discussion of holistic versus subskill theories of reading comprehension and their relationship to assessment).

Nonetheless, criterion-referenced measures are included in almost every published reading program. Their advantage over norm-referenced tests has traditionally been their close tie to instruction, making them useful for a **management system.** A management system provides a detailed record of each student's progress through an instructional program and records when mastery of specific skills occurs. Such systems are attractive to school systems that are concerned with accountability issues.

Criterion-referenced assessment can monitor a student's progress through instructional materials. For example, let's assume that a reader is learning the two-letter blend *st*. The instructional program introduces the *str* blend at a more difficult level, but only after the *st* combination has been mastered. Five items testing *st* might be administered, with the criterion set at 3. When the student answers three of the five items correctly, instruction moves on to the *str* blend. Until then, more instruction is provided on *st*, and the test (usually in a different form) is readministered. This close tie to instruction is a major reason for the popularity of criterion-referenced assessment.

One misconception about the differences between norm- and criterion-referenced scores needs to be addressed here. The statement is often made that norm-referenced assessment results in a relatively arbitrary comparison of individual students to a norm group, whereas criterion assessment examines students' performance only against their own strengths. However, criterion-referenced tests also compare student performance to an externally imposed criterion. In fact, one could argue that the criterion is more arbitrary than the norms, as norm-referenced tests provide a comprehensive and valuable discussion of the norm group and the norming procedure, whereas the rationale for a given criterion level is rarely addressed in teacher's manuals. Consequently, such questions as How is a criterion determined? are left unanswered.

Usually, a criterion is set at the level at which average students—average in relation to the students being tested—perform. Thus, the difference between a norm and a criterion is minimal. The major difference between criterion- and norm-referenced assessment lies in philosophy and in the way scores are used, rather than in any substantive difference in how appropriate performance is determined. This difference in usage

management system
A detailed, systematic record of a student's progress through an instructional program.

M O D E L   L E S S O N

Experience with a Criterion-Referenced Test in Mr. Washington's Class

Mr. Washington has just completed a lesson on cause-and-effect relationships. The lesson format came from a published reading program that includes criterion-referenced tests as part of the program. The teacher's manual suggests that the appropriate criterion-referenced test be given to see whether students have mastered the concept.

The test provided in the reading program contains 10 items, with 8 as the criterion. The teacher's guide suggests reteaching if the criterion is not met, and new lessons are provided for that purpose. An additional criterion assessment, with new items, is provided for use after reteaching.

Mr. Washington administers the test to his students, and all but five meet the criterion. His teacher's aide works with this group of students, using the reteaching lesson and then retests. On the retest all five students meet the criterion and Mr. Washington begins instruction on the next unit.

is reflected in the frequency of administration of the two types of assessment. Criterion-referenced tests are used often and are usually specifically keyed to the instructional situation, whereas norm-referenced tests are generally used only once or twice a year. The model lesson above shows how criterion-referenced tests can lead to instructional decisions.

EVALUATING MATERIALS
Readability Formulas

A **readability formula** provides a rough guideline for determining the difficulty level, or grade level, of reading material. Although useful, the results of a readability formula must be interpreted carefully. In fact, the International Reading Association and the National Council of Teachers of English (1984-1985) have noted that readability formulas, on their own, are insufficient for matching books with students. They suggest that teachers do the following:

readability formula
A formula that indicates the difficulty of textual material in terms of a reading grade level; uses factors such as the number of syllables and sentences in a passage.

- evaluate proposed texts based on knowledge of their students' prior information, experiences, reading abilities, and interests
- observe students using proposed texts in instructional settings to evaluate the effectiveness of the material
- use checklists for evaluating the readability of proposed materials, paying attention to variables such as student interests, text graphics, number of ideas and concepts in the material, length of lines in the text, and other factors that contribute to the relative difficulty of textual material

Although several readability formulas are available, all are similar in their manner of analyzing textual difficulty. Two factors are usually considered in determining difficulty level: word difficulty and sentence difficulty. To determine word difficulty, many readability formulas follow the premise that longer words are more difficult. Thus, by extension, difficult words contain more syllables than easier words. For that reason, many formulas require that the number of syllables in a given sample of text be counted. Other formulas compare the words in the sample material to a specific word list and that list guides the estimate of word difficulty.

To determine sentence difficulty, readability formulas use similar logic, reasoning that longer sentences are more difficult. Thus, many readability formulas require that the number of sentences in a given sample of material be counted. A small number suggests that the sentences are long and thus difficult. The relationship between the number of syllables and the number of sentences is often used to determine the approximate reading grade level (RGL) of the text being evaluated.

Readability formulas are more accurate at higher grade levels (that is, above second grade) because most materials written for lower grade levels use a relatively limited set of words, many words of one syllable, and relatively short sentences. In addition, reading selections for young students are usually quite short. For a readability measure to be valid, however, a continuous passage of approximately 100 words should be used, and it is strongly suggested that at least three representative passages from several sections of the material be averaged to estimate the overall reading grade level. Thus, some formulas specifically state that they are not intended for use below certain grade levels, whereas others may be used throughout a broad range of grades. (Fry [1990] has proposed a formula for use with passages as short as 80 words, but that formula must also be used with care when evaluating beginning reading materials.)

A Common Readability Measure. A popular readability measure, the Fry Readability Scale, is shown in Figure 11-12, along with directions for its use. The Fry scale's popularity results from its ease of use and its wide range of grade levels. Try using the Fry scale to estimate the reading grade level of the following passage (Williams, 1973). For your information, 100 words precede the double slash mark. (The answer is given at the end of this section.)

> That evening they all had dinner together in the enchanter's cozy kitchen. Then Albion took Petronella out to a stone building and unbolted its door. Inside were seven huge black dogs.
> "You must watch my hounds all night," said he.
> Petronella went in, and Albion closed and locked the door.
> At once the hounds began to snarl and bark. They showed their teeth at her. But Petronella was a real princess. She plucked up her courage. Instead of backing away, she went toward the dogs. She began to speak to them in a quiet voice. They stopped snarling and sniffed // at her.

FIGURE 11-12 *The Fry Readability Scale*

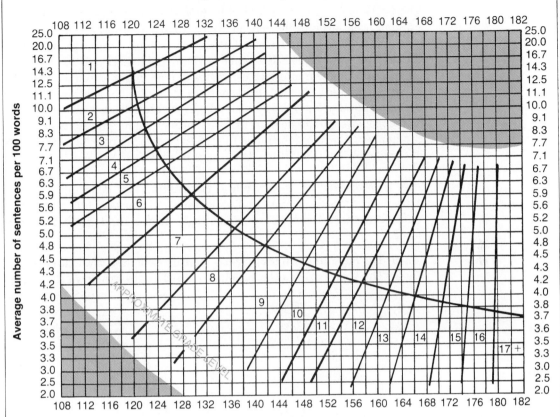

Average number of syllables per 100 words

Expanded Directions for Working Readability Graph

1. Randomly select three (3) sample passages and count out exactly 100 words each, beginning with the beginning of a sentence. Do count proper nouns, initializations, and numerals.
2. Count the number of sentences in the hundred words, estimating length of the fraction of the last sentence to the nearest one-tenth.
3. Count the total number of syllables in the 100-word passage. If you don't have a hand counter available, an easy way is to simply put a mark above every syllable over one in each word, then when you get to the end of the passage, count the number of marks and add 100. Small calculators can also be used as counters by pushing numeral 1, then push the + sign for each word or syllable when counting.
4. Enter graph with *average* sentence length and *average* number of syllables; plot dot where the two lines intersect. Area where dot is plotted will give you the approximate grade level.
5. If a great deal of variability is found in syllable count or sentence count, putting more samples into the average is desirable.
6. A word is defined as a group of symbols with a space on either side; thus, *Joe, IRA, 1945,* and *&* are each one word.
7. A syllable is defined as a phonetic syllable. Generally, there are as many syllables as vowel sounds. For example, *stopped* is one syllable and *wanted* is two syllables. When counting syllables for numerals and initializations, count one syllable for each symbol. For example, *1945* is four syllables, *IRA* is three syllables, and *&* is one syllable.

Source: From E. Fry, Fry's Readability Graph: Clarifications, Validity, and Extension to Level 17, *Journal of Reading, 21* (1977), pp. 242–252. (Reproduction permitted. No copyright.)

There are, of course, other highly regarded readability formulas: for example, the formula by Spache (1953, 1976), appropriate for Grades 1 through 3; by Dale and Chall (1948), for Grades 4 through 6; and by Flesch (1948), for Grades 5 and above. Many publishers and other private businesses offer computerized estimates of readability, based on a variety of such formulas. Readability analyses can also be performed using microcomputers. There is commercially available software, as well as free or inexpensive public domain (that is, without copyright) software, that can apply one or more formulas to a passage (see chapter 14). [The reading grade level of the Petronella passage is early fourth grade.]

The Limitations of Readability Formulas. The following sentence pairs illustrate some factors that make texts more or less difficult to read. Which sentence in each pair would be easier for a second grader to understand?

1. (a) The boy ran down the street.   (b) The boy ran down the street.
2. (a) The boy ran down the street.   (b) The boy ran down the street.

3. (a) The boy ran down the street.   (b) Down the street ran the boy.
4. (a) The boy ran down the long,   (b) The boy ran down the street.
       busy street.   The street was busy. The street
                                            was long.

In each of the pairs, the first sentence is generally considered to be easier to understand than the second. Such things as print size, supportive illustrations, and word order do affect reading difficulty, yet those factors are not considered when a formula is used. In addition, short sentences do not always facilitate comprehension: 4(a) is easier for a second grader to read than 4(b) (Pearson, 1974-1975). But readability formulas usually equate length with difficulty.

Conceptual difficulty and background knowledge are other aspects of reading that formulas do not address, and misleading estimates can sometimes result. For example, because readability formulas generally assume that more syllables imply greater difficulty, a formula would consider *television* a more difficult word than *vector,* even though second graders would have much less trouble understanding *television*. Because of these limitations several proposals are being introduced that have the potential for more precise estimation of readability, both with and without the use of formulas (for example, see Zakaluk and Samuels, 1988).

Nonetheless, readability formulas provide an easy-to-use method of estimating the relative difficulty of reading materials. If carefully and thoughtfully interpreted, readability formulas can provide an indication of the RGL of a specific piece of text. We must remember, however, that formulas can be fooled, especially at lower grade levels, where reading selections often become more difficult as the reader moves through a book. Thus, the readability of a passage at the beginning of a book might be different from that of a passage at the end—just one more reason to use multiple passages and average the results.

Additional Considerations

When evaluating materials, teachers often supplement readability formulas with other information. A form that considers readability as well as other data is presented in Figure 11-13. Such a form should be used with the realization that not all the items apply to every type of reading material. For example, deductive and inductive presentation methods would not apply to narrative reading material. Thus, only items that pertain to the material under consideration need to be addressed. In addition, when materials are compared, it is important that they be from similar domains. For example, it is not appropriate to compare a children's literature book with a content-area textbook. The form in Figure 11-13 identifies many factors that teachers might consider important in the selection of reading materials, and it can help in decision making. Others (for example, Bell & Davey, 1994) have also provided tools and procedures for evaluating the interaction of readers and textbooks.

CELEBRATING DIVERSITY THROUGH ASSESSMENT

Through informal assessment such as IRIs and think-alouds, and through formal, diagnostic tests that must be individually administered, you will come into close contact with all of the students in your class and will come to know each of your students' individual strengths, needs, and challenges. Whenever you use formal, informal, or teacher-made assessment tools, you will clearly notice the diversity in your classroom. Noticing diversity through assessment often results in teachers moving toward interactive beliefs for how people read, and toward integrated beliefs for how children learn to read. Assessment emphasizes that some children need more guidance in developing higher-level components of the reading process, such as prior knowledge, while others need more guidance in developing lower-level components such as decoding or syntactic knowledge. It is difficult to take the extreme positions on the literacy framework when acknowledging the diverse nature of learning and reading that are highlighted through assessment. Interactive beliefs imply that

FIGURE 11-13

Material analysis form

Title _____

Author _____

Publisher _____

A. *Readability*

Formula used _____

Reading grade level _____, which is

(1) appropriate	5 points
(2) more than one grade off	3 points
(3) one grade off	2 points

B. Rate all appropriate items in this section using a scale of 1 through 5, with 1 being unsatisfactory and 5 being excellent.

Literary style

Use of topic sentences _____

Use of technical terms _____

Sentence complexity _____

Appropriate summaries _____

General appearance

Total selection size _____

Print size and quality _____

Eye appeal _____

Durability _____

Comments:

Content

Suitable for chosen objective _____

Up-to-date (current and accurate) _____

Appropriate to students' readiness _____

Appropriate to students' interests _____

Treatment of controversial subjects _____

Comments:

Illustrations

Modern, generally of high quality _____

Useful for learning and discussion _____

Matching the written text _____

Comments:

Organization of content

Use of underlying theme _____

Logical units, subunits _____

Logical chapter/heading sequence _____

Comments:

Supplementary materials/learning aids

Table of contents _____

Appendices _____

Glossary _____

Suggested activities _____

References _____

Teacher's guide (appropriate) _____

Teacher's guide (easy to use) _____

Comments:

all components of reading are important, and thus facilitate modifying instruction to meet individual needs.

For example, it is clear that individuals from certain cultures are disadvantaged by standardized tests, and teachers need to closely examine standardized tests (a) to see if the norm group is reflective of the students being examined, and (b) to see if test items are realistic in their expectations for bicultural students. If either the norm group appears inappropriate, or if a significant number of test items appear to require knowledge that would not be available to certain groups of students, then that test should not be used. Realistically, however, teachers may have little

FIGURE 11-13 *continued*

C. *Presentation of content* (check primary mode of presentation)

Authoritarian presentation _____	Prescriptive presentation _____
Deductive presentation _____	Inductive presentation _____
Type of text: expository _____	Narrative _____

D. *Background knowledge demands*

Note background knowledge requirements
(e.g., prior knowledge, mathematical concepts,
prerequisite course work or reading)

_____

_____

E. *Other comments*

F. *Overall rating*

1. (a) Count the number of ratings given in Section B.   _____
   (b) Multiply by 5.   x 5 _____
   (c) Enter the result.   _____
   (d) Add 5 (from Section A).   + 5 _____
   (e) Enter the result. This is the total possible points.   _____
2. (a) Add all of the numerical ratings given in Section B.   _____
   (b) Add the appropriate points from Section A.   + _____
   (c) Enter the result. This is the raw score.   _____
3. (a) Divide 2(c) by 1(e). Enter the result.   _____
   (b) Multiply by 100.   x 100 _____
   (c) Enter the result. This percentage can be used to
       compare similar materials.   _____ %

Source: From *Effective Reading Instruction: K–8.* Second Edition, by Donald J. Leu, Jr., and Charles K. Kinzer. Copyright 1991 by Macmillan Publishing Company. Permission is granted by the publisher to reproduce Figure 11–14 for student record-keeping purposes.

choice about mandated assessments in their school districts. If this is the case, then instructional decisions should not be made solely on test scores from these instruments. You must realize that some students will be reading at levels significantly higher than their standardized test scores.

In some ways, informal assessments are more difficult to evaluate in terms of cultural bias than are formal assessment tools. When using informal reading inventories, cloze procedures, or running records it might be more difficult to determine the existence of cultural bias, especially in terms of background knowledge assumptions. For example, an IRI might include a passage about rodeos, with both factual and inferential questions asked at the end of the passage. Although factual questions can often be answered from one's knowledge of syntax, or sentence structure (syntax, for example, enables you to answer "Where is the zokat?" after reading "The zokat is in the pikzet!") students from different cultural groups or different first-language backgrounds might not be familiar with English sentence patterns. These students would have greater difficulty in answering factual questions. Different sentence structures are common, especially in English as a Second Language learners. Spanish, for example, commonly has a subject-object-verb sentence structure, while subject-verb-object order is more common in English.

Similarly, inferential questions are answered using a combination of background knowledge and text information. For example, knowing that a zokat goes into a pikzet when hungry allows one to answer the inferential question "What do you think the zokat is doing in the pikzet?" (probably eating). But students without such background knowledge would have difficulty fully comprehending such a text. To go back to the rodeo example in an IRI, students who might not have prior knowledge of rodeos, perhaps because they come from other countries or cultures that do not include rodeos, might have significant difficulty in answering the factual and/or inferential questions about a rodeo passage. Similar problems might occur in any text that is chosen for a cloze procedure or a running record.

Thus, teachers must be aware of equity issues, especially in informal performance assessments. However, addressing equity issues requires more than selecting culturally representative materials (Villegas, 1990). Consider Gitomer's (1993) comment that

> there must be a fundamental understanding and respect for the ways in which members of different social groups communicate, particularly as this affects performance. For example, the reticence of one group in certain situations may be a function of social values . . . . Cultural differences may affect the ways in which one formulates a problem or develops a solution (p. 260).

Issues of diversity in assessment might also be highlighted if your classroom includes physically challenged or learning disabled students. These students often require special arrangements in terms of environment (perhaps a quieter, less distracting area), additional time to complete a task such as a writing sample or reading passage, or leeway in interpreting pronunciation when analyzing miscues. Pronunciation factors due to dialect variation, of course, have been discussed earlier and should not be counted as miscues when assessing students who speak a nonstandard dialect.

Finally, you should take advantage of the diversity you will find in your classroom in any number of ways. Your assessment program will show that each student has strengths, and using method frameworks such as jigsaw procedures within co-operative learning groups (see chapter 10) can show students that each of them can make a valuable contribution to the class and to their own learning. This is especially true for nonnative speakers, who can extend the background knowledge of standard-English speakers while acquiring new knowledge and skills themselves.

THE ROLE OF A LITERACY FRAMEWORK IN ASSESSMENT

A literacy framework plays a significant role in selecting an assessment tool and in interpreting results. Teachers with more of a holistic language explanation of learning to read tend to be less satisfied with traditional assessment tools, especially standardized tests that use short test items and require multiple choice, fill-in-the-blank, or true/false responses. Holistic language perspectives are more consistent with measures that are more holistic, that present items in context, that are based on what students are reading, and that do not attempt to split reading into closely defined subskills. Teachers with more of a specific skills explanation for literacy learning tend to be more satisfied with assessment procedures that facilitate the examination of various reading subskills. Teachers with integrated beliefs are likely to combine assessment tools, using formal tests that examine specific skills as well as less formal, more holistic tools (see Table 11-3).

Although selecting assessment tools is clearly related to one's literacy framework, interpreting assessment results and making instructional decisions based on those results are perhaps even more closely linked to literacy frameworks. When interpreting test results, teachers with more specific skills explanations about learning are more likely to focus on specific skills that are identified as weak and then to use that information to provide instruction in that specific area. Teachers with holistic language perspectives are more likely to be flexible in scoring, focusing on whether the reader understood the intent of a passage or looking for patterns of responses across skill areas. Integrated perspectives tend to result in merging components of reading and writing processes and guiding students to build up needed skills through authentic tasks that are grounded in larger literacy contexts. Similar types of decisions result from the various beliefs that relate to how one reads (see Table 11-4).

Regardless of a teacher's literacy framework, however, a test in and of itself is relatively meaningless, whether it be informal, teacher-made or formal, a process or a product measure. It will be your clear understanding of your assessment goals, together with your interpretation and use of test results, that will determine the value of assessment in your instructional situation.

TABLE 11-3

Assessment choices based on different beliefs about how children learn to read

Explanations for how children learn to read	Beliefs	Choice of assessment tools
Holistic language learning	Students direct much of their own learning and inductive learning is emphasized. Reading experiences always take place in the context of authentic social contexts and with authentic reading materials.	Assessment tends to focus on informal and alternative assessment tools, particularly those that are grounded in authentic literacy tasks. Think-alouds during reading and writing, IRIs and cloze tests taken or developed from classroom reading materials. "Kidwatching," self assessment and assessment of interests and attitudes are especially valued.
Integrated	Both student-directed and teacher-directed experiences are used. Both inductive and deductive learning are used. Reading experiences take place in the contexts of authentic social contexts and with authentic reading materials. Specific skills are taught when needed, often in mini-lessons.	A combination of assessment tools are used, including both formal and informal tests. Alternative assessment as well as more traditional tools are used and their information examined to make instructional decisions.
Specific skills	Teacher-directed reading activities and deductive learning are emphasized. Specific skills, often organized in terms of difficulty, are frequently taught.	Assessment tends to focus on tools that can delineate subskills of reading. Formal tests, either norm- or criterion-referenced tests, as well as IRIs that focus on decoding are valued.

TABLE 11-4

Assessment choices based on different beliefs about how one reads

Explanations for how one reads	Related assumptions	Probable focus of assessment
Reader-based explanations	Meaning exists more in what the reader brings to the text. Reading is a result of expectations. Reading begins with elements of prior knowledge.	Process assessment that examines the reader's ability to access and apply prior knowledge. Aesthetic responses are evaluated.
Interactive explanations	Meaning exists in both the text and the reader. Reading is both translation and expectation. Reading uses each knowledge source simultaneously.	Both process and product assessment would occur, in relatively equal amounts. Both aesthetic and efferent responses are evaluated.
Text-based explanations	Meaning exists more in the test. Reading is translation. Reading begins with decoding.	Product assessment to determine knowledge of the structural components of literacy. Decoding and literal meaning are emphasized. Efferent responses are evaluated. Assessment to determine whether the reader is comprehending the text's message, together with supporting details from the text.

Comments from the Classroom

Nikki Robinson, Sixth Grade Teacher

At the beginning of the year I use the short passages found in informal reading inventories to help establish each student's reading level, especially the point at which they become frustrated. While I truly believe in building on a student's strengths, sometimes miscue analysis can be very revealing. Miscue analysis requires students to read longer passages (a chapter or a complete book) aloud into a tape recorder. I try to use adult volunteers to sit with the children while they read. Then I listen to the tape with a photocopy of the chapter and record each reader's miscues.

Sometimes I don't have to listen to the entire chapter before a pattern emerges. Discovering the error patterns allows me to pinpoint areas that require remediation. Grid sheets can help organize miscues into semantic (word meaning) or syntactic (grammatical structure) patterns. This method of assessment allows me to group students who share problems or pair up students with different strengths, rather than doing blanket lessons with the entire class. Then I can target groups or pairs with specific strategies that can help them. Occasionally, the analysis suggests a relatively simple strategy. For example, readers often get so caught up in decoding that they forget to look at the illustration on a page for help with context. A quick glance at the picture can alert a student that "castle" is a more likely choice than "casting" or "candle."

As with all learning, students have fewer problems with stories for which they already have background knowledge. Once I thought a student was a much poorer reader than she was because the informal reading inventory passages were about the circus and rodeos—neither of which were part of her experiences. The interest inventory that she filled out as part of the informal reading inventory indicated that she liked birds. She chose an information book about birds for her miscue analysis. I was amazed at how she breezed through that book, even decoding some of the scientific terms with ease.

I have discovered that the lines between planning, assessment, and teaching blur as I have gained more experience. Assessing students' progress is a continuous mental activity for me. Assessment no longer means "test." Tests are now just one way for me to organize and validate my "kidwatching."

- Process assessment allows teachers to infer students' underlying processes. Product assessment provides an indication of students' performance without reference to how a score was achieved.

- Portfolios consist of a wide variety of student's work, performance, self-evaluation and other informal and formal items that are collected on a regular, ongoing basis. Examining the items in a portfolio can help document a student's growth and progress as well as provide an indication of specific areas that need support.

- Measurement instruments can be categorized as informal (for example, IRIs, running records, think-alouds, cloze tests, retellings); teacher made; or formal (for example, standardized, norm- or criterion-referenced tests). Alternative assessment is often thought of as informal; traditional assessment is often thought of as formal.

- Assessment instruments are used to evaluate readers, reading materials, and the interaction between readers and materials.

- Assessment is a good indicator of the diversity found in a classroom and can provide guidelines to celebrate the challenges presented by different students' respective strengths and weaknesses.

1. At some point in your teaching career, you will probably be asked to recommend a reading test for use in your classroom, or you may be asked to serve on a committee that will choose a test for your school or school district. What would your criteria be? What should a good test do? What would you look for in a test?

2. Interview a teacher, a parent, and a school principal. Ask them to describe how they view testing and how they use or what they think about test results. How do the goals and uses of testing differ among these people? What implications do these differences have for you as a future teacher?

3. Try to find a teacher who uses portfolio evaluation (you might ask a professor or a principal to recommend someone). Interview the teacher, and ask how the portfolio is used in instructional decision making. Ask whether you might see a student's work. If so, try to describe that student's progress from what appears in the portfolio.

4. Interview both a primary and an intermediate grade teacher. Ask about the different kinds of measurement that are used in their classrooms. What are the purposes of each kind and how do they help in instructional decision-making?

5. Choose two passages from two different published reading programs, and perform a readability analysis, using the Fry scale. Compare your results with the readability information provided in the teacher's manual of each program. What are some of the reasons that a mismatch might occur?

6. Borrow a copy of a published IRI from your library. Using the checklist for IRI administration, included in this chapter, and the information provided in the IRI's manual, practice giving that IRI to a second-grade student and a fourth-grade student. How did you have to change your administrative techniques to account for the differences in the students' grade level? Practice until you feel comfortable with the scoring system.

7. Construct a cloze test for use with elementary students or with some of your college-age friends. Choose appropriate materials for your practice group. Administer your test. Analyze the results.

8. Describe your view of testing, and relate it to your literacy framework. Specify how you might use assessment to make instructional decisions in your own classroom.

Further Reading

Baumann, J. F. (1988). *Reading assessment: An instructional decision-making perspective.* Columbus, OH: Merrill.

A comprehensive paperback discussing most aspects of reading assessment. Numerous examples of tests as well as discussions of test interpretation. Includes checklists and forms for choosing tests and setting assessment goals.

Bell, R., & Davey, B. (1994). Assessing students' skills in using textbooks: The textbook awareness and performance profile (TAPP). *Journal of Reading, 37,* 280–286.

Provides a detailed tool for assessing students' use of textbooks and discusses instruction that can occur based on the findings.

Eeds, M. (1988). Holistic assessment of coding ability. In S. M. Glazer, L. W. Searfoss, & L. M. Gentile (Eds.), *Reexamining reading diagnosis: New trends and procedures* (pp. 48–66). Newark, DE: International Reading Association.

Provides a basis for holistic evaluation of coding, including several sets of guidelines that teachers can use when examining children's writing.

Farr, R., & Tone, B. (1994). *Portfolio and performance assessment.* New York: Harcourt Brace College Publishers.

A paperback that discusses issues surrounding portfolio and performance assessment, and that provides scoring systems, checklists, and guidelines for interpreting and reporting students' progress.

Glazer, S. M., & Brown, C. S. (1993). *Portfolios and beyond: Collaborative assessment in reading and writing*. Norwood, MA: Christopher Gordon Publishers.

A short paperback that examines alternative assessment. Provides background, rationale, and guidelines for alternative assessment of reading and writing, including think-alouds, retellings, and collaborative reporting that links students, teachers, and parents.

Paris, S. G., Calfee, R. C., Filby, N., Hiebert, E. H., Pearson, P. D., Valencia, S. W., Wolf, K. P. (1992). A framework for authentic literacy assessment. *The Reading Teacher, 46,* 88–98.

Summarizes a research report, initially supported as a federally funded project, that provides a framework for authentic literacy assessment.

Shearer, A. P., & Homan, S. P. (1994). Linking reading assessment to instruction: An application worktext for elementary classroom teachers. New York: St. Martin's Press.

A looseleaf-sized paperback that discusses evaluation and includes a large number of scoring / reporting forms, tests, and discussions of their use and limitations.

Traill, L. (1993). *Highlight my strengths: Assessment and evaluation of literacy learning*. Crystal Lake, IL: Rigby Education.

A teacher-oriented paperback that provides guidelines for several informal assessments and includes record-keeping forms for summarizing ongoing, cumulative learning in reading and writing.

Valencia, S. (1990). A portfolio approach to classroom reading assessment: The whys, whats, and hows. *The Reading Teacher, 43,* 338–340.

Outlines the benefit of portfolio assessment, describes what should be included, and discusses its use.

References

Allington, R. L., Chodos, L., Domaracki, J., & Truex, S. (1977). Passage dependency: Four diagnostic oral reading tests. *The Reading Teacher, 30,* 393–395.

Aulls, M. W. (1982). *Developing readers in today's elementary schools*. Boston: Allyn & Bacon.

Barrs, M., Ellis, S., Hester, H., & Thomas, A. (1989). *The primary language record: Handbook for teachers*. Portsmouth, NH: Heinemann Educational Books.

Bell, R., & Davey, B. (1994). Assessing students' skills in using textbooks: The textbook awareness and performance profile (TAPP). *Journal of Reading, 37,* 280–286.

Betts, E. A. (1946). *Foundations of reading instruction*. New York: American Book.

Bormuth, J. R. (1968). The cloze readability procedure. In J. R. Bormuth (Ed.), *Readability in 1968* (pp. 40–47). Champaign, IL: NCTE.

Burns, P. C., Roe, B. D., & Ross, E. P. (1988). *Teaching reading in today's elementary schools* (4th ed.). Boston: Houghton Mifflin.

Calfee, R. C. (1987). The school as a context for assessment of literacy. *The Reading Teacher, 40,* 738–743.

Carson, J. (1990). Unpublished manuscript.

Clark, C. H. (1982). Assessing free recall. *The Reading Teacher, 35,* 434–439.

Clay, M. (1985). *The early detection of reading difficulties* (3rd ed.). Portsmouth, NH: Heinemann-Boynton/Cook.

Cooper, J. L. (1952). *The effect of adjustment of basal reading materials on reading achievement*. Unpublished doctoral dissertation, Boston University.

CTGV (1993 March). Anchored instruction and situated cognition revisited. *Educational Technology,* 52–70.

Dale, E., & Chall, J. S. (1948). A formula for predicting readability. *Educational Research Bulletin* (Ohio State University), *27,* 11–20; *28,* 37–54.

Duffelmeyer, F. A., & Duffelmeyer, B. B. (1989). Are IRI passages suitable for assessing main idea comprehension? *The Reading Teacher, 42,* 358–363.

Dulin, K. L. (1984). Assessing reading interests of elementary and middle school students. In A. J. Harris & E. R. Sipay (Eds.), *Readings on reading instruction* (pp. 346–357). New York: Longman.

Dulin, K. L., & Chester, R. (1984). *Dulin-Chester Reading Attention Scale/Reading Interest Questionnaire.* Madison: University of Wisconsin.

Eeds, M. (1988). Holistic assessment of coding ability. In S. M. Glazer, L. W. Searfoss, & L. M. Gentile (Eds.), *Reexamining reading diagnosis: New trends and procedures.* Newark, DE: International Reading Association.

Englert, C. S., & Semmel, M. I. (1981). The relationship of oral reading substitution miscues to comprehension. *The Reading Teacher, 35,* 273–280.

Farris, J. (1989). From basal reader to whole language: Transition tactics. *Reading Horizons, 30,* 23–28.

Flesch, R. F. (1948). A new readability yardstick. *Journal of Applied Psychology, 32,* 221–223.

Flesch, R. F. (1949). *The art of readable writing.* New York: Harper.

Fry, E. (1990). A readability formula for short passages. *The Reading Teacher, 33,* 594–597.

Gardner, H., & Hatch, T. (1989). Multiple intelligences go to school: Educational implications of the theory of multiple intelligences. *Educational Researcher, 18*(8), 4–10.

Gentile, L. M., & McMillan, M. M. (1987). *Stress and reading difficulties: Research, assessment, intervention.* Newark, DE: International Reading Association.

Gentile, L. M., & McMillan, M. M. (1988). Reexamining the role of emotional maladjustment. In S. M. Glazer, L. W. Searfoss, & L. M. Gentile (Eds.), *Reexamining reading diagnosis: New trends and procedures* (pp. 12–28). Newark, DE: International Reading Association.

Gentry, J. R. (1982). An analysis of developmental spelling in GNYS AT WRK. *The Reading Teacher, 36,* 192–200.

Gifford, B. R. (1990). *Report of the National Commission on Testing and Public Policy.* Chestnut Hill, MA: Boston College.

Gitomer, D. H. (1993). Performance assessment and educational measurement. In R. E. Bennett & W. C. Ward (Eds.), *Construction versus choice in cognitive measurement: Issues in constructed response, performance testing, and portfolio assessment* (pp. 241–240). Hillsdale, NY: Lawrence Erlbaum Associates.

Glazer, S. M., & Brown, C. S. (1993). *Portfolios and beyond: Collaborative assessment in reading and writing.* Norwood, MA: Christopher Gordon Publishers.

Goodman, K. S., & Buck, C. (1973). Dialect barriers to reading comprehension revisited. *The Reading Teacher, 27,* 6–12.

Harp, B. (1989). "When you do whole language instruction, how will you keep track of reading and writing skills?" *The Reading Teacher, 42,* 160–161.

Harris, A. J., & Sipay, E. R. (1990). *How to increase reading ability: A guide to developmental and remedial methods* (9th ed.). New York: Longman.

Herman, J. L., Aschbacher, P. R., & Winters, L. (1992). *A practical guide to alternative assessment.* Alexandria, VA: Association for Supervision and Curriculum Development.

IRA, NCTE take stand on readability formulae. (December 1984-January 1985). *Reading Today, 2,* 1.

IRA/NCTE Joint Task Force on Assessment. (1994). *Standards for the assessment of reading and writing.* Newark, DE: International Reading Association.

Johns, J. L., & Kuhn, M. K. (1983). The informal reading inventory: 1910–1980. *Reading World, 23,* 8–19.

Johnson, M. S., Kress, R. A., & Pikulski, J. J. (1987). *Informal reading inventories* (2nd ed.). Newark, DE: International Reading Association.

Johnston, P. H. (1983). *Reading comprehension assessment: A cognitive basis.* Newark, DE: International Reading Association.

Johnston, P. (1987). Teachers as evaluation experts. *The Reading Teacher, 40,* 744–748.

Johnston, P. H. (1992). *Constructive evaluation of literate activity.* White Plains, NY: Longman.

Jongsma, E. (1980). *Cloze instruction research: A second look.* Newark, DE: International Reading Association.

Jongsma, K. S. (1989). Portfolio assessment. *The Reading Teacher, 42,* 264–265.

Lapp, J., & Flood, D. (1989). Reporting reading progress: A comparison portfolio for parents. *The Reading Teacher, 42,* 508–514.

Mehrens, W. A., & Lehman, I. J. (1984). *Measurement and evaluation in education and psychology* (3rd ed.). New York: Holt, Rinehart & Winston.

Morrow, L. M. (1988). Retelling stories as a diagnostic tool. In S. M. Glazer, L. W. Searfoss, & L. M. Gentile (Eds.), *Reexamining reading diagnosis: New trends and procedures* (pp. 128–138). Newark, DE: International Reading Association.

Nickerson, R. S. (1989). New directions in educational assessment. *Educational Researcher, 18*(9), 3–7.

Nitko, A. J. (1980). Distinguishing the many varieties of criterion-referenced tests. *Review of Educational Research, 50,* 461–485.

Pearson, D. (1974–1975). The effects of grammatical complexity on children's comprehension, recall and conception of certain semantic relations. *Reading Research Quarterly, 10,* 155–192.

Pikulski, J. J. (1989). The assessment of reading: A time for change? *The Reading Teacher, 42,* 80–81.

Popham, W. J. (1978). *Criterion referenced measurement.* Englewood Cliffs, NJ: Prentice Hall.

Powell, W. R. (1970). Reappraising the criteria for interpreting informal reading inventories. In J. DeBoer (Ed.), *Reading diagnosis and evaluation.* Newark, DE: International Reading Association.

Rankin, E. F. (1971). Grade level interpretations of cloze readability scores. In F. Greene (Ed.), *The right to participate.* Milwaukee, WI: National Reading Conference.

Rankin, E. F. (1974). The cloze procedure revisited. In P. L. Nacke (Ed.), *Interaction: Research and practice in college-adult reading* (23rd NRC Yearbook). Clemson, SC: National Reading Conference.

Rankin, E. F. (1978). Characteristics of the cloze procedure as a research tool in the study of language. In P. D. Pearson & J. Hanson (Eds.), *Reading: Disciplined inquiry in process and practice* (pp. 148–153). Clemson, SC: National reading Conference.

Rankin, E. F., & Culhane, J. W. (1969). Comparable cloze and multiple choice comprehension test scores. *Journal of Reading, 13,* 193–198.

Ruddell, R. B., & Kinzer, C. K. (1982). Test preferences and competencies of field educators. In J. Niles & L. Harris (Eds.), *New inquiries in reading research and instruction.* Rochester, NY: National Reading Conference.

Siegler, R. S. (1989). Strategy diversity and cognitive assessment. *Educational Researcher, 18*(9), 15–20.

Silvaroli, N. J. (1994). *Classroom Reading Inventory* (7th ed.). Dubuque, IA: Brown & Benchmark.

Spache, G. S. (1953). A new readability formula for primary grade reading material. *Elementary English, 53,* 410–413.

Spache, G. S. (1976). The new Spache readability formula. In *Good reading for poor readers* (pp. 195–207). Champaign, IL: Garrard.

Stiggins, R. (in press). *Classroom assessment for teaching and learning.* Columbus, OH: Macmillan.

Taylor, W. L. (1953). Cloze procedures: A new tool for measuring readability. *Journalism Quarterly, 30,* 415–433.

Tierney, R. J., Carter, M. A., & Desai, L. E. (1991). *Portfolio assessment in the reading-writing classroom.* Norwood, MA: Christopher Gordon Publishers.

Traill, L. (1993). *Highlight my strengths: Assessment and evaluation of literacy learning.* Crystal Lake, IL: Rigby Education.

Tuinman, J. J. (1974). Determining the passage-dependency of comprehension questions in 5 major tests. *Reading Research Quarterly, 9,* 207–223.

Valencia, S., & Pearson, P. D. (1987). Reading assessment: Time for a change. *The Reading Teacher, 40,* 726–735.

Villegas, A. M. (1990). *Culturally responsive pedagogy for the 1990s and beyond.* Princeton, NJ: Educational Testing Service.

Wade, S. E. (1990). Using think-alouds to assess comprehension. *The Reading Teacher, 43,* 44–53.

Warwick, G. E. (1978). Cloze procedures as applied to reading. In O. K. Buros (Ed.), *Eighth mental measurements yearbook* (vol. 2, pp. 1174–1176). Highland Park, NJ: Gryphon Press.

Williams, J. (1973). *Petronella.* New York: Scholastic.

Wittrock, M. C. (1987). Process oriented measures of comprehension. *The Reading Teacher, 40,* 734–737.

Wixson, K. K., Bosky, A. B., Yochum, N., & Alvermann, D. E. (1984). An interview for assessing students' perceptions of classroom reading tasks. *The Reading Teacher, 37,* 346–352.

Yancey, K. B. (Ed.). (1992). *Portfolios in the writing classroom: An introduction.* Urbana, IL: National Council of Teachers of English.

Zakaluk, B. L., & Samuels, S. J. (Eds.). (1988). *Readability: Its past, present, & future.* Newark, DE: International Reading Association.

CHAPTER

Including All Children In Your Reading Program

12

"I was so surprised after I visited an inclusive classroom today for the first time. At the end of the day I could not tell which children had been labeled as 'special education' or 'at-risk' and which had not. In fact, I wasn't even certain if there were any 'special ed' or 'at-risk' kids in this classroom, even though I knew you had me visit to observe how these students function within a regular classroom. When I asked the teacher about this after school, she beamed at me and said, 'That's just the way it should be, shouldn't it?'"

A classroom observational journal entry from a sophomore
student in a teacher education program.

Several recent trends require today's teacher of reading to be prepared to work with a wider range of students than ever before. We are witnessing an increasing respect for the unique needs of all students. Today, federal and state legislation require schools to provide a free and appropriate public education for all students, including those who are in need of special educational support. In addition, a Regular Education Initiative is being debated around the country as educators attempt to serve the needs of special education youngsters within regular classrooms. Students who were formally excluded from regular school classrooms are increasingly being served in what are coming to be called "inclusive classrooms." But the movement is not only being directed by federal legislation and policy debates. Increasingly, teachers themselves are finding important benefits for all children when they include youngsters who were previously excluded from regular classrooms. Consequently, it is imperative that teachers understand the unique reading needs of all types of students. This understanding will allow you to take advantage of the new opportunities for forming collaborative communities in your classroom. This chapter will help develop that understanding and provide instructional suggestions about how to develop a community in your classroom that supports the learning of all children.

Chapter 12 includes information that will help you answer questions such as:

1. In what way is each student a student with special needs?
2. How should I adapt reading instruction to meet the needs of children with exceptionalities and create a classroom community that is supportive of all children?
3. How can my literacy framework guide instructional decisions as I teach reading to children with special needs?

KEY CONCEPTS

children with exceptionalities
contract reading
cross-age tutoring
The Education for All Handicapped
   Children Act (PL 94-142)
emotional disturbance
enrichment program
giftedness
hearing impairment
individualized education program (IEP)
The Individuals with Disabilities
   Education Act

inquiry reading
language disorders
learning disability
least restrictive environment (LRE)
mainstreamed
mental retardation
special education
speech disorders
VAKT approaches
visual impairment

OPPORTUNITIES TO CELEBRATE DIVERSITY

Having children with special needs in your classroom provides an opportunity to celebrate and learn about diversity as you work to develop inclusive communities. Working with special children provides opportunities for both you and your students, not an additional burden. If you want to prepare your students for the realities of contemporary life in a pluralistic society, you must seek out diversity for your classroom. Diverse classrooms help each of us learn more about ourselves and our society. You can do this by including each child into the full measure of life in your classroom community.

SPECIAL NEEDS: A POINT OF VIEW

Two thoughts should guide your consideration of children with special needs. The most important is that each of your students is, in fact, a student with special needs. Each and every student has unique needs that must be acknowledged as you make instructional decisions. You must always consider each student's background and abilities as you teach reading. Nothing is more important.

Reading Recovery, one of the more successful programs for children experiencing reading difficulty in the first year of instruction, demonstrates the importance of focusing on individual needs. In fact, Reading Recovery has achieved success specifically because it focuses so carefully on the unique needs of each student (Pinnell, Fried, & Estice, 1990). Specially trained teachers in the program provide a daily, thirty-minute lesson for individual students, following a five-step method framework but adjusting the lesson on a minute-to-minute basis to meet an individual student's needs. This unique focus on individual needs may be difficult for you to completely replicate with an entire class. Nonetheless, it is most important for you to always attempt to accomplish this during reading instruction.

The second point is related to the first: categorical designations used for pedagogical, legal, or administrative purposes must never limit your instructional decisions regarding individual children or your expectations for their achievement. Categorical designations for different populations appear in this chapter for three reasons: (1) because they are used in legal definitions for categorical aid programs; (2) because they are sometimes used for administrative purposes; and (3) because they facilitate your learning as a new teacher. However, you must never allow the use of categories by others outside your classroom to interfere with the individual learning needs of any child. Your instructional decisions must always take into account the unique differences of each individual in your classroom. The use of labels has brought significant benefits to students whose needs have too long been ignored, but we must ensure that those labels do not blind us to the individuality each of us expresses in our daily lives.

UNDERSTANDING THE HISTORY AND CONTEXT OF CHILDREN WITH EXCEPTIONALITIES

children with exceptionalities
Children unable to reach their full potential without services that go beyond the requirements of the average child.

Children with exceptionalities are unable to reach their full potential without services, instructional materials, and/or facilities that go beyond the requirements of the average child. Typically, this includes those who experience learning disablity, emotional disturbance, hearing impairment, visual impairment, speech or language disorders, mental retardation, and giftedness. According to federal estimates, approximately 13 to 16 percent of school-age children fall into at least one of these categories (Hallahan & Kauffman, 1982; Lerner, 1985; U.S. Department of Education, 1984).

special education
Services, materials, and/or facilities provided to help exceptional children reach their full potential.

Special education encompasses the educational services, materials, and/or facilities provided to help children with exceptionalities reach their full potential. The specific nature of special education varies along a continuum ranging from the least to the most restrictive environments, as shown in Figure 12-1. You can see from the figure that regular classroom teachers have opportunities to work with exceptional students in more than half of the environments described. Increasingly, special educational services are being provided entirely within **inclusive classrooms.** Therefore, it is important that all teachers understand special education and the needs of children with exceptionalities.

inclusive classrooms
Classrooms where exceptional students are included in the classroom community with other, non-exceptional students and receive their special instructional support within that classroom.

FIGURE 12-1

A continuum of special educational environments and services

Least Restrictive ⟶ **Most Restrictive**

1. An inclusive classroom with a classroom teacher who is trained in both regular and special education.
2. An inclusive classroom with a classroom teacher who works in consultation with a specialist in special education.
3. An inclusive classroom with a classroom team comprising the regular classroom teacher and one or more special education teachers who work together to meet the needs of all students.
4. Itinerant services provided by a special educator who regularly visits and teaches the exceptional child within the regular classroom. Itinerant teachers also make instructional suggestions to the regular classroom teacher.
5. Resource services provided by a special educator outside the classroom. Exceptional children receive instruction in a resource center for a portion of the day. The resource teacher also consults with the classroom teacher regarding instruction within the classroom.
6. Self-contained special education classrooms within the regular school for homogeneous classes of exceptional children.
7. Hospital or home-bound instruction by itinerant special education teachers.

PL 94-142: The Education for All Handicapped Children Act

The most important influence in the education of exceptional children has been a federal law passed in 1975—The Education for All Handicapped Children Act, or **PL** (Public Law) **94-142.** The most important provision of PL 94-142 states:

> In order to receive funds under the act every school system in the nation must make provision for a free, appropriate public education for every child . . . regardless of how, or how seriously, he may be handicapped.

This law contains two other provisions affecting classroom teachers of reading: the development of individualized education programs and placement in a least restrictive environment.

Individualized Education Programs

PL 94-142 requires that a multidisciplinary team of trained specialists evaluate each exceptional student and each potential exceptional student. This team submits a report to a case conference meeting, at which a representative from the school, the teacher, the parents, and other appropriate individuals develop an **individualized education program (IEP)** for each exceptional child. The IEP is used to guide instruction and monitor student progress. According to federal guidelines, an IEP must contain the following components:

PL 94-142
Federal legislation mandating a free and appropriate public education for all children, regardless of handicap.

individualized education program (IEP)
Instructional plans for each exceptional child that are used to guide instruction and monitor progress.

An individualized education program (IEP) for each exceptional child is developed at a case conference meeting.

- a statement of the present levels of educational performance
- a statement of annual goals, including short-term instructional objectives
- a statement of the specific educational services to be provided . . . and the extent to which [each] child will be able to participate in regular educational programs
- the projected date for initiation and anticipated duration of such services, and appropriate objective criteria and evaluation procedures and schedules for determining, on at least an annual basis, whether instructional objectives are being achieved (Education for All Handicapped Children Act of 1975, p. 3).

The Least Restrictive Environment

One of the most important decisions made at the case conference is the recommended instructional environment. Participants in that conference must state in the IEP the extent to which a handicapped child will be included in the regular classroom. PL 94-142 requires that handicapped children be placed in the **least restrictive environment (LRE)** possible, where maximum opportunity is provided for those students to engage in the full measure of school life, consistent with their educational needs. Thus, children should not be educated in a separate special education classroom if their needs can be adequately met in a regular classroom with outside instruction provided by a special educator. Other children should not leave the regular classroom for special assistance if their needs can be adequately met by the regular classroom teacher. In short, exceptional children are to be included in the mainstream of educational life.

The principle of LRE has been given a recent boost by an initiative of the federal government. This "regular education initiative" is an effort to review, coordinate, and improve mainstreaming in schools (Stainback & Stainback, 1989; Wood, 1992). Increasingly, the regular classroom is being viewed as the most appropriate and least restrictive environment for special education students who had formerly been excluded from these settings. As a result, the education of special education students is increasingly taking place within inclusive classrooms as regular and special educators work together to develop supportive learning communities for all students.

How will all of this affect you as a classroom teacher of reading? Should you have the opportunity to have an exceptional child in your classroom, you will be affected in three ways. First, you will be required to attend the case conference meeting and assist in planning the student's IEP.

Second, if the multidisciplinary team decides to mainstream your student for reading instruction, you will be responsible for implementing the IEP in your classroom. You may be totally responsible for reading instruction, you may work together with a special education teacher or support

least restrictive environment (LRE)
A learning environment in which maximum opportunity is provided for exceptional students to engage in the full measure of school life, consistent with their educational needs.

·· **EXPLORING DIVERSE POINTS OF VIEW** ·······························

Support for children with special needs is often provided in either a pull-out or a push-in program. Pull-out programs take students out of their regular classrooms to provide special services such as special education or remedial reading. They provide an opportunity for students and teacher to focus on specific instructional needs outside of the hustle and bustle of the child's classroom. Push-in programs provide such services to students within their regular classrooms, working with those students and their teachers in an inclusive classroom setting. Here, students and teachers have an opportunity to always connect their learning with what takes place within the classroom community. In addition, students are likely to feel more like a full member of the classroom society. Which model of support services do you favor? Why?

person in your classroom, or you may provide the instruction in consultation with a special education teacher, who may advise you about materials and methods.

Finally, you will be responsible for evaluating the degree to which your student has met the specified instructional objectives. With the multidisciplinary team you will then decide on new instructional objectives.

Individuals with Disabilities Education Act

Recently, federal legislation has been updated by the Individuals with Disabilities Act which has added several important new requirements for schools. These include the principle of zero rejection, the principle of nondiscriminatory evaluation, procedural due process, and parental and student participation. Each is important for you to consider as you prepare to work with children in classrooms.

The principle of zero rejection prohibits schools from excluding any student with a disability from a free and appropriate public education. Schools may not exclude any child from a free and appropriate public education no matter how severe that child's disability. Each district must provide for educating all of its students.

The principle of nondiscriminatory evaluation requires each school district to fairly evaluate students as they determine which students have a disability and which do not. Often, it has been the case that children from less advantaged populations have been identified as children with exceptionalities with higher frequencies than children from more advantaged populations. Often this appears to be due to cultural and/or linguistic biases that exist in many assessment instruments used to screen students into special education programs. Schools today are attempting to ensure that the assessment process used to identify children in need of special education does not discriminate on the bases of cultural or linguistic background.

In addition, schools are now required to provide due process to parents and children from the moment they begin the screening process into special educational services. The requirement of due process is an attempt to safeguard students and parents against any action of the school that may be harmful. Due process rights include the parents' right to sue in court in order to be certain that the appropriate services are provided for their child.

Finally, the Individuals with Disabilities Education Act requires schools to provide opportunities for parents and adolescent students to participate in designing and carrying out special education programs. Parents and adolescent students will be invited to participate in IEP conferences and their insights will be sought during the implementation of these plans.

GENERAL GUIDELINES FOR INCLUDING ALL STUDENTS IN YOUR CLASSROOM READING PROGRAM

Beyond accommodating a child's particular handicapping condition, reading instruction for students receiving special educational services does not differ substantially from the materials, methods, and activities described in previous chapters. Reading instruction for every student requires judicious selection from the range of instructional suggestions presented in this text. Nonetheless, the following suggestions should guide you as you integrate students receiving special educational services into your classroom reading program.

1. *Work actively to develop a sense of community in your classroom where each member is valued.* Try, whenever possible, to structure learning experiences in cooperative learning groups. In these settings, each student is supported by the experiences and knowledge that others bring to the group. Include literature selections about exceptionalities in your students' reading experiences and in your read-aloud sessions. Use these opportunities to initiate discussions about the concerns and feelings of all members of your classroom community. This focus will help your students respect the unique qualities of each member of the class. A list of appropriate selections can be found in Figure 12-2 on page 528. Finally, help students to recognize the unique contributions each member of your classroom community makes to the class.

2. *Capitalize on individual strengths.* When necessary, work around an exceptionality by taking advantage of the individual's strengths. A child with a hearing impairment, for example, may require a more visual approach than a child without one. Pictures might be needed to complement verbal definitions during vocabulary instruction.

3. *Ensure successful learning experiences.* Try to build success into your instruction by carefully considering what each child can be expected to do.

4. *Record and chart individual growth to demonstrate gains to students and parents.* Make individual growth more visible by listing

individual achievement and keeping examples of work in a portfolio. Recording growth makes it concrete and tangible.

5. *Establish an accepting and positive environment.* Praise success with enthusiasm; accept failure with tolerance. Realize that mistakes are an important part of learning. Try to compliment each child in your class each day, and encourage your students to do the same.

6. *Discuss your students' progress regularly with parents, special educators, and other teachers.* It is important to keep others informed of your work. It is also important to learn about ideas that may work from others. Keep a list of the ideas that others have found successful.

7. *Use background knowledge to make difficult learning tasks easier.* When a student experiences difficulty, redefine the content of the task to match the child's background knowledge. This modification will make the task easier and will lead to initial success. Once children have been successful and understand the nature of the task, have them try it with less familiar content.

8. *Do not continuously repeat unsuccessful learning experiences.* Be willing to change materials, strategies, and activities when a student has not been successful. Find other approaches that work and maintain them.

9. *Do not search for a single solution to reading difficulties.* Reading is a complicated developmental process. No single set of materials or activities will ever solve a reading problem.

10. *Provide independent reading opportunities.* Do not neglect independent reading experiences. All children need time to read for pleasure or personal information.

STUDENTS WITH LEARNING DISABILITIES

The term **learning disability** was first used in 1963 by Samuel Kirk to refer to children who, despite normal intelligence, had great difficulty learning in school. Since then, a variety of definitions have evolved, including these most common characteristics:

learning disability
A substantial gap between expected and actual achievement levels, which cannot be attributed to mental retardation or emotional disturbance.

- a substantial gap between expected achievement levels (based on intelligence scores) and actual performance in at least one academic subject area

- an uneven achievement profile, with achievement very high in some areas and very low in others

- low achievement levels that do not result from environmental factors

- low achievement levels that are not due to mental retardation or emotional disturbance

....

FIGURE 12-2

A selected bibliography of exceptionalities in children's literature

General

H. Bornstein (Ed.), *The Comprehensive Signed English Dictionary* (Washington, DC: Gallaudet College Press.)

B. B. Osman, *No One to Play with: The Social Side of Learning Disabilities* (New York: Random House)

J. Quicke, *Disability in Modern Children's Fiction* (Cambridge, MA: Brookline Books)

Physical disability

P. D. Frevert, *It's OK to Look at Jamie* (Mankato, MN: Creative Education)

M. W. Froehlich, *Hide Crawford Quick* (Boston: Houghton Mifflin)

D. J. Hamm, *Grandma Drives a Motor Bed* (Chicago: Albert Whitman)

L. Henriod, *Grandma's Wheelchair* (Chicago: Albert Whitman)

R. C. Jones, *Angie and Me* (New York: Macmillan)

C. Kaufman and C. Kaufman, *Rajesh* (Atheneum)

S. Kuklin, *Thinking Big* (New York: Lothrop)

M. McDonald, *The Potato Man* (Orchard Press)

K. Muldoon, *Princess Pooh* (Chicago: Albert Whitman)

B. Rabe, *The Balancing Girl* (New York: Dutton)

R. Roy, *Move Over, Wheelchairs Coming Through!* (Boston: Houghton Mifflin)

Mental retardation

A. Baldwin, *A Little Time* (New York: Viking Press)

B. Byars, *Summer of the Swans* (New York: Viking Press)

P. Hermes, *Who Will Take Care of Me?* (New York: Harcourt Brace Jovanovich)

N. Hopper, *Just Vernon* (New York: Dutton)

A. B. Lithfield, *Making Room for Uncle Joe* (Chicago: Albert Whitman)

H. Sobol, *My Brother Stephen Is Retarded* (New York: Macmillan)

B. R. Wright, *My Sister Is Different* (Milwaukee, WI: Raintree)

....

The federal definition is the most widely used.

> "Specific learning disability" means a disorder in one or more of the basic psychological processes involved in understanding or in using language, spoken or written, which may manifest itself in an imperfect ability to listen, think, speak, read, write, spell, or do mathematical calculations. The term includes such conditions as perceptual handicaps, brain injury, minimal brain dysfunction, dyslexia, and developmental aphasia. The term does not include children who have learning problems which are primarily the result of visual, hearing, or motor handicaps, of mental retardation or emotional disturbance, or of environmental, cultural, or economic disadvantage (*Federal Register* 42, p. 65083).

FIGURE 12-2 *continued*

Learning disabilities

L. Albert, *But I'm Ready to Go* (Scarsdale, NY: Bradbury Press)
J. Gilson, *Do Bananas Chew Gum?* (New York: Lathrop)
E. Hunter, *Sue Ellen* (New York: Houghton Mifflin)
J. Lasker, *He's My Brother* (Chicago: Albert Whitman)
D. B. Smith, *Kelly's Creek* (New York: Crowell)

Hearing impairment

R. Charlip and M. B. Charlip, *Hand Talk: An ABC of Finger Spelling and Sign Language* (New York: Four Winds Press)
J. W. Peterson, *I Have a Sister. My Sister Is Deaf* (New York: Harper & Row)
M. Riskind, *Apple Is My Sign* (Boston: Houghton Mifflin)
L. Rosen, *Just Like Everyone Else* (New York: Harcourt Brace Jovanovich)
B. Wolf, *Anna's Silent World* (Philadelphia, PA: Lippincott)

Visual impairment

C. Brighton, *My Hands, My World* (New York: Macmillan)
M. Cohen, *See You Tomorrow, Charles* (New York: Greenwillow)
H. Coutant, *The Gift* (New York: Knopf)
J. Little, *Listen for the Singing* (New York: E. P. Dutton)
P. MacLachlan, *Through Grandpa's Eyes* (New York: Harper & Row)
M. Mark, *Toba* (Scarsdale, NY: Bradbury Press)
S. Pearson, *Happy Birthday Grampie* (New York: Dial)
R. Radin, *Carver* (New York: Macmillan)
S. Sargent and D. Wirt, *My Favorite Place* (Abingdon)
J. Yalen, *The Seeing Stick* (New York: Thomas Y. Crowell)

Speech and language disorders

M. Christopher, *Glue Fingers* (Toronto: Little, Brown)
P. Fleischman, *The Half-a-Moon Inn* (New York: Harper & Row)
E. B. White, *The Trumpet of the Swan* (New York: Harper & Row)

Approximately 5 percent of school-age children are considered to have learning disabilities (U.S. Department of Education, 1984).

Learning Characteristics

Students with learning disabilities do not all share a common set of learning characteristics because different psychological processes are impaired in different children. The most common characteristic found in children with learning disablities is some disruption in language processing. Because reading is a language-based process, children with learning disabilities frequently have extreme difficulty learning how to read. Consequently, they may be more than two years behind grade level in reading achievement. Often they have trouble with automatic decoding and need additional instruction to acquire that skill (Harris & Sipay, 1990).

Other characteristics are also likely to appear and should be accommodated during instruction.

- *Perceptual-motor problems.* Students may lack both fine- and gross-motor coordination. They may appear clumsy. Writing is often labored and hard to read. Many reversals appear in letter formation (for example, *d* for *b, z* for *s*) and letter order (for example, *tac* for *cat*), persisting beyond the age of seven or eight. They may often confuse similar appearing words (for example, *saw* for *was*).
- *Attention problems.* Students may have short attention spans. They may be easily distracted and have difficulty completing regular class assignments on time.
- *Lack of effective learning and problem-solving strategies.* Students may not be aware of effective strategies for learning and problem solving.

Adapting Learning Environments

At least three general categories of instructional approaches have been used to teach reading to children experiencing a learning disability: language-based approaches; visual, auditory, kinesthetic, and tactile (VAKT) approaches; and behavior modification approaches.

language-based approaches
Instruction that provides functional reading experiences with extensive writing and oral language opportunities.

Language-based approaches have recently been suggested for children experiencing reading disabilities. Such approaches provide functional reading experiences in motivating and pleasurable environments, usually with children's literature and extensive writing experiences. The most practical and clear set of recommendations for classroom teachers has been provided by Ford and Ohlhausen (1988), who make the following suggestions:

- Focus on real, meaningful learning through the use of themes.
- Maximize the participation of readers by using whole language activities which capitalize on their strong oral language skills.
- Implement whole room activities which have built-in individualization . . . [such as] Sustained Silent Reading and journal writing.
- Use open ended projects which allow students to contribute at various levels with various skills . . . [such as] the publication of a class newspaper and the production of a drama.
- Plan writing activities which allow individuals to respond at their own levels . . . [such as] using patterned stories and poetry. . . .

- Use group incentives and internal competition to motivate readers.

- Implement a cross-grade arrangement with a group of younger students.

- Organize and participate in a support group with other teachers who work with readers experiencing a learning disability. (pp. 18–22)

Students with learning disabilities typically receive additional reading instruction from a resource teacher, a learning disability specialist, or a reading specialist. The goal is to maintain the child as much as possible in a regular classroom reading program (Lerner, 1985). When an outside person and a classroom teacher are both working with a youngster, it is important that instruction be consistent (Allington & Shake, 1986; Walp & Walmsley, 1989). Otherwise children can become confused. Teacher and specialist need to communicate regularly regarding instructional approaches and materials, sharing teaching strategies that seem to be especially productive.

When **VAKT approaches** are used, children receive information simultaneously through visual, auditory, kinesthetic (movement), and tactile (touch) modalities. Receiving information through multiple channels of sensory input is thought to make learning more likely.

The most common VAKT method is one originally developed by Fernald (Fernald, 1943; Tierney, Readence, & Dishner, 1985). With that method, letters and words are first taught to students by having them simultaneously see (visual), hear (auditory), and trace (kinesthetic and tactile) words with their fingers. Sometimes sandpaper letters are used to enhance tactile input. After the letters and some words are learned, children receive reading instruction based on what they write themselves, much like language experience methods. Such writing experiences provide important language input through each of the identified modalities and thus contribute to the development of reading.

Behavior modification approaches attempt to overcome the attentional problems exhibited by some readers with a learning disability. Behavior modification involves identifying valued behaviors and the conditions under which such behaviors take place and then immediately reinforcing those behaviors with praise or tokens (Hallahan & Kauffman, 1982). Gradually, a set of discreet behaviors is developed that contributes to successful learning. Behavior modification was especially popular during the 1960s and 1970s and is seen occasionally today.

STUDENTS WITH EMOTIONAL DISTURBANCES

There is no widely accepted definition of children who are **emotionally disturbed.** However, three features are found in most definitions of emotional disturbance:

VAKT approaches
Methods of teaching reading to children through visual, auditory, kinesthetic, and tactile modalities.

behavior modification
Instruction that identifies valued behaviors, defines conditions where valued behaviors will take place, and immediately reinforces positive behaviors with praise or tokens.

emotionally disturbed
Describes individuals with normal intelligence who achieve substantially below expected levels because of chronic withdrawal, anxiety, and/or aggressive behavior.

1. behavior that goes to an extreme, that is, behavior that is not just slightly different from the usual
2. a problem that is chronic, that is, one that does not disappear
3. behavior that is unacceptable because of social or cultural expectations

According to federal estimates, approximately 1 percent of the school-age population are emotionally disturbed (U.S. Department of Education, 1984). Kauffman (1981), however, has put the actual estimate at 6 to 10 percent. Thus, teachers are likely to encounter children who experience serious and persistent emotional and behavioral problems but who have not been formally identified.

Learning Characteristics

Children experiencing emotional disturbance have at least normal intellectual ability but achieve substantially below expected levels because of withdrawal, anxiety, and/or aggressive behavior. Each of those behaviors reflects a different set of learning characteristics, often in combination, that need to be accommodated during instruction.

Withdrawal

1. May be without friends and may have difficulty working cooperatively in groups
2. Often daydreams more than is normal for a particular age group
3. May appear secretive

Anxiety

1. May cry much more frequently than is normal
2. Often appears tense and nervous; may be easily embarrassed and overly sensitive to criticism
3. May appear depressed, sad, or troubled
4. Frequently is reluctant to attempt new tasks independently
5. May be afraid of making mistakes

Aggression

1. May disrupt the classroom environment frequently
2. May be frequently involved in physical aggression
3. May intentionally destroy the property of others

Adapting Learning Environments

Several instructional approaches are often used with children experiencing emotional difficulties: contract reading, bibliotherapy, and cross-age tutoring. These approaches usually complement the regular reading program in the classroom and do not, except in extreme cases, replace it. Such approaches are not limited to students who are emotionally disturbed; they can be used with all students.

Contract reading requires both teacher and student to agree that a defined set of reading experiences will be completed in a fixed time period. Usually, a reading contract is written by the teacher and then signed by the student. Upon completion, it is evaluated by the teacher or by both the teacher and the student and sometimes by the parents also. Reading contracts can cover a single reading period or can extend over a number of periods. Contract reading can be useful in helping aggressive students control disruptive behavior and complete work on time. It can also help anxious students meet with success or can assist withdrawn children in interacting with others to complete learning experiences. An example of a contract used in conjunction with **individualized reading** is shown in Figure 12-3.

Bibliotherapy refers to an "attempt to promote mental and emotional health by using reading materials to fulfill needs, relieve pressure, or help an individual in his development as a person" (Harris & Sipay, 1990, p. 682). A reader might find comfort or a solution to a real-life problem by interacting with literature that is related to an emotional difficulty being experienced. Reading about others with similar problems and seeing how they solve their difficulties often provides important therapy (D'Alessandro, 1990).

A program of bibliotherapy requires literature selections related to the emotional difficulties that students are experiencing. A librarian might be able to suggest selections, and bibliographies by Coody (1983) and Sutherland and Arbuthnot (1986) might be helpful. Bibliotherapy also requires special care in putting children in touch with appropriate materials. Self-selection is a possibility, as is introducing a number of related books to the entire class and hoping that target children are attracted to them.

Consultation with a school psychologist should precede any program of bibliotherapy. That specialist should be informed of plans and should be encouraged to give professional guidance throughout the program. Bibliotherapy should then be followed up with discussions, retellings, journal responses, role-playing, art projects, or other activities that allow students to respond to what they have read.

Cross-age tutoring is a third approach to working with children experiencing emotional difficulties. With cross-age tutoring, older children assist younger children with reading activities, perhaps reading stories aloud to a group of younger children, listening to their oral reading, or participating in buddy journal activities. Children experiencing emotional problems can benefit from either tutoring younger children or receiving instruction from an older tutor. Children often feel special in the new roles and relationships that develop through cross-age tutoring. Nevertheless, teachers must carefully choose, train, and supervise any students who work as tutors with younger children. Clear directions regarding specific responsibilities increase their chance of success.

contract reading
An approach in which teacher and student agree to a document defining a set of reading experiences to be completed in a fixed time period.

individualized reading
A method framework that consists of selecting a book, reading it independently, having a conference, and completing a project (see chapter 2).

bibliotherapy
Using literature to promote mental and emotional health.

cross-age tutoring
Involvement of older or more proficient students in assisting younger or less proficient students.

FIGURE 12-3

A sample reading contract used in conjunction with individualized reading

READING CONTRACT

Date: __October 5__

Description of the work to be completed:

I will read Sarah's unicorn. Then I will make an ad for it and put it up on our Good Books bord.

This work will be completed on: __October 8__

Signed: __Michael T.__   __Debbie Smith__

Self evaluation: _I think I did good. Maria and Sarah liked my ad. Sarah read the book becaus it had her name._

Teacher evaluation: _Your ad encouraged someone else to read your book. That's the best kind of ad. GREAT!_

Parent Comments and Signature(s): _Thank you for all the special things you do. Mike read this to us at home and we all enjoyed it. Bob Tanner_

In addition to the use of contract reading, bibliotherapy, and cross-age tutoring, there are important guidelines to follow while working with children who are experiencing emotional difficulties.

1. Be sure to complete an interest inventory before beginning reading instruction; motivation and interest are critical for these children. Then use reading materials that are interesting and engaging.

2. Communicate regularly with the specialist who provides services to your student(s). Use consistent management and instructional approaches, and share observations regularly.
3. Communicate regularly with the parents or guardians of your student(s). Ask that you be kept informed if problems occur at home.
4. Explain clearly the rules in your classroom. Children need to understand exactly what is expected of them.
5. Provide reading instruction at the students instructional level. Begin with experiences with which your students can be successful, and gradually increase the difficulty of reading tasks.
6. Praise children in public. Reprimand them in private.
7. Maintain your classroom as a happy, calm, orderly, and protective environment for children. Model your concern for others, and expect students to treat each other with respect.

STUDENTS WITH HEARING IMPAIRMENTS

Children with hearing impairments have permanently reduced sensitivity to the sounds in their environment because of genetic factors, illness, or trauma. Usually, these children are not sensitive to sounds softer than about 26 decibels (dB). It is important for teachers to know the extent of the hearing loss. One categorization system used by the Conference of Executives of American Schools for the Deaf defines degrees of hearing impairment as follows:

children with hearing impairments
Describes individuals with permanently reduced sensitivity to sounds softer than 26 dB.

Category of impairment	Amount of loss
mild	26–54 dB
moderate	55–69 dB
severe	70–89 dB
profound	>90 dB

Individuals with hearing losses greater than 90 dB are usually considered deaf; those with a lesser loss are considered hard of hearing.

It is also important for teachers to know when the hearing loss took place. The earlier a loss occurs, the more likely it is that a child will have inadequately developed language. And since reading depends on language knowledge, a child with an early hearing loss may have great difficulty acquiring higher levels of reading comprehension, especially if the loss went undetected for a long time. Approximately 0.2 percent of school-age children are considered to be deaf and hard of hearing (U.S. Department of Education, 1984).

Learning Characteristics

Depending on the degree of hearing loss, children compensate by using amplifying devices; speechreading (lipreading); sign language; or a combination of these methods to assist them. Teachers must realize that these students are very dependent on the visual information in a classroom, which includes facial expressions, lip movements, and writing. In addition, the following considerations should be kept in mind:

- The language of children with a hearing impairment is often less completely developed than the language of other children.
- Children with a hearing impairment must concentrate very carefully on learning tasks that are presented orally. Fatigue can develop quickly, leading to inattentive behavior.
- Children with amplifying devices are distracted by extraneous noises in the environment. Such devices amplify both target and background sounds.

Even though most schools screen children for hearing impairment, some children have mild or moderate hearing losses that go undetected. Consequently, teachers should be aware of classroom behaviors associated with hearing loss and should request a hearing evaluation for a child displaying some of the following symptoms:

- frequent earaches, head colds, or sinus difficulties
- difficulty following directions or frequent requests to have explanations repeated
- quick fatigue during learning tasks
- easy distraction by external noises
- frequent mispronunciation of words
- clearly immature language

Adapting Learning Environments

mainstreamed
Placement of students with exceptionalities in inclusive learning environments with other students.

Increasingly, children with hearing impairments are being **mainstreamed** into inclusive classrooms. Of those who are mainstreamed, the majority have mild or moderate hearing losses. Most mainstreamed children with profound or severe hearing losses have sign language interpreters who accompany them in the classroom. Teachers working with children who have hearing losses should consider these instructional suggestions:

1. Phonics instruction presents special problems to hearing impaired children. Therefore, teachers should depend more on contextual analysis and sight word instruction and should present all new words in context.
2. Children with a hearing impairment should always sit close to the teacher, where they can clearly see the teacher's face and lips.
3. Lipreading is easier for students if teachers speak normally, not with exaggerated lip movements and not too quickly or too slowly. Teachers should maintain eye contact with students and should

stand still when speaking. Movement makes lipreading more difficult.

4. Because an amplifying device amplifies all sounds, teachers should attempt to limit extraneous noise in the classroom, especially during verbal instruction.

5. Periods of oral instruction should be limited. Several short sessions, separated by independent work, are better than a single long session.

6. Visual aids should be used as much as possible during vocabulary instruction and explanation of directions.

STUDENTS WITH VISUAL IMPAIRMENTS

Students with a **visual impairment** may be legally blind or partially sighted. Individuals who are legally blind have visual acuity that is less than 20/200. That designation means that with their best eye those individuals can see at 20 feet (or less) what a normally sighted individual can see at 200 feet, even with correction. Partially sighted individuals have visual acuity in their best eye that falls between 20/70 and 20/200, even with correction.

Contrary to popular opinion, being legally blind does not require being totally blind. Eighty-two percent of those who are legally blind have some vision. Often it is enough to be able to read print in large-print books or with the aid of magnifying devices (Stephens, Blackhurst, & Magliocca, 1988). Only about one in five individuals who are legally blind depend solely on Braille for reading. More than half use large- or regular-print books for most or all of their reading. One out of ten school-age children (10 percent) are thought to be visually impaired (U.S. Department of Education, 1984).

visual impairment
Describes individuals who are legally blind (20/200) or partially sighted (20/70 to 20/200), even with correction.

Learning Characteristics

It is important for teachers to recognize behaviors that indicate visual difficulty. Vision testing usually occurs in elementary schools but does not identify all vision problems, some of which go undetected. Teachers should recommend more thorough testing for children who display these symptoms:

- squinting
- holding reading materials very close or very far away from their eyes
- having red or watery eyes
- rubbing their eyes frequently
- covering one eye while reading
- having crusty material around their eyes and lashes

There are several ways in which students with a visual impairment compensate for their handicap: tactile sensation, listening skills, and greater attention. Some formal training may be required to take maximum advantage of each compensatory strategy.

Adapting Learning Environments

Students with a visual impairment are typically mainstreamed into elementary classrooms. If you have the opportunity to work with a child who is visually impaired, you should first consult your school's specialist to learn the extent of the impairment. You should also determine the most appropriate instructional methods to use, and you should find out which optical and mechanical devices your student may require when reading.

In your classroom you should try to maintain a relatively constant physical environment to help a child who is visually impaired move about. And you should always introduce children who are visually impaired to any changes in the location of materials or furniture. Classmates can help with this task, too.

New concepts often need to be more extensively defined for children with visual impairments, taking advantage of their tactile and auditory strengths. Although students with visual impairments may have had identical background experiences, their interpretation of those experiences is different because it has been determined more by nonvisual senses. One important way to develop conceptual knowledge is to provide a rich listening environment. Tape recordings of favorite literature selections are particularly useful for younger children, and you may wish to develop a listening center for all of your students, including a central tape player and individual headphones. Most publishers make audio cassettes of popular children's literature, and books on tape can be obtained through your local public library or from Recordings for the Blind, 214 East 58th Street, New York, NY 10022.

STUDENTS WITH SPEECH OR LANGUAGE DISORDERS

speech disorders
Abnormal oral language behavior due to phonological, voice, or other disorders.

Children with **speech disorders** produce oral language that is abnormal in how it is said, not in what is said. Several categories of speech disorders exist: phonological disorders, such as substituting /w/ for /r/; voice disorders, such as speaking with unusual pitch or loudness; disorders associated with abnormalities in the mouth and nose, such as orofacial clefts; and disorders of speech flow, such as stuttering. Speakers of nonstandard English dialects and children who speak English as a second (or third) language do not typically have speech disorders. Their speech needs to be compared to the speech of their language-related peers to determine whether a speech disorder exists. A speech pathologist can help make that determination.

Children who have **language disorders** have difficulty expressing their ideas in oral language or have difficulty understanding the ideas expressed by others. Students with language disorders may not have developed oral language capabilities or may use words in abnormal ways, perhaps echoing words that are spoken to them. They may also have varying degrees of delayed or interrupted language development. Children who speak nonstandard dialects or who are acquiring English as an additional language typically do not have language disorders. According to federal estimates, about 3 percent of the school-age population have speech disorders; approximately 0.5 percent have language disorders (U.S. Department of Education, 1984).

language disorders
Difficulty expressing ideas in oral language or understanding the ideas expressed by others.

Learning Characteristics

Children with speech disorders often do quite well in reading since their difficulty is associated with speech production, not comprehension. Not surprisingly, they do especially well in silent reading, rather than in oral reading experiences. Children with language disorders often have a more difficult time with reading, which is so dependent on adequate language proficiency.

At some time you may need to refer a child for formal speech and language assessment by a speech pathologist, who will appreciate specific information about the child's speech or language difficulties. Statements such as "Karen's language seems to be different" are not especially helpful. Consider the following questions before making a referral:

- Is the child's language substantially less mature than that of peers? How does the child use vocabulary and syntax differently from peers? Can the student tell a complete story with all of the appropriate elements?

- What sound substitutions or omissions does the child regularly make? These are some of the more common substitutions:
   /w/ for /r/ or /l/ as in *wead* for *read* or *lead*
   /b/ for /v/ as in *berry* for *very*
   /t/ for /k/ as in *tat* for *cat*
   /f/ for /voiceless th/ as in *wif* for *with*
   /voiceless th/ for /s/ as in *thith* for *this*
   /d/ for /voiced th/ as in *dis* for *this*
   /voiced th/ for /z/ as in *thew* for *zoo*

- Do other students in the class often have trouble understanding what the child is saying? Why?

- Does the child speak so fast that intelligibility suffers?

- Does the child use normal intonation patterns?

- Does the child experience difficulty following directions?

Adapting Learning Environments

Classrooms provide excellent opportunities for youngsters with speech and language disorders to improve their communication skills, especially when the use of oral language is encouraged, valued, and well integrated into the daily schedule. Regular sharing times, formal oral presentations, informal conversations, group discussions, and cooperative learning group tasks can all be used to foster development of effective communication skills.

Younger students with speech disorders benefit greatly from reading experiences with predictable texts. Students can practice their rhyming or rhythmic patterns while enjoying a good story (see chapters 4 and 5). For the child who stutters, both teacher and classmates need to adhere to certain guidelines.

- Attend carefully to what the child has to say.
- Let the child finish talking before you respond or interrupt.
- Do not become tense or frustrated at waiting for the entire message.
- Do not tease or ridicule the child's condition.

It is perfectly acceptable to talk about a disorder with a child. It helps greatly, though, if the condition is discussed in a matter-of-fact manner. For the stutterer, anxiety is likely to exaggerate the difficulty.

STUDENTS WITH MENTAL RETARDATION

The American Association on Mental Deficiency (AAMD) has defined **mental retardation** as follows:

mental retardation
The condition of individuals with inadequate adaptive behavior and intellectual functioning significantly below average.

> Mental retardation refers to significantly subaverage general intellectual functioning existing concurrently with deficits in adaptive behavior and manifested during the developmental period (Grossman, 1973, p. 11).

According to the AAMD, "significantly subaverage general intellectual functioning" requires an IQ score of 69 or below on the most commonly used test, Wechsler Intelligence Scale for Children—Revised (WISC-R). Children with IQ scores between 70 and 85 may learn more slowly than their peers and may be called slow learners. Typically, however, they are not formally labeled as mentally retarded. Figure 12-4 illustrates the various categories of mental retardation used by the AAMD.

When "deficits in adaptive behavior" are evaluated, the AAMD suggests that the age of the child be considered. In early childhood, sensorimotor, communication, self-help, and socialization skills are evaluated. In middle childhood and early adolescence, learning processes and interpersonal social skills are evaluated. According to federal estimates, approximately 1.9 percent of school-age children are mentally retarded (U.S. Department of Education, 1984).

FIGURE 12-4

Categories of mental retardation used by the AAMD

IQ	100	95	90	85	80	75	70	65	60	55	50	45	40	35	30	25	20	15
Categories of Mental Retardation								Mild		Moderate			Severe				Profound	

Learning Characteristics

Students with mental retardation tend to progress through the same developmental stages that normal students experience, but their rate of progress is much slower. This difference is especially evident in academic learning tasks such as reading. Other important characteristics that need to be accommodated during instruction include the following:

- *Short attention spans.* Students may be easily distracted, especially when there are many visual and auditory signals to distract them.

- *Poor short-term memory.* The ability to remember words, numbers, and ideas for short periods of time is limited. Long-term memory is less of a problem.

- *Delayed language development.* Language development is often slower than normal, although it progresses in a sequence that is similar to that of most children. A higher frequency of language and speech problems can be anticipated.

- *Difficulty in grasping abstract ideas.* Children tend to have more difficulty with abstract concepts. They do better with concrete concepts.

Adapting Learning Environments

The most important instructional consideration with students who are mentally retarded is that their development lags behind that of other children of the same chronological age. Thus, while normally developing second graders are learning new vocabulary meanings, the structure of various narrative and expository forms, and useful reading strategies, children of the same age who experience mental retardation might still be consolidating important emergent literacy/readiness skills. In fact, emergent literacy/readiness skills are often a major aspect of reading programs in the early elementary years for students who are mildly retarded. Acquiring oral language skills, learning letter names, listening to stories, completing language experience activities, and learning to read and write their own names might all be appropriate. Learning sight

....

FIGURE 12-5

Examples of functional reading strategies

 Learning to Understand Environmental Print. Teach children to understand the environmental print that they experience daily. Such print includes street signs, traffic signals, labels, children's names, and bus or transit signs. Include important safety words such as *Danger, Poison, Keep Out,* and *Caution.* Put each such word on a card, and use it in a sight word recognition game.

 Catalog Reading. Show children how to read a catalog to determine the name and price of items. Provide duplicate copies of the order form, and have students complete it. Structure this as a cooperative learning group task.

 Reading Students' Names. Give students frequent opportunities to read the names of other children in the class. Be certain to provide opportunities to have students return papers that have been corrected.

 Reading and Writing Personal Information. Teach children how to read and write their names, addresses, and phone numbers. Let them practice by filling out employment forms for favorite classroom jobs.

 Reading TV Guides. Bring in program listings for TV and show children how to read them. Have students make a TV viewing schedule for the week, allowing only one or two hours of television each day. This task could be effectively completed in cooperative learning groups.

....

words through language experience activities might be especially useful (Raver & Dwyer, 1986).

The use of cooperative learning group experiences is also appropriate. These provide supportive environments in which children can interact with print. In addition, cooperative learning group tasks have been found to be particularly effective in increasing social acceptance and positive social behavior among children (Slavin, 1984).

functional reading strategies
Reading strategies required to successfully interact with written language during daily life.

Reading instruction for children experiencing mental retardation should emphasize **functional reading strategies,** which include the reading abilities required for daily life. Such strategies enable individuals to read signs, follow simple written directions, use the yellow pages, read and order from catalogs, read names, locate bus routes on a map, and read recipes. Examples of functional reading strategies are described in Figure 12-5.

STUDENTS WHO ARE GIFTED

giftedness
The condition of individuals with high cognitive ability, creativity, and/or motivation.

A universally accepted definition of **giftedness** has yet to emerge. Creativity, intelligence, motivation, artistic talent, verbal ability, curiosity, and the ability to see unique relationships might all be used to define giftedness. However, each would identify a different population of students who are gifted.

Renzulli's (1978) definition of giftedness includes three characteristics: high cognitive ability, creativity, and motivation. Alone or in combination, these factors distinguish gifted children sufficiently from their peers to make it possible for them to contribute something of exceptional value to society. Hallahan and Kauffman (1982) estimate that approximately 2 to 5 percent of school-age students might be labeled as gifted according to this definition. The federal definition is somewhat different.

> "Gifted and talented children" means children and, wherever applicable, youth, who are identified at the preschool, elementary, or secondary level as possessing demonstrated or potential abilities that give evidence of high performance capabilities in areas such as intellectual, creative, specific academic, or leadership ability, or in the performing and visual arts and who by reason thereof require services or activities not ordinarily provided by the school. (Gifted and Talented Children's Act of 1978, PL 95-561, section 902.)

Learning Characteristics

Children who are gifted tend to demonstrate exceptional performance with most cognitive and linguistic tasks. Indeed, a teacher's first observation of a gifted child is often to note the student's precocious language use. Children who are gifted talk about topics that are advanced for their ages, and the way that they talk is noticeably more mature. Some individuals believe that early reading is a mark of giftedness. Nevertheless, even though early reading is often found among gifted children, not all read at an early age.

Adapting Learning Environments

The most common form of instructional accommodation for children who are gifted is an **enrichment program,** which provides opportunities for students to pursue special interests inside and outside the regular classroom. A popular enrichment program defined by Renzulli (1978) consists of three types of activities. Type I activities are designed to help children learn about their environment and develop particular interests. Type II activities are developed around group process tasks, such as gaming and simulations. These are designed to enhance problem-solving skills, critical thinking, and creative thinking. Type III activities allow individual or group study of actual problems, such as community reaction to a new shopping center, preservation of traditional folk knowledge, or changes in the local environment. Reading and writing experiences are a natural part of each of these tasks; in addition, research skills are often developed with Type II tasks and then applied to the solution of real-life problems with Type III tasks.

A unique aspect of this enrichment program is the "revolving door" through which students enter and leave the program. Renzulli argues

enrichment program
Learning activities provided to students who are gifted, often outside the regular classroom.

that children are gifted for particular tasks and at particular times. He advocates that children be included in a gifted program when they show an interest in and talent for the topic being covered. If they are successful and make an important contribution to the project, they may remain. If they lose interest or do not succeed in making a substantive contribution, other children are allowed to take their places. This approach opens enrichment programs to a wider population.

inquiry reading
An approach to gifted education that has students define, research, and then report on a project of personal interest.

Cassidy (1981) has described another approach for students who are gifted, one referred to as **inquiry reading.** Inquiry reading follows a week-by-week sequence of activities, allowing students in Grades 3 through 6 to define, research, and then report on a project of personal interest. This method framework, which follows a procedural sequence consisting of four steps, can be used in the classroom with all students.

1. Develop a contract (Week 1).
2. Research the topic (Weeks 2 to 3).
3. Prepare the project for presentation to the class (Week 4).
4. Present the project to the class (Week 4).

During the first week children learn the procedures, purposes, and goals of inquiry reading. Then they identify a topic of personal interest, locate the necessary resources, and specify a project that can be completed. All of this information is defined, along with a due date, in a contract developed by the student with assistance from the teacher.

During weeks 2 and 3 students research their topics independently or in small groups. Often this step requires independent library work and sometimes interviews with members of the community. Students read, listen, take notes, and otherwise acquire the necessary resources to complete their projects. Often the teacher sets aside time during this step to confer with students and review their progress.

FIGURE 12-6
Additional reading strategies sometimes used with students who are gifted and others

Establishing Mentor Relationships. Locate local experts in areas in which your students are interested. See whether they can contribute an hour or so each week to work on an independent project with your students. Then design a contract around the project and display the final results in your classroom.

Publishing a Classroom Magazine. Have a rotating group of students be responsible for gathering, editing, and printing articles written by members of the class. Encourage students to include stories, poetry, crossword puzzles, and other features, too. Consider using a computer since software is available for laying out and printing the results. Make arrangements to use the school's duplicating machine, and produce copies for each student in the class. Suggest that they share their magazines with their parents.

Cross-Age Tutoring. Involve students in tutoring situations with students in younger classes. Explain that each member of a society is obligated to contribute something of value and that tutoring younger children is one way of contributing. Help students to plan and evaluate their tutoring activities carefully.

The final week is spent completing the project and preparing it for presentation to the class. Students can present the results of their work in a variety of ways. They might choose an oral report, a play, a written report, an art project, a diorama, a slide show, or one of many other creative formats.

Additional strategies that have been found to be helpful when working with gifted students can be seen in Figure 12-6.

DEVELOPING A CLASSROOM COMMUNITY THAT SUPPORTS ALL LEARNERS

Perhaps the single most important thing you can do as a teacher of reading to support all of your students is develop a sense of community that respects the unique qualities that each one of your students brings to your classroom. There is no simple prescription for how a teacher should go about developing the respect for individual differences that is such an important part of our society. More than anything else, it takes a teacher who sees the value of diversity in everyday life and brings that concern into every aspect of the classroom community.

Clearly, one way this can be accomplished is to recall the points made at the beginning of this chapter about exceptionalities. We need to recognize that each child in our classroom is an individual with special needs. We need to continually keep in mind that the categories used in this chapter should never limit our instructional decisions regarding individual children or our expectations for their achievement. And finally, we need to recall that diversity should be viewed as an opportunity for us to exploit, not a challenge to overcome.

Another way to accomplish this is to take maximum advantage of group learning experiences as you consider the nature of each day's reading activities. Group learning activities allow your students to experience the advantages that come from diversity as each student makes a contribution to the completion of the learning task. You should use these activities to help your students see the advantages in diversity as they complete their learning activity. The method framework initially described in chapter 3 as cooperative group learning is especially useful, largely because it can be used in so many different learning activities. You will recall that this method framework consists of four procedural steps:

1. The teacher defines a learning task.
2. The teacher assigns students to groups.
3. Students complete the learning task together through cooperative group activity.
4. The results of the learning task are shared with the other groups.

While cooperative group learning may be used by itself to organize learning activities for your students it may also be combined with a wide variety of other method frameworks during reading instruction. It could,

Teachers should recognize that all students have special strengths and needs, regardless of labels and categories.

for example, be used to organize method frameworks as diverse as readers theater (chapter 4); directed reading activities (chapter 2); read-aloud response journal activities (chapter 2); literature discussion groups (chapter 4); writers workshop (chapter 5); invented spelling (chapter 7); style studies (chapters 5 and 9); or reciprocal teaching (chapter 9).

Notice, too, how cooperative group learning can be used with method frameworks that contain very different assumptions about how children best learn to read. It could, for example, be used during the final two procedural steps of either inductive instruction (chapter 3) or deductive instruction (chapter 3) which we have defined as "provide guided practice" and "provide independent practice." You could ask students to complete the learning task you have developed in a cooperative learning group as a means of providing guided practice. Students could also be asked to complete the independent practice step and have them compare their results in a cooperative group learning task. Clearly, cooperative group learning is a method framework that can be adapted to different types of literacy frameworks and provide useful opportunities for your students to experience the advantages of diversity.

OPPORTUNITIES TO CELEBRATE DIVERSITY

In the final analysis, creating a classroom community that supports all learners can only be accomplished by the example you set and the values you bring to classroom learning. This is why it is so important to carefully consider the type of community you wish to develop in your classroom. It is also the reason why it is so important to view diversity as an opportunity for both you and your students, not an obstacle to learning. Helping your students to see the benefits of working with peers who have different exceptionalities should be a central part of your instructional program.

USING A LITERACY FRAMEWORK TO GUIDE INSTRUCTION OF STUDENTS WITH SPECIAL NEEDS

Teaching reading to children with special needs presents the same types of instructional decisions that must be faced when you teach any children. You must still decide what and how to teach. As a result, you will use your literacy framework in a similar way. If, for example, you have a text-based explanation of how a person reads, you will tend to emphasize aspects such as decoding knowledge and fluent oral reading. If, on the other hand, you follow a reader-based explanation, you will emphasize aspects such as inferential reasoning, vocabulary knowledge, and other elements of prior knowledge. With a specific skills explanation of how reading ability develops, you will use more deductive instructional practices when you work with children with special needs. With a more holistic language explanation you will depend on students to learn what is important through inductive and self-selected reading experiences.

It is important to note that these generalizations do not mean that all children with special needs will receive identical instruction from one teacher. These children require individualized attention to their unique strengths and weaknesses. The approaches described in this chapter should be valuable resources as you accomplish this important goal.

Comments from the Classroom

Judy Dill, first grade teacher

In our school we are not usually able to have multiple classrooms of one grade so I have a variety of children with several different kinds of needs in one room. It is not unusual to have children with physical disabilities, emotional and behavioral needs, and special learning needs in my classroom each school year. I also have one or two children who are gifted and need challenging learning experiences. My role as a teacher is not unlike a juggler doing a delicate balancing act to meet everyone's needs.

One way I accomplish meeting the needs of my diverse group of students is to enlist the help of the fifth grade classroom. These students become our Book Buddies for the year. This program, now in its third year, has become extremely successful for both classes. The fifth graders get a chance to practice their oral reading and my first graders get a chance to listen to stories—something that is so necessary for beginning readers. As the program progresses, and the first graders begin to read, the partners change roles. As a positive offshoot, I often observe fifth graders sharing reading strategies for decoding, inferencing, and predicting.

At the beginning of each session the Book Buddies agree on a book they will share. Once in a while I have a mystery box of books where one partner reaches in and gets a surprise book to read. But most of the time one buddy brings a book he or she likes to the paired reading session, or the buddies choose a book together from the class or school library. (The school librarian is very sensitive to the needs of the students and directs partners toward books with appropriate reading levels.)

At the onset of the yearly program we agree on reading goals for the Book Buddies. To account for books read during each session, the fifth graders take the responsibility of recording the books shared. They fill out record sheets I have prepared by writing down the book title, author's name, child's name, date the book was shared, and who did the reading. The fifth graders take this responsibility very seriously.

Additionally, after completing each book the partners fill out a segment of a bookworm with their name and the title of their book. These segments are added *together and the worm begins to stretch all over the room. It becomes a visual reminder of the number of books read. (When our worm begins to outgrow our room space, we add feet instead of more segments.)*

The added benefit of this program is that nobody worries about partners who are different in any way and become quite protective and caring towards one another. Working together, the first graders and fifth graders develop a very special friendship.

Major Points

- Every student has unique needs that must be acknowledged in instructional decisions. Each student's background and abilities must be considered in reading instruction. Having children with special needs in the classroom provides an opportunity to celebrate and learn about diversity.

- Teachers can help children with exceptionalities develop reading proficiency in several ways: preparing other students, capitalizing on individual strengths, ensuring successful learning experiences, building success into instruction by carefully considering what each child can be expected to do, recording and charting individual growth to demonstrate gains to students and parents, establishing an accepting and positive environment, regularly discussing student progress with others, and adjusting background knowledge to reduce the difficulty of learning tasks.

- To support all of your students it is essential to develop a sense of community that respects the unique qualities that each of your students brings to your classroom.

- Teachers face the same types of instructional decisions with children with special needs that they face with other children. As a result, a personal literacy framework functions in a similar way as you consider each child's learning needs.

Making Instructional Decisions

1. Read a variety of literature selections that explore issues of diversity including cultural diversity, linguistic diversity, and the diversity of exceptionalities. Develop an outline for a thematic unit on

diversity that might be used at the beginning of the year. See chapters 4 and 5 for suggestions about how this might be done.

2. Your school psychologist has just informed you that you will have a new student in your room. This student was tested for mental retardation but was not admitted into the district's special education program. The school psychologist explains that the student has below-average intellectual functioning, but it is not low enough to qualify for special assistance. Identify several learning characteristics that you might look for during the first few weeks of school. Also, specify the major instructional consideration you will need to incorporate into your reading plans for this student. Finally, describe how you will provide appropriate instruction for this student without developing expectations that are too low and thereby preventing the student from developing her full potential.

3. Students with learning disabilities sometimes receive instruction from a classroom teacher with one type of literacy framework and a specialist with another type of literacy framework. What might that teacher and that specialist do to avoid confusing the child about the nature of reading?

4. It is the end of the school year and you have been told that you will have five exceptional students in your classroom in the fall: two students with learning disabilities, a student with emotional difficulties, a student who has been labeled as mildly mentally retarded, and a student who is visually impaired. You will be teaming with another teacher who is certified in special education during the mornings. What principles will guide your attempts to develop an inclusive classroom and, at the same time, meet the reading needs of these students?

Further Reading

Cousin, P. T., Weekley, T, & Gerard, J. (1993). The functional uses of language and literacy by students with severe language and learning problems. *Language Arts, 70,* 548–557.

Describes the results of a collaborative project between a university professor and classroom teachers who work with exceptional youngsters. By looking at the functional uses of language and literacy for children with language and learning problems new insights are presented about the most appropriate ways of supporting their learning needs. Presents several case studies of students in this classroom.

D'Alessandro M. (1990). Accommodating emotionally handicapped children through a literature-based reading program. *The Reading Teacher, 44*(4), 288–293.

Describes how a literature-based reading program was used in a special education classroom to support the literacy development of children who had been labeled as emotionally handicapped.

Kameenui, E. J. (1993). Diverse learners and the tyranny of time: Don't fix blame; fix the leaky roof. *The Reading Teacher, 46*(5), 376–383.

Argues that we have spent too much time and energy searching for the "best" method to teach reading to diverse learners. Suggests that what is required is simply to use what appears to work for diverse learners. Proposes six principles to guide these efforts: do not waste instructional time; intervene and remediate early, strategically, and frequently; teach less more thoroughly; communicate reading strategies in a clear and explicit manner, especially during initial phases of instruction; guide student learning through a sequence of teacher-directed and student-directed activities; and examine the effectiveness of instructional tools.

Nistler, R. J. & McMurry, H. (1993) Insights into dyslexia: Lessons from a personal struggle to overcome reading disabilities. *Language Arts, 70,* 559–566.

Describes the case history of an undergraduate student in a teacher education program who has struggled with dyslexia. It explains the nature of her struggles and the ways in which she has overcome her reading difficulties.

References

Allington, R. L., & Shake, M. C. (1986). Remedial reading: Achieving curricular congruence in classroom and clinic. *The Reading Teacher, 39,* 648–654.

Cassidy, J. (1981). Inquiry reading for the gifted. *The Reading Teacher, 35,* 17–21.

Coody, B. (1983). *Using literature with young children* (3rd ed.). Dubuque, IA: W. C. Brown.

D'Alessandro M. (1990). Accommodating emotionally handicapped children through a literature-based reading program. *The Reading Teacher, 44*(4), 288–293.

Federal Register 42, No. 250, December 29, 1977.

Fernald, G. (1943). *Remedial techniques in basic school subjects.* New York: McGraw-Hill.

Ford, M. P., & Ohlhausen, M. M. (1988). Tips from reading clinicians for coping with disabled readers in regular classrooms. *The Reading Teacher, 42*(1), 18–22.

Grossman, H. J. (Ed.). (1973). *Manual on terminology and classification in mental retardation.* Washington, DC: American Association on Mental Deficiency.

Hallahan, D. P., & Kauffman, J. M. (1982). *Exceptional children* (2nd ed.). New York: Prentice Hall.

Harris, A. J., & Sipay, E. R. (1990). *How to increase reading ability* (9th ed.). New York: Longman.

Kauffman, J. M. (1981). *Characteristics of children's behavior disorders* (2nd ed.). Columbus, OH: Merrill.

Lerner, J. (1985). *Learning disabilities: Theories, diagnosis, and teaching strategies* (4th ed.). Boston: Houghton Mifflin.

Pinnell, G. S., Fried, M. D., & Estice, R. M. (1990). Reading recovery: Learning how to make a difference. *The Reading Teacher, 43*(4), 282–295.

Raver, S. A., & Dwyer, R. C. (1986). Teaching handicapped preschoolers to sight read using language training procedures. *The Reading Teacher, 40,* 314–321.

Renzulli, J. S. (1978). What makes giftedness? Re-examining a definition. *Phi Delta Kappan, 60*(3), 180–184, 261.

Slavin, R. E. (1984). Effects of cooperative learning and individualized instruction on mainstreamed students. *Exceptional Children, 50*(5), 434–443.

Stainback, S., & Stainback, W. (1989). Integration of students with mild and moderate handicaps. In D. Kerzner & A. Gartner (Eds.), *Beyond separate education.* Baltimore, MD: Paul H. Brookes.

Stephens, T. M., Blackhurst, A. E., & Magliocca, L. A. (1988). *Teaching mainstreamed students.* Oxford: Pergamon Press.

Sutherland, Z., & Arbuthnot, M. H. (1986). *Children and books* (7th ed.). Glenview, IL: Scott, Foresman.

Tierney, R. J., Readence, J. E., & Dishner, E. K. (1985). *Reading strategies and practices: Guide for improving instruction* (2nd ed.). Boston: Allyn & Bacon.

U. S. Department of Education. (1984). *To assure the free, appropriate public education of all handicapped children.* Sixth Annual Report to Congress on the Implementation of PL 94–172. Washington, DC: Author.

Walp, T. P., & Walmsley, S. A. (1989). Instructional and philosophical congruence: Neglected aspects of coordination. *The Reading Teacher, 42*(6), 364–368.

Wood, J. W. (1992). *Adapting instruction for mainstreamed and at-risk students,* (2nd ed.) New York: Merrill.

PART 4

Instructional Patterns and Technologies

Classroom Organization

The hardest thing for me during that first year of teaching was to develop a system for working with my students in ways that would meet their individual reading needs. Initially, I thought a single organizational scheme would work best and last me all through the year. I quickly learned that what I needed to do was to use many different types of organizational patterns because my students had so many different needs. The trick was to know how to weave the different organizational patterns in and out throughout the year. At the beginning of my second year, I sat down and planned out all the patterns I wanted to use and made initial decisions about when I would use each pattern. This helped a lot, and even though I made changes in this plan as we went along, it gave me a good road map for the year.

An experienced teacher describing his first year of teaching.

How can you best organize your classroom for reading instruction? Should you teach reading to the whole class? Or should you work with separate literature discussion groups, interest groups, or achievement groups? Should you have each student pursue individualized reading projects? Or should you develop experiences for the whole class and small groups too? In earlier times, this question was an easy one to answer; everyone simply learned together as a whole class. Each year, the better readers always became even better readers and the weaker readers became even weaker readers. The situation is very different now. Organizational decisions have become more complex as we have begun to value and meet the many individual differences that exist among our students.

In this chapter you will learn how insightful decisions about classroom organization can help you to support all of your students, helping each one to become an engaged and proficient reader. Chapter 13 includes information that will help you answer questions such as:

1. Which individual differences make a difference in reading?
2. What organizational patterns do schools use to accommodate individual differences in reading? Are these effective?
3. What organizational patterns do teachers use to accommodate individual differences in reading?
4. How can a literacy framework guide decisions about classroom organization and integrate instruction focused on individuals, small groups, and the whole class?

KEY CONCEPTS

achievement groups	intraclass organizational patterns
cooperative learning groups	literature discussion groups
cross-age tutoring	reader's workshops
cross-grade grouping	reading/writing center
departmentalized reading instruction	strategy groups
grand conversations	team teaching
individualized reading	thematic units
interclass accommodations	tracking
interest groups	yearly plan

individual differences:
Ways in which students vary; in reading, specifically background knowledge, reading interests, reading achievement levels, and reading skills.

INDIVIDUAL DIFFERENCES: THE CHALLENGE AND THE OPPORTUNITY

As a developing professional, you are familiar with the concept of **individual differences** in educational settings. You know that each child in your classroom is unique in many ways. You also know that instruction must attempt to meet the unique needs of each student. Those individual differences within your classroom provide both a challenge and an opportunity. The challenge, of course, is to make instructional decisions that take into account the unique characteristics of each child in your class. The opportunity is to nurture the diversity in your classroom, modeling the respect for individual differences that is so important to our pluralistic society.

As chapter 12 pointed out, individual students differ along many dimensions. In terms of reading instruction, however, four types of individual differences are most important:

background knowledge

reading interests

reading achievement level

reading skills

These are the major differences that make a difference during reading. Each contributes in an important way to a student's interaction with a text. Consequently, each needs to be recognized in the organization of a reading program.

Let's look first at individual differences in background knowledge. Each child's previous experiences are unique; as a result, each has different background knowledge to assist with comprehension. If two readers are identical in every respect but background knowledge, they will comprehend the same story in very different ways. One child might make the required inferences, while the other struggles to understand. Classroom organization needs to recognize individual differences in background knowledge.

Reading interests also vary among students. Some prefer to read narratives; others enjoy exposition. Some prefer stories about animals; others enjoy stories about sports. Even students with the same background knowledge would comprehend the same story differently if one was interested in the topic and the other was not. Classroom organization needs to recognize individual difference in reading interests.

In addition, students vary in their reading achievement levels. What range of reading achievement do you think a teacher might expect in an average fourth-grade class? A conservative rule of thumb is that the variation in reading achievement levels equals the grade level of the class. According to Harris and Sipay (1990), we can expect to find at least four years' difference in achievement between the highest and the lowest achieving readers in a fourth-grade class. Thus, the lowest achieving reader might be reading at a second-grade level while the highest achieving reader is reading at a sixth-grade level. Because reading achievement levels vary so much within classrooms, no teacher can expect to accommodate individual differences by teaching all students with the same set of materials. Classroom organization needs to recognize these individual differences in reading achievement.

A final dimension of individual difference within the classroom is reading skill knowledge. Each student brings a unique combination of reading skills to instructional lessons. Some students may have comprehensive vocabulary knowledge but poorly developed decoding knowledge. Others may have comprehensive decoding knowledge but poorly developed metacognitive knowledge, or any one of many other combinations of well-developed and poorly developed knowledge sources. Multiplying the number of possible combinations by the number of students in a class helps us appreciate the importance of accommodating each child's instructional needs in specific skill areas.

Students are clearly unique in the background knowledge, reading interests, achievement levels, and specific skills each brings to the reading task. The challenge is to determine how best to address that diversity to further each child's development. Both schools and teachers meet this challenge through organizational decisions, attempting to accommodate the wide range of differences and provide more appropriate reading experiences for individual students. Schools work through interclass organizational patterns; teachers utilize intraclass organizational patterns.

INTERCLASS ORGANIZATION

interclass accommodations
Modifications in the organizational patterns among classes to accommodate individual differences.

Schools sometimes organize classes to accommodate individual differences in reading. However, these **interclass accommodations** address differences only in reading achievement. They do nothing to recognize differences in other areas important to reading, such as background knowledge, reading interests, or specific skill knowledge. Consequently, considerable variation among individuals still remains within each classroom. A variety of interclass accommodations exist and are described below. Most interclass organizational patterns are found in grades 4 and higher.

Homogeneous Grouping (Tracking)

homogeneously grouped classrooms
An interclass organizational pattern in which classes are formed around students who are similar in at least one dimension, such as reading achievement level.

tracking
An interclass organizational structure using classes that are homogeneously grouped according to achievement levels.

Most elementary classrooms are heterogeneous; they contain children with a wide range of reading achievement levels (Hiebert, 1983; Slavin, 1987). To reduce the range of achievement differences within any single class, schools sometimes form **homogeneously grouped classrooms.** For example, a school with three homogeneously grouped classrooms at the fourth-grade level might have one class of high-achieving readers, one class of average-achieving readers, and a third class of low-achieving readers. This approach to individual differences is sometimes called **tracking** as children are placed in different educational tracks, depending on reading achievement level.

Homogeneous grouping is more frequently found in Grades 4 through 8, seldom in kindergarten through third grade. There is not much evidence supporting its use. Low-achieving students do not do any better in such settings, although limited evidence suggests that high-achieving readers do benefit from homogeneous grouping (Harp, 1989).

Departmentalized Reading Instruction

Occasionally schools use **departmentalized reading instruction.** This approach makes one or several teachers solely responsible for reading instruction while other teachers are responsible for other subject areas. With this arrangement, which is essentially a traditional high school format, students move from one subject-area classroom to another during the day, receiving instruction from each subject-area teacher. This type of interclass accommodation is almost always limited to Grades 4 through 8 and is seldom, if ever, found in kindergarten or Grades 1 through 3.

By itself, departmentalized reading instruction does not meet the challenge posed by individual differences. Often, however, it is combined with some form of homogeneous grouping. For example, the teacher responsible for reading at the fourth-grade level might teach reading to classes that have been homogeneously grouped on the basis of reading achievement.

departmentalized reading instruction
An interclass organizational pattern in which one teacher teaches reading while other teachers teach other subject areas.

Team Teaching

There are probably as many different definitions of **team teaching** as there are groups of teachers who decide to share instructional ideas and students. Team teaching usually involves several teachers who pool their students for instruction, each teacher assuming responsibility for a specific subject area. This form of team teaching usually involves two or more teachers at the same grade level. For example, two sixth-grade teachers might decide to team teach mathematics and reading. Each teacher would then teach one of those subject areas to all the students in both classes. Typically, half the students would receive instruction in reading from one teacher while the other half received instruction in mathematics from the other teacher. After that, the students would switch classrooms and receive instruction in the other subject area. Both teachers would remain responsible for teaching their own students in all other subjects.

Like departmentalized reading instruction, team teaching by itself does not really meet the challenge of individual differences. Again, however, team teaching usually takes place in conjunction with some form of homogeneous grouping based on achievement levels. In the previous example the sixth graders might be grouped according to a combined achievement level in reading and mathematics. During one period the high-achieving students would receive reading instruction while the low-achieving students received mathematics instruction. Then, the same groups would switch subjects and teachers.

team teaching
An interclass organizational pattern in which two or more teachers cooperate for instructional purposes, sharing ideas and students.

Cross-Grade Grouping

Cross-grade grouping for reading instruction requires a school to homogeneously regroup students across several grades according to read-

cross-grade grouping
An interclass organizational pattern in which a school regroups students across several grades for reading instruction.

ing achievement levels. This plan affects only reading instruction. Students receive instruction in all other areas within their regular classrooms. According to this scheme, children in all classes leave their regular classrooms at the same time each day to go to their assigned classrooms for reading instruction. Thus, in each classroom, reading is taught to students who are reading at about the same grade level, even though their nominal levels might be anywhere from kindergarten to sixth grade. Sometimes cross-grade grouping is referred to as the Joplin Plan, after the Missouri town where it first received notice.

Split-Half Classes

split-half classes
An interclass organizational pattern in which each classroom is divided into two halves based on reading achievement levels.

Schools that use **split-half classes** divide each classroom into groups of higher-achieving and lower-achieving readers. One group comes to school an hour before the other group and receives reading instruction at the beginning of the day. After that period the remaining students arrive, and the school day proceeds normally with both groups in attendance. Then, one hour before the end of school, the early-arriving students leave, freeing the teacher for reading instruction with the late-arriving students.

Split-half classes create scheduling problems for families with several children in school and both parents working. As children leave and return home from school at different times, busy schedules must accommodate additional juggling. In addition, split-half classes require that a school devote an additional period each day to reading.

Retention and Acceleration

retention and acceleration
An interclass organizational pattern in which students either repeat or skip a grade level, based on achievement.

Retaining lower-achieving students for another year at the same grade level while accelerating higher-achieving students to a higher grade level was one of the earliest types of interclass accommodation (Harris & Sipay, 1990). In most cases of **retention and acceleration,** achievement was based substantially on reading performance. More recently, retention has found increasing favor, despite evidence that neither retention nor social promotion has been a consistently successful response to the challenge of individual differences. Whenever retention or acceleration is being considered, it is important for the teacher to carefully review the child's situation with parents, principal, and school psychologist.

Assistance by Reading Specialists or Special Educators

reading specialist
A teacher specially trained to diagnose and provide remedial assistance to children with reading difficulties.

In many classrooms children who achieve at lower reading levels are provided with additional assistance, which is the final form of interclass accommodation. Under this arrangement children receive remedial reading instruction from a **reading specialist,** a teacher with special training in diagnosing and teaching children with reading difficulties. Other children may be formally identified as students in need of special educational support and will then receive instruction from a special educator trained to work with students experiencing an exceptionality. This type of assistance was traditionally provided outside of the main classroom; stu-

Under careful teacher supervision, cross-age tutoring can benefit both the younger and the older student.

dents left the class and received instruction that was sensitive to their particular needs. Increasingly, this assistance is being provided today within the classroom by reading specialists or special educators.

The Weaknesses of Interclass Accommodations

Interclass accommodations of individual differences suffer from two weaknesses. First, they tend to give the false impression that achievement differences among students have ceased to exist when, in fact, significant achievement differences still remain. Teachers of homogeneously grouped classes often believe that since all students in the class are high-, average-, or low-ability readers, they should receive identical instruction. Seldom is that response appropriate. Nearly every classroom, despite the best attempts at homogeneous grouping, will contain a range in reading achievement of at least two years (Harris & Sipay, 1990).

A second problem is that interclass accommodations recognize only one type of individual difference that is important to reading—differences in reading achievement levels. None of the interclass accommodations address variations in background knowledge, reading interests, or reading skills. These differences will always exist in a classroom and are also important to accommodate during reading instruction.

INTRACLASS ORGANIZATION

Teachers often use **intraclass organizational patterns** to accommodate additional differences within their classes. There are three types of patterns that teachers use: individualized patterns, small-group patterns, and whole-class patterns.

Individualized Patterns

Individualized patterns provide an organizational framework to meet the multiple needs of students within a classroom (Staab, 1991). Such patterns can be used to accommodate all types of individual differences important to reading: background knowledge, reading interests, achievement levels, and reading skills. Because individualized patterns usually allow students to select their own reading materials, individual differences among students are easily accommodated. Students choose to read something that is appropriate for their own background knowledge, reading interests, achievement level, and reading skills. Individualized patterns include several different approaches.

   Individualized reading is described in chapter 3 as a method framework often used to replace or supplement a published reading program. Individualized reading uses self-selected reading experiences with children's literature, a practice that has demonstrated positive results (Tunnel & Jacobs, 1989). The process includes the following steps:

1. selecting a book to read
2. reading the book independently
3. having a conference with the teacher
4. completing a culminating experience (optional)

   During individualized reading, students have an opportunity to select their own reading materials and read at their own pace. Thus, students are able to read materials that are consistent with their background knowledge, reading interests, achievement levels, and reading skills. After students complete their books, they discuss with the teacher what they have read. During this conference they might be asked to read a short excerpt aloud and discuss the most interesting parts of the story. Teachers might also suggest that students complete a project based on the book (lists of possible projects are presented in chapter 3).

   Individualized reading can be combined with reading contracts, which are helpful reminders for students of what needs to be done. A reading contract identifies the book a child selects to read, specifies the projected completion date, and defines how the book will be presented to the class in a culminating project, when appropriate. An example of a contract used with an independent book project is illustrated in Figure 13-1.

   A **reading/writing center** is a location in the classroom where students may engage in a series of independent, self-guided, teacher-designed activities that connect reading and writing. Reading/writing

FIGURE 13-1

A sample contract used with an independent book project

Contract

I *Sarah Lewis* plan to read the following book and complete
my independent book project by *October 15*

Book: *The Giver*
Author: *Lois Lowry*

My independent book project will include:

1. Write a story about the ~~fates~~ future at our school.
2. Read my rough draft to three people.
3. ~~Ritis~~ Revise my story.
4. Read my story to the class.

Signed *Sarah Lewis*   *Mr. Callahan*
       (Student)   (Teacher)
Date *September 25*

centers take many different forms but usually share several characteristics. First, reading/writing centers usually contain all of the materials required to complete an activity. For example, the following materials were needed for one reading/writing center activity used at the third-grade level:

1. Four books containing tall tales: *Shenandoah Noah* by Jim Aylesworth, *Paul Bunyan* by Steven Kellogg, *Sally Ann Thunder*

and Whirlwind Crockett by Caron Lee Cohen, and *John Henry* by Ezra Jack Keats.

2. Writing paper, pencils, and felt-tip pens.
3. Students' writing folders.
4. A box to collect students' finished work.

Second, reading/writing centers have clear directions detailing the procedures for completing each learning activity. These directions are often displayed prominently on a bulletin board or wall. Figure 13-2 shows the directions for the reading/writing center activity just described.

Third, reading/writing centers hold students' writing folders, where students can keep drafts of writing projects. Often, a manila folder is provided for each student and these are organized alphabetically in a small box.

Finally, reading/writing centers often have a place to turn in or display completed work. There may be a collection box, as in the example, and perhaps a bulletin board nearby. Displaying completed work gives other students an idea of what can be done. Usually a teacher has a single reading/writing center and rotates the activities there. Students are expected to complete center activities as they have time.

cross-age tutoring
An approach using older, more proficient students to assist younger, less proficient students.

With **cross-age tutoring,** an older, more proficient reader assists a younger, less proficient reader in activities that are carefully organized by a teacher. Cross-age tutoring provides an opportunity to individualize reading experiences and provide a supportive reading environment for students, especially those who may require additional assistance. It is usually recommended that the older student be about two grade levels beyond the younger student.

FIGURE 13-2

The directions for a reading/writing center activity

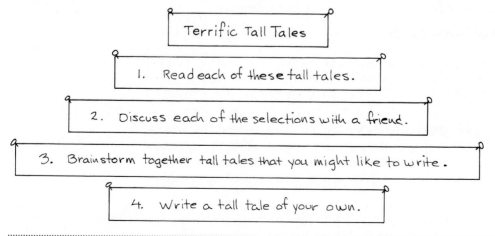

Terrific Tall Tales

1. Read each of these tall tales.

2. Discuss each of the selections with a friend.

3. Brainstorm together tall tales that you might like to write.

4. Write a tall tale of your own.

OPPORTUNITIES TO CELEBRATE DIVERSITY

Paired reading is a useful approach to support the reading of students whose first language is not English. It supports their development in a very rich social support system. Students who work as the tutor learn, too, about a language and culture other than their own, especially if you encourage the pair to sometimes read books together about the culture of the limited English proficiency (LEP) student.

Cross-age tutoring is usually associated with increases in time on task, interactive learning, positive self-concepts, and positive attitudes about reading (Topping, 1989). There is also evidence that tutors gain in reading achievement at least as much as, if not more than, the students they tutor (Sharpley & Sharpley, 1981). Topping (1989) suggests that a minimum of three periods per week for at least six weeks' duration be set aside for cross-age tutoring. Usually, each session lasts from fifteen to thirty minutes.

In **paired reading** a tutor and a student read a text together. On easy sections the tutor allows the student to read out loud independently. When a mistake is made, the tutor pronounces the word correctly and has the student do the same before continuing. On more difficult sections the two read out loud together. Then, when easier sections appear again, the student might signal the tutor to stop reading, and the student would continue reading independently.

Paired reading provides a scaffold that supports a student, especially when more challenging reading materials are encountered. It requires less training than cross-age tutoring and results in similarly positive outcomes. Paired reading is typically used at frequent intervals, with each period of use lasting at least six weeks.

Small-Group Patterns

Small-group patterns provide an organizational framework designed to meet individual needs within a group of peers. Like individualized patterns, small-group patterns can be used to accommodate all types of individual differences important to reading: background knowledge, reading interests, achievement levels, and reading skills. Differences in background knowledge are usually addressed by providing a group with a common task and encouraging all group members to contribute their unique background knowledge to solving the task. Differences in reading interests, achievement levels, and reading skills are usually handled by developing groups around common interests, achievement levels, or skill needs. A variety of small-group patterns exist to meet these individual differences.

An increasingly common small group organizational pattern is the use of **literature discussion groups.** In literature discussion groups, groups of students read the same work of children's literature on their

paired reading
An approach in which two students read a text together.

literature discussion groups
A method framework that helps students develop wider response patterns to their reading; small groups of students read a single work of literature on their own, come together to have a grand conversation, and then complete a project that is shared.

grand conversations
A method framework that helps students develop wider response patterns to their reading; involves reading, reminding students of the guidelines, engaging students in a conversation which they direct, and asking one interpretive or literary question.

own and then come together to have a **grand conversation** about what they have read. Afterwards, the students develop a project and then share their project with the rest of the class. You will recall the procedural steps of a literature discussion group from chapter 4:

1. The teacher introduces three to five different books to the class, each with multiple copies.
2. Students determine which book they want to read and form groups based on this book.
3. Students read the literature selection for their group independently.
4. The teacher and each group have a grand conversation about the work.
5. A project is developed to extend students' response and understanding of the work.
6. The results of the project are shared with the other groups.

Literature discussion groups are used to support individual differences in each of the areas important to reading. By bringing students together to work on a common reading experience, discussion, and project, differences in background knowledge, reading interests, achievement levels, and reading skills are all supported. Sometimes, teachers will use individual contracts like that shown in Figure 13-3 during the use of litera-

It is often useful to arrange seating patterns to encourage small group interactions.

FIGURE 13-3

A sample contract used in one class for literature discussion groups

---

A Contract with Ms. Clark

The commitments expressed on this page are binding on each participant as they so commit.
Revocations, modifications, and other changes should be recorded with Ms. Clark before the
ending date of the contract. Questions regarding the completion of this contract may be
referred to the law firm of Dewey, Cheatum & Howe, Inc. for final arbitration.

I _Caity Parker_ plan to read the following book as a part of my literature

discussion group experience and complete each of the activities our group has decided upon as listed below:

Our book: _Dragon's Gate by Lawrence Yep._

Other members of my literature discussion group include:

Katie McClung   _Claire Weeks_

Jessica Brewing   _Rebecca Cottrell_

Jamie Matthewson

Katie Wentink

Activities that I will complete as a member of my literature discussion group:

1. _Write at least 5 entries in my response journal and share these with my group._

2. _Discuss our book with Ms. Clark after chapter 5 and at the end._

3. _Develop a reader's theater from our book._

4. _Present the reader's theater to our class._

Signed: _Caity Parker_   _Jardi Jones Clark_
        (Student)   (Teacher)

Date: _January 15_

interest groups
An intra-class organizational pattern that allows students to explore topics that are personally interesting.

ture discussion groups to help students remember what needs to be done and when it should be completed.

It is also useful to group students by reading interests. Such **interest groups** allow students to explore topics that are personally interesting. For example, the sixth-grade class in one elementary school had been learning in social studies about the exploration of the western United States. Consequently, the teacher decided to let students select their favorite western state and then work with others who also selected that state. For one week during their reading period, students worked in their interest groups, reading, collecting information, and finally reporting to the class about their states. At the same school the third-grade class was learning about different types of mammals in science, and that teacher decided to have students get together in groups to study their favorite mammal. Each group read, collected information, and then created a bulletin board display on their favorite mammal. Other interest groups might last longer but meet less frequently. Perhaps once a week or once a month different interest groups might get together to share information and books about their favorite topics: sports, pets, science fiction, music, or computers. In each case grouping decisions are based solely on students' interests.

Interest groups can serve several different purposes in a classroom reading program. A teacher might consider it important to regularly engage students in functional reading experiences, and opportunities to discover and share new information about an interesting topic can create important learning experiences. A teacher might also want to increase interest in and motivation for reading, developing students who not only can read, but also choose to read on their own. Or a teacher might be concerned about the negative effects on self-concept that might result from the regular use of achievement groups. With interest groups even the weakest readers have a chance to contribute to a topic that they find personally interesting.

There are several ways to form interest groups in a class. Perhaps the most common is to simply set up groups on several topics and allow students to select the area that they want to pursue. Often teachers administer a reading inventory at the beginning of the school year to determine students' interests (see chapter 4 and 11). The results of that inventory can then be used to make initial decisions about interest groups. Another approach is to ask students what areas they would like to explore that are related to a discussion topic just being completed. After students have had several experiences working in interest groups, this strategy can be an effective method of turning control over to students and developing greater independence in reading.

What is a teacher's role once interest groups are functioning? Instead of providing direct instruction, a teacher should guide students, providing resources for and direction to their reading. A teacher might circulate around the room, listening to ideas, offering suggestions, and helping children implement their own plans by directing them to appropriate resources.

A third type of small-group pattern is the use of **cooperative learning groups,** which are described in chapters 3 and 10. Cooperative learning groups provide learning experiences for students in a supportive, collaborative environment, as small groups of students work together to gather information and complete a learning task. Cooperative learning groups often follow the procedural steps of cooperative learning.

cooperative learning groups
An intraclass organizational pattern that uses small groups and a cooperative learning method framework.

Cooperative learning is a method framework consisting of several procedural steps:

1. The teacher defines a learning task.
2. The teacher assigns students to groups.
3. Students complete the learning task together.
4. The results of the learning task are shared with the entire class.

The model lesson that follows reviews those steps in operation.

A fourth type of small-group pattern is the use of **achievement groups** during reading instruction, thereby providing students of similar achievement levels an opportunity to work together. Groups of high-, average-, and low-achieving readers often use published reading programs to provide developmental reading instruction. Even though the utility of achievement groups has been questioned (Berghoff & Egawa, 1991; Harp, 1989; Slavin, 1987), this grouping pattern remains one of the most common in schools today, especially among teachers who hold a specific skills belief about how children learn to read.

achievement groups
An intraclass organizational pattern that provides students of similar achievement levels with an opportunity to work together.

The first step in forming achievement groups is to gather information and determine achievement levels in the class. Two common sources of information include students' cumulative files and the informal assessment of reading achievement completed during the first few weeks of the school year.

Each student has a **cumulative file,** which contains achievement and health records. Cumulative files are typically located in the school office, but classroom teachers have access to the information and often choose to review incoming students' files before the beginning of the year. At least two types of information might be useful: placement recommendations from last year's teacher and formal and informal test scores in reading.

cumulative file
A school file that contains a student's achievement and health records.

In schools that use published reading programs, teachers are expected to record the materials that each student completes by the end of the year. The next year's teacher often combines that information with additional data and places it all on a single form. Table 13-1 includes the information collected by a fourth-grade teacher from the previous year's records of two third-grade teachers. The five students without such information are new students who transferred into the school at the beginning of the year. Notice how one of these teachers (Ms. Ayre) used a published reading program while the other teacher (Mr. Loseby) did not.

MODEL LESSON

Using Cooperative Learning Groups in Mr. Graham's Class

Mr. Graham uses individualized reading projects a lot with his sixth-grade class. He is concerned, though, that individualized reading is limiting interactions among students; he believes that his students benefit both socially and intellectually when they work together on joint projects. Consequently, Mr. Graham has decided to spend two weeks during each nine-week marking period in cooperative learning groups.

The Teacher Defines a Learning Task. Mr. Graham's class is studying Europe in social studies, and he decides to integrate social studies and reading for several weeks by using cooperative learning groups. He explains to the class that each group will study one European country in detail, exploring the history of the country as well as its economy, geography, political system, and famous people. Mr. Graham is especially excited about the potential this project has to motivate students to read newspapers and news magazines. The changes taking place in Europe will require that they read about current events. Mr. Graham explains that each group will read about its country and prepare a bulletin board display with a map of physical features and written reports on the country's history, economy, political system, and famous people.

The Teacher Assigns Students to Groups. Mr. Graham puts up a list of European countries on the bulletin board and asks students to sign up for their three favorite countries. Using that list for guidance, he puts students together in groups of four or five.

Students Complete the Learning Task Together. For the next two weeks each group gathers information and puts it together for a bulletin board display. Some groups work as a unit on each element of the task. Other groups split up, with one person responsible for the map and one person responsible for each of the reports. Mr. Graham encourages all groups to spend ten minutes at the beginning of each work period sharing the information collected the previous day. He notices that students are gathering information for each other as they come across it in their reading. The last two days are a flurry of work, excitement, and debate as each group puts the finishing touches on its bulletin board display.

The Results of the Learning Task Are Shared with the Entire Class. On the final day the recorder/reporter designated by each group makes a formal presentation to the class. Individual group members also contribute their expertise, and then members of the class get to ask questions about the group's country.

stanine scores
Norm-referenced test scores that range from 1 to 9 and allow a comparison of relative standing.

The second type of achievement information can also be found in cumulative files—formal and informal test scores in reading. Table 13-1 lists **stanine scores** for decoding knowledge, vocabulary knowledge, and comprehension. These scores came from a test administered at the end of the third grade.

Because no single test score should ever be used to make decisions about youngsters, teachers should also gather informal assessment information on each student's performance within the context of the classroom. This type of assessment is especially important at the beginning of

TABLE 13-1

Classroom assessment data collected at the beginning of the year by one fourth-grade teacher

Name	Materials completed	Stanine decod/voc/comp	IRI instructional level	Informal observation	Interests
From Mr. Loseby					
Tommy	Thematic units, literature discussion groups, individualized reading	8/9/8	*Explorations* (5th)	Fluent. Has read *The Giver*	Myths & legends
Anne	Thematic units, lit. discussion groups, individualized reading	9/9/9	*Explorations* (5th)/ *Celebrations* (6th)	Spends lunch in library. Has read *Number the Stars*	Olympics, ballet
Tama	Thematic units, lit. discussion groups, individualized reading	3/9/6	*Flights* (4th)/ *Explorations* (5th)	Excellent comprehension	Poetry
Sharon	Thematic units, lit. discussion groups, individualized reading	8/4/7	*Explorations* (5th)	Summer library reader	Basketball, sports
Brian	Thematic units, lit. discussion groups, individualized reading	8/6/8	*Flights* (4th)	Summer library reader	Mysteries
Jo	Thematic units, lit. discussion groups, individualized reading	5/5/5	*Flights* (4th)	Exposition a problem	Sports
Katie	Thematic units, lit. discussion groups, individualized reading	6/4/5	*Flights* (4th)/ *Journeys* (3-2)	Good reader	Horses, skiing
Sarah	Thematic units, lit. discussion groups, individualized reading	7/5/5	*Flights* (4th)	Fluent reader	Science, computers

TABLE 13-1 *continued*

Name	Materials completed	Stanine decod/voc/comp	IRI instructional level	Informal observation	Interests
From Ms. Ayre					
Kathy	*Journeys* (3-2)	6/7/7	*Explorations* (5th)	Excellent inferences, vocabulary	Mysteries
Nelima	*Journeys* (3-2)	7/5/7	*Explorations* (5th)	Summer library reader	Computers
Billy	*Journeys* (3-2)	6/4/5	*Explorations* (5th)/ *Celebrations* (6th)	Excellent vocabulary	Ballet, sports
Jesus	*Journeys* (3-2)	6/8/7	*Explorations* (5th)	Excellent vocabulary	Basketball, poetry
Tim	*Journeys* (3-2)	5/8/7	*Explorations* (5th)	Fluent, excellent vocabulary	Computers, sports
Roberto	*Journeys* (3-2)	5/4/5	*Flights* (4th)	Weak vocabulary, exposition a problem	Mysteries, Olympics
Jessica	*Journeys* (3-2)	4/6/5	*Flights* (4th)/ *Journeys* (3-2)	Good inferences, vocabulary	Reading, sports
Vanessa	*Journeys* (3-2)	5/3/3	*Caravans* (3-1)	Weak vocabulary knowledge	Pets, baseball
Jeff	*Journeys* (3-2)	5/3/3	*Caravans* (3-1)	Exposition a problem	Bowling, pets
Kurt	*Discoveries* (2-2)	4/3/4	*Caravans* (3-1)	Poor vocabulary, weak in exposition	Olympics
Warren	*Discoveries* (2-2)	3/2/3	*Discoveries* (2-2)	Poor decoding skills, halting reader	Basketball, dirt bikes
Becky	*Discoveries* (2-2)	2/3/4	*Caravans* (3-1)	Weak decoding skills	Magic, travel
New Students					
Erica			*Explorations* (5th)	Writes own stories at home	Adventure stories
John			*Flights* (4th)	Weak vocabulary	Science fiction

TABLE 13-1 *continued*

Name	Materials completed	Stanine decod/voc/comp	IRI instructional level	Informal observation	Interests
New Students *continued*					
Vanita			*Explorations* (5th)/ *Celebrations* (6th)	Excellent vocabulary	Ballet, sports
Gene			*Flights* (4th)	Lacks prefix/suffix knowledge	Dirt bikes
Daniel			*Carousels* (1-2)	Poor decoding skills, little comprehension	Hamsters, baseball

the year: some students read widely and make gains in reading achievement over the summer vacation, whereas others do not read anything at all and lose ground. Teachers might want to administer an informal reading inventory (IRI) at the beginning of the year to obtain informal data on achievement levels, or they might want to simply listen to children read during the first few weeks of school.

Table 13-1 indicates the instructional level for each child according to an IRI administered at the beginning of the year. This particular teacher used passages from each level in the school's published reading series, and some students' instructional levels bridged two levels in the series. Table 13-1 also includes the results of informal classroom observations and an interest inventory completed during the first few weeks of school. This information, along with IRI scores, is especially important for new students, whose cumulative files are not likely to have been transferred by the beginning of the year.

After achievement data have been gathered, teachers must consider how many groups they want to form. The most common number is three (high, average, and low). Nevertheless, teachers—especially new teachers—should consider several important factors before making that decision. First, what previous experience have students had with small-group instruction? Students with considerable small-group experience are able to handle more groups. Second, what experience has the teacher had managing several reading groups? Extensive experience makes it easier to manage more groups. Finally, what amount and quality of supplemental materials are available? Again, extensive materials for students make it easier to manage additional groups.

Teachers should also consider how many students they want to have in each group. This decision hinges on your students' ability to work independently. Often it is best to reduce the number of students in a group

EXPLORING DIVERSE POINTS OF VIEW

Using the information in cumulative files at the beginning of the school year is controversial. Some professionals argue that the use of this information biases a teacher's perception of a child and results in a self-fulfilling prophecy (Rosenthal & Jacobson, 1968). They consider this practice most damaging to the least able and suggest that achievement information in cumulative files not be used to form achievement groups. Others argue that achievement scores, used correctly, are just one source of information that a teacher should consider. These professionals consider it inappropriate to ignore any information when making a decision as important as achievement group placement. What do you think? Will you use the achievement information in a child's cumulative file? If you decide to use it, what might you do to reduce the possibility of creating self-fulfilling prophecies for your students?

that requires more individual attention. Thus, the lowest-achieving group in a classroom is often the smallest because those students frequently require more guidance and support from the teacher.

Any decisions made about placement in achievement groups at the beginning of the year should be considered tentative and open to revision. Teachers should use the first month or two to see how well individual students fit into the organizational scheme of the classroom. In addition, teachers should be conservative when making those initial placements. Placing students in a lower-achieving group lets a teacher evaluate their performance and move them to a higher group at a later time. It is much harder to move students down without disturbing their confidence and motivation. As the year progresses, teachers should continuously reevaluate their grouping decisions and be prepared to accommodate students who might benefit from a change in group assignment.

Finally, it is essential to use alternate grouping patterns during the year—perhaps interest groups, cooperative learning groups, and/or individualized organizational patterns. Flexibility is important if students' individual differences are to be accommodated.

One final small-group pattern that attempts to meet individual differences is the use of **strategy groups.** Teachers often find it useful to organize their classrooms for short periods of time on the basis of specific strategy needs. Sometimes these strategy groups will be referred to as a **readers' workshop.** During a strategy group or readers' workshop, a teacher might provide instruction to a small group on inferencing strategies, the use of contextual information during reading, effective strategies to use when reading content-area selections, or any of numerous strategies that are known to be useful during reading. This type of grouping is appropriate when skill and strategy needs cut across established achievement groups in a class or when several students in individualized reading display similar skill or strategy needs. In such situations a teacher might regroup students temporarily on the basis of skill or strat-

strategy groups
An intraclass organizational pattern in which students are grouped for a short period of time according to skill or strategy needs.

reader's workshop
A small group approach to reading instruction that uses temporary groups, formed to focus on a particular aspect of reading.

OPPORTUNITIES TO CELEBRATE DIVERSITY

Thematic units can be organized around different cultural and linguistic experiences. Several models of how to do this are described in chapter 4. You may wish to look back at this discussion. In these units, children have an opportunity to discover insights about cultural groups that exist within their class as well as cultural groups they have yet to experience.

---

egy needs or might pull together certain students for a short workshop on particular reading skills or strategies.

Decisions about how many groups to use and how many students to have in each group closely parallel the decisions made with achievement groups. The number of groups will depend on students' previous experience with group work, the teacher's experience, and the amount and quality of supplemental materials available. The number of students in each group will be determined by the number of students with similar skill or strategy needs.

Despite these similarities, two important differences distinguish the use of strategy groups from the use of achievement groups. First, strategy groups typically last for only a few reading periods before children are regrouped for instruction on new strategies. Second, not all students will require instruction in the targeted areas. As a result, teachers should plan to use other reading activities with the students who are not placed in a skill or strategy group.

Whole-Class Patterns

Whole-class experiences can be valuable in many instances of reading instruction. They are especially useful when they take advantage of the diversity inherent in any classroom.

As noted in chapter 4, **thematic units** are being used increasingly in elementary and middle school classrooms. Thematic reading experiences result when a teacher organizes reading selections around a single theme. In addition, writing activities, vocabulary study, and discussions are used to expand on the theme and generate new understanding.

thematic units
Reading experiences that include writing activities, vocabulary study, and discussions, all of which are organized around a theme.

Thematic experiences can be organized in numerous ways: around a topic, such as solving problems, helping others, winter adventures, friendship, or animal pets; around an author, such as Daniel Pinkwater, Judith Viorst, Paul Goble, or Laura Ingalls Wilder; or around a type of writing, such as science fiction, biographies, fables, or mysteries. The advantage of thematic reading experiences is that reading focuses on content. As a result, reading experiences become more significant and functional. Students read, discuss, and write about a theme in order to learn more about it, not simply to learn how to read.

In a thematic unit the entire class usually reads the same selections so that all students share a similar body of content. However, these experi-

MODEL LESSON

A Thematic Unit on Sharing in Mr. Dewey's Class

Mr. Dewey has organized a short integrated language arts unit on sharing for his entire class to enjoy. Three reading selections form the core of the unit.

The Giving Tree by Shel Silverstein
The Gift by Helen Coutant
New Year's Hats for the Statues by Yoshiko Uchida

Before each reading selection Mr. Dewey initiates a discussion about sharing that prepares students for the story. He also introduces any new vocabulary words from the selection that might be unfamiliar to students. After each selection Mr. Dewey uses cooperative learning groups to discuss it. He presents each group with a thought-provoking question about the story. After students read *The Giving Tree,* for example, he has cooperative learning groups consider the following:

If you had been this apple tree would you have acted the same? Why or why not?

During this thematic unit Mr. Dewey also conducts read-aloud sessions from the book *Chester Cricket's Pigeon Ride* by George Selden. During each session the class discusses the read-aloud story in relation to the selections they are reading themselves about sharing. Students begin to make comparisons between the characters and to apply the characters' experiences to their own experiences in the classroom and outside school.

Mr. Dewey also introduces a writing experience in order to connect reading and the writing. He suggests that everyone in the class share an important idea for making the class a better place in which to learn and to grow. He encourages students to brainstorm a list of possible ideas, and writes the list on the board. After students finish drafting, editing, and revising their work, Mr. Dewey has them all read their papers aloud from the author's chair in the room. Their ideas generate lively discussion about improving the classroom. Finally, Mr. Dewey posts each paper on a bulletin board labeled Share a Great Idea.

ences often include cooperative learning group activities and individualized writing assignments to better accommodate individual differences.

There are also a number of additional whole-class patterns that you might choose to use in your classroom. Any reading activity that requires an audience is a perfect opportunity for a whole-class experience. Oral book reports, for example, can be presented by students when they finish reading a book that they think others might enjoy. Readers theatre presentations are also especially appropriate, as are read-aloud response journal sessions.

Short sessions in which students are introduced to new materials are also perfect opportunities for a whole-class activity. The teacher might conduct a book talk to introduce a new set of books in the reading corner. Or a student might introduce the author-of-the-week bulletin board and acquaint students with a favorite author. Perhaps a new activity at the reading/writing center could be explained. Each of these provides a useful encounter with reading materials in a whole-class pattern.

Another opportunity for a whole-class experience may occur when you wish to teach a reading strategy to all students together—for example, the use of references in the library, map reading before a field trip, the use of a thesaurus as a writing aid, or a new poetic form. Another opportunity comes with current events. Often teachers have their classes subscribe to a weekly newspaper so that students can read and discuss current events together. In addition, sustained silent reading (SSR), which is often incorporated into a daily reading schedule, is an important whole-class reading experience. And choral reading provides an entire class with an opportunity to appreciate rhythm, poetry, and the stylistic conventions of unique discourse forms.

USING A LITERACY FRAMEWORK TO GUIDE DECISIONS ABOUT CLASSROOM ORGANIZATION

Decisions about classroom organization are decisions about how you will structure learning experiences for students. Will you use individualized reading, literature discussion groups, interest groups, and thematic reading experiences to provide meaningful, holistic, and functional opportunities for students to learn inductively? Will you use achievement groups and strategy groups to provide students with more direct instructional

Whatever centers or organizational systems you use for your class, they should encourage interactions between students and their literacy experiences.

experiences? Or will you integrate achievement and/or strategy groups with individualized reading, literature discussion groups, interest groups, and thematic reading experiences? Because organizational decisions determine how learning experiences will be structured, your belief about how reading ability develops can be used as a guide. These relationships can be seen in Table 13-2.

If you have a holistic language learning belief about how children learn to read, you believe that reading is learned inductively as students engage in self-directed, meaningful, and holistic experiences with authentic literature. As a result, you are most concerned about accommodating two individual differences that make a difference in reading: reading interests and background knowledge. And, because you are most concerned about accommodating these two differences you tend to favor certain types of intraclass organizational patterns. These include the use of thematic units, literature discussion groups, interest groups, and individualized reading activities.

If you have a specific skills belief about how children learn to read, you believe that differences in reading achievement levels and reading skills are most important to accommodate in your organizational plans. These differences are most important because you believe that students learn best when they are taught specific reading skills directly. As a result, you favor intraclass organizational patterns such as achievement groups and strategy groups. These allow you to focus your attention on direct instruction of specific reading skills.

If you have an integrated belief of how children learn to read, you think that all four types of individual differences are important to consider: reading interests, background knowledge, reading skills, and reading achievement level. This is because you believe that children learn best when they are exposed to authentic and holistic experiences with print and, at the same time, receive instruction in important skill areas. As a result, you favor all six types of intraclass organizational patterns: thematic units, literature discussion groups, interest groups, individualized reading, achievement groups, and strategy groups. These allow you to accommodate all of the individual differences that are important to you.

Of course, it is also important to recognize that the previous discussion represents three specific beliefs. If your beliefs about how children learn to read fall somewhere between any two of these beliefs you will modify your organizational plans accordingly.

But how would teachers with these different beliefs actually organize their reading program during the year to accommodate the individual differences they find to be most important? The following section will describe how teachers with different beliefs might develop a **yearly plan** for their classroom. A yearly plan is often used by teachers to plan out how and when they will use different organizational patterns in their classroom for the entire year. The plans in Tables 13-3 through 13-5 specify the primary grouping patterns for each week and also indicates how

yearly plan
A schedule of organizational patterns to be used during the year to accommodate individual differences.

TABLE 13-2

A summary of how a literacy framework can be used to inform decisions about intraclass organizational patterns

Beliefs about how children learn to read	Related assumptions	Most important individual differences that make a difference in reading	Favored organizational patterns
Holistic Language Learning	Students learn best in an inductive fashion as they direct their own learning and reading experiences. Students learn best during holistic, meaningful, and functional experiences with authentic literature.	Reading Interests Background Knowledge	Thematic Units Literature Discussion Groups Interest Groups Individualized Reading
Specific Skills	Students learn best when they are taught directly by the teacher in a deductive fashion. Students learn best when they master specific reading skills.	Reading Achievement Level Reading Skills	Achievement Groups Strategy Groups
Integrated	Students learn best as a result of both student-directed, inductive experiences and teacher-directed, deductive experiences. Students learn best when they engage in purposeful, functional, and holistic experiences with authentic texts and when they acquire specific reading skills.	Reading Interests Background Knowledge Reading Skills Reading Achievement Level	Thematic Units Literature Discussion Groups Interest Groups Individualized Reading Achievement Groups Strategy Groups

TABLE 13-3

An organization plan for one year consistent with a holistic language perspective

Weeks	Getting started in reading
1 & 2	Introduce and begin read alouds and response journals Introduce and begin reading/writing center activities Introduce and begin individualized reading Collect reading interest information from an interest inventory and discussions Collect background knowledge information with informal assessment Administer IRI Check cumulative files for additional assessment information

Week	Primary grouping pattern	Additional experiences
3–6	Thematic Unit #1: Human rights and responsibilities (whole class—60 minutes)	Read Aloud Response Journals (30 minutes alternate days) Sustained Silent Reading (30 minutes alternate days) Individualized Reading (as time permits) Reading/Writing Center Activities (as time permits)
7–9	Thematic Unit #2: The African American Experience (whole class—60 minutes)	Read Aloud Response Journals (30 minutes alternate days) Sustained Silent Reading (30 minutes alternate days) Individualized Reading (as time permits) Reading/Writing Center Activities (as time permits)
10–12	Thematic Unit #3: The Asian Experience (whole class—60 minutes)	Read Aloud Response Journals (30 minutes alternate days) Sustained Silent Reading (30 minutes alternate days) Individualized Reading (as time permits) Reading/Writing Center Activities (as time permits)
13–15	Literature Discussion Groups (small groups—60 minutes)	Read Aloud Response Journals (30 minutes alternate days) Sustained Silent Reading (30 minutes alternate days)
16–18	Interest groups (small groups—60 minutes)	Read Aloud Response Journals (30 minutes alternate days) Sustained Silent Reading (30 minutes alternate days)

TABLE 13-3 *continued*

Week	Primary grouping pattern	Additional experiences
19–21	Thematic Unit #4: The Hispanic Experience (whole class—60 minutes)	Read Aloud Response Journals (30 minutes alternate days) Sustained Silent Reading (30 minutes alternate days) Individualized Reading (as time permits) Reading/Writing Center Activities (as time permits)
22–24	Literature Discussion Groups (small groups—60 minutes)	Read Aloud Response Journals (30 minutes alternate days) Sustained Silent Reading (30 minutes alternate days)
25–27	Interest groups (small groups—60 minutes)	Read Aloud Response Journals (30 minutes alternate days) Sustained Silent Reading (30 minutes alternate days)
28–30	Thematic Unit #5: The Meaning of Friendship (whole class—60 minutes)	Read Aloud Response Journals (30 minutes alternate days) Sustained Silent Reading (30 minutes alternate days) Individualized Reading (as time permits) Reading/Writing Center Activities (as time permits)
31–33	Literature Discussion Groups (small groups—60 minutes)	Read Aloud Response Journals (30 minutes alternate days) Sustained Silent Reading (30 minutes alternate days)
34–36	Interest groups (small groups—60 minutes)	Read Aloud Response Journals (30 minutes alternate days) Sustained Silent Reading (30 minutes alternate days)

much time will be devoted to other organizational patterns such as read-aloud response journals, sustained silent reading, individualized reading, and reading/writing center activities.

Holistic Language Learning

Teachers with a holistic language learning perspective believe that reading ability develops as students engage in holistic, meaningful, and func-

TABLE 13-4

An organization plan for one year consistent with a specific skills perspective

Weeks	Getting started in reading
1 & 2	Check cumulative files for assessment information Introduce and begin reading/writing center activities Introduce and begin read alouds and response journals Collect reading interest information from an interest inventory and discussions Administer IRI

Week	Primary grouping pattern	Additional experiences

3–6	Achievement Groups with Published Reading Program
	(whole class—60 minutes)
	(regroup as necessary)
		Read Aloud Response Journals
		   (30 minutes alternate days)
		Sustained Silent Reading
		   (30 minutes alternate days)
		Reading/Writing Center Activities
		   (Contracts)

7–9	Achievement Groups with Published Reading Program
	(whole class—60 minutes)
	(regroup as necessary)
		Read Aloud Response Journals
		   (30 minutes alternate days)
		Sustained Silent Reading
		   (30 minutes alternate days)
		Reading/Writing Center Activities
		   (Contracts)

10	Strategy Groups
	(small groups—60 minutes)
		Read Aloud Response Journals
		   (30 minutes alternate days)
		Sustained Silent Reading
		   (30 minutes alternate days)
		Reading/Writing Center Activities
		   (Contracts)

11–18	Achievement Groups with Published Reading Program
	(whole class—60 minutes)
		Read Aloud Response Journals
		   (30 minutes alternate days)
		Sustained Silent Reading
		   (30 minutes alternate days)
		Reading/Writing Center Activities
		   (Contracts)

19	Strategy Groups
	(small groups—60 minutes)
		Read Aloud Response Journals
		   (30 minutes alternate days)
		Sustained Silent Reading
		   (30 minutes alternate days)
		Reading/Writing Center Activities
		   (Contracts)

TABLE 13-4   *continued*

Week	Primary grouping pattern	Additional experiences
20–27	Achievement Groups with Published Reading Program (whole class—60 minutes)	Read Aloud Response Journals (30 minutes alternate days) Sustained Silent Reading (30 minutes alternate days) Reading/Writing Center Activities (Contracts)
28	Strategy Groups (small groups—60 minutes)	Read Aloud Response Journals (30 minutes alternate days) Sustained Silent Reading (30 minutes alternate days) Reading/Writing Center Activities (Contracts)
29–36	Achievement Groups with Published Reading Program (whole class—60 minutes)	Read Aloud Response Journals (30 minutes alternate days) Sustained Silent Reading (30 minutes alternate days) Reading/Writing Center Activities (Contracts)

tional experiences with authentic literature and as students direct many of their own learning and reading experiences. A yearly plan for such a teacher would reflect those assumptions. Table 13-3 shows one possible arrangement.

The first two weeks of school are typically used by all teachers to develop an understanding of students' abilities, interests, background knowledge, and reading skills. This time is also used to introduce students to some of the organizational aspects of the class. Note, for example, how this teacher introduces students to read alouds, response journals, individualized reading activities, and reading/writing center activities. Introducing these more independent activities also frees the teacher to conduct Informal Reading Inventories (IRI) or other informal assessments such as running records.

Teachers with a holistic perspective would rely largely on four grouping patterns during the year: thematic units, literature discussion groups, interest groups, and individualized reading. Table 13-3 suggests how these primary grouping patterns might be scheduled during the year. Read-aloud response journal sessions, sustained silent reading, and reading/writing center activities would also be used. Teachers with a more holistic perspective would find these experiences to provide special opportunities for students to direct their own experiences in literacy learning.

Specific Skills Beliefs

Teachers with a specific skills perspective believe that reading ability develops as students learn specific reading skills through teacher-directed, deductive lessons. As a result, these teachers organize their classrooms to maximize instruction on specific reading skills. A yearly plan for reading that is consistent with a specific skills explanation is outlined in Table 13-4.

Teachers with a specific skills perspective would also want to spend the first two weeks getting acquainted with students' abilities and letting students become familiar with the organization of their new classroom. These teachers might also introduce students to read aloud response journals and reading/writing center activities. And as students are working independently, these teachers might evaluate them individually with an IRI. They might also administer an interest inventory. At the same time they would be gathering achievement information from students' cumulative files and use all of this information to make preliminary decisions about achievement groups.

Teachers with a specific skills perspective would probably rely on a published reading program for the core of their reading instruction, thereby leading to the use of achievement groups as their primary grouping pattern. According to Table 13-4, instruction would begin during Week 3. Then, during Weeks 3 to 6 these teachers would observe their students' performance and make any changes in group assignments by the end of Week 6. They would also do the same type of observation and regrouping during weeks 7–9.

We can see from the table that achievement groups are used during the first nine-week period. After that, the first week in each nine-week block is devoted to strategy groups, for which students would be regrouped according to specific strategy and skill needs and provided with appropriate instruction. The final eight weeks in each block are then spent in achievement groups.

While achievement groups and strategy groups are the primary grouping patterns used by this type of teacher, other experiences will also be provided. Read aloud response journals will be used on alternate days to make connections between reading and writing (see chapter 5). On other days, sustained silent reading will be used to help develop independent readers (see chapter 4). And reading/writing center activities will be used to provide independent practice opportunities for students. Here, a specific skills teacher is likely to use contracts to monitor students' progress. Each week the center activity is changed, and students make a contract with the teacher to complete a certain number of activities during each nine-week period.

Integrated Explanation

Teachers with an integrated explanation of development would include both holistic and specific skills perspectives in their decisions about class-

TABLE 13-5

An organization plan for one year consistent with an integrated perspective

Weeks	Getting started in reading
1 & 2	Introduce and begin read alouds and response journals
	Introduce and begin individualized reading
	Introduce and begin reading/writing center activities
	Collect reading interest information from an interest inventory and discussions
	Collect background knowledge information with informal assessment
	Administer IRI
	Check cumulative files for additional assessment information

Week	Primary grouping pattern	Additional experiences
3–5	Thematic Unit #1: Diversity and Difference (whole class—60 minutes)	Read Aloud Response Journals (30 minutes alternate days) Sustained Silent Reading (30 minutes alternate days) Individualized Reading (as time permits) Reading/Writing Center Activities (as time permits)
6–8	Thematic Unit #2: Planet Earth: Ecology (whole class—60 minutes)	Read Aloud Response Journals (30 minutes alternate days) Sustained Silent Reading (30 minutes alternate days) Individualized Reading (as time permits) Reading/Writing Center Activities (as time permits)
9	Strategy Groups or Achievement Groups (small groups—60 minutes)	Read Aloud Response Journals (30 minutes alternate days) Sustained Silent Reading (30 minutes alternate days) Individualized Reading (as time permits) Reading/Writing Center Activities (as time permits)
10–12	Thematic Unit #3: The Written Word: Literacy (whole class—60 minutes)	Read Aloud Response Journals (30 minutes alternate days) Sustained Silent Reading (30 minutes alternate days) Individualized Reading (as time permits) Reading/Writing Center Activities (as time permits)

TABLE 13-5 *cont'd*

Week	Primary grouping pattern	Additional experiences
13–15	Literature DiscussionGroups (small groups—60 minutes)	Read Aloud Response Journals (30 minutes alternate days) Sustained Silent Reading (30 minutes alternate days)
16–17	Interest groups (small groups—60 minutes)	Read Aloud Response Journals (30 minutes alternate days) Sustained Silent Reading (30 minutes alternate days)
18	Strategy Groups or Achievement Groups (small groups—60 minutes)	Read Aloud Response Journals (30 minutes alternate days) Sustained Silent Reading (30 minutes alternate days) Individualized Reading (as time permits) Reading/Writing Center Activities (as time permits)
19–21	Thematic Unit #4: Medieval Europe (whole class—60 minutes)	Read Aloud Response Journals (30 minutes alternate days) Sustained Silent Reading (30 minutes alternate days) Individualized Reading (as time permits) Reading/Writing Center Activities (as time permits)
22–24	Literature Discussion Groups (small groups—60 minutes)	Read Aloud Response Journals (30 minutes alternate days) Sustained Silent Reading (30 minutes alternate days)
25–26	Interest groups (small groups—60 minutes)	Read Aloud Response Journals (30 minutes alternate days) Sustained Silent Reading (30 minutes alternate days)
27	Strategy Groups or Achievement Groups (small groups—60 minutes)	Read Aloud Response Journals (30 minutes alternate days) Sustained Silent Reading (30 minutes alternate days) Individualized Reading (as time permits) Reading/Writing Center Activities (as time permits)

TABLE 13-5 *continued*

Week	Primary grouping pattern	Additional experiences
28–30	Thematic Unit #5: The meaning of Friendship (whole class—60 minutes)	Read Aloud Response Journals (30 minutes alternate days) Sustained Silent Reading (30 minutes alternate days) Individualized Reading (as time permits) Reading/Writing Center Activities (as time permits)
31–33	Literature Discussion Groups (small groups—60 minutes)	Read Aloud Response Journals (30 minutes alternate days) Sustained Silent Reading (30 minutes alternate days)
34–35	Interest groups (small groups—60 minutes)	Read Aloud Response Journals (30 minutes alternate days) Sustained Silent Reading (30 minutes alternate days)
36	Strategy Groups or Achievement Groups (small groups—60 minutes)	Read Aloud Response Journals (30 minutes alternate days) Sustained Silent Reading (30 minutes alternate days) Individualized Reading (as time permits) Reading/Writing Center Activities (as time permits)

room organization. Table 13-5 shows one way in which an integrated classroom might be organized.

During the first two weeks, time would again be spent collecting achievement and interest data on the students and introducing them to the organizational patterns in the classroom. Notice, too, that many of the more independent activities are introduced during this time to permit individual assessment activities.

The primary grouping patterns used by this type of teacher would include thematic units, strategy or achievement groups, literature discussion groups, interest groups, and individualized reading. Notice in Table 13-5 how this teacher weaves these different types of organizational patterns into the yearly plan.

Comments from the Classroom

Judy Dill, first grade teacher

To make reading an inviting activity, I have worked to create a reading center that has become a favorite place for my students to be. Among the truckload of books, our center is often filled with children piled into bean bag chairs, curled up in the rocking chair, or stretched out on some oversized stuffed animals. One frequent visitor to our reading center is a life-size granny doll we named Mrs. Minerva. She has velcroed hands and my first graders climb into her lap and read stories to her. Children have told me that they like to read to Mrs. Minerva because she never interrupts them when they read and she never minds hearing the same story over and over again.

I work to change certain aspects of the reading center to keep children interested in using it. One technique I use is to house the books in the center in different kinds of containers. I use baskets, an empty aquarium, or specially decorated boxes. I try to match at least one container of books to a topic we are studying. For example, when we do our ocean unit I use the aquarium. I tape fish and other interesting sea creatures facing out on the inside walls. Then I tuck a few interesting shells inside and some books about the sea and animals that live there. For a study we did on plants and flowers, I placed a number of different kinds of plants and fresh cut flowers everywhere in the center and a big empty flower pot with "blooming ideas for books to read" in the middle of the center.

At different times, I have even used a big cardboard box made into a time machine, a pirate ship, or a dragon (all of which the class made while studying certain topics) to create "great escapes" and an exciting and different reading atmosphere.

The reading center is an important part of our classroom. I try to allow more individual freedom within it. Some children enjoy reading in the center with a partner while others like to browse through the books themselves. I have a few nonreaders who choose the same book much of the time as they have memorized it and can look like they are reading. That's alright for now because that is their level.

One other key to the center's popularity is having lots of predictable books in it *because these books facilitate early reading success and the more successful the children feel, the more reading takes place.*

Our reading center has a sign in it that says, "To be a better reader you have to read, read, read, read, read, read, read, read, read," The children soon take that message to heart.

- Reading instruction should attempt to meet the individual needs of each student in the classroom. Four types of individual differences are most important to reading instruction: background knowledge, reading interests, reading achievement levels, and reading skills.

- Schools accommodate individual differences important to reading through interclass organizational patterns, such as homogeneous grouping (tracking); departmentalized reading instruction; team teaching; cross-grade grouping; split-half classes; retention and acceleration; and assistance by reading specialists or special educators.

- Teachers accommodate individual differences important to reading through intraclass organizational patterns. These include individualized patterns, such as individualized reading, reading/writing centers, cross-age tutoring, and paired reading. Small-group patterns include literature discussion groups, interest groups, cooperative learning groups, achievement groups, and strategy groups. Whole-class patterns include thematic reading experiences and other whole-class reading experiences.

- Because organizational decisions are decisions about how to structure learning experiences, a belief about how reading develops can be used to guide decision making. A holistic language perspective will favor thematic units, literature discussion groups, interest groups, and individualized reading. A specific skills perspective will favor achievement groups and/or strategy groups as the primary grouping patterns. An integrated perspective will favor using each of these grouping patterns.

Major Points

Making Instructional Decisions

1. Interview two students in an elementary grade classroom. Find out as much as possible about their background knowledge and reading interests. Then interview their teacher and find out as much as you can about their reading achievement levels and needs. Write a description of each student (without using real names), explaining how similar or different they are in areas important to reading instruction: background knowledge, reading interests, reading achievement levels, and reading skills. What can you conclude about the nature of individual differences in a classroom of 25 students?

2. According to Harris and Sipay (1990), you can expect a minimum of eight years' difference in reading achievement at the eighth-grade level. In reality, the difference is likely to be more than eight years. Let's assume that your school has departmentalized reading instruction for Grade 8, and you are responsible for assigning students to classes. You have begun by organizing three separate classes: one of lower-achieving readers, one of average-achieving readers, and one of higher-achieving readers. What is the minimum difference you should expect in reading achievement levels in each of your classes? Has a departmentalized reading program solved the challenge presented by individual differences? Why or why not?

3. Imagine that it is the beginning of the school year, and you have collected the data in Table 13-1. Use that information to form three achievement groups in your class. How confident are you in your decisions? Are there any students you should observe more carefully during the first week or so of achievement groups? Explain any concerns that you have.

4. Use the data in Table 13-1 to form several different interest groups. Describe several different reading projects that each group could complete.

5. Define your current literacy framework. If you were to begin teaching next week, what yearly plan would you follow in your classroom reading program? Describe how you would meet your students' individual differences in background knowledge, reading interests, achievement levels, and reading skills.

Berghoff, B. & Egawa, K. (1991). No more "rocks": Grouping to give students control of their learning. *The Reading Teacher, 44* (8), 536–541.

The authors describe grouping practices from more of a holistic language learning perspective. They present an excellent table describing a variety of whole class, small group, and independent patterns and explain how each supports literacy development and self-directed learning experiences.

Harp, B. (1989). When the principal asks: "What do we put in the place of ability grouping?" *The Reading Teacher, 42*(7), 434–435.

Describes two methods that can be used to replace achievement groups: flexible grouping and cooperative learning groups. Explains how each method can be used to promote reading development in the classroom.

Keegan, S. & Shrake, K. (1991). Literature study groups: An alternative to ability grouping. *The Reading Teacher, 44*(8), 542–547.

Describes the use of literature study groups, an approach to organizing classroom learning based on literature, discussions, and writing experiences. The article describes the importance of preparing students for these more independent experiences. Several useful ideas for classroom are presented including the use of a dialogue journal between the group and the teacher.

Staab, C. (1991). Classroom organization: Thematic centers revisited. *The Reading Teacher, 68,* 108–113.

Shows how the use of thematic reading centers can be used to engage students in meaningful literacy experiences within the classroom and promote self-directed learning.

Further Reading

Berghoff, B. & Egawa, K. (1991). No more "rocks": Grouping to give students control of their learning. *The Reading Teacher, 44*(8), 536–541.

Harp, B. (1989). When the principal asks: "What do we know now about ability grouping?" *The Reading Teacher, 42*(6), 430–431.

Harris, A. J., & Sipay, E. R. (1990). *How to increase reading ability* (9th ed.). New York: Longman.

Hiebert, E. H. (1983). An examination of ability grouping for reading instruction. *Reading Research Quarterly, 18*(2), 231–255.

Keegan, S. & Shrake, K. (1991). Literature study groups: An alternative to ability grouping. *The Reading Teacher, 44*(8), 542–547.

Rosenthal, R., & Jacobson, J. (1968). *Pygmalion in the classroom.* New York: Holt, Rinehart & Winston.

Sharpley, A. M., & Sharpley, C. F. (1981). Peer tutoring—A review of the literature. *Collected Original Resources in Education, 5*(3), 7–11.

Slavin, R. E. (1987). Ability grouping and student achievement in elementary schools: A best evidence synthesis. *Review of Educational Research, 57*(3), 293–336.

Staab, C. (1991). Classroom organization: Thematic centers revisited. *The Reading Teacher, 68,* 108–113.

Topping, K. (1989). Peer tutoring and paired reading: Combining two powerful techniques. *The Reading Teacher, 42*(7), 488–494.

Tunnell, M. O., & Jacobs, J. S. (1989). Using "real" books: Research findings on literature based reading instruction. *The Reading Teacher, 42*(7), 470–477.

References

CHAPTER

Supporting Literacy with Computers and Related Technologies

14

I used to be quite unimpressed with computers. I was also a little frightened of them. First, I had been teaching for a while and honestly didn't think that they would add much to what I was already doing. Then again, my experience had been largely with computer games, and I didn't think those were appropriate for classrooms. I didn't want to learn to program, and I had had several frustrating experiences with word processing and some other programs. And then, I kept hearing horror stories about how important information had been "lost." So all in all, I just didn't think it was worth it!

Now, after this class and the opportunity to experiment with some of the programs available to teachers, I must say I feel differently. I don't feel threatened and, most important, I do think that computers can help me teach children to read and write. I don't think they'll ever replace what I've been doing—but I now see them as another valuable tool that will help me do a better job as a reading teacher!

Entry in a masters student's journal.

Many teachers are frustrated or at a loss about what to do with microcomputers. In fact, many are somewhat intimidated by most of our emerging technology. Nonetheless, teachers are also generally aware that the wide range of available technology offers potential benefits for instructional practices.

This chapter discusses the use of various technologies that can benefit literacy teaching and learning. It tries to avoid discussing specific software because these are frequently updated and improved and sometimes become unavailable after a period of time. Any programs mentioned by name are used only as examples within a category. Local computer stores, educational computer publications, or a school district resource and curriculum center can recommend specific software titles for the uses we discuss.

Chapter 14 includes information that will help you answer questions such as:

1. What is an appropriate model for microcomputer use in reading instruction?
2. How can microcomputers and related technologies be used to enhance reading instruction?
3. What should be considered when choosing or evaluating software?
4. How does a literacy framework guide a teacher's use of microcomputer technology?

KEY CONCEPTS

application software	managing learning with computers
CD-ROM	multimedia
drill-and-practice software	network
graphics	program
hardware	simulations
hypertext	(speech-based) software
learning about thinking with computers	spreadsheet
learning with computers	tutorial software
Logo	videodisc

A MODEL OF MICROCOMPUTER USE IN READING INSTRUCTION

The job of the teacher of reading is a demanding one. It requires careful decision making while high-level cognitive processes are being taught. Nonetheless, some view microcomputer technology as a force that will radically change instructional practice, almost replacing teachers. Others believe that microcomputers and related technology are an expensive fad

·· **EXPLORING DIVERSE POINTS OF VIEW** ····················

The two following quotations reflect the diverse opinions about the impact of computers on education.

> There won't be schools in the future. . . . I think the computer will blow up the school. . . . The whole system is based on a set of structural concepts that are incompatible with the presence of the computer. (Papert, 1984, p. 38)

> Where favorable conditions exist, teacher use [of computers] will increase but seldom exceed more than 10 percent of weekly instructional time. . . . Where unfavorable conditions exist. . . . schoolwide

use will be spotty. . . . I predict no great breakthrough in teacher use patterns at either level of schooling. The new technology, like its predecessors, will be tailored to fit the teacher's perspective and the tight contours of school and classroom settings. (Cuban, 1986, p. 99)

Notice, however, that even the more pessimistic view acknowledges that technology will, to some extent, continue to appear in schools and that the use of technology depends on a teacher's instructional framework. Given your own literacy framework, how will you incorporate technology into your reading instruction?

that will die out as school systems reaffirm that instruction requires a human quality.

Neither of these views adequately reflects the potential benefits of a thoughtful implementation of technology in the literacy curriculum. Microcomputers are an educational tool that can be well used or badly misused, like all other technology and teaching materials. For example, neither published reading programs nor the use of children's literature provides any greater guarantee of effective instruction than do microcomputers. In all cases, *teachers* must make appropriate instructional decisions.

Goldberg and Sherwood (1983) expanded previous classifications of computer use (Taylor, 1980; Luehrmann, 1983) and presented a five-part model of computer use, highlighted in Table 14-1. This classification allows teachers to be more aware of the multiple, appropriate uses of computers in classrooms. It also enhances the awareness that software and computer use should occur in each category.

Learning from Computers

In this category the computer acts as an instructor, with communication being essentially a one-way affair—from microcomputer to student. Most of the applications in this area are drill-and-practice software, but tutorial software also falls within this category. Both drill-and-practice and tutorial software can appear as fairly formal programs that require reading and question-answering activities; game-like formats are also used. Because of the unique features of game-like software and concerns that have been voiced by parents and teachers, this format is considered as a separate category below.

TABLE 14-1

A classification system of computer use

Classification	Examples
Learning about computers	Computer literacy: includes learning about the equipment as well as learning programming languages. Learning about computers will not be the main focus in a reading classroom. However, students must know enough about the equipment to use it intelligently. For example, they need to know how to turn on and off a particular microcomputer, how to load and run specific software, how to use a printer, how to handle and store diskettes, and so on.
Learning from computers	Drill and practice: includes most games and tutorial software.
Learning with computers	Simulations: includes software that models a real-world situation and attempts to enhance problem-solving abilities.
Learning about thinking with computers	Problem solving: includes the potential influence on students' thinking skills that results from working with computers and some types of software.
Managing learning with computers	Classroom management: includes record keeping, filing, and other such functions.

drill-and-practice software
Nonteaching programs that present activities intended to reinforce knowledge.

Drill-and-Practice Software.   **Drill-and-practice software** often presents students with a series of questions. A correct response results in some form of feedback and a new question; an incorrect response results in feedback and the opportunity to try again. If the answer is still incorrect, most drill-and-practice programs give the answer and move on to a new question. Such software usually keeps track of a student's responses and provides the student, the teacher, or both with the student's overall score. Drill-and-practice software is available in all areas of reading, from decoding to vocabulary, main idea comprehension, and so on.

By definition, drill-and-practice software does not teach; like regular paper-and-pencil worksheets, it only allows students to practice what has already been taught. Nevertheless, practice can be an important step after teaching and initial learning have taken place. The question for teachers is whether drill-and-practice programs, which are often little more than computerized worksheets, offer an advantage over a regular worksheet.

In the drill-and-practice area, microcomputers may have at least three advantages over worksheets, although each drill-and-practice program must be evaluated to see whether these or other desired features are present.

1. *Motivational presentation.* Microcomputers appear to stimulate and motivate students to a greater extent than workbooks do. Even when tasks are similar, students spend more time on computer drill-and-practice activities than they do on worksheets. It is possible that this increased attention is a response to novelty rather than to some inherently motivational aspect of the microcomputer.
2. *Record-keeping functions.* The microcomputer can quickly capture and tabulate student scores, which are then usually placed in a file where teachers can easily see who has done well and who might need additional instruction. Thus, computerized record keeping can provide information needed for instructional decisions, thereby relieving teachers of the need to check students' answers manually.
3. *Branching capabilities.* The microcomputer can present drill-and-practice activities more closely matched to student ability levels than those presented in a workbook. For example, if a student answers three consecutive problems incorrectly, software can branch to similar items of less difficulty. It can also branch to items of greater difficulty if a student responds correctly a given number of times.

An additional advantage of some drill-and-practice software is that a teacher can customize what is presented, thereby more closely matching instructional objectives. For example, teachers can often enter the set of words that are to be presented in a vocabulary or spelling lesson, can vary the rate of presentation and number of repetitions, and so on.

Tutorial Software. **Tutorial software** is designed so that a student can learn as well as practice. It goes beyond a simple presentation of items to which a student responds. The critical difference between drill-and-practice and tutorial software is that tutorial programs are written so that a concept or fact is first taught and then practiced. This type of software almost always includes branches that change the difficulty of items or that provide additional instruction depending on the student's performance. In addition, explanations are included, as well as feedback.

tutorial software
Programs that attempt to teach as well as reinforce concepts.

Although tutorial software is preferred to simple drill-and-practice offerings, it, too, can be misused. The computer can patiently present a tutorial, but it cannot decide whether that tutorial includes content that is important to a student's reading development. The teacher must determine whether software content, format, sequencing of concepts, pacing, and other factors are appropriate to the instructional program, the reading process, and reading instruction in general.

Game-like Software. Most **game-like software** uses the color, sound, and animation capabilities of microcomputers to catch and hold student

game-like software
Computer programs that use games or game like formats to teach and reinforce concepts.

attention. Such software presents instruction in a format that allows a student to play against others or the computer while learning. The student is challenged to compile a high score. Software that teaches in a game format is becoming more and more prevalent, as are microcomputers that feature advanced graphics and sound capabilities. Although teachers need to be careful that the concepts being presented are not overshadowed by the peripheral aspects of the presentation, well-constructed game-like software can be pedagogically sound and is popular with both students and teachers.

Awareness of several problems associated with game-like software should help ensure that it is chosen for its educational rather than its game-like value.

- Game-like software often has violent overtones. These programs must be carefully evaluated and their consequences considered.

- Problems with reinforcement can occur if getting a wrong answer is more interesting than getting a correct one. For example, seeing something explode in full color and with sound could motivate errors.

- Game-like software is sometimes used far beyond its value. Students who like to play a particular game may continue to use the software long after mastering its concepts. In that case instructional time would be used inappropriately because students should have moved on to new items.

- Game-like software often involves eye-hand coordination and reflexes to use a joystick or control buttons, which may prompt incorrect responses due to factors unrelated to the reading process and may also make the software inappropriate for use by children with certain physical handicaps.

Learning with Computers

simulations
Presentations of events similar to those found in the real world.

Software in this category also attempts to teach, but it provides a much richer context for the student in the form of **simulations,** which are models of real-world events or situations. Microcomputer simulations place students in situations that are similar to those they would experience in reality; simulations also model events and processes. Although simulation software is less prevalent in reading education than in other subject areas, it holds tremendous potential. For example, some simulation software allows a student to learn that plot development depends on a series of decisions. That is, the student learns that later developments in a story are constrained by what happens earlier. These simulations allow the student to become a character in a story and to make decisions about that character's actions. As the plot changes according to the choices made by the student, awareness of plot development builds.

Other software simulates the world of a newspaper reporter who is sent out to get a story. The student searches for pertinent facts and

Although microcomputer technology can be motivational, teachers need to ensure that use goes beyond drill and practice.

writes the story, submitting it to the editor (the computer), who checks key words in the story to determine whether the appropriate facts have been presented. The editor then provides feedback about the logic of the facts chosen and gives hints about rewriting the story. A specific objective of this software is to teach who, why, what, when, where, and how questions.

Some software uses what we know about the reading process to require a student to approximate what a reader does. For example, we know that a reader uses context to help find the meanings of unfamiliar words or looks them up in a dictionary or glossary. We also know (1) that readers predict upcoming events, (2) that they look back to confirm their predictions, (3) that they can sometimes understand spoken words but not written words, (4) that they use syntax to aid comprehension, and (5) that quality literature is motivating. Software that incorporates these features is readily available.

Many programs on CD-ROM include books that allow a student to look up or hear a word while reading literature selections. Color illustrations and animation are included to enhance the story. Comprehension questions are asked at all levels and include questions about upcoming text, text that has just been read, and text that was read several pages before. Feedback is provided not only through the indication of a correct or incorrect response, but also through reference to the text, where syntactic and semantic connections are highlighted to make the relationships between concepts and causes explicit. The reader can reread or preview within the selection, which is longer than just a single screen of text. In addition, such integrated packages provide record-keeping functions, the capability of printing story selections, opportunities for practice, and personalized letters that can be sent to parents to indicate progress. Clearly, such programs have moved far beyond simple drill-and-practice offerings and are bordering on the realm of simulations.

Simulations intended for other subject areas can also be useful to a teacher of reading. For example, *Oregon Trail* (MECC), a simulation intended for social studies, might be used to build background knowledge before students read stories about settlers on the U. S. frontier. *Oregon Trail* puts the student in the place of an explorer moving through the frontier to a fort. The student must make decisions about where and how to travel, what supplies to buy, when and where to camp, and how to deal with dangers confronted along the way. Thus, relevant computer simulations can result in increased background knowledge and heightened interest in specific stories. Of course, appropriate prediscussion and a clear goal are important. But since simulations are most appropriate as small- or large-group activities, discussion is facilitated, and class time is used effectively even as the goal of prereading activity is met.

Simulations generally use all of the color, sound, and graphics capabilities available to the microcomputer, as well as provide record-keeping functions for the teacher. However, the same cautions that applied to tutorial software apply here. The teacher must decide whether the content is appropriate to students' needs and to the instructional program.

Learning About Thinking with Computers

There have been claims that working with computers and with certain programming languages enhances the problem-solving strategies of the user (Papert, 1980). Such claims are closely related to the tutee function originally identified by Taylor (1980). The proponents of this view argue that either the computer dominates (in effect, controlling the student) or the student dominates (thus controlling the computer). In the former case the computer can be viewed as teaching the student—presenting content, questions, and feedback, as well as branching to appropriate difficulty levels. In the latter case the student "teaches" the computer, and this teaching influences students' thought processes. Among the main advocates of the potential of microcomputers to influence thinking and problem-solving abilities are Seymore Papert and his colleagues, developers of the Logo computer language.

Simulations may also be a part of this category of computer usage. They traditionally have been developed to teach specific content, yet they require students to make decisions and anticipate the consequences of their actions. Many of the newer, CD-ROM–based interactive programs require such behaviors. Thus, it may be that general thinking skills are also being developed and that simulation software goes beyond simply imparting information. If simulation software does in fact teach specific content and expand general thinking skills, then the usage category in which it belongs depends on the instructional goal of the simulation.

Managing Learning with Computers

Teachers who have access to a microcomputer often set it aside for student use only. They forget that the machine can be used to make a teacher's job easier. An increasing amount of software is available to keep student records, indicate student progress, track lunch money, write letters to parents, find information and references useful for lesson development, and help with a variety of other time-consuming functions.

When coupled with filing system software, a microcomputer can be used to keep track of anything that would normally require entries on file cards. For example, a classroom library can be easily and quickly entered into a computerized filing system, including information about author(s), title, reading difficulty level, topic area(s), genre, and so on. Similarly, a file can be made of students' attitudes and interests, as collected on attitude/interest inventories. Figure 14-1 illustrates an entry into each of these types of files. Such a file system allows a teacher to quickly and easily choose or recommend reading material. For example, the computer could search for any books in the class library that are about pets or for any student(s) who might be interested in pet stories. Thus, the teacher can personalize supplementary reading for any student or group of students in the class. The class as a whole might decide on the categories to be included in the file system and might enter the data if that information is not confidential. If students are too young to enter data, older students might enjoy a real-world activity as a part of their computer class assignment and might help set up the class data base and enter the data.

For one more example of microcomputer assistance in lightening teacher loads, think back to the discussion of cloze tests and readability formulas in Chapter 11. Several software programs help teachers create cloze tests, either on the screen or on paper. A teacher simply types in a passage, and the computer then deletes the appropriate words and replaces them with blanks. Most such software allows the teacher to specify which words to delete (e.g., every fifth or seventh). However, a cloze test can also be customized, with specific words deleted. In either case, the test is then printed for student use or appears on the screen. If students take the test on the screen, then the program scores each test (the microcomputer "remembers" the deletions) and provides the teacher with a printout of each student's rating.

FIGURE 14-1

Sample entries in a computerized filing system

```
AUTHOR       Silverstein, Shel
TITLE        Where the Sidewalk Ends
GENRE        Poetry
RDGLEVEL     All
DESCRIPTOR   Appropriate for all students.
COMMENT      No reading level or descriptors because the
             book has a variety of poems. In previous
             use, has been of high interest across all
             students/grades.
```

```
STUDENT      Alex Smith
AGE          8
INTERESTS    Pets, Science Fiction, Poems, Cars, TV
RDGLEVEL     3.0
COMMENTS     Likes to read aloud to friends—espe-
             cially poems.
```

Readability analyses are also facilitated with a microcomputer. A teacher needs only to type in a passage, and the computer provides an analysis, often based on a choice of more than one readability formula. In addition, a listing of the number of syllables and the number of sentences in the passage is usually provided, with the result printed on either the screen or through the printer. Many people have written about readability software (much of this writing occurred in the mid to late 1980s), and interested readers are referred to work such as Standal's (1987) article, where he discusses readability formulas, presents benefits and cautions of using computers for such activities, and reviews five commercially available programs. Both cloze and readability software are available commercially but can also be found in the **public domain.** Your curriculum library and computer store can provide the names and addresses of publishers where such software can be acquired.

public domain
A term used to indicate an absence of copyright restrictions; describes software that is usually inexpensive, although frequently of high quality, and often without manuals or guarantees.

Facilitating Parental Involvement with Technology. Parents often feel helpless in the face of curricula that may be substantially different from what was in place when they were students, and some parents feel alienated from (and somewhat threatened by) schools as a result of their own negative experiences from the past. Nonetheless, many parents say that they would do more to help their children learn and to support teachers and schools if they knew what to do. Technology can be especially helpful in communicating with parents. Several schools have purchased automatic telephone dialing equipment that is interfaced with a microcomputer. Such a system is used by teachers and administrators to

M O D E L   L E S S O N

Implementing Telephone Technology in Ms. Dodson's School

It was just two years ago that I talked to our principal early in the school year about getting some additional telephone equipment. She agreed to contact the telephone company about a line for the second-grade teachers if we could find the funds to buy an answering machine. The three of us decided to contact several local businesses about the possibility of donating one to the school. We put together a brief but fairly detailed description of how the machine would be used and what it would do for us. Happily, three separate businesses agreed to donate it—two department stores and the bank our school uses. So we asked the bank to buy the machine, and the two stores, instead, to underwrite the cost of the telephone line for a year. They agreed, and we promised to report back at the end of the school year to let them know how it had worked out. Our principal was thrilled not to have to spend any school funds for our project.

Now that we've had our system operating for two years, we all wonder how we ever managed without it. Just this morning I listened to the messages several parents left for me last night. One parent said that her son was becoming interested in the basketball playoffs, and she wondered if I could suggest any books for him. So before school started, I entered that information into our microcomputer's filing system and found we had several appropriate books right in our own classroom library. Another parent had called to say that his daughter had the chicken pox and wouldn't be in school for about a week. I called him back at lunch time and talked about catch-up activities. Right now I've just finished writing out the message I'm going to put on tonight's tape.

> This is Emily Dodson. Our class will soon be reading a set of stories about pets, and I'll be asking students to bring pictures of pets to school. If your family doesn't have a pet, your child can cut out magazine pictures of a pet he or she might like to have. I have some magazines that I can send home with your child if you would like. Just let me know. It would also help if you could discuss with your child his or her feelings about your family pet and/or the responsibilities that having a pet brings. I'll be sending home a few short stories about pets, and you might want to talk about those with your child, too.

> Today I've asked the students to finish writing stories that were started in class. You might ask to see the story and have your child tell you what it's about. The story should be finished by Friday, and you might suggest that your child draw a picture to go along with it. If you would like your child to bring home some crayons, please leave me a message.

> In about a month we'll have a unit on Egypt. Please let me know if you or someone you know has traveled to Egypt and could share some pictures or could come and tell us about the trip.

> Thanks for your support.

leave messages for parents: the microcomputer can be set to dial a parent's phone number within certain hours and to keep dialing periodically until contact is made. In this way parents can be told of upcoming field trips, student tardiness, and so on. With this technology, parents also have an opportunity to leave messages.

Even without a computerized system, some schools have devised an effective alternative. Telephone lines are purchased for each grade level or each classroom, and a low-cost answering machine is hooked up to each telephone line. (Schools have been relatively successful at partnering with businesses and telephone companies to provide these resources at substantial discounts.) Then each day teachers record a message about their students—for example, upcoming assignments, homework, or class achievements—and parents can listen to the messages at their convenience, leaving their own messages if they wish.

Bauch (1988, 1990) has studied the use of inexpensive answering machine technology in a variety of schools. Without such technology he notes that the national average of parent-to-teacher contacts is approximately two per day in schools averaging 300 students. Bauch's data indicate that a telephone message system increases that average to approximately sixty per day, and the sixty calls are not all from the same parents each day. However, the majority of parents do call at least once a week.

An additional and important finding is that parents from low socioeconomic levels call just as often as do parents from average and above-average socioeconomic levels. Other data indicate that low-socioeconomic families generally do have a telephone and are most appreciative of this nonthreatening way to find out about homework and class activities and to make contact with teachers. Low-socioeconomic and single parents often have great difficulty finding time to see teachers in person, yet data indicate that they are supportive of schools and are concerned that their children achieve success.

SPECIFIC APPLICATIONS OF TECHNOLOGY

Teachers often wonder how to fairly distribute access to only one or two microcomputers among 25 or more students. In such situations teachers can allow students to work at the microcomputer in much the same way that they work at a learning center. Many people advocate that students work in groups of two or three per microcomputer (Berger, 1984; Bransford, 1984). The resulting discussion within the small group as problems are encountered and solved is valuable and can enhance learning. Small-group work is especially valuable when simulation software is being used.

With the availability of projection devices that fit on a standard overhead projector, teachers can project the computer screen and use software as a basis for discussion in whole-group situations. Think how a discussion could be enhanced if a simulation was projected, students given different aspects or points of view to think about, and then various opinions be entered and played out within the simulation. Software such as *Decisions, Decisions* (Tom Snyder Productions) incorporates such a strategy. It requires students to read and discuss within cooperative groups as part of the simulation and decision-making process, and is most appropriate for content-area reading and research assignments.

Whether classroom computers are used in whole-class or within an individual student, learning center structure, you will need to guard against allowing some students more access to the microcomputer than other students. For example, it is poor practice to allow microcomputer time as a reward for finishing assigned work. Because more advanced students often complete assignments faster than average or below-average achievers, there is a danger of increasing the gap between high and low groups. Inequities in computer use can also occur between males and females, as well as between students at high and low socioeconomic levels. In addition, teachers must ensure that those with microcomputers at home do not monopolize microcomputer time in the classroom, simply because of greater background knowledge.

Finally, teachers of reading must understand that microcomputers are appropriate for use at any grade level; they are not solely the domain of students in intermediate grades and above. Younger students may have some difficulty using keyboards to input information, but most software allows the use of a mouse or a touch pad that can be easily handled by younger children. In any case, keyboarding skills should not be the major concern in deciding whether to use a microcomputer. More important is the appropriateness of the material presented by the software—the task itself and the reading skills required.

Word Processing

Although much software is available specifically for use in reading instruction, **applications software** intended for a wide range of everyday tasks is also valuable to a teacher of reading. For example, word processing software can be used in language experience applications. As the student(s) dictate a story, it can be typed directly into the microcomputer and then quickly printed for each student. A word processor also allows students to revise or add to their stories easily. Changes can be incorporated into the original and a "clean" copy provided promptly. Printed stories can then be illustrated and either posted or made into class books. Later, teachers can create vocabulary lessons from the words that students use in their language experience stories.

applications software
Programs that are useful in everyday life, for example, word processing software.

Despite these software applications, however, students should still be provided with many opportunities to see their teachers write. Using a word processor in language experience activities should not replace the more traditional procedure. Many teachers first write their students' stories on chart paper or notebook paper and then transcribe them into the computer for distribution. At higher grade levels students often enjoy entering their stories themselves.

Students can also use word processing software to create their own stories or to access and read stories written by other class members. They might then leave messages to the other students, using the microcomputer as a form of bulletin board. They can share their reactions to other students' stories or simply leave conversational messages. As students

Technology that facilitates distance communication, learning, and multimedia applications can be incorporated into all facets of literacy instruction at all grade levels.

read and respond to such messages, they develop audience awareness in their writing and are highly motivated to read any further messages written specifically to them. Consider, for example, such a use as discussed by Myers (1993), who describes this activity with undergraduate students. Note, however, that his description could apply at any grade level.

> Undergraduates in my teacher education courses form inquiry groups to explore a topic of their choice. . . . Over the semester, they. . . discuss self-selected readings and past experiences, and write an article. Their articles are compiled into a book which we all buy, read, and discuss. . . . This curricular structure supports students' connections between ideas, similar to the intertextual linking of students in literature circles (Short, 1992). (Myers, 1993, p. 251)

Word processing software is available for varying degrees of sophistication, and even kindergarteners enjoy using the computer to write and print their stories. In addition, word processing software can help teachers make cloze tests if specific software for that purpose is unavailable. Teachers simply type a passage and then replace specific words with a blank, using a word processor's search-for-and-replace function. Software that checks spelling, which is a part of most word processing software, can also be used to generate spelling lessons. Most spelling-checker programs can create a file of words that were used in students' entries but were not recognized as correct. Teachers then access those word lists and use them as the basis of periodic spelling lessons on the words most frequently misspelled by students.

In the younger grades, students often enjoy software that allows them to easily draw illustrations for their stories, or that allows them to print notes, banners, and cards that can be given to their friends and classmates. Software such as *Kidpix* allows even young children to easily manipulate icons and "stamps" that can form elaborate illustrations, as well as allowing the addition of accompanying text. Examples of students' work with such software appear in Figure 14-2.

Spreadsheets

Other software that has been written for business use, such as spreadsheets, can also be successfully used in reading instruction. **Spreadsheets** present the user with a series of rows and columns (see Figure 14-3). The information entered in those rows and columns can then be manipulated in a number of ways. Mathematical formulas can be applied to numerical entries, allowing spreadsheets to be used as a gradebook or for other purposes that require numerical information. For reading instruction, however, the mathematics functions are less important than the row-and-column format.

spreadsheet
A type of applications software that allows entry of data in rows and columns for later manipulation.

One part of reading instruction is teaching the relationships among items. The rows and columns of a spreadsheet allow students an opportunity to classify in easily visible categories and to correct errors easily. For a lesson on action words, for example, the teacher might write on the chalkboard or on a piece of paper beside the microcomputer a series of words containing both action and nonaction words. Then at various times during the day, students could use the spreadsheet to sort the list of words into appropriate columns headed Action Words and Not Action Words. They can be encouraged to add several of their own words to each column, in addition to adding words from various selections that they read throughout the day.

Telecommunications: Accessing Bulletin Boards and Data Bases

More and more computer buyers are including a **modem** in their purchase. A modem is an inexpensive attachment that allows communication with other computers via telephone lines. This capability makes it possible to access computer bulletin boards and electronic data bases. Bulletin boards provide opportunities to leave messages for others, to browse

modem
An attachment to a computer that allows communication with other computers via telephone lines.

RE 14-2

samples of students' work

by Alexander

for Miss Goforth

My taecher is getting Merryed
With Dan. He is nice. Miss
Goforth is nice too. They have
been dateing for fuor yaers.
Miss Goforth is verey verey
verey verey verey verey
nice!!!!!!! She got picked up
in a butiful Limo and he gave
her Roseis. They were witeh
and they went to a restaurant
and she likeed it!!!! she got
a engagement ring. It was
butiful!!!!!! The class
screamed and we were
happy!!!!!!!!!!!!!!!!!!!!!!!
We get to go to her wedding.
I am happy!!!! She is butiful
!!!!! You;ve got to see her
she is number 1 teacher!!!!!!!
!!!!!!!!!!!!!!!!!!!!!!!!!!!!!
!!!!!!!!!!!!!!!!!!!!!!she is
rely nice!!!!!!!!!!!!!!

BACK
RIDING Karen
&Ashley loved to
back .Me and
Ashley named it
Stallion. One
day we went to
a field. We rode
Stallion four
hours. Karen rode
two hours and
Ashley rode two
hours. We love
Stallion very
much!

FIGURE 14-3

Spreadsheet with entries

	a	b	c	d	e	f	g	h
2					NOT			
3			ACTION		ACTION			
4			WORDS		WORDS			
5			———		———			
6								
7			RUN		THE			
8			JUMP		SHE			
9			SIT		FLOOR			
10								
11								
12		Taken from the following exercise:						
13								
14		Which of the following underlined words are action words?						
15		Which are not?						
16								
17		1. He will run to the store.						
18								
19		2. She will jump down from the chair.						
20								
21		3. Sit down on the floor.						
22								
23								

through information that has been posted, or to ask questions that others will read and respond to. Teachers have found this capability helpful, especially when evaluating software or simply discussing educational issues. Most cities and school districts have teacher networks or educational bulletin boards that facilitate such exchanges of information. Your local computer store often has a list of such bulletin boards and their access telephone numbers.

Other bulletin boards and data bases (for example, Prodigy, CompuServe) allow modem access to information from sources such as the *New York Times*, encyclopedias, travel agencies, and so on, as well as providing access to vast information sources (such as the Smithsonian data base) through the INTERNET. More specialized data bases, such as that of NASA, provide teachers with resources to develop thematic units. Prodigy and CompuServe, however, are commercial entities and charge a monthly (and sometimes hourly) fee for connecting to their service. Many schools, nevertheless, have elected to subscribe to such a service to provide their students and faculty with access to what is being called the "information superhighway."

A modem also allows teachers and students to share work or comments or to become electronic pen pals with students and teachers in other classrooms. That kind of direct communication can also occur through bulletin boards such as Kidsphere, which is supported by the University of Pittsburgh and is intended specifically for students' use.

Video and Multimedia Technology in the Classroom

In 1922 Thomas Edison stated,

> The motion picture is destined to revolutionize our educational system. . . . in a few years it will supplant largely, if not entirely, the use of textbooks. . . . we get about two percent efficiency out of schoolbooks as they are written today. The education of the future, as I see it, will be conducted through the medium of the motion picture. . . where it should be possible to obtain one hundred percent efficiency. (Cuban, 1986, p. 9)

Edison's prediction did not come to pass, yet there is increasing evidence that television and video technology can play an important role in education and may have an increasing impact in the future.

One reason that film did not have a significant impact is that it is a relatively linear medium. Even though students could watch an event occurring, it was difficult to revisit specific scenes for class discussion or to study in depth a specific item within a film. Even videotape—because of the time required for rewinding, inaccurate access to specific scenes, and poor freeze-frame capabilities—does not really allow more than a simple run-through of an entire film.

videodisc
A disk on which images are stored, allowing for easy access to specific scenes and a clear freeze-frame image.

Videodisc technology, however, is becoming increasingly available for educational purposes and allows rapid, random access to any part of the disk. It also allows clear freeze-frame images and, with its large capacity, permits the showing of approximately 50,000 still-frame pictures. The cost of videodisc players is now about equal to that of commercial-quality videotape players, and there is no difference in the cost of a videodisc as opposed to that of a videotape. In addition, a videodisc will not tear, stretch, or deteriorate in quality.

Many titles are now available on videodisc: National Geographic, Nova, and NASA all have videodisc offerings. General movies are available and can often be adapted for instructional use. In addition, specific instructional materials can frequently be applied to areas other than those for which they were created. For example, *VOTE '88, The Middle East,* and *Martin Luther King, Jr.* (available through Optical Data) are intended for social studies use but can also be used in reading instruction, much as simulations from other content areas. *The Laser Disc Newsletter* (Box 420, East Rockaway, NY 11518) provides monthly critiques of videodisc offerings and comprehensive lists of available titles.

The power of videodisc technology is enhanced even further when it is linked to a microcomputer. This combination allows specific scenes on videodisc to be accessed and shown to illustrate textual content. For example, with the disk *Designing Invitations to Thinking,* short scenes can be played that illustrate a vocabulary word being taught, thus giving the student a clearer idea of the word's meaning. This procedure is also used to teach character traits, as shown in Figure 14-4. The student indicates which word or character trait should be illustrated, and the microcomputer tells the disc player to play the appropriate scene. Available research indicates that (1) this approach enhances vocabulary learning and retention and (2) more fully developed character traits appear in students' writing when they have learned about character and plot development through videodisc presentations coupled with text (Bransford, Kinzer, Risko, Rowe, & Vye, 1989; Kinzer & CTG Vanderbilt, 1990).

A videodisc can also be used to integrate learning across a curriculum, thus providing a larger context for instruction and a common, shared background for teacher and students (Bransford, Vye, Kinzer, & Risko, 1990). Using the video as a common reference point and relating instruction to that anchor appear to facilitate students' participation as well as improving their writing and research skills (Bransford, Sherwood, Hasselbring, Kinzer, & Williams, 1990).

Many people believe that videodiscs will be supplanted by CD-ROM disks in the not-too-distant future. A number of relatively inexpensive computers that are now available, both in the Macintosh and IBM and compatible platforms, offer CD-ROM drives as part of their original equipment, and CD-ROMs will soon be able to store approximately 70 minutes of running video. This video can be played back on the computer screen in a window, surrounded by text if desired. Such playback is now feasible with documents created with current word processors, and will soon result in a new dimension for students who wish to illustrate or present. The new generation "PowerPCs" available in the RISC-based computers from Apple, and the Pentium-based computers that are identified with IBM and compatible equipment, will offer greatly increased processing speed that will allow CD-ROM multimedia applications to blossom. In fact, encyclopedias are now available, costing between $200 and $400, that include full-motion video to illustrate articles. These include encyclopedias that "pack 25,000 articles; 100 animations and video clips; eight hours of audio, including 60 spoken languages; a time line; a game; and an interactive atlas onto a single disc priced at $139." (Guglielmo, 1994, p. 46, describing Microsoft's *Encarta*); similar offerings are available from Compton's and Grolier's.

Another influence on the use of video technology in the schools is the entry of commercial vendors, who view the schools as a new market. Whittle Communication, for example, makes available to schools a satellite dish distribution network, and a television for each classroom. Each day, news programs, as well as educational offerings, can be beamed to the schools by Whittle and by other communication net-

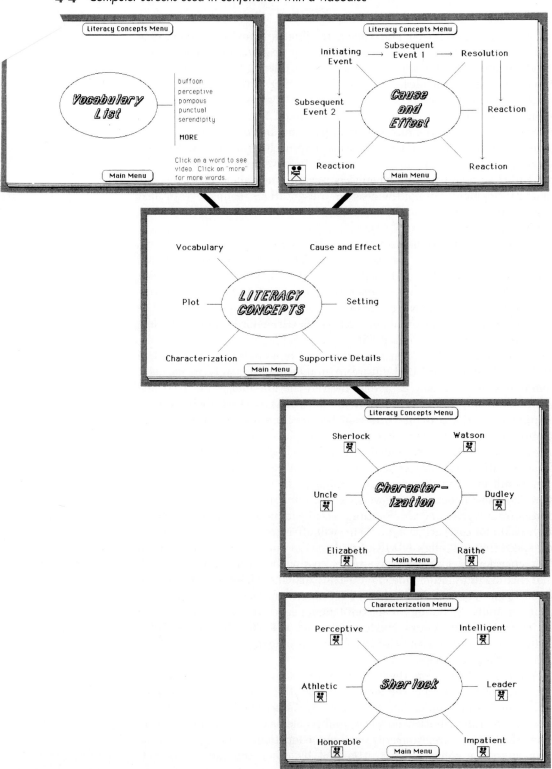

works. Nevertheless, Whittle Communication pays for its equipment and installation costs with commercials targeted specifically at school-age children. Several school boards have rejected Whittle Communication's proposal for this reason. However, other school districts believe that the Whittle approach is the only way to get such equipment into the schools because of increasingly tight budgets. For schools that already have television equipment, other agencies—for example, CNN (the Cable News Network)—offer a similar package without commercial content.

Thus, the increasing commercial presence, the availability of videodisc and CD-ROM technology, the possible link between computers and video equipment, and the specific educational programming that is becoming available indicate that video technology will be more prevalent in classrooms in the future. Although Thomas Edison was not correct in envisioning the role of motion pictures in schools, the potential of video technology is now increasingly a factor.

Hypermedia and Hypertext

An increasingly popular computer language for developers of educational software is **HyperCard.** HyperCard and similar programs (for example, *Linkway Live* and *Toolbook* for the IBM and compatible computers) allow a user to pick an independent path through material more easily. With these programs items appearing on individual computer screens are usually called cards or pages; an entire program is called a stack or book. After the stack has been created, the user can pick and choose what part to look at, where to go next, and so on. Moreover, HyperCard and similar programs can control videodisc and CD-ROM players, allowing text and video to interact, as described earlier. The general term hypermedia is often used to refer to programs that combine text and video in graphic-based animated presentations.

HyperCard and similar programs allow the use of tools to draw graphics, and programming at a basic level is relatively easy. Thus, teachers can create simple, personalized lessons for their classes or can purchase HyperCard stacks with a wide array of possibilities. A number of stacks are available that move through pieces of literature, such as *Charlotte's Web*. Those stacks are often free or are distributed at low cost, and children appear to find them highly motivating.

Hypertext refers to text that has links to further information or that allows the reader to move through it in a nonlinear sequence. For example, a hypermedia/hypertext program that presents children's literature and illustrations on the screen might allow readers to use the mouse to click on words, phrases, or pictures in order to receive more information about the item or to move to an entirely new topic or related issue. This feature provides the reader with on-line support and might well enhance background knowledge (since more information about a concept can be presented at the time of reading), but it also has an interesting side

HyperCard
A programming language that is easy to learn and use and that allows users to follow their own, nonlinear paths through a program; currently available for use on Apple's Macintosh computers.

Hypertext
Text that allows a reader, by highlighting a specific word or concept, to receive further information on the highlighted item. In a hypertext document, readers do not have to move through it in a linear manner.

Videodisc technology, often coupled with computers, can enhance group or individual instruction in reading.

effect. Because different readers might proceed through a text in different sequences or jump to different related topics, students will not all have read the same text in the same way. Indeed, it is possible that a reader might begin a text, ask for related information, become fascinated with a related topic and never return or finish the original item. The differential support that hypertext might provide good and poor readers and the effect of hypertext on classroom discussion require further research but have much potential (Alexander, Kulikowich, & Jetton, 1994).

Local Networks in School Buildings

Many schools are now beginning to network, or link, the computers in their schools to one another through local area networks. Tennessee's 21st Century Project, for example, provides schools with five CD-ROM–capable computers per classroom, a high quality printer, and a network throughout the school that links the computers to each other and to a multimedia distribution net so that teachers can access videodisc, videotape, and so on. Such networks allow enhanced possibilities for students to work cooperatively across classrooms or even across schools. Joint writing projects and multimedia presentations that supplement the more traditional assignments that take place in schools have resulted from this networked system. Networks of all types are becoming more common, and their growth is expected to continue into the future.

FINDING, CHOOSING, AND EVALUATING SOFTWARE

Literally thousands of software programs are marketed for reading instruction. Some software is intended for use on a single computer, as part of a larger reading program. Other packages (for example, IBM's *Writing to Read*) constitute a core reading program and require a number of computers in a laboratory, where intact classes go on a regular basis for reading instruction. With all the software available, teachers often ask where they can find programs that are appropriate to meet their particular instructional programs. As a starting point, search the many catalogs that are often held in the school library. Also, most school district teacher resource centers have both software catalogs, demonstration programs, and evaluations by teachers who have used specific programs.

Most educational publishers also produce software and include those offerings in their general catalogs. Such catalogs briefly describe available educational software, but usually do not evaluate what is listed. They are available from publishers on request and are automatically sent to school and university libraries and to curriculum and resource centers. Journals, too, often list and evaluate educational software. The following publications feature new product announcements, software evaluation, or similar columns.

Software Reviews on File

Educational Technology

Electronic Learning

Microcomputers in Education

Teaching and Computers

T.H.E. Journal (Technological Horizons in Education)

The Computing Teacher

One of the largest distributors of educational software is the Minnesota Educational Computing Corporation (MECC), which produces an extensive software catalog (available from 6160 Summit Dr. North, Minneapolis, MN 55408). MECC also offers a subscription service to school systems and other educational users that automatically provides every piece of software that it distributes and forwards new offerings as they appear. Many school districts subscribe to MECC, maintaining a software depository in their district resource center from which individual schools and teachers can borrow software for use in their classrooms.

After teachers have found software that interests them, they must decide whether it is appropriate for their students and their instructional program. Some software publishers will send a program (or a compressed demonstration copy) on approval so that it can be evaluated. Other publishers do not allow the return of used software. In those cases teachers should find one or more independent reviews of the software before ordering it. Reviews and articles are available in the journals mentioned previously and from agencies that evaluate educational software. EPIE (Educational Products Information Exchange, 103-3 W. Montauk Hwy., Hampton Bays, NY 11946) evaluates software and distributes those evaluations cataloged by skill and subject area. Computer bulletin boards can also be used to ask others' opinions regarding an intended software purchase or to view compilations of reviews. Additionally, most state departments of education and many school districts have collected software evaluations and make them available to teachers.

Of course, the most relevant evaluation is that of the individual teacher who may use the software. When you find yourself considering software, there are two things that you should assess. First, you must ask whether the software is appropriate to your hardware, that is, the equipment that you have available. Second, you must consider aspects of the software itself as they relate to your instructional program. Before you order any software, you should work through the following hardware-specific evaluation checklist (Kinzer, Sherwood, & Bransford, 1986). It can help identify inappropriate software before further time, effort, and money are expended, and it does not require that the software be in hand (the questions can usually be answered from information provided in catalogs or advertising brochures). A more comprehensive treatment of software evaluation is presented by Sloane, Gordon, Gunn, and Mickelsen (1989).

Hardware-Specific Software Checklist

1. Is the software available in your diskette format? For example, if your computer accepts only 3.5-inch diskettes, is the software available on such diskettes, or is it available only on 5.25-inch

diskettes? Is the software CD-ROM based and does your computer system include a CD-ROM drive?

2. Does the software require one or two disk drives, or a hard disk drive? Although virtually all computers purchased within the past three years would have a hard disk drive, older equipment in schools may have floppy drives only.

3. Is the software compatible with your brand and model of computer? Even if the software is available with your particular brand of microcomputer (for example, an Apple), it still must be compatible with the model that you have (for example, Apple II, Apple GS, or Apple Macintosh).

4. Does the software require a certain amount of computer memory? Some software must be loaded into memory before it can be used and may require additional memory during use. Find out how much memory is required for operation and whether your computer has the necessary amount.

5. Does the software require any specific input device? Are programmable, function, or special keyboard keys needed by the program? Is a special or enhanced keyboard necessary? Is a joystick or other special device required?

6. Does the software require any specific output device? Some software sends output directly to a printer and stops or "hangs up" if a printer is unavailable.

7. Does the software require any specific output capabilities? A printer with graphics capabilities, an external speaker, or a high-level color monitor are sometimes required before the full capabilities of the software are available.

8. Does the software require any other software to be useful? Some programs (for example, spelling checkers) require word processing software to input information; thus, the software might be useless without a word processing package.

After you have determined that the targeted software is suitable for your classroom microcomputer system, you should answer the questions in the following list (Kinzer, Sherwood, & Bransford, 1986). They require that you have the software in hand and will help you examine it carefully. Some software may be inappropriate for the reading level or typing skills of your students. In other cases the microcomputer's graphics and sound capabilities may draw attention to wrong answers. If your school district or school library catalogs software evaluations, you should forward yours for inclusion when it is completed. (Be sure to include title and version, publisher and address, and perhaps cost.) Additionally, because some software is developed and distributed without adequate **field testing,** you should send any suggestions for improvements or complaints regarding the software to the publisher so that modifications can be made. Hands-on evaluation is your only real safeguard.

field testing
Presale experimentation by people who typically would use a product.

Questions for Evaluating Reading and Writing
Instructional Software

1. Do you have the proper equipment to run the software?
2. What skills are targeted, according to the publisher? Do you agree?
3. Are the skills targeted by the software appropriate to your students and to your curriculum? For how many of your students would the software be useful?
4. What is the intended age/grade level, according to the publisher? Do you agree?
5. How do you intend to use the software? What would its purpose be in your overall program?
6. How many of your students are at a level at which the software would be useful?
7. In what area does the software fall: (a) learning from computers; (b) learning with computers; (c) managing learning with computers; or (d) some other area or combination of areas.
8. Does the software do more than a text could do in the same skill area? In what way?
9. Would the software be easy for your students to use and understand? Are the commands, required typing skills, or complexity of screen displays within your students' abilities?
10. Does the software make appropriate use of graphics, color, and sound to enhance motivation and learning? Are these elements necessary, given your intended use of the software?
11. Does the software make use of branching to provide instruction when errors are made? Is branching necessary, given your intended use?
12. How long would it take one of your students to go through the program? Is that an appropriate amount of time, given your goals and instructional situation?
13. Would your students have to go through the entire program, perhaps in some predetermined sequence, or would they be able to stop and start at various points?
14. Does the software provide a pretest so that students can begin at an appropriate level of difficulty? Is there a posttest to measure learning? Are these tests important, given your intended use?
15. Could your students load and use the software by themselves? How much teacher support would be needed? Is that involvement appropriate to your instructional situation?
16. Does the software provide a dictionary or glossary to explain words and/or concepts that students find difficult? Could students ask the computer for a more detailed explanation if they did not understand a word? Does the software provide help if commands are not easily understood?

17. Does the software use the computer's sound capabilities to provide speech support for unknown words? For example, can the user highlight a word or a larger part of the text and ask that it be read? If yes, which form is used: synthesized (more difficult to understand) or digitized (a good approximation of natural speech)?
18. If the software targets longer pieces of text, does it use selections that are interesting and/or drawn from good children's literature?
19. Does the software score students' work and file the results by individual names for later access by the teacher (that is, does it include record-keeping capabilities)?
20. Can the software be used by more than one student at a time? Would this usage detract from your intended use?
21. Is there overt gender, racial, or socioeconomic bias in the software?
22. What suggestions for improvement should be communicated to the publisher?

USING A LITERACY FRAMEWORK TO GUIDE TECHNOLOGICAL APPLICATIONS

Your literacy framework will determine how you use microcomputers, other technology, and associated software in your instructional program. It will also result in an emphasis on one part of the five-part model discussed at the beginning of this chapter. Teachers with a specific skills explanation of how reading ability develops tend to choose drill-and-practice or tutorial software that relates to specifically defined skills. Teachers with a reader-based view of how we read or a holistic explanation of how reading ability develops may find simulations useful or may use word processors to enhance language experience activities. Literacy frameworks based on an interactive explanation of how we read or an integrative explanation of how reading ability develops tend to incorporate a variety of software appropriate for specific learners. They may use drill-and-practice programs for some purposes and software that targets high-level knowledge sources for other purposes—for example, the selection of story endings, which uses high-level discourse knowledge.

Computers are simply tools for teachers to use in reading instruction. They are governed by the same kinds of philosophical considerations that we applied to printed materials earlier. With both new and traditional technologies you will be on the forefront of educational opportunities. Supported by the concepts, theories, and methods suggested throughout this text and guided by your own personal literacy framework, you should be ready to become a professional and effective teacher of reading.

Nikki Robinson, Sixth Grade Teacher

CD-ROM, laser disks, networks, multimedia . . . what happened to plain vanilla computers and calculators? Half the teachers in my school run in the opposite direction when technology is mentioned, the other half seem to embrace it with enthusiasm. Money is so tight in our district that it is not feasible financially to incorporate technology into every classroom. However, we do have one classroom that is equipped with 30 computers. We need to sign up to use it, so incorporating technology requires a lot of planning; it can't be spontaneous.

The other sixth grade teacher has one computer workstation in her classroom. She purchased a modem herself, and asked the PTA to purchase the computer. Ms. Harris wrote up a six page report showing how she would use the computer in order to convince the parents that it was a worthwhile investment. Now her students access information through a computer network that they use as the basis for reading related to mathematics and science projects. Some of her "technowhiz" kids can get information about weather, volcanoes, and earthquakes around the world. Ms. Harris says this "real" information motivates her students to formulate and solve problems. The mathematical and scientific calculations and formulas are a means to an end—the tools to solve the problem, not the problem itself.

I remember when pocket calculators were too expensive to purchase, and now they are very affordable. Some companies lease the equipment if schools purchase the laser disks, software, or CDs. Ms. Harris says the district has formed a committee to investigate these options. In the meantime, I'm going to attend a workshop on how to use computers effectively in my classroom. I don't want my students to be computer-phobic, but I'm just not sure how I could use computers to improve my teaching. I don't want to use the computer as a babysitter. Some drill and practice software seems like worksheets on a screen to me. It scares me a little that some students know so much more than I do about computers. I'd like to tap into that knowledge, but I don't know how. I hope the workshop will help. The brochure said that regular classroom teachers will show us what they do with computers. I'm skeptical, but willing to learn. I don't want to get run down on the information highway!

- The use of microcomputers in reading instruction falls into five general categories: learning about computers, learning from computers, learning with computers, learning about thinking with computers, and managing learning with computers.

- In addition to microcomputers and their software, various other technologies—including videodiscs, answering machines, and television—are useful in reading instruction. These other technologies can be effectively used independently or can be linked to microcomputers.

- All types of software—including drill-and-practice, tutorial, game-like, simulation, and programming software—can have a place in reading instruction, if appropriately used.

- If thoughtfully applied, software intended for use in other areas can also be used in reading instruction.

- Teachers should carefully evaluate software before using it in reading instruction.

Major Points

1. What are the role and value of drill and practice in a reading lesson? For what purpose(s) might you assign students to computer software for drill and practice?

2. Imagine the management functions that will face you as a teacher of reading. Explain how a microcomputer could be used to help you with those tasks.

3. Interview several teachers who use microcomputers in their reading instruction. Ask how they use the system specifically in their reading lessons and how they perceive the microcomputer in comparison to more traditional instructional practices, like workbooks.

4. Interview several students who have been allowed to use microcomputers as a part of their reading instruction. Ask how they feel about the microcomputer and how it has helped them learn.

5. Your curriculum library or microcomputer laboratory probably has software that is marketed as being appropriate for reading instruction. (If not, check a computer store.) Evaluate several software packages using the checklists in this chapter. How might the software be used in reading instruction?

6. How might microcomputers and related technologies fit into your instructional program and, specifically, your literacy framework?

Making Instructional Decisions

...her Reading

Balajthy, E. (1986). *Microcomputers in reading and language arts*. Englewood Cliffs, NJ: Prentice Hall.

Includes chapters on evaluating software as well as applications in emergent literacy/readiness, word recognition, vocabulary, comprehension, and study skills. Also discusses other general issues of microcomputer use in reading instruction.

Bennett, S., & Bennett, R. (1993). *The official Kidpix activity book*. Random House Electronic Publishing.

Provides activities that can be suggested to parents as well as used in the classroom by teachers. Based on Kidpix software, it includes activities that can be integrated in a wide variety of reading, writing, and art projects.

Blanchard, J. S., Mason, G. E., & Daniel, D. (1987). *Computer applications in reading* (3rd ed.). Newark, DE: International Reading Association.

A popular publication by the International Reading Association. A brief but good introduction and resource for teachers wishing to implement microcomputers in their reading programs.

Blanchard, J. S., & Rottenberg, C. J. (1990). Hypertext and hypermedia: Discovering and creating meaningful learning environments. *The Reading Teacher, 43,* 656–661.

Discusses and defines hypertext and hypermedia and explores potential benefits and uses in reading instruction.

Dillner, M. (1994). Using hypermedia to enhance content-area instruction. *Journal of Reading, 37,* 260–270.

Discusses the procedures and decisions a teacher made to create a hypermedia lesson, and gives some examples of how students used that lesson. Incorporates interesting ideas for developing lessons using hypermedia.

Dublin, P., Pressman, H., & Woldman, E. J. (1994). *Integrating computers in your classroom: Elementary language arts*. New York: Harper Collins College Publishers.

A short paperback in a readable style that provides tips for integrating computers into existing curriculum; includes some lesson plans.

Whitaker, B. T., Schwartz, E., & Vockell, E. (1989). *The computer in the reading curriculum*. New York: McGraw-Hill.

A comprehensive paperback that discusses computer applications for each component of the reading process. Includes extensive software lists, evaluations, and publishers' addresses.

References

Alexander, P. A., Kulikowich, J. M., & Jetton, T. L. (1994). The role of subject-matter knowledge and interest in the processing of linear and nonlinear texts. *Review of Education Research, 64,* 201–252.

Bauch, J. P. (1988). Communicating with parents through technology. In J. Collins et al. (Eds.), Proceedings of the Fifth International Conference on Technology and Education. Edinburgh, Scotland: CEP Consultants.

Bauch, J. P. (1990). The TransParent school model: A partnership for parent involvement. *Educational Horizons, 68,* 187–189.

Berger, C. (1984, April). *Assessing cognitive consequences of computer environments for learning science: Research findings and policy implications*. Paper presented at the National Association for Research in Science Teaching, Lake Geneva, WI.

Bransford, J. (1984, April). Personal communication.

Bransford, J. D., Kinzer, C. K., Risko, V. J., Rowe, D. W., & Vye, N. J. (1989). Designing invitations to thinking: Initial thoughts. In S. McCormick & J. Zutell (Eds.), *Cog-*

nitive and social perspectives for literacy research and instruction (38th NRC Yearbook, pp. 35–54). Chicago: National Reading Conference.

Bransford, J. D., Sherwood, R. D., Hasselbring, T. S., Kinzer, C. K., & Williams, S. M. (1990). Anchored instruction: Why we need it and how technology can help. In D. Nix & R. Spiro (Eds.), *Cognition, education, and multimedia* (pp. 115–141). Hillsdale, NJ: Erlbaum.

Bransford, J. D., Vye, N. J., Kinzer, C. K., & Risko, V. J. (1990). Teaching thinking and content knowledge: An integrated approach. In B. F. Jones & L. Idol (Eds.), *Dimensions of thinking and cognitive instruction* (pp. 381–413). Hillsdale, NJ: Erlbaum.

Cuban, L. (1986). *Teachers and machines: The classroom use of technology since 1920.* New York: Teachers College Press.

Goldberg, K., & Sherwood, R. D. (1983). *Microcomputers: A parent's guide.* New York: Wiley.

Guglielmo, C. (1994). What's happening on CD-ROM: Encyclopedias. *MacWeek, 8*(31), 45–46.

Hasselbring, T. S., & Cavanaugh, K. (1986). Computer applications for the mildly handicapped. In C. K. Kinzer, R. D. Sherwood, & J. D. Bransford (Eds.), *Computer strategies for education: Foundations and content-area applications.* Columbus, OH: Merrill.

Kinzer, C. K. (1986). A five-part categorization for use of microcomputers in reading classrooms. *The Reading Teacher, 30,* 226–232.

Kinzer, C. K., with the Cognition and Technology Group at Vanderbilt. (1990). Anchored instruction and its relationship to situated cognition. *Educational Researcher, 19,* 2–10.

Kinzer, C. K., Sherwood, R. D., & Bransford, J. D. (Eds.). (1986). *Computer strategies for education: Foundations and content-area applications.* Columbus, OH: Merrill.

Luehrmann, A. (1983). *Computer literacy: A hands-on approach.* New York: McGraw-Hill.

Myers, J. (1993). Constructing community and intertextuality in electronic mail. In D. J. Leu & C. K. Kinzer (Eds.), *Examining central issues in literacy research, theory and practice.* Forty-second yearbook of the National Reading Conference (pp. 251–262). Chicago, IL: National Reading Conference.

Papert, S. (1980). *Mindstorms: Children, computers, and powerful ideas.* New York: Basic Books.

Papert, S. (1984). Trying to predict the future. *Popular Computing.*

Short, K. G. (1992). Intertextuality: Searching for patterns that connect. In C. K. Kinzer & D. J. Leu (Eds.), *Literacy research, theory, and practice: Views from many perspectives.* Forty-first yearbook of the National Reading Conference (pp. 187–197). Chicago, IL: National Reading Conference.

Sloane, H. N., Gordon, H. M., Gunn, C., & Mickelsen, V. G. (1989). *Evaluating educational software: A guide for teachers.* Englewood Cliffs, NJ: Prentice Hall.

Taylor, R. P. (Ed.). (1980). *The computer in the school: Tutor, tool, tutee.* New York: Teachers College Press.

Whitaker, B. T., Schwartz, E., & Vockell, E. (1989). *The computer in the reading curriculum.* New York: McGraw-Hill.

Appendix A *Award-winning Children's Literature: Newbery Medal Winners*

Year	Title	Author
1922	The Story of Mankind	Hendrik Willem van Loon
1923	The Voyages of Doctor Dolittle	Hugh Lofting
1924	The Dark Frigate	Charles Hawes
1925	Tales from Silver Lands	Charles Finger
1926	Shen of the Sea	Authur Bowie Chrisman
1927	Smoky, the Cowhorse	Will James
1928	Gayneck, The Story of a Pigeon	Dhan Gopal Mukerji
1929	The Trumpeter of Krakow	Eric P. Kelly
1930	Hitty, Her First Hundred Years	Rachel Field
1931	The Cat Who Went to Heaven	Elizabeth Coatsworth
1932	Waterless Mountain	Laura Adams Armer
1933	Young Fu of the Upper Yangtze	Elizabeth Foreman Lewis
1934	Invincible Louisa	Cornelia Meigs
1935	Dobry	Monica Shannon
1936	Caddie Woodlawn	Carol Brink
1937	Roller Skates	Ruth Sawyer
1938	The White Stag	Kate Seredy
1939	Thimble Summer	Elizabeth Enright
1940	Daniel Boone	James Daugherty
1941	Call It Courage	Armstrong Sperry
1942	The Matchlock Gun	Walter D. Edmonds
1943	Adam of the Road	Elizabeth Janet Gray
1944	Johnny Tremain	Esther Forbes
1945	Rabbit Hill	Robert Lawson
1946	Strawberry Girl	Lois Lenski
1947	Miss Hickory	Carolyn Sherwin Bailey
1948	The Twenty-One Balloons	William Pène du Bois
1949	King of the Wind	Marguerite Henry
1950	The Door in the Wall	Marguerite de Angeli
1951	Amos Fortune, Free Man	Elizabeth Yates
1952	Ginger Pye	Eleanor Estes
1953	Secret of the Andes	Ann Nolan Clark
1954	. . . and now Miguel	Joseph Krumgold
1955	The Wheel on the School	Meindert DeJong
1956	Carry On, Mr. Bowditch	Jean Lee Latham
1957	Miracles on Maple Hill	Virginia Sorensen
1958	Rifles for Watie	Harold Keith
1959	The Witch of Blackbird Pond	Elizabeth George Speare
1960	Onion John	Joseph Krumgold
1961	Island of the Blue Dolphins	Scott O'Dell

Year	Title	Author
1962	The Bronze Bow	Elizabeth George Speare
1963	A Wrinkle in Time	Madeleine L'Engle
1964	It's Like This, Cat	Emily Neville
1965	Shadow of a Bull	Maia Wojciechowska
1966	I. Juan de Pareja	Elizabeth Borten de Trevino
1967	Up a Road Slowly	Irene Hunt
1968	From the Mixed-Up Files of Mrs. Basil E. Frankweiler	E. L. Konigsburg
1969	The High King	Lloyd Alexander
1970	Sounder	William H. Armstrong
1971	Summer of the Swans	Betsy Byars
1972	Mrs. Frisby and the Rats of NIMH	Robert C. O'Brien
1973	Julie of the Wolves	Jean George
1974	The Slave Dancer	Paula Fox
1975	M.C. Higgins, the Great	Virginia Hamilton
1976	The Grey King	Susan Cooper
1977	Roll of Thunder, Hear My Cry	Mildred D. Taylor
1978	Bridge to Terabithia	Katherine Paterson
1979	The Westing Game	Ellen Raskin
1980	A Gathering of Days: A New England Girl's Journal, 1830–32	Joan Blos
1981	Jacob Have I Loved	Katherine Paterson
1982	A Visit to William Blake's Inn: Poems for Innocent and Experienced Travelers	Nancy Willard
1983	Dicey's Song	Cynthia Voigt
1984	Dear Mr. Henshaw	Beverly Cleary
1985	The Hero and the Crown	Robin McKinley
1986	Sarah, Plain and Tall	Patricia MacLachlan
1987	The Whipping Boy	Sid Fleischman
1988	Lincoln: A Photo Biography	Russell Freedman
1989	Joyful Noise: Poems for Two Voices	Paul Fleischman
1990	Number the Stars	Lois Lowry
1991	Maniac Magee	Jerry Spinelli
1992	Shiloh	Phyllis Naylor
1993	Missing May	Cynthia Rylant
1994	The Giver	Lois Lowry

Appendix B *Award-winning Children's Literature: Caldecott Medal Winners*

Year	Title	Illustrator	Author
1938	Animals of the Bible	Dorothy P. Lathrop	Helen Dean Fish
1939	Mei Li	Thomas Handforth	Thomas Handforth
1940	Abraham Lincoln	Ingri and Edgar D'Aulaire	Ingri and Edgar D'Aulaire
1941	They Were Strong and Good	Robert Lawson	Robert Lawson
1942	Make Way for Ducklings	Robert McCloskey	Robert McCloskey
1943	The Little House	Virginia Lee Burton	Virginia Lee Burton
1944	Many Moons	Louis Slobodkin	James Thurber
1945	Prayer for a Child	Elizabeth Orton Jones	Rachel Field
1946	The Rooster Crows	Maud and Miska Petersham	Maud and Miska Petersham
1947	The Little Island	Leonard Weisgard	Golden MacDonald
1948	White Snow, Bright Snow	Roger Duvoisin	Alvin Tresselt
1949	The Big Snow	Berta and Elmer Hader	Berta and Elmer Hader
1950	Song of the Swallows	Leo Politi	Leo Politi
1951	The Egg Tree	Katherine Milhous	Katherine Milhous
1952	Finders Keepers	Nicholas Mordvinoff	William Lipkind
1953	The Biggest Bear	Lynd Ward	Lynd Ward
1954	Madeline's Rescue	Ludwig Bemelmans	Ludwig Bemelmans
1955	Cinderella, or the Little Glass Slipper	Marcia Brown	Charles Perrault
1956	Frog Went A-Courtin'	Feodor Rojankovsky	Retold by John Langstaff
1957	A Tree Is Nice	Marc Simont	Janice May Udry
1958	Time of Wonder	Robert McCloskey	Robert McCloskey
1959	Chanticleer and the Fox	Barbara Cooney	Translated by Barbara Cooney
1960	Nine Days to Christmas	Marie Hall Ets	Marie Hall Ets & Aurora Labastida
1961	Babouska and the Three Kings	Nicolas Sidjakov	Ruth Robbins
1962	Once a Mouse. . .	Marcia Brown	Marcia Brown
1963	The Snowy Day	Ezra Jack Keats	Ezra Jack Keats
1964	Where the Wild Things Are	Maurice Sendak	Maurice Sendak
1965	May I Bring a Friend?	Beni Montresor	Beatrice Schenk de Regniers
1966	Always Room for One More	Nonny Hogrogian	Sorche Nic Leodhas
1967	Sam, Bangs & Moonshine	Evaline Ness	Evaline Ness
1968	Drummer Hoff	Ed Emberley	Barbara Emberley
1969	The Fool of the World and the Flying Ship	Uri Shulevitz	Arthur Ransome
1970	Sylvester and the Magic Pebble	William Steig	William Steig

Year	Title	Illustrator	Author
1971	A Story—A Story: An African Tale	Gail E. Haley	Gail E. Haley
1972	One Fine Day	Nonny Hogrogian	Nonny Hogrogian
1973	The Funny Little Woman	Blair Lent	Arlene Mosel
1974	Duffy and the Devil	Margot Zemach	Harve Zemach
1975	Arrow to the Sun	Gerald McDermott	Gerald McDermott
1976	Why Mosquitoes Buzz in People's Ears	Leo and Diane Dillon	Verna Aardema
1977	Ashanti to Zulu: African Traditions	Leo and Diane Dillon	Margaret Musgrove
1978	Noah's Ark	Peter Spier	Peter Spier
1979	The Girl Who Loved Wild Horses	Paul Goble	Paul Goble
1980	Ox-Cart Man	Barbara Cooney	Donald Hall
1981	Fables	Arnold Lobel	Arnold Lobel
1982	Jumanji	Chris Van Allsburg	Chris Van Allsburg
1983	Shadow	Marcia Brown	Blaise Cendrars
1984	The Glorious Flight: Across the Channel with Louis Bleriot	Alice and Martin Provensen	Alice and Martin Provensen
1985	St. George and the Dragon	Trina Schart Hyman	Margaret Hodges
1986	The Polar Express	Chris Van Allsburg	Chris Van Allsburg
1987	Hey, Al	Richard Egielski	Arthur Yorinks
1988	Owl Moon	John Schoenherr	Jane Yolen
1989	Song and Dance Man	Stephen Gammell	Karen Ackerman
1990	Lon Po Po: A Red Riding Hood Tale from China	Ed Young	Ed Young
1991	Black and White	David Macaulay	David Macaulay
1992	Tuesday	David Wiesner	David Wiesner
1993	Mirette on the High Wire	Emily McCully	Emily McCully
1994	Grandfather's Journey	Allen Say	Allen Say

Practical Teaching Strategies and Activities Index

The following strategies and activities provide opportunities for a number of language arts experiences that support the development of literacy.

Name Index

Subject Index

Donald J. Leu is associate professor of education and director of graduate programs in Reading and Language Arts at Syracuse University. He teaches graduate and undergraduate courses at Syracuse University's Reading and Language Arts Center. He has served in the Peace Corps, teaching English in the Marshall Islands of Micronesia. He has also been an elementary teacher and a reading specialist in California. He received an Ed.M. degree in Reading at Harvard and a Ph.D in Language and Literacy at the University of California, Berkeley. Professor Leu's current research includes work on predictable texts, teacher's cognitive processes in literacy context, and the development of reading/writing software. He has published articles on reading in a variety of journals, including *Reading Research Quarterly, The Journal of Educational Psychology,* and *Curriculum Review.* He currently serves on the editorial review boards for *The Journal of Educational Psychology* and *The Journal of Reading Behavior.* He enjoys dressage, fly fishing, and spending time with his family.

Charles K. Kinzer is associate professor of education and research scientist at the Learning Technology Center, Peabody College of Vanderbilt University, where he teaches graduate and undergraduate courses in reading education and language arts. He has taught reading and remedial reading in middle and junior high schools, and has served as Language Arts Consultant (K–12) at the school district level. He received his M.A. in Education from the University of British Columbia, Canada, and his Ph.D. in Language and Literacy at the University of California, Berkeley. Professor Kinzer's research includes reading comprehension, vocabulary acquisition, teacher cognition, and the application of technology in education. He has published articles about reading education, technology, and expert systems development in journals such as *The Journal of Reading Behavior, The Journal of Reading, Reading Research and Instruction, The International Journal of Intelligent Systems,* and *Applied Cognitive Psychology.* He currently serves on the editorial boards of the *Reading Research Quarterly, The Journal of Reading Behavior,* and *The Journal of Special Education Technology.* He enjoys photography, traveling, and spending time at the beach with his wife and daughter.